Ethics and Economics
Volume II

The International Library of Critical Writings in Economics

Series Editor: Mark Blaug

Professor Emeritus, University of London
Professor Emeritus, University of Buckingham
Visiting Professor, University of Exeter

This series is an essential reference source for students, researchers and lecturers in economics. It presents by theme an authoritative selection of the most important articles across the entire spectrum of economics. Each volume has been prepared by a leading specialist who has written an authoritative introduction to the literature included.

A full list of published and future titles in this series is printed at the end of this volume.

Ethics and Economics
Volume II

Edited by

Alan P. Hamlin

Reader in Economics
University of Southampton, UK

THE INTERNATIONAL LIBRARY OF CRITICAL WRITINGS IN ECONOMICS

An Elgar Reference Collection
Cheltenham, UK • Brookfield, US

Published by
Edward Elgar Publishing Limited
8 Lansdown Place
Cheltenham
Glos GL50 2HU
UK

Edward Elgar Publishing Company
Old Post Road
Brookfield
Vermont 05036
US

British Library Cataloguing in Publication Data
Ethics and Economics. – (International
Library of Critical Writings in Economics;
No. 63)
I. Hamlin, Alan P. II. Series
333.01

Library of Congress Cataloguing in Publication Data
Ethics and economics / edited by Alan P. Hamlin.
p. cm. — (The international library of critical writings in
economics ; 63) (An Elgar reference collection)
Includes bibliographical references and index.
1. Economics—Moral and ethical aspects. 2. Utility theory.
3. Value. I. Hamlin, Alan P., 1951– . II. Series. III. Series:
An Elgar reference collection.
HB72.E782 1996
174'.4—dc20

95–45585
CIP

ISBN 1 85278 814 3 (2 volume set)

Printed in Great Britain by Galliard (Printers) Ltd, Great Yarmouth

Contents

Acknowledgements

The editor and publishers wish to thank the following who have kindly given permission for the use of copyright material.

American Economic Association for article: Daniel M. Hausman and Michael S. McPherson (1993), 'Taking Ethics Seriously: Economics and Contemporary Moral Philosophy', *Journal of Economic Literature*, **XXXI** (1), June, 671–731.

Aristotelian Society for article: John Broome (1990–1), 'Fairness', *Proceedings of the Aristotelian Society*, **LXXXXI**, 87–101.

Basil Blackwell Ltd for excerpts: R.M. Hare (1984), 'Rights, Utility, and Universalization: Reply to J.L. Mackie', in R.G. Frey (ed.), *Utility and Rights*, Chapter 5, 106–20; David Wiggins (1987), 'Claims of Need', *Needs, Values, Truth: Essays in the Philosophy of Value*, 2nd Edition, Volume 6, Chapter 1, 1–57, 319–28.

Basil Blackwell Ltd and the University of Minnesota Press for excerpt: J.L. Mackie (1984), 'Rights, Utility, and Universalization', in R.G. Frey (ed.), *Utility and Rights*, Chapter 4, 86–105.

Cambridge University Press for excerpt and article: T.M. Scanlon (1978), 'Rights, Goals, and Fairness', in Stuart Hampshire (ed.), *Public and Private Morality*, Chapter 5, 93–111; Hal R. Varian (1985), 'Dworkin on Equality of Resources', *Economics and Philosophy*, **1**, 110–25; John E. Roemer (1987), 'Egalitarianism, Responsibility, and Information', *Economics and Philosophy*, **3**, 215–44.

Journal of Philosophy, Inc. for article: Amartya K. Sen (1985), 'Well-Being, Agency and Freedom: The Dewey Lectures 1984', *Journal of Philosophy*, **LXXXII** (4), April, 169–221.

Kluwer Academic Publishers B.V. for article: Richard J. Arneson (1989), 'Equality and Equal Opportunity for Welfare', *Philosophical Studies*, **56**, 77–93.

University of Chicago Press for articles: Allan Gibbard (1985), 'Moral Judgment and the Acceptance of Norms', *Ethics*, **96** (1), October, 5–21; James Griffin (1985), 'Some Problems of Fairness', *Ethics*, **96** (1), October, 100–118; John Roemer (1986), 'The Mismarriage of Bargaining Theory and Distributive Justice', *Ethics*, **97** (1), October, 88–110; T.M. Scanlon, Jr. (1986), 'Equality of Resources and Equality of Welfare: A Forced Marriage?', *Ethics*, **97** (1), October, 111–18; G.A. Cohen (1989), 'On the Currency of Egalitarian Justice', *Ethics*, **99** (4), July, 906–44; Philip Pettit (1990), '*Virtus Normativa*: Rational Choice Perspectives', *Ethics*, **100** (4), July, 725–55.

University of Utah Press for excerpt: Amartya Sen (1980), 'Equality of What?', in Sterling M. McMurrin (ed.), *The Tanner Lectures on Human Values, Volume I*, 197–220.

Every effort has been made to trace all the copyright holders but if any have been inadvertently overlooked the publishers will be pleased to make the necessary arrangement at the first opportunity.

In addition the publishers wish to thank the Library of the London School of Economics and Political Science, the Marshall Library of Economics, Cambridge University and the Photographic Unit of the University of London Library for their assistance in obtaining these articles.

Part I
Rules, Rights and Norms

[1]

TWO CONCEPTS OF RULES*

IN THIS paper I want to show the importance of the distinction between justifying a practice [1] and justifying a particular action falling under it, and I want to explain the logical basis of this distinction and how it is possible to miss its significance. While the distinction has frequently been made,[2] and is now becoming commonplace, there remains the task of explaining the tendency either to overlook it altogether, or to fail to appreciate its importance.

To show the importance of the distinction I am going to defend utilitarianism against those objections which have traditionally been made against it in connection with punishment and the obligation to keep promises. I hope to show that if one uses the distinction in question then one can state utilitarianism

---

* This is a revision of a paper given at the Harvard Philosophy Club on April 30, 1954.

[1] I use the word "practice" throughout as a sort of technical term meaning any form of activity specified by a system of rules which defines offices, roles, moves, penalties, defenses, and so on, and which gives the activity its structure. As examples one may think of games and rituals, trials and parliaments.

[2] The distinction is central to Hume's discussion of justice in *A Treatise of Human Nature*, bk. III, pt. II, esp. secs. 2–4. It is clearly stated by John Austin in the second lecture of *Lectures on Jurisprudence* (4th ed.; London, 1873), I, 116ff. (1st ed., 1832). Also it may be argued that J. S. Mill took it for granted in *Utilitarianism;* on this point cf. J. O. Urmson, "The Interpretation of the Moral Philosophy of J. S. Mill," *Philosophical Quarterly*, vol. III (1953). In addition to the arguments given by Urmson there are several clear statements of the distinction in *A System of Logic* (8th ed.; London, 1872), bk. VI, ch. xii pars. 2, 3, 7. The distinction is fundamental to J. D. Mabbott's important paper, "Punishment," *Mind*, n.s., vol. XLVIII (April, 1939). More recently the distinction has been stated with particular emphasis by S. E. Toulmin in *The Place of Reason in Ethics* (Cambridge, 1950), see esp. ch. xi, where it plays a major part in his account of moral reasoning. Toulmin doesn't explain the basis of the distinction, nor how one might overlook its importance, as I try to in this paper, and in my review of his book (*Philosophical Review*, vol. LX [October, 1951]), as some of my criticisms show, I failed to understand the force of it. See also H. D. Aiken, "The Levels of Moral Discourse," *Ethics*, vol. LXII (1952), A. M. Quinton, "Punishment," *Analysis*, vol. XIV (June, 1954), and P. H. Nowell-Smith, *Ethics* (London, 1954), pp. 236–239, 271–273.

in a way which makes it a much better explication of our considered moral judgments than these traditional objections would seem to admit.[3] Thus the importance of the distinction is shown by the way it strengthens the utilitarian view regardless of whether that view is completely defensible or not.

To explain how the significance of the distinction may be overlooked, I am going to discuss two conceptions of rules. One of these conceptions conceals the importance of distinguishing between the justification of a rule or practice and the justification of a particular action falling under it. The other conception makes it clear why this distinction must be made and what is its logical basis.

I

The subject of punishment, in the sense of attaching legal penalties to the violation of legal rules, has always been a troubling moral question.[4] The trouble about it has not been that people disagree as to whether or not punishment is justifiable. Most people have held that, freed from certain abuses, it is an acceptable institution. Only a few have rejected punishment entirely, which is rather surprising when one considers all that can be said against it. The difficulty is with the justification of punishment: various arguments for it have been given by moral philosophers, but so far none of them has won any sort of general acceptance; no justification is without those who detest it. I hope to show that the use of the aforementioned distinction enables one to state the utilitarian view in a way which allows for the sound points of its critics.

For our purposes we may say that there are two justifications of punishment. What we may call the retributive view is that punishment is justified on the grounds that wrongdoing merits punishment. It is morally fitting that a person who does wrong

[3] On the concept of explication see the author's paper *Philosophical Review*, vol. LX (April, 1951).

[4] While this paper was being revised, Quinton's appeared; footnote 2 supra. There are several respects in which my remarks are similar to his. Yet as I consider some further questions and rely on somewhat different arguments, I have retained the discussion of punishment and promises together as two test cases for utilitarianism.

should suffer in proportion to his wrongdoing. That a criminal should be punished follows from his guilt, and the severity of the appropriate punishment depends on the depravity of his act. The state of affairs where a wrongdoer suffers punishment is morally better than the state of affairs where he does not; and it is better irrespective of any of the consequences of punishing him.

What we may call the utilitarian view holds that on the principle that bygones are bygones and that only future consequences are material to present decisions, punishment is justifiable only by reference to the probable consequences of maintaining it as one of the devices of the social order. Wrongs committed in the past are, as such, not relevant considerations for deciding what to do. If punishment can be shown to promote effectively the interest of society it is justifiable, otherwise it is not.

I have stated these two competing views very roughly to make one feel the conflict between them: one feels the force of *both* arguments and one wonders how they can be reconciled. From my introductory remarks it is obvious that the resolution which I am going to propose is that in this case one must distinguish between justifying a practice as a system of rules to be applied and enforced, and justifying a particular action which falls under these rules; utilitarian arguments are appropriate with regard to questions about practices, while retributive arguments fit the application of particular rules to particular cases.

We might try to get clear about this distinction by imagining how a father might answer the question of his son. Suppose the son asks, "Why was *J* put in jail yesterday?" The father answers, "Because he robbed the bank at *B*. He was duly tried and found guilty. That's why he was put in jail yesterday." But suppose the son had asked a different question, namely, "Why do people put other people in jail?" Then the father might answer, "To protect good people from bad people" or "To stop people from doing things that would make it uneasy for all of us; for otherwise we wouldn't be able to go to bed at night and sleep in peace." There are two very different questions here. One question emphasizes the proper name: it asks why *J* was punished rather than someone else, or it asks what he was punished for. The other question asks why we have the institution of punishment: why do people punish one another rather than, say, always forgiving one another?

Thus the father says in effect that a particular man is punished, rather than some other man, because he is guilty, and he is guilty because he broke the law (past tense). In his case the law looks back, the judge looks back, the jury looks back, and a penalty is visited upon him for something he did. That a man is to be punished, and what his punishment is to be, is settled by its being shown that he broke the law and that the law assigns that penalty for the violation of it.

On the other hand we have the institution of punishment itself, and recommend and accept various changes in it, because it is thought by the (ideal) legislator and by those to whom the law applies that, as a part of a system of law impartially applied from case to case arising under it, it will have the consequence, in the long run, of furthering the interests of society.

One can say, then, that the judge and the legislator stand in different positions and look in different directions: one to the past, the other to the future. The justification of what the judge does, *qua* judge, sounds like the retributive view; the justification of what the (ideal) legislator does, *qua* legislator, sounds like the utilitarian view. Thus both views have a point (this is as it should be since intelligent and sensitive persons have been on both sides of the argument); and one's initial confusion disappears once one sees that these views apply to persons holding different offices with different duties, and situated differently with respect to the system of rules that make up the criminal law.[5]

One might say, however, that the utilitarian view is more fundamental since it applies to a more fundamental office, for the judge carries out the legislator's will so far as he can determine it. Once the legislator decides to have laws and to assign penalties for their violation (as things are there must be both the law and the penalty) an institution is set up which involves a retributive conception of particular cases. It is part of the concept of the criminal law as a system of rules that the application

[5] Note the fact that different sorts of arguments are suited to different offices. One way of taking the differences between ethical theories is to regard them as accounts of the reasons expected in different offices.

and enforcement of these rules in particular cases should be justifiable by arguments of a retributive character. The decision whether or not to use law rather than some other mechanism of social control, and the decision as to what laws to have and what penalties to assign, may be settled by utilitarian arguments; but if one decides to have laws then one has decided on something whose working in particular cases is retributive in form.[6]

The answer, then, to the confusion engendered by the two views of punishment is quite simple: one distinguishes two offices, that of the judge and that of the legislator, and one distinguishes their different stations with respect to the system of rules which make up the law; and then one notes that the different sorts of considerations which would usually be offered as reasons for what is done under the cover of these offices can be paired off with the competing justifications of punishment. One reconciles the two views by the time-honored device of making them apply to different situations.

But can it really be this simple? Well, this answer allows for the apparent intent of each side. Does a person who advocates the retributive view necessarily advocate, as an *institution*, legal machinery whose essential purpose is to set up and preserve a correspondence between moral turpitude and suffering? Surely not.[7] What retributionists have rightly insisted upon is that no man can be punished unless he is guilty, that is, unless he has broken the law. Their fundamental criticism of the utilitarian account is that, as they interpret it, it sanctions an innocent person's being punished (if one may call it that) for the benefit of society.

On the other hand, utilitarians agree that punishment is to be inflicted only for the violation of law. They regard this much as understood from the concept of punishment itself.[8] The point of

[6] In this connection see Mabbott, *op. cit.*, pp. 163–164.

[7] On this point see Sir David Ross, *The Right and the Good* (Oxford, 1930), pp. 57–60.

[8] See Hobbes's definition of punishment in *Leviathan*, ch. xxviii; and Bentham's definition in *The Principle of Morals and Legislation*, ch. xii, par. 36, ch. xv, par. 28, and in *The Rationale of Punishment*, (London, 1830), bk. I, ch. i. They could agree with Bradley that: "Punishment is punishment only when it is deserved. We pay the penalty, because we owe it, and for no other reason; and if punishment is inflicted for any other reason whatever than because it is

the utilitarian account concerns the institution as a system of rules: utilitarianism seeks to limit its use by declaring it justifiable only if it can be shown to foster effectively the good of society. Historically it is a protest against the indiscriminate and ineffective use of the criminal law.[9] It seeks to dissuade us from assigning to penal institutions the improper, if not sacrilegious, task of matching suffering with moral turpitude. Like others, utilitarians want penal institutions designed so that, as far as humanly possible, only those who break the law run afoul of it. They hold that no official should have discretionary power to inflict penalties whenever he thinks it for the benefit of society; for on utilitarian grounds an institution granting such power could not be justified.[10]

The suggested way of reconciling the retributive and the utilitarian justifications of punishment seems to account for what both sides have wanted to say. There are, however, two further questions which arise, and I shall devote the remainder of this section to them.

First, will not a difference of opinion as to the proper criterion of just law make the proposed reconciliation unacceptable to retributionists? Will they not question whether, if the utilitarian principle is used as the criterion, it follows that those who have broken the law are guilty in a way which satisfies their demand

merited by wrong, it is a gross immorality, a crying injustice, an abominable crime, and not what it pretends to be." *Ethical Studies* (2nd ed.; Oxford, 1927), pp. 26–27. Certainly by definition it isn't what it pretends to be. The innocent can only be punished by mistake; deliberate "punishment" of the innocent necessarily involves fraud.

[9] Cf. Leon Radzinowicz, *A History of English Criminal Law: The Movement for Reform 1750–1833* (London, 1948), esp. ch. xi on Bentham.

[10] Bentham discusses how corresponding to a punitory provision of a criminal law there is another provision which stands to it as an antagonist and which needs a name as much as the punitory. He calls it, as one might expect, the *anaetiosostic*, and of it he says: "The punishment of guilt is the object of the former one: the preservation of innocence that of the latter." In the same connection he asserts that it is never thought fit to give the judge the option of deciding whether a thief (that is, a person whom he believes to be a thief, for the judge's belief is what the question must always turn upon) should hang or not, and so the law writes the provision: "The judge shall not cause a thief to be hanged unless he have been duly convicted and sentenced in course of law" (*The Limits of Jurisprudence Defined*, ed. C. W. Everett [New York, 1945], pp. 238–239).

that those punished deserve to be punished? To answer this difficulty, suppose that the rules of the criminal law are justified on utilitarian grounds (it is only for laws that meet his criterion that the utilitarian can be held responsible). Then it follows that the actions which the criminal law specifies as offenses are such that, if they were tolerated, terror and alarm would spread in society. Consequently, retributionists can only deny that those who are punished deserve to be punished if they deny that such actions are wrong. This they will not want to do.

The second question is whether utilitarianism doesn't justify too much. One pictures it as an engine of justification which, if consistently adopted, could be used to justify cruel and arbitrary institutions. Retributionists may be supposed to concede that utilitarians *intend* to reform the law and to make it more humane; that utilitarians do not *wish* to justify any such thing as punishment of the innocent; and that utilitarians may appeal to the fact that punishment presupposes guilt in the sense that by punishment one understands an institution attaching penalties to the infraction of legal rules, and therefore that it is logically absurd to suppose that utilitarians in justifying *punishment* might also have justified punishment (if we may call it that) of the innocent. The real question, however, is whether the utilitarian, in justifying punishment, hasn't used arguments which commit him to accepting the infliction of suffering on innocent persons if it is for the good of society (whether or not one calls this punishment). More generally, isn't the utilitarian committed in principle to accepting many practices which he, as a morally sensitive person, wouldn't want to accept? Retributionists are inclined to hold that there is no way to stop the utilitarian principle from justifying too much except by adding to it a principle which distributes certain rights to individuals. Then the amended criterion is not the greatest benefit of society *simpliciter*, but the greatest benefit of society subject to the constraint that no one's rights may be violated. Now while I think that the classical utilitarians proposed a criterion of this more complicated sort, I do not want to argue that point here.[11] What I want to show is that

[11] By the classical utilitarians I understand Hobbes, Hume, Bentham, J. S. Mill, and Sidgwick.

there is *another* way of preventing the utilitarian principle from justifying too much, or at least of making it much less likely to do so: namely, by stating utilitarianism in a way which accounts for the distinction between the justification of an institution and the justification of a particular action falling under it.

I begin by defining the institution of punishment as follows: a person is said to suffer punishment whenever he is legally deprived of some of the normal rights of a citizen on the ground that he has violated a rule of law, the violation having been established by trial according to the due process of law, provided that the deprivation is carried out by the recognized legal authorities of the state, that the rule of law clearly specifies both the offense and the attached penalty, that the courts construe statutes strictly, and that the statute was on the books prior to the time of the offense.[12] This definition specifies what I shall understand by punishment. The question is whether utilitarian arguments may be found to justify institutions widely different from this and such as one would find cruel and arbitrary.

This question is best answered, I think, by taking up a particular accusation. Consider the following from Carritt:

> . . . the utilitarian must hold that we are justified in inflicting pain always and only to prevent worse pain or bring about greater happiness. This, then, is all we need to consider in so-called punishment, which must be purely preventive. But if some kind of very cruel crime becomes common, and none of the criminals can be caught, it might be highly expedient, as an example, to hang an innocent man, if a charge against him could be so framed that he were universally thought guilty; indeed this would only fail to be an ideal instance of utilitarian 'punishment' because the victim himself would not have been so likely as a real felon to commit such a crime in the future; in all other respects it would be perfectly deterrent and therefore felicific.[13]

Carritt is trying to show that there are occasions when a utilitarian argument would justify taking an action which would be generally condemned; and thus that utilitarianism justifies too much. But the failure of Carritt's argument lies in the fact that

[12] All these features of punishment are mentioned by Hobbes; cf. *Leviathan*, ch. xxviii.

[13] *Ethical and Political Thinking* (Oxford, 1947), p. 65.

he makes no distinction between the justification of the general system of rules which constitutes penal institutions and the justification of particular applications of these rules to particular cases by the various officials whose job it is to administer them. This becomes perfectly clear when one asks who the "we" are of whom Carritt speaks. Who is this who has a sort of absolute authority on particular occasions to decide that an innocent man shall be "punished" if everyone can be convinced that he is guilty? Is this person the legislator, or the judge, or the body of private citizens, or what? It is utterly crucial to know who is to decide such matters, and by what authority, for all of this must be written into the rules of the institution. Until one knows these things one doesn't know what the institution is whose justification is being challenged; and as the utilitarian principle applies to the institution one doesn't know whether it is justifiable on utilitarian grounds or not.

Once this is understood it is clear what the countermove to Carritt's argument is. One must describe more carefully what the *institution* is which his example suggests, and then ask oneself whether or not it is likely that having this institution would be for the benefit of society in the long run. One must not content oneself with the vague thought that, when it's a question of *this* case, it would be a good thing if *somebody* did something even if an innocent person were to suffer.

Try to imagine, then, an institution (which we may call "telishment") which is such that the officials set up by it have authority to arrange a trial for the condemnation of an innocent man whenever they are of the opinion that doing so would be in the best interests of society. The discretion of officials is limited, however, by the rule that they may not condemn an innocent man to undergo such an ordeal unless there is, at the time, a wave of offenses similar to that with which they charge him and telish him for. We may imagine that the officials having the discretionary authority are the judges of the higher courts in consultation with the chief of police, the minister of justice, and a committee of the legislature.

Once one realizes that one is involved in setting up an *institu-*

tion, one sees that the hazards are very great. For example, what check is there on the officials? How is one to tell whether or not their actions are authorized? How is one to limit the risks involved in allowing such systematic deception? How is one to avoid giving anything short of complete discretion to the authorities to telish anyone they like? In addition to these considerations, it is obvious that people will come to have a very different attitude towards their penal system when telishment is adjoined to it. They will be uncertain as to whether a convicted man has been punished or telished. They will wonder whether or not they should feel sorry for him. They will wonder whether the same fate won't at any time fall on them. If one pictures how such an institution would actually work, and the enormous risks involved in it, it seems clear that it would serve no useful purpose. A utilitarian justification for this institution is most unlikely.

It happens in general that as one drops off the defining features of punishment one ends up with an institution whose utilitarian justification is highly doubtful. One reason for this is that punishment works like a kind of price system: by altering the prices one has to pay for the performance of actions it supplies a motive for avoiding some actions and doing others. The defining features are essential if punishment is to work in this way; so that an institution which lacks these features, e.g., an institution which is set up to "punish" the innocent, is likely to have about as much point as a price system (if one may call it that) where the prices of things change at random from day to day and one learns the price of something after one has agreed to buy it.[14]

---

[14] The analogy with the price system suggests an answer to the question how utilitarian considerations insure that punishment is proportional to the offense. It is interesting to note that Sir David Ross, after making the distinction between justifying a penal law and justifying a particular application of it, and after stating that utilitarian considerations have a large place in determining the former, still holds back from accepting the utilitarian justification of punishment on the grounds that justice requires that punishment be proportional to the offense, and that utilitarianism is unable to account for this. Cf. *The Right and the Good*, pp. 61–62. I do not claim that utilitarianism can account for this requirement as Sir David might wish, but it happens, nevertheless, that if utilitarian considerations are followed penalties will be proportional to offenses in this sense: the order of offenses according to seriousness can be paired off

TWO CONCEPTS OF RULES

If one is careful to apply the utilitarian principle to the institution which is to authorize particular actions, then there is *less* danger of its justifying too much. Carritt's example gains plausibility by its indefiniteness and by its concentration on the particular case. His argument will only hold if it can be shown that there are utilitarian arguments which justify an institution whose publicly ascertainable offices and powers are such as to permit officials to exercise that kind of discretion in particular cases. But the requirement of having to build the arbitrary features of the particular decision into the institutional practice makes the justification much less likely to go through.

II

I shall now consider the question of promises. The objection to utilitarianism in connection with promises seems to be this: it is believed that on the utilitarian view when a person makes a promise the only ground upon which he should keep it, if he should keep it, is that by keeping it he will realize the most good on the whole. So that if one asks the question "Why should I keep *my* promise?" the utilitarian answer is understood to be that doing so in *this* case will have the best consequences. And this answer is said, quite rightly, to conflict with the way in which the obligation to keep promises is regarded.

Now of course critics of utilitarianism are not unaware that one defense sometimes attributed to utilitarians is the consideration involving the practice of promise-keeping.[15] In this connec-

with the order of penalties according to severity. Also the absolute level of penalties will be as low as possible. This follows from the assumption that people are rational (i.e., that they are able to take into account the "prices" the state puts on actions), the utilitarian rule that a penal system should provide a motive for preferring the less serious offense, and the principle that punishment as such is an evil. All this was carefully worked out by Bentham in *The Principles of Morals and Legislation*, chs. xiii–xv.

[15] Ross, *The Right and the Good*, pp. 37–39, and *Foundations of Ethics* (Oxford, 1939), pp. 92–94. I know of no utilitarian who has used this argument except W. A. Pickard-Cambridge in "Two Problems about Duty," *Mind*, n.s., XLI (April, 1932), 153–157, although the argument goes with G. E. Moore's version of utilitarianism in *Principia Ethica* (Cambridge, 1903). To my knowledge it does not appear in the classical utilitarians; and if one interprets their view correctly this is no accident.

tion they are supposed to argue something like this: it must be admitted that we feel strictly about keeping promises, more strictly than it might seem our view can account for. But when we consider the matter carefully it is always necessary to take into account the effect which our action will have on the practice of making promises. The promisor must weigh, not only the effects of breaking his promise on the particular case, but also the effect which his breaking his promise will have on the practice itself. Since the practice is of great utilitarian value, and since breaking one's promise always seriously damages it, one will seldom be justified in breaking one's promise. If we view our individual promises in the wider context of the practice of promising itself we can account for the strictness of the obligation to keep promises. There is always one very strong utilitarian consideration in favor of keeping them, and this will insure that when the question arises as to whether or not to keep a promise it will usually turn out that one should, even where the facts of the particular case taken by itself would seem to justify one's breaking it. In this way the strictness with which we view the obligation to keep promises is accounted for.

Ross has criticized this defense as follows:[16] however great the value of the practice of promising, on utilitarian grounds, there must be some value which is greater, and one can imagine it to be obtainable by breaking a promise. Therefore there might be a case where the promisor could argue that breaking his promise was justified as leading to a better state of affairs on the whole. And the promisor could argue in this way no matter how slight the advantage won by breaking the promise. If one were to challenge the promisor his defense would be that what he did was best on the whole in view of all the utilitarian considerations, which in this case *include* the importance of the practice. Ross feels that such a defense would be unacceptable. I think he is right insofar as he is protesting against the appeal to consequences in general and without further explanation. Yet it is extremely difficult to weigh the force of Ross's argument. The kind of case imagined seems unrealistic and one feels that it needs to be described. One is inclined to think that it would

[16] Ross, *The Right and the Good*, pp. 38–39.

either turn out that such a case came under an exception defined by the practice itself, in which case there would not be an appeal to consequences in general on the particular case, or it would happen that the circumstances were so peculiar that the conditions which the practice presupposes no longer obtained. But certainly Ross is right in thinking that it strikes us as wrong for a person to defend breaking a promise by a general appeal to consequences. For a general utilitarian defense is not open to the promisor: it is not one of the defenses allowed by the practice of making promises.

Ross gives two further counterarguments:[17] First, he holds that it overestimates the damage done to the practice of promising by a failure to keep a promise. One who breaks a promise harms his own name certainly, but it isn't clear that a broken promise always damages the practice itself sufficiently to account for the strictness of the obligation. Second, and more important, I think, he raises the question of what one is to say of a promise which isn't known to have been made except to the promisor and the promisee, as in the case of a promise a son makes to his dying father concerning the handling of the estate.[18] In this sort of case the consideration relating to the practice doesn't weigh on the promisor at all, and yet one feels that this sort of promise is as binding as other promises. The question of the effect which breaking it has on the practice seems irrelevant. The only consequence seems to be that one can break the promise without running any risk of being censured; but the obligation itself seems not the least weakened. Hence it is doubtful whether the effect on the practice ever weighs in the particular case; certainly it cannot account for the strictness of the obligation where

[17] Ross, *ibid.*, p. 39. The case of the nonpublic promise is discussed again in *Foundations of Ethics*, pp. 95–96, 104–105. It occurs also in Mabbott, "Punishment," *op. cit.*, pp. 155–157, and in A. I. Melden, "Two Comments on Utilitarianism," *Philosophical Review*, LX (October, 1951), 519–523, which discusses Carritt's example in *Ethical and Political Thinking*, p. 64.

[18] Ross's example is described simply as that of two men dying alone where one makes a promise to the other. Carritt's example (cf. n. 17 supra) is that of two men at the North Pole. The example in the text is more realistic and is similar to Mabbott's. Another example is that of being told something in confidence by one who subsequently dies. Such cases need not be "desert-island arguments" as Nowell-Smith seems to believe (cf. his *Ethics*, pp. 239–244).

it fails to obtain. It seems to follow that a utilitarian account of the obligation to keep promises cannot be successfully carried out.

From what I have said in connection with punishment, one can foresee what I am going to say about these arguments and counterarguments. They fail to make the distinction between the justification of a practice and the justification of a particular action falling under it, and therefore they fall into the mistake of taking it for granted that the promisor, like Carritt's official, is entitled without restriction to bring utilitarian considerations to bear in deciding whether to keep *his* promise. But if one considers what the practice of promising is one will see, I think, that it is such as not to allow this sort of general discretion to the promisor. Indeed, the point of the practice is to abdicate one's title to act in accordance with utilitarian and prudential considerations in order that the future may be tied down and plans coordinated in advance. There are obvious utilitarian advantages in having a practice which denies to the promisor, as a defense, any general appeal to the utilitarian principle in accordance with which the practice itself may be justified. There is nothing contradictory, or surprising, in this: utilitarian (or aesthetic) reasons might properly be given in arguing that the game of chess, or baseball, is satisfactory just as it is, or in arguing that it should be changed in various respects, but a player in a game cannot properly appeal to such considerations as reasons for his making one move rather than another. It is a mistake to think that if the practice is justified on utilitarian grounds then the promisor must have complete liberty to use utilitarian arguments to decide whether or not to keep his promise. The practice forbids this general defense; and it is a purpose of the practice to do this. Therefore what the above arguments presuppose—the idea that if the utilitarian view is accepted then the promisor is bound if, and only if, the application of the utilitarian principle to his own case shows that keeping it is best on the whole—is false. The promisor is bound because he promised: weighing the case on its merits is not open to him.[19]

---

[19] What I have said in this paragraph seems to me to coincide with Hume's important discussion in the *Treatise of Human Nature*, bk. III, pt. II, sec. 5; and also sec. 6, par. 8.

Is this to say that in particular cases one cannot deliberate whether or not to keep one's promise? Of course not. But to do so is to deliberate whether the various excuses, exceptions and defenses, which are understood by, and which constitute an important part of, the practice, apply to one's own case.[20] Various defenses for not keeping one's promise are allowed, but among them there isn't the one that, on general utilitarian grounds, the promisor (truly) thought his action best on the whole, even though there may be the defense that the consequences of keeping one's promise would have been *extremely* severe. While there are too many complexities here to consider all the necessary details, one can see that the general defense isn't allowed if one asks the following question: what would one say of someone who, when asked why he broke his promise, replied simply that breaking it was best on the whole? Assuming that his reply is sincere, and that his belief was reasonable (i.e., one need not consider the possibility that he was mistaken), I think that one would question whether or not he knows what it means to say "I promise" (in the appropriate circumstances). It would be said of someone who used this excuse without further explanation that he didn't understand what defenses the practice, which defines a promise, allows to him. If a child were to use this excuse one would correct him; for it is part of the way one is taught the concept of a promise to be corrected if one uses this excuse. The point of having the practice would be lost if the practice did allow this excuse.

It is no doubt part of the utilitarian view that every practice should admit the defense that the consequences of abiding by it would have been extremely severe; and utilitarians would be inclined to hold that some reliance on people's good sense and some concession to hard cases is necessary. They would hold that a practice is justified by serving the interests of those who take part in it; and as with any set of rules there is understood a background of circumstances under which it is expected to be applied and which need not—indeed which cannot—be fully stated. Should these circumstances change, then even if

[20] For a discussion of these, see H. Sidgwick, *The Methods of Ethics* (6th ed.; London, 1901), bk. III, ch. vi.

there is no rule which provides for the case, it may still be in accordance with the practice that one be released from one's obligation. But this sort of defense allowed by a practice must not be confused with the general option to weigh each particular case on utilitarian grounds which critics of utilitarianism have thought it necessarily to involve.

The concern which utilitarianism raises by its justification of punishment is that it may justify too much. The question in connection with promises is different: it is how utilitarianism can account for the obligation to keep promises at all. One feels that the recognized obligation to keep one's promise and utilitarianism are incompatible. And to be sure, they are incompatible if one interprets the utilitarian view as necessarily holding that each person has complete liberty to weigh every particular action on general utilitarian grounds. But must one interpret utilitarianism in this way? I hope to show that, in the sorts of cases I have discussed, one cannot interpret it in this way.

III

So far I have tried to show the importance of the distinction between the justification of a practice and the justification of a particular action falling under it by indicating how this distinction might be used to defend utilitarianism against two longstanding objections. One might be tempted to close the discussion at this point by saying that utilitarian considerations should be understood as applying to practices in the first instance and not to particular actions falling under them except insofar as the practices admit of it. One might say that in this modified form it is a better account of our considered moral opinions and let it go at that. But to stop here would be to neglect the interesting question as to how one can fail to appreciate the significance of this rather obvious distinction and can take it for granted that utilitarianism has the consequence that particular cases may always be decided on general utilitarian grounds.[21] I want to

[21] So far as I can see it is not until Moore that the doctrine is expressly stated in this way. See, for example, *Principia Ethica*, p. 147, where it is said that the statement "I am morally bound to perform this action" is identical with the statement "*This* action will produce the greatest possible amount of good in

argue that this mistake may be connected with misconceiving the logical status of the rules of practices; and to show this I am going to examine two conceptions of rules, two ways of placing them within the utilitarian theory.

The conception which conceals from us the significance of the distinction I am going to call the summary view. It regards rules in the following way: one supposes that each person decides what he shall do in particular cases by applying the utilitarian principle; one supposes further that different people will decide the same particular case in the same way and that there will be recurrences of cases similar to those previously decided. Thus it will happen that in cases of certain kinds the same decision will be made either by the same person at different times or by different persons at the same time. If a case occurs frequently enough one supposes that a rule is formulated to cover that sort of case. I have called this conception the summary view because rules are pictured as summaries of past decisions arrived at by the *direct* application of the utilitarian principle to particular cases. Rules are regarded as reports that cases of a certain sort have been found on *other* grounds to be properly decided in a certain way (although, of course, they do not *say* this).

There are several things to notice about this way of placing rules within the utilitarian theory.[22]

the Universe" (my italics). It is important to remember that those whom I have called the classical utilitarians were largely interested in social institutions. They were among the leading economists and political theorists of their day, and they were not infrequently reformers interested in practical affairs. Utilitarianism historically goes together with a coherent view of society, and is not simply an ethical theory, much less an attempt at philosophical analysis in the modern sense. The utilitarian principle was quite naturally thought of, and used, as a criterion for judging social institutions (practices) and as a basis for urging reforms. It is not clear, therefore, how far it is necessary to amend utilitarianism in its classical form. For a discussion of utilitarianism as an integral part of a theory of society, see L. Robbins, *The Theory of Economic Policy in English Classical Political Economy* (London, 1952).

[22] This footnote should be read after sec. 3 and presupposes what I have said there. It provides a few references to statements by leading utilitarians of the summary conception. In general it appears that when they discussed the logical features of rules the summary conception prevailed and that it was typical of the way they talked about moral rules. I cite a rather lengthy group of passages from Austin as a full illustration.

John Austin in his *Lectures on Jurisprudence* meets the objection that deciding in accordance with the utilitarian principle case by case is impractical by saying that this is a misinterpretation of utilitarianism. According to the utilitarian view "... our conduct would conform to *rules* inferred from the tendencies of actions, but would not be determined by a direct resort to the principle of general utility. Utility would be the test of our conduct, ultimately, but not immediately: the immediate test of the rules to which our conduct would conform, but not the immediate test of specific or individual actions. Our rules would be fashioned on utility; our conduct, on our rules" (vol. I, p. 116). As to how one decides on the tendency of an action he says: "If we would try the tendency of a specific or individual act, we must not contemplate the act as if it were single and insulated, but most look at the class of acts to which it belongs. We must suppose that acts of the class were generally done or omitted, and consider the probable effect upon the general happiness or good. We must guess the consequences which would follow, if the class of acts were general; and also the consequences which would follow, if they were generally omitted. We must then compare the consequences on the positive and negative sides, and determine on which of the two the *balance* of advantage lies. . . . If we truly try the tendency of a specific or individual act, we try the tendency of the class to which that act belongs. The *particular* conclusion which we draw, with regard to the single act, implies a *general* conclusion embracing all similar acts. . . . To the rules thus inferred, and lodged in the memory, our conduct would conform *immediately* if it were truly adjusted to utility" (*ibid.*, p. 117). One might think that Austin meets the objection by stating the practice conception of rules; and perhaps he did intend to. But it is not clear that he has stated this conception. Is the generality he refers to of the statistical sort? This is suggested by the notion of tendency. Or does he refer to the utility of setting up a practice? I don't know; but what suggests the summary view is his subsequent remarks. He says: "To consider the specific consequences of single or individual acts, would *seldom* [my italics] consist with that ultimate principle" (*ibid.*, p. 117). But would one ever do this? He continues: ". . . this being admitted, the necessity of pausing and calculating, which the objection in question supposes, is an imagined necessity. To preface each act or forbearance by a conjecture and comparison of consequences, were clearly *superfluous* [my italics] and mischievous. It were clearly superfluous, inasmuch as the *result of that process* [my italics] would be embodied in a known *rule*. It were clearly mischievous, inasmuch as the *true* result would be expressed by that rule, whilst the process would probably be faulty, if it were done on the spur of the occasion" (*ibid.*, pp. 117–118). He goes on: "If our experience and observation of particulars were not *generalized*, our experience and observation of particulars would seldom avail us in *practice*. . . . The inferences suggested to our minds by repeated experience and observation are, therefore, drawn into *principles*, or compressed into *maxims*. These we carry about us ready for use, and apply to individual cases promptly . . . without reverting to the process by which they were obtained; or without recalling, and arraying before our minds, the numerous and intricate considerations of which they are *handy abridgments* [my italics]. . . . True theory is a *compendium* of particular truths. . . . Speaking then, generally, human conduct is inevitably *guided* [my italics] by *rules*, or by *principles* or *maxims*" (*ibid.*, pp. 117–118). I need not trouble to show how all these remarks incline to the summary view. Further, when Austin comes to deal with cases "of comparatively rare occurrence" he holds that specific considerations may outweigh the general. "Looking at the reasons from which we had inferred the rule, it were absurd to think it inflexible. We should therefore dismiss the *rule;* resort directly to the *principle* upon which our rules were fashioned; and calculate *specific* consequences to the best of our knowledge and ability" (*ibid.*, pp. 120–121). Austin's view is interesting because it shows how one may come close to the practice conception and then slide away from it.

In *A System of Logic*, bk. VI, ch. xii, par. 2, Mill distinguishes clearly between the position of judge and legislator and in doing so suggests the distinction between the two concepts of rules. However, he distinguishes the two positions to illustrate the difference between cases where one is to apply a rule already established and cases where one must formulate a rule to govern subsequent conduct. It's the latter case that interests him and he takes the "maxim of policy" of a legislator as typical of rules. In par. 3 the summary conception is very clearly stated. For example, he says of rules of conduct that they should be taken provisionally, as they are made for the most numerous cases. He says that they "point out" the manner in which it is least perilous to act; they serve as an "admonition" that a certain mode of conduct has been found suited to the most common occurrences. In *Utilitarianism*, ch. ii, par. 24, the summary conception appears in Mill's answer to the same objection Austin considered. Here he speaks of rules as "corollaries" from the principle of utility; these "secondary" rules are compared to "landmarks" and "direction-posts." They are based on long experience and so make it unnecessary to apply the utilitarian principle to each case. In par. 25 Mill refers to the task of the utilitarian principle in adjudicating between competing moral rules. He talks here as if one then applies the utilitarian principle directly to the particular case. On the practice view one would rather use the principle to decide which of the ways that make the practice consistent is the best. It should be noted that while in par. 10 Mill's definition of utilitarianism makes the utilitarian principle apply to morality, i.e., to the rules and precepts of human conduct, the definition in par. 2 uses the phrase "actions are right in *proportion* as they *tend* to promote happiness" [my italics] and this inclines towards the summary view. In the last paragraph of the essay "On the Definition of Political Economy," *Westminster Review* (October, 1836), Mill says that it is only in art, as distinguished from science, that one can properly speak of exceptions. In a question of practice, if something is fit to be done "in the majority of cases" then it is made the rule. "We may . . . in talking of art *unobjectionably* speak of the *rule* and the *exception,* meaning by the rule the cases in which there exists a preponderance . . . of inducements for acting in a particular way; and by the exception, the cases in which the preponderance is on the contrary side." These remarks, too, suggest the summary view.

In Moore's *Principia Ethica*, ch. v, there is a complicated and difficult discussion of moral rules. I will not examine it here except to express my suspicion that the summary conception prevails. To be sure, Moore speaks frequently of the utility of rules as generally followed, and of actions as generally practiced, but it is possible that these passages fit the statistical notion of generality which the summary conception allows. This conception is suggested by Moore's taking the utilitarian principle as applying directly to particular actions (pp. 147–148) and by his notion of a rule as something indicating which

1. The point of having rules derives from the fact that similar cases tend to recur and that one can decide cases more quickly if one records past decisions in the form of rules. If similar cases didn't recur, one would be required to apply the utilitarian principle directly, case by case, and rules reporting past decisions would be of no use.

2. The decisions made on particular cases are logically prior to rules. Since rules gain their point from the need to apply the utilitarian principle to many similar cases, it follows that a particular case (or several cases similar to it) may exist whether or not there is a rule covering that case. We are pictured as recognizing particular cases prior to there being a rule which covers them, for it is only if we meet with a number of cases of a certain sort that we formulate a rule. Thus we are able to describe a particular case as a particular case of the requisite sort whether there is a rule regarding *that* sort of case or not. Put another way: what the *A*'s and the *B*'s refer to in rules of the form 'Whenever *A* do *B*' may be described as *A*'s and *B*'s whether or not there is the rule 'Whenever *A* do *B*', or whether or not there is any body of rules which make up a practice of which that rule is a part.

To illustrate this consider a rule, or maxim, which could arise in this way: suppose that a person is trying to decide whether to tell someone who is fatally ill what his illness is when he has been asked to do so. Suppose the person to reflect and then decide, on utilitarian grounds, that he should not answer truthfully; and suppose that on the basis of this and other like occasions he formulates a rule to the effect that when asked by someone fatally ill what his illness is, one should not tell him. The point to notice is that someone's being fatally ill and asking what his illness is, and someone's telling him, are things that can be described as such whether or not there is this rule. The performance of the action to which the rule refers doesn't require the stage-setting of a practice of which this rule is a part. This is

of the few alternatives likely to occur to anyone will generally produce a greater total good in the immediate future (p. 154). He talks of an "ethical law" as a prediction, and as a generalization (pp. 146, 155). The summary conception is also suggested by his discussion of exceptions (pp. 162–163) and of the force of examples of breaching a rule (pp. 163–164).

what is meant by saying that on the summary view particular cases are logically prior to rules.

3. Each person is in principle always entitled to reconsider the correctness of a rule and to question whether or not it is proper to follow it in a particular case. As rules are guides and aids, one may ask whether in past decisions there might not have been a mistake in applying the utilitarian principle to get the rule in question, and wonder whether or not it is best in this case. The reason for rules is that people are not able to apply the utilitarian principle effortlessly and flawlessly; there is need to save time and to post a guide. On this view a society of rational utilitarians would be a society without rules in which each person applied the utilitarian principle directly and smoothly, and without error, case by case. On the other hand, ours is a society in which rules are formulated to serve as aids in reaching these ideally rational decisions on particular cases, guides which have been built up and tested by the experience of generations. If one applies this view to rules, one is interpreting them as maxims, as "rules of thumb"; and it is doubtful that anything to which the summary conception did apply would be called a *rule*. Arguing as if one regarded rules in this way is a mistake one makes while doing philosophy.

4. The concept of a *general* rule takes the following form. One is pictured as estimating on what percentage of the cases likely to arise a given rule may be relied upon to express the correct decision, that is, the decision that would be arrived at if one were to correctly apply the utilitarian principle case by case. If one estimates that by and large the rule will give the correct decision, or if one estimates that the likelihood of making a mistake by applying the utilitarian principle directly on one's own is greater than the likelihood of making a mistake by following the rule, and if these considerations held of persons generally, then one would be justified in urging its adoption as a general rule. In this way *general* rules might be accounted for on the summary view. It will still make sense, however, to speak of applying the utilitarian principle case by case, for it was by trying to foresee the results of doing this that one got the initial estimates upon which acceptance of the rule depends. That one is

taking a rule in accordance with the summary conception will show itself in the naturalness with which one speaks of the rule as a guide, or as a maxim, or as a generalization from experience, and as something to be laid aside in extraordinary cases where there is no assurance that the generalization will hold and the case must therefore be treated on its merits. Thus there goes with this conception the notion of a particular exception which renders a rule suspect on a particular occasion.

The other conception of rules I will call the practice conception. On this view rules are pictured as defining a practice. Practices are set up for various reasons, but one of them is that in many areas of conduct each person's deciding what to do on utilitarian grounds case by case leads to confusion, and that the attempt to coordinate behavior by trying to foresee how others will act is bound to fail. As an alternative one realizes that what is required is the establishment of a practice, the specification of a new form of activity; and from this one sees that a practice necessarily involves the abdication of full liberty to act on utilitarian and prudential grounds. It is the mark of a practice that being taught how to engage in it involves being instructed in the rules which define it, and that appeal is made to those rules to correct the behavior of those engaged in it. Those engaged in a practice recognize the rules as defining it. The rules cannot be taken as simply describing how those engaged in the practice in fact behave: it is not simply that they act as if they were obeying the rules. Thus it is essential to the notion of a practice that the rules are publicly known and understood as definitive; and it is essential also that the rules of a practice can be taught and can be acted upon to yield a coherent practice. On this conception, then, rules are not generalizations from the decisions of individuals applying the utilitarian principle directly and independently to recurrent particular cases. On the contrary, rules define a practice and are themselves the subject of the utilitarian principle.

To show the important differences between this way of fitting rules into the utilitarian theory and the previous way, I shall consider the differences between the two conceptions on the points previously discussed.

TWO CONCEPTS OF RULES

1. In contrast with the summary view, the rules of practices are logically prior to particular cases. This is so because there cannot be a particular case of an action falling under a rule of a practice unless there is the practice. This can be made clearer as follows: in a practice there are rules setting up offices, specifying certain forms of action appropriate to various offices, establishing penalties for the breach of rules, and so on. We may think of the rules of a practice as defining offices, moves, and offenses. Now what is meant by saying that the practice is logically prior to particular cases is this: given any rule which specifies a form of action (a move), a particular action which would be taken as falling under this rule given that there is the practice would not be *described as* that sort of action unless there was the practice. In the case of actions specified by practices it is logically impossible to perform them outside the stage-setting provided by those practices, for unless there is the practice, and unless the requisite proprieties are fulfilled, whatever one does, whatever movements one makes, will fail to count as a form of action which the practice specifies. What one does will be described in some *other* way.

One may illustrate this point from the game of baseball. Many of the actions one performs in a game of baseball one can do by oneself or with others whether there is the game or not. For example, one can throw a ball, run, or swing a peculiarly shaped piece of wood. But one cannot steal base, or strike out, or draw a walk, or make an error, or balk; although one can do certain things which appear to resemble these actions such as sliding into a bag, missing a grounder and so on. Striking out, stealing a base, balking, etc., are all actions which can only happen in a game. No matter what a person did, what he did would not be described as stealing a base or striking out or drawing a walk unless he could also be described as playing baseball, and for him to be doing this presupposes the rule-like practice which constitutes the game. The practice is logically prior to particular cases: unless there is the practice the terms referring to actions specified by it lack a sense.[23]

[23] One might feel that it is a mistake to say that a practice is logically prior to the forms of action it specifies on the grounds that if there were never any

2. The practice view leads to an entirely different conception of the authority which each person has to decide on the propriety of following a rule in particular cases. To engage in a practice, to perform those actions specified by a practice, means to follow the appropriate rules. If one wants to do an action which a certain practice specifies then there is no way to do it except to follow the rules which define it. Therefore, it doesn't make sense for a person to raise the question whether or not a rule of a practice correctly applies to *his* case where the action he contemplates is a form of action defined by a practice. If someone were to raise such a question, he would simply show that he didn't understand the situation in which he was acting. If one wants to perform an action specified by a practice, the only legitimate question concerns the nature of the practice itself ("How do I go about making a will?").

This point is illustrated by the behavior expected of a player in games. If one wants to play a game, one doesn't treat the rules of the game as guides as to what is best in particular cases. In a game of baseball if a batter were to ask "Can I have four strikes?" it would be assumed that he was asking what the rule was; and if, when told what the rule was, he were to say that he meant that on this occasion he thought it would be best on the whole for him to have four strikes rather than three, this would be most kindly taken as a joke. One might contend that baseball would be a better game if four strikes were allowed instead of three; but one cannot picture the rules as guides to what is best on the whole in particular cases, and question their applicability to particular cases as particular cases.

3 and 4. To complete the four points of comparison with the summary conception, it is clear from what has been said that

instances of actions falling under a practice then we should be strongly inclined to say that there wasn't the practice either. Blue-prints for a practice do not make a practice. That there is a practice entails that there are instances of people having been engaged and now being engaged in it (with suitable qualifications). This is correct, but it doesn't hurt the claim that any given particular instance of a form of action specified by a practice presupposes the practice. This isn't so on the summary picture, as each instance must be "there" prior to the rules, so to speak, as something from which one gets the rule by applying the utilitarian principle to it directly.

rules of practices are not guides to help one decide particular cases correctly as judged by some higher ethical principle. And neither the quasi-statistical notion of generality, nor the notion of a particular exception, can apply to the rules of practices. A more or less general rule of a practice must be a rule which according to the structure of the practice applies to more or fewer of the kinds of cases arising under it; or it must be a rule which is more or less basic to the understanding of the practice. Again, a particular case cannot be an exception to a rule of a practice. An exception is rather a qualification or a further specification of the rule.

If follows from what we have said about the practice conception of rules that if a person is engaged in a practice, and if he is asked why *he* does what *he* does, or if he is asked to defend what he does, then his explanation, or defense, lies in referring the questioner to the practice. He cannot say of *his* action, if it is an action specified by a practice, that he does it rather than some other because he thinks it is best on the whole.[24] When a man engaged in a practice is queried about his action he must assume that the questioner either doesn't know that he is engaged in it ("Why are you in a hurry to pay him?" "I promised to pay him today") or doesn't know what the practice is. One doesn't so much justify one's particular action as explain, or show, that it is in accordance with the practice. The reason for this is that it is only against the stage-setting of the practice that one's particular action is described as it is. Only by reference to the practice can one *say* what one is doing. To explain or to defend one's own action, as a particular action, one fits it into the practice which defines it. If this is not accepted it's a sign that a different question is being raised as to whether one is justified in accepting the practice, or in tolerating it. When the challenge is to the practice, citing the rules (saying what the practice is) is naturally to no avail. But when the challenge is to the particular action defined by the practice, there is nothing one can do but refer to the rules. Concerning particular actions

[24] A philosophical joke (in the mouth of Jeremy Bentham): "When I run to the other wicket after my partner has struck a good ball I do so because it is best on the whole."

there is only a question for one who isn't clear as to what the practice is, or who doesn't know that it is being engaged in. This is to be contrasted with the case of a maxim which may be taken as pointing to the correct decision on the case as decided on *other* grounds, and so giving a challenge on the case a sense by having it question whether these other grounds really support the decision on this case.

If one compares the two conceptions of rules I have discussed, one can see how the summary conception misses the significance of the distinction between justifying a practice and justifying actions falling under it. On this view rules are regarded as guides whose purpose it is to indicate the ideally rational decision on the given particular case which the flawless application of the utilitarian principle would yield. One has, in principle, full option to use the guides or to discard them as the situation warrants without one's moral office being altered in any way: whether one discards the rules or not, one always holds the office of a rational person seeking case by case to realize the best on the whole. But on the practice conception, if one holds an office defined by a practice then questions regarding one's actions in this office are settled by reference to the rules which define the practice. If one seeks to question these rules, then one's office undergoes a fundamental change: one then assumes the office of one empowered to change and criticize the rules, or the office of a reformer, and so on. The summary conception does away with the distinction of offices and the various forms of argument appropriate to each. On that conception there is one office and so no offices at all. It therefore obscures the fact that the utilitarian principle must, in the case of actions and offices defined by a practice, apply to the practice, so that general utilitarian arguments are not available to those who act in offices so defined.[25]

[25] How do these remarks apply to the case of the promise known only to father and son? Well, at first sight the son certainly holds the office of promisor, and so he isn't allowed by the practice to weigh the particular case on general utilitarian grounds. Suppose instead that he wishes to consider himself in the office of one empowered to criticize and change the practice, leaving aside the question as to his right to move from his previously assumed office to another. Then he may consider utilitarian arguments as applied to the practice; but

TWO CONCEPTS OF RULES

Some qualifications are necessary in what I have said. First, I may have talked of the summary and the practice conceptions of rules as if only one of them could be true of rules, and if true of any rules, then necessarily true of *all* rules. I do not, of course, mean this. (It is the critics of utilitarianism who make this mistake insofar as their arguments against utilitarianism presuppose a summary conception of the rules of practices.) Some rules will fit one conception, some rules the other; and so there are rules of practices (rules in the strict sense), and maxims and "rules of thumb."

Secondly, there are further distinctions that can be made in classifying rules, distinctions which should be made if one were considering other questions. The distinctions which I have drawn are those most relevant for the rather special matter I have discussed, and are not intended to be exhaustive.

Finally, there will be many border-line cases about which it will be difficult, if not impossible, to decide which conception of rules is applicable. One expects border-line cases with any concept, and they are especially likely in connection with such involved concepts as those of a practice, institution, game, rule, and so on. Wittgenstein has shown how fluid these notions are.[26] What I have done is to emphasize and sharpen two conceptions for the limited purpose of this paper.

IV

What I have tried to show by distinguishing between two conceptions of rules is that there is a way of regarding rules which allows the option to consider particular cases on general utilitarian grounds; whereas there is another conception which does not admit of such discretion except insofar as the rules themselves authorize it. I want to suggest that the tendency while doing philosophy to picture rules in accordance with the sum-

once he does this he will see that there are such arguments for not allowing a general utilitarian defense in the practice for this sort of case. For to do so would make it impossible to ask for and to give a kind of promise which one often wants to be able to ask for and to give. Therefore he will not want to change the practice, and so as a promisor he has no option but to keep his promise.

[26] *Philosophical Investigations* (Oxford, 1953), I, pars. 65–71, for example.

mary conception is what may have blinded moral philosophers to the significance of the distinction between justifying a practice and justifying a particular action falling under it; and it does so by misrepresenting the logical force of the reference to the rules in the case of a challenge to a particular action falling under a practice, and by obscuring the fact that where there is a practice, it is the practice itself that must be the subject of the utilitarian principle.

It is surely no accident that two of the traditional test cases of utilitarianism, punishment and promises, are clear cases of practices. Under the influence of the summary conception it is natural to suppose that the officials of a penal system, and one who has made a promise, may decide what to do in particular cases on utilitarian grounds. One fails to see that a general discretion to decide particular cases on utilitarian grounds is incompatible with the concept of a practice; and that what discretion one does have is itself defined by the practice (e.g., a judge may have discretion to determine the penalty within certain limits). The traditional objections to utilitarianism which I have discussed presuppose the attribution to judges, and to those who have made promises, of a plenitude of moral authority to decide particular cases on utilitarian grounds. But once one fits utilitarianism together with the notion of a practice, and notes that punishment and promising are practices, then one sees that this attribution is logically precluded.

That punishment and promising are practices is beyond question. In the case of promising this is shown by the fact that the form of words "I promise" is a performative utterance which presupposes the stage-setting of the practice and the proprieties defined by it. Saying the words "I promise" will only be promising given the existence of the practice. It would be absurd to interpret the rules about promising in accordance with the summary conception. It is absurd to say, for example, that the rule that promises should be kept could have arisen from its being found in past cases to be best on the whole to keep one's promise; for unless there were already the understanding that one keeps one's promises as part of the practice itself there couldn't have been any cases of promising.

It must, of course, be granted that the rules defining promising are not codified, and that one's conception of what they are necessarily depends on one's moral training. Therefore it is likely that there is considerable variation in the way people understand the practice, and room for argument as to how it is best set up. For example, differences as to how strictly various defenses are to be taken, or just what defenses are available, are likely to arise amongst persons with different backgrounds. But irrespective of these variations it belongs to the concept of the practice of promising that the general utilitarian defense is not available to the promisor. That this is so accounts for the force of the traditional objection which I have discussed. And the point I wish to make is that when one fits the utilitarian view together with the practice conception of rules, as one must in the appropriate cases, then there is nothing in that view which entails that there must be such a defense, either in the practice of promising, or in any other practice.

Punishment is also a clear case. There are many actions in the sequence of events which constitute someone's being punished which presuppose a practice. One can see this by considering the definition of punishment which I gave when discussing Carritt's criticism of utilitarianism. The definition there stated refers to such things as the normal rights of a citizen, rules of law, due process of law, trials and courts of law, statutes, etc., none of which can exist outside the elaborate stage-setting of a legal system. It is also the case that many of the actions for which people are punished presuppose practices. For example, one is punished for stealing, for trespassing, and the like, which presuppose the institution of property. It is impossible to say what punishment is, or to describe a particular instance of it, without referring to offices, actions, and offenses specified by practices. Punishment is a move in an elaborate legal game and presupposes the complex of practices which make up the legal order. The same thing is true of the less formal sorts of punishment: a parent or guardian or someone in proper authority may punish a child, but no one else can.

There is one mistaken interpretation of what I have been saying which it is worthwhile to warn against. One might think that the use I am making of the distinction between justifying a practice and justifying the particular actions falling under it involves one in a definite social and political attitude in that it leads to a kind of conservatism. It might seem that I am saying that for each person the social practices of his society provide the standard of justification for his actions; therefore let each person abide by them and his conduct will be justified.

This interpretation is entirely wrong. The point I have been making is rather a logical point. To be sure, it has consequences in matters of ethical theory; but in itself it leads to no particular social or political attitude. It is simply that where a form of action is specified by a practice there is no justification possible of the particular action of a particular person save by reference to the practice. In such cases the action is what it is in virtue of the practice and to explain it is to refer to the practice. There is no inference whatsoever to be drawn with respect to whether or not one should accept the practices of one's society. One can be as radical as one likes but in the case of actions specified by practices the objects of one's radicalism must be the social practices and people's acceptance of them.

I have tried to show that when we fit the utilitarian view together with the practice conception of rules, where this conception is appropriate,[27] we can formulate it in a way which saves it from several traditional objections. I have further tried to show how the logical force of the distinction between justifying a practice and justifying an action falling under it is connected with the practice conception of rules and cannot be understood as long as one regards the rules of practices in accordance with the summary view. Why, when doing philosophy, one may be inclined to so regard them, I have not discussed. The reasons for this are evidently very deep and would require another paper.

Cornell University JOHN RAWLS

[27] As I have already stated, it is not always easy to say where the conception is appropriate. Nor do I care to discuss at this point the general sorts of cases to which it does apply except to say that one should not take it for granted that it applies to many so-called "moral rules." It is my feeling that relatively few actions of the moral life are defined by practices and that the practice conception is more relevant to understanding legal and legal-like arguments than it is to the more complex sort of moral arguments. Utilitarianism must be fitted to different conceptions of rules depending on the case, and no doubt the failure to do this has been one source of difficulty in interpreting it correctly.

[2]

*Rights, Goals, and Fairness**

T. M. SCANLON

Critics of utilitarianism frequently call attention to the abhorrent policies that unrestricted aggregative reasoning might justify under certain possible, or even actual, circumstances. They invite the conclusion that to do justice to the firm intuition that such horrors are clearly unjustifiable one must adopt a deontological moral framework that places limits on what appeals to maximum aggregate well-being can justify. As one who has often argued in this way, however, I am compelled to recognize that this position has its own weaknesses. In attacking utilitarianism one is inclined to appeal to individual rights, which mere considerations of social utility cannot justify us in overriding. But rights themselves need to be justified somehow, and how other than by appeal to the human interests their recognition promotes and protects? This seems to be the uncontrovertible insight of the classical utilitarians. Further, unless rights are to be taken as defined by rather implausible rigid formulae, it seems that we must invoke what looks very much like the consideration of consequences in order to determine what they rule out and what they allow. Thus, for example, in order to determine whether a given policy violates the right of freedom of expression it is not enough to know merely that it restricts speech. We may need to consider also its effects: how it would affect access to the means of expression and what the consequences would be of granting to government the kind of regulatory powers it confers.

* The original version of this paper was presented at the Reisensberg Conference on Decision Theory and Social Ethics and appeared in an issue of *Erkenntnis* devoted to papers from that conference. This revised version is used with the permission of the editors of that journal and D. Reidel & Co. I am indebted to a number of people for critical comments and helpful discussion, particularly to Ronald Dworkin, Derek Parfit, Gilbert Harman, Samuel Scheffler, and Milton Wachsberg. Work on this paper was supported in part by a fellowship from the National Endowment for the Humanities.

I am thus drawn toward a two-tier view: one that gives an important role to consequences in the justification and interpretation of rights but which takes rights seriously as placing limits on consequentialist reasoning at the level of casuistry. Such a view looks like what has been called rule utilitarianism, a theory subject to a number of very serious objections. First, rule utilitarians are hard pressed to explain why, if at base they are convinced utilitarians, they are not thoroughgoing ones. How can they square their utilitarianism with the acceptance of individual actions that are not in accord with the utilitarian formula? Second, rule utilitarianism seems to be open to some of the same objections leveled against utilitarianism in its pure form; in particular it seems no more able than act utilitarianism is to give a satisfactory place to considerations of distributive justice. Third, in attempting to specify which rules it is that are to be applied in the appraisal of acts and policies rule utilitarians of the usual sort are faced with an acute dilemma. If it is some set of ideal rules that are to be applied – those rules general conformity to which would have the best consequences – then the utilitarian case for a concern with rules, rather than merely with the consequences of isolated acts, appears lost. For this case must rest on benefits that flow from the general observance of rules but not from each individual act, and such benefits can be gained only if the rules are in fact generally observed. But if, on the other hand, the rules that are to be applied must be ones that are generally observed, the critical force of the theory seems to be greatly weakened.

The problem, then, is to explain how a theory can have, at least in part, a two-tier structure; how it can retain the basic appeal of utilitarianism, at least as it applies to the foundation of rights, and yet avoid the problems that have plagued traditional rule utilitarianism. As a start towards describing such a theory I will consider three questions. (1) What consequences are to be considered, and how is their value to be determined? (2) How do considerations of distributive justice enter the theory? (3) How does one justify taking rights (or various moral rules) as constraints on the production of valued consequences?

1. Consequences and their values

Here I have two remarks, one of foundation, the other of content. First, as I have argued elsewhere[1] but can here only assert, I depart from the classical utilitarians and many of their modern followers in rejecting subjective preferences as the basis for the valuation of outcomes. This role is to be played instead by an ethically significant, objective notion of the relative importance of various benefits and burdens.

Second, as to content, the benefits and burdens with which the theory is concerned must include not only the things that may happen to people but also factors affecting the ability of individuals to determine what will happen. Some of these factors are the concern of what are generally called rights, commonly[2] distinguished into (claim-) rights to command particular things, where others have a correlative duty to comply; liberties to do or refrain from certain things, where others have no such correlative duties; powers to change people's rights or status; and immunities from powers exercised by others. I take it to be the case that the familiar civil rights, as well as such things as rights of privacy and 'the right to life', are complexes of such elements. The de facto ability effectively to choose among certain options and the de facto absence of interference by others with one's choices are not the same thing as rights, although if it is generally believed that a person has a particular right, say a claim-right, this may contribute to his having such de facto ability or lack of interference. But, however they are created, such abilities and protections are important goods with which any moral theory must be concerned, and the allocation of rights is one way in which this importance receives theoretical recognition.

Any theory of right, since it deals with what agents should and may do, is in a broad sense concerned with the assignment of rights

[1] In 'Preference and Urgency', *The Journal of Philosophy* 72 (1975), pp. 655–70.

[2] Following Hohfeld and others. See W. N. Hohfeld, *Fundamental Legal Conceptions* (New Haven, 1923), and also Stig Kanger, 'New Foundations for Ethical Theory' in Risto Hilpinen, ed., *Deontic Logic: Introductory and Systematic Readings* (Dordrecht, 1971), pp. 36–58. On the distinction between concern with outcomes and concern with the allocation of competences to determine outcomes see Charles Fried, 'Two Concepts of Interests: Some Reflections of the Supreme Court's Balancing Test', *The Harvard Law Review* 76 (1963), p. 755–78.

and liberties. It is relevant to ask, concerning such a theory, how much latitude it gives a person in satisfying moral requirements and how much protection it gives a person through the constraints it places on the actions of others. Traditional utilitarianism has been seen as extreme on both these counts. It is maximally specific in the requirements it imposes on an agent, and, since there are no limits to what it may require to be done, it provides a minimum of reliable protection from interference by others. Objections to utilitarianism have often focused on its demanding and intrusive character,[3] and other theories of right may grant individuals both greater discretion and better protection. But these are goods with costs. When one individual is given a claim-right or liberty with respect to a certain option, the control that others are able to exercise over their own options is to some degree diminished. Further, if we take the assignment of rights to various individuals as, in at least some cases, an end-point of justification, then we must be prepared to accept the situation resulting from their exercise of these rights even if, considered in itself, it may be unattractive or at least not optimal. Both these points have been urged by Robert Nozick,[4] the latter especially in his attack on 'end-state' and 'patterned' theories. What follows from these observations, however, is not Nozick's particular theory of entitlements but rather a general moral about the kind of comparison and balancing that a justification of rights requires: the abilities and protections that rights confer must be assigned values that are comparable not only with competing values of the same kind but also with the values attached to the production of particular end-results.

The same moral is to be drawn from some of Bernard Williams' objections to utilitarianism.[5] Williams objects that utilitarianism, in demanding total devotion to the inclusive goal of maximum happiness, fails to give adequate recognition to the importance, for each individual, of the particular projects which give his life content. The problem with such an objection is that taken alone

[3] See Bernard Williams, 'A Critique of Utilitarianism', in J. J. C. Smart and B. Williams, *Utilitarianism: For and Against* (Cambridge, 1973).

[4] In *Anarchy, State and Utopia* (New York, 1974), esp. pp. 32–35 and Chapter 7.

[5] In Sec. 5 of 'A Critique of Utilitarisnism'.

it may be made to sound like pure self-indulgence. Simply to demand freedom from moral requirements in the name of freedom to pursue one's individual projects is unconvincing. It neglects the fact that these requirements may protect interests of others that are at least as important as one's own. To rise clearly above the level of special pleading these objections must be made general. They must base themselves on a general claim about how important the interests they seek to protect are for any person as compared with the interests served by conflicting claims.

The two preceding remarks – of foundation and of content – are related in the following way. Since the ability to influence outcomes and protection from interference or control by others are things people care about, they will be taken into account in any subjective utilitarian theory. I will later raise doubts as to whether such a theory can take account of them in the right way, but my present concern is with the question what value is to be assigned to these concerns. On a subjective theory these values will be determined by the existing individual preferences in the society in question. I would maintain, however, that prevailing preferences are not an adequate basis for the justification of rights. It is not relevant, for example, to the determination of rights of religious freedom that the majority group in a society is feverishly committed to the goal of making its practices universal while the minority is quite tepid about all matters of religion. This is of course just an instance of the general objection to subjective theories stated above. The equally general response is that one has no basis on which to 'impose' values that run contrary to individual preferences. This objection draws its force from the idea that individual autonomy ought to be respected and that it is offensive to frustrate an individual's considered preferences in the name of serving his 'true interests'. This idea does not itself rest on preferences. Rather, it functions as the objective moral basis for giving preferences a fundamental role as the ground of ethically relevant valuations. But one may question whether this theoretical move is an adequate response to the intuitive idea from which it springs. To be concerned with individual autonomy is to be concerned with the rights, liberties and other conditions necessary for individuals to develop their own aims and interests and to make their preferences effective in shaping their own lives and contributing to the formation of social policy. Among these will be rights protecting people against various forms of paternalistic intervention. A theory that respects autonomy will be one that assigns all of these factors their proper weight. There is no reason to think that this will be accomplished merely by allowing these weights, and all others, to be determined by the existing configuration of preferences.

2. Fairness and equality

Rather than speaking generally of 'distributive justice', which can encompass a great variety of considerations, I will speak instead of fairness, as a property of processes (e.g. of competitions), and equality, as a property of resultant distributions. The question is how these considerations enter a theory of the kind I am describing. One way in which a notion of equality can be built into a consequentialist theory is through the requirement that, in evaluating states of affairs to be promoted, we give equal consideration to the interests of every person. This principle of equal consideration of interests has minimal egalitarian content. As stated, it is compatible with classical utilitarianism which, after all, 'counts each for one and none for more than one'. Yet many have felt, with justification, that utilitarianism gives insufficient weight to distributive considerations. How might this weight be increased? Let me distinguish two ways. The first would be to strengthen the principle of equal consideration of interests in such a way as to make it incompatible with pure utilitarianism. 'Equal consideration' could, for example, be held to mean that in any justification by appeal to consequences we must give priority to those individual interests that are 'most urgent'. To neglect such interests in order to serve instead less urgent interests even of a greater number of people would, on this interpretation, violate 'equality of consideration'. Adoption of this interpretation would ward off some objections to utilitarianism based on its insensitivity to distributive considerations but would at the same time preserve other characteristic features of the doctrine, e.g. some of its radically redistributive implications. Such a 'lexical interpretation' has, of course, its own problems. Its strength (and plausibility) is obviously dependent on the ranking we choose for determining the urgency of various interests.

The nature of such a ranking is an important problem, but one I cannot pursue here. Whatever the degree of distributive content that is built into the way individual interests are reckoned in moral argument, however, there is a second way in which distributive considerations enter a theory of the kind I wish to propose: equality of distributions and fairness of processes are among the properties that make states of affairs worth promoting. Equality in the distribution of particular classes of goods is at least sometimes of value as a means to the attainment of other valued ends, and in other cases fairness and equality are valuable in their own right.

Classical utilitarianism, of course, already counts equality as a means, namely as a means to maximum aggregate utility. Taken alone, this seems inadequate – too instrumental to account for the moral importance equality has for us. Yet I do think that in many of the cases in which we are most concerned with the promotion of equality we desire greater equality as a means to the attainment of some further end. In many cases, for example, the desire to eliminate great inequalities is motivated primarily by humanitarian concern for the plight of those who have least. Redistribution is desirable in large part because it is a means of alleviating their suffering (without giving rise to comparable suffering elsewhere). A second source of moral concern with redistribution in the contemporary world lies in the fact that great inequalities in wealth give to those who have more an unacceptable degree of control over the lives of others. Here again the case for greater equality is instrumental. Were these two grounds for redistribution to be eliminated (by, say, greatly increasing the standard of living of all concerned and preventing the gap between rich and poor, which remains unchanged, from allowing the rich to dominate) the moral case for equality would not be eliminated, but I believe that it would seem less pressing.

Beyond these and other instrumental arguments, fairness and equality often figure in moral argument as independently valuable states of affairs. So considered, they differ from the ends promoted in standard utilitarian theories in that their value does not rest on their being good things *for* particular individuals: fairness and equality do not represent ways in which individuals may be ***better off***.[6] They are, rather, special morally desirable features of states of affairs or of social institutions. In admitting such moral features into the evaluation of consequences, the theory I am describing departs from standard consequentialist theories, which generally resist the introduction of explicitly moral considerations into the maximand. It diverges also from recent deontological theories, which bring in fairness and equality as specific moral requirements rather than as moral goals. I am inclined to pursue this 'third way' for several reasons.

First, it is not easy to come up with a moral argument for substantive equality (as distinct from mere formal equality or equal consideration of interests) which makes it look like an absolute moral requirement. Second, considerations of fairness and equality are multiple. There are many different processes that may be more or less fair, and we are concerned with equality in the distribution of many different and separable benefits and burdens. These are not all of equal importance; the strength of claims of equality and fairness depends on the goods whose distribution is at issue. Third, these claims do not seem to be absolute. Attempts to achieve equality or fairness in one area may conflict with the pursuit of these goals in other areas. In order to achieve greater equality we may, for example, change our processes in ways that involve unfairness in the handling of some individual cases. Perhaps the various forms of fairness and equality can be brought together under one all-encompassing notion of distributive justice which is always to be increased, but it is not obvious that this is so. In any event, it would remain the case that attempts to increase fairness and equality can have costs in other terms; they may interfere with processes whose efficiency is important to us, or involve unwelcome intrusions into individuals' lives. In such cases of conflict it does not seem that considerations of fairness and equality, as such, are always dominant. An increase in equality may in some cases not be worth its cost; whether it is will depend in part on what it is equality *of*.

[6] Here I am indebted to Kurt Baier. Defending the claim that fairness and equality are intrinsically valuable is of course a further difficult task. Perhaps all convincing appeals to these notions can be reduced to instrumental arguments, but I do not at present see how. Such a reduction would move my theory even closer to traditional utilitarianism.

Economists often speak of 'trade-offs' between equality and other concerns (usually efficiency). I have in the past been inclined, perhaps intolerantly, to regard this as crassness, but I am no longer certain that it is in principle mistaken. The suggestion that equality can be 'traded-off' against other goods arouses suspicion because it seems to pave the way for defenses of the status quo. Measures designed to decrease inequality in present societies are often opposed on the ground that they involve too great a sacrifice in efficiency or in individual liberty, and one way to head off such objections is to hold that equality is to be pursued whatever the cost. But one can hold that appeals to liberty and efficiency do not justify maintaining the status quo – and in fact that considerations of individual liberty provide some of the strongest arguments in favor of increased equality of income and wealth – without holding that considerations of equality are, as such, absolute and take priority over all other values.

3. *Rights*

Why give rights a special place in a basically consequentialist theory? How can a two-tier theory be justified? One common view of the place of rights, and moral rules generally, within utilitarianism holds that they are useful as means to the coordination of action. The need for such aids does not depend on imperfect motivation; it might exist even in a society of perfect altruists. A standard example is a rule regulating water consumption during a drought. A restriction to one bucket a day per household might be a useful norm for a society of utilitarians even though their reasons for taking more water than this would be entirely altruistic. Its usefulness does not depend on self-interest. But the value of such a rule does depend on the fact that the agents are assumed to act independently of one another in partial ignorance of what the others have done or will do. If Dudley knows what others will do, and knows that this will leave some water in the well, then there is no utilitarian reason why he should not violate the rule and take more than his share for some suitable purpose – as the story goes, to water the flowers in the public garden.

I am of two minds about such examples. On the one hand, I can feel the force of the utilitarian's insistence that if the water is not going to be used how can we object to Dudley's taking it? On the other hand, I do not find this line of reply wholly satisfying. Why should *he* be entitled to do what others were not? Well, because he knows and they didn't; he alone has the opportunity. But just because he has it does that mean he can exercise it unilaterally? Perhaps, to be unbearably priggish, he should call the surplus to the attention of the others so that they can all decide how to use it. If this alternative is available is it all right for him to pass it up and act on his own? A utilitarian might respond here that he is not saying that Dudley is entitled to do whatever he wishes with the surplus water; he is entitled to do with it what the principle of utility requires and nothing else.

Here a difference of view is shown. Permission to act outside the rule is seen by the non-utilitarian as a kind of freedom for the agent, an exemption, but it is seen by a utilitarian as a specific moral requirement. Dudley is required to do something that is different from what the others do because his situation is different, but he has no greater latitude for the exercise of discretion or personal preference than anyone else does. This suggests that one can look at an assignment of rights in either of two ways: as a way of constraining individual decisions in order to promote some desired further effect (as in the case of a system of rules defining a division of labor between co-workers) or as a way of parceling out valued forms of discretion over which individuals are in conflict. To be avoided, I think, is a narrow utilitarianism that construes all rights on the first model, e.g. as mechanisms of coordination or as hedges against individual errors in judgment. So construed, rights have no weight against deviant actions that can be shown to be the most effective way of advancing the shared goal.

If, however, the possibility of construing some rights on the second model is kept open, then rights can be given a more substantial role within a theory that is still broadly utilitarian. When, as seems plausible on one view of the water-shortage example, the purpose of an assignment of rights is to ensure an equitable distribution of a form of control over outcomes, then these rights are supported by considerations which persist even when contrary actions would promote optimum results. This could remain true for a society of conscientious (though perhaps not single-minded) consequentialists, provided that they are concerned with 'consequences' of the sort I have described above. But to say that a rule or a right is not in general subject to exceptions justified on act-utilitarian grounds is not to say that it is absolute. One can ask how important it is to preserve an equitable distribution of control of the kind in question, and there will undoubtedly be some things that outweigh this value. There is no point in observing the one-bucket restriction when the pump-house is on fire. Further, the intent of an assignment of rights on the second model is apt to be to forestall certain particularly tempting or likely patterns of behavior. If this is so, there may be some acts which are literally contrary to the formula in which the right is usually stated but which do not strike us as actual violations of the right. We are inclined to allow them even though the purposes they serve may be less important than the values the right is intended to secure. Restrictions on speech which nonetheless are not violations of freedom of expression are a good example of such 'apparent exceptions'.

Reflections of this kind suggest to me that the view that there is a moral right of a certain sort is generally backed by something like the following:

(i) An empirical claim about how individuals would behave or how institutions would work in the absence of this particular assignment of rights (claim-rights, liberties, etc.).

(ii) A claim that this result would be unacceptable. This claim will be based on valuation of consequences of the sort described in section 1 above, taking into account also considerations of fairness and equality.

(iii) A further empirical claim about how the envisaged assignment of rights will produce a different outcome.

The empirical parts of this schema play a larger or at least more conspicuous role in some rights than in others. In the case of the right to freedom of expression this role is a large one and fairly well recognized. Neglecting this empirical element leads rights to degenerate into implausible rigid formulae. The impossibility of taking such a formula literally, as defining an absolute moral bar, lends plausibility to a 'balancing' view, according to which such a right merely represents one important value among others, and decisions must be reached by striking the proper balance between them. Keeping in mind the empirical basis of a right counters this tendency and provides a ground (1) for seeing that 'apparent exceptions' of the kind mentioned above are not justified simply by balancing one right against another; (2) for seeing where genuine balancing of interests is called for and what its proper terms are; and (3) for seeing how the content of a right must change as conditions change. These remarks hold, I think, not only for freedom of expression but also for other rights, for example, rights of due process and rights of privacy. In each of these cases a fairly complex set of institutional arrangements and assumptions about how these arrangements operate stands, so to speak, between the formula through which the right is identified and the goals to which it is addressed. This dependence on empirical considerations is less evident in the case of rights, like the right to life, that lie more in the domain of individual morality. I will argue below, however, that this right too can profitably be seen as a system of authorizations and limitations of discretion justified on the basis of an argument of the form just described.

This view of rights is in a broad sense consequentialist in that it holds rights to be justified by appeal to the states of affairs they promote. It seems to differ from the usual forms of rule utilitarianism, however, in that it does not appear to be a maximizing doctrine. The case for most familiar rights – freedom of expression, due process, religious toleration – seems to be more concerned with the avoidance of particular bad consequences than with promoting maximum benefit. But this difference is in part only apparent. The dangers that these rights are supposed to ward off are major ones, not likely to be overshadowed by everyday considerations. Where they are overshadowed, the theory I have described allows for the rights in question to be set aside. Further, the justification for the particular form that such a right takes allows for the consideration of costs. If a revised form of some right would do the intended job as well as the standard form at clearly reduced costs to peripheral interests, then this form would obviously be preferred. It should be noted, however, that if something is being maximized here it can not, in view of the role that the goals of fairness and equality play in the theory, be simply the sum of individual benefits. Moreover, this recognition of an element of maximization does not mean that just any possible improvement in the way people generally behave will become the subject of a right. Rights concern the alleviation of certain major problems, and incremental gains in other goods become relevant to rights in the way just mentioned only when they flow from improvements in our ways of dealing with such problems.

I have suggested that the case for rights derives in large part from the goal of promoting an acceptable distribution of control over important factors in our lives. This general goal is one that would be of importance to people in a wide range of societies. But the particular rights it calls for may vary from society to society. Thus, in particular, the rights we have on the view I have proposed are probably not identical with the rights that would be recognized under the system of rules, general conformity to which in our society would have the best consequences. The problems to which our rights are addressed are ones that arise given the distribution of power and the prevailing patterns of motivation in the societies in which we live. These problems may not be ones that would arise were an ideal code of behaviour to prevail.[7] (And they might not be the same either as those we would face in a 'state of nature'.) Concern with rights does not involve accepting these background conditions as desirable or as morally unimpeachable; it only involves seeing them as relatively fixed features of the environment with which we must deal.

[7] How much this separates my view of rights from an ideal rule utilitarian theory will depend on how that theory construes the notion of an ideal system of rules being 'in force' in a society. In Brandt's sophisticated version, for example, what is required is that it be true, and known in the society, that a high proportion of adults subscribe to these rules, that is, chiefly, that they are to some extent motivated to avoid violating the rules and feel guilty when they believe they have do so. ('Some Merits of One Form of Rule Utilitarianism' in Gorovitz, ed., *Mill: Utilitarianism, with Critical Essays* [Indianapolis, Ind., 1971].) This may not insure that the level of conformity with these rules is much greater than the level of moral behavior in societies we are familiar with. If it does not, then Brandt's theory may not be much more 'ideal' than the theory of rights offered here. The two theories appear to differ, however, on the issues discussed in sections 1 and 2 above. These issues also divide my view from R. M. Hare's version of rule utilitarianism, with which I am otherwise in much agreement. See his 'Ethical Theory and Utilitarianism', in H. D. Lewis, ed., *Contemporary British Philosophy, Fourth Series* (London, 1976). Like these more general theories, the account of rights offered here has a great deal in common with the view put forward by Mill in the final chapter of *Utilitarianism* (particularly if Mill's remarks about 'justice' are set aside).

Which features of one's society are to be held fixed in this way for purposes of moral argument about rights? This can be a controversial moral question and presents a difficult theoretical issue for anyone holding a view like rule utilitarianism. As more and more is held fixed, including more about what other agents are in fact doing, the view converges toward act utilitarianism. If, on the other hand, very little is held fixed then the problems of ideal forms of rule utilitarianism seem to loom larger: we seem to risk demanding individual observance of rights when this is pointless given the lack of general conformity.

This dilemma is most acute to the degree that the case for rights (or moral rules) is seen to rest on their role in promoting maximum utility through the coordination of individual action. Where this is actually the case – as it is with many rules and perhaps some rights – it is of undoubted importance what others are in fact doing – to what degree these rights and rules are generally observed and how individual action will affect general observance. I suggest, however, that this is not the case with most rights. On the view I propose, a central concern of most rights is the promotion and maintenance of an acceptable distribution of control over important factors in our lives. Where a certain curtailment of individual discretion or official authority is clearly required for this purpose, the fact that this right is not generally observed does not undermine the case for its observance in a given instance. The case against allowing some to dictate the private religious observances of others, for example, does not depend on the existence of a general practice of religious toleration. Some of the benefits at which rights of religious freedom are aimed – the benefits of a general climate of religious toleration – are secured only when there is general compliance with these rights. But the case for enforcing these rights does not depend in every instance on these benefits.

For these reasons, the view of rights I have proposed is not prey to objections often raised against ideal rule utilitarian theories. A further question is whether it is genuinely distinct from an act-consequentialist doctrine. It may seem that, for reasons given above, it cannot be: if an act in violation of a given right yields some consequence that is of greater value than those with which the right is concerned, then on my view the right is to be set aside.

If the act does not have such consequences then, in virtue of its conflict with the right and the values that right protects, it seems that the act would not be justifiable on act-consequentialist grounds anyway. But this rests on a mistake. The values supporting a particular right need not all stand to be lost in every case in which the right is violated. In defending the claim that there is a right of a certain sort, e.g., a particular right of privacy, we must be prepared to compare the advantages of having this right – the advantages, e.g., of being free to decline to be searched – against competing considerations – e.g., the security benefits derived from a more lenient policy of search and seizure. But what stands to be gained or lost in any given instance in which a policeman would like to search me need not coincide with either of these values. It may be that in that particular case I don't care.[8]

There is, then, no incoherence in distinguishing between the value of having a right and the cost of having it violated on a particular occasion. And it is just the values of the former sort that we must appeal to in justifying a two-tier view. What more can be said about these values? From an act-consequentialist point of view the value attached to the kind of control and protection that rights confer seems to rest on mistrust of others. If everyone could be relied upon to do the correct thing from an act-consequentialist standpoint would we still be so concerned with rights? This way of putting the matter obscures several important elements. First, it supposes that we can all agree on the best thing to be done in each case. But concern with rights is based largely on the warranted supposition that we have significantly differing ideas of the good and that we are interested in the freedom to put our own conceptions into practice. Second, the objection assumes that we are concerned only with the correct choice being made and have no independent concern with who makes it. This also seems clearly false. The independent value we attach to being able to make our own choices should, however, be distinguished from the further value we may attach to having it recognized that we are *entitled* to make them. This we may also value in itself as a sign of respect and personhood, but there is a question to what degree this value is an artifact of our moral beliefs and customs rather than a basis

[8] On the importance of establishing the proper terms of balancing see Fried, 'Two Concepts of Interests', p. 758.

for them. Where a moral framework of rights is established and recognized, it will be important for a person to have his status as a right holder generally acknowledged. But is there something analogous to this importance that is lost for everyone in a society of conscientious act consequentialists where no one holds rights? It is not clear to me that there is, but, however this may be, my account emphasizes the value attached to rights for the sake of what they may bring rather than their value as signs of respect.

If the factors just enumerated were the whole basis for concern with rights then one would expect the case for them to weaken and the force of act-consequentialist considerations to grow relatively stronger as (1) the importance attached to outcomes becomes absolutely greater and hence, presumably, also relatively greater as compared with the independent value of making choices one's self, and as (2) the assignment of values to the relevant outcomes becomes less controversial. To some extent both these things happen in cases where life and death are at stake, and here mistrust emerges as the more plausible basis for concern with rights.

4. *Cases of life and death*

From the point of view suggested in this paper, the right to life is to be seen as a complex of elements including particular liberties to act in one's own defense and to preserve one's life, claim-rights to aid and perhaps to the necessities of life, and restrictions on the liberty of others to kill or endanger. Let me focus here on elements in these last two categories, namely limits on the liberty to act in ways that lead to a person's death. An act-consequentialist standard could allow a person to take action leading to the death of another whenever this is necessary to avoid greater loss of life elsewhere. Many find this policy too permissive, and one explanation of this reaction is that it represents a kind of blind conservatism. We know that our lives are always in jeopardy in many ways. Tomorrow I may die of a heart attack or a blood clot. I may be hit by a falling tree or discover that I have a failing liver or find myself stood up against a wall by a group of terrorists. But we are reluctant to open the door to a further form of deadly risk by licensing others to take our life should this be necessary to minimize loss of life overall. We are reluctant to do this even when the effect would be to increase our net chances of living a long life by decreasing the likelihood that we will actually die when one of the natural hazards of life befalls us. We adopt, as it were, the attitude of hoping against hope not to run afoul of any of these hazards, and we place less stock on the prospect of escaping alive should we be so unlucky. It would not be irrational for a person to *decide* to increase his chances of survival by joining a transplant-insurance scheme, i.e. an arrangement guaranteeing one a heart or kidney should he need one provided he agrees to sacrifice himself to become a donor if he is chosen to do so. But such a decision is sufficiently controversial and the stakes so high that it is not a decision that can be taken to have been made for us as part of a unanimously acceptable basis for the assignment of rights. What I have here called conservatism is, however, uncomfortably close to a bias of the lucky against the unlucky insofar as it rests on a conscious turning of attention away from the prospect of our being one of the unlucky ones.

A substitute for conservatism is mistrust. We are reluctant to place our life in *anyone's* hands. We are even more reluctant to place our lives in *everyone's* hands as the act-consequentialist standard would have us do. Such mistrust is the main factor supporting the observed difference between the rationality of joining a voluntary transplant-insurance scheme and the permissibility of having a compulsory one (let alone the universally administered one that unrestricted act consequentialism could amount to). A person who joins a voluntary scheme has the chance to see who will be making the decisions and to examine the safeguards on the process. In assessing the force of these considerations one should also bear in mind that what they are to be weighed against is not 'the value of life itself' but only a small increase in the probability of living a somewhat longer life.

These appeals to 'conservatism' and mistrust, if accepted, would support something like the distinction between killing and letting die: we are willing to grant to others the liberty not to save us from threat of death when this is necessary to save others, but we are unwilling to license them to put us under threat of death when we have otherwise escaped it. As is well known, however, the killing/letting die distinction appears to permit some actions leading to a person's death that are not intuitively permissible. These are actions in which an agent refrains from aiding someone already under threat of death and does so because that person's death has results he considers advantageous. (I will assume that they are thought advantageous to someone other than the person who is about to die.) The intuition that such actions are not permitted would be served by a restriction on the liberty to fail to save, specifying that this course of action cannot be undertaken on the basis of conceived advantages of having the person out of the way. Opponents of the law of double effect have sometimes objected that it is strange to make the permissibility of an action depend on quite subtle features of its rationale. In the context of the present theory, however, the distinction just proposed is not formally anomalous. Conferrals of authority and limitations on it often take the form not simply of licensing certain actions or barring them but rather of restricting the grounds on which actions can be undertaken. Freedom of expression embodies restrictions of this kind, for example, and this is one factor responsible for the distinction between real and apparent violations mentioned above.[9]

Reasons for such a restriction in the present case are easy to come by. People have such powerful and tempting reasons for wanting others removed from the scene that it is obviously a serious step to open the door to calculations taking these reasons into account. Obviously, what would be proposed would be a qualified restriction, allowing consideration of the utilitarian, but not the purely self-interested, advantages to be gained from a person's death. But a potential agent's perception of this distinction does not seem to be a factor worth depending on.

The restriction proposed here may appear odd when compared to our apparent policy regarding mutual aid. If, as seems to be the case, we are prepared to allow a person to fail to save another when doing so would involve a moderately heavy sacrifice, why not allow him to do the same for the sake of a much greater benefit, to be gained from that person's death? The answer seems to be that, while a principle of mutual aid giving less consideration to

[9] For a view of freedom of expression embodying this feature, see Scanlon, 'A Theory of Freedom of Expression', *Philosophy and Public Affairs* 1 (1972), p. 204–26.

the donor's sacrifice strikes us as too demanding, it is not nearly as threatening as a policy allowing one to consider the benefits to be gained from a person's death.

These appeals to 'conservatism' and mistrust do not seem to me to provide adequate justification for the distinctions in question. They may explain, however, why these distinctions have some appeal for us and yet remain matters of considerable controversy.

[3]

Rights, Utility, and Universalization

J. L. Mackie

Many different forms of utilitarianism have been put forward and discussed in some detail, and several very different right-based moral and political theories have been at least outlined.[1] But I shall be concerned mainly with the contrast between one form of utilitarianism, that advocated by R. M. Hare, and one right-based view, my own. Hare's theory has been fully stated, especially in his recent book *Moral Thinking;*[2] mine has not yet been adequately presented, but I shall indicate its main outlines, using comparisons with utilitarianism for this purpose.

The fundamental point of contrast, and conflict, between utilitarian and right-based views is that the former, at least in their basic theory, aggregate the interests or preferences of all the persons or parties who are being taken into account, whereas the latter insist, to the end, on the separateness of persons.[3] For the utilitarian, the ultimate determination and the ultimate justification of every moral requirement lies in its relation—perhaps a complex and indirect relation—to something that represents the pooling of all individual purposes. The rights-theorist takes it to be morally important to respect and protect—at all levels, not at some only—the separate interests of each individual in a way that goes beyond the mere counting of them, however fairly, as elements in the pool.

Of course this does not mean that a utilitarian must literally deny that persons are separate, or that any utilitarian has ever done so. What it means is that this separateness does no work in the utilitarian method of determining what is good or just, that in the utilitarian calculus the desires, or the satisfactions, of different individuals are all weighed together in the way in which a single thoroughly rational egoist would weigh together all his own desires or satisfactions: on a utilitarian view, transferring a satisfaction from one person to another, while preserving its magnitude, makes no morally significant difference.

A right-based moral theory attempts to develop and clarify the popular notion that everyone should have a fair go. This is something more than the utilitarian principle, enunciated by Bentham and echoed by Mill, that everybody is to count for one and nobody for more than one. It is also more than Hare, as we shall see, provides by saying that the moral point of view is that in which an agent imaginatively occupies in turn the positions of all those who would be affected by his action, and gives equal weight to all the preferences that he thus, in thought, acquires. One whose interests have been thus fairly taken into account may still, in the end, have much less than a fair go: the maximizing of utility may turn out to require that his well-being should be sacrificed, without limit, in order to promote that of others. It is this that a right-based theory is meant to bar.

The formal structure of such a theory will be something like this. Having started with the assignment to all persons alike of the rather vague right to a fair go, we first make this somewhat more explicit, in the light of ordinary human needs and purposes, by an assignment of some basic abstract *prima facie* rights. These, I suggest, will include the traditional rights to life, health, liberty, and the pursuit of happiness. We also need basic rights with regard to possessions. Here I suggest a right to the products of one's own labor, insofar as these can be distinguished, but also a right to share equally in or have equal access to all natural resources. I suggest also a similar right with respect to such products of the labor of previous generations as have reverted to the status of natural resources. This applies both when special claims are untraceable and when, though traceable, they are no longer in force. Such claims gradually fade out because the recipient of a bequest has a weaker right than the original producer, and this effect is cumulative. I suggest also a right to the fulfillment of reasonable expectations based on a fairly stable system of laws, institutions, and practices; and, finally, a right—which, unlike the others, can be not *prima facie* but absolute—to equal respect in the procedures that determine the compromises and adjustments between the other, *prima facie,* rights. Any specific moral or political theory or system can then be defended or criticized (or both) by considering to what extent its provisions and workings—including, no doubt, assignments of concrete, institutional rights, but also including rules, concepts of duty, the recognition and encouragement of certain dispositions as virtues, and the discouragement of others as vices—can be seen as applying, implementing, and realizing those basic abstract rights in view of the actual purposes, choices, negotiations, actions, and interactions of persons over the course of time.

Since the ultimate rationale of such a theory is the respecting and protecting of separate interests, it seems likely that any practical system that it would endorse and defend to any significant extent would center, as do most actual working moralities, on norms of reciprocation and conditional cooperation. Among other things, it will direct us to show gratitude, to help those who help us, to join in mutually beneficial enterprises and play our part in them, and to display the various sorts of honesty, fidelity, loyalty, and agreement-keeping that are in general likely to facilitate such conditional cooperation.

As this sketch shows, a right-based theory can and naturally will incorporate the distinction on which Hare insists between two levels of moral thinking. What I have called a specific moral or political theory or system belongs to what he calls the intuitive level, whereas the basic assignment of rights belongs to what he calls the critical level. The fact that most of the suggested rights are only *prima facie* ones, capable of being overridden in particular cases, does not mean that they are, like the rights that would be recognized in many utilitarian systems, merely derived principles whose rationale lies in their tendency to promote something else, say, the general happiness. The suggested rights are basic, though defeasible. They must be defeasible, since they can in particular circumstances conflict with one another. But the conflicts are to be resolved by balancing these *prima facie* rights themselves against one another, not by weighing their merits in terms of some different ultimate standard of value, such as utility.

This notion of balancing may seem obscure and may be thought to compel recourse to utilitarian methods at some point. This obscurity can be removed, and both the character of the proposed right-based theory and the contrast between it and utilitarianism can be made plainer, if we compare it also with the Marxist slogan, 'From each according to his ability, to each according to his needs'. My proposal incorporates Locke's two principles of property: that all natural resources belong, fundamentally, to all persons equally and in common, but that each individual has a private property in his own body, energy, talents, and labor, and therefore also in the traceable products of his labor. The Marxist slogan presupposes rather that not only natural resources but also each individual's labor, talents, energy, and perhaps his body too, belong to everyone in common: the needs of other persons constitute valid claims on whatever I can contribute. However, the second part of this slogan is ambiguous: just how are goods and services to be distributed in relation to needs? This might be read as proposing a utilitarianism of needs: utility might be equated with need-satisfaction (it being assumed that we can distinguish needs from mere wants or preferences), and the total of this utility or need-satisfaction maximized. But an alternative and more natural reading would give each person an equal *prima facie* right to have his needs satisfied, so that an ideally just arrangement would be one in which everyone's needs were satisfied to the same degree: the practical principle of redistribution would be 'Your need is greater than mine'. These two interpretations are not even extensionally equivalent. Equalizing marginal need may well not minimize total unsatisfied need or maximize the satisfaction of need: when A's and B's levels of need are equal, we may be able, by transferring resources from A to B, to increase B's need-satisfaction by an amount greater than that by which A's is reduced; B may be a more efficient converter of resources into need-satisfaction than A, even when their levels of need-satisfaction are initially equal. If we were choosing simply between these two readings of the Marxist slogan, the second would be not only the more natural but also the more attractive. There is a similar choice to be made between methods of adjusting conflicts between our more Lockean rights. The two principles of property quoted above are not absolute, either in my proposal or in Locke's own theory: initial property rights have to be weighed together with the rights to life, health, liberty, and the pursuit of happiness. Locke himself says 'so . . . when his own Preservation comes not in competition, ought he, as much as he can, *to preserve the rest of Mankind*'.[4] Conflicts between these *prima facie* rights might be handled by a utilitarianism of rights, so that what would count as the ideally just arrangement would be that in which total right-fulfillment was maximized, or total right-infringement minimized. Alternatively, they might be handled by assuming that, ideally, one person's rights should not be infringed more than another's. Again the two methods are not even extensionally equivalent, and again I suggest that the second is the more attractive. Such equality of sacrifice in compromises between our Lockean rights is, of course, not equivalent to the equal need-satisfaction in our second reading of the Marxist slogan, precisely because our rights include each individual's private property in his own body, energy, talents, and labor, and because each has a *prima facie* right to be free and to pursue happiness in whatever way he chooses, doubtless with very varying degrees of success. Does this mean that what I am advocating is equality of opportunity rather than final equality? Not if this means that justice would be secured if only each young adult started with equal resources and chances, no matter what happened thereafter. Rather we should include what we might call the prodigal son principle, that even someone who has squandered his initial opportunities has, later, some claim to be helped to make a fresh start. We want a continuing or at least a recurrent equality of opportunity, not merely an initial equality of opportunity, once and for all.

These contrasts have been drawn in terms of various ideal principles of justice. In practice each of the rival ideals could be realized only approximately and indirectly through some concrete system of institutions. Nevertheless, the ideal formulations are useful, both as guiding lights for the criticism or defenses of institutions and to bring out the contrasts between the different possible views. Our Lockean proposal is, not surpisingly, more individualist and less collectivist than the Marxist one. Yet even the latter, with the second, egalitarian, reading, is, paradoxically, *less* collectivist than any utilitarian principle. For a utilitarian principle also—as William Godwin in particular made clear—presupposes that everyone's labor, talents, energy, and body are in principle common property, to be used in whatever way maximizes overall utility. The utilitarian, no less than the Marxist, is committed to the clause, 'From each according to his ability'. And whereas 'to each according to his needs' can be read as prescribing *equal* need-satisfaction between individuals, a utilitarian is committed rather to *maximum* overall satisfaction—whether of needs or of preferences—that may well be at the cost of every sort of equality except equality of consideration, the right to be taken equally into account.

Hare's theory is based on features that, he believes, conceptual analysis shows to be characteristic of moral thinking: moral judgments are prescriptive, universalizable, and overriding. The kind of universalizability on which he relies is made very clear in his recent book: to endorse something as a moral judgment is seriously to prescribe it for a whole set of possible worlds each of which is exactly like the actual world in all its general features, but in which individuals change places in all possible ways. Essentially, this means that for me morally to choose some action is for me to prefer that action to any alternative with respect to an imaginary situation in which I not only occupy in turn the positions of all the persons affected in any way by this choice, but also take on all their preferences, detaching myself completely from my own actual preferences and values and ideals, except as those of one affected person among others. What is morally right, therefore, is what would be chosen from a point of view that thus combines or amalgamates all points of view. Hare infers that this will be equivalent to the output of a preference-utilitarianism, in which the 'utility' that is to be maximized is the balance of satisfactions over frustrations of all the preferences of all the persons concerned.[5] (The range covered by this phrase 'the persons concerned' is indeterminate: it presumably includes all actual human beings, present and future, but it is not clear whether it includes merely possible people, nonhuman animals, and perhaps all sentient beings whatever. But a right-based theory suffers initially from the same indeterminacy. This is a problem common to the two approaches and therefore irrelevant to the choice between them; so I shall leave it aside.)

The practical effect of this theory is very significantly affected by Hare's stress on the distinction between two levels of moral thinking. At the lower, practical, working level—the intuitive level, as Hare calls it—various rules, principles, and dispositions are in place; but thought at the higher, critical level has the task of deciding *what* rules, principles, and dispositions are to be adopted or cultivated for use at the lower level. This distinction provides two quick answers to anyone who complains—as so many recent writers have complained—that utilitarianism, including the proposed preference-utilitarianism, has counter-intuitive consequences. One answer is that the true consequences, for a practical working morality, of this preference-utilitarianism do not conflict but rather coincide with our ordinary intuitions. A prescriptively universalizing (and therefore utilitarian) critical thinker would encourage the adoption and development of firm principles and dispositions of the ordinary moral sort, rather than the direct use of utilitarian calculation as a practical working morality. There are at least six reasons why this is so. Shortage of time and energy will in general preclude such calculations. Even if time and energy are available, the relevant information commonly is not. An agent's judgment on particular issues is liable to be distorted by his own interests and special affections. Even if he were intellectually able to determine the right choice, weakness of will would be likely to impair his putting of it into effect. Even decisions that are right in themselves and actions based on them are liable to be misused as precedents, so that they will encourage and seem to legitimate wrong actions that are superficially similar to them. And, human nature being what it is, a practical working morality must not be too demanding: it is worse than useless to set standards so high that there is no real chance that actions will even approximate to them. Considerations of these sorts entail that a reasonable utilitarian critical thinker would recommend the adoption of fairly strict principles and the development of fairly firm dispositions in favor of honesty, veracity, agreement-keeping, justice, fairness, respect for various rights of individuals, gratitude to benefactors, special concern for some individuals connected in certain ways with the agent, and so on, as being more likely in general to produce behavior approximating to that which would be required by the utilitarian ideal than any other humanly viable working morality.

Since utilitarianism itself would thus generate an apparently non-utilitarian intuitive morality, it is idle to appeal against it to just such intuitions. Hare's second answer to the common complaint grants that there may be some very unusual situations, or some fantastic imagined situations, in which this reconciliation fails, in which utilitarianism, even after all the above-mentioned considerations have been allowed for, recommends choices that are at variance with our ordinary moral intuitions. But, it says, this shows only that these are situations with which our intuitions are not competent to cope. These intuitions have been developed in the real, normal world, and they are appropriate only for it: in fantastic situations they have no authority against the implications of universalizing critical thinking, if those implications are themselves clear.[6]

These answers are powerful enough to dispose of the majority of the stock objections to utilitarianism or to the kind of overridingly prescriptive universalization that, in Hare's opinion, generates it; it would, therefore, be both misguided and tedious to reiterate them. Instead, I shall raise three other objections.

One of these is internal to Hare's theory. Let us accept, provisionally, the thesis that first emerges from his kind of universalization, that what is morally right is, ultimately, what would be chosen from a point of view that combines or amalgamates all points of view. Is there, then, a uniquely correct way of amalgamating those points of view? Does it follow that what is right is what maximizes utility defined as the balance of the aggregate of the satisfactions of preferences over the aggregate of frustrations of preferences? Or might the appropriate amalgamation still be the one that took serious notice of the separateness of persons, perhaps in a way that would be expressed by the assigning of some basic abstract rights to each individual? If I am, for the purpose of ultimate moral decision, to be everyone, must I be everyone in such a way that all are blurred together into a mere aggregate of preferences, or can I be everyone with the boundaries between all these persons still visible and important? Can I not still want *each* of my multiple incarnations to have a fair go?[7] And, if I do, will I not assign to each of them *prima facie* rights that, when conflicts arise between one incarnation's rights and another's, are to be adjusted in the way indicated above, so that the ideally acceptable compromise will not infringe the rights of one more than those of another? In contrast with this, it is not enough that in the utilitarian method, or in Hare's utilitarian way of combining points of view, each individual is fully considered and his preferences counted, all preferences being given equal weight. The boundaries between persons are here being ignored, in that one person's satisfaction can simply replace another's and outweigh that other's miseries or frustrations.

An analogy between the different personae that one would assume through universalization and the different temporal phases of the life of an ordinary individual will throw some light on this issue. Suppose that as a young adult one could look forward to a fairly long life, and had some rough idea of the various satisfactions and frustrations likely to be experienced as a result of each of several alternative choices of a plan of life. Suppose that one could also allow for probable changes in one's preferences and ideals as one grew older, and was able to detach oneself from one's present youthful purposes and values and to look fairly at the alternative plans of life from the points of view of all one's future selves as well as the present one. Is it obvious that if a reasonable person were able to do all these things, he would opt for whatever plan of life promised the greatest aggregate utility? Or might he try to ensure that no substantial phase of his life was too miserable, even if very great satisfactions at other times were to compensate for this? I am not merely saying, as Hare might concede, that in general one would be most likely to maximize the aggregate of utility by providing for one's well-being at each successive phase. I am suggesting that looking after each substantial phase might be the sensible thing to opt for in its own right, not merely as a means to maximizing the aggregate. Yet the separateness of phases, in this case, just because they are only phases of the same person, would matter much less than the separateness of persons within the whole that is created and embraced by the adoption of the universalizing procedure. I might the more readily tolerate *my* misery over one five-year period if it were compensated by *my* great happiness over another five years simply because it is the same I that will be, or has been, happy. But if I adopt a way of thinking that commits me to being, as it were, both Smith and Jones, but separately, it is not so clear that I can tolerate unmitigated misery *as Smith* merely because that will enable me, *as Jones*, to be extravagantly happy. So if there is any force at all in the suggestion that the young adult might be reasonably concerned for the well-being of *each* of his temporal phases, it follows *a fortiori* that Harean universalization might generate a persisting concern for each separate individual.

I need not insist that what Hare's universalization leads to *is* a rights-theory rather than an aggregative utilitarianism even at the critical level: it is enough to point out that it does not give unequivocal support to the latter. There is no uniquely correct or rational way of amalgamating the indefinitely many points of view that are brought together by universalization, so there is no support to be derived from Hare's basic principles for utilitarianism as contrasted with a right-based theory.

My second objection is external to Hare's theory, in that it challenges even his basic approach through prescriptive universalizability. In earlier writings, Hare has placed great weight on conceptual analysis, maintaining that a correct understanding of ordinary moral concepts and moral language shows that overridingly prescriptive universalizability is built into them, and hence that to follow any other method would be tantamount to refusing to answer the moral questions we began by asking: while one can, without incoherence, simply opt out of the moral game altogether, this is the only consistent alternative. But this approach can be questioned on three grounds. First, even if analysis of established moral concepts shows that they involve some sort of universalizability, it is far from clear that they involve the precise sort that Hare is now using. His present method embraces all three of the stages of universalization that I have distinguished, but our ordinary concepts may well involve only the first, or perhaps the first and second, without the third.[8] Secondly, since there are these complications, opting out of the moral game and ceasing to ask recognizably moral questions is not the only alternative to using Hare's method. Thirdly, even if we accepted his conceptual analysis, we might well ask why that should matter, what power the analysis of existing concepts has to constrain our thinking, if there are other coherently possible ways of thinking about choices and patterns of behavior.

These points are important, since between them they destroy whatever force there might be in Hare's reliance on conceptual analysis and linguistic intuitions. Since there are coherent ways of thinking morally other than the one he describes, and moral language does not determinately involve his specific method of universalization, we have not only the choice whether or not to speak and think morally, but also, if we choose to do so, the further choice whether to speak and think morally in Hare's style or in some other. Since he vehemently advocates one specific kind of moral thinking, he is under pressure to find further ways of recommending it.

However, I need not labor these points here.[9] Hare himself now seems willing (at a pinch) to concede them. He says:

> If anybody either does not believe that I have given a true account of the moral concepts as we have them, or thinks that investigations of the logic of words in ordinary language are unhelpful, it is open to him to proceed in a different way. He could set out the logic of an artificial language, identical in its properties with the logic which I claim our ordinary words have; then he could show that anybody reasoning in such a language would have to think in the way in which *I* say our existing concepts constrain us to think;

> and then he could, using the same arguments as I shall use, show that there would be an advantage in our adopting such a language. Though I should not like such a method as much as my own . . . I do not think that the difference between the results of the two methods would be very substantial.[10]

In short, he is now prepared to join with others in sawing off the branch on which he has been sitting all these years. But though the branch is sawn off, Hare does not fall with it: he has provided himself with alternative means of support, in the claim that 'there would be an advantage in our adopting such a language'. But what can this mean?

It might mean that adopting this as an artificial language (or retaining it if it is, after all, our ordinary moral language), and thinking in terms of it to determine a practical working morality, would do more than any alternative system of action-guiding thought to fulfill together all the preferences of all human (or perhaps all sentient) beings. Now, provided that it really is possible to think properly in terms of this language, this must be true, since what the use of the Harean moral language aims at is precisely the fulfillment of all these preferences – subject, of course, to the query in our first objection about whether there is a unique way of amalgamating them. Hare assigns his critical thinking to a class of 'archangels' presumed to be thoroughly rational and fully informed, and of course a system of thoroughly rational and fully informed thinking aimed at achieving X must be a better way of achieving X than any other sort of thinking. But precisely because this is so obvious, it is no real defense of, or support for, this kind of thinking.

Alternatively, this claim might mean that the adopting (or retaining) of such a language and way of thinking by *each* person is advantageous to *him*; in other words, that Hare is prepared to mount a prudential defense of moral thinking. And this is indeed what he does. He admits that to do what we ought to do is not always in our prudential interest and remarks that it is hard to see how anybody could have thought that it was always so in default of divine rewards and punishments. But he says that we can still 'achieve something more modest, which nevertheless is adequate for the defense of morality'. His argument is that if one were bringing up a child and had *only* the child's interests at heart, one would not inculcate in him a purely egoistic principle; rather, one would try to develop in him not only such virtues as courage but also 'moral *prima facie* principles of just the same sort as the act-utilitarian archangel would select'. The reason is that it is not easy to be a successful immoral egoist. 'Mankind has found it possible to make life a great deal more tolerable by bringing it about that on the whole morality pays'. Since 'by far the easiest way of seeming to be upright is to be upright . . .

perhaps the most effective way of bringing up our child to obey the principles would be to inculcate moral feelings'. And if this holds for the supposed case of educating a child in its own interests, it must hold also with regard to each agent on his own: it would be prudent for him, so far as he is able, to adopt or retain the moral way of thinking.[11]

What I have given here is a précis of quite a long discussion. Clearly it makes important empirical claims; but are they true? I agree that if one were bringing up this child with a view simply to its own interests one would not try to make it into a directly calculating egoist. One would try to provide it with such self-strengthening virtues as courage, perseverance, some sort of temperance, and so on. Also, one would try to provide it with the specifically moral dispositions of some sort of morality. But not, I think, exactly the same moral dispositions as would be selected by Hare's act-utilitarian archangels, even allowing for all the above-listed considerations that would make a reasonable Harean critical thinker settle for an apparently nonutilitarian practical working morality. Rather, one would develop in the child dispositions that would enable it to accept and take advantage of unequal social structures to a greater extent than would the product of an education directed by Harean critical thought. For example, if the child happened to be born into a slave-owning aristocracy, one would educate him so as to be a well-behaved member of that class, and no doubt so as to be disposed to treat his slaves reasonably well. But Hare's critical thinking might well say that we should develop even in so fortunately endowed a child principles that might lead him to support some tendency to reform this unequal social structure, rather than merely to accept it and flourish within it, if there were any real possibility of successful reform.

In short, Hare slides far too easily from the admitted point that to have some sort of morality is very likely to be to the advantage of any individual, to the conclusion that his specific sort of morality is so, and is maximally so. This thesis is, on the face of it, highly implausible; if Hare wants to make use of it, the onus is on him to defend it far more thoroughly than he has done. It is not enough simply to reiterate his belief that it holds.

However, let us suppose, merely in order to investigate a further step in the argument, that he is right in this empirical claim. Suppose, that is, that the practical morality that would be chosen with a view simply to the agent's interests coincides perfectly with that which would be chosen by a Harean critical thinker. Even so, this would not yield a prudential vindication of Hare's style of critical thinking or of its basic utilitarianism. The prudential support would go straight to the working morality, not by way of the utilitarian critical thinking. It would be at most a lucky accident that the two lines of thought led to the same practical results. Even if they did, what the prudential argument would vindicate would be something like our ordinary morality with its norms of reciprocation and cooperation, special duties of honesty and agreement-keeping, special obligations of loyalty to family and friends, gratitude to benefactors, the legitimacy of the pursuit, within limits, of one's own interests, and of resentment of injuries, and so on. It *may* be that, contrary to initial appearances, the universalizing critical thinking, interpreted in the aggregative utilitarian way, would recommend acceptance of just this same practical moral system. But this would not mean that we had thereby a prudential vindication of that sort of critical thinking; at most we would have an absence of any prudential case against such critical thinking, as a general program. In particular—and this is crucial—we should have no reason for regarding utilitarian calculation as the method on which we should fall back in really hard cases: these, like the basic method itself, would lie beyond the scope of the prudential vindication.

By 'hard cases' I mean ones in which appeal to the established principles of a practical working morality fails, either because those principles conflict with one another or because the situation is abnormal. Here, by Hare's own account, we shall have to suspend the normal operation of even the best 'intuitions', and since the assumed defense of the ordinary reliance on those 'intuitions' has been a prudential one, there is no case for saying that what we should fall back on here, to replace those 'intuitions' and principles, is the utilitarian style of critical thinking, merely because the output of this normally coincides with that of prudential critical thinking.

There is, then, no sound, nontrivial interpretation of the thesis that 'there would be an advantage' in adopting (or retaining) the moral language and the basic method of moral thinking that Hare favors. His alternative means of support gives way, and he does, after all, fall with the sawn-off branch of conceptual analysis.

But what else, he may ask, can we offer as a method of critical moral thinking? We surely need something on this level. We cannot be content simply to accept whatever morality is conventionally in force, or to respect all the threadbare 'intuitions' to which popular moralists appeal—particularly when we see how they conflict with one another and how some of them stem from religious traditions to which we have no good reason to ascribe any authority. We need some way of revising a community's working morality and of making adjustments when discrepant working moralities come into contact with one another. Certainly; but there are at least two possible rivals to utilitarianism as a guide to thinking at the critical level.

One of these, which Hare himself might on reflection find acceptable, results from my first objection, which is, as I said, internal to his theory. His thoroughgoing prescriptive universalization might amalgamate the points of view of all the individuals concerned in a way that took serious account of the separateness of persons, by assigning such basic abstract rights as I have suggested to each person. That is, we could have a right-based method of critical thinking, and it could be supported, with at least as much plausibility as the aggregative utilitarian one, by the approach through universalization.

But I would not myself support it in this way, because, as I have indicated, I do not find the argument from conceptual analysis for prescriptive universalization compelling as a method for choosing ultimate constraints on action. Rather, I would fall back on the thesis for which I have argued elsewhere, that right and wrong have to be invented, that morality is not to be discovered but to be made.[12] We have to start somewhere, simply adopting some basic practical principles, though no doubt not in an arbitrary or casual spirit, but with reflection on the range of alternative sets of principles, and on the entailments and likely consequences of each such set. I suggest that on reflection we might find an assignment of basic abstract rights to persons a more acceptable starting point for critical moral thinking than any other.

A second suggestion is harder to state succinctly. Let me approach it by way of a digression through a speculative account of the origins of morality. Hare has spoken as if our existing 'intuitive' moralities were the product of his style of critical thinking:

> It is no accident that the world and society are such that crime does not in general pay. . . . It is better for nearly all of us if social rewards and penalties are attached to socially beneficial and harmful acts; *and so it has come about that on the whole they are* (my italics).[13]

Similarly Hume, in the *Enquiry concerning Morals,* thinks that it is a sufficient explanation of moral rules and practices that they have utility:

> The rules of equity and justice owe their origin and existence to that utility, which results to the public from their strict and regular observance. . . . Common interest and utility beget infallibly a standard of right and wrong among the parties concerned.[14]

But this is emphatically not an adequate method of explanation. There is no sound general principle either of biological evolution or of sociohistorical development that tendencies or dispositions or practices will be fostered and encouraged simply because they are beneficial to the community as a whole in a utilitarian sense. The true explanation, of which this is a distortion, runs rather as follows.

Sociobiologists have outlined processes of natural selection by which genetically determined tendencies are developed in favor of 'kin altruism'—that is, helping offspring and other close relatives—and reciprocal altruism—that is, helping those who help you. Tendencies to cooperate in small groups, in which each agent's participation is conditional on that of most of the other members, can be fostered in similar ways, as can the resentment of injuries and hostile retribution. All these are what we might call spontaneous premoral tendencies: they can be found and understood in many nonhuman species as well as in humans. They are typically spontaneous, being genetically fostered, and give only an appearance of calculation: here, as elsewhere, natural selection mimics purposiveness. Further, social evolution is superimposed on biological evolution. Here the most important element is the development of conventions. These can be understood as arising out of and helping to resolve problems of several sorts: coordination problems and especially problems of partial conflict of interests, either of much the same form as the prisoners' dilemma or of nonsymmetrical variants of this form. Then the internalization of rules of behavior will turn conventions into norms. In this social evolution, as in biological evolution, mechanisms of interaction can generate spontaneous tendencies that mimic purpose and calculation, and the solutions of problems can be produced and maintained by the very forces that initially create the problems. Hume, in Book III of the *Treatise,* at least hints at this explanation of morality in terms of conventions, though in the *Enquiry* he substituted for this the simpler but less correct attempt to explain morality directly by its utility.[15]

If it is by such processes as these that first premoral and then specifically moral tendencies have actually developed, it is not surprising that actual moral systems have the features we usually find in them: norms of cooperation (including cooperation on terms that are differentially advantageous to parties of different sorts); norms of reciprocation; principles that secure various rights. In general, we find moralities that look like the product of many contractual or quasi-contractual relationships, although actual historical contracts have not as a rule contributed significantly to their development.

My second suggestion, which this digression has been designed to introduce, is that moral thinking at the critical level might resemble the processes by which practical working moralities really have developed, rather than the control by utility to which Hare, and Hume in the *Enquiry*, mistakenly ascribe their origin. That is, critical thinking might itself be a process of interaction, negotiation, and debate between diverse groups with different starting points, different traditions of thought. Rather than proceeding *de haut en bas*, being pursued by one or more detached thinkers who try to stand above the whole conflict of interests and ideals, it would work up from below, from those conflicting views and claims themselves. The details of this process would be contingent upon the input to it and are therefore not open to any precise description *a priori*. But it is reasonable to expect that any such process of interaction, negotiation, and debate would be roughly equivalent to some distribution of entitlements that are not merged into a pure collectivity—in other words, that this too would be, in effect, a right-based approach.

In criticizing an earlier draft of this essay, Hare has demanded that more should be said about the ground rules for such negotiation. This may, indeed, be a fruitful line of inquiry, but I cannot say much about it here. An attractive principle would be the above-mentioned one of equality of sacrifices in compromises between our Lockean rights, but realistic ground rules for negotiation would need to take some account of the strength of the bargaining positions of the parties. I would stress, however, that Hare's thoroughgoing universalization, which means that each party abandons his special interests, values, and point of view in taking on those of all parties alike, is not a ground rule for negotiation, but a move that would make negotiation unnecessary. Equally, Rawls's notion of a hypothetical contract made behind a veil of ignorance destroys what is characteristic of a contractual or negotiating method. In speaking of negotiation I mean real negotiation, conducted in the full light of day, while the parties retain their self-conscious individuality and divergent aims.[16]

This second suggestion is plainly different from the first, but it could be supported in the same sort of way, simply as a possibly acceptable starting point for critical moral thinking. There is, however, something else that might be said for it; and this brings me to my third main objection to Hare's theory, which, like the second, challenges his basic approach.

Hare's critically thinking archangels are supposed to be performing a task that Bishop Butler assigned more appropriately to God. (Hare has himself noted this in an earlier essay.)[17] Butler's God is presumed to have perfect knowledge and complete benevolence towards all his creatures; he therefore is in a position to choose the best practical working morality for human beings, with their limitations as he knows them, and to write it into their consciences in the form of moral intuitions. But this viewpoint that Butler plausibly ascribes to God is simply not accessible, either intellectually or emotionally, to anyone else.

It is obvious that it is not intellectually accessible. Critical thinking, it is to be remembered, is concerned primarily with the choice of sets of moral principles and dispositions, and this choice will affect indefinitely many present and future persons. No human thinker or small group of thinkers can possibly know what it is really like to be each of these people. Hare takes trouble to argue that one can really put oneself imaginatively in the place of *some* other people. This might be sufficient for universalization used as a test of the rightness of some particular choice of action; but it cannot be sufficient for the main task of critical thinking.

I would have supposed that the required viewpoint is also emotionally inaccessible, that no one can really *take on* the feelings of all persons, present and future, even if he could surmount the intellectual barriers to his discovery of them. However, Peter Singer, in a recent book, has tried to meet this challenge. His title, *The Expanding Circle*,[18] refers to the well-known thesis of Westermarck and others that the history of human moral thought has been, in part, the history of a progressive enlargement of the circle of persons towards whom altruism is morally prescribed and towards whom, to some extent, altruistic feelings and actions are really directed. Singer describes and accepts very much that same sociobiological account of the origins of morality in kin altruism, reciprocal altruism, and cooperation in small groups as has been sketched above. But he then argues that the expansion of the range of altruism is not due merely to wider practical opportunities for useful cooperation or to widening sympathies, but is rather to be ascribed to *reason* in something like a Kantian sense. This is not what Hume would have called reason: there is no strict deductive requirement to go on from altruism (or universalization) with respect to a small community, to altruism (or universalization) with respect to a large community or the human race or all sentient beings. But it is reason in a looser sense: it is the avoidance of an arbitrary cutoff. Singer appropriately compares this moral expansion with the gradual progress of arithmetic from the recognition of the integers from, say, 1 to 10, *via* the extension to an infinite sequence of integers, the introduction of negative numbers, fractions, irrationals, and so on, to the full modern development of mathematics. He connects both of these with biological theory. The growth of the ability to develop the higher mathematics could not be explained *in itself* as a product of natural selection: this ability could never itself have given its possessors a genetic advantage. But this ability may well be so closely linked with practically useful and genetically advantageous forms of intelligence that natural selection could not help introducing them together. We could not have the useful abilities to count sheep and to think conditionally without having also the useless ability and motivation that have led the mathematicians into Cantor's paradise. Similarly, Singer suggests, the kinds of moral thinking that are genetically advantageous, that would be and have been produced by the above-mentioned sociobiological mechanisms, together with the practically useful ability to generalize, tend automatically to produce the unrestricted prescriptive universalization of Hare's archangelic critical thinkers. And the latter, *unlike* the higher mathematics, may really be useful after all, although it could not have been selected genetically—or, I would add, culturally—for its usefulness.

If Singer were right, then, the archangelic viewpoint would in principle be emotionally accessible even to humans, not only to Butler's God, insofar as there would be a tendency in thinking, closely linked with reasoning powers that we already have, that would carry us from the already existing kind of morality (directly produced by biological and cultural evolution) to a Harean universalization.

However, this suggestion slides too easily over the contrast between a norm of reciprocation and conditional cooperation on the one hand and a norm of pure rational benevolence on the other. To go from the first to the second of these would be a qualitative change in moral thinking, different from a mere expansion of the circle within which altruism *of the same kind* operates. The 'reason' that avoids arbitrary cutoffs will not carry us over this gap. Also, the supposed evidence that there already is a significant amount of pure rational benevolence is weak. Singer makes much of the altruism of blood donors, but after all this is a comparatively inexpensive form of altruism. More spectacular forms of self-sacrifice typically come under the heading of the taking of risks within what is normally a cooperative enterprise, and are governed by norms of reciprocation. Despite Singer's argument, therefore, I still deny that the archangelic viewpoint is emotionally accessible to humans in any real sense, and I repeat that in any case it is not intellectually accessible.

There is, then, a good reason why critical moral thinking should take the form sketched in my second suggestion above, that of a process of interaction, negotiation, and debate rather than something closely analogous to the thinking of Butler's God, namely, that the former is humanly possible, while the latter is not.

This criticism may seem to tell not only against Hare's theory but also against my own first suggestion. But I think it is less damaging to the latter. We should need less close an approximation to divine omniscience and universal benevolence in order seriously to assign some basic abstract rights to all persons alike, and to criticize practical working moralities by reference to that assignment, than in order seriously to adopt an unqualified aggregative utilitarianism, even if we confined this to the critical level. There are two reasons why this is so. First, the right-based approach, since it keeps everyone covered to some extent, keeps *us* covered among others. And, secondly, since its aim is to keep everyone covered, it can proceed in a more piecemeal way. We can say roughly whether some local arrangement, over a finite geographical area and a modest time span, does or does not constitute a decent approximation to an application and realization of the basic rights of those directly involved, without necessitating sacrifices of the corresponding rights of persons outside this spatiotemporal region. We can say this more confidently than we can say that any scheme, however local its immediate bearing may be, is likely on the whole to come close to maximizing the aggregate satisfaction of preferences of the whole body of human (let alone sentient) beings, present and future. In effect, this means that while my first and second suggestions about possible methods of critical thinking—the first, universalization in the form of an assignment of basic abstract rights to all persons, the second, a process of interaction, negotiation, and debate—are in principle different from one another, they are still not very far apart: the second could be seen as a way of approximately realizing the first.

Let me sum up, then, the ways in which we might want to stress the role of rights in moral theory. First, it is clear that we shall want rights to be recognized and taken seriously as elements in our practical working morality. But this not a point at issue between Hare's view and mine: he would be emphatic about the importance of rights at this level, as was another utilitarian, J. S. Mill, when he wrote:

> Justice is the name for certain classes of moral rules, which concern the essentials of human well-being more nearly, and are therefore of more absolute obligation, than any other rules for the guidance of life; and the notion which we have found to be the essence of the idea of justice, that of a right residing in an individual, implies and testifies to this more binding obligation.[19]

The real dispute, then, concerns the choice between 'utility' and 'rights' as the central concepts in higher level, critical, moral thinking.

Secondly—and this is now a point at issue—I have questioned whether the analysis of moral concepts yields the precise kind of universalization that amounts to the identification of morally defensible choices with ones made from a point of view that amalgamates the points of view of all persons. But even if the analysis of existing moral concepts did have this as its output, why should this be seen as an important constraint on the kind of critical thinking whose function is to choose a practical working morality, that is, a body of rules, principles, and dispositions that would directly guide and control what people do? The authority of moral concepts is no more sacred than that of particular 'intuitions', and I have argued that Hare is not able to substitute for this authority a prudential vindication. The way, therefore, is at least open for a theory based on rights and the separateness of persons rather than on aggregative utility.

Thirdly, Hare's style of universalization assigns to his archangelic critical thinkers a point of view that belongs rather to Butler's God and is not accessible to human beings either intellectually or, despite Singer's ingenious argument, emotionally. Lacking this point of view, we could not really carry out the utilitarian critical thinking: rather, if we aimed at this, we should achieve only guesswork purporting to be an application of preference-utilitarianism. But two other methods are humanly possible. One of these accepts, as the moral point of view, one that amalgamates the points of view of all persons, but interprets this amalgamation in a way that still allows for the separateness of persons, and so issues initially in an assignment of basic abstract rights, in terms of which concrete moral and political systems and proposals can be defended or criticized. The other abandons the attempt to work down from any supreme principle or overarching point of view, and instead works up from below by a procedure of interaction, negotiation, and debate. Though different in principle, these two methods are not far removed from one another in practice. I suggest, therefore, that rights not only should be prominent in a practical working morality, but can also replace utility at the critical level.

NOTES

1. Right-based theories include those of Robert Nozick and Ronald Dworkin, and, if Dworkin is right, that of John Rawls. Another is sketched in my "Can There Be a Right-Based Moral Theory?" in *Midwest Studies in Philosophy* 3 (1978): 350–59.

2. R. M. Hare, *Moral Thinking* (Oxford: Oxford University Press, 1982).

3. Cf J. Rawls, *A Theory of Justice* (Oxford: Oxford University Press, 1972), pp. 23–27, 187.

4. J. Locke, *Second Treatise of Government*, sec. 7.

5. Hare, *Moral Thinking*, ch. 7.

6. *Ibid.*, ch. 6.

7. This point was made in discussion by Ronald Dworkin.

8. Cf J. L. Mackie, *Ethics: Inventing Right and Wrong* (Harmondsworth: Penguin Books, 1977), ch. 4.

9. Some of them are developed in the chapter referred to in note 8.

10. Hare, *Moral Thinking*, ch. 1, p. 20.

11. *Ibid.*, ch. 11.

12. Cf. chapter 1 of Mackie, *Ethics*.

13. Hare, *Moral Thinking*, ch. 11.

14. D. Hume, *Enquiries*, ed. L. A. Selby-Bigge, 2nd ed. (originally published 1902; reprint, Oxford: Oxford University Press, 1946, 1955), pp. 188, 211; see also pp. 202, 208, etc.

15. For a fuller explanation of these matters, see J. L. Mackie, *Hume's Moral Theory* (London: Routledge & Kegan Paul, 1980), chs. 6 and 9.

16. A proposal for basing a liberal theory of justice on 'constrained dialogue' has been put forward by Bruce A. Ackerman in *Social Justice in the Liberal State* (New Haven, Conn.: Yale University Press, 1980). I have criticized Ackerman's proposals in a review article, "Competitors in Conversation", in *The Times Literary Supplement*, April 17, 1981, p. 443.

17. R. M. Hare, "Principles", in *Proceedings of the Aristotelian Society* 73 (1972–73): 1–18.

18. P. Singer, *The Expanding Circle: Ethics and Sociobiology* (New York: Farrar, Straus & Giroux, 1980).

19. J. S. Mill, *Utilitarianism*, ch. 5.

[4]

Rights, Utility, and Universalization Reply to J. L. Mackie

R. M. Hare

Mr Mackie starts with a contrast between utilitarianism and what he calls 'right-based' views or theories such as he has himself advocated.[1] I must therefore first ask some questions about this supposed distinction. My trouble is partly that some of the tenets which are said to distinguish right-based theories from utilitarianism are ones which I, a utilitarian, have no difficulty in assenting to; and partly that the basic distinction which is supposed to divide the two kinds of theory is one which entirely eludes me, although, to judge by the widespread use made of it, everybody else understands it perfectly well. Or can it be that what everybody else is doing is parroting a slogan with which John Rawls ends his otherwise more or less fair statement of his disagreements with utilitarianism? He says 'Utilitarianism does not take seriously the distinction between persons'.[2] This might suggest to a careless reader that utilitarians do not realize that there are distinct people in the world, with separate interests which have to be considered. But what utilitarian has ever denied this?

Mackie, at any rate, guards against this misinterpretation. But the question remains of what, if not this obvious truth, he is accusing the utilitarians of denying. What is it to 'insist, to the end, on the separateness of persons' (p. 86)? What the utilitarian is doing is not denying this, but trying to give meaning to the requirement, on which Mackie himself lays stress, 'that everyone should have a fair go'. It is hard to see what this could mean, except, in Bentham's words, to 'count everybody for one and nobody for more than one'.[3] But Mackie attacks the utilitarians for doing this. It is indeed rather mysterious that critics of utilitarianism, some of whom lay great weight on the 'right to equal concern and respect' which all people have, should object when utilitarians show this equal concern by giving equal weight to the equal interests of everybody, a precept which leads straight to Bentham's formula and to utilitarianism itself.

It should hardly be necessary to spell this out. To have concern for someone is to seek his good, or to seek to promote his interests; and to have equal concern for all people is to seek equally their good, or to give equal weight to their interests, which is exactly what utilitarianism requires. To do this is to treat others' interests in the same way as a prudent person treats his own interests, present and future. It is thus inevitable that having equal concern for everybody will lead us, as Mackie puts it, to weigh together the interests of different individuals 'in the way in which a single thoroughly rational egoist would weigh together all his own desires or satisfactions'. To do this is not to fail to 'insist on the separateness of persons'.

We can perhaps begin to understand why advocates of right-based theories get into the paradoxical position of advocating equal concern but dismissing the theory (utilitarianism) which secures precisely this, if we notice that certain rights, or the principles safeguarding them, initially demand *un*equal concern for people. Suppose that Tom (the lecher!) is consumed with a desire for the favors of Ann, but that she resists his advances because of a preference, though only a marginal one, not to indulge him just now. We say that she has a right to refuse, and indeed to be protected in her refusal by the law. But this is to show *more* concern for her than for him: we are frustrating a consuming desire of his in order to meet what may be a mere whim of hers to accommodate him later rather than now.

It is true that we should secure *formal* equality between them by adopting a universal principle forbidding rape by *anybody*. But the right-based theorist is very reasonably not likely to be satisfied by that. A principle universally *permitting* rape, or universally requiring females to yield to the advances of males, would pass this formal test just as well. Why then do we, in spite of our belief in the right to equal concern and respect, adopt, out of these principles, all of which are formally universal, one in particular—one which in this case requires inequality of concern?

Mackie has the answer, but does not explain how it is inconsistent with utilitarianism. He says (p. 87)

> [A right-based theory's] formal structure will be something like this. Having started with the assignment to all persons alike of the

> rather vague right to a fair go, we first try to make this somewhat more explicit, in the light of ordinary human needs and purposes, by an assignment of some basic abstract *prima facie* rights. These, I suggest, will include the traditional rights to life, health, liberty, and the pursuit of happiness.

The right which stands in the lecher's way is presumably a particular case of the right to liberty: the liberty in question is the freedom not to have one's body interfered with contrary to one's wishes. As we have seen, the right demands *un*equal concern in this case.

These two stages in Mackie's account correspond closely to the two levels, critical and intuitive, in my own.[4] The explanation of how equal concern at the critical level can lead to unequal concern at the intuitive is that an impartial critical thinker equally concerned to give everybody 'the right to a fair go' would see that the right-assigning principles whose general acceptance would be most likely to achieve this aim would assign rights whose detailed observance in particular cases would sometimes require unequal concern. A two-level utilitarian theory makes this transition clear; whereas Mackie's phrase 'make more explicit, in the light of ordinary human needs and purposes' conceals the nature of the process of getting from 'the rather vague right to a fair go' to more substantial principles governing our actions in the concrete world among real people.

Is Mackie's 'formal structure' in fact different from my own utilitarian theory? The *content* of both theories might well be the same. Both, having set before themselves the aim of giving everybody a fair go, or having equal concern for all, find that the best way 'in the light of ordinary human needs and purposes' of achieving this aim is to devise a set of *prima facie* principles, some of them entrenching *prima facie* rights, for use in our moral thinking. My list of these could well be the same as Mackie's. But is the *structure* of the two theories different? I am inclined to think not.

I will not enquire what Mackie means by calling his rights 'abstract' (perhaps the point he is making is the same point as I commonly express by calling the principles used in intuitive thinking 'simple' and 'general'). But by calling them '*prima facie*' rights he seems at first sight to be accepting (as he does later accept) my division of moral thinking into two levels, and to be putting the moral judgements based on these rights into the intuitive level. This certainly seems to be their natural habitat; and that, as I have repeatedly stressed in my book, does not entail any diminution of the sanctity of the rights in question. I have given reasons why we should be extremely reluctant to let them be overridden, and even if we do, should feel bad about it.[5] Mackie himself sums up these reasons on p. 91 of his paper. But he also agrees with me that the rights have to be 'defeasible' (another word, we might almost say, for '*prima facie*'), because they can conflict in particular cases. This lays on the right-based theorist the task of giving a method for the resolution of these conflicts, as I try, in my book, to do in terms of my own theory. My account, though not entirely simple, does seem to me to yield a passably true-to-life model of the moral thinking that wise people actually do in such situations.

I am left somewhat in the dark as to the differences which he finds between a right-based theory and my own—or, which comes to the same thing, as to the sense in which his theory could be said to be 'based' on rights and mine not. For in so far as the rights are only *prima facie* and defeasible, it surely cannot be based on them; and the only right he produces which is more than *prima facie* is the right to equal concern and respect, which is preserved, at the highest level, and indeed really used as a basis, by my own theory.

This unclarity, it seems to me, infects the first of the new objections that Mackie makes against my theory. He puts it forward only after a very fair account of my suggested division of moral thought into two levels, which, he agrees, enables me to deal with the vulgar objections to utilitarianism based on counter-intuitiveness, examples of which are likely to be in evidence in this volume. He also recognizes the close relation between my version of even-handed utilitarianism and the quasi-Kantian universality of moral prescriptions on which I seek to base it. He goes on to attribute to me the view, in summary, that 'what is morally right is, ultimately, what would be chosen from a point of view that combines or amalgamates all points of view'.

We must notice that it is Mackie, and not I, who introduces the word 'amalgamate', with its suggestion, which he draws out, that 'all are blurred together into a mere aggregate of purposes', leaving the boundaries between persons no longer visible. What I actually say is rather different. In an article I published a long time ago I quoted the lines

> Momentous to himself as I to me
> Is every man that ever woman bore.[6]

My new book is full of the idea that we have in critical moral thought to think ourselves into the shoes of each of the persons affected, one by one–which is why, as we shall see when we come to Mackie's third objection, critical moral thought is so difficult for human beings. So far individual distinctions are preserved.

The question which then arises is how, when we think morally and therefore universally, we are to balance the preferences of these separate people against one another so as to be fair to them all. My answer is that we have to give equal weight to equal preferences, counting everybody for one. This is no more to *amalgamate*, let alone *blur*, the separate persons than it is when a judge, having heard what each of the parties to a suit has to say, tries to be fair to them all. As Mackie himself says, thinking this to be a point against me, 'Harean universalization might' (he implies that in my hands it does not) 'generate a persisting concern for each separate individual'. But in fact I do not in my critical thinking depart from this concern; I only seek a way in which concern for different individuals can be fairly balanced, and find it by treating their equal preferences as of equal weight.

As we have seen, this impartiality or equal concern at the critical level can yield principles which, in particular cases at the intuitive level, may require partiality or *un*equal concern, as when somebody's right has to be preserved at greater expense to somebody else. It is not clear how a right-based theory would justify this, since it purports to treat rights as 'basic'. I justify it on the ground that the general acceptance of such principles would on balance best serve the interests of all considered impartially. That is to say, there is no other set of principles which would do more for their interests in sum, when interests are counted equally in proportion to their strength.

It is the 'in sum' that Mackie is principally attacking. In the course of his attack he appeals to an analogy, which I also use, between adjudication of *inter*personal conflicts of interest and adjudication of *intra*personal but inter*temporal* conflicts. If I am now trying to decide between courses of action, of which one will in total maximally satisfy the preferences which I have at all times as to what should happen *at those times*, and the other distributes preference-satisfactions in some different way, I shall be forced into an adjudication between the interests of different phases of my own person which is analogous to that between the interests of different people. Mackie suggests that, contrary to the utilitarian solution of this prudential problem, someone in this position might 'try to ensure that no substantial phase of his life was too miserable, even if very great satisfactions at other times were to compensate for this'. How miserable is 'too miserable', and what 'compensates' for what? If we ask these questions, we see that even such a way of thinking requires us to place values on the preferences that we are going to have at the various times.

I say 'place values' and not 'assign strengths'. I shall not in this paper go into the problem of the 'interpersonal commensurability of utilities' which is discussed briefly in my book.[7] But, given that we can assess the strengths of the preferences, we still have to decide how much each of these preferences, present or future, our own or other people's, is to count for us, at the time when we are making the decision. My own answer is that, if we are prudent, they will count for us equally, strength for strength, irrespective of the times at which they are felt; and that, if we are thinking morally, other people's will count equally with each other and with our own.

The first of these theses holds because that is what we mean by 'prudent'. It has to be asked whether the person who follows the suggestion just quoted from Mackie is being prudent. On the face of it he is not; but it is perhaps possible to interpret what Mackie says in such a way that he is. All we have to say is that *by following the suggested policy*, he is showing that he places a greater negative value on the misery than the positive value he places on the sum of the spread-out satisfactions at other times that the misery makes possible. This involves taking 'compensate' in a Pickwickian sense. They do not really and fully compensate for the misery, in his present estimation, or he would not follow the policy. And he *is* being prudent in following it, if the actual values to him, at the times when they occur, of the various experiences will be the same as he now places on them (as manifested by his following the policy). If, however, they are not, he is being imprudent, most probably because he does not fully represent to himself now the values he will place upon them. Such imprudence is of course extremely common, but does not support Mackie's argument; on the other hand if, to support it, he were to allege that a *prudent* person could follow the policy in question, this, as I have just explained, will be because the satisfactions will *not* in fact compensate for the miseries; so the intrapersonal prudent calculation is, after all, analogous to the interpersonal utilitarian calculation, and the support for Mackie's argument collapses.

The second thesis, that, if we are thinking morally, other people's preferences will count equally with each other and with our own, holds because, when we make a moral judgement, we are prescribing universally for all situations of a given identical kind, irrespective of what individuals occupy the different roles in those situations (the preferences had by the individuals being part of the roles; they do not travel round with the individuals). But if we fully know what it is like to be a certain individual in a certain situation (and if we did *not* fully know, our moral thinking could be faulted for incompleteness of information) then we shall have the same preferences with regard to what should happen to us were we in that situation as the person who is actually in it and therefore actually has the preferences. For example, if I fully know what it is like to be burnt at the stake, I shall want not myself to be burnt at the stake just as much as does the person who is actually being burnt. Put these two premisses together, and it becomes inescapable that we prescribe, if we are prescribing morally, for all situations as if we were going to be in them forthwith, and therefore giving the same weight to the preferences of the people in them as *they* actually give to them. I have summarized the argument, and there is a lot more to be said about it; but it is not this part of my argument that Mackie challenges in his paper.

This, then, is my answer to Mackie's first, 'internal', objection: the objection that, even if my universal prescriptivist theory be accepted for the sake of argument, it does not lead inevitably to utilitarianism, but is consistent with his right-based theory. The answer is that, first of all, it does so lead, for the reason I have given; and that, secondly, if it is consistent with his right-based theory, then so is utilitarianism itself (as, indeed, I think it is, if 'based' is not taken too narrowly).

The first part of this answer, however, leads us directly to Mackie's second objective, which he calls 'external', because it takes issue with my underlying theory, universal prescriptivism. I myself base this theory on conceptual analysis or philosophical logic. The moral words do, as a matter of linguistic fact, have the logical properties of prescriptivity and universalizability on which my argument for utilitarianism is based. This is to be established by appeal to *linguistic* (not *moral*) intuitions: in our ordinary use of the words we do, as part of the meaning we give to them, assign to them these logical properties. We know that somebody who says 'He is in just the same situation as I am, including all his personal psychological characteristics, both occurrrent and dispositional, and yet he ought to do it but I ought not' is offending against the logical rules which give 'ought' its meaning, in just the same sort of way as we know that somebody who says 'All the books in the shelf are blue, yet there is one which isn't' is offending against the logical rules which give 'all', 'not', 'is', etc., their meanings. It is open to anybody to adopt a different meaning for the word 'ought' (provided that he advertises the fact in order to avoid misunderstandings); but if he does so, when he asks 'Ought I?', he will, because he has changed the meaning and the logical properties which are linked with it, no longer be asking the same question as we were asking when we used the same words; it would therefore not be surprising if he were able to give a different answer. Compare the person who says 'All the books on the shelf are blue', but means what most of us would express by 'Some of the books on the shelf are blue', or by 'All but one (the one written by me) are blue'.

This position can be, and has been, attacked in two different ways. First of all, it might be alleged that we do *not* use the words consistently in that way; my linguistic intuitions are at fault. But secondly, it might be alleged that although what I say about ordinary language may be true, (or may be admitted for the sake of argument to be true), we do not want to be tied and bound, in our practical reasoning, by contingent facts about ordinary language. So somebody might say 'If the ordinary uses of words commit me, if I use them in my moral thinking, to being a utilitarian, to hell with the ordinary uses of the words!'

Mr. Blackburn, who was kind enough to comment on an earlier draft of my book, advised me, in view of these possible objections, to take a course whose availability I had, indeed, already seen; and I was respectful enough to add a paragraph pointing out the alternative course. Mackie quotes this passage as 'conceding' the basis of his second objection. Actually, it concedes at most one (the third) of the three premisses that he needs (p. 94); and even concerning this one I make it clear in my book that this is not my preferred way of handling the matter. It is a long stop, in case anybody is so imperceptive as not to see the force of the arguments on which, in the main, I rely. The first and second of Mackie's three premisses I would reject, because I appeal to only one kind of universalization (*MT*, p. 108), and that has a logical and linguistic basis which I have just reiterated. For this reason his first premiss, which requires there to be different kinds of universalization, misses the target, and so, therefore, does the second, which depends on it.

The 'alternative course' into which Blackburn wished to draw me was to say 'All right, let us admit for the sake of argument either that my linguistic intuitions about ordinary language are wrong, or that it simply does not matter what logical properties ordinary language assigns to the words. Let us rather tell ordinary language to go to hell, and devise an *artificial* language whose words do have, by stipulation, the required properties. Then any user of this artificial language will have to be a utilitarian in his moral thinking. It remains open to anybody, provided that he makes his use clear, to use those words in some different way from that laid down in the rules of this artificial language, just as he could escape in the same way from the rules of our natural language. He will then not be asking the same questions as we are. But he may not want to ask those questions. What we have to show him is that there is some reason why he should use that language and ask those questions, or, contrariwise, why we should not give up using our language and ask instead the questions that he is asking.'

At the end of my new book I address myself to the task of justifying the asking of moral questions (which is the same task, whether following Mr. Blackburn's advice I treat them as questions in an artificial language, or whether, following my own inclinations, I claim that our natural language already serves to ask them). After admitting the possibility of there being a character whom I call 'the consistent amoralist', who has abandoned the moral language and its rules (whether natural or artificial), I try to show what reasons there are for us not to become amoralists, and, still more importantly, what reasons there are for not bringing up our children to be amoralists, even if we have only their interests at heart. This part of my book amounts to a prudential defence of the institution of morality. As such it will raise eyebrows, but it is not my task in this paper to lower them.

Let me make it clear, as Mackie does, that I am not merely giving a utilitarian justification of utilitarian morality; that would be trivial and easy. I am not, that is to say, only maintaining that an archangelic utilitarian thinker would come out with excellent moral reasons for inculcating the moral language with its rules. I am maintaining something much more substantial: that even a person who had nothing at heart but his own interest would do well to adopt this language and this way of thinking as a matter of ingrained habit. This, I maintain, holds for the world as it is and for people as they are; it does not hold for all logically possible worlds. The discussion, as Mackie says, is a long one, and my summary here will have to be even briefer than his. Note that I am not saying that the morally right *act* is always in the agent's interest; such a claim would be extravagant. I am maintaining that the interests of all ordinary humans (as opposed to impossibly clever devils) are likely to be furthered *in general* if they inculcate into themselves moral habits of thought – habits tenacious enough to make them actually suffer in mind if they transgress their morality, thereby giving them an added prudential reason for not doing so. The main reason, however, is that in the world as it is, and as we have helped, for reasons of self-interest, to make it, the easiest way of seeming to be upright is to be upright (an opinion which Xenophon attributed to Socrates).[8]

If anybody thinks that even this is an extravagant claim, I ask him to notice that the more thoughtful of us, when we have to think about the education of our children, and probably think much more about their good than about the good of the general public or about morality, in fact try, with varying degrees of success, to inculcate into them moral habits of thought. And it would go worse with the children if we did not.

There is, it goes without saying, room here for empirical differences of opinion as to whether this is so; for it is an empirical question what kind of education is most likely to lead to the maximal satisfaction of the children's preferences in the course of their lives. All I can say is that I believe that most thoughtful and experienced people, to judge by their practice, think it is so. The arguments which are brought against this position, like a lot of bad arguments against utilitarianism itself, rest largely on contrived examples, or too simple treatment of real ones. It is in this light that we should regard Mackie's example of the child brought up in a slave-owning aristocracy (p. 96). He suggests that critical moral thinking, such as I advocate, might lead such a fortunately endowed child 'to support some tendency to reform this unequal social structure, rather than merely to accept it and flourish within it, if there were any real possibility of successful reform'. But if there were any such real possibility, it could only be because there were factors at work, as there have been in many slave-societies before their reform, which made the foundations of the society shaky; and these same factors would very probably make it in the interest of its more fortunate members (especially if they they had regard to the interests of their posterity) to contemplate and work for a change to a more stable, because more equal, society. To substitute a more up-to-date example: does Mackie's argument commit him to saying that in present-day South Africa it is in the interest of a child to be brought up on diehard *verkrampte* rather than on more liberal *verligte* lines?

Although near the end of my book I do confront the question 'Why should I be moral?', I am not staking my reputation on the success of my answer to it. I should be content with something more modest: to have shown that the moral questions we are posing all the time are posed in terms whose meaning and logic generate a way of answering them which constrains us, once we ask the questions. If an amoralist refuses the questions themselves, that is another issue. However, I do believe that as a matter of fact there *is* a preestablished harmony between morality and prudence, to this limited extent, that if we were to bring up a child (or ourselves) to ask moral questions and answer them by means of the two-level structure of moral thinking which I say our language imposes on us, we should be acting in the child's (or in the second case our own) best interests.

Mackie's paper contains an illuminating digression about recent sociobiological theories and Peter Singer's first-rate appraisal of them in his book *The Expanding Circle*.[9] I shall not go into the question in detail, as I have discussed Singer's book elsewhere.[10] I agree with his contention that the limited altruisms which 'the selfish gene' can produce (kin-altruism, group altruism and, more generally, reciprocal altruism) tend to escalate into a more universal kind of altruism, even though genetic factors might not by themselves *directly* produce this. The explanation he gives is that the power of reason evolves because it helps us to secure, by its more selfish applications, the survival of the genes which produce it; but that, once we have this power, we cannot stop ourselves using it in ways which lead us towards universal impartial benevolence. He compares morality with mathematics: counting and adding are good for our genes; but once we can do them we are on an escalator that carries us up to topology and other pursuits which, even if useful, could not have grown up because they helped our genes to reproduce themselves. In the same way, the kinds of thinking which, within a limited kin-group or small reciprocally helpful society, conduce to the reproduction of the genes responsible for them, may tend to escalate into a morality of universal equal concern for all sentient beings. And this, though not genetically produced, might in the end, in the present world-nexus of interlocking interests, prove to be genetically useful. To Singer's invocation of the escalation of reason, I would add a mention of the escalation of the moral *language* in which we reason; but the general lines of his suggestion seem to me promising.

But Mackie could agree, and still be left with his most powerful argument against me. It might be, he concedes, that the adoption of something like the standard system of *prima facie* moral principles for use in our ordinary thinking would be recommended both by a perfect moral thinker and by a similarly perfect prudential thinker. But if it were merely a contingent empirical fact about the world that this was in general the case, it would not, he thinks, support my prudential defence of morality. For although the *prima facie* principles would be the same, the route by which a prudential and a moral thinker would arrive at them would be different. And the consequence of this would be that in all difficult cases, especially those in which morality and prudence diverge, as I have admitted that they may, the critical prudential thinker may cease to agree. Though it may be prudent to cultivate a repugnance to lying, there are surely (Mackie could argue) cases in which, once the question has been raised whether I ought to tell a lie in my own interest although it would be morally wrong, the perfect prudential thinker will say that I ought, and the perfect moral thinker will say that I ought not.

As I have already suggested, the most promising way of answering this objection is by an appeal to contingent facts about human nature and about the world in which we actually live. First, I do not think it practically possible to bring people up so that they follow the *prima facie* moral principles with the consistency which even their own interest demands, without implanting in them quite strong feelings of aversion to breaking them. But if they have these feelings, it will become to that extent contrary to their interest to break them, because it makes them feel bad. So, when the perfect prudential critical thinker takes this additional factor into account, he too will recommend telling the truth. The original aversion therapy was in our own interest, and, once we have undergone it, it makes it in our interest to avoid the aversive events (e.g., lie-telling by us) even in those cases (which for my argument will have to be rare) in which it is otherwise in our interest that they should occur.

Secondly, even if the coincidence between morality and prudence in general were purely fortuitous (which it is not, though it is not logically necessary either), it would be sufficient for my argument (which is designed to show why we should not bring up our children and ourselves as amoralists) if there were this contingent correlation. For when we are bringing them up (at a stage when they certainly cannot *distinguish* clearly between morality and prudence) we shall cultivate in them the sound moral principles in their own interest. So there is prudential justification for the original aversion therapy. But what shall we, if we have their interests at heart, include in our education on the question of what to do when in difficult cases morality and prudence conflict? The time will come when they will be able to distinguish between moral and prudential critical thinking, even if, being humans, they cannot manage either at all well. My guess is that we shall warn them against supposing too easily that they can win the prudential game by abandoning the moral one. Critical thinking of any sort is extremely difficult, and, for my part, I think it both easier and wiser to do it in the moral way, by appealing to truly universal principles, than to attempt self-interested cost-benefit analyses. I know of so many people who have erred, even prudentially speaking, by supposing otherwise.

This leads me to a discussion of Mackie's third and last main objection, which will have to be brief. It relates to what he calls the inaccessibility of critical thinking to human beings. I do not find so much difference on this point between him and myself as he does. I stress repeatedly in my book that only a perfect being (God, or the character I call the archangel) could do it perfectly. Bishop Butler therefore, as Mackie says and as I have said in the past, leaves the whole thing to God, to find out the best *prima facie* principles and reveal them to our consciences. But, as Hobbes says, 'Though God Almighty can speak to a man, by Dreams, Visions, Voice, and Inspiration; yet he obliges no man to beleeve he hath so done to him that pretends it; who (being a man) may erre, and (which is more) may lie'.[11] If we either do not believe in God, or believe in him but also think that the line of communication between him and us is fallible, what are we to do? Intuitive thinking, as I hope to have shown in my book and as Mackie agrees, cannot be self-supporting, because we cannot without circularity appeal to intuitions to justify intuitions. So critical thinking has somehow or other to be done.

The question therefore turns into one about whether Mackie's or my suggestions about the best method of critical thinking are more promising. He first considers a method which, he says, could be put forward as an amendment to my own which on reflection I might accept. But no reflection is necessary, because the suggestion is entirely consistent with my views from the beginning and is no amendment. This is that my

> thoroughgoing prescriptive universalization might amalgamate the points of view of all the individuals concerned in a way that took serious account of the separateness of persons, by assigning such basic abstract rights as I have suggested to each person. That is, we could have a right-based method of critical thinking (p. 98).

As I have already said, this is how my own method proceeds: the abstract right in question is that to equal concern and respect (which is a mere rephrasing of universalizability). All the other rights which Mackie wants he calls *prima facie*, and therefore cannot think them to be the bases of critical thinking; and anything else he wants to put in as a basis of critical thinking could, I am pretty sure, be shown to be derivative from this right to equal concern.

But Mackie rejects this approach because he wants us not to base ourselves on conceptual analysis: 'Right and wrong have to be invented . . . morality is not to be discovered but to be made' (p. 98). This is surely not a bone of contention between us. For if he is here speaking about the concepts, of course I can agree that they had to be invented (or at least, to allow for a Chomskian innate grammar, that they had to develop somehow among men); and if he is speaking about the *content* of morality, it is in accord with my prescriptivist views, which have often been attacked on this very ground, to say that we have to come to our own moral principles and cannot look them up in any encyclopedia.

However, for whatever reason, Mackie rejects this approach, and suggests instead that

> critical thinking might itself be a process of interaction, negotiation, and debate between diverse groups with different starting points, different traditions of thought. Rather than proceeding *de haut en bas*, being pursued by one or more detached thinkers who try to stand above the whole conflict of interests and ideals, it would work up from below, from those conflicting views and claims themselves (p. 100).

This gets me quite wrong, if it was intended to suggest that on my view moral thinking can be done without discussing other people's interests, ideals, claims, views, etc., with them. Why should it be thought that I wish to dispense with such discussion and negotiation? But the question is, 'When we have finished stating our claims and views, what do we do then?' Some people, perhaps, are content to leave the issue thereafter to a power struggle. Mackie, with proper caution, says

> The details of this process would be contingent upon the input to it and are therefore not open to any precise description *a priori*. But it is reasonable to expect that any such process of interaction, negotiation, and debate would be roughly equivalent to some distribution of entitlements that are not merged into a pure collectivity – in other words, that this too would be, in effect, a right-based approach.

I find this suggestion somewhat obscure; but in so far as I can understand it, it seems not too different from my own. The main difference is that I, unlike any right-based theory so far produced, provide a clear basis for the negotiation: the prescriptions they come to in the end have to be such as they can all accept for universal application whatever individual role anybody plays. This is a method often in effect used in negotiations, and it works. The use of this rule in critical thinking will lead the negotiators to assign to each other at least one 'entitlement' at the critical level, namely the right to equal concern. It will also lead them to give each other a lot of *prima facie* 'abstract' (as Mackie calls them) entitlements for use at the intuitive level. In fact the whole thing will go just as I say it does, given this ground rule. If this is not to be the ground rule, what other way is there of disciplining the negotiations?

I will end with a suggestion. My own ideas were developed *pari passu* with fairly engaged and involved thought about a lot of practical moral issues such as often divide the negotiators in such disputes. I would be willing to let my method and a right-based method (when one has been fully worked out) be tried out on such issues, to see how well they serve to resolve them. I think it would turn out that the methods, in so far as they served, were not all that different.

NOTES

1. This and the paper to which it is a reply are the fruits of the last of several seminars which John Mackie and I held at Oxford before his tragic death. I must express the feeling of personal loss that I share with many others at being bereft of the delight and illumination of discussions with him.

2. *A Theory of Justice* (Cambridge, Mass.: Harvard University Press, 1971), p. 27.

3. Cited in J. S. Mill, *Utilitarianism*, ch. 5 end.

4. See my *Moral Thinking* (Oxford: Oxford University Press, 1981), chs. 2, 3.

5. *Moral Thinking*, esp. pp. 28ff.

6. 'Community and Communication' in *People and Cities*, ed. S. E. Verney (London: Fontana, 1969); reprinted in my *Applications of Moral Philosophy* (London: Macmillan, 1972), p. 115.

7. *Moral Thinking*, ch. 7.

8. Xenophon, *Memorabilia* I, 7; see *Moral Thinking*, p. 196.

9. *The Expanding Circle: Ethics and Sociobiology* (New York: Farrar, Straus & Giroux, 1980).

10. *New Republic*, February 1981.

11. *Leviathan*, ch. 32.

[5]

THE JOURNAL OF PHILOSOPHY

VOLUME LXXXII, NO. 4, APRIL 1985

WELL-BEING, AGENCY AND FREEDOM
THE DEWEY LECTURES 1984*

MORAL INFORMATION

THE main aim of these lectures is to explore a moral approach that sees persons from two different perspectives: *well-being* and *agency*. Both the "well-being aspect" and the "agency aspect" of persons have their own relevance in the assessment of states and actions. Each aspect also yields a corresponding notion of freedom.

A second objective is to examine a set of metaethical issues, making use of an "informational" approach to moral analysis which focuses on the admissibility and use of different types of information in moral valuation (by imposing a set of "invariance restrictions" on moral judgments). The two objectives are closely related in the sense that the substantive moral analysis draws on the metaethical arguments.

The first lecture is concerned primarily with metaethical issues, the second with well-being, and the third with agency.

I. INFORMATION AND INVARIANCE

Informational analysis can be used to bring out the content, scope, and limitations of different moral principles. Each moral principle needs some types of information for its use, and—no less impor-

* These John Dewey Lectures were presented at Columbia University on September 17, 18, and 19 of 1984. They constitute the fifth series of John Dewey Lectures, which were established in 1967 to honor the late John Dewey, who had been from 1905 to 1930 a professor of philosophy at Columbia.

In preparing these lectures for publication, I have benefited greatly from extensive comments of John Bennett, G. A. Cohen, Ronald Dworkin, Richard Hare, Isaac Levi, Tom Nagel, T. M. Scanlon, Ian White, and Bernard Williams. I have also had helpful suggestions from Bruce Ackerman, Kenneth Arrow, John Broome, Partha Dasgupta, James Griffin, Peter Hammond, Ted Honderich, Susan Hurley, Hidé Ishiguro, Stig Kanger, John Mackie, Sidney Morgenbesser, Derek Parfit, and John Rawls.

0022-362X/85/8204/0169$05.30

tantly—"rules out" direct use of other types of information. In their latter role, moral principles impose "informational constraints," demanding that certain types of information should not be allowed to influence the moral judgments to be made.

Informational constraints are typically imposed implicitly—entailed by other conditions—rather than stated explicitly.[1] But some principles do take the explicit form of informational constraints. For example, typical requirements of "universalizability" of moral judgments are direct informational constraints. The necessity to make "similar" judgments in "similar" circumstances rules out the use of all types of information not included in the notion of "similarity" of circumstances.

The basic form of an informational constraint is that of an invariance requirement: if two objects x and y belong to the same *isoinformation set I*, then they must be treated in the same way J. For all x, y: $x, y \in I \Rightarrow J(x,y)$. Such an invariance requirement is specified in a particular context, involving (among other things) the characterization of "objects" (x,y, etc.) and that of being treated "in the same way" (J). The invariance requirement takes the form of specifying, in that context, a class of isoinformation sets of objects, and any two objects in a given isoinformation set I must be treated in the same way.[2] An invariance restriction is based on a reading—explicit or implicit—of some types of information as being relevant for the moral judgment in question, and others not so. It asserts that any difference between two objects x and y belonging to the same isoinformation set is *irrelevant* in the current context.

A few examples may help to illustrate the diversity of ways in which informational constraints may be used through the specification of invariance requirements. When Henry Sidgwick claimed that "if a kind of conduct that is right (or wrong) for me is not right (or wrong) for some one else, it must be on the ground of some difference between the two cases, other than the fact that I and he are dif-

[1] Implicit uses of informational conditions are examined and illustrated in my "Informational Analysis of Moral Principles," in Ross Harrison, ed., *Rational Action* (New York: Cambridge, 1979).

[2] The role of informational constraints in the form of invariance restrictions in social choice theory is examined in my *Collective Choice and Social Welfare* (San Francisco: Holden-Day, 1970; republished, Amsterdam: North-Holland, 1979), hereafter, CCSW, and "On Weights and Measures: Informational Constraints in Social Welfare Analysis," *Econometrica*, XLV (1977): 1539–1572, reprinted in *Choice, Welfare and Measurement* (Oxford: Blackwell, and Cambridge, Mass.: MIT Press, 1982), hereafter, CWM. See also Claude d'Aspremont and Louis Gevers, "Equity and the Informational Basis of Collective Choice," *Review of Economic Studies*, XLIV (1977): 199–209, and Kevin Roberts, "Interpersonal Comparability and Social Choice Theory," *Review of Economic Studies*, XLVII (1980): 421–439.

ferent persons,"[3] he used a powerful informational constraint to rule out taking note of personal identity, as such, in making these judgments of conduct. Other requirements of "universalization" of moral judgments take the form of similarly general informational constraints.[4]

Another example—rather more specialized than Kantian and other requirements of universalization—is Kenneth Arrow's condition of "the independence of irrelevant alternatives" in social choice.[5] Here the "objects" x and y stand respectively for alternative n-tuples of individual preference orderings $\{R_i\}$ and $\{R_i^*\}$. The two are seen as belonging to the same isoinformation set, in the context of choice from a given subset S of social states, if and only if each individual's preference ordering of the states in S is the same in the first case as in the second (no matter how the two preferences differ regarding states *not* in S). The interpretation of $J(x,y)$, i.e., of x and y being treated in the same way, is that the *same* social choice is made from S in the two cases.[6] The *independence condition* demands that, in the context of choice from the set S, all information *other than* the individual rankings of the elements of S by each person must be regarded as irrelevant and such information must not influence social choice over S.

Another interesting example is that of the Pareto principle, which is widely used in welfare economics. This can be defined in rather different forms, each imposing some informational constraint. One particular form—that of the *Pareto indifference rule*—is *purely* informational, and this demands that, if everyone is indifferent between two states x and y, then x and y are socially exactly as good as each other. Here the objects are states; the interpretation of $J(x,y)$ is that state x and state y are socially equally good; and the isoinformation sets are based on the congruence of x and y in individual preference rankings. The informational constraint imposed by this invariance restriction rules out the use of any information other than the placing of the respective states in individual preference orderings in the special case in which everyone happens

[3] *The Method of Ethics* (London: Macmillan, 7th ed., 1907), Book III, ch. XII, p. 379.

[4] Different types of universalization requirements are carefully distinguished by John Mackie, *Ethics: Inventing Right and Wrong* (Harmondsworth: Penguin Books, 1977), ch. 4. See also Richard Hare, *Moral Thinking: Its Levels, Method and Point* (New York: Oxford, 1981), ch. 6.

[5] *Social Choice and Individual Values* (New York: Wiley, 1951; 2nd ed., 1963).

[6] There can, however, be different interpretations of what "social choice" stands for. Some alternative ones have been explored and distinguished from one another in my "Liberty and Social Choice," this JOURNAL, LXXX, 1 (January 1983): 5–28. The independence condition can be correspondingly defined for each of the distinct interpretations.

to be indifferent between x and y. Given the congruence of two states in individual preference rankings, no *other* information can have any influence on the ranking of the two states in terms of social goodness, according to the Pareto indifference rule. Indeed, we do not have to know anything else at all about the two states to be able to make this judgment, and any other information would, in this context, be redundant and useless.[7]

II. UNIVERSALIZABILITY AND INVARIANCE

The informational constraints imposed by requirements of universalizability used in the literature have been justified in several different ways. They can be taken to be substantive moral principles, on which we have to exercise judgment, or as being necessitated by the very nature of ethics.[8] In his *Language of Morals,*[9] Richard Hare has powerfully argued that universalizability in the form of the need to make identical judgments in identical circumstances is entailed by the meaning of moral language. It can, however, be argued that if this claim is accepted, then it would follow that the so-called "Hume's law" (to wit: the impossibility of deriving moral propositions from factual premises), endorsed by Hare, among others, must be, strictly speaking, false.[10] If two actions are factually identical, then universalizability (seen by Hare as a necessity due to the meaning of moral language) will require that they be *morally* equivalent.

In fact, this can also be seen as an aspect of the theory of identity, whereby if $x = y$, then $f(x) = f(y)$. If the "theory of valuation," to use John Dewey's term,[11] indicates that moral values must be seen as a function f of factual information, then factual identity ($x = y$) must entail moral equivalence: $f(x) = f(y)$.[12] This does not depend on the nature of the function $f(.)$, except that it *is* a function.

The relevance of this line of reasoning does, however, depend on

[7] Though the Pareto principle is usually taken to be "mild" and "innocuous," its cutting power is indeed quite severe, because of the power of the informational constraint in excluding the use of nonpreference information in judging the social goodness of states of affairs. It is a demanding condition on its own and becomes remarkably exacting when combined with other conditions (such as Arrow's independence condition and "unrestricted domain," or a condition of personal liberty). These issues are discussed in my "Personal Utilities and Public Judgments: Or What's Wrong with Welfare Economics?" *Economic Journal,* LXXXIX (1979): 537-558, reprinted in CWM; and in "Utilitarianism and Welfarism," this JOURNAL, LXXVI, 9 (September, 1979): 479-487.

[8] Sidgwick took "the Kantian maxim" to be "certainly fundamental, certainly true, and not without practical importance" (*op. cit.,* p. xvii).

[9] New York: Oxford, 1952; rev. ed., 1961.

[10] This proposition was stated and defended in my "Hume's Law and Hare's Rule," *Philosophy,* XLI (January 1966): 75-79. Richard Hare's response to this point can be found in *Moral Thinking* (1981), pp. 233/4.

[11] *Theory of Valuation* (Chicago: University Press, 1939).

[12] It is sometimes argued that to say that two actions (or two states) are morally

the interpretation of the idea of "identity" in dealing with universalizability of moral judgments. There is an exacting sense in which it can be said that two factual circumstances are never exactly identical. The notion of identity used in the application of universalizability is based on some informational constraint, ruling out some differences as irrelevant. Richard Hare, in fact, concentrates on different cases being "identical in their *universal properties*".[13] There is an important problem in deciding whether the informational constraints that rule out the relevance of what are seen as *non*universal properties must not themselves be substantive moral requirements—not necessitated by the language of morals itself. What is at issue is the *scope* of the principle of universalizability (seen as a necessity due to the nature of moral language).[14] I shall not pursue this question further here. The theses presented in these lectures do not depend on taking a particular position on this question.

The possible conflict between the demands of Hume's law and the thesis that universalizability is necessitated by the nature of moral language, may well be a rather esoteric question. But in focusing on the need to relate moral valuation functionally to factual circumstances, the issue of universalizability does relate to the more general question of the "objectivity" of moral beliefs.[15] The question of ob-

---

equally good is not in itself a moral judgment. According to this view, "*x* is morally good" *is* a moral judgment, but "*x* and *y* are morally equally good" is not, since it does not specify whether either of them is "morally good." (I am grateful to Ted Honderich for forcefully raising this eminently discussable question, when responding to a version of this paper at a meeting of the Philosophical Society in Oxford.) I believe that such a view is hard to defend, since moral equivalence must be saying *something* about moral matters. In fact, there is a strong case for taking the relation "at least as good as" as the primitive concept in goodness judgments (as, say, in Arrow's framework, *op. cit.*, ch. 2). From this relation, that of being "equally good" can follow through conjunction. It can even be argued that a statement such as "This action is *good*" can be fully understood only in terms of some comparison (usually implicit) with *other possible actions*. The idea of being "equally good" belongs solidly to that inescapably comparative framework of moral judgment.

[13] *Moral Thinking* (1981), p. 108; italics added.

[14] The exact proposition put forward in my "Hume's Law and Hare's Rule" (1966) was, in fact: "*Either* Hare's principle of universalizability is empty of content, or it conflicts with Hume's Law" (79).

[15] See Thomas Nagel, *Mortal Questions* (New York: Cambridge, 1979), Essay 14, and "The Limits of Objectivity," in S. McMurrin, ed., *Tanner Lectures on Human Values*, vol. I (Salt Lake City: Utah UP, 1980). See also Simon Blackburn, "Moral Realism," in J. Casey, ed., *Morality and Moral Reasoning* (London: Methuen, 1971); David Wiggins, "Truth, Invention, and the Meaning of Life," *Proceedings of the British Academy*, LXII (1976); Donald Davidson, "Psychology as Philosophy," in *Essays on Action and Events* (New York: Oxford, 1980); John McDowell, "Noncognitivism and Rule-following," in S. H. Holtzman and C. M. Leich, eds., *Wittgenstein: To Follow a Rule* (London: Routledge & Kegan Paul, 1981); Susan Hurley, "Objectivity and Disagreement," Honderich, ed., *Ethics and Objectivity* (London: Routledge & Kegan Paul, forthcoming).

jectivity will be taken up later on in this lecture (in section VII), but what is important to stress here is the need, in this context, to examine the invariance requirements that must be imposed on moral beliefs. Objectivity of moral beliefs must require some types of invariance, but the necessity to make identical moral judgments in *exactly* identical circumstances is perhaps too "minimal" to take us very far into that question. It will be argued later that what may be called *authorship invariance* is indeed required by objectivity of moral beliefs, but this can coexist with the possibility that moral valuations of different persons (sharing exactly the *same* moral system) may vary with the different positions that they respectively occupy in the given states of affairs. Invariance conditions involving informational constraints will have to be formulated differently in that context (section VII).

III. UTILITARIANISM AND INFORMATION

It is manifest that the actual availability of information can affect the possibility of using specific moral approaches. For example, Lionel Robbins's celebrated attack on utilitarian welfare economics—an attack which had a profound influence on the direction of welfare economics for several decades—centered mostly on the unavailability of information regarding interpersonal comparison of utility, making utilitarianism allegedly unworkable.[16] That attack was rather wrong-headed, and it was based on a failure to grasp the nature and the evidential basis of utility comparisons.[17] But certainly the more difficult it is to get utility information, the more limited is the scope of application of utilitarianism. Other moral approaches are similarly constrained by the availability of information.

The dependence of the usability of moral principles on the availability of information is obvious enough. What is perhaps less obvious is the dependence of the usability of information on the particular moral principles adopted. This question of *implicit* informational constraints was briefly discussed earlier (in section I). A substantive moral system can indeed be substantially—though not

[16] *An Essay on the Nature and Significance of Economic Science* (London: Macmillan, 1932), and "Interpersonal Comparisons of Utility," *Economic Journal*, XLVIII (1938).

[17] See particularly I. M. D. Little, *A Critique of Welfare Economics* (New York: Oxford, 2nd ed., 1957); Richard C. Jeffrey, "On Interpersonal Utility Theory," this JOURNAL, LXVIII, 20 (Oct. 21, 1971): 647-656; Ilmar Waldner, "The Empirical Meaningfulness of Interpersonal Utility Comparisons," *ibid.*, LXIX, 4 (Feb. 24, 1972): 87-103; and my "Interpersonal Comparisons of Welfare," in M. Boskin, ed., *Economics and Human Welfare* (New York: Academic Press, 1979), reprinted in my CWM. See also the papers of Donald Davidson and Allan Gibbard to be included in a volume of essays edited by J. Elster and A. Hylland, provisionally called *Foundations of Social Choice Theory*, to be published by Cambridge University Press, and an unpublished paper by Robert Nozick, "Interpersonal Comparisons of Utility."

completely—characterized by specifying the informational constraints it imposes.[18]

Take simple act utilitarianism, which can be factored into: (1) *act consequentialism* (the goodness of an act is given by the goodness of its consequent states of affairs), (2) *welfarism* (the goodness of a state of affairs is given by the goodness of the utility information regarding that state), and (3) *sum ranking* (the goodness of utility information is given by the sum total of the utilities in question).[19] Other types of utilitarianism, such as rule utilitarianism, motive utilitarianism, etc., would require the replacement of act consequentialism by different consequentialist requirements such as rule consequentialism, motive consequentialism, etc. The common building block of different types of utilitarian consequentialism is given by the combination of some consequentialist form with *outcome utilitarianism,* which is produced by the union of welfarism and sum ranking, making the goodness of states of affairs be given by the utility sum total in that state.

These requirements impose a set of informational constraints, in the form of invariance restrictions linked to specific information types. The isoinformation sets are given by the factored conditions individually or jointly. For example, in judging states of affairs, *welfarism* would put two states in the same isoinformation set if they are identical in terms of utility (i.e., if they are mapped onto the same point in the *n*-dimensional utility space, in an *n*-person society). If *sum ranking* is also imposed, this requires further that two states must belong to the same isoinformation set whenever they have the same utility *total* (even if they are mapped onto different points in the *n*-dimensional utility space). Finally, additionally imposing a minimal (direction-neutral) version of *act consequentialism* will put two acts (even though they *are* different acts) in the same isoinformation set if the two states of affairs they respectively yield have the same utility total. And that, of course, takes us more or less all the way to act utilitarianism (all we need further is a "directional" axiom that says the more the better). In assessing act utilitarianism (and any other moral system), it is important to examine both what information it regards as appropriate *and* what information it constrains out as irrelevant and unusable.

IV. PLURALISM: PRINCIPLES AND INFORMATION

The informational parsimony of utilitarianism reflects its apparently "monist" rather than "pluralist" informational format. This

[18] This is discussed in my "Informational Analysis of Moral Principles" (1979).

[19] The rationale of this factorization is discussed in my "Utilitarianism and Welfarism" (1979). See also the "Introduction" to Sen and Williams, eds., *Utilitarianism and Beyond* (New York: Cambridge, 1982).

appearance of monism is somewhat deceptive because utility can be sensibly seen as a "plural" notion itself,[20] and I shall have more to say on this in the second lecture.

The issue of pluralism has been discussed a fair amount, and more specifically, the question has been seen as important in examining alternatives to utilitarianism. Is it necessary that a plausible alternative to utilitarianism be itself monist?

The idea of pluralism vis-à-vis monism not only is ambiguous, but also is sometimes viewed in a way that has no essential relation to the feature of plurality. A common approach seems to take the form of identifying the use of plurality of principles with *intuitionism*.[21] Pluralism is a claim about the *form* of moral structures, whereas intuitionism—unless radically redefined—is a claim about how the moral structure may be *derived and supported* (i.e., whether by intuition only). The two things are not essentially related. The suggestion that if there are many ultimate principles (and they are not in a hierarchy), then the balance among them *must be* struck by intuition, is, of course, completely baseless. John Rawls, who does restrict the term 'intuitionism' to pluralist moral theories, does at least make clear that "a conception of justice can be pluralist without requiring us to weigh its principles by intuition."[22]

Even when the confusing identification of pluralism with intuitionism has been rejected, there remain at least two different ways of defining pluralism. One is in terms of plurality of principles (I shall call this *principle pluralism*), and the other in terms of plurality of informational variables (to be called *information pluralism*).

It is probably not particularly worth while to try to define a metric on the space of principles (including "combining" principles) to be able to count them precisely and to be "really" sure how many principles there are in a particular moral structure. The genuine worry that seems to motivate concern about principle pluralism lies elsewhere and is easy to see; to wit, that a nonintegrated moral structure could leave many moral issues unresolved. In an often-quoted passage, John Stuart Mill put the problem thus:

> There must be some standard by which to determine the goodness or badness, absolute and comparative, of ends or objects of desire. And

[20] I have tried to discuss different aspects of this plurality of utility in "Plural Utility," *Proceedings of the Aristotelian Society*, LXXXI (1980 81): 193–215. See also Martha C. Nussbaum, "Plato on Commensurability and Desire," *Proceedings of the Aristotelian Society*, LXXXIII (1984): 50–80.

[21] See J. D. Urmson, "A Defence of Intuitionism," *Proceedings of the Aristotelian Society*, LXXV (1974 75): 111–119, where Urmson contrasts: (i) "mononomic," (ii) "hierarchical," and (iii) "intuitionist" moral structures.

[22] *A Theory of Justice* (1971), p. 34.

> whatever that standard is, there can be but one: for if there were several ultimate principles of conduct, the same conduct might be approved by one of those principles and condemned by another; and there would be need for some more general principle as umpire between them.[23]

The argument clearly has some force.[24] It is, however, interesting to note that here Mill is not disputing the case for having a principle-pluralist structure with a combining principle (what he calls an "umpire"), but rather asserting only the need for such a principle for a principle-pluralist structure. He is concerned to show that if that is how pluralism is to be dealt with, then it would again be true that there is "but one" ultimate standard. One could dispute this—the role of the "umpire" does not obliterate the continuing role of the plural principles in the final ranking of actions, states, etc. But not much really hangs on how such a system is described.

V. PLURALISM AND INCOMPLETENESS

The really important questions regarding pluralism seem to be the following. First, the scope of combining principles may be limited;[25] the "diversity of goods" may be too deep.[26] The conflicting values may be unreconcilable and may be hard to integrate, as Karl Marx argued in his well-known *Critique of the Gotha Programme*, referring to the German Workers Party's simultaneous loyalty to the principles of "equal distribution" and the worker's right to get "the undiminished proceeds of labor."[27] On a different type of problem, it has been argued, by Isaiah Berlin in particular, that elimination of value conflicts inevitably implies some loss of value, and perhaps even that "we cannot conceive of a situation in which it was true both that all value-conflict had been eliminated, and that there had been no loss of value on the way."[28]

[23] *A System of Logic*, Book VI, ch. XII, s. 7. See also Hillel Steiner, "Reason and Intuition in Ethics," *Ratio*, XXV, 1 (June 1983); 59-68.

[24] One point to note, though, is that it cannot be assumed that the existence of "several ultimate principles of conduct" *must* necessarily lead to conflict. Whether it would or not would depend inter alia on the overlap of the domains of the respective ultimate principles. Conditions of compatibility of principles are discussed in my "Informational Analysis of Moral Principles" (1979).

[25] See Bernard Williams, *Moral Luck* (New York: Cambridge, 1981), especially Essay 5 ("Conflicts of Values").

[26] See Charles Taylor, "The Diversity of Goods," in Sen and Williams, *op. cit.*, in which see also Stuart Hampshire, "Morality and Convention." For a different aspect of the issue of diversity and commensurability, see Nussbaum, *op cit.*

[27] *Critique of the Gotha Programme* (1875; New York: International Publishers, 1966).

[28] The quoted sentence is Bernard Williams' statement of one of Berlin's arguments; *Moral Luck*, p. 71. See Berlin, *Concepts and Categories* (New York: Oxford, 1980).

If value conflicts do remain unresolved and if conflicting principles are not "umpired" together (to use Mill's phrase) by some balancing principle, then the over-all ranking may well be incomplete (if such a combined ranking is sought).[29] The "intersection" of the different criteria will, of course, yield a partial order, and although that "intersection partial order" may be extendable by weights that are not fully determined (and could vary over a wide range), the "maximal" partial order, given everything, may still be quite seriously incomplete. Then there may not, quite possibly, exist any "best" action (or "best state"). Is that incompleteness an embarrassment for a principle-pluralist moral approach? That is, indeed an important question, to be faced.

Second, if we do happen to resolve the problem of incompleteness by some combining principle, leading to what Mill takes to be a unique "standard," would that integrated system be *informationally* monist, in the sense of taking only one type of information (like utility) to be intrinsically valuable?

I take up the second question first. The answer is straightforward: informational monism is a completely different issue and is not required for an integrated, complete structure. Indeed, if integration is brought about by a combining principle "umpiring" together various demands based on various informational bases, it would *have to be* information-pluralist. Even if we are entirely persuaded by the quoted argument from Mill, there would still be no particular reason for us to look for some single informational base of the kind that, say, utility allegedly provides. There is no argument in all this for expecting that moral goodness must be ultimately decidable by counting the units of some homogeneous nonmoral quantity (as utility is taken to be), rather than having to balance the relative importance of different considerations that conflict.[30] It is not so much that information pluralism can be defended, as that there is no special need for a defense.

I turn now to the first question—the alleged need for completeness. In a recent paper, "Moral Struggle,"[31] Isaac Levi has followed the lead of John Dewey in discussing the importance of conflicts of principles that may or may not get resolved, and has addressed the

[29] On the "disparity between the fragmentation of value and the singleness of decision," see T. Nagel, "The Fragmentation of Value," in *Mortal Questions.* See also R. Dworkin, "No Right Answer?" in P. M. S. Hacker and J. Raz, eds., *Law, Morality and Society: Essays in Honour of H. L. A. Hart* (New York: Oxford, 1977).

[30] See also Sen and Williams, "Introduction," pp. 16-18.

[31] Mimeographed, Philosophy Department, Columbia University, 1984; this is in fact the first chapter of a forthcoming book.

problem of decision making under those circumstances. To quote Dewey and Tufts:

> The struggle is not between a good which is clear to him and something else which attracts him but which he knows to be wrong. It is between values each of which is an undoubted good in its place but which now get in each other's way. He is forced to reflect in order to come to a decision. Moral theory is a generalized extension of the kind of thinking in which he now engages.[32]

Decision making with unresolved conflicts is part of a more general problem, viz., decision making with *incomplete* rankings.[33] We may begin by noting that incomplete rankings may have to be faced even with *one* ultimate principle of valuation. The most obvious reason for this is the limitation of informational availability. For example, partial comparability of utilities—in *interpersonal* correspondences—will make the utilitarian ranking a partial ordering.[34] It can also be argued that partial comparability of utilities may be caused not only by the actual limitation of factual knowledge, but also by the intrinsic nature of interpersonal utility comparisons. Utilities may not, in this view, be things that can, even in principle, be fully compared between persons, leading to an exact one-to-one correspondence of the utility measures (levels, units, etc.) of different persons.[35] The incompleteness of the utilitarian ranking would, on this view, be unremovable through richer factual knowledge. In these circumstances, a pure utilitarian would have to *assert* the incompleteness of moral ranking as the correct moral position.

In fact, depending on the status of the incompleteness, it is possible to distinguish between (1) open incompleteness, and (2) closed incompleteness. The former is exemplified by a partial ordering that can still be extended, e.g., by more information (as in the case of utilitarianism with contingent partial comparability), or by the use of some other supplementary principle (e.g., extending the in-

[32] J. Dewey and J. H. Tufts, *Ethics* (New York: Holt, 1932), p. 175.

[33] More generally, decision making with incomplete *valuation structures*, which may or may not be binary.

[34] See my "Interpersonal Aggregation and Partial Comparability," *Econometrica*, XXXVIII (1970), reprinted in CWM; and *Collective Choice and Social Welfare* (1970), ch. 7*. See also C. Blackorby, "Degrees of Cardinality and Aggregate Partial Orderings," *Econometrica*, XLIII (1975); B. J. Fine, "A Note on 'Interpersonal Aggregation and Partial Comparability'," *ibid.;* and K. Basu, *Revealed Preference of Governments* (New York: Cambridge, 1979).

[35] See my *Collective Choice and Social Welfare* (1970), ch. 7, and CWM, Essays 9 and 12.

complete ranking given by the Pareto criterion by some supplementary "distributional" judgment), or by moving toward the resolution of "moral struggles" (as in the case of conflicts of principles). The partial ordering stays, as it were, "ready" to be extended.

In contrast, for "closed" incompleteness, the absence of completeness is *assertive,* and there is no room for extending the partial order. In stating that x and y "cannot" be ranked vis-à-vis each other in terms of moral goodness, a substantive and definite moral assertion is being made. Though the demands of practical choice may force us to choose one or the other, there is—on this view—no additional moral criterion that can be used to rank the unranked pairs *in terms of moral goodness.*

Assertive incompleteness, like assertive completeness, has the effect of closing a substantive issue, declaring further search to be pointless. There is obviously an important problem here of decidability. It is also arguable that assertive incompleteness should never be "accepted," because that may discourage moral inquiry.[36] This methodological point (regarding search and research) might well be supportable, but it does not, of course, rule out the real possibility of assertive incompleteness.

When an incomplete ranking refers not to moral goodness as such but to some specific moral quality, e.g., justice, then the completion of that partial ranking by some *other* criterion may give a combined, complete view of moral goodness, but this would do nothing to complete the ranking of justice itself, which would continue to remain assertively incomplete. It could then be the case that while, say, state x is more just than y, states x and z simply cannot be compared in terms of justice (i.e., neither is more just than the other, nor can they be seen as equally just; they are simply noncomparable as far as justice is concerned). And that would continue to be so even if the incompleteness could be removed in the over-all ranking, or in decision making, by the supplementary use of some *other* criterion.

Yielding complete orders cannot be an a priori requirement of the legitimacy of a moral principle, or even of an entire moral approach with its full structure of principles. It is not a matter of getting metamoral passmarks. It does not determine a substantive moral approach, but rather *gets determined* by such an approach, which could yield completeness of valuations or not (possibly even *asser-*

[36] The strategic role of openness in this sense is discussed in my note, "The Nature and Classes of Prescriptive Judgments," *Philosophical Quarterly,* XVII, 66 (January 1967): 46–62.

tively not). If the appropriate moral approach produces the result that *x* and *y* are morally noncomparable, then decision making has to reckon with that.

It is often pointed out that in real life we have to choose something or other—we must decide, we must act. This is certainly so, and we must end up doing something or other, if only nothing, by default. If our actions are to be morally guided, then our incomplete moral valuations must be used to eliminate some alternatives, while permitting others.[37] We must not act like a moral counterpart of Buridan's ass—needlessly starving by default, unable to figure out which of the nonstarving alternatives happened to be the best.[38] Intelligent moral choice demands that we not choose—explicitly or by default—an alternative that we can see is morally inferior to another feasible alternative. But this does not require that the chosen alternative be seen to be "best" in that set of feasible alternatives, since there may be no best alternative at all, given the incompleteness of our moral ranking.

VI. STATES, ACTIONS, WELFARISM, AND CONSEQUENTIALISM

One source of informational pluralism is the possibility that acts themselves may have value or disvalue, distinct from the valuation of states resulting from such acts. This is an important issue in assessing consequentialism and in examining agent-relative moral approaches.

In examining states of affairs, we have to be sure of what they "contain." That actions are part of the respective states of affairs is sometimes denied, especially to draw a sharp contract between consequentialist and deontological theories. It is hard to defend this exclusion. A state of affairs in which Brutus kills Caesar is not just one in which Caesar has expired. It is one in which the killing of Caesar by Brutus (and others) figures. There is, of course, also the question as to how we choose to *describe* the state.[39] But what the

[37] The specification of "permissibility" based on an incomplete ranking of moral goodness may, of course, be used to generate a complete binary relation of its own, but the *derived* binary relation of being "equally permissible" will typically lack some of the standard properties of a preference relation, such as transitivity (see my CCSW, pp. 48/9).

[38] I interpret Buridan's ass's problem as the inability to rank the two haystacks, rather than—as in the more standard version—viewing them as equally good, in which case *both* haystacks would have been "best" (and either could have been unproblematically chosen in terms of binary optimality). See my "Behaviour and the Concept of Preference," *Economica*, XL (1973); reprinted in CWM, pp. 61–2.

[39] See Frederic Schick, "Under Which Description?" in Sen and Williams. See also Davidson, "Logical Form of Action Sentences," in *Essays on Actions and Events* (1980). I have tried to discuss some of the issues involved in description in "Description as Choice," *Oxford Economic Papers*, XXXII (1980); reprinted in CWM.

state of affairs includes is really a matter of what *in fact* happened. Caesar could have expired in many different ways, and the fact that he got knifed by Brutus must be a *part* of that state, no matter how we *choose* to describe it in one particular context or another. If we choose to leave out this fact in the description of the state of affairs, that is just a decision to be silent about one part of that state.[40]

It is, of course, true that utilitarianism *values* states of affairs in an informationally limited way, attaching no intrinsic importance to nonutility information about states, and thus inter alia ignoring actions too—except as variables for causal analysis (in linking utility to objects that yield utility), or perhaps as surrogates for utility (when utility information is hard to get). This feature of utilitarianism is welfarism, and it is a feature that is shared by some other approaches, such as utility-based "maximin" (seeing the goodness of a state as the utility level of the worst-off individual in that state.)[41]

It is important to distinguish between the respective roles of welfarism and consequentialism in making the evaluation of *actions* informationally restricted. Welfarism filters out all information other than utility information in the evaluation of *states of affairs,* and it is precisely because of that informational constraint that consequentialism has, in this compound system, the effect of ignoring everything other than utilities (in the consequent states) in *evaluating actions.* Had welfarism not been additionally imposed, consequentialism could have coexisted with taking note of such things as the values and disvalues of actions *through* the valuation of the states, which include these actions.

VII. AGENCY, POSITION, AND OBJECTIVITY

If the action information is not blocked out by welfarism or some other informational constraint) in evaluating states of affairs, the relation of the evaluator and his or her *agency* role in the state has to be considered in the moral assessment of states. It is often thought that although, in deliberating on the correctness of one's own *actions,* one must take ample note of one's responsibility for

[40] See Charles Taylor's argument for taking out actions from the assessment of consequent states ("The Diversity of Goods," 1982). On this, see my "Evaluator Relativity and Consequential Evaluation," *Philosophy and Public Affairs,* XII, 2 (Spring 1983): pp. 128-130.

[41] Inspired by Rawls's Difference Principle, this "maximin" criterion—and its lexicographic variant ("leximin")—have been much used in welfare economics; see, for example, E. S. Phelps, ed., *Economic Justice* (Harmondsworth: Penguin, 1973); Sen, *On Economic Inequality* (New York: Oxford, 1973); James Meade, *The Just Economy* (London: Allen & Unwin, 1976); A. B. Atkinson, *Social Justice and Public Policy* (Brighton: Wheatsheaf, 1983). Rawls's own Difference Principle is defined, however, not in terms of utility, but in terms of an index of "primary goods."

these actions, that issue does not arise in the evaluation of states. But since states do include one's own actions (albeit inter alia), that contrast is not sharp. One is responsible for, as it were, a part of the state, and as far as one's own actions in that state are concerned, one is responsible for them in a straightforward way. If some act—such as knifing a friend—is a bad thing to do and if the agent who did the knifing was responsible for that act, then that special badness must be a part of the over-all evaluation, *made by the knifer*, of that state. It could, of course, still be the case that, despite the badness of that action, everything considered, knifing Caesar produced a better state of affairs even from the evaluative position of Brutus ("Not that I loved Caesar less, but that I loved Rome more"). However, Brutus cannot evaluate the state, of which his killing Caesar is a part, without taking note of his own responsibility for that act.

A consistent moral approach may, therefore, require that the moral valuation function be *position-relative*. Given Brutus's role in the knifing of Caesar, Brutus cannot view the resulting state—of which that knifing was also a part—in the same way as, say, Appian, the historian, completely uninvolved in the matter, can. The difference can exist even when Appian and Brutus share exactly the same moral approach, and it arises because of the objective differences in their positions vis-à-vis the state in question. A position-relative valuation function builds in the parameter of the assessor's position *within* the valuation function itself.[42] Consider the following imaginary remark of Appian to Brutus: "If I were you, Brutus, I should have evaluated the state to be even worse than I do now, not having been involved in the knifing of Caesar myself." The statement is of the form $f(x,a,b) < f(x,a,a)$, in which $f(x,a,b)$ is the valuation of the state x by a (Appian) in the position of b (Brutus), and $f(x,a,a)$, the valuation made by Appian from his own position. Notice that the relativity in question links not to the *authorship* (the second variable), but to the position from which the evaluation is being made (the third variable), i.e., whether a's position or b's. The authorship is immaterial for "position relativity" of a moral system.

Indeed, that the approach is not subject-relative (and does not include "subjectivism" *within* the system) can be guaranteed by insisting on an invariance requirement regarding authorship. "Authorship invariance" requires that the moral valuations of a

[42] See my "Rights and Agency," *Philosophy and Public Affairs*, XI, 1 (Winter 1982): 3-39, and the exchange with Donald Regan in the same journal next year: Regan, "Against Evaluator Relativity: A Response to Sen," *ibid.*, XII, 2 (Spring 1983): 93-112.

state in a given moral system must not vary with the person making the judgment, even though it can vary with the *position from which* the valuation is to be made. Despite Appian's assertion (stated earlier) that $f(x,a,b) < f(x,a,a)$, which shows position-relativity, Appian would be bound by the requirements of authorship invariance to assert $f(x,a,b) = f(x,b,b)$.[43] "You, Brutus, should evaluate the state in the same unfavorable way as I should if I were in your position."

The possibility of combining position relativity with authorship invariance is also the reason why positionality of moral valuation is perfectly consistent with objectivity of moral values. Moral valuation can be position-relative in the same way as such statements as "The sun is setting." The truth of that statement varies with the position of the person, but it cannot vary from person to person among those standing in the same position. The aspect of objectivity related to authorship invariance, i.e., to $f(x,a,b) = f(x,b,b)$, for all x, a, and b, has to be, I believe, a part of what Thomas Nagel calls objectivity in "the primary sense"—that of "beliefs and knowledge."[44]

VIII. CONCLUDING REMARKS

This lecture has been concerned entirely with general—primarily methodological—issues. The use of informational constraints in the form of invariance requirements has been examined, both in an explicit form (e.g., in the requirement of universalizability) and in implicit ways (e.g., in utilitarianism, through the features of welfarism, sum ranking, and consequentialism). I have also argued against ruling out principle pluralism, information pluralism, and incompleteness in valuations (such as partial orderings of acts, states, or rules). The case for position relativity in moral valuation has been outlined, and it has been argued that position relativity is consistent with authorship invariance, and indeed with the corresponding aspect of objectivity in moral beliefs. The importance of the informational perspective suggests the need for improving the standard informational accounts of states of affairs. These issues will figure rather prominently in the substantive moral discussion to be presented in the next two lectures.

[43] A "subjectivist" ethical approach can deny this invariance condition. Indeed, it can even insist that *everyone* must accept the possibility of this denial. This involves authorship invariance of a different type altogether, operating at a "meta" level (invariably denying the requirement of authorship invariance of moral valuation). I am grateful to Thomas Nagel for raising this question.

[44] "The Limits of Objectivity" (1980), p. 77.

WELL-BEING AND FREEDOM

THOMAS M. SCANLON argues that "utilitarianism derives much of its appeal from alleged difficulties about the foundations of rival views."[1] He also suggests that "the wide-spread influence of utilitarian principles" derives from the "attractiveness" of what he calls "philosophical utilitarianism," which is "a particular philosophical thesis about the subject matter of morality, namely the thesis that the only fundamental moral facts are facts about individual well-being" (108). This "philosophical utilitarianism" can be taken to provide a "foundation" for utilitarianism in a rather limited sense.[2] It specifies an "informational" basis that is indeed highly attractive, but this does not, of course, indicate that there is no further need for justification of this informational basis. However, it does provide an interesting and important way of looking at utilitarianism, and provides a focus for critical assessment. That will indeed be the point of departure of this lecture. But since the term 'philosophical utilitarianism' is a little misleading (even nonutilitarian approaches can be consistent with "the thesis that the only fundamental moral facts are facts about individual well-being"), I shall call the use of this informational foundation by the more descriptive (though much less elegant) name 'well-being as informational foundation', or WAIF for short.[3]

Defending utilitarianism with the help of WAIF raises some immediate questions. (1) Is the thesis of this informational foundation really believable? Does it survive critical examination? (2) Do utilitarian principles really follow from WAIF? In fact, I shall split up the last question into two parts: (2a) Is well-being best seen as utility? (2b) Do utilitarian principles follow from WAIF if well-being is seen as utility?

I. WELL-BEING AND AGENCY

I start with the first question: Is the well-being foundation believable? It would, of course, be altogether amazing if moral goodness had nothing to do with well-being. It is easy to argue that well-being is fundamentally important. If we were tied to informational

[1] "Contractualism and Utilitarianism," in Sen and Williams, *op. cit.*, p. 103.

[2] Scanlon himself goes on to propose a rival foundational structure, of a procedural variety (involving a "contractual account"), motivated by his diagnosis that "what a successful alternative to utilitarianism must do, first and foremost, is to sap this source of strength [of utilitarianism] by providing a clear account of the foundations of nonutilitarian moral reasoning" (103).

[3] This acronym is not, I fear, very helpful (though the association of loneliness may not be altogether inappropriate for the information monism of WAIF).

monism, that elementary thought would have already pushed us much of the way to WAIF, since there would be "room" for only one thing at the top. But, as was argued in the last lecture, insisting on informational monism is a crude prejudice. By recognizing the importance of well-being, we do not close the door on the possible importance—intrinsic importance—of other things. So the question is not whether well-being is an intrinsically important variable for moral analysis, but whether it is uniquely so.

People have aspects other than well-being. Not all their activities are aimed at maximizing well-being (nor do their activities always contribute to it), no matter how broadly we define well-being within the limits of that general concept. There are goals other than well-being, and values other than goals. "Human beings," as John Dewey said in *Theory of Valuation*, "are continuously engaged in valuations" (58). It can be argued that something so central to human life—indeed to our being persons—cannot fail to be intrinsically relevant to moral analysis.

Indeed it is useful to distinguish clearly between the "well-being aspect" and the "agency aspect" of a person. John Rawls's "Kantian constructivism," in his Dewey lectures,[4] started at the agency end—with "persons characterized as rational agents of construction." Persons were seen as "having the moral power to have a conception of the good"; the agency role—broadly construed—came first, and other things followed. Although I shall not follow Rawls's route of Kantian constructivism, I would argue that the conception of "persons" in moral analysis cannot be so reduced as to attach no intrinsic importance to this agency role, seeing them ultimately only in terms of their well-being.

There is a particular sphere in which such an agency role may be especially important, and that is the person's own life. Various concepts of "autonomy,"[5] and "personal liberty,"[6] relate to this special role of agency in personal life, going well beyond considerations of well-being. The moral foundation of well-being is informationally extremely restrictive, and the agency aspect is much too crucial to leading a life for it to be intrinsically of no moral importance.

It is important to emphasize that in pointing to the informa-

[4] "Kantian Constructivism in Moral Theory: The Dewey Lectures 1980," this JOURNAL, LXXVII, 9 (September 1980): 515-572.

[5] See Jonathan Glover, *Causing Death and Saving Lives* (Harmondsworth: Penguin Books, 1977) for some interesting—and important—conflicts involving autonomy and other values, including well-being.

[6] Discussed in my CCSW (1970) and in "Liberty and Social Choice," this JOURNAL, LXXX, 1 (January 1983): 5-28.

tional limitation of WAIF, in that it gives no fundamental place to the agency aspect of a person, the assumption is *not* being made that the agency and well-being aspects of a person are unrelated. For an integrated person it is likely—possibly even inevitable—that the person's well-being will be influenced by his or her agency role. This does not, however, imply that the well-being information itself could capture the important features of agency, or act as its informational surrogate. In fact, some types of agency roles, e.g., those related to fulfilling obligations, can quite possibly have a negative impact on the person's well-being. Even when the impact is positive, the importance of the *agency aspect* has to be distinguished from the importance of the *impact of agency on well-being.*

II. WELL-BEING AND UTILITY

Is well-being best seen as utility? This is not an easy question to answer, for various reasons. The most immediate reason is that there are different interpretations of utility, in particular (1) happiness, (2) desire fulfillment, (3) choice.[7]

The *choice* view of utility, it is fair to say, is more popular among economists than among philosophers. In this view utility is seen as a real-valued (that is, numerical) representation of a person's choice behavior, i.e., what the person chooses from each subset of the set of alternatives (or would choose if such choices were to arise). This view of utility is, of course, purely "ordinal." Attempts to get "cardinal" utility from the choice approach are deeply hampered by the necessity of having to assume a much more elaborate framework, with much stronger requirements of consistency *and* the willingness to accept the influence of arbitrary elements in the numbering system (e.g., that of one's attitude to risk if cardinality is constructed from choices over lotteries). The extension to interpersonal comparisons is also very problematic, since we do not actually face the choice of becoming someone else, and it is hard to decide what importance to attach to answers that may be given when such choices are posed hypothetically. The natural domain of the choice interpretation of utility is in providing non-interpersonally-comparable ordinal valuations, as under Paul Samuelson's "revealed preference" approach.[8]

[7] See James Griffin, "Modern Utilitarianism," *Revue Internationale de Philosophie*, XXXVI.3, 141 (1982): 331–375, for an illuminating survey of different notions of utility and their use in utilitarian theory and for a critical assessment of some anti-utilitarian arguments, from a firm (but undogmatic) utilitarian perspective. See also J. C. B. Gosling, *Pleasure and Desire* (New York: Oxford, 1969).

[8] See *Foundations of Economic Analysis* (Cambridge, Mass.: Harvard, 1947). Some of these issues are discussed in my CWM (1982).

Even in this limited form, a serious problem with this approach arises from the fact that a person's choice behavior may fail to have any binary representation, or it may be representable by a binary relation that is not transitive (as the utility relation is required to be).[9] But perhaps a more basic problem with this approach comes from the fact that a person's choice may be guided by a number of motives of which the pursuit of personal well-being is only one. The well-being motivation may well be dominant in some choices, but not in others. Moral considerations may, inter alia, influence a person's "commitment."[10] The mixture of motivations makes it hard to form a good idea of a person's well-being on the basis of choice information only.[11]

The other two views of utility—happiness and desire fulfillment—undoubtedly have some plausibility. However, happiness has two basic problems in its claim to stand for well-being. First, as it is interpreted in the utilitarian tradition, happiness is basically a mental state, and it ignores other aspects of a person's well-being. If a starving wreck, ravished by famine, buffeted by disease, is made happy through some mental conditioning (say, via the "opium" of religion), the person will be seen as doing well on this mental-state perspective, but that would be quite scandalous. Second, as a mental-state concept, the perspective of happiness may give a very limited view of other mental activities. There are mental states

[9] The respective conditions for binary representability and transitive binariness (and other—intermediate—structures), are identified and analyzed in Arrow, "Rational Choice and Orderings," *Economica*, XXVI (1959): 121-127; my "Choice Functions and Revealed Preference," *Review of Economic Studies*, XXXVIII (1971): 307-317, reprinted in CWM; Hans Herzberger, "Ordinal Preference and Rational Choice," *Econometrica*, XLI (1973): 187-237; K. Suzumura, *Rational Choice, Collective Decisions, and Social Welfare* (New York: Cambridge, 1983).

[10] This issue, among others, is discussed in my "Choice, Orderings and Morality," in S. Körner, ed., *Practical Reason* (Oxford: Blackwell, 1974), and "Rational Fools: A Critique of the Behavioural Foundations of Economic Theory," *Philosophy and Public Affairs*, VI (1977): 317-344, both reprinted in CWM.

[11] See Thomas Nagel, *The Possibility of Altruism* (New York: Oxford, 1970); my "Behaviour and the Concept of Preference," *Economica*, XL (1973): 241-259, reprinted in CWM; Stephan Körner, *Experience and Conduct* (New York: Cambridge, 1974); Harvey Leibenstein, *Beyond Economic Man* (Cambridge, Mass.: Harvard, 1976); Tibor Scitovsky, *The Joyless Economy* (New York: Oxford, 1976); Kurt Baier, "Rationality and Morality," *Erkenntnis*, XI, 2 (August 1977): 197-223; Thomas Schelling, *Micromotives and Macrobehavior* (New York: Norton, 1978); Jon Elster, *Ulysses and the Sirens* (New York: Cambridge, 1979); Albert Hirschman, *Shifting Involvements* (Princeton, N.J.: University Press, 1982); Howard Margolis, *Selfishness, Altruism and Rationality* (New York: Cambridge, 1982); George Akerlof, "Loyalty Filters," *American Economic Review*, LXXIII (1983); Michael McPherson, "Economics: On Hirschman, Schelling, and Sen," *Partisan Review*, LI (1984): 236-247; Derek Parfit, *Reasons and Persons* (New York: Oxford, 1984).

other than being just happy, such as stimulation, excitement, etc., which are of direct relevance to a person's well-being.[12] Furthermore, mental activities involve *valuation* of one's life—a reflective exercise—and the role of valuation in the identification of the person's well-being obviously cannot be seen in terms merely of the happiness that such reflection itself creates. It is hard to avoid the conclusion that although happiness is of obvious and direct relevance to well-being, it is inadequate as a representation of well-being.

Consider, now, the *desire* approach. There is some possibility of doubt about whether this is also a mental-state view of well-being. There can be, of course, hardly anything more "mental" than desires. But as James Griffin has recently argued in his important survey of "modern utilitarianism," "the desire account does not require that satisfaction of desire translates itself in every case into experience" (338, *op. cit.*). Griffin sees the desire approach as one in which welfare lies in "the state of the world," rather than in "the state of mind."

I believe that Griffin underestimates the extent to which a desire account has to be concerned with "the state of mind." An account of well-being that is to serve as a basis for a utilitarian calculus must be able to present a cardinal and interpersonally comparable view of utility. Neither of these types of information can be obtained just by checking whether the person's desires have been realized in the state of the world. The metric that will be needed for an informationally adequate view of utility cannot be obtained from the observation of objects of desire. The strength of desire must come into the picture, and the desires of different people have to be compared. Thus, the desire account of well-being is also, in an important sense, a mental-state account, though it is not a *purely* mental-state account (given the need to observe the objects of desire *as well*).

Is the importance of desire mainly *evidential*, viz., that it gives evidence—*possible* evidence—of value, or does desire have a "value-giving" role? That is, is it the case that the activity of desiring *makes* the objects of desire have value? This question can be posed in the general context of value as such, and also in the context of the value of well-being in particular.

I begin with the general context. I would argue that the primary

[12] See Scitovsky, *op. cit.*, and "The Desire for Excitement in Modern Society," *Kyklos*, XXXIV (1981).

role of desire is evidential and that the immediate linkage is with what the person regards as valuable. Compare the two following statements:

(I) I desire *x* because *x* is valuable for me.
(II) *x* is valuable for me because I desire *x*.

The former statement is intelligible and cogent in a way the latter clearly is not. Valuing something is a good reason for desiring it, but desiring something is not an obvious reason for valuing it. Of course the latter can still make sense in some special way, which can be explained, e.g., "Having first formed the desire for *x*, I have come to value *x*, because being frustrated in my desire will be disappointing and disvaluable."[13] Though such—and other possible—special considerations do give desiring something more than a ***purely*** "evidential" role, it is hard to escape the conclusion that the main connection between desire and value is the evidential connection articulated in (I).[14]

If this line of reasoning is accepted, then the next step is to investigate the connection between what a person regards as valuable and the value of the person's well-being. That connection will be weakened precisely by the fact that a person may well value things other than personal well-being. Indeed, the agency aspect of a person and the power to form and pursue a conception of the good may well take a person's desires in a direction different from personal well-being, and the evidence for the person's valuation may not fully translate into evidence for his or her well-being. Nevertheless, there is a serious connection here, and the evidential importance of desires in reflecting a person's well-being may well be quite substantial.

III. INTERPERSONAL COMPARISONS OF DESIRES

The evidential role of desires is, however, deeply problematic in the context of *interpersonal* comparisons. Comparative intensities of desire may be a very dubious guide indeed to well-being intensities in comparing one person with another, since these intensities are influenced by many contingent circumstances that are arbitrary for

[13] Cf. "Well-being and distress are to be understood as two kinds of human experience, those in which desires are satisfied and those in which desires are frustrated" [Ted Honderich, "The Question of Well-being and the Principle of Equality," *Mind*, XC, 360 (October 1981): 481-504, p. 481].

[14] In third-person contexts, desire fulfillment may plausibly be seen as having much strategic importance. The fact that you desire something may be a good reason for me to value it. But this too may have an evidential base. In treating your desire as evidence of what you value, I may value your desire fulfillment *as a consequence* of my valuing your success in getting what you yourself value.

well-being comparisons. Our reading of what is feasible in our situation and station may be crucial to the intensities of our desires, and may even affect what we dare to desire. Desires reflect compromises with reality, and reality is harsher to some than to others. The hopeless destitute desiring merely to survive, the landless laborer concentrating his efforts on securing the next meal, the round-the-clock domestic servant seeking a few hours of respite, the subjugated housewife struggling for a little individuality, may all have learned to keep their desires in line with their respective predicaments. Their deprivations are gagged and muffled in the interpersonal metric of desire fulfillment. In some lives small mercies have to count big.

It may be asked whether this problem cannot be dealt with in the same way as some utilitarians have proposed in "purifying" desires of "imperfection." Hare demands "perfectly prudent" preferences—"fully informed and unconfused." Harsanyi wants that, and *more;* to wit, to "exclude all antisocial preferences, such as sadism, envy, resentment, and malice."[15] These devices raise questions about how we may decide on what "purifications" are appropriate and justifiable within the general logic of utilitarianism, but they may well be able to deal sensibly with some problems, particularly those associated with factual ignorance and thoughtless decisions.

Can such purification procedures eliminate the problem under discussion, viz., the *circumstantial* contingency of desires? It is not clear how they could. Desiring is a part of living; it plays a strategic role in making our wants credible, our aspirations viable. To ask what one would desire in unspecified circumstances—abstracting from the concreteness of *everyone's* life—is to misunderstand the nature of desire and its place in human life. Of course, we can *pretend* to answer this question. Since all this is imaginary anyway, we need not live in the fear of being proved wrong. This can be done by making—explicitly or by implication—some simple assumption, e.g., that our desires would be in line with what Scanlon[16] has called "an objective criterion" of well-being, appealing to a certain "consensus" of values about the content of well-being. But if that is

[15] "Ethical Theory and Utilitarianism," in Sen and Williams, *op. cit.*, p. 28; Harsanyi, "Morality and the Theory of Rational Behaviour," in Sen and Williams, p. 56. See also James Mirrlees, "The Economic Uses of Utilitarianism," and Peter Hammond, "Utilitarianism, Uncertainty and Information," both in Sen and Williams, *op. cit.*

[16] "Preference and Urgency," this JOURNAL, LXXIII, 19 (Nov. 6, 1975): 655–669. Scanlon is, however, primarily concerned with *moral* urgency rather than with getting a concept of well-being that may be used for other purposes as well.

what we are going to do, we could just as easily have started from the objective criterion itself, and "founded" it on the consensus of values on well-being, rather than having the imaginary exercise of *counterfactual desiring.* Since, according to the arguments presented earlier in this lecture, the importance of desiring is primarily "evidential" anyway, that imaginary exercise is particularly pointless. There is little merit in justifying interest in desire information on the ground that it gives evidence of valuation and then going on to "obtain" the "purified" desire information through the knowledge (or assumption) of a consensus of valuations.

IV. EQUALITY AND MORAL VALUATION

I turn now to question (2b): Do utilitarian principles follow from WAIF if well-being is taken as utility? It was argued in the first lecture that utilitarianism is really a combination of welfarism, sum ranking, and some—direct or indirect—version of consequentialism. Therefore, the question can be seen as being about the derivability of these different *factors* from the union of (1) WAIF and (2) the identification of utility with well-being.

Deriving welfarism, obviously, poses no challenge to this task. Nor, in fact, does welfarist consequentialism in general. If nothing other than well-being can count as a morally fundamental fact and if well-being is just utility, then it will be necessary to evaluate actions and other choice variables in terms of utility consequences only.

The factor that remains unmarshalled even in this demanding framework is sum ranking, viz., the view that the utilities are best valued aggregatively by summing them and by ignoring every other aspect of utility distributions, including the extent of inequality. Nothing in WAIF *or* in the identifiction of well-being with utility can make sum ranking follow automatically without invoking some consideration that makes us unconcerned with equality of well-being. It is, therefore, a matter of considerable interest that arguments have been presented by some utilitarians that make sum ranking allegedly inescapable simply on grounds of logic, mathematics, or rationality.[17] How is this unusual feat performed?

Consider the Vickrey-Harsanyi model[18] of "ethical preferences"

[17] See, for example, John Harsanyi, "Nonlinear Social Welfare Functions: Or Do Welfare Economists Have a Special Exemption from Bayesian Rationality?" *Theory and Decision*, VI, 3 (August 1975): 311-332; M. McDermott, "Utility and Distribution," *Mind*, 91, 364 (October 1982): 572-578.

[18] W. S. Vickrey, "Measuring Marginal Utility by Reactions to Risk," *Econometrica*, XIII (1945): 691-707; Harsanyi, "Cardinal Welfare, Individualistic Ethics, and Interpersonal Comparisons of Utility," *Journal of Political Economy*, LXIII (1955): 309-321.

based on choosing between different states of affairs in a state of primordial equiprobability in which the chooser has an equal chance of being anyone.[19] If the *as if* behavior of this chooser satisfies certain "rationality" conditions (such as the von Neumann-Morgenstern axioms[20]), then the position of being any persion i in any state x can be given a value $W_i(x)$ such that the chooser's behavior can be represented as maximizing the mathematical expectation of these individual W_i values, i.e., maximizing $\Sigma_i p_i W_i$, when p_i is the probability of being person i. With the assumption of equiprobability of being anyone, this is no different from maximizing $\Sigma_i W_i$. If W_i is seen as person i's utility, then it looks as if sum ranking has somehow been deduced simply from rational behavior. Rationality must, it would seem, preclude any concern for equality of well-being in aggregating different persons' well-being![21]

But what are these W_i values? They are simply accounting values for predicting choice under uncertainty. They need not coincide with any concept of utility that has independent meaning, such as happiness, or satisfaction, or desire fulfillment. Not only may the values of W_i differ from the utilities U_i as perceived by persion i himself (his happiness, his desire fulfillment, etc.), but they may also differ from what the *chooser* expects to enjoy in the counterfactual position of becoming person i. The fact that W is the sum

[19] I abstain in the present context from questioning the acceptability of this general approach to moral valuation, since I am concerned here only with the specific question of how it deals with the issue of inequality. For discussions of different types of problems raised by this moral approach, see P. A. Diamond, "Cardinal Welfare, Individualistic Ethics, and Interpersonal Comparisons of Utility: A Comment," *Journal of Political Economy*, LXXV (1967): 765/6; my CCSW, ch. 9; Rawls, *A Theory of Justice* (1971); P. K. Pattanaik, *Voting and Collective Choice* (New York: Cambridge, 1971); Levi, "Four Types of Ignorance," *Social Research*, XLIV (1977): 745-756; E. F. McClennen, "The Minimax Theory and Expected Utility Reasoning," in C. A. Hooker, J. J. Leach, and McClennen, eds., *Foundations and Applications of Decision Theory*, vol. I (Boston: Reidel, 1978); C. Blackorby, D. Donaldson, and J. A. Weymark, "On John Harsanyi's Defences of Utilitarianism," Discussion Paper, University of British Columbia, 1980; M. Machina, "'Expected Utility' Analysis without the Independence Axiom," *Econometrica*, L (1982): 277-324; J. Broome, "Uncertainty and Fairness," *Economic Journal*, XCIV (1984): 624-632. Harsanyi's own assessment is to be found in his *Essays on Ethics, Social Behavior, and Scientific Explanation* (Boston: Reidel, 1976).

[20] J. von Neumann and O. Morgenstern, *Theory of Games and Economic Behavior* (Princeton, N.J.: University Press, 1944). For an excellent discussion of the contents, interpretation and implications of the axioms, see R. D. Luce and H. Raiffa, *Games and Decision* (New York: Wiley, 1957).

[21] See also Harsanyi, "Non-linear Social Welfare Functions: A Rejoinder to Professor Sen," and my "A Reply to Professor Harsanyi," in Robert E. Butts and Jaakko Hintikka, eds., *Foundational Problems in the Special Sciences* (Boston: Reidel, 1977).

of the W_i values does not tell us anything at all about what the relationship is between W and the independently characterized utilities U_i of the respective persons. In terms of the language of the von Neumann-Morgenstern model of choice, we might employ the term 'utility' for W_i, but W_i has no necessary role other than yielding accounting values in terms of which the chooser's behavior can be predicted.

In fact, the numbering system of W_i works the way it does precisely by *incorporating* attitudes toward risk in the W_i values themselves. And, in this framework, these attitudes toward risk correspond neatly to attitudes toward inequality.[22] If the chooser's attitude toward inequality changes (but "consistency" of choice is retained in the form of continuing to satisfy the von Neumann-Morgenstern axioms), then the W_i functions will change correspondingly, even though the utilities U_i of the persons in the form of happiness or desire fulfillment may remain completely unaltered. The fact that W is the *sum* of the W_i values does not imply sum ranking of the utility values U_i, and it presents an additive accounting procedure only through the *devised* values of W_i. No *substantive* sum ranking result is entailed by the accounting procedure.

It is, in fact, not surprising that the relevance of equality in moral valuation cannot be settled without assessing equality itself. The informational foundation of well-being yielded by WAIF leaves it open how the well-being of different people are to be combined in assessing states and actions. And this issue is not obliterated even when "rational" behavior under uncertainty with primordial equiprobability is taken to be the basis of moral valuation. Rationality—even in the limited sense of satisfying von Neumann-Morgenstern axioms—is no enemy of valuing equality of well-being.

While the issue of equality has to be faced, the fact that there are many different notions of equality implies that conflicts among these different egalitarian views have to be faced as well. In an important study called *Equalities*, Douglas Rae has argued that the "one idea that is more powerful than order or efficiency or freedom in resisting equality" is "equality itself."[23] Peter Westen has gone further and has suggested that equality is "an empty form having no substantive content of its own."[24] It may be tempting to dismiss

[22] See A. B. Atkinson, "On the Measurement of Inequality," *Journal of Economic Theory*, II (1970): 244-263; P. Dasgupta, A. Sen, and D. Starrett, "Notes on the Measurement of Inequality," *Journal of Economic Theory*, VI (1973): 180-187; M. Rothschild and J. E. Stiglitz, "Some Further Results in the Measurement of Inequality," *Journal of Economic Theory*, VI (1973): 188-204.

[23] Cambridge, Mass.: Harvard, 1981; p. 150.

[24] "The Empty Idea of Equality," *Harvard Law Review*, XC (1982): 537-596, p. 596.

concern with equality in moral evaluation on grounds of this alleged "emptiness."

However, the multiplicity of notions of equality arises from various sources, and often enough these sources do not appear to be peculiar to equality at all. A person's advantage can be judged in many different ways, and corresponding to these different ways, there are various characterizations of equality. Utility, income, opulence, need-fulfillment, etc., provide different ways of seeing a person's success, and each of them would lead to a corresponding approach to equality. But this plurality is not special to equality. Any derivative notion for which individual advantage provides the informational base, would have this plurality. For example, the notion of "efficiency" in terms of achievements (that the situation is such that no one can be made more advantaged without reducing someone else's advantage) will have exactly the same variability. If advantage is seen in absolute terms *and* identified with utility, then the notion of efficiency immediately becomes the concept—much used in economics—of "Pareto optimality." But related to the other notions of advantage—income, opulence, need fulfillment, etc.—there will be the corresponding notions of efficiency.

In rejecting the claims of utility to represent well-being, we have outlined the need for an alternative approach. The issue of equality will again arise in whatever alternative concept of well-being we accept. I return now to the characterization of well-being.

V. FUNCTIONINGS AND WELL-BEING

It is useful to contrast two closely related ideas, which are quite clearly different. One is the idea of being "well off" and the other of being "well," or having "well-being." The former is really a concept of opulence—how rich is she? what goods and services can she buy? what offices are open to her? and so on. This refers to a person's command over things outside—including what Rawls calls "primary goods." Having "well-being," on the other hand, is not something outside her that she commands, but something in her that she achieves. What kind of a life is she leading? What does she succeed in doing and in being? Being "well off" may help, other things given, to have "well-being," but there is a distinctly personal quality in the latter absent in the former.

In looking for an appropriate approach to well-being, there are two different dangers to avoid, coming from two different directions. One problem lies in taking a basically subjectivist view in terms of one of the mental-state metrics of utility. The difficulties of this approach have already been discussed (sections II and III). Being happy may be a valuable thing to be, and not having one's desires frustrated may also have value, but there are clearly other things that are also valuable to do or be. We have to value the different types of doings and beings, but "desiring" is not a valuational activity in itself, though it may be the consequence of one. The linkage may give desiring an "evidential" value, which was discussed, but the limitations of which, especially in interpersonal comparison, also emerged clearly enough. We are, thus, pulled in the objectivist (and, in one sense, "impersonal") direction, looking for a criterion that does not get messed up by circumstantial contingencies (as the "evidential" value of desire information clearly can).

What form would an "objective" criterion of well-being take? "By an *objective criterion* I mean a criterion that provides a basis for appraisal of a person's well-being which is independent of the person's tastes and interests," says Scanlon.[25] But why should an objective criterion not take note of the objective basis of differences of different people's "tastes and interests"? As discussed in the first lecture (in the context of the quite different problem of position-relativity of moral judgments of actions and states, 183/4), the personal features that make a *relevant* objective difference (and which others too can see) can be built *parametrically* into an evaluation function without losing objectivity.

One reason why "being well off" is quite different from "being well," despite the fact that the former is causally related to the latter, is the variability of personal characteristics which makes the causal relations *person-specific*. The Charybdis of overrigidity threatens us as much as the Scylla of subjectivist variability, and we must not lose sight of the important personal parameters in developing an approach to well-being.

Consider a disabled person, who, with the same level of real income and opulence, cannot do many things that a normal person can. His tastes in commodities will be different (and typically more expensive), and his interests will make very different demands on others. In what way does this disabled person differ in terms of this issue from the person with "expensive tastes," who has received such a lot of attention recently (and, to indulge in an aside, whose taste for having expensive and exquisite attention must by now be well satisfied by what he has got from Kenneth Arrow, Ronald Dworkin, John Rawls, and Tim Scanlon, among others)?[26]

[25] "Preference and Urgency" (1975), p. 658. Scanlon qualifies the statement in several different ways (pp. 658/9). Also, his concern is primarily with what is morally significant and not with developing a notion of well-being relevant in other contexts as well.

[26] Arrow, "Some Ordinalist-Utilitarian Notes on Rawls's Theory of Justice," this

One important difference between the two cases relates to the likely fact that the expensive-taste person may be able to *do* most things a normal person can and be handicapped only in the context of achieving contentment or satisfaction, whereas the disabled person may be handicapped in terms of a much wider range of activities.[27] As Scanlon describes the refined being, he could not be raised to a "normal level of satisfaction" without very high expenditure (659). The Arrow-Dworkin creature hooked on "plovers' eggs and pre-phylloxera claret" is unhappy unless he gets these extraordinary provisions, even though there is nothing to suggest that he cannot do the usual things that other people can, except that of being happy. In contrast, the deprivation of the handicapped person relates also to his inability to do many entirely normal things (unless, of course, we are considering some exotic type of handicap). The disadvantages that he suffers in his "being" do not have to be seen in terms of utilities at all.

In fact, handicapped people are often cheerful enough, and do not lead a life of frustrated desires, since their desires adapt to the reality of their handicap (a point that relates to the issue of circumstantial contingency of desires, which was discussed earlier, 190/1). The primary disability certainly would be in matters of leading a normal life—being able to get around, being able to hear or see, or something like that. That it is reflected in a lowered utility level is secondary, if true, and it may not even be true. There is no real comparison with the "plover's egg" fan.

The primary feature of well-being can be seen in terms of how a person can "function," taking that term in a very broad sense. I shall refer to various doings and beings that come into this assessment as *functionings*. These could be activities (like eating or reading or seeing), or states of existence or being, e.g., being well nourished, being free from malaria, not being ashamed by the poverty of

JOURNAL, LXX (1973): 245–288; R. Dworkin, "What Is Equality? Part I: Equality and Welfare," *Philosophy and Public Affairs*, X, 3 (Summer 1981): 185–246; Rawls, "Social Unity and Primary Goods," in Sen and Williams; Scanlon, "Preference and Urgency" (1975).

[27] Another difference emphasized particularly by Dworkin, Rawls, and Scanlon relates to the "responsibility" of the person with expensive taste in the genesis of his disadvantage. However, although that consideration is of obvious interest in judging a person's *moral claim* for support, it may not be of direct relevance in judging a person's *actual well-being*. In terms of the categorization used in these lectures, the issue of responsibility relates immediately to the agency aspect of a person, rather than to the well-being aspect. There is a further problem arising from the fact that the responsibility may have to be traced over a long period of time, and this is made more complicated by issues of personal identity; see Derek Parfit, *Reasons and Persons* (New York: Oxford, 1984), and Michael Slote, *Goods and Virtues* (New York: Oxford, 1983).

one's clothing or shoes (to go back to a question that Adam Smith discussed in his *Wealth of Nations*[28]). I shall refer to the set of functionings a person actually achieves as the *functioning vector* (though it would have been more accurate to describe it as an *n-tuple*, since some of the functionings may not be numerically representable).

The primary feature of a person's well-being is the functioning vector that he or she achieves. The functioning vectors can be ranked and partially ordered in line with some common valuations, or in the light of what Scanlon calls "urgency," or some other acceptable criterion. This, then, is the secondary representation, in the form of the place of a functioning vector in a partial order of such vectors. If the ordering is complete, we should be able to get even a real-numbered "index" of well-being (in the absence of some technical peculiarities in that ordering[29]). In fact, even a partial order will typically have numerical representation with some "transparency" properties.[30] The "natural" form of well-being ranking is indeed that of a partial, incomplete order. It would be just as extraordinary if every possible pair of functioning vectors could be compared in terms of over-all well-being, as it would be if none of them could be. There will, of course, be many agreed valuations, and many decisive judgments, and the clarity of these cases is not compromised by the muddiness of others.

VI. OPULENCE, FUNCTIONINGS, AND UTILITY

The contrast between opulence and functioning achievements is simple enough, but its significance in the context of well-being may be worth spelling out. The example of the crippled (or otherwise handicapped person) is, in some respects, particularly misleading. It may suggest that personal variations are uncommon and unusual things. In fact, however, interpersonal variations in "transforming" goods into functionings is extremely common. Take, for example, the consumption of *food*, on the one hand, and the functioning of *being well nourished*, on the other. The relationship between them

[28] *An Inquiry into the Nature and Causes of the Wealth of Nations* (1776; Everyman's Library, London: Dent, 1954), vol. II, p. 352.

[29] An example of a non-numerically-representable complete order is a "lexicographic" order over the unit square: see Gerard Debreu, *Theory of Value* (New York: Wiley, 1959), ch. 4. Since lexicographic orderings have some interest in moral philosophy, as with the "lexicographic maximim" version of Rawls's difference principle [see my *Collective Choice and Social Welfare* (1970), p. 138; Rawls, *A Theory of Justice* (1971), pp. 42-45], it is perhaps just worth recording the elementary fact that a lexicographic order—or indeed any other order—over any *finite* set (no matter how large) will never have such a representation problem.

[30] See Mukul Majumdar and Amartya Sen, "On Representing Partial Orderings," *Review of Economic Studies*, XLIII (1976): 543-545. The real problem arises with guaranteeing the continuity of such a numerical function.

varies with (1) metabolic rates, (2) body size, (3) age, (4) sex (and if a woman, whether pregnant or lactating), (5) activity levels, (6) climatic conditions, (7) presence of parasitic diseases, (8) access to medical services, (9) nutritional knowledge, and other influences.

Interpersonal variability of the relation between goods and functionings turns out to be quite central to many important policy issues. For example, the comparison between the positions of men and women in terms of nutritional achievements in the poorer countries is often distorted by the use of food intake figures, which are not only unreliable, but also difficult to relate to well-being. The comparisons are usually made with some arbitrarily assumed sex-specific nutritional requirements, and there is some evidence that the most widely used requirements norms (the so-called "FAO-WHO standards") not only are inappropriate in a great majority of cases, but also involve a systematic sex bias, helping to conceal the extent of the relative deprivation of women in many of these countries. In contrast, direct information on the actual *functionings* achieved by men and women (in this case, avoiding undernourishment, escaping avoidable morbidity, etc.) are both easier to use and more sensibly interpreted in terms of well-being.[31]

Interpersonal variations are not, of course, confined to such elementary functionings as being well nourished, or escaping avoidable morbidity. Personal and social influences on the conversion of opulence into functioning achievements can be powerful in many other fields as well. The resource requirements of such functionings as "appearing in public without shame" (emphasized by Adam Smith), taking part in the life of the community, being able to visit and entertain friends, being acceptably well informed, and so on, vary a good deal with the nature of the community in which one lives and with other contingent circumstances.[32]

Opulence does, of course, *contribute* to functioning, and the command that it gives can indeed be important for a person's well-being and advantage. Rawlsian analysis of "primary goods" has forcefully demonstrated the usefulness of that perspective compared with reliance on the mental metric of utility.[33] But an index of opu-

[31] Some of these issues are discussed, along with presenting some empirical results, in Jocelyn Kynch and Amartya Sen, "Indian Women: Well-being and Survival," *Cambridge Journal of Economics*, VII (1983): 363–380, and in Essays 13, 15, and 16 in my *Resources, Values and Development* (Oxford: Blackwell, and Cambridge, Mass.: Harvard, 1984), hereafter, RVD.

[32] Some of these issues are discussed in my "Poor, Relatively Speaking," *Oxford Economic Papers*, XXXV (1983): 153–169, reprinted in RVD; and "The Living Standard," *Oxford Economic Papers*, XXXVI (1984): 74–90.

[33] Rawls, *A Theory of Justice* (1971), and "Social Unity and Primary Goods" in Sen and Williams. Rawls is concerned with agency as well, not just well-being, in his analysis of primary goods.

lence, or of primary goods, cannot be seen as an index of well-being as such. Nor can the "advantage" of different persons (or groups) be ranked on the basis of the primary goods index, because of interpersonal variations in what people can *do* with primary goods, depending on biological, social, and other parameters.

Nor, of course, is it a matter of utility, as we have already seen. Happiness may be a valuable part of well-being, and being happy is certainly a momentous functioning, but there are other important functionings that are not congruent with happiness and for which happiness cannot serve as a surrogate, especially in interpersonal comparisons. Desire intensities may also be relevant to the valuation of functionings for evidential reasons, but—as was discussed earlier—the problem of valuation of functionings cannot be avoided by concentrating instead on the observation of desires and their intensities. The central feature of well-being is the ability to achieve valuable functionings.[34] The need for identification and valuation of the important functionings cannot be avoided by looking at something else, such as happiness, desire fulfillment, opulence, or command over primary goods.

It is, of course, clear that the functioning approach is intrinsically information-pluralist.[35] Although some consensus of valuations and the usability of various objective criteria may take us a great distance in establishing an extensive partial ordering in the comparison of well-being, it would be quite wrong to expect anything like the kind of complete ordering that utilitarians have made us prone to demand. As was discussed in the first lecture, such a completeness requirement is neither methodologically sensible nor substantively plausible (nor in fact actually met by the utilitarian calculus itself, except under the artificial assumption of complete and unproblematic interpersonal comparability). Incompleteness is *not* an embarrassment.

VII. CAPABILITY AND FREEDOM

The information pluralism of the functioning approach to well-being has to be further extended if we shift attention from the person's actual functionings to his or her *capability* to function. A

[34] The problem of evaluation of functioning vectors has been discussed in my *Commodities and Capabilities* (Amsterdam: North-Holland, 1985).

[35] The feature of plurality can, however, be reduced by the use of "invariance restrictions" in the analysis of well-being, e.g., "being well nourished" defining an isoinformation set (ignoring differences between being well-nourished through eating bread *or* rice, etc.), and "being entertained" as another such category (ignoring differences between entertainment from the cinema or the theatre, etc.). There will, of course, be gradations in being well-nourished, being entertained, etc., with corresponding layers of isoinformation sets.

person's *capability set* can be defined as the set of functioning vectors within his or her reach. In examining the well-being aspect of a person, attention can legitimately be paid to the capability set of the person and not just to the chosen functioning vector. This has the effect of taking note of the positive freedoms in a general sense (the freedom "to do this," or "to be that") that a person has.

Importance may well be attached to checking whether one person did have the opportunity of achieving the functioning vector that another actually achieved. This involves comparison of actual opportunities that different persons have. If one person could have achieved all the relevant functioning vectors that the other could, then in some important sense the first person had at least as much freedom to live well. The general idea of the freedom to achieve well-being can be called *well-being freedom*.

To illustrate, consider two persons with identical actual functioning vectors, including—as it happens—both of them starving. Person *A* is starving because she is very poor and lacks the means to command food. Person *B* is starving out of choice, because of his religious beliefs, which have made him decide to starve and undergo the consequent suffering. In terms of the misery caused by the starvation, we learn that there is no difference between *A*'s experience and *B*'s. Even if it were plausible to say that *A* and *B* both have the same level of well-being, in terms of being undernourished, miserable, etc. (that complex issue will be examined presently), there would nevertheless remain an important difference between the two cases, viz., *B could have* in a straightforward sense, chosen an alternative life style which *A* could not have chosen. This is a difference that is relevant to assessing the well-being aspect of the two persons respectively, though it is not necessarily a difference between the *actual* well-being levels achieved by the two. In judging a person's advantage (and the kind of "deal" that he or she has got), the importance of well-being freedom must be recognized.[36]

A second reason for being interested in the capability set arises from a different type of consideration altogether. The existence of genuine choice may actually affect the nature and significance of the functionings achieved. The first—and primitive—characterization of functionings in terms of doing this or being that may have to be modified and made more sophisticated by taking note of more

[36] The problem of ranking capability sets involves many difficulties; on this see my *Commodities and Capabilities* (1985). Cases of dominance (*either* in the form of one set being a proper subset of another, *or* in the sense of one set being *element-by-element* dominated by the other in terms of the partial ordering of functioning vectors) would of course induce a *minimal* partial ordering on the space of capability sets.

complexly characterized doings, e.g., choosing to do x rather than y. *Fasting* involves an abstention from eating that goes beyond just starving, and it can be argued that in the example being considered, rich and religious *B* could choose to fast, whereas poverty-stricken *A* could not. The possibility of starving was open to both, but *fasting* by choice was open only to *B*.[37] Examining capability sets of primitive functionings may permit us to move to a richer analysis of functionings, taking note of the choices exercised.

It can be argued that the well-being that a person actually enjoys is often more closely related to such *refined* functioning achievements. This view relates to the idea that the good life is inter alia also a life of freedom.[38] It is a view that has found rather eloquent expression in the writings of many social and political philosophers.[39]

On this line of reasoning, the extent of the capability set is relevant to the significance and value of the respective functionings. This might look like introducing a circularity in the relationship between functionings and capabilities, and between well-being and well-being freedom. But what it, in fact, does is to force us to see these concepts as mutually dependent, taking note of the simultaneity of the relationships involved. The refined characterization of functionings has to take note of the capability set of the "primitive" functionings, but the refined functionings, in their turn, yield a (corresponding) refined capability set.[40]

VIII. CONCLUDING REMARKS

In this lecture I have argued (1) *against* accepting the adequacy of WAIF (well-being as informational foundation), (2) *against* the

[37] I am grateful to Ian White for helpful discussions on these issues.

[38] On related matters, see Jon Elster, "Sour Grapes," in Sen and Williams, pp. 227/8, and *Sour Grapes* (New York: Cambridge, pp. 128/9.

[39] One of them is, of course, Karl Marx, whose political philosophy gives a special role to bringing "the conditions for the free development and activity of individuals under their own control" and who outlines a vision of a liberated future society which "makes it possible for me to do one thing to-day and another tomorrow, to hunt in the morning, fish in the afternoon, rear cattle in the evening, criticize after dinner, just as I have in mind, without ever becoming hunter, fisherman, shepherd or critic" [K. Marx and F. Engels, *The German Ideology* (1845/46; republished New York: International Publishers, 1947), p. 22]. This perspective of freedom has a strong bearing also on other aspects of the Marxian tradition. Examples of different types of connections can be found in G. A. Cohen, *Karl Marx's Theory of History: A Defence* (New York: Oxford, 1978); J. E. Roemer, *A General Theory of Exploitation and Class* (Cambridge, Mass.: Harvard, 1982); G. G. Brenkert, *Marx's Ethics of Freedom* (London: Routledge & Kegan Paul, 1983); J. Elster, *Making Sense of Marx* (Cambridge: Cambridge, 1985); S. Lukes, *Marxism and Morality* (Oxford: Oxford, 1985).

[40] It is, of course, possible to do more than one round of refining, though the advantages of such extended refinement might be rather limited.

identification of well-being with utility (in any of its forms: happiness, desire fulfillment, choice), and (3) *against* treating sum ranking as trivial and equality as having no independent force. More positively, I have argued *for* seeing well-being in terms of functioning vectors and the capability to achieve them. The well-being aspect of a person leads to a particular concept of freedom, which has been called *well-being freedom*.

FREEDOM AND AGENCY

IN the last lecture it was argued that the well-being aspect of a person calls for dual accounting—in terms, respectively, of freedom and achievement. The significance of the distinction relates particularly to the agency aspect of a person. Values other than the pursuit of well-being may figure prominently in a person's assessment of choices. Not making maximal use of the freedom to pursue well-being may not reflect any failure of evaluation or action. In judging what kind of a deal a person has in terms of the opportunity to pursue his or her own well-being, the concept of *well-being freedom* is, therefore, necessary, and its role cannot be subsumed by the observation of actual *achievements* of well-being. The autonomy of the agency aspect of a person, which has the effect of making WAIF an inadequate basis for substantive moral reasoning, also has the result that the well-being aspect of a person must be seen in terms of freedom as well as actual achievement.

I. AGENCY FREEDOM

Well-being freedom is freedom of a rather particular type. It concentrates on a person's capability to have various functioning vectors and to enjoy the corresponding well-being achievements. This concept of freedom, based on the well-being aspect of a person, has to be clearly distinguished from a broader concept of freedom, related to the agency aspect of a person. A person's "agency freedom" refers to what the person is free to do and achieve in pursuit of whatever goals or values he or she regards as important. A person's agency aspect cannot be understood without taking note of his or her aims, objectives, allegiances, obligations, and—in a broad sense—the person's conception of the good. Whereas well-being freedom is freedom to achieve something in particular, viz., well-being, the idea of agency freedom is more general, since it is not tied to any one type of aim. Agency freedom is freedom to achieve whatever the person, as a responsible agent, decides he or she should achieve. That *open conditionality* makes the nature of agency freedom quite different from that of well-being freedom, which concentrates on a particular type of objective and judges opportunities correspondingly.[1]

This open conditionality does not imply that the person's view of his agency has no need for discipline, and that anything that appeals to him must, for that reason, come into the accounting of his agency freedom. The need for careful assessment of aims, objectives, allegiances, etc., and of the conception of the good, may be important and exacting. But despite this need for discipline, the use of one's agency is, in an important sense, a matter for oneself to judge. When the requirement of careful assessment cannot be fulfilled (e.g., in the case of young children, or with persons mentally ill in ways that rule out such assessment), the agency aspect will be, obviously, less important. This does not indicate that the demands of the agency aspect for such a person would have to be assessed by *others* on his or her behalf, but only that no such demands would then be made. This would not, of course, in any way compromise the importance of their *well-being aspect*. Indeed in the absence of the relevance of their agency aspect, it is their *well-being achievement* that would uniquely command attention.

The importance of the agency aspect, in general, relates to the view of persons as responsible agents. Persons must enter the moral accounting by others not only as people whose well-being demands concern, but also as people whose responsible agency must be recognized. Although well-being achievement is geared to a specific objective, and well-being freedom is seen in terms of the freedom to achieve that objective through the choice of functioning vectors, agency freedom cannot be examined in terms of any prespecified objective. The open conditionality referred to above is central to that concept.

II. PLURALITY, WELL-BEING, AND AGENCY

In terms of the analysis presented so far, we have a plural informational base for substantive moral analysis, which has to take note of several distinct considerations involving well-being and agency. These different considerations may quite possibly pull in different directions.

A person's actual well-being has intrinsic importance. This tends to give WAIF some apparent plausibility, and is reflected more

[1] Agency freedom has claims to being taken as freedom *tout court*, which well-being freedom clearly does not have.

generally in the hold of "well-being" on moral thinking (including utilitarian moral thinking, though—as was argued in the last lecture—utility provides rather limited ways of seeing well-being). For responsible adults, the concept of "well-being freedom" has a clear relevance in judging the opportunities a person has for pursuing his or her own advantage. The supplementation of well-being by well-being freedom, in the case of responsible adults, involves a refinement in the assessment of the well-being aspect of a person. But well-being freedom is only a specific type of freedom, and it cannot reflect the person's over-all freedom as an agent; we have to turn to the notion of agency freedom in that context. It is hard to see how any part of this plurality (involving both the well-being aspect and the agency aspect of persons) can fail to have some intrinsic importance.

This plurality would have been a matter of considerable embarrassment if for methodological reasons we were obliged to reject any information-pluralist framework, with "monism" as the only acceptable approach. But, as was discussed in the first lecture, there is no good reason for that monist presumption, and none for imposing monism as an a priori requirement.

Furthermore, as was also discussed in the first lecture, it is not a matter of embarrassment that there might be scope for variation in the assessment of the relative importance of the different elements in a pluralist structure. Although "dominance" reasoning will, as was discussed, be able to provide a minimal partial ordering in a pluralist structure, and variable valuations within given *ranges* of weights will extend that partial ordering further, nevertheless even such enhanced partial orderings may well remain incomplete. The need to consider both the agency aspect and the well-being aspect of persons is not compromised by the possibility that the combined structure may leave a large subset of unordered pairs. Those who see substantive moral reasoning as worthless unless it completely orders the space of all actions and states will, of course, find much to complain about in this incompleteness. But, as was seen in the first lecture, there is no good reason why we should have to yield to this external pressure for completeness.

It can, however, be argued that while plurality and incompleteness are not themselves objectionable, nevertheless in this particular case there happen to be redundant elements in the proposed plural structure. I have already discussed, in the second lecture, why well-being is inadequate as an informational basis of moral judgments, given the intrinsic importance of agency. But I have not yet explicitly provided any reason why agency information may not be adequate for moral judgment (thereby making it redundant to incorporate well-being information—in the form of achievement *or* freedom— in the basic structure). Agency information includes each person's pursuits and choices. The hypothesis of the adequacy of agency information might appear to have considerable plausibility,[2] especially since agency freedom can be seen as incorporating well-being freedom, inter alia. "Open conditionality" indicates that if a person were to pursue well-being, then assessment of the agency freedom of that person would have to include his or her well-being freedom as well. And if the person were unconcerned about pursuing his or her own well-being, then why should it matter whether the person had well-being freedom or not?

In responding to this issue, the important thing to recognize is that the well-being aspect and the agency aspect of persons have dissimilar roles in moral accounting. They invite attention in *disparate* ways. At the risk of oversimplification it can be said that the well-being aspect of a person is important in assessing a person's *advantage,* whereas the agency aspect is important in assessing what a person can do in line with his or her conception of *the good.* The ability to do more good need not be to the person's advantage.

Perhaps an illustration may help to bring out the distinction a little more clearly. You are enjoying eating a sandwich on a nice spring day, sitting on the bank of the river Avon. Meanwhile, far away, a man who cannot swim is drowning. You cannot do anything to save him—he is hundreds of miles away. Consider now a *counterfactual* situation in which that man, instead of drowning at that lonely, distant spot, is about to drown right in front of you. How are *you* affected by this counterfactual change? Your agency freedom is, in an important way, increased. You can now very likely save the man. You will, let us assume, value this opportunity highly and decide to save him, and, further, you will even succeed. You will chuck your sandwich, jump into the cold river, and haul the man out. Your agency freedom would have been well used, and the state of affairs would have been better, as you would yourself judge it.

But your *well-being* is, quite possibly, reduced. You may, of course, enjoy saving a life, and a part of your well-being may certainly be positively influenced by the opportunity to do good. But it is possible that, everything considered, your own well-being is no

[2] I am grateful to Bruce Ackerman for providing good arguments in favor of this possibility and for insisting that *either* agency freedom be regarded as adequate *or* its inadequacy be explicitly established.

higher, and let us assume (to pursue our contrasts) that it is actually lower—with the quiet lunch being replaced by a ducking in the chilling river, risking your own life in undertaking the life-saving operation. An expansion of agency freedom can go with a reduction in actual well-being, through your own choice, even though you are not, by any means, indifferent to your own well-being.

What about your "well-being freedom?" That was certainly not enhanced by the counterfactual change. The additional opportunity of saving the drowning person did not give you a better (or even as good a) way of pursuing your own well-being. In fact, in an important way, the counterfactual change actually *reduced* your well-being freedom. You were no longer free to eat your sandwich *without anxiety*, and, in terms of the "refined" functionings discussed in the last lecture (pp. 201/2), there was a genuine loss of opportunity to pursue your own well-being.

Since agency freedom includes inter alia the freedom to pursue your own well-being, it can, of course, also be said that *in that respect* your agency freedom too would have been adversely affected. But if it is the case (as it is here assumed to be) that, given the choice, you would rather have the opportunity of saving the drowning person than eat your sandwich without anxiety, and that your valuations as an agent confirm the correctness of this choice, then there is clearly a *net* gain in terms of your *agency freedom*. As an agent you value the new opportunity (saving the person) more than the lost opportunity (eating the sandwich without anxiety). But in terms of your *well-being freedom*, there *is* a net loss, since the lost opportunity is more valuable from the narrow perspective of your own well-being than the new opportunity. It is, in this sense, arguable that even though agency freedom does "include" well-being freedom, the latter can quite possibly go down when the former goes up (and, of course, vice versa). The ranking of alternative opportunities from the point of view of agency need not be the same as the ranking in terms of well-being, and thus the judgments of agency freedom and well-being freedom can move in contrary directions.[3] So, even though agency freedom is "broader" than well-being freedom, the former *cannot* subsume the latter.

Insofar as each person's advantage commands attention and respect in moral accounting, the well-being aspect of the person has to be directly considered. This role cannot be taken over by agency

[3] The relationship between the ranking of *elements* and the ranking of *sets* of elements is discussed in my *Commodities and Capabilities* (1985), ch. 7, in the specific context of judging "capability sets" and the corresponding "freedoms."

information. Although the agency aspect and the well-being aspect both are important, they are important for quite different reasons. In one perspective, a person is seen as a doer and a judge, whereas in the other the same person is seen as a beneficiary whose interests and advantages have to be considered.[4] There is no way of reducing this plural-information base into a monist one without losing something of importance.[5]

The well-being aspect may be particularly important in some specific contexts, e.g., in making public provisions for social security, or in planning for the fulfillment of basic needs.[6] In judging what a person may expect from social arrangements, the demands of well-being (and, in the case of responsible adults, also of well-being freedom) may loom rather large. On the other hand, in many issues of personal morality, the agency aspect, and one's responsibility to others, may be central. The well-being aspect and the agency aspect both demand attention, but they do so in different ways, and with varying relevance to different problems.

III. FREEDOM: POWER OR CONTROL?

Within the idea of freedom itself, there tends to be an internal plurality. There are, in fact, two distinct elements in the idea of freedom (they may be called, respectively, "power" and "control"), and the assessment of freedom has to deal with this internal plurality as well.[7] The distinction is of special relevance to particular issues of freedom, such as liberty and autonomy.

A person's freedom may well be assessed in terms of the power to achieve chosen results: whether the person is free to achieve one outcome or another; whether his or her choices will be respected and the corresponding things will happen. This element of freedom, which I shall call *effective power*, or *power* (for short), is not really concerned with the mechanism and procedures of control. It does not matter for effective power precisely *how* the choices are

[4] This dichotomy has a close connection with the contrast between "interest aggregation" and "judgment aggregation" in social choice theory, discussed in my "Social Choice Theory: A Reexamination," *Econometrica*, XLV (1977): 53–89; reprinted in my CWM (1982).

[5] However, while the agency and well-being aspects are quite distinct from each other, they are *not* independent of each other. The dependence arises from at least two obvious facts: that a person's agency may affect his or her well-being, and that being well may help a person's ability to act in pursuit of other objectives as well.

[6] This applies both to formal modeling of plan priorities [see, for example, G. Chichilnisky, "Basic Needs and Global Models: Resources, Trade and Distribution," *Alternatives*, VI (1980)] and to broader planning "strategies" [see, for example, P. Streeten, *et al.*, *First Things First* (New York: Oxford, 1981)].

[7] The contrast is discussed in my "Liberty as Control: An Appraisal," *Midwest Studies in Philosophy*, VII (1982): 207–221.

"executed." Indeed the choices may not even be directly addressed. Effective power can take note of *counterfactual choice:* things might be done because of knowledge of what the person would choose *if* he actually had control over the outcome.

In contrast, a person's freedom may also be assessed in terms of whether the person is himself exercising *control* over the process of choice. Is he actively doing the choosing in the procedure of decision and execution? This element of freedom may be called *procedural control,* or *control* (for short). It does not matter for freedom as control whether the person succeeds at all in achieving what he would choose.[8]

It is fair to say that, in the literature on liberty and freedom in political philosophy, it is the control element that has tended to receive the lion's share of attention. There is, of course, the related but distinct question of whether freedom should be seen in positive or negative terms, and whether one's obligations should take the form of not interfering with other people's control over spheres of their lives rather than the form of duties to help positively. I shall take up these questions later, but the distinction between effective power and procedural control is, in a sense, more elementary. While the control view is often combined with a constraint-based approach (to wit: *do not interfere* with other people's control over some specific matters), there is a general issue of whether the control view is *itself* an adequate approach to freedom, even when its use is not restricted to the negative perspective. I would argue that this concentration on control tends to produce an unacceptably narrow conceptualization of liberty and freedom.

To illustrate the contrast, I begin with a shortened version of an example I have used elsewhere.[9] Your friend is injured in an accident and is unconscious. The doctor says that either treatment *A* or treatment *B* can be used and one would be just as effective as the other, but that your friend would suffer less from *A* because of its

[8] In commenting on an earlier version of this text (and on the paper cited in fn 7), G. A. Cohen has argued that the terms 'power' and 'control' may be misleading. When a person has "effective power" in the sense specified, even if he does not have control over the process of selection, it *could be said* (Cohen points out) that he *had*, in fact, exercised control. This point might well be correct, but, if the basic distinction is accepted, it may not matter much whether we see it as a contrast between "procedural control" and "control" in some suitably broad sense, or between "procedural control" and "effective power", as it is presented here. The important issue relates to the fact that in modern society many powers are indirectly exercised, and, in that context, concentration on the levers of control provides an inadequate approach to freedom.

[9] "Liberty and Social Choice," (1983), pp. 18–20.

smaller side effects. However, you happen to know that your friend would have chosen treatment *B*, since treatment *A* is associated with some experiments on live animals of which your friend disapproves totally. He would, in fact, agree that treatment *A* would have been better for his well-being, but as a free agent he would have nevertheless chosen treatment *B*, if he were given the choice. If you now decide to ask the doctor to give your friend treatment *B*, you are giving your friend effective power even though he is not exercising the control himself. And your ground for choosing treatment *B* for him is surely not his well-being (he too agrees that *A* would be better for that), but his freedom (in the general form of *agency freedom*). It is also worth noting that your decision regarding what treatment your friend gets is *dependent* on what your friend would himself have chosen. It is not only that he happens to be getting what he would have chosen; he is getting it *because* he would have chosen it.

The contrast between effective power and procedural control is important in practice. It is often not possible to organize society in such a way that people can directly exercise the levers that control all the important aspects of their personal lives. To try to see freedom exclusively in terms of control is to miss out on the demands of freedom when control cannot feasibly be exercised by the persons themselves.

If, for example, we want the freedom not to be mugged in the streets and the liberty to move about without being so treated, we are looking for effective power. Precisely who exercises the control may be less important than the ability to achieve what we would have chosen. If the streets are cleared of the muggers *because* we would choose not to be mugged,[10] our freedom is being well served, even though we have not been given control over the choice of whether to be mugged or not.

To avoid possible misunderstandings, it may be useful to clarify what is being asserted here, and what is not. First, it is, of course, typically the case that not being mugged also serves our well-being. But in asserting that our freedom—even *agency freedom*—is well served by the streets being cleared of the muggers, something more is being asserted. It is that we would have *chosen* not to be mugged, and the streets are being cleared precisely because that is what we would have chosen.

Second, with the streets cleared of the muggers, we have, of

[10] While the dependence of the choice of antimugging policy on what we would choose is important for the "power" view of freedom, it is not necessary for that approach that this be achieved though some formal *procedure* of referendum-based execution.

course, the opportunity to walk as we please. This reflects the positive freedom, in most cases, to walk or not. But in that part of the story there is *no* contrast between control and power. We have the power to walk and also control over *that* decision. The contrast arises in considering the alternatives of being mugged and not being mugged. We do not control *this* choice ourselves, and we do not have the option of "being mugged" once the streets are cleared. But though that control is not ours, it was exercised in line with what we would have chosen and because of it.[11] It is in this sense that we have effective power, though no procedural control.

Third, in the example of mugging, the power is enjoyed not by each individual separately, but by the individuals taken together. There are other examples in which the individual on his own has effective power without control, e.g., in the example of your friend getting the treatment he would have chosen. Given the interdependences of social living, many liberties are not separately exercisable,[12] and effective power may have to be seen in terms of what all, or nearly all, members of the group would have chosen, e.g., in this case *not* to be mugged. What Isaiah Berlin calls "a man's, or a people's, liberty to choose to live as they desire"[13] has implications for effective power of individuals taken together *as well as* separately.

Concentrating on the control view of freedom and liberty has a long history. But in recent years it has tended to be particularly emphasized in the context of criticizing the practice in social choice theory of seeing freedom and liberty in terms of effective power only.[14] Robert Nozick, Peter Bernholz, Peter Gärdenfors, Robert

[11] There can, however, be *directional asymmetries* in effective power. For example, although the choice of "not being mugged" may be respected and executed, that of "being mugged" may not be similarly guaranteed. The real way to check whether we are getting *x because* we would have chosen *x*, is not so much to examine whether we would invariably have got "*not x*" if that is what we would have chosen, but to ascertain whether *x* is guaranteed in the first case but not in the second. Many standard liberties do, of course, have directional asymmetries; e.g., Miss *A* has the liberty *not to marry* Mr. *B* no matter what he wants, but not the liberty *to marry* Mr. *B* irrespective of his decisions.

[12] The issue of interdependence is well discussed by Christian Seidl, "On Liberal Values," *Zeitschrift für Nationalökonomie*, XXXV (1975): 257–292, and Jonathan Barnes, "Freedom, Rationality and Paradox," *Canadian Journal of Philosophy*, X (1980): 545–565.

[13] Isaiah Berlin, *Four Essays on Liberty* (New York: Oxford, 1969), p. 170.

[14] See my CCSW, ch. 6; and Allan Gibbard, "A Pareto-consistent Libertarian Claim," *Journal of Economic Theory*, VII (1974): 388–410. The "social choice" literature on this subject is now quite vast. For references, see the bibliographies in W. Gaertner and L. Krüger, "Self-supporting Preferences and Individual Rights: The Possibility of Paretian Libertarianism," *Economica*, XLVII (1981): 241–252; Sen, "Liberty and Social Choice" (1983); K. Suzumura, *Rational Choice, Collective Decisions and Social Welfare* (New York: Cambridge, 1983); and J. Wrigglesworth, *Libertarian Conflicts in Social Choice* (New York: Cambridge, forthcoming).

Sugden, Brian Barry, and others have pursued the control view, and though their formulations have differed from one another, there seems to have been solid agreement on the folly of seeing liberty in terms of power rather than procedural control.[15] It is not my intention to deny that the control element of freedom is indeed important in many contexts. But it is not the only important element in freedom. The power element cannot be neglected in any adequate formulation of freedom or liberty.

One may, of course, attach importance to having control over certain mechanisms of decision making and procedures of choice. In matters of what to eat, what to drink, what to wear, etc., it may not be adequate just to get what one would have chosen; one must actually do the choosing oneself. However, it is, in fact, also possible to argue that if achievements are characterized in a more articulate and apposite way than they are in the conventional formulations, then the motivation underlying any intrinsic concern with the control element of freedom can be *subsumed* within the notion of the power to achieve results. This question relates to the issue of the contents of states of affairs, which was discussed in the first lecture (181-183). Since states of affairs include actions and since agency information is part of the information regarding the states, the power to achieve particular states of affairs may have to include the power to use specific controls as well. Thus, the power view can be broadened to make room for attaching importance to control in the assessment of outcomes. The evaluation of the power to achieve different states of affairs may be control-sensitive, and the power view of freedom can, inter alia, accommodate whatever is important in the control view.

IV. AGENCY AND CONSEQUENTIALISM

Taking note of actions, agency, and control in the valuation of states of affairs raises an important question regarding the status of

[15] Nozick, *Anarchy, State and Utopia* (1974); Peter Bernholz, "Is a Paretian Liberal Really Impossible?" *Public Choice*, XIX (1974): 99-107; Peter Gärdenfors, "Rights, Games and Social Choice," *Nous*, XV (1981): 341-356; Robert Sugden, *The Political Economy of Public Choice* (Oxford: Martin Robertson, 1981); Brian Barry, "Lady Chatterley's Lover and Doctor Fischer's Bomb Party: Liberalism, Pareto Optimality and the Problem of Objectionable Preferences," mimeographed, 1982, to be published in J. Elster and A. Hylland, eds., *op. cit.*, forthcoming. A somewhat similar view is taken by Allan Gibbard, "Rights and the Theory of Social Choice," in *Logic, Methodology and Philosophy of Science*, VI (Amsterdam: North-Holland, 1982), in which volume contrast the analysis of Peter Hammond, "Liberalism, Independent Rights and the Pareto Principle." See also Isaac Levi, "Liberty and Welfare," and Peter Hammond, "Utilitarianism, Uncertainty and Information," in Sen and Williams, and Peter Bernholz, "A General Social Dilemma: Profitable Exchange and Intransitive Group Preferences," *Zeitschrift für Nationalökonomie*, XL (1980): 1-23.

that influence. If the moral approach in question incorporates "welfarism" (as the standard versions of utilitarianism do), then the value that can be attached to actions, agency, and such, must be entirely derivative. They must be based on their influence on utilities, since welfarism insists that the valuation of states must be a function of the utility information regarding the respective states. In the first lecture, this derivative view was disputed (sections VI and VII). In particular, arguments were presented against the "invariance restriction" which insists on *positional invariance*, i.e., the requirement that within a given moral approach the valuation of a state must be independent of the evaluator's position vis-à-vis the state, including his agency.

Positional invariance raises some difficult issues. It may look superficially like a condition of elementary consistency. How can two persons, sharing exactly the same moral approach, value the same state differently? The issue of consistency can be dealt with in formal terms easily enough. The valuation of the state may take note of such positional information as the agency of persons involved in bringing about that state, and the influence of that agency can vary *parametrically* depending on whether the evaluator is one of the agents involved (and if so, what has been his specific role). The real issue is not formal consistency, but cogency.[16] *Why* should the evaluator's own agency make a difference to the valuation made by him?

The issue of cogency relates to the recognition (discussed in the first lecture) that action and agency are integral parts of the state, and furthermore, that agency can be an important aspect of the person (a question also discussed in the second lecture). It would be extraordinary to require that a person himself must take no more note of his own agency in evaluating a state of affairs than others should and that a morally relevant assessment of the state can be made in this oddly detached way. When the evaluator happens to be also the agent whose action helped to bring about the state in question and when the action for which the person is peculiarly responsible is an integral part of that state, it is not at all clear why the evaluator must ignore this important connection in assessing the state, for moral reasoning. Lady Macbeth may well have got a little carried away in the state of affairs resulting from the murder

[16] I have argued elsewhere that "consistency conditions" used in the literature of rational choice and decision theory often make it difficult to see the real issues involved; and that there are no "natural" conditions—universal in scope—of "internal consistency of choice" ("Consistency," Presidential Address to the Econometric Society, 1984; to be published in *Econometrica*).

she committed when she asked, "Will these hands ne'er be clean?", but on the other hand we might mislead her a little if we were to inform her that, in the post-murder state, the perfumes of Arabia *would* sweeten her "little hand" as easily as any other hand. The responsibility of agency surely extends to evaluating states including the evaluator's own role, and that responsibility cannot suddenly disappear in the morally relevant evaluation of the state.

One reason why agency invariance may appeal, is a tendency to confuse this type of invariance with "authorship invariance," which was discussed in the first lecture. Authorship invariance does have some claims to being a reasonable requirement of moral evaluation (and, as was argued in the first lecture, can also be seen as a requirement of objectivity of moral beliefs). This is because the authorship of a statement is a very contingent fact. *A* can easily consider what he should say if he were in fact in *B*'s position rather than in his own. But the *positions* themselves are not without significance in evaluating the states, and this position relativity can be combined with authorship invariance and indeed objectivity of the corresponding type. The general thesis was presented in a broad way in the first lecture, but the gravity of the agency aspect of a person (further pursued later) has the implication of underlining the substantive importance of the position of being an agent, without in any way affecting the case for authorship invariance. The agency position has to be parameterized in the evaluation of states in a way that authorship need not be.

There is an interesting question whether these considerations require that the much-discussed condition of "consequentialism" should also be rejected. I don't believe that the outlined considerations entail either a rejection or an endorsement of consequentialism. The introduction of position relativity does have the effect of relaxing the overtight informational constraints imposed by the traditional combination of welfarism and consequentialism, and in this sense, it does make room for less blind judgments under consequentialist evaluation. But it does not require either the acceptance or the rejection of consequentialism as such.

Take Bernard Williams's famous example of Jim having to consider killing one person himself to save nine lives; the one to be killed by him would be killed anyway.[17] Whereas others have a straightforward reason to rejoice if Jim goes ahead, Jim has no option but to take serious note of his own responsibility in that state

[17] "A Critique of Utilitarianism," in J. J. C. Smart and B. Williams, *Utilitarianism: For and Against* (New York: Cambridge, 1973).

and his agency in killing someone himself. Position relativity will certainly be adequate to bring in a deep asymmetry between Jim's position and those of others even in consequential evaluation.

Nevertheless, even with this modification, Jim's decision may be ultimately straightforward in a consequentialist framework. In the state that will result from his killing one person, nine people are saved, and the one who is killed would have been killed anyway. Jim would have to attach an extraordinary degree of importance to the position of not being a killer himself to come to the conclusion that the value difference between one person being killed by Jim rather than by someone else is enough to outweigh the gain of nine people being saved from sure death. Even with position relativity, the decision is fairly straightforward. If, in fact, Jim's decision problem is *not* straightforward, as Williams argues it is not, then the difference must rest somewhere else.

It is possible to argue that there *is* a difference between an *action* being right and *the state resulting from that action* being the best feasible state, after taking note of the value or disvalue of the action itself (including agency). The first judgment concerns an *action*, and the second a *state* (*including* inter alia that action). There is no *necessity* that the two must correspond to each other in the rigid way that consequentialism would demand.[18] Whether they should, in fact, be linked in this way or not is a matter for further moral analysis, and the need to examine this link remains even after position relativity has been incorporated in the evaluation of states of affairs. Jim could still ask: "Can it be right for me to kill this man, just because the state of affairs resulting from that would be better (even after taking note of the disvalue of my action, judged as a *part* of the state of affairs)?"

The question of consequentialism will have to be settled by other arguments, since this one leaves that issue open. It is certainly true (as can easily be shown[19]) that agent relativity of every kind that has been proposed in the literature (by such authors as Bernard Williams, Thomas Nagel, and Derek Parfit[20]) can be accommodated *within* a consequentialist structure, once position relativity in the evaluation of states is admitted and used. But the *force* of the deontological considerations may not be fully captured in this way,

[18] See my "Evaluator Relativity and Consequential Evaluation," *Philosophy and Public Affairs*, XII (1983): 113-132.

[19] Discussed in my "Rights and Agency," *Philosophy and Public Affairs*, XI (1982): 3-39.

[20] Williams, "A Critique of Utilitarianism" (1973), and *Moral Luck* (1981); Nagel, "Limits of Objectivity" (1980); Parfit, *Reasons and Persons* (1984).

since part of that argument rests on distinguishing between the nature of action judgments and that of state judgments, no matter how inclusively (and position-relatively) the states are judged. The approach to moral reasoning utilized in these lectures does not force us to take a position one way or the other on this question. The welfarist part of utilitarianism (scrutinized in this lecture and the last) and the requirement of sum ranking (examined in the last lecture) stand rejected in a way that consequentialism is not; but neither is it positively endorsed.

However, the exacting demands of consequentialism must be distinguished from the requirement of "consequence sensitivity," and a firmer view can be taken about the latter. The analysis presented in these lectures would certainly be hard to reconcile with moral approaches that try to judge actions in a consequence-*independent* way. Given the intrinsic importance of well-being, and indeed of agency, it is not credible that a person can morally evaluate his or her actions without taking note of their effects on the well-being and agency aspects of others (including their well-being freedom and agency freedom).

Even the attempt to get a limited sphere of consequence-independent evaluation of actions by declaring some particular types of action to be invariably rejectable, no matter how good their consequences are, leads to problems. This "openness" is relevant even in assessing acts that are terrible judged on their own, e.g., killing. In fact, even in Williams's example involving Jim's problem, the dilemma would amount to nothing at all if some unexceptionable deontological constraint were definitively to rule out Jim's killing anyone. Whereas a nonconsequentialist Jim is *not* obliged to go ahead and shoot, simply because the resulting state of affairs (including his having killed someone) would be better, the dilemma with which Williams is concerned arises also because Jim cannot decide, in an equally straightforward way, that he *must not* shoot under any circumstances. The decision is difficult because there *is* a case for doing *either* alternative, and no unexceptionable constraint. That indeed is precisely the problem. Consequences *are* relevant even if consequence judgments do not enjoy a hegemony over action judgments.

V. RIGHTS AND NEGATIVE FREEDOM

This issue becomes particularly relevant in examining the possibility of having a substantive moral system that gives absolute priority to certain constraints related to rights, as, for example, in the system explored by Robert Nozick in *Anarchy, State and Utopia*. In such a system rights impose unrelaxable constraints, which have the effect of excluding certain alternatives. People must obey these constraints, no matter what else they may or may not do.

I have discussed elsewhere[21] why we may have good grounds for violating someone's rights if that prevents even worse consequences, e.g., a worse violation of the rights of others, arguing that this type of consideration is inescapable given the problems of interdependence that moral analysis has to face. For example, the violation of the property rights of some can prevent a developing famine and decimation.[22] Or, to take a different type of example, the violation of the rights of privacy of someone may yield the necessary information to prevent someone else from being battered, kidnapped, raped, or murdered. It is not at all clear why violating property rights, privacy, etc., must still remain rejectable, everything considered, in the cases specified. This necessity of considering, as it were, "everything" makes the proposals of consequence-independent absolute rights hard to defend. And the considerations of well-being and agency discussed in these lectures are impossible to reconcile with any proposal of consequence independence.

The nature of the rights considered by Nozick raises two different types of question. One concerns their *force,* in particular, their irresistibility; and the other relates to their *form,* namely their focus on "control" and more specifically their concentration on the "negative" perspective—imposing constraints on what others are permitted to do. The question of force, which has already been briefly addressed, must be distinguished from the issue of the appropriate form.

Considerations of well-being freedom and agency freedom need not, of course, have this negative concentration. Concern for well-being, well-being freedom, and agency freedom can all figure in a system in which conflicting positive contributions have to be weighed against each other when we are faced with a choice. Some of the relevant freedoms can also yield straightforward notions of rights. For example, minimal demands of well-being (in the form of basic functionings, e.g., not to be hungry), and of well-being freedom (in the form of minimal capabilities, e.g., having the means of avoiding hunger), can well be seen as rights that command attention and call for support. This perspective, which is close to the traditional format of the pursuit of positive freedoms, emerges naturally from the analysis that I have tried to present in these lectures.

[21] "Rights and Agency" (1982).

[22] Discussed, and empirically illustrated, in my *Poverty and Famines: An Essay on Entitlement and Deprivation* (New York: Oxford, 1981).

Some demands of *agency* freedom can also be seen as rights. The importance of self-agency has easily recognized urgency, and the force of such considerations as autonomy and liberty relate to the capability to take decisions in certain personal spheres in one's own life and to choose for oneself certain basic features of one's personal existence.[23] Although, as has been argued earlier in this lecture, the formulation of these freedoms requires us to look beyond control at effective power, this reformulation does not change the reasons for which such rights are taken to be important. One's ability to decide on certain matters in one's own personal life is given general support, and this support is not confined only to valuing procedural control or merely to wanting others not to violate these controls.

It is, in this general context, legitimate to ask: Where does *negative* freedom fit into this picture? Or does it not at all? The identification of the *source* of negative freedom has to be distinguished from that of its relative *strength* and its comparative force in a pluralist approach. In particular, the possibility that the source may be entirely *instrumental* is not ruled out by the general recognition that considerations of negative freedom may limit other people's actions very forcefully. Giving people powerful rights of, say, immunity from interference by others may help in furthering various intrinsic goals, including that of enhancing well-being freedom and agency freedom. Focusing on instrumentality (vis-à-vis utility) is, of course, precisely the way Jeremy Bentham reconciled attaching importance, on the one hand, to negative freedom (and to institutionalized rights) and, on the other hand, also regarding "natural rights" as "simple nonsense" and "bawling upon paper," and "natural and imprescriptible rights" as "rhetorical nonsense, nonsense upon stilts".[24]

It is, in fact, quite possible that much of the actual force of negative freedom and the rationale of institutional rights come from instrumental considerations of one kind or another. But without trying to rival the "instrumental" approaches through an alternative ("intrinsic") view that would yield these rights with *comparable force*, it is possible to argue that there are other—more intrinsic—sources of value in negative freedom. A violation of negative

[23] I have discussed some of these issues in "Liberty and Social Choice" (1983).

[24] For an interesting and useful analysis of Bentham's treatment of moral and natural rights, see Ross Harrison, *Bentham* (London: Routledge & Kegan Paul, 1983), ch. IV. The instrumental approach need not, of course, be utilitarian. On this see Scanlon, "Rights, Goals and Fairness," in S. Hampshire, ed., *Public and Private Morality* (New York: Cambridge, 1978), pp. 104/5.

freedom involves a direct failure on the part of the violator as a moral agent. And this failure of agency can be seen as having some significance of its own.

Consider a case in which person *A* pushes person *B*, who does not swim, into the river. *B* in fact drowns, and *A* cannot justify his action, we assume, in terms of some greater good that would follow from this drowning. It is possible to distinguish between two bad things that have happened. First, *B* is drowned and his positive freedom to live on and not to die prematurely has been violated. Second, *A* has failed rather badly as a responsible moral agent. So something worse than *B*'s drowning has occurred, especially as it should be viewed from the position of *A*.

This way of seeing the problem can appear to be erroneous, involving double-counting. Everything follows, it can be argued, from the bad thing happening to *B*. But is such an objection really sustainable? *A*'s failure is, of course, not unrelated to the bad thing happening to *B*, but there is a source of badness in *A* as well, in terms of his agency aspect, since he has failed so badly as an agent. Indeed, *A*'s failure as a responsible agent could have taken place even without the same bad thing happening to bedraggled *B*. For example, *A* pushes *B* with all his might, but unexpectedly *B* somehow does manage to stay on land; *or B* does fall, but is saved by the accidental presence nearby of a good swimmer. *B*'s positive freedom is, thus, very little affected, but *A*'s agency failure remains serious, if the saving happened to be unexpected and accidental.

In evaluating the states and actions, agent *A* cannot but take note of his own agency in the attempted drowning. His moral assessment must take note of both *B*'s loss, if any, and his own failure as a moral agent (if he were to take the step of pushing *B* into the river). Once the agency aspect of a person is given a central place in moral accounting, there is no escape from including this type of consideration in evaluating states and actions, and what looks like double-counting is, in fact, the union of two different, though not independent, bad things. The state in which *B* drowns accidentally—not pushed by anyone—cannot be as bad, especially as it should be seen by agent *A*, as the state in which *B* drowns after being deliberately pushed by *A* himself into the river. Thus, negative freedom does have some intrinsic importance of its own, *in addition to* its instrumental role in the pursuit of positive freedom.

There are many ambiguities in analyzing responsibility, and it is not my intention to suggest that this way of seeing negative freedom is unproblematic. But the coupling of agency considerations with well-being considerations does provide a much wider basis for analyzing the moral value of various traditional concepts—negative freedom among them.

To prevent a possible misunderstanding, I should also say that this type of agency-based consideration is not specifically confined to negative freedom only. The agency failure may well take a different form. For a variant of this case, consider one in which *B* falls accidentally into the river, with swimming champion *A* standing close to the spot, doing absolutely nothing to save *B*. Though *A* has not violated *B*'s negative freedom, it can be argued that this is also a case of agency failure on the part of *A* and that the state of affairs is, in a morally relevant way, worse for agent *A* than it would have been had *B* drowned without *A* standing nearby, or had *A* tried to save *B* unsuccessfully (with, of course, exactly the same result, so far as *B*'s life is concerned). Agency failure is a more general consideration than failure to respect negative freedom, which does not stand, by any means, alone in supplementing considerations of positive freedoms. But the relevance of agency failure provides some reason for intrinsic interest, inter alia, in negative freedom, in addition to whatever instrumental relevance negative freedom may have.

VI. CONCLUDING REMARKS

In these lectures I have tried to explore some of the implications of seeing persons from two different perspectives, viz., well-being and agency, neither of which can subsume the other. The substantive moral discussions drew on the examination of methodological issues in the first lecture, using an informational approach to ethical questions, and dealing with such matters as pluralism, incompleteness, positionality, agent relativity, and objectivity.

The adequacy of the foundational structure that Scanlon calls "philosophical utilitarianism" (more descriptively renamed here as "well-being as informational foundation"—WAIF for short) was examined and rejected. But that informational foundation provided one of the two major bases of moral reasoning used in the second and the third lectures. While the attractiveness of well-being as a foundation accounts for a good deal of the appeal of utilitarian moral approaches, it was argued in the second lecture that the identification of well-being with utility fails for each of the three main interpretations of utility (in the form of choice, happiness, and desire fulfillment). It was further argued that even if such an identification were, for the sake of argument, to be accepted, utilitarianism still could not be derived substantially from WAIF. Contrary to some claims, the issue of sum ranking is not trivial nor unproblematic.

More positively, it was argued that a more plausible view of well-being is provided by the accounting of functioning vectors, refined by considerations of capabilities to function. This approach yields partial orderings which are typically incomplete but eminently usable.

The third lecture has been largely concerned with examining the relevance of agency and the nature of freedom. Each of the two basic aspects of persons, viz., well-being and agency, leads to a particular concept of freedom. Using this dual base, I have tried to comment on a number of related issues concerning control, power, rights, consequences, agency, and positive and negative freedoms. Both well-being freedom and agency freedom have important—though disparate—relevance to the assessment of states of affairs and actions. And the informational base of the moral approach explored in these lectures cannot, in general, dispense with either agency information or well-being information, each of which has intrinsic interest—in the form of freedom as well as that of achievement. These lectures have been much concerned with examining these plural informational elements and their respective roles in moral valuation and judgment.

AMARTYA SEN

All Souls College, Oxford

[6]

Claims of Need*

David Wiggins

The art of our necessities is strange.
SHAKESPEARE (*King Lear* III:3:70)

O, I have ta'en
Too little care of this! Take physic, pomp;
Expose thyself to feel what wretches feel,
That thou mayst shake the superflux to them
And show the heavens more just
(*Ibidem*, III:4:32)

1. It has been felt for a long time that there must be some intimate connection between the needs of human beings and their abstract rights. H.L.A. Hart was giving voice to a strong and widespread intuition when he wrote:

> A concept of legal rights limited to those cases where the law . . . respects the choice of individuals would be too narrow. For there is a form of the moral criticism of law which . . . is inspired by regard for the needs of individuals for certain fundamental freedoms and protections or benefits. Criticism of the law for its failure to provide for such individual needs is distinct from, and sometimes at war with, the criticism with which Bentham was perhaps too exclusively concerned, that the law often fails to maximize aggregate utility.[1]

In practice, however, the connection between needs and rights

* In a slightly different form, this essay originally appeared in a tribute to John Mackie, *Morality and Objectivity*, ed. Honderich (London: Routledge & Kegan Paul, 1985). Sections 4, 5, 6, 7, 8, and 14 are adapted from work on needs which will appear elsewhere and in another form in the *Journal of Medical Ethics*, under joint authorship with Sira Dermen, to whom I am greatly indebted. I benefited greatly from letters that Bernard Williams and Ronald Dworkin kindly sent to me about the penultimate draft. I am grateful too for advice and suggestions given by Jennifer Hornsby, Susan Hurley, Robert Gay, Michael Smith, Margery Eagle, and Roger Scruton and Anthony Price (who both made many more suggestions than I was able to do justice to).

[1] 'Bentham on Legal Rights' in *Oxford Essays in Jurisprudence* II ed. Simpson, 1973, p. 200.

has proved elusive. Of course it ought not to have been expected that a linkage of this kind would be simple or hard and fast, or provide the one missing clue to everything that still puzzles us in the idea of justice. But if the connection is not only complicated but important too, and what validates it is there to be discovered among the sentiments that actually sustain our various ideas about justice, it will be a great shame if the failure to be simple or hard and fast continues to stand in the way of our trying to understand the special force and political impact of a claim of serious need. To postpone the problem is to postpone the day when we attempt to get ourselves an account of justice that is based on as many distinct ideas as justice itself may prove to contain within itself.

In advance, however, of all questions of justice and entitlement, where I have been happy to work within a framework rather similar to J.L. Mackie's, not presupposing the welfare state but reasoning positively and point by point about the kind of entitlement that needing creates,[2] it will be necessary to attend for its own sake and at some length to the question what needing is—a precaution disregarded almost equally by champions and by critics of the idea that there is something serious to be made of this notion in political philosophy. One can hardly explain the special force of a claim when one will not first determine what exactly one who makes it says, or in what contexts it seems particularly natural to make it, or what conceptions and misconceptions these contexts especially lend themselves to.

2. Those who complain that the question of what it is to need something is relatively neglected in our tradition are sometimes directed to the writings of Hegel and Marx. But there one is likely to be disappointed. It is true that each of these writers makes heartening acknowledgement of the familiarity and importance of the concept of need, and true again that in Marx one will encounter the famous or infamous formula 'From

[2] 'Can there be a rights-based moral theory?' in *Midwest Studies in Philosophy* Volume 3, 1978, pp. 350–9; 'Rights, Utility, and Universalization' in Frey ed. *Utility and Rights* (Oxford: Blackwell, 1984). See also his 'Rights, Utility, and External Costs' and other papers in his *Collected Papers* II, Oxford 1985, Essays XII–XVI.

each according to his ability; to each according to his need'[3] (though Marx did not in fact invent this principle).[4] But neither Marx nor Hegel says what a need is, or indicates what it really turns on in a given case whether this or that is needed by someone. In Hegel, there is a strong tendency for needs to be simply run together with desires: needs are first placed with desires on the side of subjectivity, in opposition to the objects of needing and desiring and the reality that resists them (as in the description of the evolution of self-consciousness in the *Phenomenology of Spirit*); and then they are put with desires again, on the social level, in the totality comprehending *all* interests and motivations that constitutes civil society as a 'system of needs' (as in the *Philosophy of Right*). Marx can be read as innocent of this conflation: but what we encounter in his case is the philosophically debilitating refusal to say anything that will forejudge any part of the substance of the public criterion of need that it is supposed history will supply or to anticipate in any other way the needs that some future 'consciousness exceeding its bounds' will acknowledge as properly expressive of 'human essence'.

Analytical philosophers are not as constrained here as it seems Marx was. But in our kind of philosophy, sensitive though it always is to questions of the form *what is it to φ?*, the idea of needing something suffers from guilt by association. Either the idea smells of *dirigisme*, state interference in the processes of production, and distaste for 'consumer preference',[5]

[3] *Critique of Gotha Programme* (towards the end of Marx's third comment on the document). For further references to Marx and Hegel, see Patricia Springborg, *The Problem of Human Needs and the Critique of Civilization* (London: George Allen and Unwin, 1981). See also Agnes Heller's important study, *The Theory of Need in Marx* (London: Allison and Busby, 1976).

[4] Cp. Shakespeare *Lear* 'So distribution should undo excess/And each man have enough', 4.1.66. And for nineteenth century pre-Marxian formulations of the abilities/needs principle, L. Blanc's and others', see pp. 147–8, note 3, of Del Vecchio *Justice: an Historical and Philosophical Essay*, ed. A.H. Campbell, (Edinburgh, 1952).

[5] Cp. Anthony Flew, *The Politics of Procrustes* (London: Temple Smith, 1981), p. 117:

> An emphasis upon needs as opposed to wants . . . cannot but appeal to those who would like to see themselves as experts qualified both to determine what the needs of others are, and to prescribe and enforce the means appropriate to the satisfaction of those needs.

Or compare Jeremy Bray, *Decision in Government* (London: Gollancz, 1970), p. 72, quoted in note 5 of essay VI. For criticisms of a very different tone and tenor, see James Griffin 'Modern Utilitarianism', *Revue Internationale de Philosophie*, no. 141, 1982, pp. 340–343.

or it revives bad memories of the 'means test' and numerous earlier attempts to restrict the number of indigent persons entitled to the outdoor relief provided by the Poor Law of 1601 and its more recent counterparts (social security, etc.). Or else it somehow contrives to arouse both sorts of association. And, in case that is not a sufficient disadvantage for the idea to labour under, those who have been willing to experiment with it have been dismayed to find, seeing the problem of justice in the way they were apt to see it, that, instead of simplifying things, the separate consideration of need only complicated them. It also infected certain questions with an indefiniteness that these philosophers were reluctant to accept as inherent in this subject matter.

3. However inhibiting these doubts and suspicions and difficulties have been within philosophy itself, it is a surprising and most important fact that they operate only at the level of theory. In practice—and to an extent that could not be predicted or even suspected on the basis of an examination of present day political theory—the political-cum-administrative process as we know it in Europe and North America could scarcely continue (could scarcely even conclude an argument) without constant recourse to the idea of need:[6]

> 'The outstanding object of the Beveridge Plan is to provide as far as possible a unified system of income maintenance to cover needs arising from a variety of causes.' (G.D.H. Cole, pamphlet explaining the Beveridge Plan.)
>
> 'Scientists are almost unanimous that in spite of the development of *in vitro* methods of testing and experiment, and in spite of

[6] Although it is official ratiocination and argument rather than legislative enactment that displays the most frequent employment of the word 'need', it is by no means unknown even in Acts of Parliament. For instance, Clause 2 of the 1978 Transport Act requires County Councils in England and Wales to prepare and publish annually a five year public transport plan reviewing existing services 'in relation to need'. (For the source of this use, compare the White Paper *Transport Policy* 1977 *Cmnd.* 6836, which lays it down as one objective of official policy to 'meet social needs by securing a reasonable level of mobility'.)

Note that in the third example given in the sequel below we find as often, the form '*x* needs to be V-ed', which may be presumed to be a transformation from 'it needs to be that *x* is V-ed', which presumably comes from '[we] need to V *x*' or '[we] need *x* to be V-ed'.

advances in tissue culture techniques, we still need to perform experiments on live animals.'

'The United Kingdom Atomic Energy Authority . . . has told the Government that it thinks that a fast reactor needs to be built and it is naturally keen to move on from the experience gained on the two small-scale plants it has operated at Dounreay in Scotland and to the logical next stage of development.' (*The Times*, March 18, 1981.)

'The minister decided not to reopen the inquiry, and in his decision he said that he had taken into account the general changes relating to design flow standards and traffic forecasts since the inquiry, and he was satisfied that they did not affect the evidence on which the inspector made his recommendation. He was convinced the schemes were needed and the road should be constructed.' (*The Times*, Law Report, December 10, 1977.)

An economist once said to me—and since that time I have gathered that this is a standardized professional reaction—'What do you mean by a need? Is a need just something you want, but aren't prepared to pay for?' This is witty, as well as perceptive of something (cp. §§26–7). But the literal inaccuracy of the suggestion will appear plainly to anyone who makes the experiment of reformulating 'needs' claims like those cited above and replacing 'need' by 'want', 'desire', 'prefer' or their nominal derivatives. No matter how one does this, the result lacks not simply the rhetorical force of the original, but even its particular meaning, coherence and argumentative point. And this is something that we have to explain, rather than rail against the idea of need and accuse it of trying to force our hand or of aiding and abetting some illicit transition from a statement of what is to a statement of what must be.[7] Indeed, I should say that, given the special force

[7] Cp. Springborg *op. cit.* Appendix. All else apart, the accusation conceded much too much to the word. There is no real contradiction at all in saying: 'This patient needs a blood transfusion. But she can't have one. The only suitable blood has been allocated to someone else'. (E.D. Watt in 'Human Needs, Human Wants, and Political Consequences', *Political Studies*, vol. 30, 1982, p. 541, imputes the same error to K.R. Minogue, who wrongly characterizes a need as something that has by definition 'a right to satisfaction'. See *The Liberal Mind* (London: Methuen, 1963), pp. 46, 103.)

carried by 'need', we ought to try to grasp some special content that the word possesses in virtue of which that force accrues to it. It would be a sort of word-magic if so striking a difference as that between 'want' and 'need' could arise except from a difference of substance.

4. The last contention might be defended on general grounds relating to meaning and force. But, where someone is seriously tempted by the idea that needs are a certain class of strong desires or preferences or strong unconscious desires or preferences,[8] more particular considerations can be adduced. If I want to have x and $x = y$, then I do not necessarily want to have y. If I want to eat that oyster, and that oyster is the oyster that will consign me to oblivion, it doesn't follow that I want to eat the oyster that will consign me to oblivion. But with needs it is different. I can only need to have x if anything identical with x is something that I need. Unlike 'desire' or 'want' then, 'need' is not evidently an intentional verb. What I need depends not on thought or the workings of my mind (or not only on these) but on the way the world is. Again, if one wants something because it is F, one believes or suspects that it is F. But if one needs something because it is F, it must really be F, whether or not one believes that it is.[9]

5. The apparent distinctiveness of needing being registered in this way, we may now move one step closer to a positive

[8] Or desires or preferences that I should have if I were rational? But who can say what it is rational for someone to want in advance of knowing what he needs? There must of course be many other ways of arriving at rational wants otherwise than via needs; but insofar as rationality comes into the matter at all—i.e. rationality as conceived independently of given actual motivations—the idea of need surely has to be at least *coeval* with the idea of want, and should be accorded its own semantic identity.

[9] See A.R. White's telling criticisms of the assimilation of needs and desires in *Modal Thinking* (Oxford: Blackwell, 1971), p. 114. There are numerous other ways of bringing out this sort of difference. But one way of making the distinction can and must be firmly dispensed with, and is certainly superfluous. This is the claim that a man who needs *x eo ipso* lacks *x* and ails without *x*, whereas a man who wants *x* may not lack *x*. The trouble with this is that it isn't true that I lack whatever I need: all sorts of things that I already have are things that I need. See again here White, p. 107. For the other view, see *e.g.* Benn and Peters, *Social Principles and the Democratic State* (London: Allen & Unwin, 1959), p. 143.

elucidation. Something that has been insisted upon in most analytical accounts of needing[10] is that needing is by its nature needing for a purpose, and that statements of need which do not mention relevant purposes (or 'end-states' as White calls them) are elliptical—some will say dishonestly elliptical—for sentences that do mention them.[11]

One thing seems right with this claim, and another seems wrong.

The thing that seems right concerns what may be called purely instrumental needing. Someone may say 'I now need to have £200 to buy a suit', or, speaking elliptically, 'I need £200'. If he can't get the suit he has in mind for less than £200, then it is true, on an instrumental reading of his claim, that he needs £200. All that has to hold for this to be the case is something of the form:

> It is necessary (relative to time *t* and relative to the *t* circumstances *c*) that if (. . . . at t″) then (___ at t′).[12]

[10] The exceptions are (1) G.E.M. Anscombe 'Modern Moral Philosophy', *Philosophy*, 1958, p. 7: 'To say that [an organism] needs that environment is not to say, e.g. that you want it to have that environment, but that it won't flourish unless it has it. Certainly, it all depends whether you *want* it to flourish! as Hume would say. But what "all depends" on whether you want it to flourish is whether the fact that it needs that environment, or won't flourish without it, has the slightest influence on your actions'; (2) Joel Feinberg in *Social Philosophy* (Prentice Hall, 1973), p. 111: 'In a general sense to say that S needs X is to say simply that if he doesn't have X he will be harmed'. (Cp. David Miller, *Social Justice* (Oxford University Press, 1976), p. 130; David Richards, *A Theory of Reasons for Action* (Oxford University Press, 1970), pp. 37–8; Honoré, *op. cit.*, at note 29 below, his p. 78.)

The main difference between these analyses or elucidations and the one we shall propose consists in the fact that we propose to see *need* as an explicitly modal notion, which leads us to insist that Anscombe's conditional be governed by 'necessarily'. For other works which appear to be under the direct or indirect influence of Anscombe's formulation see D. Wiggins, *Sameness & Substance* (Oxford: Blackwell, 1980), p. 183, and J. Finnis, *Natural Law and Natural Rights* (Oxford, 1980), *passim*.

[11] This is the common point in the otherwise very different (and differently modulated) accounts of Flew and White and Barry. See Flew, *Politics of Procrustes*, p. 120: ('If I say that I need something, it is never inept to ask what for. . . . There is always something hypothetically imperative about my need'); White, *op. cit.*, ('To say that A needs to V is elliptical for saying that A needs to V in order to F [where to F is the end state] (p. 105), . . . a failure to notice the elliptical nature of statements about what A needs leads to arguments at cross purposes (p. 106) . . . "Does A need X?" is an elliptical not a normative question' (p. 106)); Brian Barry, *Political Argument* (London: Routledge & Kegan Paul, 1965), Ch. III, §5a.

[12] Strictly speaking, we have to add something here entailing that whatever '. . . .' holds a place for is a *matter of concern*. But very shortly, when we come to the non-

In the present case, the antecedent of the conditional relates to the man's having the suit and the consequent to his having £200.

So far so good. If something like this is right, then it makes excellent sense of the claim that certain uses of 'I need to have *x*' are elliptical (*e.g.* the claim 'I need £200' as made by this man); and one whole class of non-elliptical *need* sentences receives a plausible treatment. But there is something else the elucidation fails to make sense of. This is the fact that, if we have already been through everything this man can say about his need, then we can properly and pointedly respond to his claim with: 'You need £200 to buy that suit, but you don't need £200—because you don't need to buy that suit'. The ellipse theory suggests that he ought then to insist that there is an end of his for which the suit is necessary. But it is plain that without deliberate misunderstanding of what we are now saying, he cannot make this retort. If he did respond in this way, then it would be open to us, meaning our remark to him in the only way we could mean it, to say that he was simply missing the point. What he has to show, if he wants to make more than the instrumental

---

instrumental needs, which are our real interest, the addition will be superfluous, because we shall supplant the '. . . .' in the antecedent by a sentence representing something the person cannot help being concerned with. I draw attention to this, nevertheless, because, even if there is a usage according to which the antecedent need not endorse some end as a matter of concern ('to do something totally pointless knowing that it is totally pointless you need a lot of patience'—can one truly say that?), the common elliptical usage discussed in the next paragraph is only available when the suppressed antecedent *does* relate to something that is a matter of concern.

For more on the necessity invoked in the formula, see below §8. The three time variables t, t', t'', are all needed in the full form of the 'need' sentence as given without any ellipse or abbreviation (even though, evidently, they do not vary entirely independently). t'' need not be t', because the goal mentioned in the antecendent may be achieved later than the prerequisite mentioned in the consequent. t need not be t'', because the end-state, a child's having good second teeth for instance, may create an earlier necessity that certain measures be taken. And t need not be t' either, because it may be necessary *now* (t) that certain measures be taken next year (t') for the subsequent (t'') good of the second teeth—even though it was not necessary last year (before t) that these measures be taken at t'. Before t there was a chance of dispensing with these t' measures, e.g. by taking proper or better care of the first teeth.

It is well beyond my present scope to trace the relationship of the time indicators in this sort of elucidation to the tenses that appear in the various natural language forms that it seeks to elucidate.

claim, is that he *cannot get on without that suit*, that *his life will be blighted without it*, or some such thing.

What is suggested by the existence of this extra, more problematical requirement? It suggests that, although there is an instrumental sense of 'need' where we can ask for some purpose to be specified in a non-elliptical version of the 'needs' claim and there are no limits on what purpose this is (except the limits of what can be of any conceivable concern to anyone), there is another sense of 'need' by which the purpose is already fixed, and fixed in virtue of the meaning of the word. What is more, this must be the sense of the word employed by the majority of scientists, the UKAEA, the Minister, and the other makers of needs claims quoted in §3.[13] These people are representing, and the meanings of their words commit them to representing, that we simply can't get on without more roads, more reactors, or more animal experiments or whatever. ('We have no alternative.') They might be wrong. There might be minor obscurity in what exactly is intended by this. But the thing that is controversial in what is said is not the necessity for the avoidance of harm to human beings—it is precisely the fact that such avoidance is not a controversial purpose that lends needs claims their *prima facie* special practical and argumentative force—, but the claim that our prior adherence to this end *commits us* to have more roads, more fast reactors, more animal experiments or whatever. What is controversial is the claim that there is no alternative.

6. We have then to assign at least two senses to 'need' if we are to assign the right significance to the sorts of thing people use the word to say and to understand the special argumentative force of needs claims. But of course there is a connection between the purely instrumental and the not purely instrumental sense, or what we may call (simply for the sake of a name, not

[13] The hazards of claiming the strict lexical distinctness of senses are now familiar. We are claiming that the considerations in the text will suffice for a proof of distinctness of sense of 'need' that comes up to the standard proposed in David Wiggins 'Sentence Sense, Word Sense and Difference of Word Sense' in *Semantics: an Interdisciplinary Reader*, ed. Steinberg and Jacobovits (Cambridge University Press, 1971) or Bede Rundle, *Grammar in Philosophy* (Oxford University Press, 1981), pp. 14–5.

to exclude the relativities to be set out in §7) the absolute or categorical sense of the word. Thus:

> I need [absolutely] to have *x*
> if and only if
> I need [instrumentally] to have *x* if I am to avoid being harmed
> if and only if
> It is necessary, things being what they actually are, that if I avoid being harmed then I have *x*.

What distinguishes the second sense of 'need', so defined by reference to the first, is that it is in virtue of what is carried along by this sense itself of the word 'need', not in virtue of context (whatever part context plays in determining that this is the sense intended), that appeal is made to the necessary conditions of harm's being avoided. If so, the identity of the antecedent '. . . .' of the conditional 'Necessarily, since circumstances are what they are, if . . . ., then ___' is fixed by the presence of the word 'need' taken in this absolute sense.[14] It must follow that there is then no question of ellipse in this case. (One does not have to supply again what is already there.)[15]

Given this account of the word's content, it becomes unsurprising that 'need' taken in the absolute sense should have the special point and force it appears to have both in the individual case and in the case of the community's needing something. (I postpone *sine die* the neither easy nor impossible

[14] What might possibly confuse one is that if someone says that he needs something [absolutely] then he may perfectly well explain himself (as our equivalences indeed suggest) by reference to what he needs [instrumentally] to stay alive or avoid harm.

[15] The feeling that this proposal imports a semantical singularity of some sort may be substantially reduced by reference to a certain more familiar and uncontroversial example of ambiguity, where there is a similar nesting of one sense of a word in the account of another sense of the same word: where 'V' holds a place for a verb or verb-phrase, and 'iff' abbreviates 'if and only if',

> *z* has a [liberty] right to *V* iff *z* has no duty not to *V*; *z* has a [claim] right to *V* iff *z* has a [liberty] right to *V* and some person or agency has no [liberty] right not to secure to *z* the opportunity and ability to exercise his [liberty] right to *V*.

Cp. Joel Feinberg, *Social Philosophy*, p. 58: 'One can have a liberty which is not also a [claim] right but one cannot have a [claim] right which is not also a liberty'.

task of explicating the relation of these two cases of needing.) It is also to be expected that, so understood, 'need' should be normative or evaluative, and normative or evaluative *in virtue of its content.*

7. Normativeness apart, there are at least three distinct ways in which needs-statements of the simple singular variety we have elucidated must appear to be *relative* (notwithstanding the other respect, see §5, in which they are absolute).

First, the suggested elucidation in terms of harm exposes a certain parameter that is always there to be discovered within claims of absolute needing. This is the idea, not innocent of the metaphysics of personhood, of well-being or flourishing, by reference to which we make judgments of harm.

What follows from this relativeness? Relativeness to something else is no obstacle in itself to the most extreme or perfect kind of objectivity. Indeed making such relativeness fully explicit sometimes has the effect of revealing the subject matter in question as a candidate for unqualified or absolute truth.[16]

The first relativeness was only a matter of *need*'s involving a parameter. The second and different way in which need-sentences may appear to be relative qualifies any hopes that might be inspired by this account of the first.—What constitutes suffering or wretchedness or harm is an essentially contestable matter, and is to some extent relative to a culture, even to some extent relative to people's conceptions of suffering, wretchedness and harm. Obviously there is much more to be said about that (even if it is doubtful how much of it involves the idea of 'relative deprivation'—a relativity we have ventured to omit altogether from the argument); but instead let us hurry on, simply insisting that, even when the instability is conceded of some of the opinions that have been reached within our culture about absolute needs, some needs claims are so far from being indeterminate or seriously

[16] For instance, relativizing length, duration and motion and reformulating Newton's laws to render them relative to the reference frame of the observer and all reference frames in uniform motion with respect to him, and then qualifying the laws in certain ways suggested by the Special Theory of Relativity, made of a theory that was not previously unqualifiedly true a theory that may yet prove to be absolutely true.

contestable that they are more or less decidable. We shall return briefly to this point after making mention of a third relativity.

The third relativity is relativity to the particular circumstances of the time or times (see note 12, paragraph 2) associated with the need and the background of (no doubt normative) assumptions associated with those circumstances. When we make a claim of the form *Necessarily at t if such and such then so and so*, where t is a moment for which this *necessarily* is temporally indexed, we thereby confine our consideration to all alternative futures from t onwards, and what we are saying is equivalent to the claim that every alternative in which such and such holds is one in which so and so holds. If pure historical necessity at t, $\Box_t$, were our concern, then a future would count as an alternative for times $\geqslant t$ just if it could coherently be described, and every correct description of it was compatible with the conjunction of (i) the state of the world that actually obtained at t and (ii) all true laws of nature. Thus $\Box_t(p)$ is true if and only if p is true in every alternative world whose history is indistinguishable from the history of the actual world up to the moment t, natural laws being counted as part of the history of the world and fixed as of t.[17] But where needing is concerned, it seems that the definition of alternativeness must be modified to restrict the class of alternative futures to futures $\geqslant t$ that (i) are economically or technologically realistically conceivable, given the actual state of things at t, and (ii) do not involve us in morally (or otherwise) unacceptable acts[18] or interventions in the arrangements of particular human lives or society or whatever, and (iii) can be envisaged without our envisaging ourselves tolerating what we do not have to tolerate.

This relativity to circumstance imports one more feature that deserves special comment. The fixed antecedent of the whole conditional that is governed by the modal operator

[17] Cp. David Wiggins, 'Towards a Reasonable Libertarianism', Essay VIII in this volume, §4.

[18] Note that we have already had implicit recourse to this thought in the discussion of the instrumental sense in so far as we allowed that *N* needed £200 to buy a suit. The fact that there is a future in which he has a suit without paying £200, because he steals one, was not allowed to count against this claim.

'necessarily relative to the circumstances *c* obtaining at *t*' speaks of avoidance of harm. This is not in itself obscure, but it will not give quite the sense we require to cover all the kinds of absolute (more than merely instrumental) needing that usage allows, unless some associated standard is thought of as supplied for harm to be judged according to the context, the standard creating the presumption that it is itself suggested by *some however minimal level of flourishing that is actually attainable here*. Avoidance of harm can then be understood always by reference to a norm of flourishing that is relative to *c*, and this in its turn can import the entailment or implicature that, if *y* non-instrumentally needs *x* at *t* under circumstances *c*, then there *exists* some alternative future in which *y* does flourish to some however minimal extent.[19] (When I am utterly doomed however the future is realistically envisaged, then I can begin to lose some of my ordinary needs, even as I acquire very special short term needs.)

For non-instrumental or categorical needing, this third species of relativity furnishes more of what was already furnished by the second. It is not just that the idea of harm, or the norm of flourishing by reference to which harm is judged, is historically conditioned and essentially contestable. It is also circumstantially conditioned *as of some time t* what futures are to count as realistic, morally acceptable alternatives, how long a forward view we have to take of flourishing in considering what counts as harm, and what the relevant standard of harm ought to be with respect to the time-span that is agreed to be the right one to apply in the given case. It may even be contestable—before we consider how much the present constrains the future—what exactly the circumstances are that prevail at *t*. The second and third sorts of relativity interact.

There is plenty here for an objectivist to face up to. And yet, in spite of the real and manifold contestability of most of these things, some may be tempted to conclude (as I do) that the

[19] Thus for our conditional in §6 governed by the specially indexed modality the problem simply does not arise that the impossibility of the antecedent will make the conditional true vacuously.

For the reasons for preferring the 'harm'-formulation to a direct formulation in terms of 'flourishing' ('Necessarily (if *z* flourishes then. . . .)'), see below §14, on Aristotle.

agreement that can be reached about the truth or falsity of a wide variety of needs claims (when they are seriously and correctly construed as making the contextually much constrained but very strong claims they do make) is far more striking than the disagreement some others will arouse. The temptation exists, though I shall not try to evaluate it here, to claim that objectivity is a matter of degree and that some significant degree of it can coexist even with the second of the three kinds of relativity we have distinguished.

8. The thought we have now arrived at is that a person needs *x* [absolutely] if and only if, whatever morally and socially acceptable variation it is (economically, technologically, politically, historically . . . *etc.*) possible to envisage occurring within the relevant time-span, he will be harmed if he goes without *x*. A proper development of this that enabled us to try to measure the relative public weights of various claims of need would have to make room for certain obvious and essential refinements. And it would have to prepare the ground for these by distinguishing certain distinct questions.

There is the question of the *badness* or *gravity* of needs. How much harm or suffering would be occasioned by going without the thing in question? And there is a consequential question of *urgency*: given that some not inconsiderable harm or suffering would be occasioned by going without the thing in question, how soon must this thing be supplied? And then there is the question of the *basicness*, the *entrenchment*, and the *substitutability* of needs. Being technical terms, however, these categorizations all require more elaborate introduction.

When we attempt to survey the class of alternative possible futures and then, restricting this to envisageable acceptable futures, we ask whether every future in which person *y* is not harmed is one in which he has *x*, we shall often discover that it is a matter of degree how difficult it is to envisage realistically some alternative in which *y* will escape harm without having *x*, or how morally acceptable it would be to propose—or to acquiesce in—that alternative's being deliberately brought about. Often we shall then have to resolve such difficulties by imposing a threshold on what departures from the familiar we are to regard as realistically envisageable, as morally acceptable or as practical politics. The lower such thresholds are set, the more futures then count as real alternatives, and the harder it will then become for a need statement to count as true. Seeing the effects of lower settings of the thresholds but being reluctant to deny that *y* really needs *x* at all, we shall often have to choose between (i) raising the threshold of moral and social possibility again; (ii) quite differently, lowering (relaxing) the standard by which the harm to *y* is judged, allowing more things to count as harm; and (iii) keeping the lower threshold of moral and political possibility, together with the more exigent truth-condition it imports, but disjoining having *x* with having some slightly inferior potential substitute for *x*.

In the light of all this, it will be a useful stipulation to say that *y*'s need for *x* is *entrenched* if the question of whether *y* can remain unharmed without having *x* is rather insensitive to the placing of the aforementioned threshold of realistic envisage-ability-cum-political and moral acceptability of alternative futures. When we are concerned with the problem of arbitration between general needs claims or arbitration between general needs claims and other claims, it will then be important to distinguish between entrenchment with respect to the shorter term (where extant arrangements create definite requirements that cannot be escaped immediately but may be in due course escaped) and entrenchment with respect to the longer term. Some desirable disruptions of the established order that would enable people to escape harm without having *x* cannot be envisaged happening as it were overnight; but in many cases the change can be coherently and easily described and can be quite realistically envisaged taking place gradually and by stages.

Developing a special case of entrenchment, one might then stipulate that *y*'s need for *x* is *basic* just if what excludes futures in which *y* remains unharmed despite his not having *x* are laws of nature, unalterable and invariable environmental facts, or facts about human constitution.[20] And within the basic, one might try to discriminate between (1) that which is owed to unchangeable tendencies of things to turn out in one rather

[20] 'Basic' will be here, as in all the schemes we have encountered in other writers, a technical term to be grasped in the first instance by the definition of the category, and in the second instance by reference to the *point* of setting up such a category. (To forget

than another specifiable kind of way (either in general or given the particular place, time or culture) and (2) that which is owed to something non-negotiable in the various ideas about human harm and flourishing that condition our sense of the socially possible (as well as our sense of what *y* must have).

Finally, we may find it useful to be able to say that *y*'s need for *x* is *substitutable with respect to* *x* if some slight lowering of the standard by which *y*'s harm is judged permits us to weaken claims of need by disjoining *y*'s having *x* with his having *u* or *v* or *w* or whatever.

It should be obvious that these labels correspond to overlapping but independent categorizations. A need for *x* can be not very bad but basic, for instance; or bad and also urgent yet substitutable with respect to *x*; or bad in the extreme and highly entrenched insofar as it is urgent, but, insofar as it is not urgent, relatively superficially entrenched in the mid term and not entrenched at all in the long term. It should be equally obvious how important it is to be clear whether the need we are talking about stems from a judgment about a particular human being, or about all human beings in specified kinds of circumstances, or (making the truth-condition most exigent of all) all human beings under all actual variations of circumstance.

9. How then are needs and desires and needs and interests related? Perhaps we had better see needs themselves (contrast things needed) as *states of dependency (in respect of not being harmed)*, which have as their proper objects things needed (or, more strictly, *having* or *using* . . . *x*). In that case our categorization in §8 is a categorization of states of dependency. Such states can often be expressed by desire or striving (or avoidance or whatever): and often the propositional object of

---

this, and to dispute as if the categories were antecedently given, is to engage in the sort of logomachy that gives philosophy a bad name.) In particular, we would remark that our basic category is not the same in definition or point as the category of *survival needs*, or biological needs as Benn and Peters call them (*op. cit.* pp. 144–146, see also Stanley Rosen's criticisms in *Mind*, vol. 86, 1977, p. 88). Nor is it the same in definition or point as Benn and Peter's own category of *basic needs*, which simply concerns a decent standard of living; or the same as the modern Marxist category of *really human needs*, or *one's needs as a human being*, which are usually introduced to make a contrast with *false needs*. (A contrast we have partially but only partially absorbed by bringing out the full exigency of the truth-conditions of statements of need.)

the desire or striving will be the same as that which we find in some correct statement of the need. But even in this special case it is not perfectly obvious that the desire ought to be simply identified with the need. A more plausible identification is between someone's having a certain need and his having a certain interest. If a person needs *x*, then he has an interest in *x*'s being or becoming available to him. And if he very badly needs at *t* to have *x* at *t*, and the need is also significantly entrenched as of *t* and scarcely substitutable at all, then his having *x* may be said to represent a *vital interest* of his. His having the need for *x* is then the same as his having a vital interest in having *x*. This is a good ruling, I believe, but only if we use the word 'interest' to mean what it means in English, where its connection with 'want' or 'desire' is complicated and indirect (cp. White, *op. cit.*, p. 120.), and if the proposed equivalence is without prejudice in favour of any general alignment between needs and interests.

10. So far so good. Inasmuch as the idea of need has begun to appear at least clarifiable and intelligibly related to familiar notions, its champions will now hasten to point out what an important part it played in the motivation of the later 19th and 20th-century humanitarian efforts that have transformed the living conditions of so many 20th-century city-dwellers.

Yet it is important that there is another side to this picture. Detractors of the *need* concept will point out that, among those who know the failures as well as the successes of modern planning, the regulations and minimum standards which ideas about what people need have inspired national and municipal governments to lay down and impose with the effect of law are now widely blamed for urban blight, the bleak monotonous environment, the graceless stereotyped architecture, and even the economic inertia of that which has come to replace the city of slums and smoking factories. Over and over again, these critics will say, rigid housing standards, building regulations, public health regulations and zoning restrictions, all founded in the idea of human need and many of them supposed to afford particular protection to the poorest and wretchedest members of society, have combined in a singular and unforeseen way to their conspicuous disadvantage. In operation, these standards and restrictions have first reduced the housing stock actually available at any time for human habitation, thus raising rents and house-prices against those least able to afford them; then conspired to inhibit all individual efforts at piecemeal improvement in neighbourhoods that will probably be condemned in their entirety; and then narrowed the choice, where new building is concerned, to the meanest and least flexible of conceptions (excluding from consideration almost all that we are wont to admire when we encounter them in the architecture and town-planning of the past). Thus a quarter of alleys, tenements and terraces that long ago replaced a semi-rural slum of huts and hovels built on small plots is not itself replaced gradually, or at a pace that corresponds to what can be practically envisaged or anticipated by anyone with a direct interest there, but—such is the power of an idea like *need*—is demolished and swept away in its entirety. Inhabitants and local industries are dispersed. And then, to a lengthening list of statutory specifications and on a shrinking budget (itself ill-defended from corruption), the towers or blocks we now see in the East End of London (or Liverpool, or Glasgow or, more benignly, Sheffield) are built upon the vast space that has been swept clear, connected only by windswept walkways or (where new, higher capacity roads dictate this) pedestrian underpasses, in an environment that repels all human attempts to come to terms with it and almost paralyses practical initiative. It can still be hoped that trees or grass will catch root somewhere and grow where they can. But otherwise, and surely at least in part as a result of an official determination of need, a whole quarter is sterilized against all beneficial adaptation, initiative or change. And, except in the rare cases where industry and business reestablish themselves there in strength, it will be beyond the powers of most of the tenants of the place to escape from the client condition to which they have been reduced.

11. Anyone who wants to take needs seriously would not be well advised to deny that such occurrences are familiar in practice, or simply to counter by pointing to outrageous schemes that governments of different complexion now instigate *in defiance* of local need. For where need really was the dominant motivation, the indictment he faces must be a serious

one, and attributions of need are deeply implicated in the charge. He may of course declare that so many different misapprehensions and oversights lie buried in the dense history of shortage, emergency and unreasoning optimism that makes up the record of the early post Second World War reconstruction—while the later history of the idea of need is overlaid by so much unconscious corruption,[21] dogmatism and megalomania (all sustained by the in practice nearly limitless ambiguity of the expression 'the public interest')—that his opponent can not really claim to have laid bare the one mistake that explains everything that he deplores and laments here. There is some justice in that. But, given the original motivation and the need-oriented thoughts that were expressed in good faith by statesmen, public officials and the experts they relied upon, a more substantial defence is required. Unless we can find some serious misconception of need among the ideas that motivated these people, or can, as I suspect, identify some definite coarseness in their appreciation of it, the case for superseding the idea of need altogether in political philosophy will be extremely hard to rebut. (Indeed I expect that some new Tory thinkers will already have blamed the dismal scenes just described on the very attempt to give the idea of need any positive place at all in politics beyond the residual role of determining minimum levels of social security.)

The first thing I should say myself in defence of the idea of need is that, as we have elucidated statements about what is needed by a given person or set of persons, they commit us, not only to answers for certain general questions about harm, about what can be tolerated or not, and about what sort of thing can and cannot be realistically envisaged, but also to something highly particular and special to the given circumstances of the people, whoever they are, who will not, it is said,

[21] Corruption flourishes in a special way when nobody quite knows what *counts* as corruption, and even honest men do not know what distance to keep from certain other men of entrepreneurial energy and flair. For one part of the reason for this state of doubt and confusion see §24 following below. This is a state of doubt and confusion that makes room for methods of persuasion and promotion that represent corruption in a further moral/intellectual (not legal) sense. (Cp. Francis Gladstone, *The Politics of Planning* (London: Temple Smith, 1976), p. 105 on rhetorical use of the 'have-nots' as a means of dressing up the desiderata of those who 'have'.)

being placed just as they are placed, escape harm without the thing stated to be needed. This combination of particular and general is one of the most important and intriguing features of particular non-instrumental needs. And it is open to question whether it has been properly grasped by those who have been happy to think in terms of codes of minimum standards. Certainly, the rigid standard is in constant danger of institutionalizing the neglect of such differences. It threatens the distinction between particular needs that are *bad* (even amount to the vital interest of certain particular people at a particular time) and something yet harder to identify and formulate, *viz.* needs that are *basic* or *deeply entrenched* and susceptible of being *generalized* to arrive at practical precepts that it is safe and sensible to have enforced by public officials over indefinitely many cases in indefinitely many kinds of circumstances.[22]

[22] For the inherent indefiniteness of the subject matter of practice, cp. Aristotle *Nicomachean Ethics* V.x. 4–5.

Somewhat similar remarks to those in the text ought probably to be directed at the Marxists' conception of 'truly human needs', needs that are 'expressive of human essence' etc. Countless needs, under any conceivable state of affairs, will always be both urgent and non-basic—i.e. put there by particular circumstances. And there will always be particular circumstances, however admirable the new condition of man. To the extent then that we cannot confront the problem that 'Under private property . . . every person speculates on creating a new need in another' (Marx *1844 MSS.*, London: Lawrence and Wishart, 1970, p. 147) by insisting on the proper interpretation of claims of need, the problem of false needs is much too hard to be simply solved by identifying the class of basic or essentially human needs.

The poignancy of the contrast between the thin set of universal needs that *nature* will underwrite and the set of things that may be needed by someone placed in a particular situation is brought out, however obliquely to Shakespeare's intention, most vividly in *Lear* (2.4.262):

> Allow not nature more than nature needs,
> Man's life is cheap as beast's.

Plainly, there is no 'human need' to have a retinue of a hundred knights. But an abdicated king in Lear's position needed such a retinue—and, to judge by what happened to him, much else besides.

There is a closely related difficulty in bringing Rawls' theory of primary goods to bear upon the problem of needs, as I conceive this. For one of the things we have to be prepared to attempt here is to look behind social arrangements defined in terms of primary goods, and behind representative positions of representative kinds of person, to the actual circumstances of particular persons—all in a manner apparently forbidden by Rawls in *A Theory of Justice*. On this point, see Brian Barry *The Liberal Theory of Justice* (Oxford University Press, 1975), especially pp. 54–5, 114–15.

In the second place, I should say that, if the relativities set out in §7 were imperfectly understood by those charged with post war reconstruction, it was not likely that there would be much understanding of the interaction of the second and third species of relativity. Many claims of needing depend crucially for their acceptance or rejection on our being ready to try to find the practically envisageable standard of flourishing or well-being by reference to which questions of harm (or lesser or greater harm) can be judged and questions of substitutability can be resolved in a way that respects real political possibility. Of course every necessary condition of a possible state of affairs of not being harmed is consistent with every other necessary condition whenever harm is not inevitable. But if, in pride or a spirit of would-be revolution that will in fact come to nothing, or for whatever other reason, statesmen or managers pitch the standard too high (and this has already happened in effect wherever the replacement of what is condemned will *in fact* represent no real improvement), or if they fail to be realistic about what futures are practically envisageable, then, in the limited space which is all there really is here, one condition of harm's being avoided will be met at the expense of another condition. (Even at the expense of a condition that is more important and nothing less than a prerequisite for an even more minimal state of not being harmed.) If the standard is set impossibly high in one sphere of concern,[23] and we fail at the same time to heed or respect (if only by *not* doing things) the totality of other needs (and if we do not recognize that we don't know too much about many of these things), then something like this is pretty well bound to happen. The more resources that are then diverted to the task of meeting the standard of need that has been set in one sphere, the worse this tendency is likely to become, and the greater the danger that one specific

[23] For some connected observations, based on the experience of developing countries, see Paul Streeten, *First Things First* (Oxford: OUP for World Bank, 1981), pp. 190–91. I must however qualify the claims I make in the text. Under special conditions—and when the *immediate* result is not in itself very costly—it may be heuristically indispensable to set the standard too high (even shameful not to). When anaesthetics did not exist, certain sorts of suffering and harm were inevitable. Yet there was a point in saying anaesthetics were needed; and, had our ancestors not felt some such thing, they would not have striven as hard as they did to make such things realistically envisageable or to discover them.

requirement will eventually crowd out other less specific, less behaviourally transparent, but perhaps equally or even more important requirements (especially requirements such as choice and independence); or the greater the danger that what is provided may suit some people and not suit others—an outcome that is not inconsistent with the objectivity of value, but reflects the tendency for values to compete with one another and for the lives of different people to represent widely different responses to irreducibly distinct value claims. (A different emphasis or value focus.)

12. If we have enough faith in this defence to persist in the wish to take needs with a seriousness at all proportionate to the frequency with which they are actually invoked in political and administrative argument (cp. §3), then it seems that, having grasped the complexity and stringency of the truth-condition, we must start to see any statement of the form '*y* needs *x* [absolutely]' as tantamount to a challenge to imagine an alternative future in which *y* escapes harm or damage without having *x*, or an alternative where *y*'s vital interests are better adjusted to others' vital interests than they would be if *x* were what he had. We must proceed like this not because to be concerned with needs is to take up an attitude of stinginess or meanness (if it connotes any particular attitude, the attitude is much closer to the concern for *all* rights, 'counter-rights', cp. §20 below, and right-like claims), but because, if we do not, some vital needs and interests may not be properly determined, or may go unheeded. It is without prejudice one way or the other to the satisfaction of desires for things that are not needed.

Sometimes (as we have noticed) this sort of challenge to the imagination will not lead to outright rejection of a statement, but to a weakening of the specification of the thing said to be needed: 'He will get by if he has *x* or *w* or *v*'. This is a very familiar move, and the elucidation of needing given here explains why that is. Overspecificity in a 'needs' sentence makes it false.[24] But what our elucidation equally predicts is

[24] A good example of this is provided by modern transport planners' ingrained habit of speaking of 'mobility' (by car) as a standing need of western civilization. There is no doubt that, with present tendencies towards concentration of facilities, closure of

that often the thing that survives the weakening (the introduction of disjunctions *etc.*) will still be a very strong statement—most especially where the particular judgement of *y*'s non-instrumental need results from a process in which the actuality of *y*'s concrete situation and the constraints that this puts upon the future are fully apprehended (taking into account the real, however hypothetical, intentions of all relevant other persons or groups of persons), and where the process clarifies both the worst and the best that can befall *y* and *y*'s vital interests. (Perhaps prompting us to climb down from '*y* needs *x*', where *x* is the best but most expensive remedy, well out of *y*'s reach unless he forgoes everything else, to 'what *y* really needs [given the circumstances] is *w*', where absence of *w* will blight even that minimal level of well-being that is the best real possibility for *y*.) It seems certain that, even when claims of need are scrutinized in this way, we shall be left with much more than a tiny handful of needs statements. If so, there need be no further postponement of the question whether vital needs are better or worse satisfied now than they once were, why they are worse satisfied (wherever they are), and whether they can be better satisfied.

13. It is sometimes held that it is the role of government to make itself as responsive as possible in as many ways as possible to as many of its subjects' desires as possible. But obviously the more strongly someone inclines to the opposing view that what prudence and justice demand is that public policy be selective in what it attempts positively and be primarily based upon needs, the more important he must think it is for governments, insofar as they are directly or indirectly involved in some matter, not to specify needs incorrectly, and to be careful to take the greatest advantage of all alternative ways of satisfying them (and/or letting them go on being

---

smaller shops and offices and more dispersed patterns of development, such mobility approximates to a short or medium term need with a considerable and rising degree of entrenchment. But, if alternative tendencies can be envisaged, we shall get a fairer view of all the available options if we realize that the right name for the standing, invariable need (the need that underlies the shorter term need) is not 'mobility' but, more plastically and indefinitely, 'access [to facilities that are frequently needed]'.

satisfied, however they already were satisfied). Among needs that such a policy concerns itself with, the more plastic must make accommodation for the less plastic, and (what is different) the less bad must give way to the worse. A proper balance must be found between present needs and future needs. And *ceteris paribus* desires as such must cede rank to what emerge from careful scrutiny as grave, entrenched, non-substitutable needs. Nobody's grave, entrenched, non-substitutable need, or as one might say (exploiting the ambiguity in the adjective that was surely made for just this purpose) nobody's *vital interest*, must be sacrificed by society to the mere desire of anybody else, or of any however large group of other people.—Or as we have this contention stated in Del Vecchio's formulation of what is called, in his classic study of the history of the idea of justice, *providential*, *assisting* or *social* justice:

> It is a requirement of justice, that, before being assigned to any other purpose whatever, all the means which the state has legally at its disposal should be assigned by it to the protection of the life and physical and moral integrity of its members, especially of those who are not in a position to provide for this by their own means or by means of persons particularly obliged thereto.[25]

Del Vecchio is no friend of *need*. I have singled him out here as one who is explicitly hostile in principle to that way of making claims upon society.[26] But what we may now suspect is that the indispensable role of the concept of need is precisely to assist us in singling or marking out those very interests that have to be the *special* concern of social justice, both where the State has to intervene on their behalf and also in the cases where it is the business of the State to insist on some pause or hesitation, e.g. in connection with grand projects (private or public) that will serve the actual or hypothetical desires of millions but sacrifice to them the present or future vital interests of other identifiable or unidentifiable people.[27]

[25] Del Vecchio, *Justice*, *op. cit.* p. 148.

[26] See his criticisms at p. 148 (note), somewhat mitigated at p. 143.

[27] Cp. §23 below and cp. Mackie 'Can There be a Rights-based Moral Theory?', *op. cit.* Note also the discrepancy with Mackie, who uses the notion of a right for what we use *right, counterclaim* and *vital need* together to accomplish.

If this suspicion can be shown to be well-founded, it will certainly put in a new light the ineliminable vagueness, contestability, or non-effectiveness for which the idea of need is so often criticized. The true situation may really be that these charges against it are an indirect tribute to the idea's actual importance and indispensability to us. It may be that, *pace* some liberal and conservative critics, one aspect of its indispensability concerns the defence it can afford to the individual, in a community that has found a way of adjusting its institutions to its sentiments, against the arbitrary use of State power. (Cp. §23 below.)

14. Having thus arrived at the frontier of political philosophy and canvassed—so far without much attempt at precision or argument—a priority principle about true needs that is either an inchoate political principle (a principle of social justice) or nothing, not a principle of individual morality as such, I want to pause for the space of one section and try to see more clearly where we have come from, before moving further forward.

We have taken Anscombe's and Feinberg's part against White, Barry and Flew (see notes 9, 10, 11) in seeking to identify an absolute sense of 'need'. We have been with White, however, in insisting that *need* is a modal notion. And here again we are not the first to take up such a position.

Aristotle is not usually credited with having any view of what a need is; but in his philosophical lexicon at *Metaphysics V* he has the following entry for 'necessary':

> 1015a20: We call NECESSARY (a) that without which, as a joint cause, it is not possible to live, as for instance breathing and nourishment are necessary for an animal, because it is incapable of existing without them: and (b) anything without which it is not possible for good to exist or come to be, or for bad to be discarded or got rid of, as for instance drinking medicine is necessary so as not to be ill, and sailing to Aegina so as to get money (trans. Kirwan).

For good reasons (especially the importance of the chapter's being seen as Aristotle's single entry for several senses of the Greek word for 'necessary'), the word ἀναγκαῖον has never been translated here as 'needed'. But, in another way, it is a shame that it was not. In the presence of an Aristotelian elucidation, the reductive, rationalized strong desires conception of need might not have passed so long without serious challenge.

Aristotle's (a)-paraphrase appears too restrictive to exhaust what we have called the absolute sense. (The case for some relaxation of the condition is, of course, of long standing. Cp. Adam Smith, *Wealth of Nations* [V.2.2], 'By necessities I understand not only the commodities which are indispensably necessary for the support of life, but whatever the custom of the country renders it indecent for creditable people even of the lowest rank to be without'.) And Aristotle's (b)-paraphrase is in danger of causing us to classify certain absolute occurrences of 'need' (needing to drink medicine for instance) with other occurrences of the word that it may be better to treat as elliptical and purely instrumental (*e.g.* needing to sail to Aegina). These two faults, if they are faults, are better corrected in the 'harm' formulation of Feinberg, I suggest, than by substituting 'flourishing' for 'living' in Aristotle's (a)-paraphrase. (One is bound to think that they are better corrected by the 'harm' formula if one is reluctant to be led by the tautology that flourishing is a necessary condition of flourishing to say that human beings *need to flourish*, but one does not mind being led by the same form of argument to the conclusion that human beings need to avoid harm.) But the value of Aristotle's contribution to this subject is not obscured by the necessity to make the case for these amendments. It resides in his having signalled (even if only to those already open to the thought) that *need* is a modal concept of a special kind[28] and imports the linked ideas of a situation and a non-negotiable (or in-the-circumstances-non-negotiable) good, which *together* leave no real alternative but to . . . . .

15. Even those who urge us to dispense with the idea of need concede the *prima facie* compelling character of a true unexaggerated statement of need. Hence, I suppose, their

[28] The point is of course unaffected even if one supposes that the natural conditional is *already* secretly modal. This would hardly make the modality indexed for time and circumstance, as in §7, redundant.

animus against it. But what sort of claim is made upon society by such a statement? And is this really a claim of justice, or sometimes a claim of justice and sometimes an appeal to something beyond or beside justice? Or what is it? The rest of the paper will be devoted to these questions.

It is a marked tendency in most of the writers in whom one can discover an interest in the force of claims of need to subsume them for all purposes of justice under the general category of equality-claims (claims of equality of treatment, or claims about the intolerability of certain *in*equalities).[29] Many liberal conservatives, as well as seeing the concern with needs as such as symptomatic of an ill-conceived, busy-body or interventionist attitude to public policy or of a simple-minded idea of justice, distrust the idea of a need because they view it as indissolubly linked with conceptions of equality that they find deeply suspect. And the same linkage between needs and equality claims would appear to be assumed by radical or anti-conservative writers. Indeed, in so far as there are differences of opinion between radicals in the matter of needing, the significant divergence seems to turn on the question whether they see the idea of need as a positive help[30] or as a hindrance in

[29] Cp. V. Pareto *Les Systèmes Socialistes* (Paris 1901–2) vol. ii, pp. 167–8: 'La formule: *à chacun selon ses besoins*, devient . . . un travestissement métaphysique de la formule: *à chacun part égale, avec certaines corrections*'; Gregory Vlastos 'Justice and Equality' in Brandt, ed. *Social Justice* (Prentice Hall, 1962): ' "To each according to his need" . . . is in fact the most perfect form of equal distribution' (p. 40); A.M. Honoré, 'Social Justice' in *Essays in Legal Philosophy*, ed. R.S. Summers (Blackwell, 1970) p. 78: 'The principle of social justice . . . lays down that men have a claim to advantages and an equal share in advantages. Therefore the principle of justice according to need may be regarded as one aspect, or one corollary, of the principle of social justice. From the point of view of this principle, those who are in need are entitled to point to the fact that they lack advantages to which the principle of social justice entitles them'; Honoré quotes here D.D. Raphael 'Justice and Liberty' in *Proceedings of the Aristotelian Society*, 1951: 'Thus the basis of the claim of social need is really a recognition of the claim to equality'; Feinberg, *op. cit.* at note 10 above, p. 111; A. Sen 'Equality of What?' in *Tanner Lectures on Human Values* (Utah/Cambridge, 1980), ed. McMurrin, especially pp. 217–19; David Miller, *Social Justice* (Oxford University Press, 1976), 'One could say that the principle of need represents the most urgent part of the principle of equality' (p. 149). See also Peter Singer in *Reading Nozick*, J. Paul ed., (Oxford: Blackwell, 1981), p. 49; Flew, *op. cit.* at note 4 above; R.H. Tawney *Equality* (London: Allen and Unwin, 1952), p. 42.

[30] Cp. Williams, *Problems of the Self* (Cambridge University Press, 1973), p. 240 following, and *e.g.* Vlastos, Honoré, Miller, cited at note 29.

the justification and further elucidation of the idea of equality.[31]

There is nothing to be gained by denying how natural and appropriate it is, where a writer already has a strong, positive argument in support of the idea of men's having a title and an equal title to all advantages that are generally desired and are in fact conducive to well-being (*a fortiori* where he has an argument in support of the idea of men's having a title to an equal share in such advantages),[32] for him to call on the concept of need to help him articulate his proposal. (A redistribution of everything—if that were thinkable—in accordance with need would no doubt be a more efficient approach to equality of welfare than, say, assigning everyone an equal share of goods.) The thing that does deserve to be denied is that need claims are essentially, or by their nature, claims to be treated in accordance with the precepts of the distinctive sorts of social justice that are advocated by egalitarians. There are several ways of seeing that, as such, they are not. I shall offer two considerations. Neither is a proof. Each points I hope at something the reader is already able to see.

The first consideration I advance is this: claims of vital need can be satisfied (or satisfied to a great extent at least) in a society where there is considerable inequality of wealth and even some appreciable inequality of economic opportunity[33] (especially—however big an *if* this may be—if economic inequalities are prevented from undermining legal rights and effective equality before the law). When one looks at how matters stand within such a society, and what it will involve on the levels of thought and action and refraining from action (cp. §§7–13) to maintain this happy state of affairs, nothing appears

[31] It may be surmised that Ronald Dworkin would regard it as a hindrance, at least so far as elucidation goes. See 'What is Equality? (Part One)', *Philosophy and Public Affairs*, vol. 10, no. 3, 1981. (Marx, having no patience with the idea of equality as such, is of course an exception to the general claim in the text.)

[32] I lean heavily here, and below, on the useful formulations of Honoré, *op. cit.* at note 29 above.

[33] And even perhaps inequality of respect? (Cp. H.L.A. Hart, *The Concept of Law*, Oxford University Press, 1961, p. 158.) Some may be tempted to say that equality of respect is a need. This is not something I shall deny. But note that if *this* is wherein the urgency of equal respect resides, then there is a danger, not that equality considerations will swallow considerations of need, but that the latter will swallow the former.

rationally inevitable in the progression from taking claims of need as deeply seriously as this society does to taking similarly seriously everyone's claim to a level of well-being effectively equal to that of anyone else.[34]

In the second place, needs claims and claims to equal treatment are sustained by and appeal to interestingly different sentiments. The matter is clearest perhaps where disappointment is in question. Under such conditions, claims to equal treatment typically proceed out of feelings of being affronted, insulted, belittled or (more generally) left out, or slightingly used; and, in their debased or pathological form, they may lapse into simple envy. What these claims demand is for those who advance them to be treated with the respect due to a human being who is accepted, simply *qua* human being, as an equal participant with an equal stake in what is seen under the aspect of a common venture.[35] Claims of need on the other hand, even when tinged with moral indignation, may be pressed from a simple passion to subsist (or for one's dependents to subsist) under tolerable conditions—a passion that lapses in its extreme or pathological form not into envy necessarily, but into self-pity or helplessness or self-absorption. When claims of need go unheeded, that which is disappointed is the expectation that it would be taken into account that the claimant's actual survival or most minimal well-being was at issue. The appeal of need depends of course on recognition of the claimant as equally a participant in society; but what sustains the appeal of the claimant and lends it strength may

[34] And if so, then here at least even some conservatives could afford to relax their guarded attitude towards needing. If the attitude towards need that I shall propose is taken just as it stands, and no more is then read into it by the force of habitual political association, then it is left open whether the proper province of state action or interference is wide or narrow, except insofar as there is strong pressure for such intervention from the quarter of otherwise unsatisfiable vital human need. But the final import of such claims of need will then depend on the totality of justice claims that are invoked. What is more, considerations of need will themselves suggest principles of limitation of the scope of action by the state. (See §23 below.)

[35] This is not to say that, by simply knowing that the relevant feelings and sentiments were drawn from this store, one could determine the content or character of the claim for equal treatment. What matters for the argument is only that there should be some distinctive difference or other in the feelings characteristically involved in the making or the recognition of the two kinds of claim.

have to comprise simple compassion or sympathy (on the part of the recognizer of the claim, and the expectation of this on the part of the claimant), or a particularized form of what Hume called the 'resentment of the misery of mankind'—a much more powerful sentiment, as Schopenhauer and others have truly observed, than even-handed benevolence or humanity. It is true of course that, insofar as claims of equality and claims of need are accepted as claims of justice, the acceptance must involve the recognition of the claimant as party to a whole network of intersubjectively established interrelations between selves which create actual duties and entitlements.[36] But for purposes of any special entitlement or expectation that is conferred by need, this network or system does not have to legitimize the expectation of substantive equality of title to all advantages. The most that it validates is the expectation that wherever rights are themselves formulated in terms of needing as such equal *needs* for φ will import equal titles to φ-derived benefit: but that is not the title to economic equality *per se*, or in general. We do not have to speak here of the claimant's equal stake in anything, for instance.

16. What then, if it is *sui generis*, and not to be reduced to the claim that inequality as such ought to be removed, is the distinctive political force of a statement of a serious need? The positive answer to be offered to that question will depend on dividing it in a way corresponding to three phases or levels. Phase one justice will be justice as the guardian of rights as narrowly and strictly construed; phase two justice will be justice as the definer of the limits of aggregative reasoning and vigilant arbitrator between rights and other claims (to be called counter-rights) which are not themselves rights; phase three justice will be justice as the custodian and distributor of public goods. Phase three justice will operate only within the area allowed to it by a certain principle of phase two justice, limiting the operation of aggregative reasoning.

This is to anticipate, however; and we must begin by excogitating the prerequisites of something's counting as a

[36] Cp. Del Vecchio's treatment of *alteritas*, in *Justice* Ch. VII. And compare H.L.A. Hart, *Concept of Law*, p. 155.

possible social morality and try to identify the role that such a thing must give (at phase or level one) to the idea of a right. Some needs will then appear as special candidates to make abstract claim-rights (claim-rights that ought to be recognized and realized concretely); and some others that do not attain to this status will appear at the second phase or level as candidates to represent abstract *counter-claims*. But these counter-claims will lie well within the province of justice, however strictly it is conceived, and will rest upon the same sort of foundation as abstract rights rest upon.

There are two necessary preliminaries to this approach. First, although need statements, when they weigh with us at all, do always weigh at least in part *as* statements of need, yet we must note that their public force is highly variable, even when their truth is not being questioned. Certainly this force is not always proportional to the need's admitted seriousness. Any account of these matters must explain or allow for this variability, and leave room for the influence or countervailing influence of factors other than need itself. Secondly, it is still worth insisting, against one kind of positivist, that the moral force of a claim of need cannot be identified with its being acknowledged to have this force, or with society's acting upon it or having regard to it—just as the social morality that a claim of need depends on for its force ought to be clearly distinguished both from the actual norms of reciprocity and cooperation that the morality makes possible and from the extant laws and social institutions that regulate these norms. (I take it that such a morality cannot properly coincide with any of these things if it will sometimes muster criticisms of existing social arrangements, and will also serve to *sustain* mores, institutions and laws, weakly or strongly, even as it subjects them to scrutiny.)

17. These preliminaries being completed, the first part of my answer to our question is this: that, in the case of some needs-statements, they report a need for something whose being needed is one part of what precisely creates the abstract right or entitlement to it. I suggest that, for purposes of a social morality *S* that is actually lived and succeeds in proposing to agents shared concerns that they can make their own, there is

an *abstract claim-right or entitlement to x under conditions* C just where *x is something the denial or removal of which under conditions* C *gives (and can be seen as giving)*[37] *the person denied or deprived part or all of a reason, and a reason that is avowable and publicly sustainable within S, to reconsider his adherence to the norms of reciprocity and cooperation sustained by S*. This is to say that, if in such a case the victim who is deprived of *x* disappoints us in some spoken or previously unspoken expectation of co-operation, then that counts as something morally intelligible within the shared sensibility that depends on this expectation.[38]

To grasp the full import of this very exigent condition for the existence of a right it will assist to state the assumption it rests upon. This is the assumption that unless there existed *some* condition under which withdrawal of consensus was found intelligible and natural *even within S—i.e.* some condition under which *S* at least allowed someone party to *S* to think of himself as having been unjustly (even unjustifiably) sacrificed—, then *S* could scarcely count as a social morality at all. For a

[37] Note that the *non-availability of x* is not sufficient. The condition is limited to the denial or deprivation or removal of *x*.

Strictly we need to add after 'seen' some such words as these: both within S and within any recognizable transformation of S that continues to define a point of view can be 'common to each man with others' as he departs from his 'private and particular situation'. (Cp. Hume, *Inquiry Concerning the Principles of Morals*, IX part 1, 222.)

It suffices for this construction if, where there are interestingly different moral sensibilities to be discovered within a historically given culture, there is some minimal shared components or nucleus of differing sensibilities.

For the claim (neither required by nor inconsistent with anything that is urged here) that what is timelessly essential to the core of morality as such can be reached by factoring *ethos* out from morality itself, within what he sees as only superficially different moralities, see Aurel Kolnai 'Moral Consensus', *Proceedings of the Aristotelian Society*, 1969/70.

For another account of rights that is complementary and would deliver substantially the same account as this of the connection between needs and rights, see note 45.

[38] In connexion with this whole approach, compare *e.g.* J.L. Mackie, 'Rights, Utility and Universalization', *op. cit.*, J.L. Mackie, *Ethics* (Harmondsworth: Penguin, 1977), Bernard Williams, *Moral Luck*, p. x and *passim e.g.* 'Internal and External Reasons' pp. 101–113. In so far as my treatment differs from Mackie's and Williams', it is mainly in respect of the crucial importance I should attach in these matters of motivation to judgments of value being what they seem to be, viz. statements about features of reality, albeit essentially anthropocentrically categorized, that are discovered to us by our interest in them. Cp. Essays III and V, below.

For certain aspects of social morality equally neglected by Williams, Mackie and myself, see A.M. Honoré, 'Groups, Law and Obedience' in *Oxford Essays in Jurisprudence* II, 1973.

social morality, as conceived for these purposes, is not just any old set of abstract principles. It is something that exists only as realized or embodied (or as capable of being realized or embodied) in a shared sensibility, and in the historically given *mores* and institutions that are themselves perpetuated by it. It is only by virtue of participating in this sort of thing, and seeing one another as participating in it, that ordinary human beings as actually constituted are able to embrace common concerns and common goals that will take on a life of their own or be perceived as enshrining values that possess what Hume sometimes called 'moral beauty'. A social morality cannot of course give any particular person a guaranteed title to wealth, health, happiness, or security from ordinary misfortune. But equally it must not be such as to threaten anyone who is to be bound by it that it will bring upon him or any other individual participant, as if gratuitously, the misfortune of having his vital interests simply sacrificed for the sake of some larger public good.[39] What sustains and regulates or adjusts a social morality and what rebuts objections to it, must be something intelligible to all its individual participants, in human (never mind archangelic or ideal observer) terms.[40] It must engage with the passions of those who are to live by it—or at least not *dis*engage with those passions.

[39] Cp. J.L. Mackie, 'Can there be a rights-based moral theory?', *op. cit.*

> 'A central embarrassment for the best known goal-based theories, the various forms of utilitarianism, is that the well being of one individual should be sacrificed without limits, for the well being of others (p. 352) . . . Why should it not be a *fundamental* moral principle that the well being of one person cannot be simply replaced by that of another? There is no proof of purely aggregative consequentialism at any level (p. 354)'.

For a lawyer's formulation of what is almost the same point see Arnold Goodman, *Not for the Record* (London: Deutsch, 1972), pp. 18–19:

> 'The popular proposition that we must sink our selfish self-interest in the public good . . . requires the closest scrutiny and the strongest scepticism. For it is the proposition which can justify any hardship or injustice to a private person, and the one most prone to ignore the arithmetical truism that the community is the sum of its individuals. That injury to an individual—inequitable or unrequited—is, in the absence of strong contrary proof, an injustice to the community in whose name it is so lightly committed. But [this proposition] is invoked with monotonous ruthlessness by governmental systems.'

[40] States go to war, and in fighting them they have exacted the sacrifice of millions of lives. But states that deserve the loyalty of their subjects do not go to war 'to maximize the public good'—rather to avoid invasion or national humiliation or subjugation or to defend vital interests that subjects can identify with.

18. It is only a small step from requiring that a social morality lack this licence to requiring, more positively and definitely: (i) that it should place explicit limitations on the social goals it promotes or tolerates, on the burdens individuals can normally be asked to endure in the common pursuit of this or that kind of public goal, and on the scope and ambit of any modes of aggregative reasoning it countenances: (ii) that it should sustain rights under a rule of law, securing individuals from arbitrary arrest, imprisonment or punishment, and assuring them of other civic and legal protections; and (iii) that it should uphold the right to make certain sorts of agreement with other individuals, to buy the necessities of life, sell the product of one's labour, and be not dispossessed of that which one has appropriated or mixed one's labour with in ways seen as worthy of being accorded legal recognition.

Items that find a place in this enumeration do not find it *simply* because they are needed. But as Hart anticipated (§ 1), the idea of need plays its own distinctive and recognizable role in helping to generate and constrain the enumeration. What is more, its presence helps to render the idea of an abstract claim-right unmysterious. Certainly the derivation is not obliged to represent itself as *a priori* or *pre-moral* or as resting upon natural law (a concept it needs neither to invoke nor to denounce). In a very general way it is *a posteriori*. No doubt the *a posteriority* of the question what social moralities have to be like in order to be possible will appear to many philosophers of some temperaments to disqualify the entire approach. But surely *a posteriority* is what we ought to have predicted if we expect morality to have the hold upon motive and action that Hume argued that it must. Morality must have this hold intelligibly, by virtue of the content of the judgements it delivers, and by virtue of the possibility of the values and concerns that it proposes to agents becoming for them nothing less than ends in themselves, furnishing them with what they can see as reasons for being concerned or affected in certain particular ways.[41]

[41] *A posteriority* is again what we ought to predict if we will allow that the relation between social morality and its embodying social institutions needs to be a reciprocal one. It needs to be reciprocal if the morality is to take up from *mores* and institutions the distinctive colouration and distinctive emphases that will characterize the

This whole view of rights may provoke the accusation that I say there is a right wherever there is an opportunity for blackmail, or that I submit morality itself to what Nietzsche called 'the trading mentality', and might equally well, with almost equal moral ugliness, have called 'the contracting mentality'. But wherever else this accusation may be appropriate, it does not belong here. The view of rights that I am defending is consistent with a morality's *not* being something whose force, nature or content is supplied from any kind of prudence. Not only does the view respect the fact that we do not opt or contract into a social morality. No weight at all has had to attach to the possibility (which I wholly discount) of reconstructing the reasons we would or might, as pre-socially conceived, have had for so opting or contracting. A social morality, as conceived here, is not even something which *it is as if* we have opted or contracted into.[42] It is simply the sort of thing that we find ourselves in the midst of. By virtue of being what it is and having the content it does have and deserving to command the consensus of those who live within it, it is something that does *not* furnish its adherents with what they would have to regard as decently avowable reasons to *opt out of it*. It is neither here nor there if there are all sorts of other

---

communal ends and socially conditioned individual ends that the morality recognizes as intelligible ends of human endeavour and concern. (In fact both logically and historically speaking, social morality and social institutions must come into being simultaneously.) To reject *a posteriority* here is to reject the idea that values and shared concerns need to have a historical aspect. But without a historical aspect most values and concerns that go beyond simple human survival are simply arbitrary and, in every relevant sense of the phrase, rationally unintelligible.

[42] If we suppose that it is even a bit like something to opt into, then we immediately find ourselves forced to think that it ought to be possible to reconstruct the reasons (it is now as if) we once had for the choice that (it is now as if) we once made when we opted into it. But surely, if such reasons had to be found, none could possibly be provided. How could any candidate to be such a reason both show, as it would need to show, that this was the morality we would have been most *prudent* or *rational* to adhere to, and also respect the status as a morality of what it is as if we should have chosen? Any consideration at all that promised to be suitable to count as a reason of the required sort would *either* employ a notion of rationality and prudence that begged the question (this I insist is the innocent, fruitful way with the matter in all other connexions) *or* depend on a conception of rationality that would have us as choosing virtue or justice not for what it is in itself but in the expectation of a return of another sort.

moralities that pass this test and that we might have found ourselves in the midst of. Our attachment does not depend on that's not being so, or on our satisfying ourselves that there is no other social morality that might have offered someone in our position a better package of rights.

19. Principles (i), (ii) and (iii) are concerned with great goods, and what they presuppose is already an enormous charge on the State. But consideration of what it takes to ensure their persistence in the real world is certain to lend colour to an independent demand for certain much more specifically political rights, as well as for publicly provided systems of education, legal aid and basic health care. These things are intelligible extensions, of which I shall say more later, in what it is still just possible to recognize as the same spirit. I should say that these things were at most one step beyond the rights whose non-realization gives men good reason for disaffection from society, because (i) (ii) (iii) and their proper extensions are simply the preconditions of someone's securing his own material survival in his own way, or in the best way relative to his circumstances, by his own efforts. Someone who demands such rights as these asks for scarcely any strictly first order goods—only for that with which to get his own, within a community that recognizes him as a participant with this right and that he in his turn recognizes as conferring, guaranteeing and limiting that right, and as presupposed, in some condition or other, to any life that he can fully value. Still less does he ask for an equal title to an equal share of first order goods.

However familiar or unfamiliar our general method of justification may have appeared, the embryo rights that it generates are familiar enough. What will be noted, however, is that, although some needs have now turned up as generating rights and/or liberties with a protective fence of claim-rights, we still have no *general* vindication of the force of serious needs claims as such. It is true of course that some who set store by rights are apt to insist on more numerous and stronger rights than any afforded under (i), (ii) and (iii), and it is also true and important that, in practice, many extant social moralities will recognize, and impress upon the institutions and laws that they sustain, more rights than the abstract things one can demonstrate by the general method we have sketched.[43] (In their special circumstances, they may have to. See below §21 foll.) But that is not enough for our purposes. For, having rejected the idea of a social contract, and what one is *owed* for one's accord in the same, because we rejected the idea of a reconstruction of any however hypothetical, prudence-based reasons for opting into morality, we dare not see first order benefits that go too far beyond (i) (ii) (iii), or all needs simply as such, under the aspect of moral rights or abstract entitlements—lest they appear under the guise of a sort of *quid pro quo* for the retention of participative adherence or consensus. No idea could more quickly subvert a social morality, or more effectively despoil the achievement that it represents. (Cp. Schopenhauer, *On the Basis of Morality*, §7.)

There is a second reason not to find rights, or what have sometimes been called 'claim-rights in the making' or 'manifesto rights', wherever there happen to be some serious needs, and this reason will hold good even for cases where certain needs are far harder to ignore than some unproblematical, acknowledged rights are. If we hold onto the conception of rights introduced in §17, then it will be natural to suppose that a categorical abstract claim-right only exists where there could in principle be some institutional obligation upon someone or something to arrange for people to have the chance to take official or legal action against some specific defendant or legal entity in order to require some specific performance of him or it.[44] But however we rearrange society and its processes, there will always be claims of dire need that fail this test. If we use the idea

[43] Historically some have recognized rather fewer. But the reader will have guessed that I shall claim this does not matter. What people will put up with is an *a posteriori* question, one dependent on factors of human psychology and awareness that change gradually but constantly through time. These changes are for the most part irreversible. As in all matters of awareness, a kind of ratchet mechanism operates.

What people will acquiesce in is to some degree a moral question. For what people can acquiesce in depends on what they think is fair to them. And what they think fair must depend however indirectly or minimally on what *is* fair. If our explanations in these sections were intended as reductive or eliminative, this would be fatal to them. But our aim here is only to exhibit the *inter-connections* of the concepts *claim-right, need, participants' consensus, social justice* . . . .

[44] On claim rights, cp. note 15 above; and see also Alan Ryan 'Overriding Interests', *Times Literary Supplement*, 22 April 1983, p. 411.

of right to prevent these from falling into oblivion, then we risk having to do without any criterion at all for right-hood and losing all sharpness in the idea of a right.[45] Given the nature of the opposition, that is not a risk that it is wise to take.

There will be a temptation at this point to try to find room for needs in our picture by seeing needs that are not good candidates to be simple rights as having a force somehow comparable to a claim-right, and as requiring that whoever has this or that serious need should be recognized as owed *special consideration* when the mass of claims that bear upon any particular matter is reviewed. But, although this is correct enough for certain kinds of claims of needing, it is too vague. What is far worse, it still leaves everything unexplained. Why *should* these kinds of needing deserve special public consideration?

The general form of the answer that I shall offer to this question, in what I shall number the second phase of the explanation promised in §16, is that serious non-instrumental

[45] Cp. also the question put by Charles Fried, *Right and Wrong* (Cambridge Mass: Harvard, 1978), p. 122:

> The major objection to a theory of rights based on needs [is that] though needs and their satisfaction have an objective quality, the fact is that any commitment, via the recognition of positive rights, to meet need also makes us hostages to vastly varied and voracious needs. . . . How to contain this voraciousness? If needs create rights to their satisfaction, how are we to prevent them from claiming so much that there is no energy left to pursue other goals?

Having given an account of rights that answers Fried's question—see §17 above—, let me refer to a complementary and no doubt better account of rights, which I did not know when I formulated mine, namely Joseph Raz's version of the so-called beneficiary theory of rights as given in his 'On the Nature of Rights', *Mind* vol. 93, 1984, pp. 192–214. The careful adherent of a position like Raz's may certainly hold that to say a person has a right is to say that some interest of that person's is a sufficient reason for holding another person or body to be subject to some duty that serves the interest. But not just any old interest will count, or just any old ground. Everything depends on what kind of interest, with what provenance, and (if the interest passes that test) what protection, if any, is not only stably and foreseeably beneficial to the right-holder in society, but also nearly invariably indispensable to the protection and enjoyment of that interest. What the Aristotelian account explains is how needs can be important enough *in certain classes of case* to be indispensable to the justification for imposing such duties, not how needs automatically generate rights *wherever* needs ought to impinge as needs on the determination of public policy. Compare also E.D. Watt, *op. cit.* (note 7 above): 'What it is important to insist . . . is that it can make good sense to speak of needs without implying an active obligation on the part of any person to meet these needs'.

needs that do not constitute rights or entitlements can sometimes stand in a certain counterpoise relation, first with straightforward rights actually recognized, and then (in a potentially contrasting way) with the ends of concerted public action. Especially, vital needs (as defined p. 17) can do so.

20. Principles (i), (ii) and (iii) of §18 start life as scarcely more than the preconditions of men's securing their own survival in their own way, or in the best way relative to their circumstances. But they have a tendency to outgrow their beginnings. And on our *a posteriori* consensual approach, the strength and status of class (iii) rights and entitlements to property, inheritance etc. is not fixed exactly or for all places and times. What *is* determined about them—given the finitude of the world's natural resources, the long term impossibility of each man's appropriation from natural resources leaving behind as much and as good for the next, and the accumulation of power that has inevitably accrued in a finite social space to those who stand at the end of long chains of inheritance of property and influence—is only that the stronger the support and confirmation that a given social morality provides for entrenched entitlements, and the greater the legal and political protection accordingly extended to those exercising a large number of class (iii) rights, the greater will be the State's and its servants' moral duty to respect in all legal and political deliberation the needs and vital interests of the people there will always be who have not got themselves into a position to acquire or exercise very many such rights and entitlements. And the readier the State must then be, having marked out property and other entitlements, to diminish the extent to which such entrenched rights can countervail against true claims of vital need that must otherwise go unsatisfied. Surely needs must offset property rights *at least* to the extent that the appropriations and transfers of the centuries render ineffective all present efforts to command the resources that one requires to live by one's own efforts.[46] But one ought to go

[46] Cp. J.L. Mackie *Ethics, op. cit.* pp. 175–6: and 'Rights, Utility and Universalization', *op. cit.* And for a relatively ancient statement of the relevant (still neglected) platitude, see J. von Neumann, *Collected Works VI*, p. 505: 'Literally and figuratively we are running out of room. At long last, we begin to feel the effects of the finite actual size of the earth in a critical way.'

further. The stronger the property rights that are politically recognized and legally enforced, and the greater the efficacity of the social morality in sustaining the institutions that protect these rights, the more self-conscious society must become (at least under the conditions we are now used to in all the more populated, civilized and economically exploited parts of the earth) about the *inflexibility* and *possible failure* of the systems of entitlement relations that govern possession and use,[47] and the readier it must be to give practical expression to this self-consciousness, by the regulation of commerce, by ministering directly to unsatisfied vital needs, or (better) by ensuring that wealth should be created closer to the point where there are vital interests that will otherwise go unsatisfied. Society must cultivate this self-consciousness on pain of being seen as precisely worsening the plight of those who have least and who might otherwise have combined to take by force what they needed for self-sufficiency.[48]—Or on pain of the State's finding itself forced to subdue these people by methods that will in the end subvert morality itself.

21. It would be a great mistake to suppose that the public perception of the failure of entitlement relations is wedded even historically (let alone philosophically, see §15) to the ideal of equality (in the sense of everyone's having an equal title to all advantages), or that this failure is a new thing, and somehow the problem child of the welfare state as such. Classical and medieval anticipations aside, even nineteenth century capitalism hard-headedly recognized what was nothing other than a failure of entitlement relations when it saw a problem in the housing of the poor (the employed and industrious poor

[47] I am indebted in this formulation to important general ideas expounded by Amartya Sen in his *Poverty and Famines* (Oxford University Press, 1983) and, later, to his contention that what famine dramatizes is not so much the power of natural disaster as the failure or weakness of systems of entitlement relations.

[48] I say 'otherwise'. But of course they may do this anyway. And they may do it in a way that goes well beyond taking by force what they need. What is being urged here without prejudice to any of those questions is simply the weakest claim: that, if under these circumstances men combine to take what they need by force, then moral justification may be available for that, whatever condemnation may also be possible for whatever else they do.

For the way in which phase two justice (I now see) makes ineliminable use of one distinctively egalitarian (but restricted) idea, see now *Postscript*, note 13.

especially).[49] It is true that *de facto*, and perhaps inevitably, philanthropy entered in here. But even if it takes emergency to make us attend to what is intolerable in certain failures of entitlement, *e.g.* in famine as Amartya Sen has anatomized that, we must still distinguish that mixed sort of disaster from natural disasters like flooding, earthquake or hurricane. Society intervenes there as well, but in the cause of philanthropy. Whereas in the case of simple starvation or lack of shelter, the duty to ask whether these are failures of entitlement, and to be prepared, if necessary, to abridge or modify various type (iii) rights is a requirement of justice, and will remain so even where we cannot characterize the situation either correctly or illuminatingly in terms of specific rights. (Of course, in the context of a given system of law and administration that has grown sensitive to counterclaims, it may come about that citizens acquire certain legal rights to certain sorts of benefits, in money or in kind, *e.g.* health-care, or subsidized housing or even subsidized transport. And, as we have seen, there can be backing in justice for these rights, as conditionally considered, at least in the presence of certain now familiar social conditions arising from distortions of various heterogeneous kinds. But this backing can scarcely comprise any categorical abstract rights to such goods or services, however badly they are needed.)

22. With counterclaims and everything they involve, one enters immediately into an area of conflict, of revolution even. So it is not surprising how hard it is to say anything, however theoretical, to satisfy all parties to the conflict. One half of the difficulty is that rights like those of class (iii) give rise to entirely legitimate expectations about the character and extent of the interventions against historical contingency and luck that society will undertake in the name of justice. Not only are rights like those falling in class (iii) founded in a special way in a human need. It is also a deep human need to be *able* to frame such long term expectations of tenure and security. (To remove the possibility of these is to abandon one of the most distinctive advantages of the very civilization that almost everyone aspires

[49] For an illuminating account, see for instance J.N. Tarn *Five per cent Philanthropy* (Cambridge University Press, 1973).

to enjoy who looks to ordinary politics for the redress of injustice.) The other half of the difficulty is of course that in certain cases the situation of those whom a certain system of rights impedes from living by their own efforts may be nothing short of desperate.

Sticking to what our approach suggests ought to be least controversial, I would urge (1) that the clearest case, both for rights falling within the kinds (i), (ii), (iii) and for counterclaims, reposes upon vital needs that men will not otherwise be able to satisfy by their own efforts; (2) that, however strong the case in need for however stringent an abridgement of rights of acquisition or tenure, the correction or redistribution ought to be gradual and non-retrospective lest considerations of social justice invade and annihilate the very idea of a right. Again (3), when the satisfaction of counter-claims makes it necessary to abridge rights or raise taxes above levels that were justified by the expense of providing and protecting rights and benefits falling within categories (i), (ii), (iii), this should be done in a manner that is (a) perspicuous in intention; (b) generally consistent with a man's original title to what he earns;[50] (c) such as to force upon us the question whether enough (or too much) is being attempted, and whether in the right way.[51] Otherwise we lose sight of the terms of the original conflict, and blur the distinction between that issue and other issues that arise at a later phase of the evolution of social justice (namely, phase three, see below, §26). Finally (4) I note that the more complicated and diverse the admissible counter-claims that can appear under the aspect of claims in justice, and the more complicated and diverse the response to them that is attempted in society's name, the more likely this public response is to get

[50] A citizen is taxed, surely, on what he has earned and made his own. He ought not to be deemed not even to have earned the portion he gives up. He cannot give *back* to society what is never his.

[51] Consider for instance subsidized, publicly owned housing. Is this a better solution to the problem than subsidizing rents of those of low income in a flourishing, properly regulated private sector? For a powerful but wholly neglected argument that public or special housing was not the best or the only solution to the problem, see Jane Jacobs *Death and Life of the Great American City* (London: Jonathan Cape, 1962), pp. 323–7. And *why* in any case (we must always ask) are the incomes of some hard-working industrious persons doing essential work too low for them to be able to afford adequate housing?

muddled up with different kinds of public projects whose rationale is not vital need based at all.

Justice mediates between rights and counter-rights on the principle that, when the rights system leaves insufficient room for everyone to satisfy vital needs, rights may have to be abridged on a principle of equal concern for anyone's and everyone's vital need. But this concern will often itself lead to collective reasoning designed to increase the overall sum of opportunities —which may in its turn threaten vital needs of some individuals.

23. Perhaps the limitative principle that must regulate both rights/counter-rights arbitration *and* collective reasoning conducted in pursuit of public goods is this. Even if there is nothing unjust in actions of the State or its agencies making one man poorer in a way that makes another man less poor than he was (in kind or money)—and even if there need be no injustice as such (whatever pause it suggests for thought) if among those who suffer thereby one will find some who are already the least fortunate among all the parties involved—, *it is pro tanto unjust* if the State or an agency of the State intervenes against contingency, or changes its policy, or confounds citizens' sensible expectations, in a way that sacrifices anyone's strictly vital interests to the mere desires of however many others; and (more speculatively) *it is pro tanto unjust* if, among vital interests actually affected by such interventions, the greater strictly vital need of anyone is sacrificed in the name of the lesser needs of however many others.

Such a principle—which must be based, as always, in the connexion between justice, consensus and citizens' sense of the legitimacy of government (and should be adjusted or corrected and weakened or strengthened in the light of that connexion)— is still in the spirit of the arguments of §§20–21. A society that allows type (iii) rights to outgrow their proper rationale does precisely threaten vital interests. And the same applies to a society that is uncritical of the counter-claims it finds valid. But let it be clear that not only the fortunate need to be protected by the operation of a limitative principle, and it is not only the question of counter-claims that gives rise to the need for it. Almost invariably, actual societies' perception of the duty of governments to intervene in the name of counter-claims has coincided with (or even been preceded by) a perception of quite different reasons for public intervention, *e.g.*, the necessity to solve coordination problems or provide benefits that coordination problems prevent the market from providing. It is hard to show any objection in principle to this, even where the resulting projects are not vital needs-based. But all experience suggests that, as society's public actions become more heterogeneous, as lower incomes begin to be heavily taxed, and as public projects impinge more and more severely upon the environment, displacing citizens for public works such as schools, hospitals, parks and public road building (the last having an understandable tendency always to seek out the areas of lowest rateable value), those who stand in the direst need of the Principle of Limitation are almost never the rich or the fortunate. And the more it then begins to seem proper for the State to undertake, the smaller the probability that all consensually requisite protection of every individual's vital interests will be available already, in the shape of effective, recognized legal and/or constitutional rights and remedies, like those falling in our classes (i), (ii), (iii), that can be opposed to the actual or prospective, direct or indirect effects of public action.

24. In the face of this sort of problem, some have suggested that accepted methods such as cost-benefit analysis be more widely used and simultaneously strengthened to reflect the observed fact that the most a person will pay for a benefit he has not got, or to avert an evil he already suffers, is a smaller amount than the smallest amount he would accept to be deprived of the benefit or be forced to put up with the evil; or that such methods ought to give a special weighting to burdens and benefits that will accrue from a scheme to the poorer sections of the community. But this palliative[52] scarcely goes to the middle of the difficulty, which is that a sufficient number of mere desires can always swamp any however heavily weighted need; and that a sufficient number of needs of the non-vital

[52] Cp. *mutatis mutandis* Sen's remark at *op. cit.* pp. 156–7 ('As a category for causal analysis *the poor* isn't a very helpful one').

variety can always outweigh any however heavily weighted vital need.[53]

Others have considered that what was required was a new sensitivity to the common law rights of individuals and some legislative strengthening of individual rights. But in practice this would almost certainly have been ineffective in some cases and too effective in others—if it means that certain sorts of public project, even projects justified by the direst need, could always be obstructed (*e.g.* by the refusal or threatened refusal by the victims of a public project to accept proffered compensation as adequate).[54] I do not of course deny that there may be a case for some strengthening in individual rights. But as a general response, this sort of approach does not address

[53] Soberer theorists like E.J. Mishan have always been unequivocally clear that projects admitted on cost-benefit analysis are 'consistent with transparent inequity', and that 'for a project to be socially acceptable it is not enough to show that the outcome of a cost-benefit analysis is acceptable . . . it must also be shown that no gross inequities are committed'.

Mackie had an idea which might seem to help here, in 'Can there be a rights-based Moral Theory' *op. cit.*

> [We shall] not allow the vital interests of anyone to be sacrificed for the advantage of others, to be outweighted by an aggregate of less vital interests. Rather we might think in terms of a model in which each person is represented by a point-centre of force, and the forces (representing *prima facie* rights) obey an inverse square law, so that a right decreases in weight with the remoteness of the matter on which it bears from the person whose right it is. There will be some matters so close to each person that with respect to them his rights will nearly always outweight any aggregate of other rights.

The mathematical model is suggestive, and it will be plain that I am indebted to it (however doubtful I am that it will quite work). But I fear it will provoke ingenious, disobliging persons to miss the whole point of holding some position such as Mackie's; and, if the model were applied to the exposition of the present proposal (which complicates the picture by bringing in needs-based counter-claims as vital interests that do not necessarily correspond to rights), it would no doubt provoke the same persons to misunderstand the basis and intention of the Principle of Limitation. In my treatment, that Principle is not, of course, part of an outline decision procedure but one of the several principles comprised in justice, with the special property of essentially contestably demarcating the area in which certain others can operate.

[54] Yet nothing less than the possibility of refusing what was offered would have been sufficient in the case of many of the injustices that have actually been committed in this area.

It is instructive in this connexion and in all sorts of connected ways to read command paper Cmnd. 5124 (October 1972) *Development and Compensation*—especially if one is moved beyond anything that is actively encouraged by the cool correct language of the document itself to try to remember or imagine the countless actions that eventually gave rise to the need for this, by the going standards, extraordinarily frank official confession of past injustice.

the real problem. *What* new rights are to be found or created, and on what principle? And how can these ever be arranged to anticipate the *indefinite* number of possible future injustices that will be committed against identifiable and non-identifiable people in the name of the public interest?[55]

Another slightly different approach has proposed the institution of a procedural-cum-constitutional right to have one's vital needs or interests taken as vital interests when public schemes are mooted, this right being backed by the legal power to force relevant officials either to prove at a hearing that these interests have been taken into account and treated in accordance with some relevant principle or to abandon their project. But, however impressive this may sound, it would be curiously ineffective in the absence of any agreed principles about how vital interests that are not legal rights are to be treated, as well as suffering from the same difficulties with unidentified or unidentifiable victims as beset the common law and new statute law approach.

So the direction in which one is finally inclined is along the path that leads not through rights as such but directly back to what starts to appear as nothing less than a necessity of political culture, namely the explicit acknowledgement as a constituent principle of justice (along with whatever other principles we can muster) of some principle like the ones I

[55] It may be well to give an example where common law rights give out before the concerns of justice can. When public works lay a whole neighbourhood waste and some or all of its inhabitants are to be resettled, the only legal claim-right anyone has normally had to compensation has derived from the legal ownership of land or a house. But there are always many who own neither. It is true that in more recent times those who actually live there at a specified date have been given some legal right to be resettled by the local authority, and may even qualify under recent provisions for some grant for 'disturbance' (a sum that it was proposed in 1972, on the basis of some vague sense of its inadequacy, simply to double). These are improvements in justice, even though the local authority is not necessarily the landlord of their choice, nor will they necessarily be rehoused at the rent they paid previously. It is possible to imagine these and other deficiencies being remedied. It is even possible, I suppose, to imagine a code of compensation that made good in real terms what a scheme actually took away from owners and non-owners who could be *identified*. Note however that even this would by no means exhaust those whose vital interests were actually affected, *e.g.*, by the contribution that such public projects may make to shortage (pushing up rents and house-prices), to blight, and to the dereliction of local employment. Any approach that will stress the openness of the class of persons to be affected in these ways must go well beyond the concern with common law rights and codes of compensation.

stated in §§22–3. (Cp. also §13.) Administrative and legal details are important but secondary. What matters first is that something like what I shall call the Principle of Limitation should be confirmed in the status of a principle of fairness, and should come to be taken so much for granted as a principle of fairness that it be normally impossible for administrative practice and political decision-making to proceed in apparent defiance of the Principle. (By 'normally' I mean 'under conditions where there is no strong case for overriding considerations of justice'.) In the presence of the expectation of this, it will be largely a matter of legal tradition whether or not citizens have the envisaged procedural-constitutional rights or how else the operation of the principle is guaranteed.[56] In the absence of the expectation that vital needs will rank in this way, the long term prospects are not very good, in the world as it is now, for government with the full consent of the governed. There will be things that stick in the throat when we seek to justify what government is forced to say and do to those who take exception to its encroachments.

25. If the Limitation Principle is an attempt to spell out, in terms of a vagueness suited to the subject matter, one of the prerequisites for the adherents of a workable social morality to lack avowable reasons to abdicate from it, then in all modern societies that are governed by consent, men's moral consciousness ought to concur in the Limitation Principle. But perhaps one should not expect to find any very direct practical or phenomenological test for the Principle or the correctness of the argument that I have offered for it. For we must be prepared to accept that different societies may differ considerably in the interpretation they put on 'vital' as it figures in 'vital interest or need'. (Cp. §9.) One would predict that these and other differences in interpretation or emphasis will combine

[56] A compromise might make provision for appeal against such procedures as Compulsory Purchase Order or Power of Eminent Domain, and might permit those directly affected to secure a formal hearing for themselves at which it was relevant and appropriate to refer to the Limitation Principle. Indeed I believe that the strong official predisposition in favour of the language of need, pointed out in §3, precisely rests on some inchoate, partial understanding of this appropriateness.

with divergent conceptions of the interventive role of government to issue in many important variations in the practice and sentiments of justice. The existence of these variations is perfectly consistent with the correctness of the Limitation Principle, whose operation is in any case highly sensitive, even at a particular time in a particular context, to where exactly the frontier of vital interests is seen as lying. Where a need is (as correctly formulated) vital and is specially protected as such by the principle, then it limits the space within which it is just for society to seek to maximize aggregated social advantage. If on the other hand the need falls short of that threshold, then it takes its chance with other needs, and there are conditions under which it may be sacrificed, and sacrificed without injustice, to the aggregated weight of other interests.

This discontinuity may seem strange. But reflection suggests that things have to be like this. There are some things we cannot justly do to a man, however much in aggregate other men may benefit.[57] (Almost nobody thinks that it can be just to kill one innocent man simply in order that millions should each receive some less than vital benefit.) The only question is how far this special protection extends beyond life itself. And of course there must be *some* cut-off. Otherwise we could scarcely ever reason aggregatively without incurring the charge of being to some extent unjust to someone.

What one ought to hope then is not that we can dispense with the threshold just mentioned, but that, given a place, a time, a climate of opinion and a set of expectations, the placing of the threshold will not be arbitrary but at worst essentially contestable. One might also expect that, as a society grows richer—and as it enlarges its sympathies to treat as if they were counter-claims in justice the claims of those who are prevented by natural handicap rather than by the power or prior appropriations of others from living through their own efforts—, the members of that society will construe 'vital interests' more generously. Perhaps in feeling they do. In

[57] It is worth remembering here that if we allow ourselves to be forced by some imaginable but appalling circumstance to override the claim of justice, it will be better to say 'We had to be unjust' than to say 'What we did was, in the circumstances, just' (or 'just in the circumstances'). (For a good statement of the impact of emergency upon criteria of vital need, see Finnis, *Natural Law and Natural Rights*, *op. cit.*, p. 174.)

practice, however—even if the human sentiments are prepared in principle for this, and are also prepared to understand the Limitation Principle more generously than I did in assigning it the excluding role I proposed for it—, the bureaucratic consciousness construes 'vital interests' extremely narrowly, so narrowly sometimes as to include little more than the bare prerequisites of life.[58]

The long term dangers of this narrow construal are the same, I believe, as the dangers of an outright rejection of the Principle of Limitation. But the chief reason for the narrow interpretation is not, I think, any particular wickedness of bureaucrats, but the intense competition that they are apt to find themselves witnessing at close quarters (or involved in as the recipients of lobbying, special pleading, pressure from newspapers about particular cases *etc.*) between considerations like the Limitation Principle (understood as a principle of justice, but not properly understood as a principle of limitation, and almost always *under-represented* because very few projects clearly endanger the vital interests of a larger number of people than the number they benefit) and very different kinds of need-based claims. The rationale of these other claims (which should not be lightly assumed to be a rationale in justice) arises at what is logically (if not historically) a third phase, after the two phases I have described in the preceding sections.

26. A society reaches the third phase, by my count, when government not only sees itself as the guardian of rights (the first phase) and counter-claims (the second phase), but also confirms itself in its role as the agent of coordination and the

[58] Nobody who does not already have some knowledge of the desolate scenes touched upon in *Cmnd* 5124 (*op. cit.* note 54 above) will want to take this on my say so. But to those who do I will remark how rare it is for a public agency bent on a large project with many direct and indirect consequences to pause to consider all the legal and moral obstacles that a private promoter would have had to face if he had tried to realize the same project as a commercial venture.

Postscript (1990) The decade just concluded, dense as it has been with socially and aesthetically destructive schemes promoted by private Act of Parliament or by other special procedures, has not been kind to the assumption that is made in the last sentence, namely that private or mixed private and public schemes will be scrutinized with greater care or with greater thought for legitimate expectations of the kind expressed by the Principle of Limitation than public schemes were. What the decade has reinforced is the case for recognizing such a principle as the Limitation Principle.

indispensable minister (at least in certain particular spheres) to human needs that will otherwise go unsatisfied. (And desires too, no doubt, though, as we noticed at the beginning, once taken on board, desires are usually accorded the official title of needs.) Here the numbers who benefit from any project and the quantity of need that can be satisfied by a given resource are felt to be a strong consideration—and, given the shortage of resources, rightly so. For what the administrator is now involved with is aggregative or agglomerative reasoning—i.e. subject to some constraint, he is maximizing something—, and what presumably matters most *within the proper sphere of such reasoning* is accurate measurement and prediction of consequences, and the will to jump off the treadmill whenever necessary for the imaginative exploration of alternatives that will bring greater total satisfaction and avoid the projection into the future of situations already giving rise to dissatisfaction and the mounting consumption of resources.[59]

Once a society is launched into phase three (and launched there for reasons having nothing specially to do with justice) and has instituted corresponding rules and practices, it moves into a whole new range of possible unfairness. And protestation at unfairness is sure to become unprecedentedly shrill and rancorous, giving even an obsession with the older and more important part of justice the unjustified reputation of enviousness and stridency. 'If *z* with need *x* had such and such done for him, why is nothing done for me with my need *w*?' What every administration that has entered the third phase requires is a range of defensible answers to such questions. It seems it must always be able to reply either 'Yes, we will!' or '*z*'s need is greater', or 'Your need is more expensive to satisfy'. Whatever

[59] It is not very useful to predict how people would behave, and what preferences they would thereby reveal, in a future state of affairs that inherits most of the unsatisfactory features they seek to escape from in the present. ('We always plan too much and think too little', as Schumpeter says in another connection.) But of course to escape from that dead end, we must understand better on the levels of reason and constituent beliefs, desires, needs, vital interests . . . what people avoid or seek in the present, and what alterable features of the present condition these beliefs, desires, needs, vital interests . . . (and how they condition them). (See my *Sameness and Substance*, pp. 180ff.; also 'Deliberation and Practical Reason' in J. Raz, *Practical Reasoning* (Oxford University Press 1981), which is an extract from Essay VI below.) And this may interest us afresh in considerations of justice that antedate phase three.

it gives to anyone placed in such and such a way, it must also give to anyone else so placed; and then (for given only finite resources, this must result from the same policy) it must be careful never to give anyone anything before it has looked to the ends of the earth to ensure that there are not too many others who will be able to represent that they have the very same entitlement.

27. There is no going back from phase three. We are too used to the benefits we attribute to it. And our feelings are commendably (however confusedly) fixed upon at least one small but conspicuous concomitant of it, namely our new willingness to intervene against contingency to help remedy certain entitlement failures that are in no way society's fault or strict responsibility. We did not have to feel this, but we do in fact. What was claimed about the distinction between claims of need and claims of the intolerability of inequality still holds good; but that distinction leaves room for an idea (not itself lacking some link with consensus but without any *special* tie to need) that there can be such a thing as too great a gap between people's life-chances.[60] It does not enforce or entail this idea, but it allows it.

But if there is no going back, and phase three is where we resolve to take our stand, then the time has arrived to try to understand much better the essential instability of the conception of social justice that we have got ourselves. And this we can scarcely do if we will never try to decipher the palimpsest of divergent ideas that it comprises.

In the first place, *need* itself now figures not only on the side of *justice as limitative, protective, and remedial*, (phases one and two), but also on the frequently conflicting side of *justice as the keeper and distributor of public goods.* In the conversation with the economist that I reported at §3, we could barely understand

[60] It may be worth contrasting this relatively weak principle with stronger formulations such as Richard Norman's 'Comprehensive Egalitarian Principle' in *Contemporary Political Philosophy: Radical Studies* (Cambridge, 1982), ed. K. Graham, p. 102: 'satisfaction of the basic needs of all, plus equality of monetary incomes over and above that (though this might need further qualifying if it were desired to increase some incomes to compensate for particularly dangerous or unpleasant work)'.

one another because he was preoccupied with the second of these roles and I was so preoccupied with the first. Had we realized this, and had I then expressed my concurrence in his belief that claims of need are often found in the company of abuse and special pleading, we could have got a little further and might even have found ourselves discussing vital interests, the limits of compensation and the problem of bequeathing to our descendants a world with at least as many tolerable niches for individual human existence as the one we inherited. Few questions are more urgent. But no progress at all can be made on them without some public understanding of the distinctness of these ways in which need claims impinge on us, and some sense of the putative priority in justice itself of phase one and phase two considerations over phase three considerations.

In the second place, we must learn to acquiesce in a tension there will always be *within* our way of thinking of phase three justice as keeper and distributor of whatever wealth is deemed public.

Consider the two following principles of justice:

(U) *Ceteris paribus* it is unjust not to have equal regard to equal needs, and subject to possibility and cost, it is just to accord equal weight to equal needs.

(E) *Ceteris paribus* it is unjust to accord different weight to people in respect of their needs; and, subject to possibility and cost, it is just to satisfy people equally in respect of their needs.

Each will seem compelling, especially in the absence of the suggestion that the other is compelling.

(U) looks like just the kind of principle the hard pressed bureaucrat or manager requires. What he is there for is to rid the world from all the various kinds of unsatisfied need, starting presumably with the worst among those unsatisfied. At any stage he reaches in the process[61] he must identify all outstanding needs that are as bad as or worse than (equal to or greater than) those so far attended to, and attend to them—*subject* of course *to cost*. But what effectively can that mean? The

[61] Recall here Beveridge's 'five giants' on the road of reconstruction: 'Want, Ignorance, Squalor, Idleness and Disease'.

answer that suggests itself is: Consider the resources available, and do the most you can with them by way of need satisfaction. And of course the next thought is: Needs do after all shade off into desires, so it would be less arbitrary to do the best one can with the resources available to satisfy all unsatisfied needs *and* desires. And then having reached that point—that is, act utilitarianism with respect to public policy—even the Limitation Principle must begin to seem anomalous, or ripe to be swallowed by the new doctrine. Indeed, the Limitation Principle, in so far as it suggests any policy at variance with what is suggested by the diminishing marginal usefulness to individuals of public largesse, will now seem simply irrational. It can only appear to stand in the way of the war against unsatisfied needs and desires.

But the principle (E) can initiate its own progression. Surely when we treat people differently, there must be a reason to treat them differently. And what better reason to treat them differently than that one of them has more unsatisfied needs? So we must proportion the largesse people receive to how much they stand in want of. Or rather we must do this subject to the cost. We cannot spend a million pounds on making one paraplegic's life just appreciably less bad simply because his suffering is greater than that of others who also have serious needs, or in spite of the fact that the same money would have given these others a very great deal of what they need. So, as we said, it is all subject to cost. But what effectively can that mean? The manager will want a rule. And if he must have a rule, then perhaps the only possible rule is to allocate the same to each person for his needs (or, since they shade off into desires, for his needs and desires) for him to do the best he can with.—Or rather, remembering the starting point and the anxiety that some had more unsatisfied need and others less, the rule must be to allocate public resources in such a way that the total that each person eventually enjoys (of public and private resources taken together) is equal to that which anyone else eventually enjoys. And having got to that point, or to some further sophistication of it—that is to a public philosophy of pure equality—it must seem anomalous and absurd to recognize a separate Limitation Principle. Since we are doing the best we can for each, everybody's vital interests will be intact if anyone's are. The distributive principle (E) simply swallows the limitative protective principle.

28. (U) and (E) so developed stand in stark opposition to one another. Each initiates a progression or simplification that seems within its own terms of reference irresistible. But each then loses touch with the original impulse that placed it there. (U) prepares us in principle to sacrifice individuals without limit, as Mackie would put it. (E) serves up a notion of equality of resources that is so abstract that it can scarcely impinge at all upon the sentiments that made needs seem important in the first place.

If the prospect seems unbearable of living with this conflict or tolerating the essential contestability of the frontier that contains it and is intended to prevent (U) and (E) from overrunning phase one and phase two reasoning about justice, then, having deciphered the palimpsest I spoke of, we could, I suppose try to retrace the marks we have made and contemplate the restoration (by deletion of the most recent) of the simpler moral universe in which the State undertakes the minimum and in which rights and counter-claims make up the whole of justice. It seems certain that it could induce a sense of proportion to think through the moral advantages of this. But this is not to say that it is really possible to get back to that point.

A much more characteristic response on the part of philosophers and political scientists is to tinker and try to find a principle that mediates or compromises somehow between (U) and (E), and then to make the new principle absorb everything that we have subsumed under phases one and two. And there is no end I am sure to the ingenuity that can be brought to bear upon the task of qualifying and adjusting the arguments that lead (U) and (E) from the state of tension into the state of outright practical incompossibility. But perhaps it would be better to learn to live with (U), (E) and the Limitation Principle as making out three separate, mutually irreducible sorts of claim upon us, and to prevent the deafening noise of the conflict between (U) and (E) from drowning the pleas of other more important and prior demands of justice. It would be better to refrain from assimilating limitative protective justice (phase one and two) to distributive justice (phase three), not taking protective justice (properly understood as protective and limitative and not as presupposing phase three) to be in any conflict at all with aggregative public rationality. Surely they cannot be in conflict. One simply defines the other's proper theatre of operation, essentially contestably.

Why then might the prospect of living with these irreducibilities seem unbearable—or any more unnerving than the prospect of riding a bicycle? I suspect that it will seem unbearable only if we see it as the task of a theory of justice to hit on suitable principles or axioms that generate a description or blueprint for a just state or society, *e.g.* in the manner Plato adopts in the *Republic*, relying upon the non-self-sufficiency of men and the supposed truism that each kind of man should do what he does best, or in the manner of John Rawls, who arrives at a just order of things by working out what departures from strict equality would have been written into a social contract drawn up under ideal conditions, in ignorance of social reality as we have it and of the positions of particular people therein. In the thought-experimentation that is characteristic of these approaches, nothing is left to chance, and nothing is *prima facie* anybody's (even if the thing in question would never have existed at all but for him) until it is *assigned* to him as his share.—Though of course the exactitude of the theoretical calculations that the procedure purports in some variants to make possible is diminished out of all recognition when we reach the problem of social criticism and we attempt concrete comparison of actual holdings with hypothetically just holdings, a baffling and multiply counterfactual problem.

So long as one is committed to this approach, one will think one has to try to construct a sort of *model* of justice. Our own attempt has been quite different—indeed almost opposite in intention. We have started out with the historical contingency that men live in societies, societies being things that we discover in existence possessing whatever nature they do possess, completing and conditioning the lives of men in all sorts of different ways and manifesting different degrees of cohesion and consensus. And we have then speculated on what it now takes for societies that exist by consensus to perpetuate themselves on terms and by means that their participants can avow to themselves without having to unlearn their instinctive capacity to recognize other men as conscious subjects and objects of reciprocity and interpretation[62]—and what it takes for them to continue to do so even as the awareness grows among these societies' members of their own power. In this consensual, evolutionary approach, the philosophy of justice does not have to invent and hold up for comparison some contractualist (or whatever) *ideal polity* with which reality can be confronted for purposes of adjustment and criticism. It has to try to draw upon the various potentially divergent and discrepant ideas and feelings we already have, in order to describe how and to what extent historical contingency, and whatever other goals besides justice we may pursue, will have to be offset by deliberate regulation and intervention, sometimes despite men's legitimate expectation, to secure some accord with our evolving sense of what it is fair for people to be asked to do and endure, with our sense of the entitlement that must normally accrue to effort or achievement or inheritance or settled expectation or whatever, and with our untheoretical sense of the relative strengths of the various classes of need claims. Justice here is only the lack of a certain sort of evil. (A theory of it does not need to furnish a determinate paradigm for the legal and constitutional arrangements of a country.) And not only are there many other matters a society must concern itself with besides justice (the security of the state, economic survival, *etc.*) Not only must these other considerations limit how just it is possible to be. But also justice is *itself* a complex and many rooted idea; and it can even conflict with itself—or so our approach prepares us to expect—in ways for which there may be no predetermined mode of resolution.

When it comes to applying such a conception of justice as this to social reality, whether in policy-making or in criticism, its practical application is at once direct, underdetermined and contextually constrained (leaving much to be decided by something like Aristotelian *aisthesis*).[63] There is no difficulty in

[62] Cp. *Sameness and Substance*, *op. cit.* Chapter Six, with addenda for pp. 174–184, *Longer Note* 6.36 §3; Peter Winch, Presidential Address, *Proceedings of the Aristotelian Society*, 1980–81, stressing correctly the pre-rational character of this recognition.

[63] Cp. J.R. Lucas 'The Lesbian Rule' *Philosophy* 1954, Essay VI below, §4–5. In correction and amplification of what is said here, the issue of underdetermination is treated further at pp. 318 and 348.

seeing that certain things are clearly just and that certain others are clearly unjust. But room is left even for one and the same society at a given time to choose between several different ways of answering certain sorts of question.

Nor is it a positive point in favour of accepting some other picture that it eliminates this under-determination, either within justice itself or in the competition between justice and other values. Given a social morality as determinate as you like (as determinate even as such a thing can be), it is not demonstrably rational to look confidently for the elimination of essential contestability. But then, if we pause a little longer on the point, maybe we shall find not hopelessness but comfort—even some obscure hope for politics itself (does one *have* to think of one's political opponents as wicked or morally deranged?)—in the thought that I shall end by quoting from another colleague to whom, as to Mackie, this essay owes much:

> The basic moral intuitions of mankind—which Right and Left alike cannot but take for granted as a premise for their moral appeal—provide no solution except in a prohibitive and limiting sense, for the permanent and topical problems of political organization and choice.[64]

[Postscript. These questions are resumed and certain related themes pursued at pp. 314–28 below.]

[64] Aurel Kolnai, 'The Moral Theme in Political Division', *Philosophy*, 1960. For other references to Kolnai's thinking on this and related matters, see Bernard Williams' and David Wiggins' Introduction to his *Ethics, Value and Reality* (London: Athlone, 1973).

2.1 As I look back at Essay I, what now disturbs me most is the suspicion that I have gravely underestimated the resistance that anyone must expect who defends a principle of justice like the Limitation Principle given at the beginning of §23.[8] If he puts it forward to be one of the limits of the area within which

[8] The relevant passage runs as follows:

> Perhaps the limitative principle that will regulate both rights/counter-rights arbitration *and* collective reasoning conducted in pursuit of public goods is this. Even if there is nothing unjust in actions of the State or its agencies making one man poorer in a way that makes another man less poor than he was (in kind or money) . . ., it *is pro tanto unjust* if the State or an agency of the State intervenes against contingency, or changes its policy, or confounds citizens' sensible expectations, in a way that sacrifices anyone's strictly vital interests to the mere desires of however many others; and (more speculatively) *it is pro tanto unjust* if, among vital interests actually affected by such interventions, the greater strictly vital need of anyone is sacrificed in the name of the lesser needs of however many others.

It is an urgent matter to improve all such formulations, but I believe that the improvement must be made in the light of the question discussed in Essay I §17. This is a far more sensible focus for the dialogue between conservatism and socialism, I claim, than the question of equality. By socialism I suggest one then ought to mean a position whose central preoccupation is with *counter-claims*, as these are defined in Essay I.§12 following. For the way in which the idea of counter-claims will make better sense of some of the more promising questions about equality, see below note 13.

For my use of the expression *pro tanto* in the passage cited, and elsewhere, see Susan Hurley 'Conflict, Akrasia, and Cognitivism', *Proceedings of the Aristotelian Society*, vol. 86 (1985/6), pp. 23ff. For the need for such a term see Bernard Williams' critique of the term '*prima facie*' in 'Consistency and Realism', *The Aristotelian Society Supplementary Volume* 40, 1966.

aggregative reasoning can operate without injustice and announces, as I have, that this principle is to be part of a fence between the justice that concerns rights or counter-rights and a kind of justice that is treated with less respect in that essay and called 'phase three justice' or 'the rest of justice', then he must expect to be closely cross-examined about what vital interests are. When the proponent of the limitation principle goes on to reveal that vital interests are due to be defined in terms of needs that are grave, deeply entrenched, and scarcely substitutable (§9), he is bound to be pressed very hard to face the question exactly how such needs are to be determined, and who is to determine them.

It is often assumed that simply to ask the last question in the right tone of voice suffices to dissipate the whole force of the suggestion that needs are an urgent or central constituent in the idea of justice. Who wants other people to tell him what he needs?

Among the first to have seen this as the difficulty was Pareto. What Pareto wrote was:

> La formule: *à chacun selon ses besoins* se change ainsi en l'autre: *à chacun selon ce que décide l'autorité:* et elle vaut en général ce que vaut l'autorité.[9]

Pareto's objection has not lost its power. Variants of it are still directed with the same expectation of dialectical triumph against champions of the need concept who, unlike Pareto's, have never proposed 'From each according to his ability: to each according to his need' as part of some supreme or all-embracing principle of all justice, are quite innocent of all totalitarian or authoritarian aspirations in politics, and have as their principal transgression nothing worse than this: to find nothing compelling or convincing in any of the descendants or mitigations of the Greatest Happiness Principle that have been intended to minister to our ideas of justice and injustice.

Perhaps the only way to come to terms with the sneer 'And who then is simply to determine vital interests, or needs?' is to pretend that no sneer is intended, to overlook the rhetorical

[9] *Les Systèmes Socialistes* (Paris, 1901) vol. II, p. 167.

intentions with which such questions are so often uttered, and try to provide a literal answer to them, just as they stand, attending *en route* to all the supplementary questions that would be bound to arise in a political or philosophical exchange on the subject. Those not in the grip of Pareto's objection may feel that they wish at this point to skip to §3.1 below.

2.2 How are needs to be determined? Confronted with this question our first task, but not our only one, is surely to say what the question of needing *turns on*, and what is relevant to it, and what is not.

Sections 3–7 of Essay I attempt this task. What the question of needs turns on depends in the first instance on what needing is, and on what people mean when they speak seriously about needs (in the absolute or categorical sense, see §6). So the first part of the first task is the question of meaning. The correctness of §§3–7 and of the use they make of such ideas as harm and necessity chiefly depends on whether the proposals put forward there make better sense of the data than any rival semantical hypothesis.

Once we emerge from that semantical question, if we do, it will appear that the idea of harm is correlative with ideas of human life and flourishing that each age, community and culture has to make the best it can of. These are public property and the fit subject of constructive argument; but, like so many ordinary ideas, they are also metaphysical and essentially contestable. And to some theorists of politics that will seem both dangerous and unnerving. They will search about for reasons to displace these notions by more technical, supposedly more operational, counterparts whose application will occasion less heart-searching and less argument.

If the principles of need comprised some political principle to the effect that a person was to have only what he or she needed, then the essential contestability of need claims would be a troublesome point and the public determination of needs and vital interests would represent an intolerable violation of personal autonomy. But the thing I must emphasize is that no such principle is being offered in Essay I. What is being offered there is a principle that is designed to safeguard the space around the individual, and to protect him and his life chances from certain kinds of injustices that might otherwise be committed against him on some specious pretext of public interest.

In fact even more protection could be afforded to individuals' interests within the needs framework if the protection of the individual from aggregative reasoning were the only sort of protection that was at issue here. But legitimate purposes of the State, most conspicuously the requirements of phase two justice, cannot help but circumscribe what ought to be attempted in this connexion. That which is really required is a way of arbitrating between all sorts of claims—the individual's claim, the community's claim, other individuals' claims.[10]

That this last end has to be achieved *somehow* is common ground. What is controversial is whether the concept of need is somehow pernicious in this connexion. I am claiming that it is not, and that in these conflicts it often clarifies what is at issue on both sides. Surely the idea of need is not disabled from its conceptual role on either side of the argument by the essential contestability that statements of vital interest inherit from the essential contestability of statements of need. For in this area, essential contestability is the condition of all important ideas. Its presence does not entail that just anything goes, or that the process of determination of harm (either to the individual or by the individual) is simply a matter of counting ayes and noes. These ideas of life, harm, flourishing are the focus of wide-ranging, open-ended controversy and of a rich variety of

[10] And once phase two justice enters explicitly, we can find a reading that nobody need find too sinister for such familiar observations as Wade's in his *Administrative Law*: 'social needs and ancient liberties are frequently hard to reconcile'; though this is not to say that the phase two interpretation of 'social needs' has been consistently accorded any actual priority by all the great departments of State in which writers on administrative law such as W. Robson were prepared to place such confidence. Not only have phase three considerations come slowly but surely to outstrip all others. These departments have been slow to see the conceptual basis of the profound truth that what real justice usually requires is not that utility should be maximized by whatever means and then 'redistributed' (for the strangeness of this verb see Essay I §17), but that (however hard this is to achieve) it should be made possible for the wealth on which vital interests depend to be produced closer to the point where it is to confer its benefit, and that its presence there, when once it is present, should be actively protected by use of all the judicial and other resources of the State from predations of all kinds, not excluding predations by agencies of the State itself.

opposing analogies which it can still be hoped will converge in an agreement over essentials (either a general agreement, or an agreement among a majority of representatives properly elected) that is both principled and capable of justifying itself. In the present we have to draw credit upon the prospect of drawing closer to that auspicious state of affairs in the future. Certainly the ideas of flourishing and harm are not rendered inapplicable by virtue of being temporally and culturally conditioned. For one might think that notions that are conditioned by one's own time and culture are the ones that it ought to be easiest to criticize in a practical way and, after refinement by criticism, to apply in action.

2.3 But *why*, I may now be asked, are vital interests in *x*, *y*, *z* to be defined in terms of needs that are grave, non-substitutable with respect to *x*, *y*, *z*, entrenched *etc?* To this I answer that these categories, as defined in §§8–9 of Essay I were designed to catch something that I hoped that everyone would recognize as the grounds for a certain sort of concern for an individual whose interests are gravely threatened by our pursuit of some supposedly common good, a concern further enlarged upon in §12 following. But the categories can be displaced by any others that are better designed to fulfil this task and that engage better with the relevant sentiments.

2.4 All right, someone may say. I hear all that. But what states then, with what objects, will deserve the title of grave, non-substitutable, entrenched needs? Once you answer this question, you will be seen in your true colours as an autocrat, or as the willing slave of the autocrat.

I would reply that §12 following give some indication of the states I should single out for this special title: but that it is philosophically important to distinguish here (and I have already assumed that one must distinguish) between the question of how to specify these states, *i.e.* to enumerate them, and the logically prior question of what it *turns on* in a given case whether, under circumstances *c*, *x* is a vital need or interest of such and such persons. In so far as the theorist has any privileged standing here, it only consists in his claim to have tried to articulate this logically prior thing, and in the liberty (which is not exclusively his) to issue reminders of this, if nobody else will, whenever and wherever argument breaks out over such things as needs, rights and counter-claims. Apart from this, the theorist has no privileged standing. Nor wili any other supposed expert, appointed, self-appointed or elected necessarily have a privileged position. The question of the norms of flourishing or harm, and of the subclassification of these, is the exclusive intellectual property of nobody, except in so far as what is proposed is the creation or perpetuation of a system of government that *makes* these questions into someone's mystery or exclusive preserve.

2.5 Who then is to determine, either in a given case or more generally, what are harms, what are needs, what are vital interests?

Pareto envisages that the answer to that sort of question will be 'the authority'; and then he rightly points out that the answer we shall get from that authority about our needs cannot be expected to be worth more than that authority is worth. But since 'from each according to his ability: to each according to his need' is not being put forward by me as the single supreme principle of justice, and all that is being said (contrast the contentions of some of Pareto's opponents) is that the idea of need figures essentially in constituent principles of phase one and phase two justice, it will be apparent that no proposal is in question here to set up some unitary dictatorial authority to determine the needs and/or abilities of each and every person.

Facing the questions we actually face then, let us make the thought-experiment of envisaging in some detail the present pattern of government, judiciary *etc.*, and let us speculate what is the least institutional change that would be required to enforce the Limitation Principle and to make counter-claims stick. I claimed in Essay I that the first necessity here was a further (by no means novel or unexpected) development of our moral and political culture; and that the second necessity might be to make provision (or to take seriously some old provision) by which government or its agencies would be legally required on certain sorts of occasion to demonstrate that this or that public practice or project did not infringe the principles of justice.[11]

Who then would judge that? Well, suppose that on these occasions it was for some member or members of the judiciary to determine the question of infringement or non-infringement. Then on this sort of occasion, the question of determination of vital need would be one for judges. What then would judges themselves rely upon? In the last resort, they would have to rely (as they sometimes have to in matters of equity) on the more durable deliverances of our shared moral and political culture. But what would those deliverances themselves depend upon? Well, indirectly but ultimately, these would surely depend on *us*, on how careful we ourselves were to listen to what we were saying and think what we meant by it, and on how careful we were both singly and collectively to keep track of our own judgments and our reasons for making them.

In this area it turns out that, if public policy were more need-orientated and less preference-orientated, and if the emphasis were shifted from phase three to phase two justice, it would sometimes fall to judges, or legislators or their public servants to determine the substance of certain vital needs. That is in line with Pareto's gloomy general prediction. But note now that the substance of vital needs is not very different from what legislators and their public servants *already* claim to determine. See Essay I, §3. The difference I am interested in is that, under the happier state of affairs I am trying to describe, these legislators and their servants would have not to use the words 'need' or 'vital interest' so lightly or without thinking what they meant by what they said: and that in order to administer phase two justice, they would then have to aim to articulate for this or that particular purpose that which was soundest and most durable in the ideas of needs, vital interest, *etc.* that passed muster then. Hence the importance (already urged) of our understanding as well as we can now what we are talking about

[11] Where counter-claims are concerned, it will probably be necessary to envisage yet a third thing: some sort of procedure designed to draw attention to the condition to which certain people have been reduced by the existing systems of entitlement relations. I shall not weigh down the argument by seeking to specify such a procedure. It will be sufficient to suppose, for the sake of determinacy, that those arbitrating the outcome might be members of the judiciary, or members of the first or second chamber of the legislature.

now when we make arguments in the area of needs, rights and counter-claims—and of our not permitting moral or political philosophers or political scientists or economists to cheat us of our conceptual birthright by reducing questions of social choice and justice to questions that can be dealt with in the impoverished terms of bare desire, revealed preference *etc.*, however mitigated or tempered by the superposition of radical or inspiratory after-thoughts of equality or fraternity. If our own way of thinking becomes over-schematized or over-simplified, or insensitive to the vital interests of the outvoted or outnumbered, then that of our public servants is bound to do so.

2.6 At certain points in the last answer I pass close to the fear that is sometimes voiced that expert opinion or some wide public consensus about what is a good or wretched life or a vital need might work against the interests of those not party to the consensus and license massive interference in their freedom.

Of course the determination of practical matters by those who represent majorities, or by educated consensus, or (what is different again) by experts subject to educated consensus is always dangerous. It is a dangerous necessity (once given the greater danger of dispensing with government altogether). The only real question is whether, under the condition I have called the happier state of affairs, such things as majorities or experts or consensus would be more dangerous than they have to be, or less answerable to rational control. For, as I have said, this happier state is not a new political arrangement by which some single person or body is newly charged with realizing any supreme principle or with butting into every detail of everyone's life. It is simply a state of affairs differing at specific points from the present by virtue of certain thoughts about justice being taken more seriously, and then followed through.

My claim, as I have said, is that at present experts and ministers or their public servants purport (in effect) to determine what preferences *have* been revealed and then (within limits and constraints no doubt, but with only fitful regard for phase two justice) devise the policies that will optimize relative to these. The great choice we need to find a way to make is not whether a large variety of things will continue to be determined for us, but whether those who determine them shall continue to work to maximize the satisfaction of preferences within the framework of what I call phase three justice: or whether they shall leave rather more of these preferences to find their own satisfaction and concentrate instead, in the frameworks of phase one and phase two justice, on our grave, unsubstitutable, entrenched needs, interpreting our vital interests in the light of what people pursue and say they pursue qua needed, and in the light of what appear as the best ideas to be had about these things. In this matter, *pace* Pareto, the champion of needs has as good a right as anyone else to declare himself as an opponent of despotism and authoritarianism. He can join with others in the contention that it would be a good thing if social deliberations in which appeal is made to our behaviour as evidence of how we conceive of our interests were more often obtruded upon by our own interpretations of our own doings—albeit in defiance of the behaviourism that has shaped the development of our theories of political economy and has made these theories so blind to the question what people might have chosen had there been the option to act out some other choice, in behaviour the economist could then have observed.[12] On any sane view, the human voice is required in any case. But the human voice, where permitted, is no worse adapted to the revelation, expression and constructive criticism of needs than it is to that of preferences (preferences themselves often notoriously failing in any case to effect any unique determination of the correct, or the 'democratic', decision).

2.7 Finally then freedom, and the threat to freedom that is sometimes apprehended from any theory of needs. Here perhaps one can only have recourse to a question. In operation within a non-authoritarian, critical society in which discussion was both free and effective, why should not principles like the Limitation Principle, explicated in terms of vital interests and needs, *restore* freedom or choice or independence to classes whose freedom is now intolerably restricted and narrow, or has

[12] Cp. David Wiggins, *Sameness and Substance*, p. 180.

been substantially diminished? What is more, freedom, choice, and autonomy are themselves vital human needs, and are candidates for precisely the kind of protection that is accorded *qua* needs to other real needs. Is it not within the power of the idea of need to suggest limitations on the purposes of the State, as well as to suggest the desirability, in certain well understood cases that can be carefully defined, of the State's raising taxes for the purpose of giving education, health or self sufficiency (requirements of phase one and phase two justice) to its citizens?[13] The real enemy of human freedom is not the idea of a need—or any other ordinary moral or political idea that we can sustain in a determinate distinctive use—but conceptions of political science that will reduce or simplify the complex vocabulary of politics and political evaluation that is second nature to us and will give undeserved assistance to those already bent on narrowing ignobly the range of political possibilities that can be sufficiently visible even to be considered. (Cp. Essay VIII §3; Essay VI §4; Essay VII §8.)

2.9 Over and over again in these matters, one will find oneself referring to what can by effort be discovered within *us* or *our* valuational consciousness. Who is this *we*? Anyone and everyone is included in it until explicitly (and for good reasons, cp. p. 66) he or she is excluded. To see another as disagreeing is precisely to see him or her as *party* to the effort to construct the point of view that shall be common to one person with another. If things go well, then everyone is party. But even where things go well, we are not simply counting heads. Rather we have concerted our efforts to make it possible for the best considerations to prevail—*as* the best considerations.

[13] With all these things in place, I gladly mitigate some of my strictures on the idea of equality. For what has emerged as a plausible requirement of phase two justice is that in the pursuit of that sort of justice, where it does pursue it, the State must not only delimit the sphere of aggregative calculation but must have regard and equal regard, in its actions as well as its deliberations, for each person's equally vital interest *as* his or her vital interest. Note however that this strong principle still leaves it open what the scope of State intervention is to be, and what further commitment if any the State must have to the further aspects or dimensions of equality. And what I cannot retract is my claim that it is a gratuitously weak (and *de facto* ineffective) criticism of most actual acts or public injustice to say that what is being done is inegalitarian. (Or else it is a gratuitously obscure criticism.) Always so much else is wrong too. Can that not be articulated?

[7]

SYMPOSIUM ON RATIONALITY AND MORALITY

Moral Judgment and the Acceptance of Norms*

Allan Gibbard

In recent years, various ethical theorists have turned to considering the nature of rationality.[1] How, after all, might we best seek out a promising line of approach to fundamental moral questions? A possible stratagem is to ask first why moral questions matter. The chief reasons must surely lie in what their answers can tell us of how to live—and in this response may lie hints of a way to proceed. Look for what, in a general prescription for living, plays the role of morality and take that itself to constitute morality. Deciding how to live, after all, is in effect deciding how it is rational to live. Begin, then, by developing a theory of rational conduct, and then in that theory, see if there is anything that fits our ordinary, vague picture of the demands of morality. If there is, call that morality—for whether or not it is what we initially conceived morality to be, it is what we can rationally treat in much the way we initially treated morality in our thinking.

This broad approach evidently requires a theory of rational conduct. What does it mean for something to be "rational"? To call a thing "rational" is to endorse it in some sense, and that in turn suggests a scheme for eliciting the meaning of 'rational.' Instead of seeking to define a property, "rationality," by giving the conditions under which a thing would have that property or lack it, start with the use of the term. Fix on the dictum

The articles in this issue of *Ethics* are the proceedings of the twenty-fourth annual Oberlin Colloquium in Philosophy, held April 13–15, 1984. The topic of the colloquium was "Rationality and Morality." Following the colloquium, each main speaker was invited to revise his paper for publication; and commentators prepared the published versions of their comments from this final version. Main speakers were also invited to prepare rejoinders to their commentators. The 1984 Oberlin Colloquium was the first to be partially funded by the Gertrude Dahl Philosophy Colloquium Fund.

* Much of this article is drawn from work done while I was a Fellow of the Center for Advanced Study in the Behavioral Sciences, with support from a National Endowment for the Humanities Fellowship for Independent Study and Research and from the Andrew W. Mellon Foundation.

1. I have in mind, among other people, Richard Brandt and aspects of recent work by R. M. Hare and John Rawls. See R. B. Brandt, *A Theory of the Good and the Right* (Oxford: Oxford University Press, 1979); R. M. Hare, *Moral Thinking: Its Levels, Method, and Point* (Oxford: Oxford University Press, 1981), esp. pt. 3; and John Rawls, "Kantian Constructivism in Moral Theory," *Journal of Philosophy* 77 (1980): 515–72.

Ethics 96 (October 1985): 5–21

"To call a thing rational is to endorse it" and search for a sense of the term 'endorse' for which the dictum holds true.

The word 'rational' has a learned flavor, but the concept I am tracking is familiar enough. It is the one we use when we talk about "what it makes sense" to do or to believe, or when we speak of actions as "reasonable" or "unreasonable," or when we search for the "best thing to do" in a way that does not presuppose that we are searching for the morally best thing to do. There does seem to be a common notion involved in all these turns of phrase; one test is that to affirm one of an action while denying another would be to invite puzzlement, not to invoke a distinction we could expect the audience to grasp antecedently. When we use the more learned term 'rational,' it is often this notion we are trying to apply.

I try in this article to give some inkling of a larger project. What I say will thus be sketchy and incomplete, but I hope it will suggest directions for thought. I begin by laying out some characteristics of rationality as it appears in ordinary thought, suitably refined. These are characteristics we might want an analysis of the term 'rational' to capture. I then turn to the relation of morality to rationality and develop a proposal that stems from Mill. Questions of morality, on this proposal, are questions concerning the rationality of certain specifically moral emotions: guilt and resentment. Only after this do I return to the concept of rationality and broach the analysis I want to combine with Mill's proposal. Cryptically put, the analysis is that to call something rational is to express one's acceptance of norms that permit it. That leaves much to be explained: among other things, what it is for a person to accept a norm. In the last part of the article I speculate on the psychological nature of the acceptance of norms. I sketch how the psychic mechanisms involved might be explained naturalistically; they can be understood, I suggest, as devices for interpersonal coordination. Normative discussion coordinates emotions and actions, and in the life of a social animal such coordination can be vital.

The analysis I broach is noncognitivistic, in the narrow sense that on the analysis, to call a thing "rational" is not straightforwardly to attribute a property to it, but to do something else. I have argued elsewhere that leading cognitivistic accounts of what 'rational' means fail; the same kinds of arguments as G. E. Moore used to discredit "naturalistic" definitions of moral terms apply to 'rational' as well.[2] I shall not repeat these arguments here, but I should say at the outset that what I say here presupposes that attempts to treat rationality as a straightforward property fail. They miss a crucial element of endorsement that the term connotes.

My analysis is not meant to capture a substantive view on the nature of rationality; rather it is meant to capture the common element in dispute when people disagree on the nature of rationality. It is supposed to tell us what it is to debate what is rational and to wonder what is

2. See my "A Non-Cognitivistic Analysis of Rationality in Action," *Social Theory and Practice* 9 (1984): 199–221, esp. 200–206.

rational. If I am right, deciding what sorts of things are rational is in effect deciding what norms to accept for a given domain of appraisal.

I. WHAT IS APPRAISED AS RATIONAL OR IRRATIONAL

In everyday life we appraise a wide variety of human attributes as "rational" or "irrational." Not only can a person act rationally or irrationally, but he can also believe rationally or irrationally, and he can be angry or grateful or envious rationally or irrationally. It is irrational, for example, to be angry at the messenger who brings bad tidings but rational to be angry at the miscreant who deliberately wrongs one. Or at least this, I take it, is what we tend to think in the normal course of life. If the word "rational" seems overly learned here, I suggest close substitutes with a more homely flavor: "It doesn't make sense" to be angry at the person who brings bad news he had no part in making. You "shouldn't be grateful" to someone who benefited you only inadvertently in seeking his own gain.

It is this family of appraisals I seek to interpret. Do they make genuine sense, and if so, how are they to be understood? If the term 'rational' can be applied intelligibly to as wide a range of human attributes as we seem to think, does it have the same meaning in all these contexts?

It might be thought that for something to be rational is for it to be desirable or advantageous. Such a crude pragmatism, though, would leave ordinary thought about rationality mysterious: it fits actions, perhaps, but not beliefs and attitudes. Take the stock example of the man who has some evidence his wife is unfaithful. Whether it is still *rational* for him to believe her faithful depends on his evidence, and on his evidence alone. Whether it is *desirable* for him to believe her faithful, and whether his believing her faithful is *good for him,* depend as well on how his beliefs would affect his feelings toward her. The rationality of a belief and its desirability, then, are different, if ordinary thought is to be trusted. Likewise, it might be disadvantageous for one of Cleopatra's courtiers to be angry at her, even if she ordered an execution unjustly, and it thus "made sense" to be angry at her. For the courtier might want to ingratiate himself with her, and he might rightly fear that anger would cloud his countenance and spoil his charm. In that case, he would have every reason to want not to be angry, and still, we seem to think, it would make sense for him to be angry. It made no like sense for Cleopatra to be angry at the slave who brought news of Antony's defeat—however therapeutic or palliative her anger might have been. For anger to make sense is not for it to be advantageous.

In all this we must distinguish saying that it makes sense for a person *to be* angry from saying that it makes sense *that* the person *is* angry. If I have had a bad day and now face a new disappointment, it "makes sense that I am angry"—we can expect me to be angry in the circumstances, for reasons we understand—even if it doesn't "make sense for me to be angry" because the new disappointment is no one's fault. Likewise, it makes sense that Cleopatra was angry at the messenger, but it made no sense *for* her to be angry at him. Misdirected anger in the circumstances was to be expected, but the bad news was not the messenger's fault.

Are these ordinary distinctions truly intelligible? Can we really distinguish anger's making sense from anger's being desirable? If we understood the word 'rational,' we could put the distinction as follows. In the case of the courtier and the queen, even though it is rational for him to be angry with her for ordering an execution unjustly, it may also be rational for him to want to ingratiate himself with her, for his own good or for that of her subjects. If anger would prevent that, then it may be rational for him to *want* not to be angry with her. Thus in such a case, it is rational *to be angry* but also rational *to want not to be angry.* This pattern applies not only to emotion but also to belief. Take the stock case of a deceived husband: his evidence may make it rational for him *to believe* his wife unfaithful, but the way the belief would affect his feelings toward her may make it rational for him *to want to believe* her faithful. Rationally *feeling* or *believing* something is distinct from rationally *wanting* to feel or believe it.

Talk of emotions as "rational" or "irrational" will strike many readers as dubious. True, we may say the kinds of things I have been claiming we say: that it "makes sense to be angry" in certain cases and "it makes no sense to be angry" in others. It may still be asked, though, whether these judgments can bear scrutiny. It may well seem that we can appraise as rational or irrational only what is under a person's voluntary control. Emotions fail this test, since they are not under a person's direct voluntary control. True, they can be nurtured or repressed, but a person cannot simply be angry at will, or grateful at will. Nor can a person refrain from any of these things simply at will. What can be appraised as rational or irrational is not an emotion itself, it may be said, but taking measures to nurture or repress it.

Now I accept, of course, that emotions cannot be had or cast off at will. What I deny is the dictum "Only the voluntary can be appraised as rational or irrational." Beliefs seem prime examples of what we can appraise as rational or irrational, but beliefs, like emotions, cannot be had or cast off at will. We may be able to "make believe" at will, but that is not the same as really believing at will.

None of this is to say that when we call an act, belief, or emotion "rational" we are saying something intelligible; that remains to be seen. I am saying that we talk and think as if such appraisals are intelligible. It may be worthwhile, then, to see if we can interpret them as intelligible.

II. RATIONALITY AND MORALITY

Before I proceed to hunt for an account of what 'rational' means, I turn to morality and its relation to rationality. In what follows, I shall naively suppose that we know what 'rational' means; only later will I be broaching an analysis of the term.

In the history of moral philosophy, there seem to be at least two sharply different conceptions of what morality is. On what I shall call the "broad" conception, morality is simply practical rationality in the fullest sense: to say that an act is morally right is to say that it is rational. Kant and Sidgwick are prime exponents of this broad conception, which is shared by many current writers. On this conception, it makes no sense to ask, "Is it always rational to do what is morally right?" for 'the morally right' simply means "the rational." On a "narrow" conception of morality, in contrast, moral considerations are just some of the considerations that bear on what it makes sense to do. Nonmoral considerations matter too. On the narrow conception, for instance, it is normally wrong to injure others, to steal, or to break one's word. It would normally not be morally wrong, though, to fritter away a day for which one had planned an enjoyable hike—however irrational that might be. On the broad conception of morality, morally right action simply is action that is truly rational, whereas on the narrow conception, an act may be truly irrational without being morally wrong.

In chapter 5 of *Utilitarianism*, John Stuart Mill uses the term 'morality' in this narrow sense and offers an account of what is distinctive about "morality" so taken. "Morality," he says, "pertains to what is wrong or not wrong, and to say that an act is wrong is to say that there ought to be a sanction against it, a sanction of law, of public opinion, or of conscience." The 'ought' here, Mill proposes, should be judged by the standards of the greatest happiness principle—but that is part of Mill's normative theory, not his theory of meanings. What I propose to do is to take over Mill's analysis of what "morality" is in the narrow sense, with various interpretations and modifications.[3]

When Mill says there "ought" to be a sanction, let us read him as saying that a sanction is rational—or, perhaps, rationally required. Let us also drop talk of legal sanctions. Suppose, say, we think that people who overpark at parking meters ought to be fined, but that they ought not to feel guilty and ought not to be resented by others for overparking. In that case, it seems to me, we do not think overparking morally wrong; we merely think that a price should be charged. That leaves sanctions of conscience and of public opinion: sanctions of guilt and remorse, on the one hand, and of blame, resentment, and moral outrage, on the other. Thus as the proposal now stands, what a person does is *morally wrong* if and only if it is rational for him to feel guilty for doing it, and for others to resent him for doing it.

As it stands, the analysis is more plausible for 'blameworthy' than for 'morally wrong.' The term 'wrong,' it is often said, has two distinct moral senses, the objective and the subjective. The difference between the two is displayed through stories like this: Yesterday, I had the brakes

3. It was David Lyons who brought Mill's theory to current philosophical attention in a series of articles. See esp. his "Mill's Theory of Morality," *Nous* 10 (1976): 101–20.

of my car checked. Today, I drive a friend to the supermarket, but on the way, my brakes fail and I kill a pedestrian. Driving my car, then, has turned out to be wrong in the "objective" sense, but not in the "subjective" sense—since I had every reason to think my brakes reliable, and my friend needed to get to the store. Thus an act is wrong in the objective sense if it is wrong in light of all the facts, knowable and unknowable, whereas it is wrong in the subjective sense if it is wrong in light of what the agent had good reason to believe. More precisely, an act is wrong in the subjective sense if it is wrong in light of the degrees of plausibility (or "subjective probabilities") the agent has reason to ascribe to relevant propositions.

Now the analysis I have proposed will clearly not work for 'wrong' in the objective sense. In the story, my driving my car turns out to be wrong in the objective sense, but it would not make sense for me to feel guilty over it, or for others to resent me for it. What about the subjective sense? It is this sense that really matters, for a theory for the subjective sense can offer moral guidance: even when we know we are ignorant of the relevant facts, we can use the theory, together with what we think we do know, to decide what acts to avoid on moral grounds.[4] Might the analysis I have proposed work, then, for 'wrong' in the subjective sense? Might an act be wrong in the subjective sense if and only if it is rational for the agent to feel guilty over the act and for others to resent him for it?

I think not. Wrongness, even in the subjective sense, is not the same as blameworthiness, and when the two diverge, the proposal seems most apt as an analysis of 'blameworthiness.'[5] Imagine that, in a paroxysm of grief, I speak rudely to a friend who offers condolences and so hurt his feelings. My rudeness is unprovoked but understandable in the circumstances. I have thus acted wrongly, but because of my agitated state, it may not make sense to blame me. If it does not, then my act is wrong in the subjective sense, but not blameworthy. An act is *blameworthy*, we might say, if and only if it makes sense for the agent to feel guilty over it, and for others to resent him for it—but we still need to ask what it means to call an act "morally wrong."

Why, then, should we need a distinct concept of "wrong" in the subjective sense, as opposed to "blameworthy"? The answer seems to be that the concepts of "right" and "wrong" are forward looking in a way that the concept of blameworthiness is not. The morally conscientious agent is one who asks himself which of the acts open to him are right and which are wrong and then rules out any act he judges wrong. That

4. This is argued in my "Act-Utilitarian Agreements," in *Values and Morals*, ed. Alvin I. Goldman and Jaegwon Kim (Dordrecht: D. Reidel Publishing Co., 1978), pp. 95–96.

5. R. B. Brandt, in *Ethical Theory* (Englewood Cliffs, N.J.: Prentice-Hall, 1959), argues that 'reprehensible' cannot be defined in terms of 'moral obligation' (p. 458) and then offers a definition of 'reprehensible' that is quite close, in some respects, to the one I am offering.

means, among other things, that the rightness or wrongness of an alternative does not depend on the agent's motives. Rather, conscientious motivation consists in trying to confine one's actions to what is right. Blame, in contrast, attaches to the agent in retrospect; the agent is blamed for acting with insufficient morally desirable motivation. Rightness is prospective; blame is retrospective.

What, then, might it mean to call an act wrong? Roughly, we might say, the standards of right and wrong are the standards we demand an agent use to rule out certain alternatives. In assessing blame, we apply two kinds of tests. First, we ask whether the agent's level of morally desirable motivation was satisfactory. If not, we ask whether there are extenuating circumstances that render the agent not fully responsible. Standards of right and wrong pertain to the first part: an agent's motives are morally acceptable if he is sufficiently motivated to avoid wrong acts. Standards for wrongness, then, are the standards such that an agent is prima facie blameworthy if he does not use them to rule out acts that violate them. The reason the blameworthiness is only prima facie is that facts about the person's motivational state may be extenuating. Blame thus depends both on standards of wrongness in the subjective sense and on standards for responsibility. Formally put, then, the definitions I propose are these: an act is *wrong* if and only if it violates standards for ruling out actions, such that if an agent in a normal frame of mind violated those standards because he was not substantially motivated to conform to them, he would be to blame. To say that he would *be to blame*, here, is to say that it would be rational for him to feel guilty and for others to resent him.

What I have done in my discussion so far is to suppose that we know what 'rational' means and to propose a way of interpreting the relation between rationality, on the one hand, and concepts that are "moral" in the narrow sense. In the next section, I propose in rough terms an analysis of 'rational' and plug it into the analyses I have given these moral concepts.

III. AN ANALYSIS OF 'RATIONAL' APPLIED TO MORAL TERMS

What does it mean to call something "rational"? One way of tackling such a question is to psychologize it. What, we may ask, is the psychological state of regarding something as rational, of taking it to be rational, of believing it rational? The answer I want to give is noncognitivistic. To call an action, belief, or attitude "rational," if I am on the right track, is not to express a proposition; it is to do something else. What that "something else" is I shall try to explain psychologistically, by saying what it is to think something rational.

Put cryptically, the hypothesis I shall develop is this: that to *think something rational* is to accept norms that permit it. This rough analysis needs much elucidation and refinement, and I will not be able to say here nearly all I think should be said. I do hope to give you some intimation of what I hope can be done along the lines I am suggesting.

Take first my use of the word 'norm.' By a "norm" here, I mean a possible rule or prescription, either general or specific. The prescription need not actually be made by anyone, or accepted by anyone, to count as a "norm" as I am using the term; I am thus using the term as a short way of saying "possible norm." The main thing to be explained, then, is not what a "norm" is, but what "accepting a norm" is—or more precisely, what it is for something to be permitted or required by "the norms" a person "accepts." I mean these latter notions to be psychological: they are meant to figure in an explanatory theory of human experience and action.

Consider next some schematic illustrations. Delilah, let us suppose, is pondering whether various of Samson's acts, beliefs, and emotions are rational. What is it, on the proposal, for her to conclude that one of Samson's acts, beliefs, or emotions indeed is rational? It is for her to accept norms that, as applied to Samson's situation as she thinks it to be, permit that act, belief, or emotion. Thus when Samson destroys the Philistine temple, Delilah considers the act rational if and only if she accepts norms that permit—for Samson's situation as she takes it to be—destroying the temple. She might, for instance, accept the norm, "When in the hands of one's enemies with no hope of escape, kill as many of them as possible, even if you must kill yourself in the process." Then if she believes that Samson is in the hands of his enemies with no hope of escape and that destroying the temple will kill as many of his enemies as possible, then she considers his action rational. Earlier, Samson believed Delilah loyal to him. Delilah, then, thinks this belief to have been rational if and only if she accepts norms for belief that, for Samson's situation at the time as she now conceives it, permit believing one's woman loyal to one. Samson hates the Philistines, and Delilah considers his hatred rational if and only if she accepts norms that, for his situation, permit such hatred.

Nothing I have said here, I stress, speaks to whether Samson's actions, beliefs, and emotions really were rational. My hypothesis is not that a person's action, belief, or emotion really is rational if someone—be it I, or the person in question, or a commentator—accepts norms that prescribe it for that person's circumstances. It is not directly a hypothesis about what it is for something to be rational at all. It is a hypothesis about what it is to *think* or *believe* something rational, to *regard* it as rational, to *consider* it rational. An observer believes an action, belief, or emotion *A* of mine to be rational, the hypothesis is, if and only if he accepts norms that permit *A* for my circumstances. It follows that, if we want to decide what really is rational, we shall have to decide what norms to accept ourselves—for that is what it is to form an opinion as to the rationality of something.

To believe something rational, I have said, is to accept norms that permit it. In this cryptic form, the proposal says very little, and even what little it says will need to be refined and modified in various ways.

Many of its problems I shall not be able to address here. I will, though, try to say a little about two sets of problems: first, what a norm is and what it is to accept one, and second, what distinguishes norms of rationality from other kinds of norms, such as norms of morality, norms of etiquette, and aesthetic norms.

I turn first to moral norms, and the narrowly moral notions, "blameworthy" and "wrong." In analyzing these notions in the previous section, I took the term 'rational' as understood. If we now combine these analyses with our rough analysis of 'rational,' we can derive an account of the distinction between moral norms and norms of rationality. All norms, we can say, are norms of rationality, but moral norms in particular are norms for guilt and resentment. Consider first what it is for an action to be "blameworthy." The analyses given so far tell us this: (1) An observer thinks an act blameworthy, or morally reprehensible, if and only if he thinks it rational for the agent to feel guilty over the act, and for others to resent the agent for it. (2) To think something 'rational' is to accept norms that prescribe it. Therefore, we may conclude, to think an act morally reprehensible is to accept norms that prescribe, for such a situation, guilt on the part of the agent and resentment on the part of others.

Next consider the term 'morally wrong' (in the subjective sense). The standards for whether an act is wrong, we have said, are the standards such that guilt and resentment are prima facie rational if the agent is not disposed to rule out alternatives that violate them. Thus to *think* an act *wrong* is to accept norms for guilt and resentment that, prima facie, would sanction guilt and resentment if the act were preformed. 'Prima facie' here means before questions of the psychological peculiarities of the agent are raised—the psychological peculiarities, that is, that bear on whether the agent is to be considered fully responsible. Norms for wrongness are thus explained in terms of norms for guilt and resentment.

This proposal as it stands smacks of circularity; the terms 'prima facie blameworthy' and 'responsible' seem to be defined in terms of each other. The psychic makeup of the agent, after all, has some bearing not only on whether the agent is responsible, but on what acts open to him are wrong. Suppose, for instance, that an act is the only one that is eligible, in the sense that all alternatives to it would leave the agent desperately unhappy. That fact may, in our opinion, tend to justify the act morally: it might be that even though the act would otherwise be wrong, this consideration renders it right. A moral adviser, after all, might sincerely advise the agent not to regard the action he was contemplating as wrong, even though it is of a kind that would normally be wrong, and do so precisely because of the psychological effects the alternatives would have on the agent. That, in any case, is what we might well think, and an analysis should allow for the possibility. In what ways, then, are we saying that the "psychological peculiarities" of an agent bear on his degree of moral responsibility, as opposed to the rightness and wrongness of the acts open to him? So far, there is no clear answer. Standards for responsibility, I have said, are standards for when an agent is to blame for acting on prima facie blameworthy motivations. Prima facie blameworthy motivations are motives for which an agent is to blame if he is fully responsible. Hence although 'blameworthy' itself has been defined independently, the terms 'prima facie blameworthy' and 'responsible' have been defined only in terms of each other.

This circularity, I think, can be eliminated as follows: consider an agent who has various psychological peculiarities, and an act for which I would consider the agent to blame if I thought him normal. Our problem, recall, is to untangle whether, because of his psychological peculiarities, I regard the act as right, or whether, rather, I consider the act to be wrong but excusable. The test I propose is this. Imagine the agent for the moment rendered normal but expecting to reacquire his "psychological peculiarities" once he had decided how to act on this occasion. He thus must take these psychological peculiarities into account in deciding what to do, though he is not presently subject to them apart from his belief that he has them. Whether I consider the act to be wrong, then, is a matter of whether I accept norms that would sanction guilt and resentment if the agent, while temporarily rendered normal, were to perform that act.

A moral norm forbidding an action, I have proposed, is a norm of rationality governing guilt and resentment. We might likewise speculate that all norms are primarily norms of rationality, and the various different kinds of norms governing, say, a given action—moral norms, aesthetic norms, norms of propriety—are each norms for the rationality of some one kind of attitude one can have toward an action. Just as moral norms are norms for the rationality of guilt and resentment, the aesthetic norms that apply to an action might be norms for the rationality of kinds of aesthetic appreciation of actions, and norms of propriety might be norms for the rationality of shock at an action. Norms of moral praiseworthiness, we can say, are norms for the rationality of an emotion of moral approbation. To call an action praiseworthy, on this proposal, is to say that it would make sense to feel moral approbation of the agent for having performed it. To say that, in turn, is to express one's acceptance of norms that permit that feeling, given the facts of the situation as one takes them to be.

IV. ACCEPTING A NORM AND BEING IN ITS GRIP

To think something rational, I have been proposing, is to accept norms that permit that thing. This is cryptic and incomplete in many ways, and I shall be able to take up just one central respect in which it is incomplete. The analysis as I have stated it gives the meaning of 'rational' in terms of another notion that has so far been left unexplained—in terms of a person's "accepting norms." This places great demands on the notion of accepting a norm.

The most straightforward way to elucidate the "acceptance of norms" would be further analysis: we might look for an analysis of what it means to say things like "Mary accepts the following norms: . . ." I doubt, though, that such an analysis is possible. Instead of trying for an analysis, I shall engage in incipient psychological theorizing. "Accepting a norm," I want to suggest, is a significant kind of psychological state that we are far from entirely understanding. What we can hope to do is not define this state precisely but to point to it.

Start by considering a case of "weakness of will." Suppose I "can't get myself to stop" eating nuts at a party. What is happening? One commonsense description is this: I think it "makes sense" to stop eating the nuts—indeed that it doesn't "make sense" to go on eating them—but I nevertheless go on. In this case, it seems, I accept a norm that prescribes eating no more nuts but go on eating them even so.

In this commonsense account, it is assumed that the acceptance of a norm is motivating, at least to a degree: believing I ought to stop tends to make me stop. On this occasion, though, the motivation that stems from my accepting a norm is "overpowered" by motivation of another kind: my craving or appetite for nuts. The craving is not itself a matter of my accepting norms; indeed such cravings are sometimes referred to as "animal": we think that they are motivations of a kind we share with beasts.

This is a picture of two motivational systems in conflict. One system is of a kind we think peculiar to human beings; it works through a person's accepting norms. We might call this kind of motivation *normative* motivation, and the putative psychological faculty involved the *normative control system*. The other putative system we might call the *animal control system*, since it, we think, is the part of our motivational system that we share with the beasts. Let us treat this picture as a vague psychological hypothesis.

"Weakness of will" involves conflict, and so far in my discusion, the conflict has been one between the norms a person accepts and an appetite. Many apparent cases of "weakness of will," though, are not of this kind. Often what we experience is not a conflict between the norms we accept and a bodily appetite but a conflict between our "better judgment" and powerful social motivations. We are paralyzed by embarrassment, or a desire to ingratiate, or some other motivation that is peculiarly social. Examples abound: I may be unable to get myself to walk out of a lecture, even though it is important for me to be somewhere else. I may find myself unable to say something that will be painful to my listener, even though I think it needs to be said. My discussion of "normative control" seems not to have addressed cases like these.

An especially powerful demonstration of the kind of conflict I have in mind lies in Milgram's series of experiments on compliance. Subjects of his experiments were told to administer electric shocks—shocks that were increasingly painful and eventually lethal—to another subject (who in fact was not being shocked but was acting as a confederate of the experimenter). Roughly two-thirds of the subjects eventually did all they were ordered to do, although they were upset and protested vigorously.[6]

Now when we read about these experiments, we are appalled by what the subjects did. Their actions violate norms that we accept. The near uniformity with which the subjects substantially acquiesced, however, should suggest to each of us, "Had I been a subject in one of these experiments before I first read or heard of them, I too would have cooperated with the experimenter—perhaps fully, and almost certainly more than I would like to acknowledge. I would have felt immensely disturbed about the situation in which I found myself, and I would have protested vigorously and regarded the experimenter as a madman. Nevertheless, I probably would have complied."

A typical subject in one of these experiments clearly experiences conflict of some sort; that is shown by his protests and his extreme agitation. The conflict, though, is not between a norm he accepts and a bodily appetite. It seems rather to be a conflict between one norm and another. The subject accepts the norm against intentional harm in terms of which we ourselves, as we read about the experiment, condemn his behavior. Nevertheless, he obeys an experimenter who tells him to violate that norm, and he does so, it would appear, because he is strongly motivated to be polite and cooperative—because to refuse, having originally agreed to participate in the experiment, would be uncooperative and insulting to the experimenter. The conflict, we might therefore say, is between opposing norms: a norm of nonharm, on the one hand, and norms of politeness and cooperativeness, on the other.

What is the role of norms here? The conflict is between one set of norms and another, true enough, but that suggests a symmetry that is specious. The two sets of norms play different psychological roles. The norm of noninfliction of harm prevails in the judgments of detached observers, whereas the norms of cooperativeness and politeness control the agent in the heat of social encounter. Ordinary language has devices that come close to labeling this contrast. We, as judges, accept a norm against infliction of harm and accept that this norm, in the situation of Milgram's subjects, overrides those norms of politeness and cooperativeness that we also accept. The subjects, on the other hand, do not genuinely accept that, in their situation, norms of politeness and cooperativeness override all other norms. Rather, we might say, they are *in the grip* of these norms. In common language, then, the contrast is between *accepting* a norm (or, more precisely, *accepting* that one set of norms outweighs another in a given situation) with *being in the grip of* a norm.

6. Stanley Milgram, *Obedience to Authority* (New York: Harper & Row, 1974). A fascinating discussion of these experiments and their implications is to be found in John Sabini and Maury Silver, *Moralities of Everyday Life* (Oxford: Oxford University Press, 1982), esp. chaps. 3–5, 9–11.

Now presumably, whatever happens when I am "in the grip" of a norm that I do not "accept" happens also, much of the time, when I do accept a norm. Take again our ordinary norms of politeness and co-operativeness. In my usual dealings with people, I not only accept these norms as having some weight; I accept them as having enough weight to override any conflicting norms that apply to my situation. I normally give people directions when asked, even if I am in a slight hurry, and this I do not out of weakness of will, but because I accept that it makes sense to help people who need it when the cost is small. In these cases, we would not say that I am "in the grip" of the norms of politeness and cooperativeness that guide my conduct, since I accept them as reasonably controlling in the situation. It may well be, though, that these norms would control my behavior even if I did not accept them or did not accept them as having greatest weight in my situation. In this respect, my psychological state is like the state of being in the grip of a norm.

We need, then, some term for what is common to situations in which I am "in the grip" of a norm and situations of the more usual kind: situations in which I accept a norm as rightly controlling on balance but would be in its grip if I did not. I propose the colorless, rather technical term *internalizing* a norm.

I have pointed to three sources of motivation that can be teased out of commonsense acounts of weakness of will: appetites, the internalization of norms, and the acceptance of norms. If there are distinctions of this kind to be drawn, how are they tied to ascriptions of rationality? I proposed that rationality has something to do with norms: to call something rational is to express one's acceptance of norms that, on balance, permit it. Once "accepting" a norm has been distinguished from "internalizing" it, we need to ask which of the two belongs in the analysis of 'rational.' Now in the examples, the answer seems clear: it is "accepting" norms that matters here, not "internalizing" them. What, after all, does a subject in one of Milgram's compliance experiments think it rational to do? If his plight is genuinely one of "weakness of will," that is presumably because he thinks that it makes no sense to cooperate but finds himself cooperating nevertheless. In other words, he does what he thinks irrational. Now what he actually does, in this case, is a matter of the norms that have him "in their grip"—norms of politeness and cooperativeness that he has internalized. What he thinks it "rational" to do, on the other hand, is what is required by norms against inflicting pain and danger—and these are the norms he "accepts" as having most weight in his situation. Thinking something rational or irrational thus seems to be a matter not of internalizing norms but of accepting them.

V. THE NATURE OF ACCEPTANCE

How might we explain the acceptance of norms as a psychological phenomenon? I shall only be able to give the briefest sketch of some lines for investigation that strike me as promising.

In the first place, I have distinguished "accepting" a norm from "internalizing" a norm, and so let me say briefly how I think we should understand internalizing a norm. The capacity to do so, I suggest, is one we share with other mammals, especially those who live in groups. Two dogs meeting on neutral ground will engage in elaborate "rituals," and this anthropomorphic language suggests that something akin to humans' internalizing norms may be in play. As in the human case, these animal interactions follow certain regular patterns, and the patterns seem, in a way, to have a rationale. They presumably constitute adaptations; that is to say, they are the result of natural selection favoring these patterns. Internalizing a norm, I suggest, involves tendencies toward action and emotion, tendencies that are coordinated with the tendencies of others in ways that constitute matched biological adaptations, or are the results of matched adaptations. We share the capacity to internalize norms with other animals, although the greater complexity of human social life may well mean that our capacities to internalize norms are more refined than those of any other animal.[7]

If that is what it is to "internalize" a norm, what is it to "accept" one? To understand acceptance, I suggest, we should look to language. Think of what language has to do with motivation, apart from simply making us aware of the states of affairs we confront. Although the most obvious function of language is to convey information, much of language is more than merely informative. Language is used to exhort, to criticize, and to summon up emotions. Language influences actions and emotions not only by conveying information that prompts those actions or emotions but in many other ways as well.

A central way in which language affects human motivation is by enabling people to share a picture of an absent situation. Reactions can then be shared—not only reactions to the immediate situation but to past, future, and hypothetical situations as well. Various kinds of reactions can be expressed in various ways: emotional responses can be shared simply by evincing them. Hypothetical decisions—decisions on what to do in the place of someone who is in the situation being discussed—can be expressed in language. Emotionally laden words can be used to label actions and characters. Explicit precepts can be formulated. Discussion, then, allows for shared evaluation.

A capacity for shared evaluation would be biologically fitness-enhancing in a species with a complex social life. Those who can work out together reactions to an absent situation—what to do and what to feel—are ready for similar situations. They are better prepared than they would

7. The classic discussion of coordination in the broad sense I have in mind is Thomas Schelling, *The Strategy of Conflict* (Cambridge, Mass.: Harvard University Press, 1960), chap. 2. It is, of course, a theme that runs through the political theories of Hobbes and Hume. Matched adaptations are treated in John Maynard Smith's theory of "evolutionarily stable strategies" (see "The Evolution of Behavior," *Scientific American* 239 [1978]: 136–45, and *Evolution and the Theory of Games* [Cambridge: Cambridge University Press, 1982]).

otherwise be to do what is advantageous in a new situation, and they can rely on complex schemes of interpersonal coordination. On general evolutionary grounds, then, we might expect shared evaluation to figure centrally in a complex social life.

Working out, in community, what to do, what to think, and how to feel in absent situations, if it has these biological functions, must presumably influence what we do, think, and feel when faced with like situations. It is in such control of action, belief, and emotion, I suggest, that we can find a place for phenomena that constitute acceptance of norms, as opposed merely to internalizing them. When we work out at a distance, in community, what to do or think or feel in a situation we are discussing, we come to accept norms for the situation. This is the tentative hypothesis I want to propose; I shall be calling the discussion involved "normative discussion."

We evaluate in community, but part of what goes on is individual. Groups do, to be sure, reach normative consensus in many situations, but sometimes they do not. Even when consensus is reached, it may well emerge from individuals' taking positions and then, to some degree, persuading each other. Acceptance of norms is tied not only to a consensus that emerges from normative discussion but also to individuals' taking positions in normative discussion. This taking of normative positions I shall call "normative avowal." By 'avowal' here I mean to include a wide range of kinds of expression we might count as taking a position in normative discussion—in the discussion of absent states of affairs. The simplest kind might simply be the evincing of an emotion toward an absent situation. Other kinds of avowal are linguistically more explicit: we may express a hypothetical decision in words or label an action in emotively charged words. To understand acceptance of norms, we need to look to such avowal—the kind of avowal from which consensus emerges when it does and which may persist even without approach to consensus.

What is the connection of avowal to acceptance? As a first approximation, we might say that to accept a norm is to be prepared to avow it in normative discussion—at least when the discussion is reasonably unconstrained, so that the avowal would be spontaneous rather than calculated. Acceptance, though, involves more than this; it involves a response to demands for consistency. Normative discussion consists of taking positions; even a conversational groan stakes out a position. Consensus may then be reached by a mechanism that is incipiently Socratic. Discussants hold each other to consistency in their positions and thus force each other to shift positions by exposing inconsistency. A person, then, must take positions in order to engage in normative discussion responsibly, and in doing so, he exposes himself to pressures toward consistency. To accept a norm, we might say, is to be disposed to avow it in unconstrained normative discussion, as a result of the workings of demands for consistency in the positions one takes in normative discussion.

To prepare oneself to meet demands for consistency requires a strong imaginative life. A person will engage in imaginative rehearsal for actual normative discussion; he practices by holding himself to consistency. I do not mean to suggest that the pressure for consistency will be as strong as it is in good philosophical discussion, but there will be some demand for consistency, and it may exert a significant pressure. From this imaginative rehearsal, a kind of imaginative persona may emerge, an "I" who develops a consistent position to take in normative discussion. It is then, perhaps, that we can speak more clearly of what the person accepts; he then has a worked out normative position to take in unconstrained contexts.

Why expose oneself to these demands for consistency? We do so naturally, but what selection pressures might have shaped us to do so? The answer should be clear from what I have said. The demands for consistency are reciprocal, and the system of mutual demands is part of a coordinating device. It is partly because of these mutual demands that there is any hope of reaching consensus in normative discussion. A person who refuses these demands must therefore be a poor candidate for cooperation of any kind—and in human life, cooperation is vital. It is fitness enhancing, then, to stand ready to engage in normative discussion and so to accept the demands for consistency that involves.

In the picture I have sketched, the difference between accepting a norm and internalizing it is this. Accepting a norm is something that we do primarily in the context of normative discussion, actual and imaginary. We take positions and thereby expose ourselves to demands for consistency. Normative discussion of a situation influences action and emotion in like situations. It is then that we can speak of norms as "governing" action and emotion, and it is through this governance that normative discussion serves to coordinate. The state of accepting a norm, then, is a syndrome of tendencies toward action and avowal—a syndrome produced by the language-infused system of coordination peculiar to human beings. The system works through discussion of absent situations, and it allows for the delicate adjustments of coordination that human social life requires. Internalizing a norm is also a matter of coordinating propensities, but propensities of a different kind: these propensities work independently of normative discussion.

VI. CONCLUDING REMARKS

There remains much to be done before the kind of analysis I am proposing could stand much chance of seeming plausible. To call something rational, I have proposed, is to express one's acceptance of a system of norms that permits that thing. I have speculated on the psychological nature of accepting norms, in an attempt to lend plausibility to my claim that there is such a state and that it plays an important part in human life. Many other things I have not discussed. I have not talked about what it is to express a state of mind—be it belief in a straightforwardly factual proposition or acceptance of a system of norms. I have not said how we can give the meaning of a term by talking about the state of mind a speaker expresses when he uses that term.

Other problems will no doubt leap to mind. An observer may accept many different norms that apply to a situation, and some of these norms may weigh in opposing directions. Norms of rationality apply to a person's subjective situation, in that facts a person has no way of knowing do not affect whether an action, belief, or attitude of his is rational. A person who contemplates the rationality of another person's acts, beliefs, or emotions normally does not take himself to know everything about the other person's situation. An explanation of what it is to think an act rational does not automatically yield an account of what is involved in thinking more complicated things about rationality, such as "Samson would never do anything so irrational as *that!*" Handling these considerations will require not only elucidation of the analysis but also elaboration and revision.

Moreover, I have said nothing here about a central problem for any theory of rationality: what constitutes the "objectivity" we sometimes want to attribute to judgments of rationality. Much of what is involved in claims of objectivity for normative judgments, I think, can be explained in terms of conversational demands in normative discussion. Normative discussion, as I have pictured it, is a communal activity: we subject ourselves to mutual influence and form a partial community of judgment. To put a judgment forth as objective, I want to say, is to make an appropriate response a requirement for membership in one's community of judgment—or at least this gives as much of ordinary claims to objectivity as is tenable.

All this, however, is for other occasions. What I have done here is to sketch part of a program. Moral judgments, I have suggested, concern the rationality of certain specifically moral emotions. To judge something rational is to accept a system of norms that permits it, in the circumstances as one thinks them to be. The psychological state of accepting a norm is partly to be understood in terms of the ways it underlies normative discussion. In biological terms, the capacities that underlie normative discussion are coordinating devices; they allow for the kinds of flexible, complex coordination that is peculiar to human social life. That is the rough hypothesis I have sketched in this paper, and I hope it is worth further exploration.

[8]

SYMPOSIUM ON NORMS IN MORAL AND SOCIAL THEORY*

Virtus Normativa: Rational Choice Perspectives†

Philip Pettit

Norms are an important species of social institution, on a par with conventions, customs, laws, and other brands of established regularity. They often overlap with those other institutions, so that the same regularity can be both a norm and a law, for example. But still, they retain a distinctive profile. Like the other institutions norms reinforce certain patterns of behavior, but they do so in their own way, by representing those patterns as peculiarly desirable or obligatory. Norms are generally operative, for example, in supporting patterns of behavior like truth-telling, promise-keeping, and abstinence from theft, fraud, and violence. They also play a role in supporting familiar virtues like loyalty, fairness, integrity, and courtesy, as indeed they play a role in supporting less attractive dispositions like conformism and vengefulness.[1]

Most visions of the good society allot an important job to certain norms, relying on their presence to generate or reinforce crucial features of the society: features such as the dedication of public officials to the common interest, the acceptance by people at large of certain sorts of official decision, their participation in different forms of social and political

* The articles for this symposium were generated by a conference on norms, held at the University of Chicago, May 19–21, 1989, with support from the National Endowment for the Humanities, the Center for Ethics, Rationality and Society at the University of Chicago, and Jerry Knoll of Washington, D.C.

† I am grateful for helpful comments received from Alan Bellett, John Braithwaite, Geoffrey Brennan, Bob Goodin, Alan Hamlin, Chandran Kukathas, and Fred Schick. I am also grateful for the many useful remarks made at seminars where the article was presented including the *Ethics* symposium in Chicago, where Brian Barry and Karen Cook were commentators. I made use in particular of remarks by Larry Becker, Josh Cohen, Jon Elster, Allan Gibbard, Maggie Gilbert, Ned Hall, Russell Hardin, David Lewis, Steven Lukes, Michael Otsuka, and Michael Smith. The article was finalized while I held a Visiting Fellowship at Corpus Christi College, Oxford, with visiting facilities at Nuffield College, and I am grateful to both institutions for their support.

1. Thus I follow Jon Elster in acknowledging "Norms of Revenge" (see his article in this issue). But I differ from Elster, in so far as he seems to think that norms cannot double in other roles, say as laws. He apparently thinks that a norm is operative only when people actually deliberate or are led to action in a certain way. This is the source of his objection to a rational choice account of norms, for he also thinks that rational choice requires a particular path to action. I differ from him on both points, as will be clear later.

Ethics 100 (July 1990): 725–755

activity, and their contribution to the achievement of public goals that are of benefit to everyone. True, other visions imagine the desired social pattern emerging, as by an invisible hand, from the interactions of individuals who may themselves lack any sense of that outcome, and in these pictures norms play no role in the generation of order. But even those visions, like the ones that give pride of place to norms, assume at least that the order they envisage will not be undermined by the emergence of antisocial norms, say norms of cooperation among manipulative or criminal subgroups.

This inevitable appeal to norms raises the question motivating my article. The question is, What, if anything, makes certain norms resilient; what ensures that in suitable circumstances those norms can be relied on to emerge and persist? In a phrase, what constitutes *virtus normativa*? Unless this question can be answered, then the visionaries who hail certain norms as desirable, for example, can never be sure that the norms are dependable; thus they can never be sure that they are not indulging impractical utopian dreams. The visionaries who are challenged include at one extreme anarchists and at the other those who believe in a strong state, say a state of a social democratic kind. Anarchists have to show that people would behave in a manner conducive to social life without a state to restrain them.[2] Social democrats need to show that the public officials and politicians whom they would empower can be relied on to pursue the public interest.[3]

The article is written within the tradition of rational choice theory. That theory starts from the assumption that two sorts of factor explain a good deal of human behavior. The assumption is almost canonically formulated by John Harsanyi. "People's behavior can be largely explained in terms of two dominant interests: economic gain and social acceptance."[4] The theory suggests that norms will be resilient if—though not necessarily only if—circumstances are such that it is in people's individual interest, economic or social, to honor them. It will be in their economic interest, broadly conceived, if the direct self-interested benefit of honoring the norms, in particular the sort of benefit that can be assigned monetary value, exceeds the cost; it will be in their social interest if honoring the norms promotes the esteem, affection, or pleasure with which they are viewed and this indirect self-interested benefit exceeds the cost.[5] The

2. See Michael Taylor, *Anarchy and Cooperation* (London: Wiley, 1976).

3. See Philip Pettit, "Towards a Social Democratic Theory of the State," *Political Studies* 35 (1987): 42–55.

4. John Harsanyi, "Rational Choice Models of Behavior versus Functionalist and Conformist Theories," *World Politics* 22 (1969): 513–38. The postulate is quoted with approval in Michael Taylor, "Rationality and Revolutionary Collective Action," in *Rationality and Revolution*, ed. Michael Taylor (Cambridge: Cambridge University Press, 1987), p. 66.

5. Here I am suggesting a reading of Harsanyi's postulate under which only current social acceptance matters. What is also undoubtedly important is the social acceptance given to an agent in the past—say, by parents—for certain forms of behavior and the good feeling therefore promoted by such behavior. See John Braithwaite, *Crime, Shame and Reintegration* (Cambridge: Cambridge University Press, 1989).

task of showing whether certain norms are resilient in certain circumstances comes down to that of seeing whether it is possible to derive those norms, under these circumstances, from the assumption that people satisfy Harsanyi's postulate.

Harsanyi's postulate requires some comment even at this early point. As I interpret it, it says that the fact that an option promises to promote an agent's economic gain or social acceptance makes it *pro tanto* desirable. Although the postulate represents gain and acceptance as dominant interests, it does not weight them against other goods or against each other. Thus it enables us to make firm predictions about an individual only for choices where one option does better by gain or acceptance and is not otherwise very costly.[6] In predicting in this way that people will not generally frustrate their economic and social interests, the postulate does not allege that they explicitly calculate about gain and acceptance. The idea is that, whatever the basis on which they make their choices, the fact that a sort of choice which they are in the habit of making becomes inimical to those interests will at least make them pause. No choice of a kind they commonly make is likely to undermine both their economic and social prospects.

This article is not intended as an impartial overview of the different rational choice ways of deriving norms, though an overview is sketched in passing. The main point is to defend a partisan thesis: that the standard mode of derivation adumbrated, if not always spelled out, in the rational choice literature is only one possibility and that we should also pay attention to a sort of derivation which that literature generally derides. The standard strategy of derivation is behavior-based; the strategy identified here is attitude-based. They are not incompatible approaches, and my case for the attitude-based strategy is not meant to cast doubts on the more standard alternative. The intention is to open doors, not to close them. I believe that some norms may only be derivable by the standard strategy, others only by that which I propose, as I believe that some norms may be derivable by both strategies, and some by neither.

The article is in five sections. In the first I offer a definition of norms, elaborating on the observations made above. In the second I distinguish the two strategies of derivation and try to explain why the attitude-based strategy has been ignored. Then in the third section I show how an attitude-based derivation might go. In a short fourth section I look at the definition and derivation of norms, if norms are assumed to require not just fulfillment of the conditions mentioned in the first section but also the common belief that those conditions are fulfilled; this section is something of an appendix to the main paper and may be skipped without serious loss. Finally, in a short conclusion I summarize results so far and show that those who think the rational choice approach cannot make

6. Even without weighting of course, the postulate will enable us to make the prediction that as a sort of option becomes more hostile to either interest, it is less likely to be chosen by a random individual, and it will be chosen less often in the relevant population.

room for the moral aspect of many norms may be mistaken; I sketch an attitude-based derivation for a norm of moralizing about conformity to other norms.

How original is the attitude-based style of derivation that I propose in this article? The derivation will be a novel offering in rational choice circles, as already mentioned; it assumes a rejection of the view, hallowed within those circles, that enforcing a norm necessarily imposes costs on the enforcers. But if the thesis is an original offering in this context, I should stress that it will not appear so in the broader historical picture. The thesis links up with the line about norms which Adam Smith defends in *The Theory of Moral Sentiments*. I might have taken this passage, for example, as my text. "What reward is most proper for promoting the practice of truth, justice and humanity? The confidence, esteem and love of those we live with. Humanity does not desire to be great, but to be beloved."[7]

THE DEFINITION OF NORMS

Almost all accounts of norms emphasize at least these two requirements. First, that if a regularity is a norm in a society, then it must be a regularity with which people generally conform; lip service is not enough on its own.[8] And second, that if a regularity is a norm, then people in the society generally approve of conformity and disapprove of deviance: they may believe, for example, that everyone ought to conform, that conformity is an obligation of some sort.[9]

My inclination is to honor both of these requirements in defining norms. Perhaps the best argument for the first is suggested by the opening sentence of R. M. Hare's *Language of Morals*: "If we were to ask of a person 'What are his moral principles?' the way in which we could be most sure of a true answer would be by studying what he *did*."[10] If we want to identify a society's norms, then equally the best way is surely by studying what people do there. And that means that a norm is a regularity with which most people in the society must conform. There are regularities which fail this requirement while meeting the second but we shall not cast them as social norms; we might describe them as social standards.

7. Adam Smith, *The Theory of Moral Sentiments*, ed. D. D. Raphael and A. L. Macfie (Indianapolis: Liberty Classics, 1982), p. 166.

8. See David Shwayder, *The Stratification of Behavior* (New York: Humanities Press, 1965), p. 253; Kent Bach and R. M. Harnish, *Linguistic Communication and Speech Acts* (Cambridge, Mass.: MIT Press, 1979), p. 271; Robert Sugden, *The Economics of Rights, Co-operation and Welfare* (Oxford: Basil Blackwell, 1986), p. 166; Robert Axelrod, "An Evolutionary Approach to Norms," *American Political Science Review* 8 (1986): 1097; and Michael Taylor, *The Possibility of Cooperation* (Cambridge: Cambridge University Press, 1987), p. 29.

9. See David Lewis, *Convention* (Cambridge, Mass.: Harvard University Press, 1969), p. 97; plus Shwayder; Bach and Harnish; Sugden; Axelrod, "An Evolutionary Approach to Norms"; and Taylor, *The Possibility of Cooperation*.

10. R. M. Hare, *The Language of Morals* (Oxford: Oxford University Press, 1952), p. 1.

The second requirement hardly needs defending, since a regularity would clearly fail to be a norm of a society unless it commanded general commendation in the society.[11] But there is a question about how precisely to define it. In fact there are a number of questions. Ought we to allow the approval or disapproval to be based, say, on the benefit or harm to the agent himself or should we require that it be based on the public interest, at least as the agent sees that? Should we think of approval and disapproval as something which anyone can give anyone else or as something only available in any instance from designated others? Ought we to require that everyone approves of conformity, and disapproves of deviance, in relation to everyone's behavior, his own included, or only in relation to everyone else's? Should we be content if everyone approves or disapproves case by case—*in sensu diviso*—or do we stipulate that everyone has an attitude to the general state of affairs: everyone approves or disapproves *in sensu composito*?[12] Finally, do we really want the requirement to stipulate "everyone all of the time" or is "nearly everyone most of the time" going to be enough?

It would be exceedingly tedious to argue these questions one by one, trying to find the answer which best honors common usage. I propose to identify the right answer in each case by a methodological consideration: that we should make it as easy as possible in this regard for a regularity to count as a norm. The matters raised in these questions are ones to which we commonly pay no attention—we overlook the distinctions in play—and it would be bad practice to define a norm in a way which required that we took a stricter rather than a more relaxed view of those matters. Applying this principle then, and letting "nearly everyone" stand for "nearly everyone most of the time," the second requirement will be this: that nearly everyone, on whatever basis, approves *in sensu diviso* of nearly everyone else he finds conforming—that is, approves of his conforming, approves of him so far as he conforms—and disapproves of nearly everyone else he finds deviating.

Many will object that this lax version of the second requirement employs a notion of approval—and equally disapproval—which is not to be found in everyday usage. The objection is that if I approve of an action only because it suits my particular purposes, then that is not approval, properly speaking; approval proper must be based on principle or must be suited to the social role of the approver.[13] I am not worried about this objection, since I do not care very much about picking up everyday usage. But in any case I think that my generous notion of

11. It might be a norm of course of a subgroup in the society without being generally commended; it would only be required to be commended in the subgroup (see Axelrod, "An Evolutionary Approach to Norms").

12. On this distinction, see Lewis, *Convention*, pp. 64–66.

13. See Philippa Foot, "Approval," in her *Virtues and Vices* (Berkeley: University of California Press, 1978).

approval does have everyday resonance. We speak of someone's expressing approval, not just when he judges an action right or best all things considered but also when he simply likes it. Approval in my sense is nothing less than that broad sort of attitude to which acts of expressing approval testify; it is what expressions of approval express.

But though my lax formulation of this second requirement makes it as easy as possible for a regularity to count as a norm, it does not make it as easy as you might think. Notice in particular that not only must conformity attract approval; equally, deviance must elicit disapproval. Indeed the negative claim is the crucial one, for if we disapprove of someone's not Φ-ing and do not disapprove of his Φ-ing, that is tantamount to approving of the Φ-ing. The claim means that a practice of supererogatory virtue, even one that becomes fairly general, is not going to count as a norm of the society. Why this restriction? Because here we reach a limit where further laxity would put us misleadingly out of line with everyday usage. That a sort of action is normative in a society is not compatible in ordinary parlance with its being regarded as supererogatory. And so I prefer the stricter formulation. The strictness in question may not come to much of course. It is unlikely that a supererogatory type of act will be so commonly performed as to meet the first requirement of general conformity.

Do these first two requirements call for any obvious supplement in the definition of a norm? I believe they do, though the supplement I have in mind is almost universally ignored in the literature. It is surely not going to be enough for normative status that a regularity commands general conformity and that conformity attracts approval, deviance disapproval. For what if there is no connection between these two facts; what if the approval and disapproval are epiphenomenal, playing no part in ensuring the conformity? In such a case I think it is clear that we would hesitate to regard the regularity as a norm. Not that there are any obvious examples of such a case in the offing.[14] It's just that with all the regularities we actually regard as normative, we see the pattern of approval and disapproval as contributing, at least in some way, to the conformity. That is why we lay stress on this pattern in trying to inculcate the norms in our children.

We should add therefore a third requirement to our first two. This is a requirement to the following effect: that the fact that nearly everyone approves appropriately of conformity and disapproves of deviance helps to ensure that nearly everyone conforms. The requirement is not, of course, that people are moved by the consideration that nearly everyone approves and disapproves in the appropriate pattern. It does not matter

14. We do describe rules of logic as norms of reason, and it is sometimes urged that our conformity to these is explicable in evolutionary terms (see Neil Tennant, "Two Problems for Evolutionary Epistemology," *Ratio* 1 [1988]: 47–63). But surely our conformity is not wholly explicable in these terms; surely we are responsive also to the approval which conformity wins and the ridicule which deviance hazards.

what considerations move people deliberatively, what considerations come up in their practical reasoning. At least it does not matter so long as the fact that nearly everyone approves and disapproves appropriately helps to ensure that nearly everyone conforms. That condition would certainly be fulfilled were people to be moved by the consideration of what others approve and disapprove but such reasoning is not required. The condition will be fulfilled, for example, if the considerations that move agents to conform are ones whose relevance or weight is due to the pattern of other people's approval and disapproval; they might be considerations which have been made salient by the approval and disapproval of others, such as considerations as to the goodness and badness of certain options. Equally the condition will be fulfilled if the approval or disapproval of others would come into play and help to produce conformity in the event of a failure by whatever considerations are operative now—say, economic ones—to support such conformity: that is to say, if the approval and disapproval of others serve as standby supports for conformity.[15]

We have identified three requirements that certainly ought to be built into the definition of a norm, two of them commonly recognized, one—perhaps because it is so obviously necessary—not. Recent accounts of norms also tend to build in a further sort of requirement. This is that not only should requirements like those we have canvased be fulfilled, it should also be a matter of common belief that they are fulfilled. I find this requirement congenial, but I propose to ignore it for the moment. We will return in the fourth section below to the case for honoring it in the definition of norms and to the possibility of deriving norms, thus redefined.

The requirements assembled so far are sufficient to give us a workable definition of norms. It goes like this.

> A regularity, R, in the behavior of members of a population, P, when they are agents in a recurrent situation, S, is a *norm* if and only if, in any instance of S among members of P,
>
> 1. nearly everyone conforms to R;
> 2. nearly everyone approves of nearly anyone else's conforming and disapproves of nearly anyone else's deviating; and
> 3. the fact that nearly everyone approves and disapproves on this pattern helps to ensure that nearly everyone conforms.[16]

This definition is modeled on David Lewis's definition of a convention, differing from some versions of that definition only in clauses 2 and 3. Lewis's corresponding clauses are that nearly everyone expects nearly

15. Notice that my formulation of the third requirement allows me to think that a norm may also be a law, even a law such that people's actual reason for conforming to it is the penalty attached. Here there is a contrast with Elster's approach in "Norms of Revenge."

16. If norms are thought to come in degrees, the phrase "if and only if" can be replaced by "to the extent that" (see Axelrod, "An Evolutionary Approach to Norms," p. 1097).

everyone else to conform and nearly everyone prefers to conform on condition that the others do, since universal conformity solves a coordination problem.[17] It is important to recognize, however, that these definitions are in no way exclusive of one another. It is more than likely that a regularity which is a convention in a society will also be in our sense a norm. The point comes up again in the next section.[18]

Beyond my earlier remarks I have little to say in defense of this definition of norms. I believe that the definition catches an interesting category of regularities, even if the category does not fit exactly with everyone's conception of a norm. Thus I hope that even those who question the definition in some manner will still find it a useful way of identifying a topic for discussion. They may not see the topic as involving norms, but the difference need not be more than terminological.

The only thing I will add in defense of the definition is that it includes the sort of regularities that H. L. A. Hart had in mind in his classic discussion of rules of obligation, though it also encompasses more. Hart characterizes such rules by a number of features: they are supported by serious social pressure; they are thought necessary for social life or some prized feature of social life; and they may be individually burdensome, despite being thought to be collectively beneficial.[19] These features are not all mentioned in my definition, but it is a fair bet that anything that has them will satisfy the definition.

TWO STRATEGIES FOR DERIVING NORMS

David Lewis's account of conventions, the model for any work in this area, does more than offer us a definition. It also helps to show why certain regularities can be depended on to emerge and persist as conventions. The key to this aspect of his account is, first, that in a certain sort of coordination predicament it will be rational for each to prefer to follow any one of the regularities possible there if he expects others to follow it; and second, that factors like precedent, salience, and agreement will often identify one regularity as that which others may be expected to follow. Thus it will be rational for each to drive on the left rather than the right if precedent—and perhaps precedent only—means that he expects others to drive on the left. Everyone's driving on the left will emerge as an equilibrium in the sense that no one benefits by unilateral defection from it, and as a coordination equilibrium in the sense that no one benefits by anyone else's unilaterally defecting from it either.

17. See Lewis, *Convention,* p. 42.

18. Margaret Gilbert, "Notes on the Concept of a Social Convention," *New Literary History* 14 (1982–83): 225–51, taxonomizes things so that social conventions are a larger subclass of the class of norms than Lewis would make them.

19. H. L. A. Hart, *The Concept of Law* (Oxford: Oxford University Press, 1961), pp. 84–85. See also Edna Ullmann-Margalit, *The Emergence of Norms* (Oxford: Oxford University Press, 1977), pp. 12–13.

Lewis does not say that rational calculation in such a case is what makes each conform to the regularity; the immediate trigger may be the training received, a habit ingrained by the training, even a compulsion to be conformist. His claim is best taken as follows: that so far as it is rational for each to conform to any regularity that constitutes a convention, that makes it very probable that he will conform. He may actually conform from habit, but the rationality of conforming makes it likely that even if the habit disappeared, the conformity would tend to continue, if only after a lapse.[20] The rationality of conforming programs for the resilience of the conformity, even if it does not produce the conformity; it more or less ensures that whatever productive mechanism generates the agent's behavior—habit, rule of thumb, calculation—it will generate behavior in conformity to the convention.[21]

Our definition of norms does not serve on its own, unlike Lewis's definition of conventions, to show that certain regularities can be depended on in certain conditions to constitute norms. Such a derivation would provide us with an understanding of why certain norms emerge and/or persist and perhaps why other norms fail to do so. It might not shed light on the precise process of emergence or persistence—here socialization is probably the most important factor—but it would do something as good or better. It would show why in certain conditions those norms more or less had to emerge or more or less have to persist. The challenge then is to supplement our definition of norms with a derivation, or at least a derivation for some of the norms defined: a story as to why those norms can be depended upon to emerge and persist under certain circumstances.

Looking at our definition of norms, two strategies of derivation suggest themselves. One strategy would be to show first why certain behavioral patterns are intelligible and then to explain why, having appeared, they should attract the sort of approval that constitutes them as norms. The other would take the contrary path, explaining first why certain attitudes of approval are intelligible and then showing how they might generate the patterns of behavior required for norms. The first strategy is behavior-based, the second is attitude-based. In terms of Harsanyi's postulate, the first would tend to show that the behavior is economically rational and, being performed by nearly all, comes to be socially

20. Lewis makes a complementary point: "If that habit ever ceased to serve the agent's desires according to his beliefs, it would at once be overridden and corrected by conscious reasoning" (David Lewis, "Languages and Language" [1972] in his *Philosophical Papers*, vol. 1 [Oxford: Oxford University Press, 1983], p. 181). On related matters, see Philip Pettit and Michael Smith, "Backgrounding Desire," *Philosophical Review* (in press).

21. On this notion of programming, see Frank Jackson and Philip Pettit, "Functionalism and Broad Content," *Mind* 97 (1988): 381–400, "Program Explanation: A General Perspective," *Analysis*, vol. 50 (1990), and "Structural Explanation in Social Theory," in *Reductionism and Anti-reductionism*, ed. D. Charles and K. Lennon (Oxford: Oxford University Press, in press).

rational too; the second would show that it is socially rational from the start.

David Lewis indicates how we might pursue the behavioral strategy in arguing that conventions, once established, are likely to constitute norms; as well as the first, they are likely to meet the second and third clauses in our definition of norms. Lewis's conclusion, in his own words, is that "one is expected to conform, and failure to conform tends to evoke unfavorable responses from others. . . . These are bad consequences, and my interest in avoiding them strengthens my conditional preference for conforming."[22] Without going into the detail of his argument, we may note that it turns crucially on propositions like these.

> 1. Universal conformity with a convention like driving on the left is a coordination equilibrium in the sense that not only does no one benefit by unilaterally defecting himself, equally no one benefits by anyone else's unilaterally defecting either: in fact everyone is usually made worse off by anyone's unilateral defection.[23]
>
> 2. Everyone therefore will tend to disapprove of anyone else's defecting from such an outcome, so that the second condition in our definition of norms will be effectively fulfilled.
>
> 3. Since everyone is in a position to realize this, everyone has an extra motive not to defect from the outcome, over and beyond the fact that it would bring him no benefit: namely, that he would thereby attract the disapproval of others. Thus the third condition in our definition of norms will also be fulfilled.

The rational choice literature of the past decade or so supports the behavioral strategy for deriving norms in two ways. First of all, it makes explanatory claims sufficient to support such a strategy.[24] And second it presents an argument against the alternative attitude-based approach. In this section I will look at those explanatory claims, suggesting that in some ways they may be overblown, and I will show that the argument against the attitude-based strategy is almost certainly misconceived. Thus I prepare the way for the attitudinal derivation of certain norms explored in the next section. I should stress again that there is no need to reject one strategy of derivation because of recognizing the other. I think that the attitude-based strategy deserves more attention than it has received, but I do not hold that it is uniquely right. Some norms may be derivable in the one way, some in the other; some norms may be subject to both sorts of derivation, as some will be subject to none.

The norms that have been at the focus of concern in the rational choice literature are those such that conformity to them enables people to resolve free-rider problems, in particular problems that are also many-

22. Lewis, *Convention*, pp. 99–100.

23. The equilibrium, in Lewis's terminology (*Convention*), is a proper equilibrium, so far as everyone does worse by unilaterally defecting. Such a proper equilibrium is an instance of what Sugden defines as a stable equilibrium (p. 28).

24. Sugden explicitly develops a behavior-based strategy of derivation.

party prisoner's dilemmas.[25] In a prisoner's dilemma each party faces options of cooperating or defecting in some way and the following two conditions are fulfilled: universal cooperation is Pareto-superior to universal defection, being better for some—perhaps for all—and worse for none; but defecting is the dominant option, being better for each regardless of what others do. Arguably, conforming to norms like the following is equivalent to cooperating in a many-party prisoner's dilemma, so that universal conformity—though, in most cases, just fairly general conformity will do—represents an escape from the predicament.

1. Telling the truth reliably rather than expediently, randomly, or whatever.
2. Keeping promises reliably.
3. Refraining reliably from theft or fraud or violence.
4. Reliably discharging any publicly assigned duties.
5. In general, reliably contributing to goals that are of benefit to everyone.

How might we explain the emergence and persistence of behavior in accordance with such norms, abstracting for the moment from how the behavior comes to attract approval? That universal behavior of the kind in question would enable people to resolve prisoner's dilemmas does not itself furnish an explanation of emergence and persistence, though some authors write, misleadingly, as if it did. Thus Edna Ullmann-Margalit writes, "Such situations 'call for' norms. It can further be said that a norm solving the problem inherent in a situation of this type is generated by it."[26] In an individual prisoner's dilemma all do better if all conform to a normative resolution than if all defect, but each does better still if he defects while the others conform. So why should universal conformity emerge or persist?

One now standard answer is motivated by the observation that the parties who conform, if they do conform, face an indefinitely extended sequence of prisoner's dilemmas, not a single one, and that in such a sequence permanent defection is not a dominant option; it is not the best for each regardless of what others do. Permanent defection by all may be an equilibrium outcome, in the sense that no one can unilaterally depart from it with benefit. Equally permanent conformity or cooperation by all may not be an equilibrium outcome. But, as Michael Taylor has shown, there are equilibrium outcomes besides permanent defection by all, at least under plausible assumptions such as that people do not severely discount future benefits. And some of the other outcomes are Pareto-

25. This trend is breaking down (see Sugden; and Taylor, *The Possibility of Cooperation*). On the relation between free-rider problems and prisoner's dilemmas, see my paper, "Free Riding and Foul Dealing," *Journal of Philosophy* 83 (1986): 361–79, reprinted in *The Philosopher's Annual* 9 (1986): 149–67.

26. Ullmann-Margalit, p. 22. For a discussion of other such views, see Anthony Heath, *Rational Choice and Social Exchange* (Cambridge: Cambridge University Press, 1976), chap. 7.

superior to permanent defection by all.[27] The most salient example of such an outcome is that under which each tit-for-tats in some way: he begins by cooperating but only cooperates in a later round if no one defected (nonpunitively) in the previous round. This is an equilibrium, because anyone who unilaterally defects will be punished by the defection of others and will have to cooperate while they defect (in punishment for a previous defection of his) before they return to cooperation; thus any one who unilaterally defects will suffer through doing so. The outcome of universal tit-for-tat is Pareto-superior to that of permanent defection by all because it means that everyone is better off, benefiting from universal cooperation rather than universal defection at each round.

The fact that joint tit-for-tat is an equilibrium outcome which is Pareto-superior to permanent defection by all suggests an explanation for why universal tit-for-tat behavior should emerge and persist. It will emerge if each can persuade others that he is a tit-for-tatter, so that it is to their advantage to tit-for-tat with him. It will persist if each recognizes that a unilateral defection will attract the punitive defection of others, so that he does better continuing to tit-for-tat and therefore, assuming that others tit-for-tat with him, continuing to conform.

If this explains why people might evince tit-for-tat behavior, what might explain the approval for that behavior which is required if it is to constitute a norm? Here the crucial fact is not that universal tit-for-tat is an equilibrium but, as Russell Hardin has emphasized, that it is also a coordination equilibrium.[28] It is an outcome such that each is made worse off by anyone else's unilateral defection, since each is forced to defect at the next round in punishment, thereby jeopardizing the benefits of general cooperation. Hence it is a coordination equilibrium: no one benefits—in fact each suffers—by anyone's unilateral defection, his own or someone else's. That being the case, we can invoke propositions like those mentioned in discussing Lewis's argument that conventions are likely to be norms, in order to explain why people may be expected to disapprove of anyone else's unilaterally defecting, giving everyone extra reason not to defect himself.[29] People will disapprove of anyone else's unilateral defection, since any such defection harms each of them.[30] That is a fact which everyone is in a position to recognize and, since disapproval

27. See Taylor, *Anarchy and Cooperation*, and *The Possibility of Cooperation*.

28. Russell Hardin, *Collective Action* (Baltimore: Johns Hopkins University Press, 1982), p. 171.

29. The point is not generally recognized. It would have helped Russell Hardin himself at pp. 105–6 of *Morality within the Limits of Reason* (Chicago: University of Chicago Press, 1988), as it would those theorists who rely on the adage that the customary becomes obligatory; they are discussed in Heath, pp. 65–67, 161–62. One writer, however, who defends a similar claim is Sugden, p. 166.

30. If this claim seems questionable, see the discussion in the next section. Notice in particular that disapproval is an attitude: a disposition to express disapproval, if the circumstances are suitable.

is generally a bad, the recognition will give everyone an extra motive not to defect. Hence it appears that any tit-for-tat regularity will constitute a norm. Not only will it attract general conformity. Everyone will approve of anyone else's conforming, at least to the extent of disapproving of anyone else's unilateral defection, and this will help to ensure that there is indeed general conformity.[31]

We have sketched a behavior-based derivation, not of a norm like that of reliably telling the truth or keeping promises, but of a closely related norm: that of truth-telling or promise-keeping in a tit-for-tat way. The derivation is of interest because if everyone tit-for-tats in truth-telling everyone will behave as he would do were he telling the truth reliably: it will be as if everyone were telling the truth reliably. The derivation works, notice, on lines parallel to those explored by Lewis. In the Lewis case, agents have to identify a regularity on which to coordinate among a set of equally attractive conventions: say, driving on the left or the right. In this case things are set up so that they have the parallel problem of coordinating on one of those regularities that yield a superior equilibrium outcome to permanent defection. They have to coordinate on strict tit-for-tat, for example, or on any of the equally attractive variations: say, tit-for-double-tat, tit-for-tat-by-a-certain-number, and so on.

This is sufficient to show that the explanatory claims of recent rational choice theory serve to underpin a behavior-based derivation of certain norms. How successful that derivation is depends on how plausible those claims are. It is not a part of my brief to undermine such claims, but I would like here to mention two reservations about the tit-for-tat derivation. A first is this. A rational-choice derivation need not posit rational calculation—we saw this in discussing Lewis—and a tit-for-tat derivation need not therefore impute tit-for-tat reasoning. But a tit-for-tat derivation predicts that people will break norms punitively, in order to punish those who break them for convenience, even if the punishment is not explicitly rationalized in tit-for-tat terms. And this disposition is not generally manifested among those who honor norms; it is present, at most, only in certain sorts of cases.

My second reservation stems from a distinction, on which I have written elsewhere, between type A and type B prisoner's dilemmas.[32] In a type B dilemma, defection by even a single individual plunges at least one cooperator, and perhaps many more, below the baseline of universal defection. In a type A dilemma this is not so and, at the limit, the lone defector may have only an imperceptible negative effect on cooperators: the effect, say, of the one remaining person who continues to use chlorofluorocarbon sprays. My reservation about tit-for-tat derivations is that

31. Notice of course that under this derivation everyone will approve of defecting—and disapprove of conforming—when the defection is a tit-for-tat punishment.

32. See Philip Pettit, "Free Riding and Foul Dealing," and "Foul Dealing and an Assurance Problem," *Australasian Journal of Philosophy* 67 (1989): 341–44.

in a type A dilemma, it is not clear that anyone will be able to make it credible to the potential free rider that he is a tit-for-tatter. In particular it is not clear that he will be able to make credible the threat to defect—and put at risk all that has been achieved—just in order to punish a lone, barely irritating defector. The answer to this may be to accept that the only norms which can be derived under the tit-for-tat approach resolve type B dilemmas: roughly, what I have called "foul dealer" as distinct from free rider problems. But it seems clear that that would be a substantial concession.[33]

We have seen that the explanatory claims of recent rational-choice theory are naturally deployed to support a behavior-based derivation of norms, in particular a derivation of norms other than just the conventions covered in Lewis's treatment. That may be one reason why rational-choice theorists have not given much thought to the possibility of an attitude-based derivation. But there is a second reason that has certainly been of importance in directing attention away from such a derivation. This is that, within rational-choice theory, it has become established wisdom that any attitude-based approach falls foul of a decisive objection.

An attitude-based derivation of norms would try to show that a certain sort of behavior is bound to attract approval, its absence disapproval, and that such sanctions ought to elicit the behavior required, thus establishing norms. The objection is that any derivation of this kind supposes, illicitly, that the enforcement of norms—the sanctioning of conformity and deviance—is costless and will be happily conducted by people in general. James Buchanan puts the opposite, standard view. "Enforcement has two components. First, violations must be discovered and violators identified. Second, punishment must be imposed on violators. Both components involve costs."[34]

The objection in play is often developed in the form of a paradox. Norms may often serve to get us out of collective action predicaments like the prisoner's dilemma: they elicit a sort of action such that everyone is better off if everyone adopts it, and they do this even when each is

33. Notice, however, that the tit-for-tat story considered here is only one of a number of related accounts (see Taylor, *Anarchy and Cooperation*). One account of particular interest would explain behavior like general truth-telling or promise-keeping as the outcome, not of tit-for-tatting in a single many-party dilemma, but of tit-for-tatting in various two-party dilemmas (see R. Hardin, *Morality within the Limits of Reason*, p. 105). Such a possibility should not surprise us, since two-party dilemmas are by definition of type B: the lone defector makes the cooperator worse off than he would be under joint defection. On tit-for-tat in two-party dilemmas, see Robert Axelrod, *The Evolution of Cooperation* (New York: Basic, 1984). On how a tit-for-tat type of strategy may even be rational in a sequence of such dilemmas of known finite length, see Philip Pettit and Robert Sugden, "The Backward Induction Paradox," *Journal of Philosophy* 86 (1989): 169–83; and Christina Bicchieri, "Self-refuting Theories of Strategic Interaction," *Erkenntnis* 30 (1989): 69–80.

34. James Buchanan, *The Limits of Liberty* (Chicago: University of Chicago Press, 1975), pp. 132–33. See too Heath, pp. 156–58; and Axelrod, "An Evolutionary Approach to Norms," p. 1098.

motivated to choose a different option. But the objection suggests that norms can persist only if we find some other way of escaping a similar predicament which is raised by their enforcement. Everyone is better off if everyone enforces a norm, but because enforcement is costly each is motivated not to bother enforcing it himself. And so norms can solve certain collective action predicaments only if the collective predicaments they in turn generate can be solved by something else.

Anthony Heath makes the point in connection with a norm of output-restriction among a large group of workers. "Enforcement of the norm is assuredly a public good: I will get the benefits whether or not I actually do the enforcing and will hence prefer to leave the embarrassing task of disciplining the rate-busters to others. So will everybody else. And so the rate-busters will go unchecked."[35] Michael Taylor makes the point more generally: "The maintenance of a system of sanctions itself constitutes or presupposes the solution of another collective action problem. Punishing someone who does not conform to a norm—punishing someone for being a free rider on the efforts of others to provide a public good, for example—is itself a public good for the group in question, and everyone would prefer others to do this unpleasant job. Thus, the 'solution' of collective action problems by norms presupposes the prior or concurrent solution of another collective action problem."[36]

This line of objection, common though it is, rests on a mistake. It assumes that the enforcement of norms must involve intentional action and since action always generates at least time costs that it must therefore be potentially costly for those who conduct it. The surprising thing however is that this is false. Buchanan mentions two sorts of enforcement costs: those of identifying violators and those of disciplining them. But people do not have to identify violators intentionally; they just have to be around in sufficient numbers to make it likely that violators will be noticed. And equally, people do not have to discipline violators intentionally, going out of their way for example to rebuke them or report them to others;[37] they just have to disapprove of them—or at least be assumed to disapprove of them—whether that attitude ever issues in intentional activity.

It will be readily conceded that given sufficient numbers, enforcement need not involve intentionally seeking out the violators of a norm. What will come as a shock to many, however, is the claim that a violator can be punished—or of course a conformer rewarded—by the attitudes of others, even when those attitudes are not intentionally expressed, say,

35. Heath, p. 158.

36. Taylor, *The Possibility of Cooperation*, p. 30.

37. Braithwaite has suggested (*Crime, Shame and Reintegration*) that in any case reporting violators to others is generally something people enjoy and that the argument may also break down here. In order for the suggestion to work, of course, people must not enjoy falsely reporting violations nearly as much as doing so truthfully. On related matters, see the essay on gossip in John Sabini and Murray Silver, *Moralities of Everyday Life* (Oxford: Oxford University Press, 1982).

in censure or praise. Yet the point, once put, is fairly obvious. We care not just about the rebukes and commendations we receive from others but also about whether they take a negative or positive view of what we do: look at the eagerness with which we search for cues as to the view they actually take. We care about their dispositions to rebuke or commend us, even if the costs—say, the costs of social embarrassment—mean that those dispositions are not much exercised. How can we know about other people's dispositions if they are not exercised? Easy. We know what they know of us and, ascribing similar standards to them, we know whether they are likely to think well or badly, to take a favorable or unfavorable attitude.[38]

But not only is it fairly obvious that even in the absence of praise or censure the attitude of approval is a good that I can savor and the attitude of disapproval a bad under which I may smart; the claim is also supported by tradition. As with many other propositions in this article, Adam Smith can be invoked as a relevant authority: "We are pleased to think that we have rendered ourselves the natural objects of approbation, though no approbation should ever actually be bestowed upon us: and we are mortified to reflect that we have justly merited the blame of those we live with, though that sentiment should never actually be exerted against us."[39]

The rational choice tradition has been blind to the fact that the goods which we seek from others include goods that they do not intentionally bestow, in particular attitude-dependent goods like approval and disapproval. One reason may be that in giving us the distinction between strategic and parametric rationality, rationality exercised respectively with and without the assumption of rationality in the causally relevant environment, the tradition naturally suggests that parametric rationality is suited for dealings with nature, strategic for dealings with other people. Even though he doesn't endorse the suggestion fully, the distinction leads Jon Elster, for example, to the following view. "Strategic rationality is defined by an axiom of symmetry: the agent acts in an environment of other actors, none of whom can be assumed to be less rational or sophisticated than he is himself."[40]

38. If further explanation is needed, then one way of explaining why we care about covert as well as overt approval is that someone's covert attitudes affect how he will later speak of us and deal with us. This explanation may be given a sociobiological gloss, accounting for why we care even about the views of those we may never knowingly meet again: for example, the pedestrian who sees me driving through a red light and clearly regards me in a negative way. More on this in the next section.

39. A. Smith, p. 116. Here and elsewhere Smith wants to be able to say that we desire not only to be such that others are disposed to praise us but also to be such that others are rightly disposed to praise us. I suspect that he illicitly uses the first claim to make the second, intuitively stronger, thesis seem plausible. See also p. 310 where he makes three distinctions when four are obviously being offered.

40. Jon Elster, *Explaining Technical Change* (Cambridge: Cambridge University Press, 1983), p. 77. Notice that Elster, in going on to taxonomize social interdependencies, fails

If strategic rationality is thought uniquely suitable for dealings with other actors, in particular other actors who know as much as the agent knows, then the assumption is that any goods which one agent can seek from others are goods which the others rationally and therefore intentionally bestow. It means, as is indeed often explicitly maintained, that if one agent acts rationally with a view to securing such goods from others, then what he is trying to engineer is a rational exchange. But this emphasis on exchange is not always appropriate. The benefit which an agent seeks from certain others may be a benefit involuntarily provided, as when he gets them to think well of him or at least not to think ill. There need be no element of exchange in the interaction. Thus people can be more or less involuntary enforcers of norms, automatically providing suitable rewards and punishments for acts of conformity and deviance. Buchanan, thinking of electric fences and gun traps, says this: "We need not reach into the extremities of science fiction to think of devices that could serve as automatically programmed enforcers."[41] We may readily agree, for we can imagine ourselves as enforcers of that kind.

In conclusion, I would like to add a thought to bolster the point. Reflecting on the automatic way in which we sanction one another's actions by approving and disapproving, you may well think that what the rational self-interested agent should do is take over this sanctioning in an intentional way and try to drive a harder bargain for the goods he offers or the bads he reserves. But here we confront an extremely interesting and indeed pervasive paradox. When I elicit someone else's approval for an action, without intentional action on that person's own part, I enjoy a good which would not be in the offing were I to realize that the approval was provided intentionally, or at least was provided intentionally on grounds other than that it is deserved. The good of having someone else's esteem or gratitude for an action, even the good of just having him look on the action with pleasure, is something that that person therefore cannot intentionally use in exchange. If it is not enough for him to approve that he understand the merits or attractions of what I have done, if he approves only because he has an extraintentional reason for doing so, or only in part because of this, then the approval loses its significance and value. The point will be familiar. You cannot sell your approval any more than you can sell your friendship or love or trust.[42]

---

to notice the possibility that the action of each may depend on the preference structures—the attitudes—of all: this is the possibility exploited in the argument of section 3.

41. Buchanan, p. 131.

42. See Jon Elster, *Sour Grapes* (Cambridge: Cambridge University Press, 1982), chap. 2, on "essential by-products." On similar points, see Philip Pettit and Geoffrey Brennan, "Restrictive Consequentialism," *Australasian Journal of Philosophy* 64 (1986): 438–55; Philip Pettit, "The Consequentialist Can Recognise Rights," *Philosophical Quarterly* 35 (1988): 537–51, and "The Paradox of Loyalty," *American Philosophical Quarterly* 25 (1988): 163–71.

AN ATTITUDE-BASED DERIVATION

Many norms may lend themselves to a behavior-based derivation. In other words considerations to do primarily with economically rational behavior may explain why certain norms are resilient: why they can be relied on to emerge and persist in certain conditions. But I suspect that the set of derivable norms is larger than the set of norms derivable in that way, and in this section I look at the possibility that certain norms may lend themselves to an attitude-based derivation. The set of norms derivable in this way may overlap with the other set, but it certainly extends beyond it.

The norms of particular interest in moral and political theory are those which would enable people to solve collective action problems, whether problems that arise for the society at large or for particular subgroups. Such problems arise when it appears, usually in the light of considerations of economic gain, that if agents are individually rational then they will generate a Pareto-inferior member of the set of possible outcomes.[43] To solve such a problem is to succeed in getting a Pareto-optimal outcome instead: an outcome which is not Pareto-inferior to any other, there being no other that is preferred by some and that is not preferred by none. In looking at the behavior-based strategy we concentrated, as is usual, on norms that solve one species of collective action problems, namely, prisoner's dilemmas. Here we shall maintain that focus, since it has the virtue of being familiar and our aim is only to see how the attitude-based derivation might go, not to provide a survey of all the norms that are so derivable. It should be remembered, however, that there may well be norms that solve no collective action problems at all, even for a relevant subgroup—say, norms of revenge—and that among those that solve such problems there are certainly norms that solve problems other than prisoner's dilemmas. Conventional norms are of this kind, since even coordination predicaments count as collective action problems: under conditions of ignorance, rational action can lead to a Pareto-inferior outcome.[44]

The key to the attitude-based strategy of derivation is the recognition that there is a cost-benefit structure operative in social life which rational choice theory has generally neglected: the structure associated with people's thinking ill or well of an agent—or being thought to think ill or well—whether they actually censure or praise. I hypothesize that once these approbative costs and benefits are put into the equations, then we can see our way to explaining why the emergence and persistence of otherwise puzzling norms may be unsurprising. In order to support that hypothesis I shall set out a number of fairly plausible assumptions and argue that given those assumptions we should expect the approbative costs and benefits to encourage the emergence and persistence of certain norms.

43. See Taylor, *The Possibility of Cooperation*, p. 19.

44. Here I break with Taylor, *The Possibility of Cooperation*, p. 30.

In effect I shall argue that in conditions where those assumptions are satisfied the norms in question are derivable in an attitude-based way. There are five assumptions in all. I first present the assumptions, indicating briefly why I think that each is plausible. Then I show why we may expect to find certain norms in operation wherever they are satisfied.

The Interaction Assumption

Assumption 1 is that in all human societies there are collective action predicaments with these characteristics. First, among the options available to any agent in the sort of situation involved nearly everyone is better off if everyone else takes one particular option than if everyone else rejects it: the option in question is, in that sense, a collectively beneficial one. Second, and more strongly, everyone is made better off in at least one respect—and better off therefore in most cases, I shall assume—by anyone else's taking the collectively beneficial option: either that person increases or ensures the collective benefit being offered or he makes it more likely that the collective benefit will be or remain an offer.[45] The second condition is stronger than the first because it rules out the possibility that the absolute best result for everyone is not that everybody else takes the option in question but that a certain percentage do so.[46]

This first assumption is satisfied in a variety of interactions, most importantly in various prisoner's dilemmas. If everyone else tells the truth reliably, everyone is better off than if everyone else does so randomly and in one respect everyone is made better off by anyone else's being a reliable truth-teller; he benefits at least indirectly, so far as that person's conformity to the truth-telling norm reinforces truth-telling overall. The case is similar for reliably keeping promises and similar for revealing the nature of your wares, refraining from violence to others, and generally adopting a nonmalevolent stance. Again everyone is better off if everyone else contributes to the provision of nonexcludable goods like a quiet neighborhood or a clean environment than if no one does so and in the relevant respect everyone is made better off by anyone else's contributing to such a good. The examples being offered are familiar, and they need not be further elaborated to vindicate our initial assumption. Note that we have only mentioned examples of predicaments involving the society as a whole. There are bound to be analogous situations for subgroups in any society, but we will not consider them here.

The Publicity Assumption

Assumption 2 is that in at least many of the sorts of predicament described some people will be in a position to know, or be in a position where they

45. This might be weakened, so that what is required is at least that everyone is not made worse off in most cases. The weakening will not affect the argument, provided assumption 4 is strengthened so as to compensate.

46. For complicated possibilities of this kind, see Thomas Schelling, *Micromotives and Macrobehavior* (New York: Norton, 1978), esp. chap. 7.

are likely to come to know, of anyone who acts in a way that promotes the collective benefit that he does so and of anyone who fails to act in that way that he fails. This is an assumption of exposure or publicity. Clearly it is not always satisfied, since there are many occasions when we can fail to do our collective bit and successfully cover our tracks. We can litter the park at night or supply defective goods under cover and so reasonably hope to get away without having the offense put down to us. But equally clear is that the assurance of being able to keep an offense hidden from the eyes or ears of our compatriots is only rarely available. If we choose to offend then in most cases we do so at our own risk.

The Perception Assumption

Assumption 3 spells out something that is implicit on one reading of the last assumption. This is that nearly everyone who knows of someone that he has done or failed to do his collective bit in some way will perceive that that person has acted in a way that is collectively beneficial or non-beneficial and indeed in a way that is in at least one respect beneficial or nonbeneficial to him in particular. Not only does he know that the person has told the truth, he also knows that this is a sort of action such that everyone is better off if everyone else reliably does it. And he knows that he in particular is better off in one respect for the other person's doing it. The other person's telling the truth may benefit him directly but at least it will benefit him by increasing or making more secure the sort of good he would enjoy through everyone else's telling the truth. Again, to take another example, not only does he know that another person has littered the park, he also knows that this is a collectively nonbeneficial action and he knows that he in particular suffers in some measure from it: his environment is not as clean as it would be if no one else was a litterbug. Such examples should make it clear both that the perception assumption is distinct from the publicity assumption and that in many cases it is equally uncontroversial.

The Sanction Assumption

Assumption 4 is that nearly everyone approves of nearly everyone who benefits him in some respect through performing a collectively beneficial action and disapproves of nearly everyone who harms him through performing a collectively nonbeneficial action. To approve or disapprove in the broad sense adopted here is to be disposed respectively to encourage or discourage the agent in question. That the action is personally beneficial or harmful certainly provides a ground for approval or disapproval: only saints could fail to give it weight. And that the action is collectively at the same time as personally beneficial, collectively at the same time as personally harmful, means that even saints can indulge themselves. They may count their personal gain or loss into their reasoning and, even if that is totally uncongenial—even if they are perfect altruists—they may be moved by the consideration of collective benefit and harm to match the rest of us in our postures of approval and disapproval.

This assumption will not be satisfied in every case. If the beneficial action is very burdensome, for example, then while it may attract approval, many people will not disapprove of the harmful alternative; they will see it as natural and understandable. But it is surely plausible to think that the assumption will be satisfied for at least some of the collective benefits and harms invoked in the interaction assumption. Remember in this connection that while approval and disapproval require an appropriate disposition to encourage or discourage, the property required can be extremely weak. It may be the disposition to do those things only in circumstances where there are no costs whatever involved: that is, in circumstances of a kind unlikely to arise, where the acts in question are not found embarrassing or judgmental, for example, and they do not cost any time or effort that could be better spent. I smart under the gaze of the most uncensorious of my fellows if I realize that, while he will never rebuke me, he would do so were he less unassuming or were social life more conducive to such activities.

The Motivation Assumption

The last of my five assumptions is that people are moved in great part, though not exclusively, by a concern that others not think badly of them and, if possible, that they think well of them. They may not calculate by explicit reference to the opinions of others but what opinions they ascribe will affect what considerations they find salient in deliberation or what considerations they would find salient if the operative considerations supported actions that are offensive to others. This assumption is intuitively acceptable, as we have already emphasized, fitting for example into that long tradition of European thought in which the love of esteem, affection, and acceptance in general is hailed as one of the great human passions.[47] Adam Smith gives forceful expression to the assumption: "Nature, when she formed man for society, endowed him with an original desire to please, and an original aversion to offend his brethren. She taught him to feel pleasure in their favourable, and pain in their unfavourable regard. She rendered their approbation most flattering and most agreeable to him for its own sake; and their disapprobation most mortifying and most offensive."[48]

This assumption should also recommend itself nowadays, for it is built into at least two major schools of contemporary social theory. It is part of the theory of rational choice, as appears from the emphasis in Harsanyi's postulate on social acceptance. And it should also be congenial to those in the sociological tradition of theory. Within that tradition the desire for status ranks with the desire for wealth and power as one of the basic human motives and to enjoy status is to enjoy a special kind of acceptance: specifically, a greater acceptance than relevant others.

47. See, e.g., Arthur O. Lovejoy, *Reflections on Human Nature* (Baltimore: Johns Hopkins Press, 1961), lecture 5.

48. A. Smith, p. 116.

For those who are less impressed than I am with the plausibility, and the traditional endorsement, of the motivation assumption, it may be useful to point to an instrumental reason why people should care about what others think of them, even others who do not say or do anything by way of face-to-face rebuke or punishment. That someone comes to think ill of me for having done something gives me reason to believe that, even if no immediate penalty is forthcoming—the costs are too high to that person—still, the person is thereby made more likely, if the costs are right, to speak unfavorably of me to others and damage my prospects of being favorably treated at their hands, or to damage my prospects directly by treating me unfavorably himself: say, by preferring another in the exercise of some patronage. This is to say that someone's thinking ill of me represents an increased probability of my being ill-treated, so that no one should be surprised that we care about what others think of our actions, even when those others say or do nothing in immediate censure. I actually believe, and I assume here—though not a lot depends on the difference—that what others think is a matter of intrinsic and not just instrumental concern to most of us. Otherwise it is hard to see why we worry, as we surely do, about being noticed doing compromising or demeaning things by complete strangers say, being noticed peeping through a hotel keyhole, running a red light, or just picking your nose. It may be that this intrinsic concern for what others think is implanted in us for instrumental reasons—reasons that may not themselves make any impact on us—by evolution or by training.

It may be said against the motivation assumption that we only care about acceptance when it is given for reasons of a certain kind or by people in a certain category. The saint does not care for the knave's acceptance, the sadist does not care for the victim's. But this objection is misleading. The saint is put off by the cost of the knave's approval, the sadist by the cost of the victim's: in the one case wrongdoing, in the other kindness. The assumption regains plausibility when we realize that it postulates a desire for the property of being accepted, not a desire for every prospect that involves acceptance. Would the saint or sadist like to continue to act as he does and now in addition have the acceptance of the relevant party? That is the question to be asked and the motivation assumption, plausibly enough, says that, impossible though it might be, the saint and the sadist would each prefer that alternative.[49]

With the five assumptions in place, I am now in a position to argue that under conditions where those assumptions are satisfied, certain norms can be depended on to emerge and persist.

Stage 1. The interaction, publicity, and perception assumptions mean that in any society there will be certain action types that satisfy the conditions

49. On the distinction between desiring properties and prospects, see Philip Pettit, "Decision Theory and Folk Psychology," in *Essays on the Foundations of Decision Theory,* ed. Michael Bacharach and Susan Hurley (Oxford: Blackwell, in press).

they lay down. The action types will be collectively beneficial options such that everyone is better off in some measure for any one else choosing one, worse off for any one else choosing something different. They will be options which no one can choose or reject without someone else being likely to notice. And they will be options such that anyone who notices will recognize the collective and personal benefit or harm occasioned by such a choice.

Stage 2. By the sanction assumption, many of these action types will be such that the choice of an action type will usually attract approval, the choice of an alternative disapproval. Thus the second condition in our definition of a norm will be fulfilled by those action types. Each will be a regularity such that nearly everyone approves of nearly anyone else's conforming and disapproves of nearly anyone else's deviating.

Stage 3. By the motivation assumption, this approval and disapproval constitutes a potential motive for people generally to evince such actions. It seems reasonable to take it that at least if people were not to evince the action types in question, then the motive would become actual: people would become aware of the approval they had lost, the disapproval they had attracted, and this awareness would generate a corresponding concern. Assume for the moment that if the potential motive were to become actual in this way, then that motive would also be generally effective, eliciting the appropriate action types; we redeem this assumption in stage 4, below. It will follow in that case that the existence of the pattern of approval and disapproval in question makes it relatively certain that the first and third conditions in our analysis of a norm will be fulfilled for those action types. Each type will be a regularity to which nearly everyone conforms: either he will have reasons to conform independently of the approval and disapproval or, lacking such reasons and tending not to conform, he will be brought into line by the consequent loss of approval, the consequent attraction of disapproval. And each will be a regularity such that people's conformity to it is more or less ensured—if not actually produced in every case—by the approval given to conformity, the disapproval given to deviance.

Stage 4. The action types will constitute norms, therefore, in any circumstances where the motive in question—the desire to have the approval of others and, in particular, to avoid their disapproval—can be expected to outweigh competing motives, including motives related to the immediate costs of conformity, the threats of powerful agents, the operation of other norms, the feelings of guilt derived from past patterns of approval, or whatever. Among many-party prisoner's dilemmas, we cannot expect the motive to triumph in foul dealer problems, for example, since cooperating exposes each to the risk of being plunged beneath the baseline of universal defection, even by a lone defector. Indeed cooperating may be so burdensome in such a predicament that defecting does not attract disapproval, so that the derivation fails at stage 2. Other things being equal, however, we can perhaps be more sanguine with prisoner's dilemmas of the other type: for example with free rider problems in which cooperation certainly costs something but at least does not involve the foul dealer risk; so long as a certain minimum of others cooperate too, the cooperator is better off than under universal defection.[50] It would seem that with many action types that represent cooperative options in such predicaments, if the action types satisfy all the conditions mentioned earlier, then they are likely to emerge and persist as norms of the society.

An example will breathe life into this abstract derivation. A particularly appropriate example, given Garrett Hardin's famous analysis of the tragedy of the commons, is a norm of not overgrazing such shared land. According to Hardin we ought to expect a commons to be overgrazed, so far as overgrazing is a dominant option for each: better if others choose it, better if others do not choose it. The tragedy is that overgrazing by all is worse for all than refraining; the situation is a many-party prisoner's dilemma.[51] It turns out, however, that the case is one where our assumptions would lead us to expect a norm of not overgrazing to emerge and persist. Such a norm may explain why, as a matter of fact, the commons system was generally very successful in medieval Europe.[52]

Under commons conditions we have a collective action predicament in which not overgrazing is collectively beneficial and in which each is benefited in some measure by anyone else's not overgrazing: thus the interaction assumption is fulfilled. But the publicity and perception assumptions are also satisfied, for anyone who overgrazes is likely to be noticed and anyone who notices is bound to understand the collective and personal harm done. Thus we may expect, as the sanction assumption has it, that nearly everyone will disapprove of anyone else's overgrazing and approve of anyone else's not overgrazing. Since there is no great cost in not overgrazing, at least if enough others also refrain, the desire which the motivation assumption postulates ought to weigh sufficiently with people to elicit a general pattern of restraint. The upshot will be a norm of not overgrazing. Nearly everyone will conform to this regularity. Nearly everyone will approve of nearly anyone else's conforming and disapprove of nearly anyone else's deviating. And this pattern of approval and disapproval will help to explain why nearly everyone conforms.

I hope that this example will serve to show that it is possible to have norms whose emergence and persistence are derivable in an attitude-based way. The possibility is significant. With a norm like that of not overgrazing, a behavior-based derivation, or at least one which relies on tit-for-tat, is unlikely to be persuasive. The predicament is a type A dilemma, in which the lone defector will not put anyone below the baseline

50. Other things may not be equal with free rider problems such as those raised by truth-telling and promise-keeping, where the action type in question often represents, not just the cooperative option in such a many-party dilemma, but also the cooperative option in a two-party dilemma with one's interlocutor. See n. 33 above.

51. Garrett Hardin, "The Tragedy of the Commons," *Science* 162 (1968): 1243–48.

52. Taylor, *The Possibility of Cooperation*, pp. 26–27.

of universal defection. Why, therefore, should the potential defector or free rider expect others to stick with tit-for-tat? In particular, why should he expect them to risk all they have achieved and punish his lone defection by defecting themselves in response? The availability of an attitude-based derivation with a norm of this kind is therefore something of significance. The availability of the derivation means that political theorists may have a novel basis for identifying resilient norms, social theorists a novel hypothesis for explaining the rise and fall of norms that have appeared in history.

In identifying feasible norms, or in explaining why certain norms emerged and persisted, the idea suggested is that we should look to see how far the norms involve action types that engage our five assumptions. If the action type provides a collective and personal benefit, as required by the interaction assumption, does it satisfy the publicity and perception requirements? If it does, is the action type such as to attract approval, its omission disapproval, as in the sanction assumption? Is it, for example, sufficiently undemanding on the individual for people not to shrink from such disapproval? And if the action type satisfies all those conditions, is it the sort where the desire which the motivation assumption postulates—the desire to have approval rather than disapproval—is likely to outweigh conflicting motives? These questions represent a miniature research program for political and social theory.

Consider a norm such as that which most of us would hope to find operating in juries: the norm of taking seriously the question of whether the evidence establishes guilt beyond reasonable doubt. The behavior required by that norm is hardly independently motivated as a behavior-based derivation would have to suppose. And so the question of whether we can really rely on such a norm assumes some urgency. In dealing with a question of this kind, it will be useful to bear in mind the lesson of this article. We should explore the possibility that the norm is derivable in an attitude-based way. If it proves to be derivable, or derivable given certain additional constraints, this will reinforce our attachment to the institution of the jury, perhaps guiding us on particular issues of reform. If it proves not to be derivable in this way, then that raises doubts about the whole institution, at least for someone in the rational-choice tradition.

In fact, I would suggest, the jury norm does promise to be derivable in an attitude-based way. The activity required is collectively beneficial and in some measure beneficial to nearly everyone individually: it reinforces an institution from which almost everyone stands to gain. Thus our first assumption is fulfilled in this case. And so, more obviously, are the other four: everyone embracing or resisting the behavior is subject to the publicity and perception of other jurors; everyone is subject therefore to approval or disapproval; and everyone has a potential motive to display the behavior. Would the motive be effective, if actualized? We may hope so, especially given that juries are vetted to eliminate those with an interest in the outcome and that jurors are relatively protected from the threats of those with such an interest.

The vindication of the jury norm that I have sketched foreshadows other possibilities. It may be, for similar reasons, that norms of serving the public interest are feasible, or can be made to be feasible, in the realms of bureaucracy and academia. After all, the promotions committee, the lynchpin of such organizations, closely parallels the jury. And it may be too that professional norms, such as those to which doctors and lawyers subscribe, are or can be made resilient in a similar manner. Again the norms that have to be exemplified if patterns of self-regulation are to operate successfully in business and industry may prove to be feasible, in the light of our analysis, under appropriate conditions. Finally, and less congenially, the attitude-based strategy of derivation may enable us to understand why certain subgroup norms that are inimical to the large society—the norms of manipulative elites or criminal subcultures, for example—prove so enduring that no policy-making initiative should assume they can be displaced.

The possibilities are tantalizing. They make an interesting research agenda for political theorists who are concerned with which attractive norms are feasible, which unattractive norms inevitable, and under what conditions. And equally they point to an agenda for social theorists whose primary concern is explanation rather than evaluation. The fulfillment or nonfulfillment of assumptions like those listed may be very important in explaining the emergence or nonemergence, the persistence or nonpersistence, of the norms that interest social theorists. For the explanatory questions teem. How important a factor is size in affecting publicity? How far does publicity matter if the agent remains anonymous? Does popular understanding of the benefit or damage attending a certain activity—say, the damage done by smoking in public—encourage the appearance of a suitable norm? Does group conflict in a society—say, on a Left-Right or feminist-nonfeminist axis—undermine common norms such as those that we might expect to govern appointments and promotions? Does it mean that patterns of approval shift, for example, or that people come to care only for the approval of their own group? I hope that by adverting to issues like these I can at least signal the possibility that the attitude-based strategy for deriving norms is of more than just philosophical interest.

ONCE MORE, WITH COMMON BELIEF

It has been fashionable to argue that norms require not just the fulfillment of conditions like those given in the first section of this article but also the common belief that such conditions are fulfilled. People each believe that they hold, they each believe that they each believe this, and so on. Or at least they approximate to such common belief. Perhaps they have the belief but only *in sensu diviso*.[53] Perhaps they have the belief but only

53. Lewis, *Convention*, p. 66.

up to three levels.[54] Or perhaps they just lack at each higher level the contrary disbelief: they do not disbelieve that the basic matters hold, they do not disbelieve this, and so on.[55]

The reason for building a requirement of this kind into the definition of norms is that we would probably hesitate to describe a regularity as a norm if it were not fulfilled. Suppose for example that with a regularity, R—say, the regularity whereby people marry outside their families—the three requirements are fulfilled, but people do not generally believe they are: say, they generally believe that conformity is wholly explained by genetic predispositions. We might well hesitate to say in such a case that R was a norm. It would not be something that people thought it important for them to approve, since they would see their approval as epiphenomenal; thus it would not be something which served the ordinary role of a norm in their lives. Again suppose, a level up, that each person believed that the three requirements were fulfilled but believed that others did not believe this: say, each believed that others believed that conformity was genetically produced. Here too we would perhaps hesitate to say that R was a norm, for it would also fail to serve the ordinary role of a norm in the society: it would not be something each believed that others thought it important for them to approve.[56] Similar considerations would seem to carry weight, though progressively lighter weight, at higher levels. They suggest that norms do involve common belief, at least in the weakest sense that people do not disbelieve the relevant proposition at any higher level.

The requirement of common belief forces us then to tighten up our definition of norms.

> A regularity, R, in the behavior of members of a population, P, when they are agents in a recurrent situation, S, is a norm if and only if it is true that, *and it is a matter of common belief that*, in any instance of S among members of P,
>
> 1. nearly everyone conforms to R;
> 2. nearly everyone approves of nearly anyone else's conforming and disapproves of nearly anyone else's deviating; and
> 3. the fact that nearly everyone approves and disapproves on this pattern helps to ensure that nearly everyone conforms.

The question raised by this redefinition is whether the two strategies for deriving norms are capable of supporting a derivation of norms under this tighter analysis. I believe they can, and I would like briefly to show how.

54. Bach and Harnish, p. 269.

55. See Lewis, "Languages and Language," p. 166; and Gareth Evans and John McDowell, eds., *Truth and Meaning* (Oxford: Oxford University Press, 1976), pp. xx–xxi.

56. Notice that these considerations are not undermined by Tyler Burge's arguments in "On Knowledge and Convention," *Philosophical Review* 84 (1975): 249–55.

In arguing that conventions involve common knowledge David Lewis introduces the notion of a basis for common knowledge.[57] A basis of common knowledge that *q* is a proposition *p* such that everyone has reason to believe that *p*; *p* indicates to everyone that everyone has reason to believe that *p*; and *p* indicates to everyone that *q*. Given this, and given the mutual ascription of common information and inductive standards, *p* will indicate to everyone not only that everyone has reason to believe that *p* but also that everyone has reason to believe that *q*; and iterating again, not only that everyone has reason to believe that *q* but also that everyone has reason to believe that everyone has reason to believe that *q*; and so on. In such a situation it would seem reasonable to ascribe a common belief that *q*, at least under the negative construal of such belief. It is plausible that everyone believes that *q*, that no one disbelieves that everyone believes that *q*, that no one disbelieves that this disbelief is generally absent, and so on.

The notion of a basis of common knowledge suggests a nice way of showing that a derivation of a norm under our original definition also provides a derivation of the norm under the tighter analysis. This would be to show that the propositions involved in the derivation are the analogue of '*q*,' providing a basis for common knowledge that *p*, where '*p*' stands for the proposition that nearly everyone conforms to the regularity involved, nearly everyone approves and disapproves appropriately, and nearly everyone's conformity is ensured in part by that pattern of approval and disapproval. It turns out that this can be shown, or at least this can be made plausible, both for the behavior-based sort of derivation and for the attitude-based one.

Consider the propositions involved in the behavior-based tit-for-tat derivation of a norm of cooperating in some way with others. These are the crucial claims.

1. Universal tit-for-tat is a Pareto-optimal equilibrium.
2. Everyone adopts the tit-for-tat strategy, so far as it is the salient alternative.
3. And so everyone cooperates.
4. Universal tit-for-tat is also a coordination equilibrium.
5. Therefore everyone disapproves of anyone else's unilaterally defecting and approves of anyone else's defecting in this way.
6. And so, given that everyone is in a position to recognize the truth of 5, everyone has an extra motive not to defect unilaterally.

If we imagine a situation in which these propositions hold, then it is plausible to say that everyone there has reason to believe they hold; if he thinks about the matter, then he is likely to endorse the propositions or at least some less technical counterparts. Not only does everyone have reason to believe that the propositions hold, but the propositions also

57. See Lewis, *Convention*, p. 56.

indicate to everyone—they provide everyone with reason to believe—two distinct things: that everyone has reason to believe they hold, the evidence being equally available to all, and that tit-for-tat cooperation will satisfy the earlier conditions for being a norm, attracting general conformity and a general reinforcing pattern of approval for conformity. This means in turn, iterating, that they indicate to everyone, given that everyone has the same information and follows the same inductive standards, that everyone has reason to believe that cooperation will satisfy those conditions. And so on up the hierarchy.

That everyone has reason to believe that cooperation satisfies the conditions, that everyone has reason to believe that everyone has reason to believe that it does so, and so on, does not mean in itself that the common belief requirement is fulfilled. But it makes the requirement extremely likely to be met. It makes it likely, on our construal, that nearly everyone will believe that cooperation satisfies the conditions, that no one will disbelieve that nearly everyone believes this, that no one will disbelieve that this disbelief is generally absent, and so on. Thus we can see how a behavior-based derivation of a norm under the old definition can yield a derivation of the norm under the new.

The line of argument just run with the behavior-based strategy can be run also, as ought to be obvious, with the attitude-based approach. All that needs to be done is to replace the six propositions mentioned above with the claims involved in the four-stage derivation described in the last section. Thus we may conclude that the omission of the common belief requirement in our earlier discussions does not vitiate any of our results. What we did in defining and deriving no-frills norms, we can also do for norms in full dress.

CONCLUSION; AND A LAST OBJECTION RESOLVED

In conclusion, but before addressing one last objection, it will be useful to highlight the main claims made and defended so far.

1. Rational choice theory postulates that the things people generally do, whatever the basis on which they are chosen, are consistent with a major interest in economic gain and social acceptance; people do not generally flout such self-interest, even if they rarely think about it.

2. Norms are regularities such that nearly everyone conforms; nearly everyone approves of nearly anyone else's conforming and disapproves of his deviating; and this pattern of approval helps to ensure general conformity: whatever the basis on which people actually conform, the pattern of approval makes it unlikely that they will deviate.

3. Many norms will probably be inexplicable from a rational choice point of view. But it is still an important question whether we can identify certain norms such that, under suitable circumstances, rational choice theory predicts that they will emerge and/or persist. Such a rational choice derivation would identify those norms as significantly reliable; with some norms that will be good news, with others bad.

4. The definition of norms suggests that there ought to be two major styles of derivation available. One, the behavior-based strategy, would first explain the behavior of conformity and then explain the attitude of approval for that sort of behavior, given it is in place. The other, the attitude-based strategy, would first explain the attitude of approval for the kind of behavior at issue, whether or not it is in place, and would then explain the conformity in terms of a desire for approval.

5. The standard derivation attempted in rational choice circles is the behavior-based kind. The main examples are David Lewis's derivation of conventional norms and the derivation of tit-for-tat norms associated with a number of recent thinkers.[58] The Lewis derivation is impressive but the tit-for-tat variety has problems, at least for the many-party case.

6. Despite such problems, rational choice theorists have shied away from the other, attitude-based, strategy for deriving norms. They have been impressed, it seems, by the objection that people will find the giving of disapproval costly and will each abstain from the activity, seeking to free ride on the giving of disapproval by others to offending types of behavior. But while this objection may apply to the overt activity of disapproval—or indeed approval—it does not apply to the covert attitude of disapproval. The point is of relevance, because we care about the attitudes, including the unexpressed attitudes, of other people toward us, not just about their overt censure or punishment.

7. This observation shows the way to an attitude-based derivation of certain norms. There are five conditions such that where they are fulfilled rational choice theory predicts that certain norms will emerge and persist. The conditions seem to be fulfilled for some norms in every society—and for some norms in many social subgroups—and the derivation is therefore of practical significance. Just to mention two socially desirable examples, we are pointed toward a norm of not overgrazing the commons and a norm of conscientiousness in jury service.

8. There is a case for enriching our definition of norms, so that the conditions given are a matter of common knowledge. But the derivations discussed here can be extended to make such common knowledge also intelligible.

So much for the ground gained. To finish off our discussion, I turn to an objection: that neither sort of rational choice derivation can make sense of the fact that with many norms people are disposed to approve of conformity and disapprove of deviance on a moral or at least impartial basis, not just on a basis of self-interest. People overtly and covertly censure one another's failures on the basis that they are inimical to the common interest, are unfair, or whatever; they moralize about one another's transgressions. The objection is that rational choice theory cannot explain this and that it does not enable us to derive the presence of any moralized

58. These norms would count as conventions in Sugden's sense. They each represent one of a number of stable equilibria.

norms, as distinct from the norms that fit our comparatively undemanding definition.

The attitude-based derivation identified in this article enables us, happily, to counter the objection. Suppose that an unmoralized norm, N, is in place in a society or group, being explicable in a behavior-based or attitude-based way. It turns out that in that case there is an attitude-based derivation available for the norm of moralizing about N in the society or group: that is, for praising conformity and censuring deviance on an impartial basis, at least in a certain sort of context.

The five conditions under which we would expect a derivation to go through are fulfilled for any such moralizing. Everyone is better off if everyone else moralizes, since the N promoted by moralizing is to everyone's advantage, by the assumption that conformity with it is independently derivable; for similar reasons, everyone is better off in one respect for anyone else's moralizing in that way.[59] Thus the interaction assumption is fulfilled. The publicity and perception assumptions go through smoothly, at least for moralizing that is done in front of third parties. The sanction assumption goes through also, since each person will have reason to approve of anyone else's moralizing and disapprove of his failing to moralize, at least in an appropriate context. Finally, this should give each a motive to moralize that we may expect generally to be effective.

If there is a norm of moralizing about N in place then an offender need not expect everyone who notices him to offer moral censure: the context may not be of the sort appropriate. However, he is in a position to expect that the observer would censure him in the appropriate context, at least were costs low enough. And that means that he is in a position to know that the observer has an attitude of disapproval, specifically of moral disapproval, toward him for what he has done: he may not lay blame on him overtly, but he is bound to be covertly censorious.

This is a nice note to end on. It suggests that resort to the attitude-based strategy does more than extend the domain of rational-choice derivations, targeting norms that would otherwise be underivable. Resort to the attitude-based strategy may also deepen the reach of rational-choice derivations, enabling us to see why the norms derived may come to have a quasi-moral status in the relevant society or subgroup. This is not to derive the "ought" of morality from the "is" of rational self-interest. But it is to say that declaiming about what morally ought to be may be an activity which often makes rational self-interested sense.

59. On the point of moralizing as a practice, see Michael Smith, "Dispositional Theories of Value," *Proceedings of the Aristotelian Society,* supp. vol. 61 (1989).

Part II
Fairness and Equality

[9]

Equality of What?

AMARTYA SEN

Discussions in moral philosophy have offered us a wide menu in answer to the question: equality of what? In this lecture I shall concentrate on three particular types of equality, viz., (i) utilitarian equality, (ii) total utility equality, and (iii) Rawlsian equality. I shall argue that all three have serious limitations, and that while they fail in rather different and contrasting ways, an adequate theory cannot be constructed even on the *combined* grounds of the three. Towards the end I shall try to present an alternative formulation of equality which seems to me to deserve a good deal more attention than it has received, and I shall not desist from doing some propaganda on its behalf.

First a methodological question. When it is claimed that a certain moral principle has shortcomings, what can be the basis of such an allegation? There seem to be at least two different ways of grounding such a criticism, aside from just checking its *direct* appeal to moral intuition. One is to check the *implications* of the principle by taking up particular cases in which the results of employing that principle can be seen in a rather stark way, and then to examine these implications against our intuition. I shall call such a critique a *case-implication critique.* The other is to move not from the general to the particular, but from the general to the *more* general. One can examine the consistency of the principle with another principle that is acknowledged to be more fundamental. Such prior principles are usually formulated at a rather abstract level, and frequently take the form of congruence with some very general procedures. For example, what could be reasonably assumed to have been chosen under the *as if* ignorance of the Rawlsian "original position," a hypothetical primordial

NOTE: For helpful comments I am most grateful to Derek Parfit, Jim Griffin, and John Perry.

state in which people decide on what rules to adopt without knowing who they are going to be — as if they could end up being any one of the persons in the community.[1] Or what rules would satisfy Richard Hare's requirement of "universalizability" and be consistent with "giving equal weights to the equal interests of the occupants of all the roles."[2] I shall call a critique based on such an approach a *prior-principle critique.* Both approaches can be used in assessing the moral claims of each type of equality, and will indeed be used here.

1. Utilitarian Equality

Utilitarian equality is the equality that can be derived from the utilitarian concept of goodness applied to problems of distribution. Perhaps the simplest case is the "pure distribution problem": the problem of dividing a given homogeneous cake among a group of persons.[3] Each person gets more utility the larger his share of the cake, and gets utility *only* from his share of the cake; his utility increases at a diminishing rate as the amount of his share goes up. The utilitarian objective is to maximize the sum-total of utility irrespective of distribution, but that requires the *equality* of the *marginal* utility of everyone — marginal utility being the incremental utility each person would get from an addi-

[1] J. Rawls, *A Theory of Justice* (Cambridge: Harvard University Press, 1971), pp. 17–22. See also W. Vickrey, 'Measuring Marginal Utility by Reactions to Risk', *Econometrica* 13 (1945), and J. C. Harsanyi, 'Cardinal Welfare, Individualistic Ethics, and Interpersonal Comparisons of Utility', *Journal of Political Economy* 63 (1955).

[2] R. M. Hare, *The Language of Morals* (Oxford: Clarendon Press, 1952); 'Ethical Theory and Utilitarianism', in H. D. Lewis, ed., *Contemporary British Philosophy* (London: Allen and Unwin, 1976), pp. 116–17.

[3] I have tried to use this format for an axiomatic contrast of the Rawlsian and utilitarian criteria in 'Rawls versus Bentham: An Axiomatic Examination of the Pure Distribution Problem', in *Theory and Decision* 4 (1974); reprinted in N. Daniels, ed., *Reading Rawls* (Oxford: Blackwell, 1975). See also L. Kern, 'Comparative Distributive Ethics: An Extension of Sen's Examination of the Pure Distribution Problem', in H. W. Gottinger and W. Leinfellner, eds., *Decision Theory and Social Ethics* (Dordrecht: Reidel, 1978), and J. P. Griffin, 'Equality: On Sen's Equity Axiom', Keble College, Oxford, 1978, mimeographed.

tional unit of cake.[4] According to one interpretation, this equality of marginal utility embodies equal treatment of everyone's interests.[5]

The position is a bit more complicated when the total size of the cake is not independent of its distribution. But even then maximization of the total utility sum requires that transfers be carried to the point at which the marginal utility gain of the gainers equals the marginal utility loss of the losers, after taking into account the effect of the transfer on the size and distribution of the cake.[6] It is in this wider context that the special type of equality insisted upon by utilitarianism becomes assertively distinguished. Richard Hare has claimed that "giving equal weight to the equal interests of all the parties" would "lead to utilitarianism" — thus satisfying the prior-principle requirement of universalizability.[7] Similarly, John Harsanyi shoots down the non-utilitarians (including this lecturer, I hasten to add), by claiming for utilitarianism an exclusive ability to avoid "unfair discrimination" between "one person's and another person's equally urgent human needs."[8]

The moral importance of needs, on this interpretation, is based exclusively on the notion of utility. This is disputable, and having had several occasions to dispute it in the past,[9] I shall not shy away

[4] The equality condition would have to be replaced by a corresponding combination of inequality requirements when the appropriate "continuity" properties do not hold. Deeper difficulties are raised by "non-convexities" (e.g., increasing marginal utility).

[5] J. Harsanyi, 'Can the Maximin Principle Serve as a Basis for Morality? A Critique of John Rawls' Theory', *American Political Science Review* 64 (1975).

[6] As mentioned in footnote 4, the equality conditions would require modification in the absence of continuity of the appropriate type. Transfers must be carried to the point at which the marginal utility gain of the gainers from any further transfer is *no more than* the marginal utility loss of the losers.

[7] Hare (1976), pp. 116–17.

[8] John Harsanyi, 'Non-linear Social Welfare Functions: A Rejoinder to Professor Sen', in R. E. Butts and J. Hintikka, eds., *Foundational Problems in the Special Sciences* (Dordrecht: Reidel, 1977), pp. 294–95.

[9] *Collective Choice and Social Welfare* (San Francisco: Holden-Day, 1970), chapter 6 and section 11.4; 'On Weights and Measures: Informational Constraints in

from disputing it in this particular context. But while I will get on to this issue later, I want first to examine the nature of utilitarian equality without — for the time being — questioning the grounding of moral importance entirely on utility. Even when utility is the sole basis of importance there is still the question as to whether the size of *marginal* utility, irrespective of *total* utility enjoyed by the person, is an adequate index of moral importance. It is, of course, possible to define a metric on utility characteristics such that each person's utility scale is coordinated with everyone else's in a way that equal social importance is simply "scaled" as equal marginal utility. If interpersonal comparisons of utility are taken to have no descriptive content, then this can indeed be thought to be a natural approach. No matter how the relative social importances are arrived at, the marginal utilities attributed to each person would then simply reflect these values. This can be done explicitly by appropriate interpersonal scaling,[10] or implicitly through making the utility numbering reflect choices in situations of *as if* uncertainty associated with the "original position" under the additional assumption that ignorance be interpreted as equal probability of being anyone.[11] This is not the occasion to go into the technical details of this type of exercise, but the essence of it consists in using a scaling procedure such that marginal utility measures are automatically identified as indicators of social importance.

This route to utilitarianism may meet with little resistance, but it is non-controversial mainly because it says so little. A prob-

---

Social Welfare Analysis', *Econometrica* 45 (1977). See also T. M. Scanlon's arguments against identifying utility with "urgency" in his 'Preference and Urgency', *Journal of Philosophy* 72 (1975).

[10] For two highly ingenious examples of such an exercise, see Peter Hammond, 'Dual Interpersonal Comparisons of Utility and the Welfare Economics of Income Distribution', *Journal of Public Economics* 6 (1977): 51–57; and Menahem Yaari, 'Rawls, Edgeworth, Shapley and Nash: Theories of Distributive Justice Re-examined', Research Memorandum No. 33, Center for Research in Mathematical Economics and Game Theory, Hebrew University, Jerusalem, 1978.

[11] See Harsanyi (1955, 1975, 1977).

lem arises the moment utilities and interpersonal comparisons thereof are taken to have some independent descriptive content, as utilitarians have traditionally insisted that they do. There could then be conflicts between these descriptive utilities and the appropriately scaled, essentially normative, utilities in terms of which one is "forced" to be a utilitarian. In what follows I shall have nothing more to say on utilitarianism through appropriate interpersonal scaling, and return to examining the traditional utilitarian position, which takes utilities to have interpersonally comparable descriptive content. How moral importance should relate to these descriptive features must, then, be explicitly faced.

The position can be examined from the prior-principle perspective as well as from the case-implication angle. John Rawls's criticism as a preliminary to presenting his own alternative conception of justice took mostly the prior-principle form. This was chiefly in terms of acceptability in the "original position," arguing that in the postulated situation of *as if* ignorance people would not choose to maximize the utility sum. But Rawls also discussed the violence that utilitarianism does to our notions of liberty and equality. Some replies to Rawls's arguments have reasserted the necessity to be a utilitarian by taking the "scaling" route, which was discussed earlier, and which — I think — is inappropriate in meeting Rawls's critique. But I must confess that I find the lure of the "original position" distinctly resistible since it seems very unclear what precisely would be chosen in such a situation. It is also far from obvious that prudential choice under *as if* uncertainty provides an adequate basis for moral judgment in *un*-original, i.e., real-life, positions.[12] But I believe Rawls's more direct critiques in terms of liberty and equality do remain powerful.

Insofar as one is concerned with the *distribution* of utilities, it

[12] On this, see Thomas Nagel, 'Rawls on Justice', *Philosophical Review* 83 (1973), and 'Equality' in his *Mortal Questions* (Cambridge: Cambridge University Press, 1979).

follows immediately that utilitarianism would in general give one little comfort. Even the minutest gain in total utility *sum* would be taken to outweigh distributional inequalities of the most blatant kind. This problem would be avoidable under certain assumptions, notably the case in which everyone has the *same* utility function. In the pure distribution problem, with this assumption the utilitarian best would require absolute equality of everyone's total utilities.[13] This is because when the marginal utilities are equated, so would be the total utilities if everyone has the same utility function. This is, however, egalitarianism by serendipity: just the accidental result of the marginal tail wagging the total dog. More importantly, the assumption would be very frequently violated, since there are obvious and well-discussed variations between human beings. John may be easy to please, but Jeremy not. If it is taken to be an acceptable prior-principle that the equality of the distribution of total utilities has some value, then the utilitarian conception of equality — marginal as it is — must stand condemned.

The recognition of the fundamental diversity of human beings does, in fact, have very deep consequences, affecting not merely the utilitarian conception of social good, but others as well, including (as I shall argue presently) even the Rawlsian conception of equality. If human beings are identical, then the application of the prior-principle of universalizability in the form of "giving equal weight to the equal interest of all parties" simplifies enormously. Equal marginal utilities of all — reflecting one interpretation of the equal treatment of needs — coincides with equal total utilities — reflecting one interpretation of serving their overall interests equally well. With diversity, the two can pull in opposite directions, and it is far from clear that "giving equal weight to

[13] The problem is much more complex when the total cake is not fixed, and where the maximization of utility sum need not lead to the equality of total utilities unless some additional assumptions are made, e.g., the absence of incentive arguments for inequality.

the equal interest of all parties" would require us to concentrate only on one of the two parameters — taking no note of the other.

The case-implication perspective can also be used to develop a related critique, and I have tried to present such a critique elsewhere.[14] For example, if person A as a cripple gets half the utility that the pleasure-wizard person B does from any given level of income, then in the pure distribution problem between A and B the utilitarian would end up giving the pleasure-wizard B more income than the cripple A. The cripple would then be doubly worse off: both since he gets less utility from the same level of income, *and* since he will also get less income. Utilitarianism must lead to this thanks to its single-minded concern with maximizing the utility sum. The pleasure-wizard's superior efficiency in producing utility would pull income away from the less efficient cripple.

Since this example has been discussed a certain amount,[15] I should perhaps explain what is being asserted and what is not. First, it is *not* being claimed that anyone who has lower total utility (e.g., the cripple) at any given level of income must of necessity have lower marginal utility also. This must be true for some levels of income, but need not be true everywhere. Indeed, the opposite could be the case when incomes are equally distributed. If that were so, then of course even utilitarianism would give the cripple more income than the non-cripple, since at that point the cripple would be the more efficient producer of utility. My point is that there is no guarantee that this will be the case, and more particularly, if it were the case that the cripple were not only worse off in terms of total utility but could convert income into utility less efficiently everywhere (or even just at the point of

14 *On Economic Inequality* (Oxford: Clarendon Press, 1973), pp. 16–20.

15 See John Harsanyi, 'Non-linear Social Welfare Functions', *Theory and Decision* 6 (1976): 311–12; Harsanyi (1977); Kern (1978); Griffin (1978); Richard B. Brandt, *A Theory of the Good and the Right* (Oxford: Clarendon Press, 1979), chapter 16.

equal income division), then utilitarianism would compound his disadvantage by settling him with less income on top of lower efficiency in making utility out of income. The point, of course, is not about cripples in general, nor about all people with total utility disadvantage, but concerns people — including cripples — with disadvantage in terms of both total *and* marginal utility at the relevant points.

Second, the descriptive content of utility is rather important in this context. Obviously, if utilities were scaled to reflect moral importance, then wishing to give priority to income for the cripple would simply amount to attributing a higher "marginal utility" to the cripple's income; but this — as we have already discussed — is a very special sense of utility — quite devoid of descriptive content. In terms of descriptive features, what is being assumed in our example is that the cripple can be helped by giving him income, but the increase in his utility as a consequence of a marginal increase in income is less — in terms of the accepted descriptive criteria — than giving that unit of income to the pleasure-wizard, when both have initially the same income.

Finally, the problem for utilitarianism in this case-implication argument is not dependent on an implicit assumption that the claim to more income arising from disadvantage must dominate over the claim arising from high marginal utility.[16] A system that gives some weight to both claims would still fail to meet the utilitarian formula of social good, which demands an exclusive concern with the latter claim. It is this narrowness that makes the utilitarian conception of equality such a limited one. Even when utility is accepted as the only basis of moral importance, utilitarianism fails to capture the relevance of overall advantage for the requirements of equality. The prior-principle critiques can be supplemented by case-implication critiques using this utilitarian lack

[16] Such an assumption is made in my Weak Equity Axiom, proposed in Sen (1973), but it is unnecessarily demanding for rejecting utilitarianism. See Griffin (1978) for a telling critique of the Weak Equity Axiom, in this exacting form.

of concern with distributional questions except at the entirely marginal level.

2. Total Utility Equality

Welfarism is the view that the goodness of a state of affairs can be judged entirely by the goodness of the utilities in that state.[17] This is a less demanding view than utilitarianism in that it does not demand — in addition — that the goodness of the utilities must be judged by their sum-total. Utilitarianism is, in this sense, a special case of welfarism, and provides one illustration of it. Another distinguished case is the criterion of judging the goodness of a state by the utility level of the worst-off person in that state — a criterion often attributed to John Rawls. (*Except* by John Rawls! He uses social primary goods rather than utility as the index of advantage, as we shall presently discuss.) One can also take some other function of the utilities — other than the sum-total or the minimal element.

Utilitarian equality is one type of welfarist equality. There are others, notably the equality of total utility. It is tempting to think of this as some kind of an analogue of utilitarianism shifting the focus from marginal utility to total utility. This correspondence is, however, rather less close than it might first appear. First of all, while we economists often tend to treat the marginal and the total as belonging to the same plane of discourse, there is an important difference between them. Marginal is an essentially *counter-factual* notion: marginal utility is the additional utility that *would be* generated if the person had one more unit of income. It contrasts what is observed with what allegedly would be observed if something else were different: in this case if the income had been one unit greater. Total is not, however, an inherently counter-factual concept; whether it is or is not would

[17] See Sen (1977), and also my 'Welfarism and Utilitarianism', *Journal of Philosophy* 76 (1979).

depend on the variable that is being totalled. In case of utilities, if they are taken to be observed facts, total utility will not be counter-factual. Thus total utility equality is a matter for direct observation, whereas utilitarian equality is not so, since the latter requires hypotheses as to what things would have been under different postulated circumstances. The contrast can be easily traced to the fact that utilitarian equality is essentially a consequence of sum *maximization*, which is itself a counter-factual notion, whereas total utility equality is an equality of some directly observed magnitudes.

Second, utilitarianism provides a complete ordering of all utility distributions — the ranking reflecting the order of the sums of individual utilities—but as specified so far, total utility equality does not do more than just point to the case of absolute equality. In dealing with two cases of non-equal distributions, something more has to be said so that they could be ranked. The ranking can be completed in many different ways.

One way to such a complete ranking is provided by the lexicographic version of the maximin rule, which is associated with the Rawlsian Difference Principle, but interpreted in terms of utilities as opposed to primary goods. Here the goodness of the state of affairs is judged by the level of utility of the worst-off person in that state; but if the worst-off persons in two states respectively have the same level of utility, then the states are ranked according to the utility levels of the second worst-off. If they too tie, then by the utility levels of the third worst-off, and so on. And if two utility distributions are matched at each rank all the way from the worst off to the best off, then the two distributions are equally good. Following a convention established in social choice theory, I shall call this *leximin.*

In what way does total utility equality lead to the leximin? It does this when combined with some other axioms, and in fact the analysis closely parallels the recent axiomatic derivations of the Difference Principle by several authors.[18] Consider four utility levels *a*, *b*, *c*, *d*, in decreasing order of magnitude. One can argue that in an obvious sense the pair of extreme points (*a*, *d*) displays greater inequality than the pair of intermediate points (*b*, *c*). Note that this is a purely *ordinal* comparison based on ranking only, and the exact magnitudes of *a*, *b*, *c*, and *d* make no difference to the comparison in question. If one were *solely* concerned with equality, then it could be argued that (*b*, *c*) is superior — or at least non-inferior — to (*a*, *d*). This requirement may be seen as a strong version of preferring equality of utility distributions, and may be called "utility equality preference." It is possible to combine this with an axiom due to Patrick Suppes which captures the notion of *dominance* of one utility distribution over another, in the sense of each element of one distribution being at least as large as the corresponding element in the other distribution.[19] In the two-person case this requires that state *x* must be regarded as at least as good as *y*, *either* if each person in state *x* has at least as much utility as himself in state *y*, *or* if each person in state *x* has at least as much utility as the *other* person in state *y*. *If*, in addition, at least one of them has strictly more, then of course *x* could be declared to be strictly better (and not merely at least as good). If this Suppes principle and the "utility equality preference" are combined, then we are pushed in the direction of leximin. Indeed, leximin can be fully derived from these two principles by requiring that the approach must provide a com-

[18] See P. J. Hammond, 'Equity, Arrow's Conditions and Rawls' Difference Principle', *Econometrica* 44 (1976); S. Strasnick, 'Social Choice Theory and the Derivation of Rawls' Difference Principle', *Journal of Philosophy* 73 (1976); C. d'Aspremont and L. Gevers, 'Equity and Informational Basis of Collective Choice', *Review of Economic Studies* 44 (1977); K. J. Arrow, 'Extended Sympathy and the Possibility of Social Choice', *American Economic Review* 67 (1977); A. K. Sen, 'On Weights and Measures: Informational Constraints in Social Welfare Analysis', *Econometrica* 45 (1977); R. Deschamps and L. Gevers, 'Leximin and Utilitarian Rules: A Joint Characterization', *Journal of Economic Theory* 17 (1978); K. W. S. Roberts, 'Possibility Theorems with Interpersonally Comparable Welfare Levels', *Review of Economic Studies* 47 (1980); P. J. Hammond, 'Two Person Equity', *Econometrica* 47 (1979).

[19] P. Suppes, 'Some Formal Models of Grading Principles', *Synthese* 6 (1966).

plete ordering of all possible states no matter what the interpersonally comparable individual utilities happen to be (called "unrestricted domain"), and that the ranking of any two states must depend on utility information concerning *those* states only (called "independence").

Insofar as the requirements other than utility equality preference (i.e., the Suppes principle, unrestricted domain, and independence) are regarded as acceptable — and they have indeed been widely used in the social choice literature — leximin can be seen as the natural concomitant of giving priority to the conception of equality focussing on total utility.

It should be obvious, however, that leximin can be fairly easily criticised from the prior-principle perspective as well as the case-implication perspective. Just as utilitarianism pays no attention to the force of one's claim arising from one's disadvantage, leximin ignores claims arising from the *intensity* of one's needs. The *ordinal* characteristic that was pointed out while presenting the axiom of utility equality preference makes the approach insensitive to the magnitudes of potential utility gains and losses. While in the critique of utilitarianism that was presented earlier I argued against treating these potential gains and losses as the only basis of moral judgment, it was *not* of course alleged that these have no moral relevance at all. Take the comparison of (a, d) vis-à-vis (b, c), discussed earlier, and let (b, c) stand for $(3, 2)$. Utility equality preference would assert the superiority of $(3, 2)$ over $(10, 1)$ as well as $(4, 1)$. Indeed, it would not distinguish between the two cases at all. It is this lack of concern with "how much" questions that makes leximin rather easy to criticise *either* by showing its failure to comply with such prior-principles as "giving equal weight to the equal interest of all parties," *or* by spelling out its rather austere implications in specific cases.

Aside from its indifference to "how much" questions, leximin also has little interest in "how many" questions — paying no attention at all to the number of people whose interests are overridden in the pursuit of the interests of the worst off. The worst-off position rules the roost, and it does not matter whether this goes against the interests of one other person, or against those of a million or a billion other persons. It is sometimes claimed that leximin would not be such an extreme criterion if it could be modified so that this innumeracy were avoided, and if the interests of *one* worse-off position were given priority over the interests of exactly *one* better-off position, but not necessarily against the interests of *more than one* better-off position. In fact, one can define a less demanding version of leximin, which can be called leximin-2, which takes the form of applying the leximin principle *if* all persons other than two are indifferent between the alternatives, but not necessarily otherwise. Leximin-2, as a compromise, will be still unconcerned with "how much" questions on the magnitudes of utilities of the two non-indifferent persons, but need not be blinkered about "how many" questions dealing with numbers of people: the priority applies to one person over exactly one other.[20]

Interestingly enough, a consistency problem intervenes here. It can be proved that given the regularity conditions, viz., unrestricted domain and independence, leximin-2 logically entails leximin in general.[21] That is, given these regularity conditions, there is no way of retaining moral sensitivity to the number of people on each side by choosing the limited requirement of leximin-2 without going all the way to leximin itself. It appears that indifference to *how much* questions concerning utilities implies indifference to *how many* questions concerning the number of

[20] Leximin — and maximin — are concerned with conflicts between positional priorities, i.e., between ranks (such as the "worst-off position," "second worst-off position," etc.), and not with interpersonal priorities. When positions coincide with persons (e.g., the *same* person being the worst off in each state), then positional conflicts translate directly into personal conflicts.

[21] Theorem 8, Sen (1977). See also Hammond (1979) for extensions of this result.

people on different sides. One innumeracy begets another.

Given the nature of these critiques of utilitarian equality and total utility equality respectively, it is natural to ask whether some *combination* of the two should not meet both sets of objections. If utilitarianism is attacked for its unconcern with inequalities of the utility distribution, and leximin is criticised for its lack of interest in the magnitudes of utility gains and losses, and even in the numbers involved, then isn't the right solution to choose some mixture of the two? It is at this point that the long-postponed question of the relation between utility and moral worth becomes crucial. While utilitarianism and leximin differ sharply from each other in the use that they respectively make of the utility information, both share an exclusive concern with utility data. If non-utility considerations have any role in either approach, this arises from the part they play in the determination of utilities, or possibly as surrogates for utility information in the absence of adequate utility data. A combination of utilitarianism and leximin would still be confined to the box of welfarism, and it remains to be examined whether welfarism as a general approach is *itself* adequate.

One aspect of the obtuseness of welfarism was discussed clearly by John Rawls.

> In calculating the greatest balance of satisfaction it does not matter, except indirectly, what the desires are for. We are to arrange institutions so as to obtain the greatest sum of satisfactions; we ask no questions about their source or quality but only how their satisfaction would affect the total of well-being. . . . Thus if men take a certain pleasure in discriminating against one another, in subjecting others to a lesser liberty as a means of enhancing their self-respect, then the satisfaction of these desires must be weighed in our deliberations according to their intensity, or whatever, along with other desires. . . . In justice as fairness, on the other hand, persons accept in advance a principle of equal liberty and they do this without a knowledge of their more particular ends. . . . An individual who finds that he enjoys seeing

others in positions of lesser liberty understands that he has no claim whatever to this enjoyment. The pleasure he takes in other's deprivation is wrong in itself: it is a satisfaction which requires the violation of a principle to which he would agree in the original position.[22]

It is easily seen that this is an argument not merely against utilitarianism, but against the adequacy of utility information for moral judgments of states of affairs, and is, thus, an attack on welfarism in general. Second, it is clear that as a criticism of welfarism — and *a fortiori* as a critique of utilitarianism — the argument uses a principle that is unnecessarily strong. If it were the case that pleasures taken "in other's deprivation" were not taken to be wrong in itself, but simply *disregarded*, even then the rejection of welfarism would stand. Furthermore, even if such pleasures were regarded as valuable, but *less* valuable than pleasures arising from other sources (e.g., enjoying food, work, or leisure), welfarism would still stand rejected. The issue — as John Stuart Mill had noted — is the lack of "parity" between one source of utility and another.[23] Welfarism requires the endorsement not merely of the widely shared intuition that any pleasure has some value — and one would have to be a bit of a kill-joy to dissent from this — but also the much more dubious proposition that pleasures must be relatively weighed *only* according to their respective intensities, irrespective of the source of the pleasure and the nature of the activity that goes with it. Finally, Rawls's argument takes the form of an appeal to the prior-principle of equating moral rightness with prudential acceptability in the original position. Even those who do not accept that prior principle could reject the welfarist no-nonsense counting of utility irrespective of all other information by reference to other prior principles, e.g., the irreducible value of liberty.

[22] Rawls (1971), pp. 30–31.

[23] John Stuart Mill, *On Liberty* (1859), p. 140.

The relevance of non-utility information to moral judgments is the central issue involved in disputing welfarism. Libertarian considerations point towards a particular class of non-utility information, and I have argued elsewhere that this may require even the rejection of the so-called Pareto principle based on utility dominance.[24] But there are also other types of non-utility information which have been thought to be intrinsically important. Tim Scanlon has recently discussed the contrast between "urgency" and utility (or intensity of preference). He has also argued that "the criteria of well-being that we actually employ in making moral judgments are objective," and a person's level of well-being is taken to be "independent of that person's tastes and interests."[25] These moral judgments could thus conflict with utilitarian — and more generally (Scanlon could have argued) with welfarist — moralities, no matter whether utility is interpreted as pleasure, or — as is increasingly common recently — as desire-fulfilment.

However, acknowledging the relevance of objective factors does not require that well-being be taken to be independent of tastes, and Scanlon's categories are *too* pure. For example, a lack of "parity" between utility from self-regarding actions and that from other-regarding actions will go beyond utility as an index of well-being and will be fatal to welfarism, but the contrast is not, of course, independent of tastes and subjective features. "Objective" considerations can count along with a person's tastes. What is required is the denial that a person's well-being be judged *exclusively* in terms of his or her utilities. If such judgments take into account a person's pleasures and desire-fulfilments, but also certain objective factors, e.g., whether he or she is hungry, cold, or oppressed, the resulting calculus would still be non-welfarist. Welfarism is an extremist position, and its denial can take many different forms — pure and mixed — so long as totally ignoring non-utility information is avoided.

[24] Sen (1970), especially chapter 6. Also Sen (1979).

[25] T. M. Scanlon (1975), pp. 658–59.

Second, it is also clear that the notion of urgency need not work only *through* the determinants of personal well-being — however broadly conceived. For example, the claim that one should not be *exploited* at work is not based on making exploitation an additional parameter in the specification of well-being on top of such factors as income and effort, but on the moral view that a person deserves to get what he — according to one way of characterizing production — has produced. Similarly, the urgency deriving from principles such as "equal pay for equal work" hits directly at discrimination without having to redefine the notion of personal well-being to take note of such discriminations. One could, for example, say: "She must be paid just as much as the men working in that job, not primarily because she would otherwise have a lower level of well-being than the others, but simply because she is doing the *same* work as the men there, and why should she be paid less?" These moral claims, based on non-welfarist conceptions of equality, have played important parts in social movements, and it seems difficult to sustain the hypothesis that they are purely "instrumental" claims — ultimately justified by their indirect impact on the fulfilment of welfarist, or other well-being-based, objectives.

Thus the dissociation of urgency from utility can arise from two different sources. One disentangles the notion of personal well-being from utility, and the other makes urgency not a function only of well-being. But, at the same time, the former does not require that well-being be independent of utility, and the latter does not necessitate a notion of urgency that is independent of personal well-being. Welfarism is a purist position and must avoid any contamination from either of these sources.

3. Rawlsian Equality

Rawls's "two principles of justice" characterize the need for equality in terms of — what he has called — "primary social goods."[26] These are "things that every rational man is presumed to want," including "rights, liberties and opportunities, income and wealth, and the social bases of self-respect." Basic liberties are separated out as having priority over other primary goods, and thus priority is given to the principle of liberty which demands that "each person is to have an equal right to the most extensive basic liberty compatible with a similar liberty for others." The second principle supplements this, demanding efficiency and equality, judging advantage in terms of an index of primary goods. Inequalities are condemned unless they work out to everyone's advantage. This incorporates the "Difference Principle" in which priority is given to furthering the interests of the worst-off. And that leads to maximin, or to leximin, defined not on individual utilities but on the index of primary goods. But given the priority of the liberty principle, no trade-offs are permitted between basic liberties and economic and social gain.

Herbert Hart has persuasively disputed Rawls's arguments for the priority of liberty,[27] but with that question I shall not be concerned in this lecture. What is crucial for the problem under discussion is the concentration on bundles of primary social goods. Some of the difficulties with welfarism that I tried to discuss will not apply to the pursuit of Rawlsian equality. Objective criteria of well-being can be directly accommodated within the index of primary goods. So can be Mill's denial of the parity between pleasures from different sources, since the sources can be discriminated on the basis of the nature of the goods. Furthermore, while the Difference Principle is egalitarian in a way similar to leximin, it avoids the much-criticised feature of leximin of giving more income to people who are hard to please and who have to be deluged in champagne and buried in caviar to bring them to a

[26] Rawls (1971), pp. 60–65.

[27] H. L. A. Hart, 'Rawls on Liberty and Its Priority', *University of Chicago Law Review* 40 (1973); reprinted in N. Daniels, ed., *Reading Rawls* (Oxford: Blackwell, 1975).

normal level of utility, which you and I get from a sandwich and beer. Since advantage is judged not in terms of utilities at all, but through the index of primary goods, expensive tastes cease to provide a ground for getting more income. Rawls justifies this in terms of a person's responsibility for his own ends.

But what about the cripple with utility disadvantage, whom we discussed earlier? Leximin will give him more income in a pure distribution problem. Utilitarianism, I had complained, will give him *less*. The Difference Principle will give him neither more nor less on grounds of his being a cripple. His utility disadvantage will be irrelevant to the Difference Principle. This may seem hard, and I think it is. Rawls justifies this by pointing out that "hard cases" can "distract our moral perception by leading us to think of people distant from us whose fate arouses pity and anxiety."[28] This can be so, but hard cases do exist, and to take disabilities, or special health needs, or physical or mental defects, as morally irrelevant, or to leave them out for fear of making a mistake, may guarantee that the *opposite* mistake will be made.

And the problem does not end with hard cases. The primary goods approach seems to take little note of the diversity of human beings. In the context of assessing utilitarian equality, it was argued that if people were fundamentally similar in terms of utility functions, then the utilitarian concern with maximizing the sum-total of utilities would push us simultaneously also in the direction of equality of utility levels. Thus utilitarianism could be rendered vastly more attractive if people really were similar. A corresponding remark can be made about the Rawlsian Difference Principle. If people were basically very similar, then an index of primary goods might be quite a good way of judging advantage. But, in fact, people seem to have very different needs varying with health, longevity, climatic conditions, location, work

[28] John Rawls, 'A Kantian Concept of Equality', *Cambridge Review* (February 1975), p. 96.

conditions, temperament, and even body size (affecting food and clothing requirements). So what is involved is not merely ignoring a few hard cases, but overlooking very widespread and real differences. Judging advantage purely in terms of primary goods leads to a partially blind morality.

Indeed, it can be argued that there is, in fact, an element of "fetishism" in the Rawlsian framework. Rawls takes primary goods as the embodiment of advantage, rather than taking advantage to be a *relationship* between persons and goods. Utilitarianism, or leximin, or — more generally — welfarism does not have this fetishism, since utilities are reflections of one type of relation between persons and goods. For example, income and wealth are not valued under utilitarianism as physical units, but in terms of their capacity to create human happiness or to satisfy human desires. Even if utility is not thought to be the right focus for the person–good relationship, to have an entirely good-oriented framework provides a peculiar way of judging advantage.

It can also be argued that while utility in the form of happiness or desire-fulfilment may be an *inadequate* guide to urgency, the Rawlsian framework asserts it to be *irrelevant* to urgency, which is, of course, a much stronger claim. The distinction was discussed earlier in the context of assessing welfarism, and it was pointed out that a rejection of welfarism need not take us to the point in which utility is given no role whatsoever. That a person's interest should have nothing directly to do with his happiness or desire-fulfilment seems difficult to justify. Even in terms of the prior-principle of prudential acceptability in the "original position," it is not at all clear why people in that primordial state should be taken to be so indifferent to the joys and sufferings in occupying particular positions, or if they are not, why their concern about these joys and sufferings should be taken to be morally irrelevant.

4. Basic Capability Equality

This leads to the further question: Can we not construct an adequate theory of equality on the *combined* grounds of Rawlsian equality and equality under the two welfarist conceptions, with some trade-offs among them. I would now like to argue briefly why I believe this too may prove to be informationally short. This can, of course, easily be asserted *if* claims arising from considerations other than well-being were acknowledged to be legitimate. Non-exploitation, or non-discrimination, requires the use of information not fully captured either by utility or by primary goods. Other conceptions of entitlements can also be brought in going beyond concern with personal well-being only. But in what follows I shall not introduce these concepts. My contention is that *even* the concept of *needs* does not get adequate coverage through the information on primary goods and utility.

I shall use a case-implication argument. Take the cripple again with marginal utility disadvantage. We saw that utilitarianism would do nothing for him; in fact it will give him *less* income than to the physically fit. Nor would the Difference Principle help him; it will leave his physical disadvantage severely alone. He did, however, get preferential treatment under leximin, and more generally, under criteria fostering total equality. His low level of total utility was the basis of his claim. But now suppose that he is no worse off than others in utility terms despite his physical handicap because of certain other utility features. This could be because he has a jolly disposition. Or because he has a low aspiration level and his heart leaps up whenever he sees a rainbow in the sky. Or because he is religious and feels that he will be rewarded in after-life, or cheerfully accepts what he takes to be just penalty for misdeeds in a past incarnation. The important point is that despite his marginal utility disadvantage, he has no longer a total utility deprivation. Now not even leximin — or any other notion of equality focussing on total utility — will do much for him. If we still think that he has needs as a cripple that should be catered to, then the basis of that claim clearly rests neither in high marginal utility, nor in low total utility, nor — of course — in deprivation in terms of primary goods.

It is arguable that what is missing in all this framework is some notion of "basic capabilities": a person being able to do certain basic things. The ability to move about is the relevant one here, but one can consider others, e.g., the ability to meet one's nutritional requirements, the wherewithal to be clothed and sheltered, the power to participate in the social life of the community. The notion of urgency related to this is not fully captured by either utility or primary goods, or any combination of the two. Primary goods suffers from fetishist handicap in being concerned with goods, and even though the list of goods is specified in a broad and inclusive way, encompassing rights, liberties, opportunities, income, wealth, and the social basis of self-respect, it still is concerned with good things rather than with what these good things *do* to human beings. Utility, on the other hand, *is* concerned with what these things do to human beings, but uses a metric that focusses not on the person's capabilities but on his mental reaction. There is something still missing in the combined list of primary goods and utilities. If it is argued that resources should be devoted to remove or substantially reduce the handicap of the cripple despite there being no marginal utility argument (because it is expensive), despite there being no total utility argument (because he is so contented), and despite there being no primary goods deprivation (because he has the goods that others have), the case must rest on something else. I believe what is at issue is the interpretation of needs in the form of basic capabilities. This interpretation of needs and interests is often implicit in the demand for equality. This type of equality I shall call "basic capability equality."

The focus on basic capabilities can be seen as a natural extension of Rawls's concern with primary goods, shifting attention from goods to what goods do to human beings. Rawls himself motivates judging advantage in terms of primary goods by referring to capabilities, even though his criteria end up focussing on goods as such: on income rather than on what income does, on the "social bases of self-respect" rather than on self-respect itself, and so on. If human beings were very like each other, this would not have mattered a great deal, but there is evidence that the conversion of goods to capabilities varies from person to person substantially, and the equality of the former may still be far from the equality of the latter.

There are, of course, many difficulties with the notion of "basic capability equality." In particular, the problem of indexing the basic capability bundles is a serious one. It is, in many ways, a problem comparable with the indexing of primary good bundles in the context of Rawlsian equality. This is not the occasion to go into the technical issues involved in such an indexing, but it is clear that whatever partial ordering can be done on the basis of broad uniformity of personal preferences must be supplemented by certain established conventions of relative importance.

The ideas of relative importance are, of course, conditional on the nature of the society. The notion of the equality of basic capabilities is a very general one, but any application of it must be rather culture-dependent, especially in the weighting of different capabilities. While Rawlsian equality has the characteristic of being both culture-dependent and fetishist, basic capability equality avoids fetishism, but remains culture-dependent. Indeed, basic capability equality can be seen as essentially an extension of the Rawlsian approach in a non-fetishist direction.

5. Concluding Remarks

I end with three final remarks. First, it is not my contention that basic capability equality can be the sole guide to the moral good. For one thing morality is not concerned only with equality.

For another, while it is my contention that basic capability equality has certain clear advantages over other types of equality, I did not argue that the others were morally irrelevant. Basic capability equality is a partial guide to the part of moral goodness that is associated with the idea of equality. I have tried to argue that as a partial guide it has virtues that the other characterisations of equality do not possess.

Second, the index of basic capabilities, like utility, can be used in many different ways. Basic capability equality corresponds to total utility equality, and it can be extended in different directions, e.g., to leximin of basic capabilities. On the other hand, the index can be used also in a way similar to utilitarianism, judging the strength of a claim in terms of incremental contribution to *enhancing* the index value. The main departure is in focussing on a *magnitude* different from utility as well as the primary goods index. The new dimension can be utilised in different ways, of which basic capability equality is only one.

Last, the bulk of this lecture has been concerned with rejecting the claims of utilitarian equality, total utility equality, and Rawlsian equality to provide a sufficient basis for the equality-aspect of morality — indeed, even for that part of it which is concerned with needs rather than deserts. I have argued that none of these three is sufficient, nor is any combination of the three.

This is my main thesis. I have also made the constructive claim that this gap can be narrowed by the idea of basic capability equality, and more generally by the use of basic capability as a morally relevant dimension taking us beyond utility and primary goods. I should end by pointing out that the validity of the main thesis is not conditional on the acceptance of this constructive claim.

[10]

Some Problems of Fairness

James Griffin

WHAT THE PROBLEMS ARE

Cooperation raises severe and well-known problems. The most famous example of a problem of cooperation is the Prisoner's Dilemma. But there is another overlapping sort. Sometimes what matter are cumulative effects of actions, effects that singly make only a small, often imperceptible difference, and occasionally no difference at all, but together make a great difference. If one person living in the center of my town burns logs on his fire, the deposit that the smoke makes on the buildings will be imperceptible, and the next rain will wash it away. But if enough people do, the buildings will be permanently damaged and everyone will be worse off. This category only overlaps the Prisoner's Dilemma because cases of this type can involve only one person. If I once cut across your lawn, no damage is done; if I do it often enough, I wear a path. The trouble in these cases, whether involving one or many persons, arises simply from the fact that each consequence on its own is slight or, with time, entirely reversed. Whatever the other people living in the center of my town do, *my* burning a log fire will make no difference. Whatever I do at other times, my *now* cutting across your lawn will make no difference.

Cooperation raises many more problems than I want to talk about. I want to talk about two terribly familiar ones. Cooperation raises problems of *fairness.* What should the terms of cooperation be? If I voluntarily benefit from cooperation, should I not myself cooperate? And should I not even if nothing bad would happen if I did not? And cooperation raises problems of *moral perspective.* How wide does our perspective have to be to take in everything that matters morally? The problem of perspective is distinct from the problem of fairness because, although it arises in cases of fairness, it also crops up in cases where fairness does not. If a moral theory tells me to look only at the consequences of the act that I am contemplating and to compare them to the consequences of the alternatives open to me here and now, I shall miss the fact that acts can be parts of series, of practices, of activities. What matters are the consequences not just of my now cutting across or not cutting across your lawn but of my making a habit of it.

These are difficult problems, one way or another, for all moral theories, but they are thought to be particularly worrying for utilitarianism, at

Ethics 96 (October 1985): 100–118

least for common forms of it. There is the problem of moral perspective. If no one in my town burns logs, then I do no harm by doing so myself and, what is more, I get the benefit of a log fire. If everyone does, the same is true. Whatever number between "all" and "none" burn logs,the same is true. So utility, it seems, will be maximized if I do.[1] And there is a problem of fairness. Suppose I know that virtually no one else will burn logs, although they would like to. Then it will produce no harm

1. It is a contentious matter whether any kind of utilitarian reasoning, even the kind that I imagine here in which the agent ignores the effects of what groups do and concentrates on his own action in isolation, would lead to the conclusion that I ought to burn logs. Mancur Olson has argued, as I do here, that the conclusion "holds true whether behaviour is selfish or unselfish, so long as it is strictly speaking 'rational'. Even if the member of a large group were to neglect his own interests entirely, he still would not rationally contribute toward the provision of any collective or public good, since his own contribution would not be perceptible" (*The Logic of Collective Action* [Cambridge, Mass.: Harvard University Press, 1965], p. 64). To which Brian Barry has replied, "This is surely absurd. If each contribution is literally 'imperceptible' how can all the contributions together add up to anything?" (*Sociologists, Economists and Democracy* [Chicago: University of Chicago Press, 1978], p. 32). The fullest discussion that I know of is Donald Regan's in *Utilitarianism and Co-operation* (Oxford: Clarendon Press, 1980). He thinks that a person who argues as I do is committed to "logically inconsistent assumptions. On the one hand, he is committed to the assumption that a single crossing never makes a difference to the state of the grass. From this it follows that there is no difference (as far as the state of the grass is concerned) between the consequences of no one's crossing and one person's crossing . . . [or] between the consequences of one person's crossing and two persons' crossing . . . and so on. Since the relation of 'there being no difference between the consequences of . . .' is transitive, we can conclude that there is no difference (as far as the grass is concerned) between the consequences of no one's crossing and the consequences of everyone's crossing. But this is inconsistent with another premiss of the argument, the premiss that the overall consequences of everyone's crossing are much worse than the overall consequences of everyone's walking around" (pp. 59–60). But the relation "there being no *perceptible* difference between the consequences of . . ." is nontransitive. And the value at stake with lawns and buildings is aesthetic; perception is necessary for change in the sort of value that here concerns a utilitarian. Besides, not every single act (crossing the lawn, burning a log fire) has to make, over time, an actual difference. It may be that four or five crossings/fires have an effect that the lawn/buildings will entirely recover from (the grass will revive in a few hours; the next rain will wash a certain amount of deposit off the buildings) and that we shall get back to the status quo ante. But a hundred crossings/fires, let us say, will do permanent perceptible damage—though, since the grass will revive a bit and the buildings have some of the deposit washed off by the next rain, the damage might be done by only ninety-five of the crossings/fires. And from the fact that the damage of n crossings is indistinguishable from the damage of $n + 1$, and so on, it does not follow that the damage from n crossings is indistinguishable from the damage from $n + 50$. A series of imperceptible changes can grow into a perceptible change, and so a change in value, even when any individual one is reversed in short order. Regan is well aware that the important relation might be thought to be "there being no *perceptible* difference. . . ." But of this he says that there must be some point at which a single crossing either produces a recognizable change in the grass or at least changes the likelihood that the persons around will enjoy the grass less. "If this were not so, then the whole string of changes together could make no difference" (p. 61). But this is just to assert that there could not be a series of minute changes each of which, singly, made no perceptible difference but enough of which, in aggregate, did. It is simply the claim that such changes are impossible. But he gives no reason for thinking so, and there do seem to be cases.

and some benefit if I do. But then I am just free riding, exploiting the constraint of other people.

HOW RICH AN ACCOUNT OF FAIRNESS CAN UTILITARIANISM PROVIDE?

I want to start by asking what resources utilitarianism has at its disposal to deal with these problems—not whether they are up to it, but simply what they are. And here, I think, we tend to underrate utilitarianism a bit. It is easy to distort utilitarianism by misunderstanding how it uses aggregation. The distributive principle in utilitarianism is maximization; what justifies directing benefit to you instead of to me is that you benefit more. The principle of utility *is* a distributive principle. It is a view, right or wrong, about when sacrificing one person for another is allowed. It is just a modern muddle to contrast sharply distributive and aggregative principles, as if an aggregative principle could not also be fully deliberately distributive. This contrast crops up commonly, for instance, in economics, when an aggregative principle is regarded as a principle of "efficiency" and other principles are seen as ones of "fairness." Similarly, no plausible principle of equality—think of Rawls's Difference Principle—could be purely distributive, without a maximizing element, as if reducing everyone to the same level of misery could satisfy it. Every plausible principle of equality is based on the thought that everyone matters and matters equally, and to stress only formal features of distribution is to recall the "equally" but to forget the "matters." Even a principle of a minimum acceptable level of welfare has, if not a maximizing, at least a quantitative element. And the principle of utility, too, represents another conception of the distribution that the deep notion of equal regard requires.

What I am calling "equal regard" is something entirely familiar (though also, I admit, rather vague). Treating people with equal regard is looking at them from the moral point of view, seeing them as holding equal moral status. So every moral theory has some conception or other of equal regard at its heart. Different moral theories parlay this vague notion into different moral principles. Contractualists parlay it into the principles that agents with certain characteristics would agree on. Utilitarians parlay it into their principle of trade-offs: maximizing well-being, counting everybody for one and nobody for more than one.[2]

What would utilitarians say, though, animated as they are by a certain conception of equal regard, about cases where maximization gives no result? Imagine a case where the welfare total stays the same, and only chances of having it vary.[3] Suppose, for instance, that a government finds

2. It is not at all clear how this root notion of equal regard stands to the various, more specific conceptions that grow out of it. I say more about this in my reply to Kurt Baier's comments (in this issue).

3. The problem is raised by P. A. Diamond, "Cardinal Welfare, Individualistic Ethics, and Interpersonal Comparison of Utility: A Comment," *Journal of Political Economy* 75 (1967): 765–66, and the example I use is adapted from his. My thoughts have been much

itself able to act in either of two ways. If it acts in the first way, then, depending on matters outside its control, either one group will be helped or another group will be equally helped. If it acts in the second way, then the first group is bound to be helped as before, but the second group will get nothing. What should the government do? Whatever it does, the total help it gives will be the same; so the welfare sum provides no ground for choice. Yet there does seem to be an obvious ground: the first way of acting gives each group a chance.

What does utilitarianism say about this case? The utilitarian principle of trade-offs (maximization) has no implications for the case. The fault in that principle is not that it gives the wrong answer but that it gives none.

What answer, then, should utilitarianism give? That question comes down to the question, What deep, animating conception of equal regard do we think utilitarianism contains? All that I want to claim for the answer that I shall now suggest is that it is one natural development of the elements of that deep conception that are already there in utilitarianism. That is, what I want to propose will rest not on the familiar principle of trade-offs (maximization), nor on its constituent principle of equal weight (everybody to count for one), but on the conception of equal regard behind them both.

Suppose that you care equally about the welfare of your two children. You count each for one and neither for more than one; other things being equal you would have them at the same level of welfare; you would accept a loss of welfare for one of them only if, but also if, the gain to the other were greater. But then one day you find yourself confronted with a choice about which your view about trade-offs tells you nothing: the benefit will be the same whatever you do, the only choice being between directing it to only one of them or giving each a 50 percent chance at it. From your moral views, as spelled out so far, it is unclear what you would do. There is no account of utilitarianism that provides reasons for doing either. You would have to think out your principles further. You might conclude that your deep conception of equal regard can give no further guidance, that either some entirely new moral notion is needed or that the question is unanswerable. Or you might conclude that your deep conception, when developed further, gives the answer that the options are morally equal. Or you might conclude that your deep conception, when developed, points toward giving each child an equal chance.

The last seems to me the most natural development. And there is this further explanation (I do not pretend that it is anything as conclusive as an argument). You as a parent would not be choosing between acts that determine the substantive well-being of your children. You would

---

clarified by reading John Broome's paper "Selecting People Randomly" (1982, typescript) and by conversation with him.

be choosing simply between acts that affect their chances. But chances may affect one's well-being. If one child's welfare matters just as much as the other's, then it seems in the same spirit to say that, when it comes to chances of welfare, the one child's matter as much as the other's too. Where the notion of "greatest sum" provides no criterion, it does not follow that utilitarianism is without one; there is no reason why it cannot be taken to be rich enough to cover this case.

So if a utilitarian parlays equal regard in the way that I suggest, he will have, first, a principle of maximization; and next, when maximization does not rank options, a principle of equal well-being; and finally, when equalization does not rank options, a principle of equal chances at well-being. It is, as principles of equality go, a modest addition to the principle of maximization. Still, no doubt some persons will want to deny that utilitarianism has even this modest egalitarian implication. What I want to say is that I can find no good reason for their doing so. They might argue that, if one adopts maximization as the principle governing trade-offs, as all utilitarians do, then one accepts that, in a certain sense, individuals do not matter: the sum matters; which particular individuals get which part of it does not. But that individuals do not matter in this sense does not imply that they cannot matter in the sense that these further, tie-breaking egalitarian principles require. The sort of concern for individuals that is displayed in maximization is not inconsistent with the sort of concern displayed in this modest egalitarian addition.

Yet if a utilitarian spells out his notion of equal regard in this way, what is it that he has added to his views? It might, of course, really be an entirely independent principle. The most powerful objection to utilitarianism is that it cannot account for fairness. So it is not surprising that its principle of trade-offs is silent on the sort of case that we have been looking at. But what I charitably call "spelling out" the deep utilitarian conception of equal regard may look to others suspiciously like recognizing its inadequacy and adding to it an independent principle of fairness that will turn around and start qualifying the principle of utility itself in cases of other sorts. But I do not think that this is so. The addition is made within the constraint of the utilitarian principle of trade-offs: loss is justified if and only if gain is greater. And though the derivation is not especially tight, it stands to the principle of utility as a corollary. Each person's chance at welfare matters and matters equally because each person's welfare matters and matters equally and because of the causal connection between chance at welfare and welfare itself. The principle plus the corollary constitute a combination of views that is no less natural, and no more or less puzzling, than any other important view about equality. It is little reassurance, for instance, to be able to get such a view out of a contractualist framework because there are many such frameworks, yielding principles on trade-offs that range from the quite strict to the quite permissive. Contractualists have to choose one particular framework, and that choice is itself the choice of a particular conception of equal regard. Nor is my finding a corollary to the principle of utility any more puzzling or in need of justification than making a principle of equal chance an independent principle in some Ross-like pluralist kit. We all know that this sort of pluralism is very incomplete, that it has still to explain how we are to trade off, say, a principle of utility maximization against a separate principle of equality. To explain that would simply be to spell out this deep notion of equal regard. The spelling out that a pluralist has to do is the same sort of project as the spelling out that I have just done—neither one more natural or theoretically deeper than the other, and neither one different in kind from the spelling out that a contractualist has to do. All such spellings out are conducted in much the same way and uncomfortably close to present theoretical bedrock.

However, I hope that my disclaimers about the tightness of the derivation do not suggest that my argument is identical in form to certain arguments for rule utilitarianism: namely, start with (usually conventional) results that you want the principle to yield and then tinker with the principle till it does yield them. On the contrary, my argument moves from the utilitarian notion of equal weight in calculating trade-offs to a notion of equal chance; it tries to spell out in a natural way the deep notion of equal regard that underlies both.[4]

The corollary may seem very weak.[5] After all, it can help only where total welfare is the same whatever we do, and it is merely chances that differ; and cases like this may seem of great rarity and little importance. But that is really not so. The corollary has implications for procedures. For instance, in all cases where benefit or burden is about the same for each member of a group but only some can, or need to, have it, it suggests that we ought to select randomly. Conscription is a good example. When the national, or other, interest points in no particular direction, then the chance of being selected should be made equal. And it should be made equal not because, say, any other procedure would cause resentment and unrest, although they matter too, but for a much more fundamental reason: each person's fate matters and matters equally and random selection is demanded simply by that. And a lot of cases of cumulative effects are

4. It is this deep notion that would also animate ranking, say, taking turns above tossing coins. Suppose the situation will recur. You as the parent might always opt for a 50 percent chance for each child, or you might, because this sort of randomizing could just result in a freak run of benefits for one of them in particular, prefer directing it once to one child and next to the other. The second approach does seem better—better because safer, and safer precisely in more surely producing the fairer or equal distribution that seems to be at the heart of this principle. Does this not show, after all, that there is a powerful independent principle of fairness? I do not think so. Utilitarianism's basic, original equipment is a commitment to equal distribution and a standard to govern deviations. The standard governing deviations does not sanction any in this case. So there is no justification here to deviate. This is what the deep conception of equal regard at work in utilitarianism would say. I am indebted here, and elsewhere in this section, to conversations with R. M. Hargrave.

5. Broome thinks it is.

also examples. If I were to burn a log fire, I would get about the same benefit as you would. So long as there is only one exception, whoever the exception is, the welfare sum will be the same; all that changes is the chance of having the benefit.

Whether this corollary of the principle of utility is strong enough to solve the many problems of fairness is quite another matter. So let me turn to some of those problems now.

THE CONSEQUENTIALIST'S PROBLEM OF FINDING A BROAD ENOUGH PERSPECTIVE

A while ago, I mentioned two problems that would be my subject—first a problem about the width of the moral perspective and, second, the problem of free riders.

The first is a problem for consequentialists. And virtually all of us are consequentialists in the relevant sense; for virtually all of us believe that some consequences matter morally in some way. But, then, how are we to take in all the consequences that matter?

One source of trouble is a plausible, and sometimes it seems even inescapable, notion of agency—the notion of each of us as an isolated agent, cut off from other agents whose actions we are driven to treat as part of what is given, cut off even from our own long-term, life-structuring aims. For what is the central concern of moral evaluation except evaluation of acts? And what are acts except what each of us can do here and now each time an opportunity to act arises? So an isolated agent, to the extent that consequences matter to him, reasons by listing his options occasion by occasion and calculating which provides the best outcome.

An example of an isolated agent is an act utilitarian, at least in a tight construal common now;[6] let me call him a "strict act utilitarian." Such a utilitarian reviews his options case by case and plumps for the one that has, impartially considered, the best outcome. But that form of reasoning does not, in the end, produce the best outcome.[7] For most people, one of the things that gives most value to their lives is deep

6. An intriguing historical question is how act utilitarianism ever became the dominant interpretation. Bentham, Mill, and Sidgwick were pretty certainly not act utilitarians, in this tight construal. When did this construal edge the others out? Was it with G. E. Moore? See e.g., Moore, *Ethics* (Oxford: Oxford University Press, 1966), p. 121: "It must always be the duty of every agent to do that one, among all actions which he can do on any given occasion, whose *total consequences* will have the greatest intrinsic value." For recent definitions of what looks like the tight construal, usually (not surprisingly) by authors who do not find much to say for it, see D. H. Hodgson, *Consequences of Utilitarianism* (Oxford: Clarendon Press, 1967), p. 1; B. Williams, "A Critique of Utilitarianism," in *Utilitarianism: For and Against*, ed. J. J. C. Smart and B. Williams (Cambridge: Cambridge University Press, 1973), p. 128; R. B. Brandt, *A Theory of the Good and the Right* (Oxford: Clarendon Press, 1979), chap. 14, sec. 2, chap. 15, sec. 3; Regan, p. 12; etc.

7. For excellent discussions, see R. M. Adams, "Motive Utilitarianism," *Journal of Philosophy* 73 (1976): 467–81; D. A. Parfit, *Reasons and Persons* (Oxford: Clarendon Press, 1984), chap. 1, sec. 6.

attachments to particular people. And these attachments are incompatible with strict act utilitarian reasoning; they do not leave one able, occasion by occasion, to review all actions that are within human capacity and then to choose the best. Of course, a strict act utilitarian can include among his options becoming a person of deep attachments. But that is not a mere action of the sort that the isolated agent passes in review. It changes the whole source of his action. We are naturally inclined to form deep attachments, and if we know what makes life valuable we will refine and reinforce this already strong inclination. But such an inclination forms part of the long-term, life-structuring features of one's character, and it undercuts the strict act utilitarian's whole mode of deliberation.

The perspective adopted by the isolated agent could not be the right one, for any form of consequentialism. There seem to me to be three reasons for this.

For one thing, such a perspective ignores too much of our real situation of choice. Typically, we are short of time, facts, and fellow feeling. Therefore, what guides our choice must take these shortcomings into account. And those things that guide choice are not just principles and beliefs but also feelings, emotions, habits, dispositions, and policies. Modern moral philosophy has largely ignored the towering importance of moral education: we are set on a moral course early in life, changing which, except in small ways, is not often or easily done. It is always tempting to think oneself or one's situation an exception, so moral dispositions, to do their job, must go fairly deep. And dispositions have to be shaped to what usually happens, not to the exceptional case. So a moral person will be moved by inclinations that have to be, for good reason, to some degree insensitive to exceptions. Another important feature of our real situation of choice is our lack of agreement on matters on which, for the survival of our life together, we have to agree. Sometimes we need agreed practices. Sometimes a deal must be struck, even at the cost of one's own moral beliefs. I may think that *I* have the better moral principle to apply in a certain case; others may think that *they* have and we cannot here agree to differ;[8] so perhaps the best we can do is to let the toss of a coin or a majority vote decide.

These thoughts prompt some distinctions. We ought to distinguish the criteria of right and wrong from a moral decision procedure.[9] The criteria are the features that make acts right or wrong, while a moral decision procedure is the thinking one should go through to decide what morally to do. Obviously we should want a person's moral thinking as much determined by consideration of right-making features as possible. But there are good reasons, some of which we have just seen, why moral thought cannot be so pure. Then it is worth distinguishing different sorts

8. See the discussion by B. J. Diggs, "Utilitarianism and Contractarianism," in *The Limits of Utilitarianism*, ed. H. B. Miller and W. H. Williams (Minneapolis: University of Minnesota Press, 1982), pp. 103–4.

9. See R. E. Bales, "Act Utilitarianism: Account of Right-making Characteristics or Decision-making Procedure," *American Philosophical Quarterly* 8 (1971): 257–65.

of moral decision procedures. There is a practical decision procedure: what should guide one in everyday life when one is short of time, facts, and fellow feeling. Then there is an ideal decision procedure: what should guide us on the rare occasions when those shortcomings are absent. When they are absent, then, clearly, since the procedures designed for the typical case no longer fit, we should be dim not to look for new ones. I shall come back to this distinction in a moment, but it is clear that part of morality at least is a practical decision procedure. And as far as that part goes, the deliberation appropriate to it is nothing like the deliberation of the isolated agent.

There is a second reason why the isolated agent's outlook cannot be right. The value theory at the base of consequentialism rules it out. We naturally expect prudential value theory to be neutral as between different versions—say, between act and rule utilitarianism—but I think that it is not so. This is because, with the shift from a hedonist account of prudential value to an informed desire account, the focus of evaluation shifts from short to long periods of time, and in many cases to whole lives. For instance, a person may find that what would give his life value would be rich, loving relationships or some measure of achievement, or living autonomously. Even valuable short-term pleasures have to be fitted into a fairly long-term context; a person would have to decide how much place to give to living for day-to-day pleasures compared to other ways of living. Therefore the isolated agent does not properly identify the primary object of evaluation; the primary object is the quality of lives, not what we do occasion by occasion (which a hedonism of short-term experiences fits better). In a plausible theory of prudential values, the important values are what give life point, structure, or weight.

But then this must influence how moral thinking can be conducted. A person who centers his life on deep attachments to certain people adopts a whole way of living. He makes commitments that themselves become a powerful source of action; they reduce psychological freedom. The same is true of a person who tries to lead a life that accomplishes something. He makes a commitment that changes his feelings and attitudes, that takes up his time and narrows his attention. These large-scale decisions are the ones that, for the most part, determine action, and they demote the occasion-by-occasion decisions of the isolated agent to a modest corner of deliberation.

There is a third reason why the isolated agent's outlook could not be right for any sort of consequentialism. It fails to see the outcome of acting in concert with others. If the isolated agent is a utilitarian living in my town, he will, following the pattern of deliberation we have already traced, conclude that he ought to burn a log fire. And if this is the model for moral deliberation, then ideally everyone would think the same, and the buildings will be badly damaged and everyone will be worse off. This tunnel vision clearly misses too much. Before it missed the importance of whole lives; now it misses the importance of whole groups.

I have mentioned three reasons why a consequentialist would not adopt the isolated agent's outlook. Let me return for a moment to the distinction between a practical decision procedure and an ideal one. The first of the three reasons is that the isolated agent's outlook is not right for the practical decision procedure. That leaves it open whether it is right for the ideal procedure. However, the second and third arguments show that it is not right there either. When, very rarely, we are not short of time, facts, and fellow feeling, we clearly should not use decision procedures made for normal times. Should we then use strict act utilitarian thinking? Well, "act utilitarian" is a loose term, too loose to make an answer obvious, but there is at least some reason to answer no.

With time, facts, and fellow feeling, we can sit back and ask whether a certain rule of the practical decision procedure applies in a particular case, and if we decide that it does not, we can sometimes free ourselves from its grip. The rules of good citizenship, for instance, are like that; it does not take much effort to miss a vote, if one is convinced that it is all right to do so. One thing that makes it easy is that what many duties of citizenship require has value only as a means to other values, which sometimes are not at stake. Admittedly, the practices that form our practical decision procedure differ a lot in the strength of their grip on us. Still, some of the things we value are very different indeed from the rules of good citizenship. The central values of our lives always retain their value. Furthermore, they get a firm grip on our lives. For example, our deepest commitments to particular people go so deep that we never recover our original freedom of action, if ever we had much. Some are genetically based; many that are learned still go deep. If the training starts early, we can to some degree overcome our nature. But if we see no reason to overcome it, if indeed we see every reason not to, then we allow it permanently to shape, and to limit, our action. We are no longer able to enter into, and exit from, the behavior occasion by occasion.

Then there is another kind of central prudential value. If making some sort of contribution to knowledge is a large part of what gives weight to my life, this goal would then take a lot of my time. I might, if I had become a different sort of person, have been caught up, say, in politics. Indeed, as it is, I still might, even as I actually turned out, promote well-being more, all things considered, by taking time off now and then to serve some good political cause. But I should first have to find out how good the cause is, spend even more time discovering how to be effective in helping it, and spend much more time in doing the job. It is not that I have not, strictly speaking, got the time. And, of course, I ought not to sit quietly at my desk, if I could help avert some political disaster. But there comes a point where I draw a line, even knowing that I shall be missing chances to do better. But once the line is drawn, my policy to get on with my work is not shaped by the normal shortcomings we have mentioned. The policy gets its point not because time is short to reach a decision but because life is short.

These points about the ideal decision procedure raise again the question of exactly how ideal it is thought of as being. My points all rest on the assumption that it is not so ideal that it imagines human nature away; a decision procedure is, I assume, a procedure that people would sometimes use. This means that we may imagine people with ample time to reflect, in possession of the relevant facts, and finding their self-interest quiet because all of this sometimes happens. But it also means that we cannot just imagine people emotionally tied to others at one moment and detached at the next, or the human life span other than it is, or a person in society untouched by whether cooperation occurs. Any decision procedure ideal in such an extreme sense would lose interest for us.

So the practical decision procedure is this: I ignore case by case consequences and, in deciding what to do, consult the principles that express the habits, dispositions, and practices that have the best long-term consequences in the light of normal human shortcomings. The ideal procedure is this: when the shortcomings are absent, I assess the consequences occasion by occasion to determine whether a particular case is an exception to my general rules; I also assess consequences occasion by occasion at those early times when I choose the general features of my way of life; but then, having chosen them, I give up act by act deliberation in large parts of my life and settle what to do by appealing to my goals and commitments.

As you must have noticed, this contrast between the practical and the ideal decision procedure is like R. M. Hare's contrast between two levels of moral thinking, the intuitive and the critical.[10] It is a mistake to regard these two procedures, or these two levels, as merely something to smarten up dowdy old utilitarianism. They are, as Hare claims, part of the structure of moral thought. I have not got time to go into the difference between Hare's two levels and the two procedures that I am talking about. The differences, anyway, have largely to do with where act consequentialism fits into deliberation, and I should say something more in a general way about that.

It seems that, although some thought that goes on in the ideal decision procedure is act consequentialist, some is not. Our commitments and life-structuring aims largely take away our freedom to deliberate occasion by occasion; this loss of freedom is not made appropriate by the normal shortcomings that shape the practical decision procedure, so it does not disappear when they do. I spoke earlier of *strict* act utilitarianism, but it is hard to see how the ideal decision procedure could be thoroughly act utilitarian even in broader senses. Just as act-by-act deliberation is barred from the practical decision procedure, it is at times barred from the ideal procedure. If that is enough to say that the practical procedure is not act utilitarian, it is enough to say the same about parts of the ideal

10. The main sources are R. M. Hare, "Ethical Theory and Utilitarianism," *Contemporary British Philosophy*, ed. H. D. Lewis, 4th ser. (London: Allen & Unwin, 1976), and *Moral Thinking* (Oxford: Clarendon Press, 1981), chap. 2, sec. 1, chap. 3.

procedure. This conclusion does not mean that consequentialist deliberation is not, ultimately, at some particularly deep level, act by act. In a sense it has to be. There are various departments of moral thought. One deals with assessing people's characters; another with assessing their responsibility. Those are indeed proper objects of moral judgment, but not the business of the department with which we now deal. Its business is assessing behavior, not exactly what people do but what they choose to do. What they do often comes not from choice but from habits, emotion, and so on. But we want to get moments of choice, and in the case of emotions and habits the relevant choices lie back in such acts as those that formed the habits or did not curb the emotions. Act consequentialism is true simply in virtue of the proper object of assessment in this department of moral thought. But the choices that matter are often not only in the background but also far in the background. Ultimately a consequentialist has to be an act consequentialist, but it is often very ultimate indeed. Where act consequentialism has its unqualified place is not in the decision procedures we have spoken about but in the criterion of right and wrong. To the extent that consequences determine right and wrong, what makes an act right is there being no other possible act with better consequences. But even this role for act consequentialism has to be taken in a way compatible with prudential value theory. And there the primary object of evaluation is, as we have seen, lives looked at in a long-term way. So, to the extent that consequentialism has a hand in assessing what people do, it has to look at how what they do affects the quality of life. And what a person does can affect the quality of lives in very many different ways: by the disposition he encourages or discourages, by the goals he sets himself, by cooperating with others, by adopting conventions, and so on. These are all things that we choose to do. We do not just look from an act outward, toward its further and further consequences; the prudential value theory shows that we should also look from the whole of life inward, to find the acts that give it its general contours. This means abandoning the narrow perspective that sees acts as making ripples, some of which admittedly last a long while, but also as having to be repeated again and again, with the deliberation appropriate initially appropriate repeatedly. Some of our most important acts are not like that; they are important because they alter the character of deliberation; they relegate act-by-act deliberation to a relatively small segment of life.

So, no consequentialist would want to adopt the outlook of the isolated agent. It would certainly be wrong for his practical decision procedure; it would also be wrong for his ideal decision procedure. He would want to adopt an outlook that took in not only the effects of individual acts but also ways of life, commitments, aims of life, and the cumulative effects of what groups do. This is still a consequentialist outlook, only not the isolated agent's.

Once a consequentialist focuses on the proper object of evaluation, Prisoner's Dilemmas look different. A narrow consequentialist outlook gets one into troubles; shifting to a broader consequentialist outlook gets one out of many of them.[11] But how many? In particular, how much does it help with the problem of free riders?

THE FREE-RIDER PROBLEM

Broadening the consequentialist outlook, on its own, is no help with free riders. If enough people follow the rule not to burn log fires, the buildings in town escape harm, and I should increase welfare, impartially considered, by making myself an exception.

Perhaps, therefore, the fully moral outlook requires one more step back. Perhaps we should look at hypothetical as well as actual outcomes. "What if everyone burned a log fire?" The reply "Not everyone will" seems to miss the point. Of course, if they are decent sorts, they will not. But the point is that a few of us can burn log fires without damage only because the rest of you are constraining yourselves. This line of argument obviously has some force.

However, the move to hypothetical outcomes seem to drain consequentialism of its intuitive plausibility. What matters morally is actual change to people's lives. If the town council came to believe that not everyone's constraint was necessary to avoid the bad outcome and hatched a workable scheme to let us take turns burning log fires, there would be no moral objection to it. "Not everyone will" seems not to miss the point. And this second line of argument has force too.

These two arguments seem to me to make up a deeper dilemma than the Prisoner's. The pull of each is a cause—not the only one, but nowadays an important one—of the deep split between Kantians and utilitarians.

What seems right in the first argument is that it is objectionable that my life can be made better with a log fire only because your life will in that respect be worse. I am being a parasite and so violating equal regard on some conception that we should not want to lose. And, in a way, what the rest of you actually do is morally irrelevant. It is besides the point that you will actually restrain yourselves. And that is because the point is my behaving like a parasite. But what is morally pertinent about my behaving like a parasite is not a hypothetical outcome either; what would

11. I do not mean to suggest that the broader perspective is all that is needed to solve Prisoner's Dilemmas. I think that it gives us, or makes accessible, the ingredients we need for a solution, but just what those ingredients are and exactly how they are to be assembled into a solution is a large issue that I leave aside. One important question is whether, besides moral intentions and the broad perspective, we need social rules backed by sanctions. See the exchange between Sen and Baier: A. K. Sen, "Choice, Orderings and Morality," in *Practical Reason*, ed. S. Körner (Oxford: Basil Blackwell, 1974); K. Baier, "Rationality and Morality," and A. K. Sen, "Rationality and Morality: A Reply," both in *Erkenntnis* 11 (1977): 197–223, 225–32. A central issue here is how much simple savvy and self-interest lead us to evolve fairly successful strategies in iterated Prisoner's Dilemmas. On that, see Robert Axelrod, *The Evolution of Cooperation* (New York: Basic Books, 1984), esp. pt. 4.

happen if you all behaved differently from the way you will?[12] What seems right in the second argument is that the outcomes here are all real enough: I actually get the cream of life because the rest of you are actually making do with the skimmed milk.

How much do we have to do to get fairness back in the picture? If I have the log fire because I need it and the rest of you do not, then my benefit does not rest objectionably on your burden. That is because the introduction of need also introduces equal regard: people's actual interests matter and matter equally. But if I benefit because it is my turn or because it is my name that came out of the hat, then my benefit also ceases to rest, in any objectionable sense, on your burden.[13] Chance at an actual benefit also matters. If I simply award myself the benefit, then not everyone has an equal chance at it. If, on the other hand, it is simply my turn, then everyone will in time have his chance. If my name came out of the hat, then everyone has had a chance. These modal matters—neither actual consequences nor hypothetical ones—also count.[14] I think that it is the corollary of consequentialism that I spoke of earlier—namely, if equal weight in calculating welfare matters, equal chance at having it also matters—that is also important in explaining what is objectionable in free riding. To check free riding, to get fairness back in the picture, we do not have to stop me from having the benefit while you suffer the burden. That still happens, but now unobjectionably. And it is fair when it happens now because of the availability of one of a set of reasons for my getting the benefit: I needed it; I won the toss; it was my turn; et cetera. In other words, we need only show, by citing one of these reasons, that equal regard has not been violated. Equal weight in calculating

12. This way of speaking is, of course, very loose. Before I choose what to do, all consequences are hypothetical; and after I have chosen, only one set of consequences will be actual. In that sense, I never choose between actual consequences. So by "actual" consequences I mean what would actually happen if I were to act in a certain way (and "hypothetical" consequences must be understood accordingly). But this looseness of speech does not matter because it is eliminable. This looseness of speech is well pointed out by M. G. Singer, "Incoherence, Inconsistency, and Moral Theory," *Southern Journal of Philosophy* 20 (1982): 375–91.

13. There are different kinds of free riding. Sometimes my free riding adds a real, though often very small, extra burden on others (e.g., my taking my private car on the roads at rush hour, when the rest of you use buses; I may slow things up so little for each of you that you do not even notice; but I do slow things up a bit). Other times my free riding adds no extra burden (e.g., when I have a log fire, and the next rain washes the deposit away). Still, in both kinds of cases there is a steady burden that all the rest of you bear, namely a benefit forgone. I can get my questionable justification going for my having the benefit ("no harm done") only because the rest of you are denying it to yourselves.

14. This point has been made before; a good discussion is L. S. Sumner, "Cooperation, Fairness and Utility," *Journal of Value Inquiry* 5 (1971): 105–19, esp. p. 109; but he holds that a fair procedure such as random selection stands outside utilitarianism as something that though it might often be adopted on utilitarian grounds (e.g., if it were the only procedure that a group would consent to), might sometimes not be (e.g., if one could get away with loading the dice).

different people's interests would show it. Equal chance at a benefit would also show it. Do we need anything else? It seems not. We do not need that extra step backward to hypothetical consequences: "What if everyone . . . ?"

This has consequences for both those who frame and those who follow rules. To allow no one to burn log fires, when some could without harm and there are feasible ways of letting them, is senselessly stern. Those who frame laws could, as we have seen, give everyone an equal chance to have a fire; or they could amend the rules so that fires could be burned in public buildings on special occasions. Sometimes they will have to play safe because they do not know how often the rule will be broken or because what is at stake is so important. Sometimes they will have come to the point where finer calculation costs more than it is worth. But they should get as close to the edge as possible.

If they do, then those who follow the rule will not be left much room to maneuver. If the rule embodies the best estimate of compliance and of the importance of what is at stake, then generally I am in no position to conclude otherwise. That is why the practical decision procedure is so important in discussing fairness. Most of the rules, the breach of which is unfair, are rules of the practical decision procedure. They are framed for the usual context of choice.

But when, unusually, the context changes, those rules clearly suit less. There cannot be any easy move from the rules of a practical decision procedure to those of an ideal one. Do I have a duty to vote? Well, suppose I ask as a citizen of a large marginal state in the United States, where the chance of my vote's making a difference is about one in one hundred million and where the population is two hundred million.[15] Suppose, also, that whether the better person wins matters; if he does, there will be some average net benefit to each citizen's life over a certain period. Then, I will have to reason roughly like this. There is only a very slight chance of my vote's making a difference. On the other hand, the expected benefit of my voting will be twice the average net benefit,[16] less the costs of my voting. So unless my case is most unusual, this sum will turn out positive. In general, in situations of that sort, I ought to vote. One does not have to look beyond outcomes to find a reason to vote or to justify a rule about voting. But if I ask as a member of a much smaller body, say my college's governing body, and it is a case where I know perfectly well how other people will vote and that my vote clearly will

15. Here I just follow Derek Parfit's powerful reply to those who argue that in a nationwide election the consequences of my act can never explain why I ought to vote; see Parfit, pp. 73–75.

16. Expected benefit is actual benefit multiplied by the chance that one will produce it, i.e.,

$$\frac{\text{average net benefit per citizen} \times \text{200 million}}{\text{100 million}}.$$

make no difference, then outcomes may give me no reason to vote. But there seems still to be a consideration of fairness: may *I* excuse myself from voting? May I, even if there are no other outcomes that matter? Why should I be the one to get the afternoon off? Perhaps I should toss a coin over lunch with you. It is easy to make what Derek Parfit calls mistakes in moral mathematics, such as ignoring small chances or small benefits.[17] But the free-rider problem is not solved just by avoiding these mistakes.[18]

This takes us on to the ideal decision procedure, where deliberation gets complicated. There is the consideration of fairness, which can go beyond actual consequences: for instance, who should get the chance? On the other hand, only actual outcomes matter; maybe it is not worth the bother of tossing a coin with you, and since my vote will make no difference I need not go. We have also to keep in mind that although actually we have only partial compliance to our rule the ideal would be full compliance: burdens, let us say, would be fairest and outcomes best if we all faithfully voted; and my voting, joined with other people's, now and later, might be a break for higher moral ground. And we have to recognize that our attachments, commitments, and life-structuring aims limit the freedom of our occasion-by-occasion deliberation. So deliberation on the ideal level has many sides.

I know that many people will find this solution of the free-rider problem simply too weak.[19] They will think that it still allows too many exceptions, and they will insist that the free-rider problem shows that we need other, tougher principles. I want now to explain why the tougher principles seem to me to be too tough.

THE POSSIBILITY OF TOUGHER, KANTIAN SOLUTIONS

Kant himself is not a consequentialist of the familiar modern variety. Consequences do enter his theory, but his test is not to determine first the consequences of everyone's doing such and such ("what if everyone . . . ?") and then their value ("it would be disastrous").[20] The test looks elsewhere: in one formulation, it asks each of us to see whether he can act on his proposed policy and simultaneously accept everyone's acting

17. Parfit, chap. 3.

18. Nor does Parfit say that it is.

19. It is certainly too weak to solve all problems of "fairness." All that I am proposing is that it solves the free-rider problem. That still leaves other, central problems; e.g., a society with a small group of rich exploiters and a large group of poor exploited has a structural unfairness that is not removed just by giving all entrants into the society (say, babies at birth) an equal chance of being among the exploiters.

20. For a good discussion of how consequences enter the Categorical Imperative test, see H. J. Paton, *The Categorical Imperative*, 5th ed. (London: Hutchinson, 1965), chap. 7, sec. 4; chap. 14, secs. 4, 5; chap. 17, sec. 4. For a contrary view, see M. G. Singer, *Generalization in Ethics* (London: Eyre & Spottiswoode, 1963), chap. 9, sec. 3.

like that.[21] The question is not, Would it be disastrous? but, Would a contradiction appear? But obviously, the appearance of the sorts of contradiction that Kant has in mind will turn largely on how we describe a person's policy. What I propose doing may be "skipping votes," or it may be "skipping a vote when there is one spare," et cetera. How specific can my description get?

If it cannot get as specific as we want (providing, of course, that it avoids any essential mention of particular persons, places, or times), and especially if it has to be kept at a fairly high level of generality, then perhaps one of the sorts of contradiction Kant has in mind will appear.[22] Even so, however, the test would not account for fairness. If it is kept at a fairly high level of generality, then the test would not allow me, or anyone else, to miss the vote, no matter how the lucky person was chosen. It would not allow me, or anyone else, to burn a log fire, even if the city council drew names out of a hat. It is not only senselessly stern; it does not get to grips with what fairness is.

Perhaps, then, the account of a person's policy can be as specific as needed. It can mention anything morally relevant, and the fact that I do no harm by skipping the vote seems at least *that.*[23] You and I know perfectly well how the vote will go: the motion that we support will pass by two votes, when a one-vote margin is just as good. But I am quicker off the mark in the parking lot. "There is a vote to spare, so I'm leaving," I say and beetle off. You would not have minded a free afternoon either, but now you are stuck. My departure means that you cannot reason, "If I skip the vote, no harm will be done." Yet, my behavior, on a fully specific account of it, does not seem to lead to any contradiction. Still, what I do may be unfair. And not only does the test seem to allow the unfairness, but also, worse, it does not locate its source. The intuitive thought behind this test is this: if it is morally all right for *me* to do it, then it is all right for everyone, similarly placed. Nearly all of us accept that; we disagree only over how to fix what it is to be "similarly placed." But your situation might be like mine in all relevant respects—your capacity to enjoy an afternoon off just the same; your need for extra time just as great; your absence no more harmful than mine. What is important to fairness need not lie in any features of you and me, nor in any of our circumstances. It lies in the availability of one of a set of reasons for *one* of us getting the benefit. If you and I toss for the free

21. This is Paton's Formula 1, or "The Formula of the Universal Law"; see Paton, chap. 14. For another good discussion of the test, see Onora Nell, *Acting on Principle: An Essay on Kantian Ethics* (New York: Columbia University Press, 1975), chap. 5.

22. Since fairness is a "perfect duty," what ought to appear is a contradiction in conception, rather than a contradiction in the will; see Paton, pp. 148, 171–72. But it is hard to see how to make a convincing case for the appearance of either sort of contradiction.

23. The much discussed problems raised by talk of "moral relevance" I pass by. They are satisfactorily answered only by constructing a complete substantive moral theory, which then settles what has moral weight and what does not.

afternoon, or if I do indeed need it more, or . . . , my missing the vote is fair. If not, it is not. Indeed, that is why the case Kantians sometimes put up for banning consequences from mention in one's policy (not allowing one to state it as, for instance, "skipping a vote, *when no harm will be done*" [my emphasis]) is weak.[24] They rightly say that each of us would be able to argue that *his* skipping the vote would not be harmful and so each of us would be an exception. Nor does it help, they correctly add, that in fact not everyone will, because the rest may be decent sorts paying their moral fare while I ride free. However, the most that this shows is that the mere fact that I would do no harm in skipping the vote does not of itself justify skipping it. Justification needs more. What more, however, need not be, as they conclude, that my policy, formulated without mention of consequences, passes the universality test. It could instead be the availability of one of the reasons that I just began listing.

Suppose, then, we amend the test to accommodate this point. We now include how the benefit is distributed as part of the relevant circumstances. We might even find grounds in Kant's test for doing so. We could appeal to another and, according to Kant, equivalent formulation of the Categorical Imperative, the "respect for persons" formulation: persons should always be treated also as ends and never merely as means.[25] And when I speed out of the parking lot, then whether or not I am conscious of using you as a means, I am nonetheless using your attendance in order to justify my freedom. I certainly give you no chance to exercise your rational will; I do not ask you, as a free and rational person, to consent. The "respect for persons" formulation brings us very close to modern contractualism; the test is less immediately "Would a contradiction appear?" than "Would free and rational persons agree?"[26] And it seems at first sight as if this test is just what we need to generate the list of reasons that would justify exceptions. If you could do with a free afternoon just as much as I, then you are not likely to agree to my unilaterally awarding it to myself. What we both could agree to, however, would be some procedure, such as taking turns or tossing coins. We are likely also to agree, on maximin grounds, to give a place to greater need. What more would we give a place to? The answer depends on how rich a

24. The case is elegantly stated by M. G. Singer; see Singer, *Generalization in Ethics*, pp. 91, 189, 196, 209, and also his articles "Generalization in Ethics," *Mind* 64 (1955): 361–75, p. 375, and "The Principle of Consequences Reconsidered," *Philosophical Studies* 31 (1977): 391–410, p. 406. I have somewhat changed his arguments but think that what I present is still in their spirit.

25. In Paton's classification, Formula 2, "The Formula of the End in Itself"; see Paton, chap. 16.

26. There is textual support for this reading of Kant: e.g., *Grundlegung*, trans. H. J. Paton as *The Moral Law*, 3d ed. (London: Hutchinson, 1956), pp. 67–68 (marginal pagination); "the man who has a mind to make a false promise to others will see at once that he is intending to make use of another man *merely as a means* to an end he does not share. For the man whom I seek to use for my own purposes by such a promise cannot possibly agree with my way of behaving to him, and so cannot himself share the end of the action."

notion of rationality we are using. If we use the spare notion of self-interested rationality from modern contractualism, the answer is: nothing more than I have already proposed could be on the list. If we use Kant's potentially richer notion of a rational will governed by the objective ends of life, the answer is, It is hard to say. What makes my skipping the vote fair is my having the right sort of reason for being an exception, and it is hard to see how the Kantian test, made richer by his teleological account of life, identifies which reasons are of the right sort. It would be able to if its key terms "Categorical Imperative," "rational will," and "respect for persons" had more content. It is true that it is a perfectly good thing to say of my giving you an equal chance, or of my weighing your needs impartially against mine, that I thereby show respect for your person. It is a good way to sum it all up. Still we have to know how to fix the content of this respect; we have to know which substantive reasons for my getting the benefit will make it fair and which will not. It is determining what constitutes fairness that puts content into the vague formula "respect for persons," not the formula "respect for persons" that discloses to us what constitutes fairness. The potentially richer, Kantian notion of rationality is so indeterminate that it does virtually no work.

These are, in outline, three ways of understanding Kant's test. If one of them is indeed correct, then in a sense it does not matter which it is: none of them helps enough with the problem of fairness. What seems most promising is taking the "respect for persons" formulation in the direction that contractualists do. This might, depending on whether the particular form of contractualism uses a narrower index of well-being, lead to slight differences from my proposal, but only slight ones. With something like health, say, it is hard to see how they could differ. For many diseases the optimum rate of inoculation is 90 percent; inoculation beyond that brings no benefit to public health, and any inoculation imposes a real (small) risk on the child of serious illness. What rational agents would be likely to agree to, either directly or through the political structure, is inoculation to the safe threshold and a fair procedure for excepting people. This way of developing Kant's test produces a solution, but not the tough one that we set out looking for.

[11]

Economics and Philosophy, 1, 1985, 110–125. Printed in the United States of America.

DWORKIN ON EQUALITY OF RESOURCES

Hal R. Varian
University of Michigan

This essay is a review of Ronald Dworkin's recent essay on equality of resources (Dworkin, 1981b). Many of the ideas discussed by Dworkin have also been examined by economists with, I believe, considerable insight. Unfortunately, economists tend to write for economists, not for philosophers, and their insights are seldom communicated properly to noneconomists. Of course, the same criticism can be levied on philosophers! But perhaps legal theorists are less subject to this criticism. One of the great contributions of Dworkin is that he is very readable; and the quality of his exposition makes these ideas accessible to a wide audience of philosophers, lawyers, and social scientists in general.

Dworkin's discussion on equality comes in two parts. In the first (Dworkin, 1981a) he discusses equality of welfare (in the sense of "equal utilities") and compares this to the idea of equality of resources. In the end he concludes that: ". . . equality of welfare is not so coherent or attractive an ideal as it is often taken to be. We therefore have reason to consider with some care the alternative ideal of equality of resources" (p. 244).

I agree with Dworkin's conclusion in this matter, as would most economists, but for rather different reasons than Dworkin. Economists for the most part don't believe in interpersonal comparisons of utility; or, at least they don't believe that anyone has come up with an *operational* way to compare utilities across people. Thus they would reject "equality of utility" from the outset as being a nonoperational theory of justice, and turn to the idea of equality of resources by default. Perhaps this is simply limited vision on the part of economists, but they are much more

I wish to thank the participants of the Political and Legal Theory Workshop at the University of Michigan for several useful comments; Allan Gibbard and Don Regan were especially helpful. This work was supported in part by the National Science Foundation.

comfortable with goods than with utilities, and consequently their contributions to theories of distributive justice lie more in the area of equality of resources than in equality of welfare.

In this essay I want to provide a selective review of Dworkin's work on equality of resources from the viewpoint of an economist. We start with an analysis of the "envy test" for an equitable distribution and its relation to the market mechanism. As we shall see the envy test has certain problems when abilities differ across individuals, and we will consider Dworkin's suggestions as to how one might extend the spirit of the envy test to these situations, as well as review some other contributions to these issues. Dworkin's proposal is to consider a kind of "ability insurance" scheme; this in turn raises other problems that economists have investigated and which we will briefly describe.

The spirit of this review is to provide a bridge between Dworkin's work and the related work in the economics literature. I will not attempt to provide much in the way of new ideas here, but rather I intend only to present a guide to the literature that I hope can be of benefit to both philosophers and economists. Perhaps the mutual stimulation that arises from such interdisciplinary investigations can help resolve some of the difficult conceptual issues that have arisen in investigating the concept of distributive justice.

1. EQUALITY OF RESOURCES AND THE MARKET MECHANISM

Dworkin certainly recognizes the importance of economic ideas to a discussion of equality of resources. Indeed he begins his essay with a discussion of the concept of an economic market. He suggests that "the idea of an economic market, as a device for setting prices for a vast variety of goods and services, must be at the center of any attractive theoretical development of equality of resources" (p. 284).

In the conventional economics literature one finds several justifications for markets as a social institution. The dominant strand in the modern literature is no doubt the claim that under certain conditions a perfect market gives rise to a Pareto efficient allocation of resources. (By this I mean an allocation of goods such that no consumer can be made better off without making some other consumer worse off.) Dworkin's role for the market is somewhat different. He starts with a criterion for an equitable allocation he calls the *envy test*: "No division of resources is an equal division if, once the division is complete, any [person] would prefer someone else's bundle of resources to his own bundle" (p. 285).

This concept was first proposed by Foley (1967) and has been extensively treated by Pazner and Schmeidler (1974), Varian (1974, 1975, 1976) and many others; a bibliography from Thomson and Varian (1984) is given at the end of this article.

If one agent does prefer what some other agent has, we will say that the first agent *envies* the second. If no agent envies any other agent at some given allocation we will say the allocation is *envy-free*.

The concept of an envy-free allocation is meant to capture an operational concept of equal or symmetric treatment. The problem with the criterion of envy-free allocations is that it is too easy to satisfy! Any equal division is by definition envy-free and there are a large number of other envy-free allocations as well. So economists have added the additional requirement that an "equitable" allocation be Pareto efficient as well.

I believe that the initial stimulus for this additional requirement was that economists view Pareto efficiency as a desirable thing in and of itself. After all, if a given allocation is Pareto *inefficient* that means that there is a way to make someone better off without hurting anyone else . . . so why not do it? Isn't society fundamentally better off by moving from an inefficient allocation to a Pareto superior allocation where everyone is at least well off and some people are strictly better off? I recognize that this view is open to debate, but I am merely asserting that this is a view that most economists would accept.

If we accept the dual criteria of envy-free and efficient allocations we need to ask whether these criteria ask for too much. Under what conditions will such allocations exist? Are these criteria logically compatible?

Fortunately the conditions are compatible. Suppose that initially we divide the goods equally among the economic agents and then allow them to set up a market and trade to a competitive equilibrium. It is well known that under standard assumptions such an equilibrium must be Pareto efficient. Now we have started from an equal, and therefore envy-free, allocation and we have traded to a Pareto efficient allocation. But is this final allocation still envy-free? Or has the trading process itself destroyed the symmetry of the original allocation?

There is a simple argument to show that the final allocation is still envy-free. We simply note that by definition of a competitive equilibrium each agent is choosing the best bundle he can afford. But they all can afford the same set of bundles since they all have the same resources and they all face the same prices. Thus no agent can envy any other agent in the final allocation.

This is the argument in the economics literature; see e.g., Varian (1974). Dworkin follows the same line, but for a different reason. He argues that the initial equal division is "arbitrary" in the sense that there could be many different allocations that were envy-free in the sense defined above. "So the divider needs a device that will attack the two distinct foci of arbitrariness and possible unfairness" (p. 286). Dworkin proposes a Walrasian auction as the device to choose among the envy-free allocations.

The trouble with this argument, as I see it, is that there isn't really any justification for using that particular way of resolving the arbitrariness. As far as Dworkin is concerned there might well be other ways to choose among the envy-free allocations that would be just as suitable. Later on in the essay Dworkin says:

> The market character of the auction is not simply a convenient or ad hoc device for resolving technical problems that arise from the equality of resources . . . It is an institutionalized form of the process of discovery and adaptation that is at the center of the ethics of that ideal. The auction proposes what the envy-test in fact assumes, that the true measure of the social resources devoted to the life of one person is fixed by asking how important, in fact, that resource is for others. It insists that the cost, measured in that way, figures in each person's sense of what is rightly his and in each person's judgement of what life he should lead, given the command of justice. (p. 289)

This passage suggests to me that Dworkin *feels* that the market mechanism is central to the notion of justice . . . but I don't think that he has really *argued* for it.

I think that one can provide an argument that the market mechanism is an especially appropriate way to select among the envy-free allocations. Here is how the argument would go. Assuming that we are willing to accept the notion of an envy-free allocation as being a reasonable formulation of equality of resources, we must admit that we would not be satisfied with only an *initial* allocation that was envy-free. What we want is a *final* allocation that is envy-free. So we have to consider how the agents' holdings might change over time. One obvious way is that the agents might engage in voluntary trade. Now if we start with an envy-free allocation and engage in voluntary trade, will the envy-free nature of the allocation be preserved? It is not hard to see the answer is no. Consider the following example.

We have two twin brothers who have exactly the same tastes, and a third person who has quite different tastes. Suppose that we give each of these three agents the same initial endowments of goods. Imagine then that the first twin meets the third person and makes a trade, thus making both of them better off. But this sort of trade would then destroy the envy criterion, for the second brother would necessarily envy the first since by assumption they have the same tastes.

This simple example shows that not just any kind of trade or auction will preserve the symmetry of the initial endowment. Everybody gains from trade — but some people may gain more than others. Unless we are willing to outlaw "capitalist acts between consenting adults," to borrow a term from Nozick (1973), we must seek an institution that allows agents to trade in a way that *preserves* the envy-free nature of the initial allocation.

As we have seen above, the market mechanism does precisely that. Basically this is because the market mechanism is itself a symmetric mechanism in the sense that everyone faces the same prices and thus has the same opportunities to trade. In this sense the market mechanism is not just an arbitrary way to effect an equitable and Pareto efficient division, but it provides the special property of preserving the symmetry of the initial endowment. (The fact that the market mechanism allows for "equality of opportunity to trade" has been recognized as a virtue in both the informal and the formal economics literature. Conservative economists such as Friedman and Hayek often refer to this property of the free market. More formal treatments are available in Schmeidler and Vind, 1972, Thomson, 1983, or Varian, 1976.)

In fact, the market mechanism is even more special than the above argument suggests. It turns out that in a large economy with tastes that vary continuously across the population, the only envy-free and efficient allocations are market equilibria with equal incomes. This result was first proved by Varian (1976) and later generalized by Kleinberg (1978, 1980), and Champsaur and Laroque (1981). The proof is somewhat technical, but the intuition can be conveyed easily.

Suppose first that we have an economy with *identical* individuals. Then it is clear that in an envy-free efficient allocation all agents must have the same income; for if any had higher income, he would choose a bundle of goods that would be preferred by the others — since they all have the same tastes.

Now consider a large economy where each agent has just *slightly* different preferences from his neighbors; i.e. where tastes vary continuously across the population. Then if one agent had a higher income than his neighbor he would choose a bundle that his neighbor envied — since both of them have similar tastes. Thus the *only* envy-free and efficient allocations in a large economy are those with equal incomes. In this sense equal incomes — and Dworkin's auction — are central to the notion of envy-free allocations.

Of course equal income allocations would not have to arise from equal division. But given an equal income allocation any rearrangement of endowments that preserved the equality of income would not change the allocation — this is because a consumer's demands depend only on the *value* of his or her initial bundle, not on its composition. In this sense, equal income in the final allocation is operationally indistinguishable from an equal division of the initial resources.

Thus equal income market equilibria are privileged allocations in the class of envy-free Pareto efficient allocations. They are also privileged in several other ways. For example, if the notion of individual envy is extended to a kind of "group" envy it turns out that the only envy-free Pareto efficient allocations in a large economy are the equal income competitive equilibria (Vind, 1973; Varian, 1974). Also it can be shown that such allocations involve minimal information requirements in the class of envy-free efficient allocations (Thomson, 1982a). For some more reasons why equal income allocations are especially privileged envy-free allocations, see Thomson and Varian (1984) and the references contained therein.

2. VARIATIONS IN TALENT

After his discussion of the simple auction described above, Dworkin goes on to ask how it might be generalized to more complex cases involving labor, investment, trade, and so on. He is most concerned with the problems posed by labor. This has also been the focus of considerable interest in the economics literature, so we turn to a discussion of some of the problems involved in this framework.

Dworkin argues that the original envy test — now covering both the distribution of goods and the distribution of labor — is still valid in an economy involving production. He uses the example of a hard worker who accumulates more than the others and thus has a consumption bundle that is envied by the others. However:

> If we look at envy differently, as a matter of resources over an entire life, and we include a person's occupation as a part of the bundle of his goods, then no one envies Adrian's bundle, and the distinction can not be said to be unequal on that account. (p. 304)

I agree with Dworkin on this issue. The envy test seems just as appropriate when occupation and labor choices are involved as when only goods are involved. The problem is that the envy test and Pareto efficiency may now be in conflict. Pazner and Schmeidler (1974) discovered the remarkable fact that there may be no envy-free and Pareto efficient allocations at all in an economy involving labor and production! Such examples can arise when tastes and abilities "fit together" in unfortunate ways. Schmeidler and Pazner present some examples of how this can happen using quite plausible utility functions and technologies. Although their discussion is somewhat mathematical, we can convey the spirit of their examples with a simple story. Suppose that there are two people, *A* and *B*. *A* has a comparative advantage in being a chicken farmer, and *B* has a comparative advantage in being an actor. Thus productive efficiency requires that they be assigned to these activities. It can easily happen that at this equilibrium each might envy the other's life. But if they changed places, the resulting reduction in the output of chicken and theatre would make them both worse off. The problem here is that the envy comparison as originally formulated does not require the agents to consider the question of *feasibility* of the overall allocation when they compare their occupations. In the example given above efficiency dictates one occupational choice and envy dictates another. Which is the better outcome?

Although this example is suggestive, it is not at all clear how it fits in with the idea of starting with an equal division and trading to a market equilibrium. The problem comes in how we define an equal division when labor is present. Do we divide the goods equally, and allow people control over their own labor? Or do we try to correct for the original arbitrary distribution of ability by giving some control over each person's labor power to the others? Each of these proposals leads to a different outcome and it is not apparent how to choose between them. I have already written on these ideas in several places (Varian, 1973, 1977; Thomson and Varian, 1984) so I will not discuss them in great detail here.

The first treatment of a *fully* equal division — of labor power as well as goods — is due to Pazner and Schmeidler (1978b). They imagine an economy with n people where each person is issued a coupon that gives him property rights in $1/n$th of each other person's labor. Given this fully equal division, each person sells this initial endowment of goods and labor to the highest bidder. In particular the labor can be sold to firms who will use it in producing goods, or to the original owner of the labor who will use it for his own purposes — e.g. as leisure time. At the final market equilibrium each agent will hold some bundle of goods and some amount of his own leisure. Note that the value of this final bundle — using the market prices for both the goods *and each individual's leisure* must be the same across all people, since they all started with exactly the same endowment of goods and labor time. Thus this process will achieve a market equilibrium with equal "full income" — that is, income where we value each person's consumption of his own leisure at the market wage. For this reason, I have termed it an "income fair" allocation (Varian, 1974).

The other notion of equal division, where we simply divide the goods equally without any correction for the differences in ability, I termed a "wealth fair" allocation. This is because the usual definition of wealth refers only to physical property and not in general to the "human capital" from earnings potential. (Although this may well be regarded as a defect of the usual definition.)

How can we compare these two concepts? As I have argued elsewhere (Varian, 1974, 1975) income fair allocations seem to favor the untalented, while wealth fair allocations seem to favor the talented. For in an income fair allocation a talented person finds that his own leisure time is a relatively expensive commodity to acquire while the untalented find their leisure relatively cheap. If all agents happened to have the same tastes for goods and their own leisure, the talented would definitely be worse off — since they would have to spend a much larger component of their initial resources simply to purchase their own leisure time. They would be "slaves to their maximum earning power" (p. 320).

On the other hand, wealth fair allocations seem to favor the talented overly much. It can be shown that an equal division of goods alone will lead to an allocation in which no agent envies another's consumption-*output* bundle. That is, if we extend the envy test by requiring that each agent considers how much he would have to work to match each other agent's production and make the envy comparison on these adjusted bundles, then this test will be satisfied in a wealth fair allocation. (See Varian, 1974.) Note that this kind of comparison forces the agents to take account of feasibility considerations when they make the envy comparison. But of course this means that if one agent is *unable* to match another agent's output, then he has no grounds for complaint. It seems that there should be some sort of correction for the initial ability distribution.

Dworkin also considers these two possible interpretations of equal division in the presence of different abilities, although not by these names. In the end he rejects both of them. To quote:

> So the starting-gate theory [i.e. equal division of resources alone which results in a wealth fair allocation], that the [agents] should start off equal in resources but grow prosperous or lean through their own efforts thereafter, is an indefensible combination of very different theories of justice. (p. 310)

On the other hand, the income fair allocation suffers from the problem that it leads to "slavery of the talented" (p. 312). He argues instead for the original concept of an envy-free allocation. But he does recognize that the presence of untradeable goods such as ability or talent might require some modifications of the original concept: "If equality of resources is understood to include some plausible version of the envy test as a necessary condition of an equal distribution, then the role of talent must be neutralized in a way that no simple addition to the stock of goods . . . can accomplish" (p. 312).

His approach here is to consider what kind of insurance one might buy in some original position against the possibility of ending up without a particularly desirable bundle of abilities. Dworkin suggests that this kind of thought experiment will fix "at least the lower bounds of a tax-and-redistribution program satisfying the demands of equality of resources" (p. 315).

Dworkin considers this kind of hypothetical insurance market in some detail and in my opinion his discussion here is perhaps the most novel contribution of his essay. He actually considers two types of insurance in two separate places in the essay; the first is an examination of insurance against handicaps, and the second is insurance against lack of ability. Dworkin recognizes that these two types of insurance are much the same and can be discussed in parallel. As he remarks that "someone who cannot play basketball like Wilt Chamberlain, paint like Piero, or make money like Geneen, suffers from an (especially common) handicap" (p. 315).

What can economics say about such "original position" insurance markets? The simplest model would be the following. Each person draws from a sample of abilities and receives some ability that is worth \$$w$ with probability $f(w)$. He can purchase an insurance policy that pays off $t(w)$ dollars if his wealth turns out to be w. We will consider policies that break even in the sense that the total expected payoffs are zero. Thus if low ability people receive a positive payoff for being unlucky, high ability people will receive a negative payoff — i.e. will have to pay taxes — in exchange for being lucky. Letting E denote mathematical expectation and $u(w)$ his von Neuman-Morgenstern utility function (assumed to exhibit risk aversion), we can pose the agent's insurance problem as:

$$\max Eu(w + t(w))$$
$$\text{s.t. } Et(w) = 0$$

It is straightforward to show that the expected marginal utility of a dollar must be the same at each ability level — if not, it would pay to purchase a little more insurance at some wealth level and give up a little insurance in another. But this in turn implies that $w + t(w)$ must be constant across ability levels: i.e., that people will purchase *complete* insurance against having different wealth levels! This is reminiscent of the earlier discussion of income fair allocations which Dworkin rejected as being "slavery of the talented" (p. 312).

Indeed, this result seems to go against Dworkin's intuition. He seems to feel that ability insurance is ". . . likely to be a very bad bargain . . ." (p. 320). He argues that the insurance decision offers the ". . . bet of a very small chance of a very great loss in return for the very large chance of a very small gain . . ." (p. 320). But I believe he forgets that the small gain comes when people turn out to be disadvantaged; — that is, the insurance scheme pays off in those circumstances where the individuals have low ability, and thus low earning power. Thus the *marginal* utility of a small amount of extra income may be large indeed. And similarly the large loss comes when people turn out to be advantaged, and thus the *marginal* utility of a decrease in wealth is small.

Our assumption of risk aversion — which translates into an assumption of diminishing marginal utility of wealth in our context — implies that an individual will be willing to sacrifice a large of amount of wealth if he turns out to be wealthy in order to be assured a small amount of wealth if he turns out to be poorly endowed, simply because the loss of a dollar when you are wealthy involves a much smaller loss in utility than the gain in utility that a dollar provides if you turn out to be poor. It is precisely the desire to equalize the *marginal* utility of wealth across the possible outcomes that leads to the equalization of *total* wealth levels in this auction.

However, it can be argued that this kind of "wealth" auction is too simple to describe the "ability" auction that Dworkin actually proposed. Indeed one aspect of the ability auction is that the lucky people — who end up with high ability — are actually *unlucky* in the sense that their own leisure will turn out to be quite expensive to consume. This interplay between the value of the endowment (which depends on ability) and the market value of the agent's leisure (which also depends on ability) is not captured in the simple one-dimensional model described above.

Roemer (1984) has also considered this sort of one-dimensional wealth auction model and reached the same conclusion. But he has gone much further in examining the consequences of Dworkin's ability auction. One of his most interesting results is that: ". . . the talented agents can end up *worse off* under the insurance mechanism than under the equal-division-of-labor method . . . [thus] a person is more 'enslaved' by the insurance agreement, if he is born talented" (p. 37).

Thus it seems that Dworkin's insurance market is not necessarily the answer to the problem of how to correct for differences of ability. Roemer's paper goes a long way in examining various facets of ability insurance, with for the most part negative results . . . but perhaps there is some modification of Dworkin's idea that can yet provide a satisfactory solution.

3. INSURANCE AND INCENTIVES

Let me turn now to a side issue that was only briefly addressed by Dworkin. At one point he states: "I have neglected the question of the technology that will be available for the insurance firms to decide and prove who has what level of talent, and the cost of that technology" (p. 319f).

This question has been the subject of several recent investigations in the optimal tax literature, stimulated by the seminal work of Mirrlees

(1976), which ask what kinds of taxes on *income* (as opposed to ability) might maximize some social objective. This work has mostly been couched in the framework of a social welfare function but that welfare function could easily be interpreted as an expected utility function for a representative consumer.

A pure ability tax of the sort Dworkin discusses has no influence on incentives to work. If the state — or Dworkin's insurance firm — can observe ability costlessly, then individuals are forced to cough up their taxes or their premiums, as the case might be. But if true ability is not observable and a tax must be levied on some proxy for ability such as income, consumers will in general have an incentive to reduce the level of income that they exhibit. This is nothing but the commonplace observation that high taxes discourage effort.

Mirrlees and other economic theorists have examined the design of taxation schemes that take such shirking into account. This literature is unfortunately quite technical and far beyond the scope of this essay, so I can only refer the interested reader to Mirrlees (1976) for the details of the analysis.

One rather surprising outcome of these theoretical investigations has been that an optimal redistributive income tax must necessarily be regressive at high levels of income. The intuition behind this result goes something like this.

It can be shown that the optimal tax scheme must have the property that the higher ability individuals will end up having higher incomes. Suppose that the highest ability individual has some income y^* and faces a positive marginal tax rate $t'(y^*)$. I claim that this sort of tax policy can not be Pareto efficient. For suppose that we consider lowering the marginal tax rate to zero for levels of income y^* or higher and keeping the tax rates on all other levels of income constant. Then the highest income individual can now choose to work more and pay no taxes on the additional income. But his *total* tax payments — and the total tax payments of all other individuals will not change. Thus we have devised a change that makes the highest income individual better off, and hasn't harmed anyone else; that is, we have constructed a Pareto improvement. It follows that in an optimal tax system — one that is Pareto efficient — high income individuals must face low marginal tax rates.

This result arises because the only reason that individuals have different incomes is because they have different abilities. If we allow for other sources of income differences this result becomes substantially weakened.

Suppose, for example, that differences in income arise only because of differences in luck. Some people are lucky in life and end up with high income and others are unlucky and end up with low incomes. If there is no incentive effect from redistribution then the optimal policy involves complete "social insurance" — everyone ends up with the mean income regardless of their actual circumstances. This is the result described in the last section in the discussion of the wealth auction.

But if there are incentive effects this policy may be undesirable. If everyone were guaranteed the mean income, regardless of their actions, no one would have the incentive to work. Again the difficulties come in deciding what is observable. If we could tell what part of someone's income is due to luck alone, and what part is due to effort, we could tax the luck component and redistribute it to provide social insurance. This would provide an unambiguous gain in welfare. But if we can only tax observed income — the sum of effort and luck — we have to trade off the desirable insurance effects from taxing luck against the undesirable effects of discouraging effort.

This problem can be posed in a formal framework — at least in simple cases — and analyzed by the methods of optimal control theory; see Varian (1980) for a treatment. In most cases of interest an optimal tax scheme in this framework tends towards progression: higher income individuals get taxed at a higher rate, despite the adverse incentive effects. The intuition behind this result is the fact that if there is only a low probability of becoming a millionaire, there are only small disincentives from taxing million dollar incomes at a high rate. But there are considerable gains from the insurance aspect since we will then be able to subsidize major occurrences of bad luck.

So the optimal tax literature presents two polar results: if differences in income are solely due to differences in ability, high income people should face a low marginal tax rate. If differences in income are due to differences in luck, then high income people should face a high marginal tax rate. Of course in reality differences in income are due to both effects but the properties of an optimal redistributive tax system will depend crucially on the relative importance of these two effects.

To summarize this brief review of Dworkin on equality of resources: the idea of envy-free allocations is an appealing one, especially when coupled with the idea of Pareto efficiency. Dworkin's case for the equal income market equilibrium can be substantially strengthened through the use of some of the existing results in the economics literature. However, the problems involved when labor and ability differences are introduced still remain. Roemer (1984) has shown that ability auction proposed by Dworkin apparently does not give a completely satisfactory solution to the problem but this point certainly warrants further investigation. Finally, some of the recent results in the theory of optimal taxation may offer interesting extensions of the redistribution problem that Dworkin considers.

REFERENCES

Dworkin, R. (1981a). "What is Equality? Part 1: Equality of Welfare," *Philosophy and Public Affairs*, 10, 3, 185–246.

———. (1981b). "What is Equality? Part 2: Equality of Resources," *Philosophy and Public Affairs*, 10, 4, 283–345.

Mirrlees, J. (1976). "Optimal Tax Theory: A Synthesis," *Journal of Public Economics*, 6, 327–358.

Nozick, R. (1973). *Anarchy, State, and Utopia*. New York: Basic Books.

Roemer, J. (1984). "Equality of Talent," University of California at Davis, Working Paper No. 239.

Thomson, W. & H. Varian (1984). "Theories of Justice Based on Symmetry." In L. Hurwicz & H. Sonnenshein, eds., *Social Goals and Social Organization: Volume in Memory of Elisha Pazner*, Cambridge University Press.

Varian, H. (1980). "Redistributive Taxation as Social Insurance," *Journal of Public Economics*, 14, 49–68.

SUGGESTED READING

(NOTE: *This bibliography contains a list of works in economics that are concerned with envy-free theories of justice and related topics. It is taken from Thomson and Varian, 1984.*)

Allingham, M. (1977). "Fairness and Utility," *Economie Appliquée*, 29(2), 257–266.

Archibald, P. and D. Donaldson (1979). "Notes on Economic Inequality," *Journal of Public Economics*, 12(2), 205–214.

Austinsmith, D. (1979). "Fair Rights," *Economics Letters*, 4(1), 29–32.

Baumol, W. (1980). "Theory of Equity in Pricing for Resource Conservation," *Journal of Environmental Economics*, 7(4), 308–320.

———. (1982). "Applied Fairness Theory and Rationing Policy," *American Economic Review*, 72(4), 639–651.

———. (1983). "Applied Fairness Theory: Reply," *American Economic Review*, 73(5), 1161–1162.

Brock, W., & J. Scheinkman (1976). "On Just Savings Rules," Chicago: University of Chicago Press.

Campbell, D. (1975). "Income Distribution under Majority Rule and Alternative Taxation Criteria," *Public Choice*, 22(Sum), 23–35.

Champsaur, P., & G. Laroque (1981). "Fair Allocations in Large Economies," *Journal of Economic Theory*, 25, 269–282.

Crawford, V. (1977). "A Game of Fair Division," *Review of Economic Studies*, 44(2), 235–247.

———. (1979). "A Procedure for Generating Pareto Efficient Egalitarian Equivalent Allocations," *Econometrica*, 47, 49–60.

———. (1980). "A Self-Administered Solution to the Bargaining Problem," *Review of Economic Studies*, 47(2), 385–392.

Crawford, V. & W. Heller (1979). "Fair Division with Indivisible Commodities," *Journal of Economic Theory*, 21(1), 10–27.

Daniel, T. (1975). "A Revised Concept of Distributional Equity," *Journal of Economic Theory*, 11(1), 94–100.

———. (1978). "Pitfalls in the Theory of Fairness — Comment," *Journal of Economic Theory*, 19(2), 561–564.

Damange, G. (1982). "Implementing Efficient Egalitarian Equivalent Allocations," Ecole Polytechnique discussion paper, A244.

Dubins, L. E., & E. H. Spanier (1961). "How to Cut a Cake Fairly," *American Mathematical Monthly* 68, 1–17.

Feldman, A., & A. Kirman (1974). "Fairness and Envy," *American Economic Review*, 64(6), 995–1005.

Feldman, A., & D. Weiman (1979). "Envy, Wealth and Class Hierarchies," *Journal of Public Economics*, 11(1), 81–91.

Foley, D. (1967). "Resource Allocation and the Public Sector," *Yale Economic Essays*, 7, 45–98.

Gaertner, W. (1982). "Envy-free Rights Assignments and Self-oriented Preferences," *Mathematical Social Sciences*, 2, 199–208.

Gardenfors, P. (1978). "Fairness without Interpersonal Comparisons," *Theoria*, 44(10), 57–74.

Goldman, S., & C. Sussangkarn (1978). "On the Concept of Fairness," *Journal of Economic Theory*, 19(1), 210–216.

———. (1980). "On Equity and Efficiency," *Economics Letters*, 5, 29–31.

Graff, J. (1978). "Equity and Efficiency as Components of General Welfare," *South African Journal of Economics*, 19(2), 561–64.

Hammond, P. (1976). "Equity, Arrow's Conditions and Rawls' Difference Principle," *Econometrica*, 44(4), 793–804.

———. (1979). "Straightforward Individual Incentive Compatibility in Large Economies," *Review of Economic Studies*, 46, 263–282.

Hayashi, T. (1979). "On a Positive Theory of Fair Allocation," Kobe University.

Henry, J. (1977). "Efficiency, Equality, Equity, and Personal Income Distribution," *Actualité Economique*, 53(2), 154–192.

Hurwicz, L. (1979a). "On Allocations Attainable through Nash Equilibrium." In J. J. Laffont, ed., *Aggregation and Revelation of Preferences*. Amsterdam: North-Holland, 397–419.

———. (1979b). "Outcome Functions Yielding Walrasian and Lindahl Allocations at Nash Equilibrium Points for Two or More Agents," *Review of Economic Studies*, 46, 217–225.

Jaskold-Gabszewicz, J. (1975). "Coalitional Fairness of Allocations in Pure Exchange," *Econometrica*, 43(4), 661–668.

Kleinberg, N. (1978). "Three Essays in Mathematical Economics," Doctoral thesis, M.I.T.

———. (1980). "Fair Allocations and Equal Incomes," *Journal of Economic Theory*, 23(2), 189–200.

Kolm, S. (1972). *Justice et Equité*, Editions du Centre National de la Recherche Scientifique, Paris.

Kuhn, H. (1967). "On Games of Fair Division." In Shubik, M., ed., *Essays in Honor of Oskar Morgenstern*. Princeton: Princeton University Press 29–37.

Leffler, K., J. Long, & T. Russell (1979). "Signaling — Efficiency and Equilibrium," *Economics Letters*, 4, 215–220.

Luce, D. & H. Raiffa (1957). *Games and Decisions*. New York: Wiley.

Mas-Colell, A. (1982). "On the Second Welfare Theorem for Anonymous Net Trades in Exchange Economies with Many Agents." (mimeograph).

Maskin, E. (1977). "Nash Equilibrium and Welfare Optimality," in *Mathematics of Operations Research*, forthcoming.

McLennan, A. (1980). "Fair Allocations," Doctoral thesis, Princeton University.

Moulin, H. (1980). "Implementing Efficient, Anonymous and Neutral Social Choice Functions," *Journal of Mathematical Economics*, 7, 249–269.

———. (1981). "Implementing Just and Efficient Decision Making," *Journal of Public Economics*, 16, 193–213.

Musgrave, R. (1959). *The Theory of Public Finance*. New York: McGraw-Hill.

Nozick, R. (1974). *Anarchy, State, and Utopia*. New York: Basic Books.

Otsuki, M. (1980). "On Distribution According to Labor — A Concept of Fairness in Production," *Review of Economic Studies*, 47(5), 945–58.

Pazner, E. (1977). "Pitfalls in the Theory of Fairness," *Journal of Economic Theory*, 14(2), 458–466.

———. (1979). "Individual Rationality and the Concept of Social Welfare," *Theory and Decision*, 10(1-4), 281–292.

Pazner, E. & D. Schmeidler (1974), "A Difficulty in the Concept of Fairness," *Review of Economic Studies*, 41, 441–443.

———. (1976). "Social Contract Theory and Ordinal Distributive Equity," *Journal of Public Economics*, 5, 261–268.

———. (1978a). "Egalitarian Equivalent Allocations: A New Concept of Economics Equity," *Quarterly Journal of Economics*, 92(4), 1–45.

———. (1978b). "Decentralization and Income Distribution in Socialist Economies," *Economic Inquiry*, 257–264.

Rawls, J. (1971). *A Theory of Justice*. Cambridge, Mass: Harvard University Press.

Rae, D. (1979). "Egalitarian State–Notes on a System of Contradictory Ideals," *Daedalus*, 108(4), 37–54.

Roberts, K. (1980). "Possibility Theorems with Interpersonally Comparable Welfare Levels," *Review of Economic Studies*, 47(2), 409–420.

Samuelson, W. (1980). "The Object Distribution Problem Revisited," *Quarterly Journal of Economics*, 85–98.

Schick, F. (1980). "Towards a Logic of Liberalism," *Journal of Philosophy*, 77(2), 80–98.

Schmeidler, D. (1980). "Walrasian Analysis via Strategic Outcome Functions," *Econometrica*, 48, 1585–1593.

Schmeidler, D., & K. Vind (1972), "Fair Net Trades," *Econometrica*, 40(4), 637–642.

Schmeidler, D. & 36Yaari (1973), "Fair Allocations," unpublished.

Sen, A. (1977). "Social Choice Theory–Re-Examination," *Econometrica*, 45(1), 53–77.

Sen, A. (1979). "Welfare Basis of Real Income Comparisons," *Journal of Economic Literature*, 17(1), 1–45.

Singer, E. (1962). "Extension of the Classical Rule of 'Divide and Choose'," *Southern Economic Journal*, 38, 391–394.

Sobel, J. (1979). "Fair Allocations of a Renewable Resource," *Journal of Economic Theory*, 21(2), 235–248.

Steinhaus, H. (1948). "The Problem of Fair Division," *Econometrica*, 101–104.

Suppes, P. (1966). "Some Formal Models of Grading Principles," *Synthése*, 6, 284–306.

Sussangkarn, C. & S. Goldman (1980). *Dealing with Envy*, Berkeley: University of California Press.

Suzumura, K. (1980). "On the Possibility of 'Fair' Collective Choice Rules," Kyoto Institute of Economic Research, Kyoto, Japan.

———. (1981a). "On Pareto-Efficiency and the No-Envy Concept of Equity," *Journal of Economic Theory*, 25, 267–379.

———. (1981b). "Equity, Efficiency and Rights in Social Choice," Kyoto Institute of Economic Research, Kyoto, Japan.

Svensson, L. (1980). "Some Views on a Fair Wage Structure," *Ekonomiska Samfunddets Tidskrift*, 33(3), 385–392.

Tamaklowe, E. (1980). "Spatial Equity in Regional Transportation Investment Policies," *Traffic Quarterly*, 34(4), 605–626.

Thomson, W. (1979). "On Allocations Attainable through Nash-Equilibria, a Comment." In J. J. Laffont, ed., *Aggregation and Revelation of Preferences*. Amsterdam: North-Holland, 420–431.

———. (1982a). "An Informationally Efficient Equity Criterion" *Journal of Public Economics*, 18, 243–263.

———. (1982b). "The Manipulation of Mechanisms Designed to Select Equitable and Efficient Allocations," Harvard Institute of Economic Research Discussion Paper, no. 909.

———. (1983). "Equity in Exchange Economies," *Journal of Economic Theory*, 29(2), 217–244.

Ulph, D. (1978). "Labor Supply and the Measurement of Inequality," *Journal of Economic Theory*, 19(2), 492–512.
Varian, H. (1974). "Equity, Envy, and Efficiency," *Journal of Economic Theory*, 9, 63–91.
———. (1975). "Distributive Justice, Welfare Economics, and the Theory of Fairness," *Philosophy and Public Affairs*, 4, 223–247.
———. (1976). "Two Problems in the Theory of Fairness," *Journal of Public Economics*, 5, 249–260.
Vind, K. (1973). "Lecture Notes in Mathematical Economics," Stanford University. (Mimeograph)
Wittmean, D. (1979). "Diagrammatic Exposition of Justice," *Theory and Decision*, 11(2), 207–239.
Yannelis, N. (1981). "Approximate Coalitionally Fair Allocations in Large 'Mixed' Economies," Wayne State University, Discussion Paper, No. 130.
———. (1982). "Nondiscriminatory Allocations in Finite Mixed Markets," Wayne State University. (Mimeograph)
Yaari, M. (1982). "A Remark on Competitive Equilibrium with Equal Incomes," Research Memorandum No. 49, Center for Research in Mathematical Economics, The Hebrew University, Jerusalem.
Yaari, M. & M. Bar-Hillel (1983). "On Dividing Justly," Economic Theory Discussion Paper No. 63, Cambridge University.

[12]

The Mismarriage of Bargaining Theory and Distributive Justice*

John Roemer

DISTRIBUTIVE JUSTICE AND BARGAINING THEORY

Bargaining theory studies the division of utility between or among agents who, if agreement is not reached, each receive a utility designated by a threat point. For example, if there are two agents, then a bargaining problem is specified by a pair {S, d} where S is usually taken to be a convex, comprehensive[1] set in the plane (representing possible utility pairs for agents) and d is a point in S specifiying the utilities each gets in the absence of agreement. A *bargaining mechanism* is a function F which assigns to each bargaining problem {S, d} a point s in S, the agreement point under that mechanism:

$$F(\{S, d\}) = s .$$

The axiomatic approach to bargaining proceeds by specifying a set of axioms which acceptable mechanisms must obey and characterizes the class of acceptable mechanisms. For a comprehensive review of the area, see Roth;[2] a more recent survey is provided by Kalai.[3]

* I have benefited from the comments of many people on matters discussed in this paper. I acknowledge especially Roger Howe, Aanund Hylland, Louis Makowski, and William Thomson. I gratefully acknowledge, as well, support from the National Science Foundation grant SES-8509695.

1. A comprehensive utility possibilities set is one which models the idea that utility is freely disposable. Thus, if a point x is in a comprehensive set S, and $y \leq x$, then y is in S. All points to the southwest of a given point in S lie in S. Comprehensiveness is not an innocuous assumption. In particular, it rules out the typical problems which arise due to incentives, when a skilled person withholds his labor due to a high tax, thus decreasing the utility of both agents below what it otherwise could have been. The utility possibilities set for a 'Rawlsian' problem is typically not comprehensive. Problems of incentives and asymmetric information are ignored in this article; this is reflected, in part, in the comprehensiveness assumption.

2. Alvin Roth, *Axiomatic Models of Bargaining* (Berlin: Springer-Verlag, 1979).

3. Ehud Kalai, "Solutions to the Bargaining Problem," *Social Goals and Social Organization*, ed. L. Hurwicz, D. Schmeidler, and H. Sonnenschein (New York: Cambridge University Press, 1985).

Ethics 97 (October 1986): 88–110

Various writers have argued that bargaining theory provides the appropriate formal apparatus for studying distributive justice. A classical example of this approach is Braithwaite.[4] More recently, Yaari and Bar-Hillel[5] have applied various solution concepts of bargaining theory in an empirical study of respondents' attitudes toward problems of distributive justice. Brock[6] advocates a particular solution concept from bargaining theory (the Nash solution) as implementing the 'just' division. Perhaps the most sustained advocacy for the application of bargaining theory to distributive justice is that of Gauthier[7] who argues that justice should be viewed as a bargaining problem and that a particular mechanism (the Kalai-Smorodinsky solution)[8] is the most accurate conception of what bargaining is.[9] In a recent paper, Binmore[10] applies new developments in game theory to bargaining theory and supports the Rawlsian maximin criterion as the outcome of a bargaining game.[11] These authors all advocate the application of bargaining theory, as formally described above, to problems of distributive justice. In addition, other writers advocate a contractarian approach to justice (e.g., Harsanyi, Rawls, Howe and Roemer, and Scanlon),[12] without endorsing the formal apparatus of bargaining theory. While contractarianism could be considered to be related to bargaining, I shall not be concerned with that approach as my interest is in the application of the formal apparatus of bargaining theory to distributive justice.

I will argue in this paper against the application of bargaining theory to problems of distributive justice on grounds that the domain which

4. R. Braithwaite, *Theory of Games as a Tool for the Moral Philosopher* (Cambridge: Cambridge University Press, 1955).

5. M. E. Yaari and M. Bar-Hillel, "On Dividing Justly," *Social Choice and Welfare* 1 (1984): 1–24.

6. Horace Brock, "A Game Theoretic Account of Social Justice," *Theory and Decision* 11 (1979): 239–65.

7. David Gauthier, "Bargaining and Justice," *Social Philosophy and Policy*, vol. 2 (1985).

8. Ehud Kalai and M. Smorodinsky, "Other Solutions to Nash's Bargaining Problem," *Econometrica* 43 (1975): 513–18.

9. Actually Gauthier, in "Bargaining and Justice," advocates a solution which is a slight variant of the Kalai-Smorodinsky solution. For two-person bargaining games, the two solution concepts coincide.

10. K. G. Binmore, "Game Theory and the Social Contract, Part 1" (London School of Economics and Political Science, Department of Mathematics, 1984).

11. Binmore introduces into the bargaining problem the additional issue that the time elapsed in reaching a bargaining solution is costly to the agents. He also gives a new axiomatic foundation for the Nash solution, using axioms which take into account the costliness of bargaining.

12. John Harsanyi, "Morality and the Theory of Rational Behavior," *Social Research* 44 (1977): 623–56; John Rawls, *A Theory of Justice* (Cambridge: Belknap Press, 1971); R. E. Howe and John E. Roemer, "Rawlsian Justice as the Core of a Game," *American Economic Review* 71 (1981): 880–95; T. Scanlon, "Utilitarianism and Contractarianism," in *Utilitarianism and Beyond*, ed. A. Sen and B. Williams (Cambridge: Cambridge University Press, 1982): 103–28.

bargaining theory takes—objects of the form {S, d}—is informationally too impoverished to capture the important issues in distributive justice. Bargaining theory admits information only with respect to utilities of the agents once the threat point has been determined, while distributive justice is concerned with issues of rights, needs, and preferences as well. Note that *preferences,* which are not specified in the set S, and utility *numbers,* as specified in the set S, are very different objects. Being told only what the utility possibility set is differs from being told what agents' preferences are over allocations or alternatives of various kinds. The class of mechanisms which can be defined on the informationally impoverished domain of bargaining theory is very 'thin' since the objects in that domain have little structure. By defining a domain of 'economic environments,' which can include information on resources, preferences, needs, skills, and so on, the class of possible allocation mechanisms becomes much richer because the objects on which the mechanisms act are ones containing complex information. Bargaining theory, I will claim, is too simple an apparatus for studying distributive justice.

It is important to mention the fallacy of one apparently appealing argument against the application of bargaining theory distributive justice. Some might say that bargaining theory is 'welfarist' in the sense that it admits only utility information; Sen[13] and others have argued, persuasively in my opinion, against welfarism as an adequate approach to distributive justice. But bargaining theory, contrary to appearances, is not welfarist. For the threat point of a bargaining game, although described as a pair of utilities, can (and, indeed, one might say, must) be specified from knowledge of the underlying rights, needs, and so on. Thus, specification of the bargaining game *may* take account of underlying rights and justice-relevant attributes described in some richer environment. What utilities the agents receive, failing a bargain, might be defined in many different ways, each corresponding to a different conception of their rights. Hence, my criticism of bargaining theory as a tool for studying distributive justice will not be that it is welfarist. (Nevertheless, one might say the application of bargaining theory to distributive justice is almost welfarist in that nonutility information is dispensed with very early on, as soon as the threat point has been determined.)

As well as make my negative argument, I will propose a new technique for studying problems of distributive justice: mechanism theory performed on a domain of economic environments instead of on environments of the form {S, d}. Several examples will be given of how to formulate problems of distributive justice using this tool, and the relation of the approach to a bargaining-theory approach will be discussed. I think the weakness of the bargaining-theory approach to justice can only be fully appreciated after seeing this alternative method.

13. Amartya Sen, "Utilitarianism and Welfarism," *Journal of Philosophy* 76 (1979): 463–89.

It is important to distinguish what can be called the positive and normative applications of bargaining theory to distributive justice. The *positive* approach argues that justice should be viewed as a bargaining problem; that being determined, it tries to discover the best characterization of rational bargaining. This approach is associated, for instance, with Gauthier and Binmore. In this approach, the axioms on the bargaining mechanism are probed only for their accuracy in capturing how people rationally bargain. But many writers, at various times, fall into what I would call the *normative* approach, which views the bargaining axioms as capturing, directly, our moral intuitions.

I will give several examples of how writers in the area present normative justifications for axioms intended to describe positive bargaining. There are several variants of a 'monotonicity' axiom in bargaining theory. One version says: consider two bargaining problems {S, d} and {T, d} where $S \subset T$. Then neither agent should receive a lower utility at the solution in T than he does in S. It is appealing to justify this axiom on ethical grounds (if the size of the pie increases, neither should suffer in utility terms), although that would be inappropriate in bargaining theory. The question must be, Is there a reason for *bargaining* solutions to be so characterized? (Kalai and Samet[14] give proper bargaining foundations, based on considerations of incentive compatibility, for certain monotonicity axioms, although not for the particular axiom I have mentioned.) A second example of a normatively motivated axiom in bargaining theory comes from the recent work of Thomson[15] who, in a series of interesting papers, has studied an axiom he calls 'population monotonicity.' Suppose we have a solution to a bargaining problem {S, d} with two people, and there is an associated problem {T, d′}, with three people, having the property that the slice of T in the coordinate plane in which the utility of the first two agents is specified is the set S. That is, in the three-person problem, three agents share the same pie, so to speak, that is available in the original two-person problem. The axiom says: neither of the first two people should get more utility in the solution to the problem {T, d′} than they got in the solution of {S, d}. Thomson's justification of this axiom is on ethical, not positive, grounds—that it models solidarity. When the third person appears on the scene, bringing 'no additional resources,' both of the first two people must chip in to give him some utility in the new three-person problem. This may be an appropriate motivation for that axiom in a theory of justice, but not for bargaining theory. It would be pleasant to show that rational bargaining has this property, but it should not be an axiom of bargaining.

14. Ehud Kalai and Dov Samet, "Monotonic Solutions to General Cooperative Games," *Econometrica* 53 (1985): 307–28.

15. William Thomson, "Problems of Fair Division and the Egalitarian Solution," *Journal of Economic Theory* 31 (1983): 211–26, and "Axiomatic Models of Bargaining with a Variable Population: A Survey of Recent Results" (University of Rochester, Department of Economics, 1984).

I do not evaluate in this article whether the theory of rational bargaining has, as its proper informational domain, the space of objects which just admit utility information, {S, d}. I will not discuss what constitutes the correct theory of bargaining. My argument is against those who claim the same formal apparatus properly models problems of distributive justice. Against those who take the normative approach, my argument is fairly straightforward: I must only exhibit the loss of relevant information for justice considerations which occurs in the bargaining theory environment. This is most easily done by example; I will present two extended examples, in the second and fourth sections of this article. I will provide some argument against the positive application of bargaining theory to distributive justice in the third section. Others have discussed the informational poverty of bargaining theory as a model of the bargaining process.[16]

In the interest of concreteness, I proceed by presenting in the next section an example of a problem in distributive justice and the approach I find natural to take in studying the problem. This approach involves studying mechanisms on a class of economic environments. In the third section, I return to my criticism of the bargaining-theory approach to distributive justice by indicating how bargaining theory might approach the same problem. In the fourth section, I present a second example of a problem in distributive justice and show how it can be studied using mechanism theory.

PRIVATE AND PUBLIC DOMAINS: CONFLICTING CLAIMS

Consider the problem of Able and Infirm, who jointly own all the land in the world, and who each own themselves. The land is used to produce corn, which they each need or want to consume. There is a known technology for producing corn; Able is skilled in producing corn, and Infirm is less skilled or unable to produce corn. How much corn should be produced, who should produce it, and how should it be divided between them if we are to respect two principles: (1) the two agents' self-ownership of skill and labor and (2) their joint ownership of the land? Assume, for the moment, the extreme case that Infirm cannot work at all. Since they jointly own the world, Able cannot use any land to produce corn until he and Infirm have agreed upon that use, which presumably will only occur (assuming Infirm can enforce his joint property right in the land) after Infirm has assured for himself some of the corn which Able produces. On the one hand, is this an incursion against Able's self-ownership? On the other hand, if Able turns over none of the corn produced to Infirm, does that not violate Infirm's joint ownership of the land?

16. Alvin Roth, "Toward a Theory of Bargaining: An Experimental Study in Economics," *Science* 220 (1983): 687–51; Alvin Roth and Françoise Schoumaker, "Expectations and Reputations in Bargaining: An Experimental Study," *American Economic Review* 73 (1983): 362–72.

I call this the Cohen problem after G. A. Cohen, who poses it (although not in quite this form) in two recent papers.[17] The Cohen problem is a fundamental one in the debate on the legitimacy of capitalist inequality. Suppose the world is populated by people who, we deem, should have equal opportunities insofar as the resources in the external world permit but unequal opportunities insofar as their 'personal' assets, such as skills, make available. (Such equality of opportunity should hold, at least, before agents have mixed their labor with external resources in such a way as may entitle them to appropriate external resources as their own assets.) Various conceptions of such equal opportunities in respect to external assets can be put forward. Nozick[18] puts forth one such conception: that a person has the right to appropriate any amount of the external asset (land) so long as others are made no worse off by such appropriation. Other versions of the Lockean proviso can be expressed. Cohen suggests that the appropriate counterfactual to private ownership of the land might not be Nozickian no-ownership, but joint ownership. Thus, no one could use the land, if it is jointly owned, unless the owners agree to that use by whatever procedure is taken to define agreement. How much inequality in final welfares of the agents is permissible if we adhere to these two principles? Will self-ownership of skill effectively nullify any appropriation by Infirm of the corn Able produces, or will joint ownership of the land trump Able's right to the lion's share? Are there, even, any distributions of corn and labor between the agents which will respect the claims which follow from these apparently competing domains of rights? Of course, one might not agree that justice requires the delineation of the private and public domains as I have outlined them; but if one does, what allocations of corn and labor between the agents will be acceptable?

A bargaining-theory approach would take as initial data the preferences of the two agents for bundles of corn and leisure, the technology, the skill levels of the agents, and the amount of land. From this, the utility possibilities set S would be calculated. Deciding what the threat point should be, however, is a major problem for which bargaining theory has no standard solution. This problem is extraneous to bargaining theory as such. Even should a threat point be decided upon, I think bargaining theory cannot properly use the given information on joint and private rights, as will become evident below.

To capture fully the relevant information, I propose another approach, which begins by defining an *economic environment*, a vector

$$\xi = \{\overline{W};\ u(C, l);\ f(W, L);\ s^1, s^2\}\ ,$$

17. G. A. Cohen, "Nozick on Appropriation," *New Left Review*, no. 150 (1985), pp. 89–107, and "Self-Ownership, World Ownership, and Equality: Part 2," *Social Philosophy and Policy* 3 (1986): 77–96.

18. Robert Nozick, *Anarchy, State and Utopia* (New York: Basic Books, 1974).

where $\overline{W}$ is the amount of land in the world, u(C, l) is a utility function representing the (common) preferences for bundles of corn and leisure of the two agents, f(W, L) is a production function which specifies the amount of corn which can be produced from bundles (W, L) of land and labor, and s^i is the skill level of agent i. It is also given that each agent is in possession of one unit of leisure, which can be converted into labor at will. Assume there are constant returns to scale in production, so that if agent 1 expends L^1 units of labor and agent 2 expends L^2 units of labor on W acres of land, then total production of corn is $f(W, s^1L^1 + s^2L^2)$. That is, skill level is defined as the labor in efficiency units which an agent is capable of performing per unit of time. The economic environment defined above is a simple one: for instance, it assumes both agents have the same preferences, that only leisure, and not skill level, is an argument of the utility function, and that skill is defined in a simple way.

Let $\Omega(\xi)$ be the set of feasible allocations of corn and leisure available to the two agents in environment ξ. A *mechanism* is a mapping which associates to an economic environment a feasible allocation:

$$F(\xi) \in \Omega(\xi) .$$

By specifying various axioms on F's behavior, one can restrict its action to conform to requirements which respect the two agents' joint ownership of the land and their private ownership of skill. The problem is: we do not have any well-defined conception of what joint ownership means, and so the axioms can only express necessary conditions for joint ownership, whatever it means. Similarly, it is not entirely clear what private ownership of skill means when another asset which must be used in conjunction with skill is jointly owned. The advantage of the axiomatic approach, once again, is that it commits one only to necessary properties of private ownership, not to a complete characterization of what that ownership must entail. Not knowing precisely what these rights entail makes it problematical to define the threat point in a bargaining game between Able and Infirm. With the present axiomatic approach, we need not fully resolve these hazy issues; perhaps they will be resolved to some extent for us, in spite of this agnosticism.

In the following, let ξ and ξ' be two economic environments where

$$\xi = \{\overline{W}; f; u; s^1, s^2\} \text{ and } \xi' = \{\overline{W}'; f'; u'; s'^1, s'^2\} .$$

Let $F^i(\xi)$ be the allocation of corn and leisure to agent i which the mechanism assigns in the environment ξ. Thus $u(F^i(\xi))$ is the utility of agent i under F's action in the environment ξ. It is convenient to name one particular mechanism, called E, which implements welfare egalitarianism. $E(\xi)$ is that allocation of corn and leisure assigned to the two agents which is Pareto optimal and equalizes their utilities.

I propose that any mechanism F which respects private ownership of self and joint ownership of the external world should satisfy the following axioms.

C1: Unrestricted Domain. F is defined on a domain of environments ξ where u can be any (concave) utility function, f any (constant or decreasing returns to scale) production function which is increasing in both of its arguments, and W, s^1 and s^2 can be any nonnegative numbers.
C2: Pareto optimality. $F(\xi)$ is a Pareto optimal allocation in $\overline{\Omega(\xi)}$.
C3: Land monotonicity. Let ξ' and ξ differ only in that $\overline{W'} > \overline{W}$. Then for $i = 1,2$: $u[F^i(\xi')] \geq u[F^i(\xi)]$.
C4: Technological monotonicity. Let ξ' and ξ differ only in that the production function f' dominates f. (For all (W, L), $f'(W, L) \geq f(W, L)$. Then for $i = 1,2$: $u[F^i(\xi')] \geq u[F^i(\xi)]$.
C5: Self-ownership of skill. In ξ, suppose $s^i \geq s^j$. Then $u[F^i(\xi)] \geq u[F^j(\xi)]$.

The next axiom is perhaps most controversial.

C6: Protection of Infirm. Let $s^1 \geq s^2$. Then:
$u(F^2(\{\overline{W}, f, u; s^1, s^2\}) \geq u(F^2(\{\overline{W}; f; u; s^2, s^2\})$.

Call a mechanism F which satisfies these axioms[19] *acceptable*.

Axiom C1 says that the mechanism can be seen as a constitution which prescribes an allocation for 'any' economic environment. Axiom C2 is clearly desirable and requires no motivation. Axioms C3 and C4 are the necessary conditions for joint ownership of the land and the technology. Whatever joint ownership means, they say, it requires at least that an increase in the amount of the jointly owned resource (or jointly owned technology) should not harm either agent. Since land and technology are 'goods' and not 'bads,' if we jointly own them, an increase in their availability should not be to the detriment of either of us. Axiom C5 is necessary for self-ownership of skill. Able will always be at least as well-off as Infirm. This is the only axiom which requires interpersonally comparable utility to be sensible. For note that C5 implies *symmetry:* if the two agents are equally skilled, then they are assigned an allocation, under F, which equalizes their utility. (On the subclass of environments where $s^1 = s^2$, any acceptable F must coincide with the egalitarian mechanism E.) Such symmetry is defensible only if the utility which the function u measures is interpersonally comparable and in fact is 'level comparable.' Axiom C6 is designed to protect Infirm from invasion of his rights to welfare on account of the other agent's ability. The environment which appears on the left-hand side of the inequality in axiom C6 is the given environment upon which F's action is here being restricted. Axiom C6

19. The axioms contain some redundancy, which I have left in to give the flavor of this approach. In fact, C4 implies C3 because an increase in the amount of land can, alternatively, be viewed as a 'land-augmenting' technical change.

says that Infirm should not be worse off, in the given environment, than he would have been in an environment where Able were as unskilled as he. That is, *Infirm should not suffer on account of Able's ability.* I do not have a compelling justification for axiom C6 from the two fundamental principles, although perhaps it can be justified on those grounds. I think, in any case, the axiom is appealing, as it assures that Infirm does not suffer a negative externality from the fact that the other's skill is more than his own.

The somewhat remarkable theorem is that only one mechanism satisfies the six axioms, C1–C6: the welfare egalitarian mechanism E. If a mechanism is acceptable, it must, for each economic environment admitted by the domain assumption, assign that allocation of corn and labor to the two agents which is Pareto optimal and equalizes their utility levels.[20] If the axioms represent necessary conditions for a mechanism to implement public ownership of the land and technology (i.e., the external world) and private ownership of skill, then the rights of public ownership effectively trump rights of self-ownership in the sense that no outcome equality is, in the end, acceptable.

One can challenge whether these axioms indeed represent the agents' rights that they purport to represent; there is some discussion of that issue in the papers referred to in the previous footnote. The interpretation of the theorem is that even a relatively conservative socialist program, which requires joint ownership of the external resources but respects (at least a priori) some rights of agents to benefit from their skills, achieves the radical outcome of welfare equality. My purpose here is not to defend or criticize the particular axioms I have proposed or to evaluate the theorem. It is, rather, to illustrate the method and to contrast it with the approach which bargaining theory might take to the same problem.

Before doing so, it is worth remarking that the mechanism 'equal division–competitive equilibrium' (ED-CE) is not acceptable; it cannot be, by the theorem stated, since ED-CE does not, in general, assign equal utilities to the agents, and only the welfare-egalitarian mechanism satisfies all the axioms. Equal division–competitive equilibrium assigns that allocation which would have been achieved by dividing the land and ownership rights in the technology equally between the two agents and letting them trade to Walrasian equilibrium. Equal division–competitive equilibrium has been viewed, by various writers, as a good implemenation of fair division (see, e.g., Varian, and Thomson and Varian[21] for a review

20. For a proof of the theorem, see H. Moulin and J. Roemer, "Public Ownership of the External World and Private Ownership of Self," Working Paper no. 275 (Davis: University of California, Department of Economics, 1986); or J. Roemer, "An Axiomatic Approach to Marxian Political Philosophy," forthcoming in a volume of papers edited by George Feiwel in memory of Joan Robinson.

21. Hal Varian, "Equity, Envy, and Efficiency," *Journal of Economic Theory* 9 (1974): 63–91, and "Distributive Justice, Welfare Economics, and the Theory of Fairness," *Philosophy and Public Affairs* 4 (1975): 223–47; William Thomson and Hal Varian, "Theories of Justice Based on Symmetry," in Hurwicz, Schmeidler, and Sonnenschein, eds. (n. 3 above).

of the literature on 'envy-free' allocations, which are closely associated with the ED-CE mechanism). Equal distribution–competitive equilibrium might appear to implement an appropriate conception of joint ownership of land and private-ownership skill; but it is easily shown that ED-CE violates axioms C3 and C4. Hence ED-CE cannot implement *this* conception of joint ownership.

THE INFORMATIONAL POVERTY OF BARGAINING THEORY

How might one try to capture axioms C1–C6 of the Cohen problem, limiting oneself to the domain, which bargaining theory admits, of utility possibilities sets and threat points? One cannot. For an economic environment ξ contains much more information than a utility possiblities set S, and the axioms of the Cohen problem restrict the action of mechanisms on economic environments, while bargaining theory restricts the action of mechanisms on utility possibilities sets. Still, one might propose something like the following as the bargaining theory analog to the formalization of the Cohen problem. We wish to characterize a mechanism F which maps bargaining pairs {S, d} into a point of S and respects the private and joint property domains of agents as outlined in the previous section.

B1: Unrestricted domain. F acts on a domain {S, d} where the S is any strictly convex, comprehensive set which contains a strictly positive utility pair (or n-tuple, if we do the problem in R^n).
B2: F is individually rational. F assigns a utility allocation in the nonnegative orthant, when the point d is chosen as origin.
B3: F(S) is Pareto optimal in S.
B4: If S is symmetric (with d chosen as origin), then $F^1(S) = F^2(S)$.
B5: Monotonicity. If $S \subset T$ than $F^i(S) \leq F^i(T)$, for $i = 1, 2$.

As I said, there is no exact translation of the axioms C1–C6 into a bargaining-theory environment (that, indeed, is the point of this paper), but the above represents a canonical attempt at translation. Axiom C5 is translated as axiom B4. Axioms C3, C4, and C6 are all implied by axiom B5. These three axioms are highly restricted versions of 'utility monotonicity' B5, and it is hard to think of a weaker bargaining axiom than B5 which would imply them. Each of C3, C4, and C6 says that if the underlying economic environment changes *in a certain way* so as to increase the set of utility possibilities, then neither agent's utility falls. B5 is not capable of referring to economic environments since they do not exist for it; but if there were underlying economic environments to which B5 were implicity referring, it would require that *no matter what changes* in the environment give rise to the increasing utility possibilities, neither agent's utility should fall.

I have not discussed how to define the threat point for the Cohen problem in the bargaining-theory context. In the treatment of the second section, such discussion was unnecessary. That issue is, for now, tangential to my purpose, which is to observe the following:

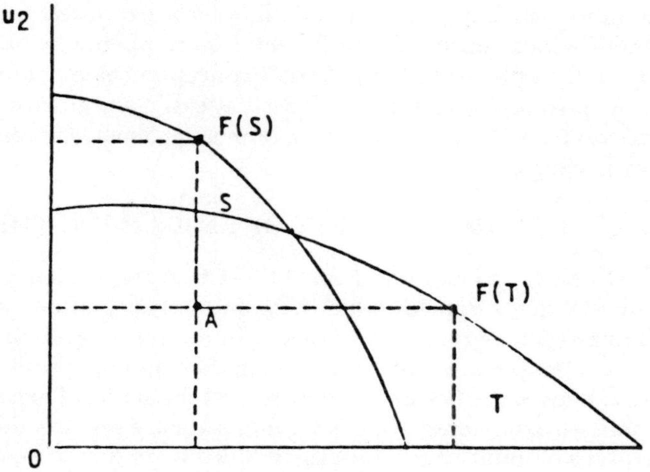

FIG. 1

Theorem: There is a unique F which satisfies axioms B1–B5: equal utility split from the threat point. F assigns that Pareto optimal point in S at which utilities are equalized, taking d as the origin.[22]

To illustrate the simplicity of this approach (which I do for a reason), I give a proof. First:

Lemma: If F satisfies axioms B1, B2, B3, and B5, then F must be a *monotone-path* solution. That is, given any threat point d, there exists a monotone path which characterizes the acceptable solutions for all problems {S, d}.

(A monotone-path solution is constructed by drawing some monotone nondecreasing path, in utility space, from the threat point d as origin; the solution is the intersection of that path with the Pareto frontier of S.)

Proof of lemma.—I do the proof for two dimensions. It generalizes to n dimensions. Suppose there is an F satisfying the listed axioms which is not a monotone-path solution. Then there must be two utility sets with the same threat point, called S and T in figure 1 such that F(S) lies to the northwest of F(T). Neither S nor T contains the other; for if S ⊂ T, for example, then by axiom B5, F(T) would lie to the northeast of F(S). Consider the utility set S ∩ T, which is in the domain by B1. By monotonicity, F(S ∩ T) lies to the southwest of both F(S) and F(T) since S ∩ T is a subset of both S and T. Hence F(S ∩ T) must lie in the rectangle

22. The bargaining theory version of this theorem is essentially equivalent to Ehud Kalai, "Proportional Solutions to Bargaining Situations: Interpersonal Utility Comparisons," *Econometrica* 45 (1977): 1623–30.

whose diagonal is OA. But this contradicts the Pareto optimality of F(S ∩ T) in the set S ∩ T. (To make this "proof" into a proof requires using the comprehensiveness and strict convexity of the sets S and T and also axiom B2.)

Proof of theorem.—Any acceptable F must be a monotone-path solution. But we know for symmetric sets by B4 that the solution lies along the 45° ray from d as origin. Hence the 45° ray is the only acceptable monotone path. Hence, any acceptable solution is equal utility split from d. Q.E.D.

This theorem might appear to be appealing from the point of view of distributive justice, if we could resolve the threat-point issue. But I claim it is not, even if we could settle on the determination of the threat point, for two reasons: (1) the axioms are too strong, and (2) the class of acceptable mechanisms is too thin. Why, for instance, is B5 too strong? Thinking back to economic environments, there are all kinds of ways an environment ξ could change into an environment ξ' so that their associated utility possibilities sets are nested: $S \subset T$. There might, for example, be a change in the utility function from ξ to ξ', combined with some non-dominating change in the production function. I have no moral intuition regarding how a justice-implementing mechanism should change its assignment as a consequence of such a change in the economic environment; but axiom B5 commits the mechanism to a monotonic change in utilities, as long as the first utility set is contained in the second one. Axioms C3, C4, and C6, in contrast, commit the mechanism to a monotonic change in the utility vector only when the economic environment changes in ways which our 'bill of rights' refers to specifically. The same criticism can be leveled against the symmetry axiom B4. Imagine an economic environment where agents have different preferences, different skills, and so forth, but it happens that the utility set S is symmetric (about the threat point). Axiom B4 commits the mechanism to an equal utility split. But surely this is too strong a moral commitment. Axiom C5, in contrast, commits us only to a clear (and weak) notion of self-ownership, which implies, in particular, that when agents are identical with respect to all the economic information, they are equally treated.

These criticisms amount to a point which is well known in the social-choice theory context (see, e.g., Sen) that axioms of the type B1–B5 are *welfarist* in that they treat two environments as identical if they have the same utility possibilities sets. In contrast, the setup of the Cohen problem in the second section is what can be called *resourcist* in that it allows information not just on final utilities but on the resources and preferences which enter into forming utility. All welfarist theories are resourcist since welfare is derived from resources and preferences, but not conversely. Many contemporary theories of justice are resourcist but not welfarist in that they take account of information concerning resources which is not summarized in the utility possbilities set. Rawls's theory is resourcist and not welfarist in the attention it pays to primary goods, independent of their utility-generating capacity, and Dworkin's interest in equality of resources is, similarly, a resourcist nonwelfarist one.[23] Sen's interest in basic capabilities is of the same nature, and Barry's emphasis on equal division of time in the Braithwaite problem is a special case of a resourcist, nonwelfarist approach.[24] The Marxian theory of exploitation is, I think, best viewed as a resourcist nonwelfarist theory, in which agents are viewed as exploited because of their lack of access to certain kinds of resources, alienable means of production.[25] In general, any theory which emphasizes equality of opportunities will require information available in economic environments but not available in utility possibility sets. For opportunites are stated in terms of initial resources of some kind—whether they be primary goods, capability-fulfilling goods, alienable means of production, talents, or time. Economic environments are required even to open discussion on these problems.

The second criticism I enumerated two paragraphs ago is that the class of mechanisms acting on the domain of objects {S, d} is too thin. There is so little structure on objects {S, d} that one is severely limited in describing the action of mechanisms on them. For instance, it is impossible to define the mechanism ED-CE given only the information {S, d}. To be precise, it is easy to write down two economic environments ξ and ξ' which give rise to the same utility possibilities set S, but in which ED-CE carried out in ξ and ξ' will lead to allocations associated with different points in S. Thus even if we view all utility sets S as coming from economic environments, we cannot construct a function which implements the equal division mechanism given only the information in S. Many conceptions of how to implement distributive justice in economic environments simply cannot be discussed given only utility information.

The combination of these two criticisms makes the proof of the theorem above simple. The axioms are too strong, and the space of mechanisms to too thin, so it is too easy to eliminate most of the feasible mechanisms. To state the contrapositive, doing mechanism theory on a space of economic environments is delicate since the appropriate axioms are weaker and the class of feasible mechanisms is richer.

It is terribly easy to fall into the error of justifying axioms made in a bargaining-theory framework by illicit reference to underlying resources which do not exist in that framework. For instance, Thomson[26] justifies

23. Rawls; Ronald Dworkin, "What Is Equality? Part 1: Equality of Welfare," *Philosophy and Public Affairs* 10 (1981): 182–246, and "What Is Equality? Part 2: Equality of Resources," *Philosophy and Public Affairs* 10 (1981): 283–345.

24. Amartya Sen, "Equality of What?" in *Tanner Lectures on Human Values*, ed. S. McMurrin (Cambridge: Cambridge University Press, 1980), vol. 1, pp. 197–220; Brian Barry, "Don't Shoot the Trumpeter—He's Doing His Best!" *Theory and Decision* 11 (1979): 153–80.

25. For discussion, see John E. Roemer, *A General Theory of Exploitation and Class* (Cambridge, Mass.: Harvard University Press, 1981), and "Should Marxists Be Interested in Exploitation?" *Philosophy and Public Affairs* 14 (1985): 30–65.

26. Thomson, "Problems of Fair Division . . ." and "Axiomatic Models . . ."

his 'population monotonicity' axiom, which I described in the first section, by asking the reader to imagine the following experiment. Recall his framework is bargaining theory. There is a population with some resources, making available some utility, summarized in the set S, and then a newcomer arrives on the scene, bringing with him no additional resources. The same resources must now generate utility for more people. Population monotonicity requires that no one from the original population end up better off in the second situation than in the first; everyone in the original group chips in to subsidize the impoverished newcomer. But such a motivation cannot be allowed because Thomson's environment is not economic; it includes no specification of resources and utility functions. Consequently, Thomson's axiom is much stronger than the above thought experiment suggests. It will implement not only the kind of solidarity described in that story but far more, just as the monotonicity axiom B5 does far more than implement the kinds of resource-generated monotonicity which axioms C3, C4, and C6 describe. 'Population monotonicity' commits us to 'welfare solidarity' in situations where no resource-based intuition justifies it. One can justify the axiom from a normative point of view only if one is an unabashed welfarist. I think hardly anyone has intuitions which are that welfarist; rather, those who find axioms like population monotonicity attractive are applying their real moral intuitions, which are resource based, to situations where they are inappropriate.[27]

In the first section, I said my purpose is to criticize the application of bargaining theory to distributive justice because of its informational impoverishment, and this applies to the *normative* use of bargaining theory. But there remains what I called the positive application of bargaining theory to distributive justice, which claims nonnormative justification of axioms and argues simply for justice as bargaining; this approach is represented by Gauthier and Binmore. Others have criticized this approach for reasons which appear to be quite orthogonal to what I have been discussing, namely, the irrelevance of bargaining power for considerations of justice (see Barry for this argument and a summary of other pertinent literature). I will limit myself to a criticism of the positive approach in the spirit of this paper. As I said, it is too facile to characterize the positive approach as welfarist because nonutility information is admitted in determining the threat point of the bargaining game whose outcome is called just. If rights are important, they must be fully incorporated into the threat point. I do not think all the rights-relevant information can be summarized in the threat point. As I have shown, once the threat point is determined, then the class of definable mechanisms on the space {S, d} immediately shrinks to a thin one. Thus, much maneuverability

27. These criticisms of Thomson's work should not be misconstrued. Thomson is an extremely careful worker. That even he could be guilty of this methodological peccadillo demonstrates the pervasiveness of this kind of error.

which we might want for the implementation of justice is immediately lost once the threat point is determined. I think this puts an unsupportably heavy informational burden on the threat point. To be precise: given any procedure for deciding upon the threat point from underlying economic information, I think it would be possible to construct two economic environments leading to the same object {S, d} but which our ethical intuitions would treat differently. I do not present this argument as a proof against the positive use of bargaining theory in distributive justice but as a conjecture (of which I am quite confident). It may, indeed, turn out to be equivalent to the criticisms which Barry and others have made, in this sense. Is it possible, for any given economic environment, to define a threat point which appropriately sterilizes the ethically unacceptable bargaining advantages that some players have over others? If so, then Barry's criticism would be neutralized. But my claim is that there is not sufficient informational density in objects of the form {S, d} to do that. Hence one *must* use axioms which have normative content; and, having admitted that, I have shown that such axioms must be defined on a domain of economic environments, not utility possibilities sets.

The recent empirical paper of Yaari and Bar-Hillel provides evidence for the misuse of bargaining theory in distributive justice. The authors propose various stylized problems of fair division to a group of 150 respondents, who are instructed to choose the fair allocation in each case. The framing of the problems differs. In some cases, the issue is to divide foods which contain nutrients, which the two agents in the problem process differentially. In some cases, it is a question of dividing luxury goods between agents who have different tastes. In some cases, goods must be divided between people who have different (and perhaps erroneous) beliefs about the true size of the total endowment available, or about what they want or what is good for them. Classes of problems are cleverly constructed so that, although they involve different environments—in the sense that the 'utility functions' describe needs, tastes, or beliefs about different kinds of goods—the bargaining objects {S, d} associated with all problems in one class are the same. The respondents choose very different allocations as 'fair' for different problems which are 'bargaining equivalent.' Thus, they are using information which is not summarized in the object {S, d}. One could say that the respondents are unjustifiably imposing their 'value judgments' on the little societies in these stories. One could say they are being tricked by the framing of the problems in the sense that Kahneman and Tversky[28] discuss. But I think it is more natural to say that bargaining theory cannot capture the information relevant for considerations of justice.

28. Daniel Kahneman and Amos Tversky, "The Psychology of Preferences," *Scientific American* (January 1982), pp. 160–73.

EQUALITY OF WELFARE VERSUS EQUALITY OF RESOURCES

In this section, I present a second example of how mechanism theory on a space of economic environments can tackle problems in distributive justice.

The problem in political theory I formalize in this section has a long history. If one is an egalitarian, what should one aim to equalize? Resources available to members of the society, or their final welfares? Slightly paraphrased, should one aim to equalize opportunities or outcomes? A thorough contemporary statement of this problem is Dworkin's, who argues that a philosophically coherent egalitarianism must call for resource equality, not welfare equality. There are far too many nuances in those papers to summarize here.[29] The key idea which Dworkin wishes to capture is the civil libertarian one, that people are responsible for their preferences but not responsible for their environments. Thus, a palatable egalitarianism should seek to equalize resources (those being the things which constitute the environment) and then let people choose what to do with them, given their preferences. Even if utility is interpersonally comparable, there is (of course) no guarantee that resource equality will imply welfare equality.

The problem is that not all resources are transferable. Some resources come with persons; I call these, generically, talents. Dworkin wants to 'equalize' these nontransferable resources as well, if their distribution is morally arbitrary. Since one cannot physically divide up talents (although one could divide up property rights in them), the problem becomes to distribute the transferable resources in such a way as to compensate appropriately people for their endowments of nontransferable resources. Dworkin proposes this be accomplished by a hypothetical insurance scheme. Knowing their preferences but not their resources, behind a 'thin' veil of ignorance, agents take out insurance against the possibility of being born with 'low' talents. I have discussed this scheme extensively elsewhere;[30] its particular merits and demerits are not germane here. What is germane is this: since there is no obvious definition of what 'equality of resources' means when some resources are nontransferable, what we require is a mechanism which maps economic environments into allocations. Equality of resources can then be defined, or at least constrained in its definition, by requiring the resource-equalizing mechanism to satisfy various axioms.

Let a two-person *economic environment* be defined as a vector

$$\xi = \{n; \bar{x}; u, v\} ,$$

where n is a positive integer, $\bar{x} \in R^n_+$ is an aggregate endowment of commodities, and u and v are in U^n, where

29. For a longer discussion, see John E. Roemer, "Equality of Talent," *Economics and Philosophy* 1 (1985): 151–87.

30. Ibid.

U^n = {all continuous, monotone, concave functions defined on R^n_+ normalized with $u(0) = 0$} .

Thus, the members of U^n are to be thought of as utility functions, with more structure than one assumes in ordinal preference theory. Let $\Omega(\xi)$ be the set of feasible allocations for the economic environment ξ. Then an *allocation mechanism* is a mapping:

$$F(\xi) \in \Omega(\xi) .$$

I suggest that, for F to qualify as a resource equalizing mechanism, it should satisfy the following axioms.

D1: F is a function defined on an unrestricted domain of environments (i.e., F is defined for all $n \geq 1$, for all $x \in R^n_+$, for all $u, v \in U^n$).

D2: $F(\xi)$ is Pareto optimal in $\Omega(\xi)$.

D3: F is symmetric. If $\xi = \{n; \bar{x}; u, u\}$ then $F(\xi) = (\bar{x}/2, \bar{x}/2)$.

D4: Resource monotonicity (RMON). Let ξ and ξ' be two economic environments which differ only in that $\bar{x}' \geq \bar{x}$. Then $F(\xi')$ weakly Pareto dominates $F(\xi)$.

D5: Consistency of resource allocation across dimensions (CONRAD). Consider an environment $\xi = \{m + n; (\bar{x}, \bar{y}); u, v\}$ with $\bar{x} \in R^m$, $\bar{y} \in R^n$, $u, v, \in U^{m+n}$.

Let $F(\xi) = ((\bar{x}^1, \bar{y}^1), (\bar{x}^2, \bar{y}^2))$ be the allocation assigned. Define: $u^*(x) = u(x; \bar{y}^1)$ and $v^*(x) = v(x, \bar{y}^2)$, noting that $u^*, v^* \in U^m$. Consider the environment $\xi^* = \{m; \bar{x}; u^*, v^*\}$. *Then* $F(\xi^*) = (\bar{x}^1, \bar{x}^2)$.

D6: Continuity. F is continuous in the appropriate topology in its arguments x, u, and v.

Theorem: If F satisfies axioms D1–D6, then F is unique. It assigns that allocation which is Pareto optimal and equalizes the utilities of the agents (i.e., F is 'welfare egalitarian').

The theorem is proved in another paper.[31]

Before discussing the axioms, I provide some interpretation. We begin with an environment which includes aggregate resource endowments $\bar{x}$ as well as preferences, and the axioms capture necessary conditions for what it must mean for an allocation of resources to be resource equalizing. We do not intend to equalize utilities. But the theorem says any acceptable mechanism for equalizing resources must, indeed, equalize welfares. Thus, any coherent notion of equality of opportunity (if resources can be thought of as equivalent to opportunities) implies equality of outcome. Although we do not begin with a welfarist assumption, we conclude that in the end only utility information matters, and, indeed,

31. John E. Roemer, "Equality of Resources Implies Equality of Welfare," *Quarterly Journal of Economics* (1986), in press.

no distinction can be drawn between equality of resources and equality of welfare.

The really new axiom is CONRAD (D5), and I discuss it last. Axiom D1 states that we are looking at economies, objects where agents have diminishing marginal utility. Utility is assumed to be fully interpersonally comparable and measurable. (It would be meaningless to try to discuss equality of welfare were it not so.) There are no axioms which require invariance of the F-acceptable allocation with respect to transformations of the utility functions. In particular, this full comparability is reflected in the symmetry axiom. If the two agents have the same utility function, the aggregate bundle $\bar{x}$ is split evenly between them under F. Thus, they are viewed as having not just the same preferences but deriving the same degree of pleasure (or whatever) from goods. I defend resource monotonicity as a necessary requirement for an equality-of-resource mechanism. Whatever equality of resources means, it must at least mean that if the total bundle of resources increases, neither agent's utility falls. (This axiom is analogous to C3 of the Cohen problem.) The continuity axiom is only needed to extend the theorem to economic environments on the boundary of the domain. It can therefore be viewed as a minor, technical axiom.

CONRAD is the only axiom which gives coherence to the mechanism as the dimension of the commodity space varies. It is a powerful axiom and brings to mind Nash's independence of irrelevant alternatives (IIA). In fact, if one tries to draw CONRAD in utility space, one gets precisely the Nash IIA picture. Formally, CONRAD is implied by IIA, just as the monotonicity axiom B5 implies resource monotonicity C3. One might justify CONRAD on the basis of what Sen[32] calls 'consistency,' but such justification is weak. Instead, I offer a justification for CONRAD which derives quite explicitly from the attempt to capture what equality of resources should require.

To motivate CONRAD, I will give an example which shows why I think the mechanism equal division–competitive equilibrium (ED-CE) is not a good resource-equalizing mechanism. The undesirable property that ED-CE has is its violation of CONRAD.[33] That is, I prescribe CONRAD as the natural way to eliminate this behavior of the ED-CE mechanism which is perverse from the resource-equalizing point of view. Imagine an economic environment $\xi = \{1; \bar{x}; u, v\}$ with one good (call it rice), and two agents, Andrea and Bob, with utility functions u and v for rice. Suppose that, for all x, $u(x) > v(x)$; Andrea gets more pleasure from rice than Bob. If we apply ED-CE, the rice endowment $\bar{x}$ is divided evenly

32. Amartya Sen, "Consistency," *Econometrica* (1986), in press.

33. The formulation of the CONRAD axiom as the appropriate formal incarnation of the economic ideas which I present below was due to a discussion with Roger Howe. Howe's theorem on concave monotone extensions, which I describe below, was a product of that same discussion.

between Andrea and Bob, and that is the final allocation which the mechanism assigns since there will be no trade with only one good. Now suppose we discover the *reason* that Andrea gets more pleasure from rice than Bob gets is that, in fact, they are each consuming another good, called endorphins. They have different amounts of endorphins which they consume. The endorphins are not transferable between them, but resource-equalization might still require that their endorphin endowments be taken into account in deciding upon the proper distribution of the rice. Over endorphins and rice, let us say, Andrea and Bob in fact have the 'same' preferences. Thus:

$$u(x) = w(x, \bar{E}_A) \text{ and } v(x) = w(x, \bar{E}_B) ,$$

where $\bar{E}_A$ and $\bar{E}_B$ are Andrea's and Bob's personal endowments of their endorphins, and $\bar{E}_B < \bar{E}_A$. w is itself a concave monotone function. It is now clear why Andrea gets more utility than Bob from any positive amount of rice: she has a higher level of endorphins than he, and otherwise they have the same tastes.

In fact, there are really now three goods: rice, Andrea's endorphins, and Bob's endorphins, and formally, we should define each of their utility functions on this space of three goods. That is why I said their preferences over rice and endorphins were the 'same' and not the same. To be precise, define Andrea's and Bob's preferences over the full space of three goods as:

$$w^A(x, E_A, E_B) = w(x, E_A) \text{ and } w^B(x, E_A, E_B) = w(x, E_B) .$$

Now consider the problem of equalizing resources in the 'extended' environment $\xi' = \{3; (\bar{x}, \bar{E}_A, \bar{E}_B); w^A, w^B\}$. How will the mechanism ED-CE distribute the three goods? It 'distributes' an initial endowment of $(0.5\bar{x}, 0.5\bar{E}_A, 0.5\bar{E}_B)$ to each agent, finds the Walrasian prices, and then assigns the equilibrium allocation. By Pareto optimality, Andrea will buy back all of her endorphins, and Bob will buy back of all his endorphins: for neither of them gets any utility from the other's endorphins. Thus the mechanism will, in fact, not end up trying to do what is impossible, trying to give Bob some of Andrea's endorphins. Each will be assigned all of the good for which he or she alone has a personalized 'taste.' *But it is not in general true that each will end up with one-half of the rice.* This is because Bob has to buy back one-half of his endorphins from Andrea, and Andrea has to buy back one-half of her endorphins from Bob, and the relative prices may be such that Bob and Andrea will not then have left over exactly the same amount of income with which to buy rice. In fact, it is easy to display cases when Bob will end up with less than one-half the rice. (This situation can be characterized on certain families of utility functions, such as constant-elasticity-of-substitution [CES] functions.)[34]

What is noteworthy is that ED-CE violates CONRAD. For we know that ED-CE assigns all of $\overline{E}_A$ back to Andrea and all of $\overline{E}_B$ back to Bob. Fixing the allocation of these two goods, CONRAD instructs the mechanism to distribute the rice in the enrivonment ξ' in exactly the same way as it distributes the rice in the environment ξ. To see this, simply check that the environment ξ is the 'restricted' environment derived by fixing the allocation of the last two goods (his or her endorphins) at their acceptable levels in ξ', as CONRAD prescribes.

Why is this violation of CONRAD an undesirable property of a resource-equalizing mechanism? In the example I gave, it seems clearly true that if we wish to equalize *all* resources, which is to say we wish to compensate Bob for his low endowment of endorphins relative to Andrea's, then he should end up not worse off, in terms of welfare, than he would end up if we only tried to equalize the rice. That is, ED-CE can be perverse in that it harms the agent whom resource-equalization is designed, presumably, to compensate. More generally, a mechanism which violates CONRAD changes its mind concerning how to distribute *some* resources as we extend the jurisdiction of resource equalization to include *other* resources. But if our object is to 'equalize all resources,' including internal ones, then I contend the mechanism must implicitly take account of all the resources which exist in the (external and internal) environment, *whether or not they are explicitly listed in the specification of the environment.* This is what CONRAD accomplishes. Regardless of the resources we list, a CONRAD-respecting mechanism must take account of all 'hidden' resources.

The philosophical implications of CONRAD are important. The reader will immediately gather from the Andrea-Bob story that CONRAD renders the distinction between preferences and resources extremely hazy. This is, indeed, the intuitive idea behind the drive to deduce welfare equalization from resource equalization. The idea of 'fundamental preferences' has been discussed in the literature for some time.[35] If two people differ in their preferences, there must be a reason. They must be consuming different internal resources. Extend the domain of commodities to include these internal resources. Then, over some sufficiently large dimension of commodity space, the agents will have the 'same' preferences in the sense of Andrea and Bob. There is a recent theorem of R. Howe which

34. See Roemer, "Equality of Talent."

35. Serge-Christophe Kolm, *Justice et équité* (Paris: Centre National de la Recherche Scientifique, 1972); G. J. Stigler and G. S. Becker, "De gustibus non est disputandum," *American Economic Review* 67 (1977): 76–90; John Rawls, "Social Unity and Primary Goods," in *Utilitarianism and Beyond*, ed. A. Sen and B. Williams (Cambridge: Cambridge University Press, 1982), pp. 159–86.

makes this precise.[36] Given any r monotone, concave 'utility' functions defined on R^n, can we view them as projections of some one (monotone, concave) utility function on a larger dimensional space? Howe's answer is: the r functions can always be so embedded as projections of a utility function on R^{n+r}. Thus, two agents always have the 'same' preferences if we include two more 'personalized' goods which they are consuming in different amounts. (In the Andrea-Bob story, only one more personalized good was needed since one utility function dominated the other in rice. The surprising fact is that even if one function does not dominate the other, only two goods are required to do this extension.) Thus, a group of agents can be reduced to their fundamental preferences rather quickly. This concave extension theorem is used in proving the theorem under discussion.

I wish to underscore the point about the appropriate strength for axioms, which was discussed in the previous section. Axiom D4 says that if the utility possibilities set increases *as a consequence of a particular kind of change in the environment,* namely because of an increase in resources, then neither agent's utility should fall. But axiom B5 says that, regardless of the change in the implicit, underlying environment which causes the utility possibility set to increase, neither agent's utility should fall. That point has been discussed. Similarly, D5 says that if one economic environment is the 'restriction' of another *in a particular fashion,* and if the F-acceptable allocation for the big environment lies in the utility set for the small environment, then it must be F-acceptable in the small environment. But Nash's IIA axiom says that *regardless* of the change in environments which produces the nested utility sets, the allocation chosen in the big set must be chosen in the little set if it is in the little set. From a normative point of view (as opposed to a positive one), this is not justifiable. There are all kinds of changes in underlying economic environments which can give rise to nested utility possbilites sets, and, for most of those changes, we have no moral intuition concerning the appropriate change in the just allocation. I have justified, in my discussion above, only the CONRAD axiom, not the IIA axiom.[37]

My purpose is not to discuss fully the Dworkin problem here. It is methodological, to illustrate the application of mechanism theory on a domain of economic environments to problems in distributive justice. Lest I be misinterpreted, it may be prudent to state that the theorem of this section does not convince me that no coherent distinction exists between equality of resources and equality of welfare—although the

36. R. E. Howe, "Sections and Extensions of Concave Functions," Discussion Paper no. 760 (New Haven, Conn.: Yale University, Cowles Foundation, 1985).

37. In fact, the theorem of this section is true with a weaker version of the CONRAD axiom. I choose not to muddy the waters here with this technical point, although it turns out to be one of some importance for bargaining theory. For full detail, see John E. Roemer, "Axiomatic Bargaining Theory on Economic Environments," Working Paper no. 264 (Davis: University of California, Department of Economics, 1985).

theorem purports to demonstrate that. Rather, axiomatic analysis forces one to concentrate attention on more narrowly delineated issues than one started off with. In this case, I think the philosophically disputable axiom is the domain assumption, which I discuss briefly in the concluding section. That domain assumption allows us to represent aspects of a person's preferences as if they were resources, and the CONRAD axiom enforces a certain consistency between the allocation mechanism's treatment of these two representations of a given world. The domain assumption enforces upon us a reductionist, determinist program. The substantive questions remain. When should a trait be considered part of what determines a person's preferences, and when should it be considered a resource in his environment? When should a person be responsible for a trait, and when should it be viewed as morally arbitrary? (Perhaps 'responsibility' and 'moral arbitrariness' are not properly antonymous.) The theorem of this section leaves us with a new set of precise questions and a somewhat new language. There are no cheap ways of solving the deepest problems, but new language often sharpens the discussion.

CONCLUSION

Bargaining theory is context free. All that matters is the utility possibilities set and the threat point, specified in terms of utilities. I claim this is an inappropriate apparatus with which to study problems of distributive justice. Many contemporary theories of distributive justice are resourcist, not welfarist, and require explicit language with which resources and preferences can be discussed, a language which bargaining theory lacks. It is impossible to make any statements regarding property rights in the bargaining-theory model since property does not exist in the domain of environments which bargaining theory posits. This is what I have called the informational poverty of bargaining theory. I propose to replace bargaining theory with the study of allocation mechanisms defined on a domain of economic environments for the purpose of studying questions of distributive justice and political philosophy.

There is information important for ethical considerations which I have not modeled. The Yaari–Bar-Hillel paper shows that people treat ethical problems differently depending on whether the issue at hand is one of needs or tastes or beliefs. One can say, people consider not only the amounts of the goods and the utility functions, but the *names* of the goods and the *name* of what the utility function measures. Notice that information on these names does not exist in the economic environments I have specified. We might define an *ethical environment* as a list of names of goods, names of what the 'utility' functions measure, amounts of the goods, and specifications of the utility functions. Then two different ethical environments could give rise to the same economic environment. For example, a particular economic environment $\xi = \{3; (\bar{x}^1, \bar{x}^2, \bar{x}^3); u, v\}$ refers to a situation with three goods in amounts specified by the $\bar{x}^i$, and two people with utility functions given by u and v. ξ could come from two ethical environments; in the first, the goods might be Scotch, champagne, and beer, and u and v represent tastes for alcohol; in the second, the goods might be milk, education, and shelter, and u and v represent the effectiveness with which the two people process those goods into the probability of realizing (or even forming) a life plan. We might wish to render different judgments on the just way to distribute the goods in these different ethical environments, but given the domain of economic environments, we cannot do so: for the economic environments do not specify names of goods, and these two ethical environments are, by hypothesis, represented by one economic environment. Just as the welfarist is not willing to impose his 'value judgment' to distinguish between two different economic situations which give rise to the same utility configuration, so the resourcist (according to my definition) is not willing (or able) to distinguish between ethical environments which give rise to the same economic environment.

The domain assumption of the models I describe in this article eliminates the names of goods. The only information that is recognized in an economic environment is 'economic' information: endowments, utility functions, production functions, but not names of goods. Economic environments represent a significant advance in making available ethically relevant information which is not in utility possibilities sets. Furthermore, they are still mathematically tractable, while ethical environments (where names are included) may not be. There is a cost, that is, to including more information in the domain of objects to be studied: it becomes harder to state any general rules about how considerations of justice should treat those objects. One moves from theory to thick description. I suggest that mechanism theory be carried out on economic environments before one attempts to model ethical environments.[38] I have discussed more thoroughly elsewhere the hierarchy of domains which can be postulated—from the bargaining-theory domain of utility sets, to economic environments, to ethical environments.[39]

It is finally necessary to mention the issues of asymmetric information and incentive compatibility which I have ignored in this paper. I think the main compromises a theory of justice will have to make are on account of these issues. My concern here has not been with institutions which will implement the just allocation, in which case incentive problems would have to be considered, but simply with what allocation is desirable. This is first-best normative analysis. Before one begins to compromise, it would be nice to know what the goal would be, if everyone knew everything.

38. In work in progress, I am modeling issues in political philosophy on a domain of environments where goods are named.

39. For a more detailed discussion, see Roemer, "Axiomatic Bargaining Theory on Economic Environments."

[13]

Equality of Resources and Equality of Welfare: A Forced Marriage?*

T. M. Scanlon, Jr.

There are many points in John Roemer's paper which I would like to discuss. Since I am in general agreement with his criticisms of bargaining theory as an approach to distributive justice, I will focus on the question of equality of welfare versus equality of resources and the striking theorem which Roemer states in the fourth section of his paper. This theorem purports to show that, insofar as it claims to differ from equality of welfare, the idea of equality of resources is incoherent: there are elements within this idea itself which lead inexorably to the conclusion that any acceptable allocation mechanism must be welfare equalizing. In addition, Roemer suggests that his axioms render "the distinction between preferences and resources extremely hazy" (p. 107) and "force upon us a reductionst, determinist program" (p. 109).

Roemer's conclusion is not that we must advocate equality of welfare but, rather, that adequate principles of distributive justice must move beyond "economic environments" and be sensitive to the "names" of goods: they must take into account which goods are being distributed, not merely the level of utility (preference satisfaction) that is produced. I agree with this conclusion, and I imagine that any defender of equality of resources would have agreed from the outset. This leads me to look back at Roemer's axioms with a more critical eye.

In what follows I will argue, first, that the axioms which Roemer puts forward as a characterization of resource egalitarianism in fact include principles which only a welfarist would accept. Second, I will argue that the welfarism which these axioms require is not as extreme as Roemer suggests: they do not "force upon us a reductionist, determinist program" unless all forms of welfarism do so. Finally, in the concluding sections of the paper, I will consider some problems which Roemer's discussion raises for resourcism and discuss the issue of "ideal" versus "second-best" theory.

* This is a much revised version of comments on John Roemer's "The Mismarriage of Bargaining Theory and Distributive Justice" (in this issue), delivered at the Weingart conference in March 1985. I am grateful to Joshua Cohen and John Rawls for helpful comments on an earlier draft.

Ethics 97 (October 1986): 111–118

AXIOMS: RESOURCIST OR WELFARIST?

A natural suspicion is that Roemer's axioms somehow incorporate welfarist intuitions which are not part of the idea of equality of resources but alien to it. Consider, for example, axioms D2, Pareto optimality, and D4, resource monotonicity, both of which employ a utility-based notion of Pareto dominance. Any principle of resource equality requires some means of comparing bundles of resources as "larger," "smaller," or "equal," and it would be question begging to assume at the outset that this standard of comparison must just be the amount of utility which a bundle produces. Employing a resourcist notion of "size," we could formulate resource-based analogues to D2 and D4. Call these axioms D2r and D4r. Axiom D2r says that a mechanism must not choose an allocation a if there is another, a', which assigns some person a "larger" bundle and no one a "smaller" bundle than that assigned by a. Axiom D4r says that when the available resources increase, no one's assigned bundle may become "smaller."

Since the "size" of a resource bundle will depend on which goods it contains, that is, on what Roemer calls the "names" of these goods, this notion cannot even be formulated within the system which Roemer provides. It is excluded by the domain axiom D1, which requires mechanisms to be defined on economic environments. Nonetheless, D2r and D4r are requirements which any proponent of resource egalitarianism ought to accept. It may be that under plausible assumptions about the idea of resource bundle "size," and given the usual assumptions about utility functions, D2r and D4r imply their utility-based correlates. Nonetheless, D2 and D4 could reasonably be thought to be no part of the idea of equality of resources. A resource egalitarian may believe that "the usual assumptions" about utility do not always hold or, more generally, may reject utility as a standard for measuring distributive shares. The idea that "if the total bundle of resources increases, neither agent's utility falls" (Roemer, p. 105) might be thought to express an optimistic (welfarist) attitude toward the consequences of economic development rather than a necessary tenet of resource egalitarianism.

Consider now Roemer's axiom D5, consistency of resource allocation across dimensions (CONRAD). What is the rationale for including this consistency requirement as part of a characterization of resource egalitarianism? The moral of the Andrea and Bob story is that whenever there are "hidden resources" (such as endorphin levels) which influence individual utility these must be included as part of the resource bundles which are to be equalized. This idea has intuitive force, and I will return to it later. But the effect of CONRAD is much broader. Since CONRAD is formulated in terms of economic environments, it is blind to matters of causal dependence. Suppose that, in some environment ξ involving $m + n$ goods, once n of these goods have been distributed in a certain way the utility consequences of possible distributions of the remaining m goods are exactly the same as the utility consequences of distributions of *m* goods in some other (*m* = good) environment ξ*. Then CONRAD requires that (assuming the original distribution of *n* goods is accepted) the remaining *m* goods in ξ and the *m* goods in ξ* must be distributed in exactly the same way *whether or not these are the same goods and whether or not the* n *additional goods are in any sense present as "hidden resources" influencing individual utility levels in the smaller environment.*

Note that, given the richness of the domain of economic environments, for any environment ξ* and mechanism F, there will be many "extended" environments ξ related to ξ* in the way just described. Not all of the extra resources in these extended environments will represent "hidden resources" present in societies represented by ξ*. Nonetheless, CONRAD requires "consistency" between each of these environments and ξ*. Why should this be required? The most natural answer is that utility sums up all relevant reasons for distinguishing between distributions from the point of view of justice; therefore, when the utility consequences of possible distributions in two situations are the same, the same distributions must be selected as just in each case. This rationale fits CONRAD exactly, but it is clearly a welfarist intuition, one which a resource egalitarian is unlikely to accept.

Another rationale for CONRAD, perhaps the one Roemer has in mind, would be this: whenever two environments ξ* and ξ are related in such a way that it is *possible* that the additional goods in ξ represent "hidden resources" in a society represented by ξ*, then the two should be treated in a way that is "consistent." (In this argument, the expressive poverty of the language of economic environments serves as an excuse for what lawyers call "overbreadth.") Does this rationale provide grounds for a resource egalitarian to accept CONRAD? It would do so *if* the resource egalitarian agreed with the moral of the story of Andrea and Bob as Roemer describes it, and *if* the resource egalitarian accepted the restrictions of the language of economic environments. These are, however, two fairly large "ifs."

To sum up: because of the limited expressive power of the language of economic environments, the "fit" between CONRAD and an arguably resourcist response to the story of Andrea and Bob is only approximate. Indeed, there is so much slack here that a resourcist who accepts CONRAD as a way of dealing with such examples will have adopted an axiom the most natural rationale for which is a broad welfarist principle which he would hardly accept on its own.

PREFERENCES AS RESOURCES?

Let me turn now from the rationale for CONRAD to the philosophical implications of adopting it. The effect of CONRAD, Roemer says, is to render "the distinction between preferences and resources extremely hazy" (p. 107). This remark is followed by a discussion of "Fundamental Preferences," and Roemer later observes that "the domain assumption allows us to represent aspects of a person's preferences as if they were resources, and the CONRAD axiom enforces a certain consistency between the allocation mechanism's treatment of these two representations of a given world. The domain assumption forces upon us a reductionist, determinist program" (p. 109).

I take it that what Roemer has in mind here is that when two economic environments $\xi = \{m + n; \bar{x}, \bar{y}; u, v\}$ and $\xi^* = \{m; \bar{x}; u^*, v^*\}$ are related in the way described in the antecedent of CONRAD, the preferences underlying u^* and v^* are "represented as if they were resources" because these preferences are seen as resulting from a particular allocation of the resources represented by $\bar{y}$. It is by including, for any ξ^*, an environment ξ related to it in this way that the domain assumption "forces on us a reductionist, determinist program."

But this involves reading into these axioms a meaning that is not really there. To begin with, the conditions laid down in CONRAD do not insure that ξ^* and ξ are two representations of a single "given world." Moreover, in the absence of "names," these conditions tell us very little about the resources involved. Since $\bar{x}$ is only an m-tuple of real numbers until ξ^* and ξ are identified with more fully described societies there is no answer to the question whether the resources represented by $\bar{x}$ in these two environments are the same or different. All that is required by the abstract characterization of ξ^* and ξ is that these goods give rise to utility in the same way.

Suppose, however, that we take ξ^* and ξ to represent (possibly identical) societies s* and s in which the resources measured by $\bar{x}$ are the same. Call these "*x* goods" and the additional resources in s "*y* goods." Even given this assumption, the descriptions of ξ^* and ξ taken together with Roemer's axioms commit us to no claim whatever about the relation between *y* goods and individual preferences over *x* goods (or about the presence of *y* goods as hidden resources in s*). For all that is said by D1 and CONRAD, this relation might be any of the following.

1. It might be no relation at all. People in s may have the same preferences for *x* goods that people in s* do, but it may be that these preferences would be the same whatever level of *y* goods the people in s were consuming. (Perhaps *y* goods have significance only within certain social practices which add "an extra dimension" to life in s but do not interact with other consumption patterns.)

2. It might be a relation like that between my preferences for certain kinds of crackers and the availability of certain kinds of cheese. If people in s enjoy consuming certain *x* goods only in conjunction with certain *y* goods, then their preferences for *x* goods will depend on the amounts of *y* goods they are consuming. In particular, these preferences will be like those of people in s* only when *y* goods are being consumed in certain quantities.

3. Finally, it might be like the relation assumed to hold in the story of Andrea and Bob between the utility derived from corn and the presence of endorphins.

Only the last of these possibilities involves anything like "a reductionist, determinist program." This last interpretation of the relation between ξ^* and ξ is consistent with the axioms D1–D6 but is not forced upon us by them since they are equally compatible with the other two interpretations I have described.

What "forces upon us a reductionist, determinist program," if anything does, is the story Roemer tells to motivate the CONRAD axiom. The situation here appears to me to be this. Roemer wants to push a resource egalitarian toward equalizing welfare. To do so, he considers a case in which the preferences of a person with less than equal utility are the result of a particular allocation of "hidden" resources. (The resource egalitarian might be indifferent to Bob's utility level per se, but is supposed to pay attention when it is seen that this results from an allocation of "hidden" resources.) Having used the story of Andrea and Bob to give a resource egalitarian reason to adopt CONRAD, Roemer then reads the circumstances of this example into the interpretation of that axiom. But this is illicit. As I have argued in the previous section, the most natural interpretation of CONRAD (and of the other axioms) is a straightforwardly welfarist one. This interpretation is quite understandably not of interest to Roemer. Given the purposes of his argument, the question which interests him is whether there exists a compelling resourcist rationale for the axioms he needs. But the natural welfarist rationale is there nonetheless. It follows, therefore, that these axioms do not "force upon us a reductionist, determinist program" unless welfarism does so. Perhaps it does, but given the range of possible readings of Roemer's axioms I do not believe that they help to show that this is the case.

WHICH RESOURCES?

Which goods and conditions should be counted as resources in a resource-egalitarian conception of justice? The pressure toward "determinism" in Roemer's paper arises from the answer to this question which is implicit in his discussion of the example of Andrea and Bob: anything which affects individual utility levels should be counted as a resource (and conditions which do this by altering preferences are no different from goods which do it by satisfying them).

This is an answer which a resourcist might well wish to reject, but some alternative must be provided. It would be arbitrary simply to begin an account of justice with some list of resources taken as given and in need of no defense. A reasonable desire to avoid this kind of arbitrariness, I believe, is what lies behind Roemer's wariness about "names" and his concern that a theory employing them would "impose" values on people who need not share them. No list of resources can be taken as fundamental; any list must be defended with reference to the needs and interests of the people to whom the theory is meant to apply. If we take this to mean that it must be defended with reference to their *preferences,* then it seems to follow that any theory of justice must, at base, be welfarist. If we add the observation that welfare—that is, utility—can be increased by resources which modify preferences as well as by those which satisfy them, then we seem to have opened the door to "treating preferences like resources" and hence, at least potentially, to what Roemer called "a determinist program." But these conclusions would be premature.

The question at issue is the selection of a standard for measuring distributive shares, where this standard is to be used by people with differing and malleable tastes and preferences. This fact of differing preference is part of our reason for being concerned about the threat of "arbitrary" or "imposed" standards. One response to this fact is to look for some common ground behind our disagreement: we may have different preferences, but we are all concerned to have these preferences satisfied to the greatest possible degree—that is, concerned with our own utility. A second approach is to look for common elements in what we prefer: we share general interests in having food, shelter, opportunities for education, and so on. A list of resources is a fair standard according to this approach if it adequately measures people's ability to advance these general categories of shared interests.

Resources which advance these interests may thereby "increase utility." But a resourcist conception of justice need not regard the importance of these interests as subsumed within that of a larger whole, utility. The reasons against doing so are particularly clear in the case of resources such as education, which contribute to preference change. People want to have preferences be ones which stand up in the light of reflection and the available facts. But they do not view preferences as things which they have reason to change whenever this would yield greater utility. A justification of preference-changing resources which appeals to shared general interests is thus more consistent with the view people take of their own preferences than a welfarist justification would be.

Consider another example. Assume we live in a society marked by sharp differences in religious belief. Aware of these differences, we can also recognize "the opportunity to pursue one's religious convictions" as a shared general interest in the sense just discussed. Appealing to this interest, one can then argue for the importance of certain resources: protection against discrimination, opportunities for religious observance, freedom to read, and disseminate literature on religious topics, and so on. If these resources are fairly distributed, however, that is all that a resourcist view of justice requires as far as religion is concerned. The choice of religion (or no religion) is entirely up to each person, and the amount of utility resulting from this choice is specifically not an object of public policy.

Consider an alternative. What religion a particular person belongs to is a contingent matter: I might have grown up in circumstances in which it would never have occurred to me to be a Catholic (or never occurred to me not to be one). Such differences in religious belief are one thing that can produce differences in utility level, and someone who regarded equality of welfare as the standard of interpersonal justification would have to regard these differences as being grounds for compensation: compensation for having acquired a particularly onerous or guilt-inducing religion or one particularly unsuited to one's own personal strengths and weaknesses. This strikes me as distinctly odd. Quite apart from the fact that it might destroy the point of religious burdens to have them lightened by social compensation, the idea that these burdens are grounds for such compensation (a form of bad luck) is incompatible with regarding them as matters of belief and conviction which one values and adheres to because one thinks them right.

I have suggested that argument about justice employs "names" of specific resources and that these are justified with reference to "names" of shared general interests. I have argued that the use of such a standard of distributive shares is not arbitrary and that it is more compatible with the view people take of their own preferences and interests than a notion of utility would be. A list of "shared general interests" is, of course, not simply given; it is something whose fairness in a particular situation has to be argued for. This argument, in turn, does not reach "beyond names," but involves mentioning specific further interests and arguing that they are insufficiently recognized by the currently accepted way of measuring bundles of resources. In this respect, argument about justice involves names "all the way down."

Another way of putting the point would be to say that "preference" is itself a "name," and not a particularly potent one. Simply to say "But I would strongly prefer . . . " is not yet a very strong argument for revising the list of resources. It is only when the interest at stake is given a more informative "name" that we can see what would be involved in recognizing it as having special force as a claim of justice.

IDEAL THEORY?

At the end of his paper, Roemer remarks, "My concern here has not been with institutions which will implement the just allocation, in which case incentive problems would have to be considered, but simply with what allocation is desirable. This is first-best normative analysis. Before one begins to compromise, it would be nice to know what the goal would be, if everyone knew everything" (p. 110).

I believe, on the contrary, that the terms in which it is appropriate to argue about justice inevitably reflect "nonideal" features of our world, such as our lack of full knowledge and the kinds of agreement, disagreement, and conflict which are common among us. In particular, it seems to me that institutions are not a matter of "compromise" but have a fundamental place in determining which outcomes are just. There are many reasons for holding institutions to be prior in this way. Here I will mention only one, a reason which is strengthened by the conclusions which Roemer reaches elsewhere in his paper.

If one believes, as Roemer suggests, that a person's preferences are largely shaped by outside factors, presumably in particular by social institutions, then the choice of such institutions takes on special importance. What one wants is to have institutions which provide a favorable environment in which to develop preferences and make choices in pursuit of the goals one has adopted: a favorable environment in which to develop and live as a "self-steering mechanism" among other such individuals. We do not have a complete view of what counts as a "favorable environment" of this kind, but we do have a partial account given by a list of the kinds of "resources" it is important to have and the kind of dangers it is important to avoid. As I have indicated above, moral and political argument is a continuing process of debate about these lists. Beyond this, there is no characterization of "the ideal" from which political argument could begin. What each of us, personally, regards as the ideal depends on how we develop within the institutions in which we are placed and is therefore, at any given time, incompletely determined. This openness of possibilities—the idea that what we do and what we value remains to be determined by how we react to and reflect upon our environment—is the freedom which remains to us even as "determined" beings. Moral argument, then, even among such beings, cannot begin from an answer to the question of what would be ideal for us individually and collectively and proceed from there to ask what institutions would realize that ideal. All we can ask of one another is a favorable environment in which to work out and pursue our own differing and as yet incompletely defined conceptions of "the ideal."

[14]

Economics and Philosophy, 3, 1987, 215–244. Printed in the United States of America.

EGALITARIANISM, RESPONSIBILITY, AND INFORMATION

JOHN E. ROEMER
University of California, Davis

1. OUTCOME- VERSUS RESOURCE-EQUALIZING THEORIES

Radical and liberal theories of egalitarianism are distinguished, in large part, by the differing degrees to which they hold people responsible for their own well-being. The most liberal or individualistic theory calls for equality of opportunity. Once such "starting gate equality," as Dworkin (1981a) calls it, is guaranteed, then any final outcome is justified, provided certain rules, such as voluntary trading, are observed. At the other pole, the most radical egalitarianism calls for equality of welfare (assuming that interpersonal welfare comparisons can be made, so that such equality makes sense). In between these two extremes are egalitarian proposals that equalize more than conventional opportunities, yet less than full welfare. Sen (1980) speaks of equality of basic capabilities as a goal; implementing that requires more than starting gate equality, because some will require more resources than others to attain the same capabilities. Meeting basic needs is another objective. Equality of needs fulfillment is perhaps less radical than equality of basic capabilities and more radical than equality of opportunity. Rawls (1971) takes equality of primary goods as a benchmark; he distinguishes primary goods from welfare, but includes among them goods that are more complicated than conventional resources and opportunities, all of which are supposed inputs into any conception of welfare. One could imagine proposing an egalitarianism that equalized some quite measurable outcome across populations, such as infant mortality. That would be an outcome-

I thank Thomas Scanlon and G.A. Cohen, from whom I have learned a great deal on these questions. The editors and referees of this journal made helpful suggestions. I am indebted to the National Science Foundation for supporting this research.

equalizing theory where the rate of infant mortality is a proxy, presumably, for some more complicated maximand, such as the degree of well-being of a population. A prominent opportunity-equalizing theory is that of Dworkin, who calls for equality of resources, and argues that equality of welfare is not a cogent egalitarianism. His conception of resources is comprehensive: It includes some aspects of people that are inalienable, their talents and propensities of various kinds. Dworkin's egalitarianism is more thorough than that which would be achieved by equalizing conventional resources only.

This survey is not exhaustive; the point I wish to illustrate is the varying degree of responsibility that these theories assign to individuals. Full equality of welfare holds a person responsible for nothing about himself: Any trait that detracts from his ability to process worldly resources into welfare is to be compensated for by the distribution that effects welfare equality. Equality of opportunity, conceived of in the usual sense, holds individuals responsible for a great deal – their own skills, including the ability to truck and barter, their rates of time preference, and their attitudes towards risk. Other theories take an intermediate stance concerning responsibility. Dworkin does not want to equalize welfare, but does want to compensate people for certain kinds of bad luck in the birth lottery, which assigns inalienable traits. He believes that people should be responsible for certain aspects of themselves, in particular, their conceptions of welfare. I do not claim that these theories hold people morally responsible (in varying degrees) for traits that they possess, just that individuals are effectively responsible for these traits, because society will not take account of them in its egalitarian calculus.

A. Economic Environments

I propose to think of outcome-equalizing theories, quite generally, in the following way. The world consists of some fixed bundle of resources, and of individuals who have ways of processing these resources into the outcome under consideration: Whether it is welfare, the fulfillment of basic needs, or the realization of capabilities. I summarize these personal technologies with a processing or outcome function $u^i(\mathrm{x})$, where x is a vector of resources, and u^i describes the effectiveness with which the ith individual processes resources into the outcome in question. In the infant mortality example, the "individual" i is a country, and u^i measures the infant survival rate in that country as a function of the resources its population consumes. If the outcome is welfare, then u^i is the ith person's utility function. An *economic environment* is a vector $\xi = \langle n, \bar{\mathrm{x}}; u^1, u^2, \ldots u^r \rangle$ where n is the number of resources in the environment (the dimension of the resource space), $\bar{\mathrm{x}}$ is the aggregate endowment of resources (a vector in R^n), r is the number of agents, and u^i is the processing function of the ith agent. This representation is sufficiently abstract to allow for discussion of the theories outlined above, where the functions u^i take on different meanings, depending on what the outcome is.

In particular, this representation allows one to contrast an equality-of-resource approach with an equality-of-outcome approach. A first pass at resource egalitarianism would propose, in the environment ξ, to give each of the r agents the vector $\bar{x}/r$ of resources: equal split. But I claim below (in Section 2) that this is an unsatisfactory way of implementing equality of resources, at least if resources are taken to include some internal traits that people have, such as talents. Outcome egalitarianism would imply dividing the social endowment $\bar{x}$ in such a way that final outcomes are equal for all: give agent i vector $\bar{x}^i$ such that $\bar{x} = \Sigma\, \bar{x}^i$ and $u^1(\bar{x}^1) = u^2(\bar{x}^2) = \ . \ . \ . = u^r(\bar{x}^r)$, if such an assignment is possible.

B. Allocation Mechanisms

How should resources be allocated in a given economic environment? For the sake of simplicity in exposition, from now on I assume that there are just two agents, and so the notation introduced above can be collapsed to $\xi = \langle n; \bar{x}; u, v\rangle$ where u and v are the outcome functions of the agents. Let the domain of possible economic environments be Σ. I choose Σ to consist of all environments ξ, where n is any positive integer, $\bar{x}$ is any nonnegative vector in R^n, and u and v are arbitrary continuous, weakly monotone increasing, concave real-valued functions of n variables, with $u(0) = v(0) = 0$. Monotonicity of the utility functions guarantees that the resources in question are goods (not bads); concavity guarantees that there is diminishing marginal productivity from each resource. Insisting on concavity is not necessary for the theory I will outline, but it imposes a reasonable economic restriction on the processing technologies. Thus, the domain of economic environments posited consists of sensible possible worlds. For simplicity, I have not represented the possibility of production in the model. The theory can be replicated if production is allowed.

An *allocation mechanism* F is a function, defined on Σ, which assigns to each economic environment ξ an allocation of the resources in that environment, that is:

$$F(\xi) = (\bar{x}^1, \bar{x}^2) = (F^1(\xi), F^2(\xi)),$$

where $F^i(\xi) = \bar{x}^i$ is the share of resource vector $\bar{x}$ assigned by F to person i. Specifying an allocation mechanism amounts to naming a rule for distributing resources in any environment. Moral beliefs about egalitarianism, or about distributive justice more generally, can be represented as requirements on the behaviour of the allocation mechanism. We might view requirements on F's behaviour as constraining an economic constitution, which should apply to any possible world.

C. Welfarism, Outcomism, and Resourcism

A common position in social choice theory, at least until a decade ago, has been that a desirable allocation mechanism use information only on the possible outcomes. When the outcome is welfare, this position has been coined "welfarism" by Sen (1979). Although formal social choice theory is different from the theory of allocation mechanisms on economic environments that I describe here, welfarism means the following in the present context. Let the outcome described by the functions u and v be utility. Then associated with any economic environment $\xi = \langle n; \overline{x}; u, v\rangle$ is a *utility possibilities set*, the set of possible welfare levels $(\overline{u, v})$ that can be generated by dividing the resource vector $\overline{x}$ between the two agents in all possible ways. Let $A(\xi)$ be the utility possibilities set for the environment ξ. Suppose that there are two environments, ξ and ξ', that give rise to the same utility possibilities set. (These environments may even have different numbers of resources, and therefore surely different utility functions in them, but the sets of welfare pairs $(\overline{u,v})$ they generate are identical.) Welfarism requires that an allocation mechanism assign the same welfare pair $(\overline{u,v})$ in both environments.

Axiom of Welfarism. Let $\xi = \langle n; \overline{x}; u^1, v^1\rangle$ and $\xi' = \langle m; \overline{y}; u^2, v^2\rangle$ be two economic environments in Σ such that $A(\xi) = A(\xi')$. Then:

$$u^1(F^1(\xi)) = u^2(F^1(\xi')) \text{ and } v^1(F^2(\xi)) = v^2(F^2(\xi')).$$

The Axiom of Welfarism is a strong restriction on the nature of the allocation mechanism. Suppose that ξ and ξ' generate the same set of possible outcomes (utility pairs). A welfarist mechanism must ignore the underlying resource and preference structures that differentiate these environments, as it assigns the same pair of utility levels in the two worlds. Utilitarianism is an example of a welfarist allocation mechanism. Indeed, any allocation mechanism that can be represented as maximizing a function of the utilities of the agents is welfarist.

Since we are allowing the processing functions to represent outcomes other than welfare, welfarism can, more generally, be thought of as a special case of *outcomism*. I will use the terminology of outcomism, recalling that welfarism is a special and important case. In particular, the Axiom of Welfarism becomes the Axiom of Outcomism.

Contrasted with outcomism is what might be called *resourcism*, the position that the economic structure (of resource availabilities and preferences) underlying the outcome possibilities set matters. A resourcist wants to pay attention to all the information given in the economic environment ξ. Consider, for example, an egalitarian who believes that splitting the aggregate resource endowment equally among the agents and then letting them trade to equilibrium is a good procedure. This is not a welfarist proposal. It is generically the case that if two economic environments give rise to the same utility possibilities set, then assigning the Equal Division Walrasian Equilibrium (ED-WE) allocation will not generate the same pair of utility levels in the two environments.

Although it is not clear whether the Rawlsian proposal can be represented in this model, it appears to be a resourcist and nonoutcomist proposal. Rawls wants to equalize (so far as incentive considerations permit) the distribution of primary goods, which are viewed as inputs into various kinds of outcomes (welfare, capability, etc.). This equalization cannot be implemented, given only the information of the utility or outcome profiles that are possible (that is, the specification of the relevant outcome possibilities set). This explains why the Rawlsian proposal differs from its common misinterpretation by economists, "maximin utility."

Indeed, any theory that assigns importance to property rights, or to rights over resources that individuals are deemed to have for reasons other than the outcome those resources will generate, must be a resourcist, nonoutcomist theory. For outcomism discards all the information about the resource structure, and limits its judgments to ones made with knowledge only of the outcomes that can be generated. Hence, resourcist, nonoutcomist positions comprise a major part of political philosophy. (For further criticisms of welfarism, see Sen (1979); for elaboration on the informational poverty of welfarist theories, see Roemer (1986b).)

D. Purpose of This Paper

It is difficult to say what resource egalitarianism consists in, if resources are taken to include inalienable traits, for how can one equally divide and distribute these important resources? The key to the approach that I describe is to change the question from "What is a resource egalitarian allocation?" to "What properties must an allocation mechanism have in order that it implement resource egalitarian allocations on a domain of possible worlds?" One can take a minimalist and somewhat agnostic approach to this problem by specifying certain necessary features that an allocation mechanism defined on the class of economic environments must have in order to qualify as resource egalitarian. In Sections 2 and 3, I propose several such necessary features, which appear formally as axioms on the behavior of the allocation mechanism.

The central theorem states: there is a unique allocation mechanism that satisfies several necessary conditions for resource egalitarianism; that mechanism divides the resources in such a way as to equalize *outcomes*. That is, a resource egalitarian who takes a comprehensive view with respect to resources is committed to outcome egalitarianism. In the language used earlier, if one endorses comprehensive resource egalitarianism, then one cannot preserve a realm of responsibility for people that permits differential outcomes. In the case of utility, the theorem is interpreted as saying that one cannot hold people responsible for their conceptions of welfare to the degree that left-liberal theory would like, if a sufficiently comprehensive view is taken with respect to what attributes of a person constitute resources.

A theorem like this does not settle the issue. It provides an occasion to examine the model in which it is proven in order to sharpen analysis of the underlying philosophical question. Sections 4 through 9 of the paper examine features of the model that I think are the main candidates for chinks in its armor. How is this unreasonable result smuggled in?

For exposition's sake, not all the details of the model are presented here, nor are the proofs of theorems. A rigorous presentation is available in Roemer (1986a), which contains the proofs of the theorems discussed here, unless otherwise indicated. Some insights are lost by sacrificing mathematical detail; for example, assumptions that appear to be merely technical often hide indefensible positions about underlying issues. I have tried to report fully those aspects of the model that are germane to a critical evaluation, but such decisions are, of course, matters of judgment.

E. What Does Equality of Resources Consist In?

Once an interpersonally comparable outcome is specified, it is clear what equality of outcome means in an economic environment, but, as Dworkin points out, it is much less clear what equality of resources might mean. For the following, suppose we are discussing welfare as the outcome. The first pass, proposed in Section 1.C, is to implement equality of resources in an environment ξ by equal division of the aggregate endowment $\bar{x}$. There are two immediate problems with this proposal. First, in general the equal division allocation is not Pareto optimal. If Pareto optimality is desirable, one might modify the equal division proposal into ED-WE. This is the allocation mechanism that assigns to the individuals that allocation which is the Walrasian or competitive equilibrium generated from equal initial endowments. The mechanism ED-WE is Pareto optimal, and seems to implement starting gate equality. It is the canonical envy-free mechanism (see, for example, Varian, 1975). Cohen

(1986) characterizes this mechanism as the Steiner constitution, after Steiner (1977).

But ED-WE is not obviously an attractive implementation of resource egalitarianism, even when the outcome is welfare, if one takes the broader view proposed by Dworkin with respect to what characteristics of an environment constitute resources. In the description of an economic environment $\xi = \langle n; \bar{x}; u, v \rangle$ not all the things we might want to consider resources necessarily appear in the $\bar{x}$ vector. Perhaps some attributes of the agents which should be considered resources are reflected only in the processing functions.

To see this, consider the case of Andrea and Bob, who have processing functions u and v, respectively, for turning rice (x) into useful nutrition. The only resource listed is rice and it is the case that for all x, $u(x) > v(x)$. The most natural resource egalitarian proposal is to divide the rice equally between Andrea and Bob. This is, of course, the ED-WE in a one-good world. But then we learn that Andrea's superior rice-processing technology is due to her possession of an enzyme that Bob lacks. The enzyme is not a listed resource. Is it not reasonable, nevertheless, to treat the enzyme as a resource, which cannot be redistributed from Andrea to Bob, but of which account should be taken by a resource egalitarian in deciding how to allocate the rice?

If so, then ED-WE does not implement resource egalitarianism, for it only "equalizes" those resources that appear explicitly in the x vector. What if the enzymes of Bob and Andrea are explicitly listed as resources in the specification of the economic environment? Then ED-WE requires us to divide the property rights in enzymes so that each agent owns, as part of his initial endowment, one-half the enzymes of the other one and one-half of his "own" enzymes. This appears to foster an unattractive kind of dependence of each agent on the other one, the consequences of which will be elaborated in Section 2.

Thus the most obvious resource-equalizing mechanism may not be attractive to a resource egalitarian. What allocation mechanisms allocate the transferable resources in a way that compensates the agents appropriately, from a resource-egalitarian viewpoint, for the endowments of inalienable resources they have?

2. AN EXAMPLE AND AN AXIOM

In this section, I propose one necessary condition for an allocation mechanism to implement an acceptable kind of resource egalitarianism. Continuing with the above example, it is discovered that Andrea has an amount $\bar{E}_A$ of the enzyme and Bob an amount $\bar{E}_B$. In fact, upon further investigation we can represent Andrea and Bob as each consuming two resources, rice and their enzyme, and their differential success at forestalling starvation, given the same amounts of rice, is the consequence of their differential enzyme consumption. Andrea and Bob can both be viewed as having the same nutrition function $w(x,E)$ over rice and the enzyme, and

$$(1) \qquad u(x) = w(x, \overline{E}_A),\ v(x) = w(x, \overline{E}_B), \text{ and } \overline{E}_A > \overline{E}_B.$$

Because the greater enzyme consumption produces more nutrients for a given level of rice consumption (because the function w is monotone increasing in its arguments), the existence of the enzyme implies in the economic environment where only rice is explicitly listed as a resource that $u(x) > v(x)$.

To model the enzyme's inalienability, we must view Andrea's and Bob's enzymes as two different resources: Bob's enzyme is useless to Andrea, and conversely. (These enzymes are not like kidneys, which can, perhaps, be transmitted from one person to another; they are truly inalienable resources.) Letting E_A stand for Andrea's enzyme and E_B for Bob's enzyme, consider the extended outcome functions w_A and w_B defined by:

$$(2) \qquad w_A\,(x, E_A, \cdot E_B) = w(x,E_A) \text{ and}$$

$$w_B(x, E_A, E_B) = w\,(x, E_B).$$

The functions w_A and w_B have been defined over rice and the two personalized enzymes; Andrea with nutrition function w_A gets benefits from consuming only rice (x) and her enzyme (E_A), while Bob with nutrition function w_B benefits from consuming only rice and his enzyme (E_B). The reader might naturally ask why Andrea's enzyme should be included as an argument of Bob's nutrition function, from which he derives no benefit; this is a technical trick whose purpose will become clear in a moment. Now consider the economic environment $\xi' = \langle 3;(\overline{x},\overline{E}_A, \overline{E}_B); w_A, w_B\rangle$. This environment is similar to ξ; the difference between ξ and ξ' is that in the latter, the enzyme endowments of Andrea and Bob have been explicitly represented as resources. We may now ask of the resource egalitarian: How should the resources be allocated in ξ'?

It is quite clear that all of the enzyme that only Andrea can consume, $\overline{E}_A$, should be assigned to her and all of the enzyme that only Bob consumes, $\overline{E}_B$, should be assigned to him, for to deprive either person of the full consumption of a good that only he or she can use would be spiteful. (One can imagine that the resource allocator has a switch by which he can control the amount of an enzyme that a person consumes.)

More formally, if Pareto optimality is one requirement of resource egalitarianism, then the allocation mechanism must assign all of the personalized enzymes to the right people. So Pareto optimality rules out spitefulness of a certain kind. (I am here borrowing the term "Pareto optimality" and using it in any outcome context, not simply the classical case where the outcome is utility.) It is to guarantee that the allocation mechanism gives all of $\overline{E}_B$ to Bob and all of $\overline{E}_A$ to Andrea that the trick of defining the two enzymes as different goods is introduced.

As I wrote, it is not obvious that in ξ' the rice should be divided equally between Andrea and Bob. Because the enzymes cannot effectively be equalized, due to their inalienability, resource egalitarian accounts should perhaps be squared by an unequal division of the rice. I will not suggest exactly how to resolve the rice allocation problem yet. My aim is to call into question the initial decision of the resource egalitarian, to divide the rice equally between Andrea and Bob, in the one-dimensional economic environment ξ. For if we decide that resource egalitarianism requires an unequal division of the rice in ξ', should it not require that same division of the rice in ξ? After all, ξ and ξ' are environments representing the same world, where resources have been uncovered in ξ' which were not visible in ξ. ξ is an incomplete description of the "actual" world, from the point of view of someone who wishes to include enzymes as resources within the jurisdiction of egalitarian compensation. This suggests that *however a resource-egalitarian allocation mechanism F divides the rice in ξ', it should divide the rice in the same way in ξ.*

I call this necessary condition on resource egalitarianism Consistency of Resource Allocation Across Dimension (CONRAD). Formally, it is defined as follows:

Axiom CONRAD. Let $\xi' = \langle n + m; (\overline{x}, \overline{y}); u(x,y), v(x,y)\rangle$ be an economic environment where there are n dimensions of the x goods and m dimensions of the y goods. Suppose that each y good is useful to, or liked by, only one person. Let $F(\xi') = ((\overline{x}^1, \overline{y}^1), (\overline{x}^2, \overline{y}^2))$. Consider the restricted outcome functions defined as follows:

$$u^*(x) = u(x, \overline{y}^1),\ v^*(x) = v\,(x, \overline{y}^2)$$

and examine the n-dimensional environment

$$\xi = \langle n; \overline{x}; u^*(x), v^*(x)\rangle.$$

Then $F(\xi) = (\overline{x}^1, \overline{x}^2)$.

That is, in the environment ξ', the m y-goods are completely personalized in their use to the two people. By Pareto optimality, which I will assume below, the allocation mechanism must assign the various y-

goods to Andrea and Bob in the obvious way, so that each gets all of the goods that only he or she derives benefit from. CONRAD then instructs us to examine the environment that is induced, once those personalized goods have been assigned, over just the x-goods; it requires that the allocation mechanism assign the x goods in exactly the same manner in the smaller-dimension environment ξ as it assigned them in the larger-dimension environment ξ'. If, in the "big" environment ξ', proper account was taken, in distributing the x goods, of the relative availabilities of the various personalized consumption goods (the enzymes), then CONRAD guarantees that in the dimensionally reduced environment ξ, proper account will be taken of personalized consumption goods, which there appear only implicitly in the processing functions of the agents. CONRAD is agnostic in not telling us exactly how to distribute the x goods in ξ'; it merely requires *consistency* between the distribution of the x goods in ξ and ξ'.

It is not immediately clear how F may allocate the resources in ξ, if F must satisfy CONRAD. We must consider all possible environments ξ' of which ξ is a reduced environment in the CONRAD sense. Say $\xi = \langle n; \bar{x}; u, v\rangle$. There may be many "CONRAD extensions" of ξ into dimensionally larger environments ξ' – environments with personalized consumption goods whose CONRAD restrictions are just ξ. CONRAD requires consistency between the allocation of $\bar{x}$ in ξ and the allocation of $\bar{x}$ in all those possible extensions ξ'.

Consider again the mechanism Equal Division Walrasian Equilibrium which assigns that allocation which is the Walrasian equilibrium from an initial equal division of all the resources between the agents. (One thinks of this allocation mechanism as a natural one when the context is utility and welfare, but it is well defined no matter what the outcome is called.) Consider the rice–enzyme environment $\xi' = \langle 3; (\bar{x}, \bar{E}_A, \bar{E}_B); w_A, w_B\rangle$. How would ED-WE divide the resources here? It would act as if property rights had been assigned, initially, of $(\bar{x}/2, \bar{E}_A/2, \bar{E}_B/2)$ to each of Andrea and Bob (that's the initial equal split). Of course, Andrea has no use for Bob's enzyme, nor does Bob have any use for Andrea's – except in trade. Thus, at Walrasian equilibrium, which is Pareto optimal, Bob will buy back all of "his" enzyme, which Andrea initially owns, and Andrea will buy back from Bob all of "her" enzyme, which he initially owns. No other final allocation of the enzymes would be Pareto optimal. But the "prices" of these two enzymes will not in general be the same in terms of rice. It may be the case that Bob has to sell some of his initial rice stock to buy back all of his enzyme (or it could be the other way around, that Andrea has to trade some of her rice to get back all of her enzyme). The point is that the allocation mechanism ED-WE will assign all of $\bar{E}_A$ to Andrea and all of $\bar{E}_B$ to Bob, since no other allocation of those goods would be Pareto optimal, but it will not in general divide the rice equally between them in the three-dimensional environment ξ'.

Now consider the original one-dimensional rice environment $\xi = \langle 1; \bar{x}; u, v \rangle$. Equal Division Walrasian Equilibrium, acting on ξ, simply splits the rice equally between Andrea and Bob. But the one-dimensional rice environment ξ is just the CONRAD-restriction of the three-dimensional rice-enzyme-enzyme environment ξ' that is induced by holding fixed the allocation of the two enzymes. We therefore conclude that ED-WE violates CONRAD, because it changes the allocation of rice it recommends when passing from ξ' to ξ. For the previous paragraph argued that in ξ', the rice is in general not equally split between Andrea and Bob under ED-WE.

One reason to reject ED-WE as a resource-egalitarian mechanism is its violation of CONRAD. ED-WE does not take proper account of the personalized resources that may exist in an environment, but have not been explicitly recorded in its description. (As well, ED-WE violates the Resource Monotonicity axiom, to be introduced in Section 3.)

This discussion may lead the reader to believe that CONRAD is an unrealistically strong requirement to place on an allocation mechanism, in the sense that it may be difficult to find allocation mechanisms that satisfy CONRAD. This, however, is not the case. There are many allocation mechanisms that satisfy CONRAD. One may object to the claim that CONRAD is a necessary condition for resource egalitarianism, but one cannot object to it on the grounds that no mechanism satisfies it.

3. EQUALITY OF RESOURCES: MORE AXIOMS AND A THEOREM

In this section I propose three other axioms which are arguably necessary conditions for the implementation of resource egalitarianism.

Axiom Pareto Optimality (PO). F should allocate the resources in any environment ξ in a "Pareto optimal" way. (The quotation marks appear because the outcome might not be utility.)

Axiom PO does not require much discussion. If it is possible to satisfy Pareto optimality, it would seem spiteful not to do so. Strictly speaking, one might say that Pareto optimality is not required for a mechanism to be resource equalizing, but if a mechanism that satisfies other necessary conditions for resource equality is also Pareto optimal, so much the better.

Axiom Symmetry (Sy). If $\xi = \langle n; \bar{x}; u, u \rangle$ then $F(\xi) = (\bar{x}/2, \bar{x}/2)$.

Symmetry says that if the two agents have the same processing function, then the resources should be divided equally between them. Whatever resource egalitarianism means, it should at least mean this. There is one perhaps contentious feature to be noted. This justification of the axiom is only plausible because outcomes have been postulated to be interpersonally comparable. If two people have the same utility function, for example, that means they get exactly the same degree of welfare from the same bundle of resources. If outcomes were interpersonally noncomparable, then I do not think the symmetry axiom would be justifiable. For in that case, the fact that two persons had the same outcome function would only represent their having the same ordinal outcome rankings over bundles of resources; it would not mean they had the same resource processing capability in an absolutely measurable sense.

Interpersonal comparability is easier to accept in some interpretations of the model than in others. If the outcome functions represent the rate of infant survival in different countries, comparability is clear; if they represent the degree of satisfaction that different people receive from consuming goods, comparability is a contentious assumption. For this reason, the model is easiest to accept when the functions measure some objectively comparable outcome across agents.

Axiom Resource Monotonicity (RMON). Let $\xi = \langle n; \bar{x}; u, v\rangle$ and let $\xi' = \langle n; \bar{\bar{x}}; u, v\rangle$ where $\bar{\bar{x}} \geqslant \bar{x}$. Then neither person's outcome level should be less under the action of F in ξ' than in ξ. That is:

$$u(F^1(\xi)) \leqslant u(F^1(\xi')) \text{ and } v(F^2(\xi)) \leqslant v(F^2(\xi')).$$

Resource monotonicity says that if the aggregate resource endowment increases from one environment to another, but nothing else about the environment changes, then the resources should be distributed in the more abundant environment in such a way that neither person ends up worse off, in outcome level, than he was in the environment in which resources were unambiguously scarcer. The motivation for RMON as an axiom is of the same minimalist sort: whatever equality of resources means, it should at least require RMON.

Finally, the domain axiom should be stated explicitly:

Domain Axiom (D^Σ). The allocation mechanism is defined on all economic environments $\xi = \langle n; \bar{x}; u, v\rangle$ where n is any positive integer, $\bar{x}$ is any nonnegative vector in R^n, u and v are any continuous, weakly monotone increasing, concave functions defined on R^n, with $u(0) = v(0) = 0$. The class of such economic environments is Σ.

As I wrote earlier, the assumptions on the processing functions imbue the model with some economic content. In this kind of axiomatic characterization of mechanisms, it is desirable to keep the domain as small as possible, for that disciplines the model to represent our intuitions more precisely. If, for example, one allowed nonmonotonic outcome functions, that would require discarding the interpretation of resources as "goods." It is a virtue of this theory that it is true on this relatively restricted domain of economic environments. This is to be contrasted, for example, with classical social choice theory which posits a domain with utility functions that are entirely arbitrary. The unrestricted domain assumption of social choice theory is that any ordering of the social states be admitted as a possible preference ordering for each agent. Here, the social states are distributions of a given resource vector, and only certain reasonable, "economically plausible" orderings are admissible according to the domain axiom.

The main result is:

THEOREM 1. *There is a unique allocation mechanism F that satisfies the axioms D^{Σ}, PO, Sy, RMON, and CONRAD. F(ξ) assigns that Pareto optimal resource allocation in ξ which equalizes the outcome levels of the agents.*

The interpretation is that if a resource-equalizing mechanism must satisfy at least the necessary conditions summarized by the axioms, then it can only do one thing: equalize outcomes. Hence, if resource egalitarianism entails the five axioms, then no distinction between equality of resources and equality of outcomes can be sustained.

Consider what the theorem says in the case where agents are countries, and each outcome function registers the rate of infant survival as a function of the resources a country consumes. The planner is directed to allocate an aggregate resource endowment to countries, restricted only by the axioms. An allocation of those resources is not acceptable if it would be possible to choose another allocation that increases the rate of infant survival in some countries without lowering it in others (PO). If the vector of aggregate resources becomes more abundant, then the planner must recommend an allocation that does not increase the rate of infant mortality in any country, compared with what it was when resources were scarce (RMON). If it so happens that all countries are identical with respect to their ability to use resources to reduce infant mortality, then resources should be evenly divided among them (Sy). Finally, suppose that in our description of the countries and the resources, certain nontransferable resources are listed, such as the climates, water supplies, and geographical locations of the countries. Listed as well are transferable resources, such as food and medicine. The planner decides upon an allocation of the transferable resources, taking account of the climates and geographical locations of the countries, which influence what their rates of infant mortality will be. Then he must allocate the transferable resources in exactly the same way, were

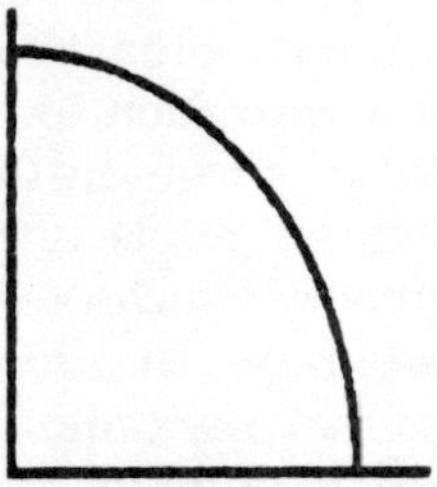

FIGURE 1A

FIGURE 1B

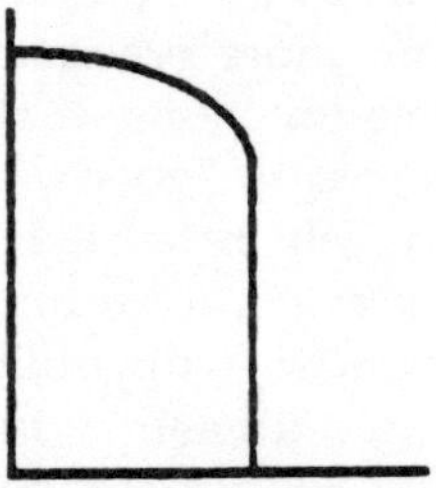

FIGURE 1C

he to face a description of the world in which climate and geographical location were not explicitly specified, but affected the rates of infant mortality of the countries nonetheless through their infant survival functions (CONRAD). If the planner respects these rules, and he is required to propose an allocation rule that will work for all possible worlds (Domain Axiom), then he has no option but to distribute resources in that way which equalizes the rates of infant mortality in all countries.

Perhaps one point should be made, to avoid some confusion about the possibility of equalizing outcomes. The usual utility possibilities set for an economic environment is the one depicted in Figure 1A – a strictly comprehensive, convex set. Utility sets like the one in Figure 1B, which are familiar from Rawlsian discussions, do not occur in this model. In Figure 1B, the interpretation must be that the first agent has a failure of incentive if he is taxed too much, and both agents become worse off. In the model here, the utility (or outcome) possibilities frontier consists of points that are either Pareto optimal or at worst "weakly Pareto optimal." Thus the utility set of Figure 1B would in fact appear as depicted in Figure 1C, with a vertical line segment dropped from the point at which the first agent's incentive fails. Strictly speaking, since there is no production in the model I have outlined, this incentive problem does not appear. But if production were incorporated, as it can be, then utility possibilities sets like Figure 1C can occur. In that case, the axiom Pareto Optimality must be replaced with the axiom Weak Pareto Optimality and then Theorem 1 states that the unique mechanism which obeys the stated axioms plus a continuity axiom is the outcome-equalizing mechanism. But considerations of incentives are not a concern of this article, and I will not pursue this issue further.

4. CRITICISMS

Theorem 1 performs a reduction that is disagreeable. There should be a distinction between equality of resources and equality of outcome. I will examine several aspects of the model, which comprise what seem to me to be the most compelling criticisms against it.

A. Nameless Goods

In the economic environments I have described, the resources have no names. Thus the same "economic information" depicted in the vector $\langle n; \bar{x}; u, v\rangle$ describes many different worlds, each with n goods, but in which the identities of the goods differ among worlds. In one world the goods may be shelter and food, and u and v are functions that describe how the agents transform these resources into welfare; in another, the goods might be beer and champagne, while the agents in that world have the same pleasure or inebriation functions, u and v, over these resources. The resource egalitarianism that many advocate would require us to distinguish between the treatment of these two worlds, depending upon the names of the goods in them, but such differential treatment is ruled out by the domain axiom of this model.

B. The Domain Axiom

I wrote above that the domain of economic environments is smaller than the usual unrestricted domain of social choice theory. Monotonicity and concavity of the processing functions ensure that the domain consists of objects in which outcome is related to resources in a nonperverse and classic way. On the other hand, it might be too much to assume that any concave, monotone function should be admitted as a possible processing function, for some interpretations. This criticism is related to the namelessness of goods.

C. CONRAD and hidden goods

As discussed in Section 3, CONRAD is a strong axiom. In Section 6, I describe what CONRAD commits us to, with respect to goods, like enzymes, that are perhaps hidden inside people.

D. Resource Monotonicity

Resource monotonicity is a powerful axiom which perhaps commits us to more than our intuitions warrant. In Section 7, I discuss how this axiom can be weakened, still preserving the outcome-egalitarian conclusion of Theorem 1.

E. Interpersonal Comparability

It is an assumption of the model that the outcome levels measured by the processing functions in an economic environment are interpersonally comparable. One way out of Theorem 1 is to remove this assumption. Without interpersonal comparability, the symmetry axiom has no inherent appeal as a resource-egalitarian axiom; and so one might ask what allocation mechanisms satisfy all the axioms except Sy, plus an axiom enforcing the noncomparability of outcomes of agents in an environment. Indeed, Dworkin (1981b) has argued that one reason to be a resource egalitarian as opposed to a welfare egalitarian is that people have such different conceptions of welfare as to be interpersonally noncomparable. In Section 8, a theorem is reported showing that if a resource egalitarian is committed to making no interpersonal welfare (outcome) comparisons, then there is *no* mechanism that satisfies the axioms. Given the rest of the structure of this model, interpersonal comparability of outcome is required to have any general conception of resource equality.

F. Full Information

It is assumed in this model that the outcome functions (and the resource availabilities) are known to whatever agency is implementing the allocation mechanism *F*. Suppose, to the contrary, that there is incomplete or asymmetric information: only the individual knows his processing function, and the agency must propose a mechanism for dividing the resources that will be compatible with the privacy of individual information. In Section 9, I propose that our ethical conception of responsibility depends upon the incompleteness of information.

5. NAMING GOODS

A. The Anonymity of Goods

There are two issues of namelessness in the model of economic environments: neither the goods are named, nor is a name given to the kind of outcome measured by the outcome functions (whether it is utility, fulfillment of needs, or the degree of achievement of basic capabilities). The namelessness of outcome may be an important issue for resource allocation, for it is reasonable to think that the kind of outcome involved makes a moral difference. This is illustrated, for example, in an article by Yaari and Bar-Hillel (1984), who asked a survey population to decide upon the appropriate division of resources in a number of hypothetical cases. In particular, the respondents' opinions about what division of resources was fair depended quite strongly on whether the problem was phrased in terms of fulfilling needs or desires. That is to say, opinions about fair division of a resource bundle in two "worlds" differed when their descriptions as economic environments were identical, but the names given to what the processing functions measured in the two worlds were not the same.

Indeed, one can criticize the model of economic environments because only one kind outcome is represented, the kind measured by the functions u and v. Since there are many kinds of outcome, perhaps each should be represented with its own function in a fuller description of an environment. (As I noted, Dworkin points out that one of the problems for welfare egalitarianism is that the kinds of welfare that are of concern to people may differ: one cares about pleasure, the other about living a worthwhile life.) I propose, instead, to interpret the model more narrowly, as follows. Imagine that we have decided upon the outcome that is of concern for the analysis at hand, and let u and v be the processing functions for the two agents representing that kind of outcome. Then the axioms reflect resource-egalitarian requirements, given that we are concerned about this particular kind of outcome. The model applies to analyzing resource egalitarianism once some particular kind of outcome has been decided upon as the relevant one. If the kinds of outcome for different people are not the same then the axioms are less convincing. What, for example, would justify the symmetry axiom if the processing function u, for Bob, measures his happiness and the same function u, for Andrea, measures her healthiness?

To discuss the namelessness of resources in the model, some additional formal structure is useful. Economic environments can be viewed as equivalence classes of informationally denser objects, descriptive of possible worlds, called environments with named goods. To describe environments with named goods, we begin with an infinite list of named goods, called Ω, which might include goods named beer, champagne, rice, Bob's enzymes, Andrea's enzymes, and so on. An *environment with named goods* is a vector $e = \langle N, n; \bar{x}; u, v\rangle$ where $N \subset \Omega$ is a finite list of n goods, $\bar{x}$ is the aggregate endowment of those goods, and u and v are the outcome functions of the agents over those goods. Let the class of all such environments with named goods be Δ.

Let $e' = \langle N', n; \bar{x}; u, v\rangle$ be another environment with named goods in which the "economic information" is the same as in e but the list of goods N' differs from N. The theory of allocation mechanisms defined on the class of economic environments Σ, as outlined in Section 3, can be re-done as a theory of resource allocation mechanisms acting on Δ, with one additional axiom: that the mechanism F, now defined on Δ, should allocate the resources in the same way between the agents in the two environments e and e' when those two environments with named goods differ, as above, only in the names of their goods. This is an Anonymity of Goods axiom, for it says the allocation mechanism looks just at "economic information" and ignores the names of the particular goods. Formally:

Anonymity of Goods (AnonG). Let e = $\langle N, n; \bar{x}; u, v\rangle$ and e' = $\langle N', n; \bar{x}, u, v\rangle$ be two economic environments with named goods in Δ. Let F be an allocation mechanism defined on the space of environments with named goods. Then F(e) = F(e').

AnonG is palatable if we think that all relevant information about goods is summarized in the processing functions, whose outcome has been named, and the endowment vector. This might not hold if, for example, the agents in e have views about certain rights that people in e have with respect to some of the goods in N, which do not apply if the goods are in N'. These views are not represented in the processing functions. For instance, N might contain certain internal goods, like personalized enzymes, while N' might contain only goods in the external world, and people's opinions about proper egalitarian compensation might differ in these two cases, even if all the economic information is the same.

The anonymity of goods can be defended as follows. Once the type of outcome that is our concern has been named, then the names of resources that generate it should not count further. Resources are, by presumption, instrumental only insofar as they produce outcomes, and this is captured by the processing functions. Distinguishing among goods in an allocation decision on the basis of their names, once the outcome has been named, would be gratuitous.

The position against AnonG is bolstered by our opinions about our own world, in which the names of goods appear to matter in our ethical judgments.[1] But it is not so clear they should, given the hypothesis that the type of outcome that the processing functions measure is named and fixed for all environments in Δ. The results of Yaari and Bar-Hillel depended upon changing the names of the outcomes across economic environments, not changing the names of goods while holding the notion of outcome fixed. Once we agree that we are studying the realization of basic capabilities, let us say, should it matter whether the resources are apples and oranges or shelter and education? If our opinions do change as the names of goods change (but the name of the outcome remains fixed), that may be due to cognitive errors on our part, to framing. Appealing to our beliefs about our own world is not a foolproof test.

I am undecided about the moral appeal of the anonymity of goods in

1. This point was communicated to me by T. Scanlon.

the present context. It is worth giving a more concrete example of what such anonymity commits one to, because it is such an important, but until now, implicit assumption. Consider again the rice–enzyme environment $\xi = \langle 3; (\bar{x}, \bar{E}_A, \bar{E}_B); w_A, w_B \rangle$ where $\bar{x}$ is the amount of rice and $\bar{E}_A$ and $\bar{E}_B$ are the enzyme endowments of Andrea and Bob, and $\bar{E}_A > \bar{E}_B$. The same economic description could apply to an environment in which the second and third goods are not enzymes, but scotch and gin. Andrea likes only rice and scotch, Bob likes only rice and gin, and there is more scotch in the world than gin. The rice-scotch-gin economic environment is also described exactly by ξ. (One point of the example is that goods whose use in consumption is completely personalized need not be internal goods.) In the second world, all the scotch goes to Andrea and all the gin to Bob, by Pareto optimality, just as in the first world Andrea and Bob were each assigned all of their own enzymes by the mechanism. And because of the anonymity of goods, the allocation of rice under the mechanism F must be the same in these two worlds.

Is it correct that resource egalitarianism should take no account of whether goods are internal or external? Perhaps so, in the radical kind of resource egalitarianism under discussion, where all resources, independent of their physical location, are within the jurisdiction of social compensation. Once a conception of welfare or outcome has been identified, then anonymity claims the only relevant attribute of a resource is the manner in which it enters into the production of benefit for the people in that world. Even relative to a single kind of outcome, this is a weaker statement than an endorsement of welfarism, or outcomism, which requires that two economic environments that give rise to the same set of outcome possibilities should not be distinguished with respect to the final outcome levels assigned.

Being undecided about the appeal of the Anonymity of Goods axiom, I proceed on two fronts. One, now concluded, has been to defend anonymity.

B. Dropping the Anonymity of Goods Axiom

The second front is to study resource-egalitarian mechanisms defined on Δ where the Anonymity of Goods is not imposed. It will turn out it is possible to recover the main theorem while working on the domain Δ, and without the Anonomity of Goods axiom, but at a cost.

The axioms necessary for a mechanism to be resource egalitarian, when defined on the class Δ, can be written as follows. These axioms are, with one exception, each weaker than their counterparts in Section 3, since no longer are all environments in Δ lumped together, whose economic descriptions are the same.

N1. (Domain D^{Δ}) F is a function assigning an allocation to each e in Δ.

N2. (PO) F assigns a Pareto optimal allocation for each e in Δ.

N3. (Symmetry) If $e = \langle N, n; \bar{x}, u, u\rangle$ then $F(e) = (\bar{x}/2, \bar{x}/2)$

N4. (Resource Monotonicity – RMON*). Let $e = \langle N, n; \bar{x}, u, v\rangle$ and $e' = \langle N, n; \bar{\bar{x}}; u, v\rangle$ be two economic environments with named goods, identical except that $\bar{\bar{x}} \geqslant \bar{x}$. Then $F(e')$ weakly Pareto dominates $F(e)$.

N5. (Consistency–CONRAD*) Let $e = \langle N \cup M, n + m; (\bar{x}, \bar{y}); u, v\rangle$ be an economic environment with $(n + m)$ named goods comprising the union of two disjoint sets N and M, where M consists of personalized consumption goods, and let $F(e) = ((\bar{x}^1, \bar{y}^1), (\bar{x}^2, \bar{y}^2))$. Consider the n-dimensional environment in Δ defined by $e^* = \langle N, n; \bar{x}; u^*, v^*\rangle$ where $u^*(x) = u(x, \bar{y}^1)$ and $v^*(x) = v(x, \bar{y}^2)$. Then $F(e^*) = (\bar{x}^1, \bar{x}^2)$.

THEOREM 2. *Exactly one allocation mechanism satisfies axioms N1–N5; F chooses a Pareto-optimal allocation for each environment in Δ which equalizes the outcome levels of the agents.*[2]

Note the sense in which axioms N4 and N5 are weaker than their counterparts in Section 3. Axiom RMON says that if the processing functions of the agents in two environments are the same, but the resources in one environment are more abundant than in the other, then the allocation mechanism must make everyone better off in the more abundant environment – even if the resources in the two environments have different names. But Axiom RMON* only requires that benefits be (weakly) increasing for all agents when, in addition, the resources in the two environments have the same identities. It is therefore a weaker axiom than RMON. Similarly, CONRAD* only requires consistency between the resource allocation in the $(m + n)$–dimensional environment and the induced n-dimensional environment when the two environments are specified as having the same n goods in common, from the set N. CONRAD, however, requires consistency even when no assurance is given that the two environments share the same set of n goods. Thus, RMON* and CONRAD* capture more faithfully the resourcist intuitions that I used to motivate RMON and CONRAD.

It would seem that Theorem 2 patches up a chink in the model's armor, for it shows that the result of outcome egalitarianism is preserved when the allocation mechanisms act on the domain of objects Δ, and the anonymity axiom is not imposed. But that is not quite the case: for the ability to name goods has been purchased at the expense of a domain axiom that is less palatable than the domain axiom of the model Σ.

2. The proof of Theorem 2 is available from the author.

C. The Domain Axioms

The domain Σ of Theorem 1 consists of all economic environments, all objects $\xi = \langle n; \bar{x}; u, v \rangle$. The domain Δ of Theorem 2 consists of all objects $e = \langle N; n; \bar{x}; u, v \rangle$ where N is any subset of size n of the universal set of named goods Ω, and the other economic information $\bar{x}$, u, and v is arbitrarily specified from the relevant families of objects. The crucial point is that while it may be palatable to accept a domain Σ, it is much less so to accept the domain Δ. The domain axiom D^{Σ} states that for any positive number n, and any vector $\bar{x}$ and functions u and v, there is *some* set N, of n resources, with respect to which $\langle n; \bar{x}; u, v \rangle$ represents a possible world. But the domain axiom D^{Δ} requires that for any n and *any* set, N, of named goods of size n, and for any vector $\bar{x}$ and functions u and v, there is a possible world represented by $\langle n; N; \bar{x}; u, v \rangle$. The force of naming goods is due, in large part, to our belief that certain goods enter into the outcome functions of all people in fairly restricted ways, for a fixed kind of outcome. Is it reasonable to suppose that there is a possible world in which the trade-offs between caviar and shelter can be specified in an arbitrary way? This is what the domain axiom of Theorem 2 requires. If there are some constraints on human biology and nature, then for any kind of outcome, the domain of possible processing functions that can be associated with a particular set of named goods N will not be the universal class of concave, monotonic functions. To make the axiom N1 palatable, we have to relax these human nature constraints: but that seems equivalent to sterilizing the identification of goods of the meaning it has. Naming goods is meaningful just because the way specific goods enter into the production of any outcome is restricted by human nature.

I have argued that AnonG is more acceptable than might first appear, because I am interpreting the type of outcome which the processing functions measure as fixed and named. If anonymity is unacceptable, we have learned more precisely why the names of goods are important, by seeing which axioms strain credibility when goods are named. It is our belief in the restriction on possible worlds by virtue of human nature, once goods are named, which can vitiate Theorem 2.

6. CONRAD AND HIDDEN GOODS

I motivated CONRAD in Section 2 with the story of Andrea's and Bob's enzymes. CONRAD was presented as a necessary condition for assuring that an allocation mechanism charged with the assignment of compensating people for their endowments of personalized nontransferable resources carries out its mandate. There is another motivation for CONRAD that derives from considering the limited information available to the planning agency, which implements the resource allocation. The planner is assigned the task of allocating a certain set of resources among agents. Some resources, in particular personalized goods of various kinds, are not in this set; indeed, the planner does not even know what these resources are, or, *a fortiori*, who has how much of each. Surely, the planner should allocate the transferable goods in such a way that, were he to gain further information about the personalized goods that were not in the original set, the decision about the allocation of the resources that has been made would not have to be altered. CONRAD assures this. Thus CONRAD enables the planning agency to economize on information. If the allocation mechanism satisfies CONRAD, the allocating agency can distribute its incomplete set of resources, knowing that the full allocation that will be realized is the one that would be chosen with fuller information about the nontransferable resources. It does not matter how many nontransferable resources there are, in what amounts they exist, nor what their identities are.[3]

This motivation for CONRAD derives from our ignorance of what personalized consumption resources may exist in the world in which our allocation mechanism must act. Scanlon (1986a), however, believes that the resource egalitarian rationale I offered for adopting CONRAD depends on claims about what goods are *actually* hidden in the world under consideration. I will paraphrase his argument using the named goods axiom CONRAD*, because the adoption of named goods responds to part of Scanlon's criticism. Consider two environments referred to by CONRAD*, e = $\langle N \cup M; n + m; (\bar{x},\bar{y}); u, v\rangle$ and e* = $\langle N; n; \bar{x}; u^*, v^*\rangle$, the CONRAD*-restriction of e. Scanlon writes that the Andrea and Bob story provides no reason to enforce consistency between the mechanism's action in distributing the goods $\bar{x}$ in e* and its distribution of the goods $\bar{x}$ in e, unless we know that the goods in the set M (the enzymes) are *actually hidden goods* in the environment e*. Although in the construction carried out to define e*, that environment materializes as a restriction of an environment e with more goods, the allocation mechanism is directed by CONRAD* to allocate the goods $\bar{x}$ in a certain way in e*, even if e* were to have no relationship to e, with respect to the goods M. Once e* is defined, it exists as an environment unto itself, with no necessary relation to e in the terms of goods that may or may not be "actually" hidden in the world described by e*.

It is possible to formalize this criticism, with the introduction of more notation, which will specify for a given environment which goods in it are "actually hidden" and which are "visible." Consider a class of "named environments with hidden goods," called Γ, whose generic

3. I am grateful to David Donaldson for this interpretation of CONRAD.

member is $f = \langle n, N; h, H; (\bar{x}; \bar{z}^1; \bar{z}^2); u, v\rangle$. The interpretation is that the set of goods N comprises the visible goods explicitly listed for allocation, and there are n of them with aggregate endowment $\bar{x}$; the set of goods H is the actual, hidden goods, there are h of them, and they are being consumed by the two agents in amounts $\bar{z}^1$ and $\bar{z}^2$ respectively; and the processing functions u and v are defined only over the set of visible goods, N. Thus, the environment we see in Δ if the hidden goods are ignored in f is e $= \langle n; N; \bar{x}; u, v\rangle$. We can now define a version of CONRAD*, which pays attention to which goods are hidden, as follows:

CONRAD (CONRAD* with actually hidden goods).** In Γ, consider the environment $f = \langle N \cup M; n + m; 0, \phi; (\bar{x}, \bar{y}); u, v\rangle$ where the goods $N \cup M$ are visible and there are no hidden goods (ϕ is the empty set). Suppose the goods in M are personalized in their use for the agents in f, and let $F(f) = ((\bar{x}^1, \bar{y}^1), (\bar{x}^2, \bar{y}^2))$ be the allocation. Consider the environment f^* in Γ defined by $f^* = \langle n, N; m, M; (\bar{x}; \bar{y}^1, \bar{y}^2); u^*, v^*\rangle$, where the hidden goods are now M, their allocation to the agents is $(\bar{y}^1, \bar{y}^2)$ and the visible utility functions are $u^*(x) = u(x; \bar{y}^1)$ and $v^*(x) = v(x; \bar{y}^2)$. Then $F(f^*) = (\bar{x}^1, \bar{x}^2)$.

CONRAD** enforces consistency of the distribution of the visible goods $\bar{x}$ in the environment f^* with the distribution of those goods in f only when we are told that the smaller-dimensional environment f^* is one in which the goods in M, which appeared explicitly in f, are actually hidden in f^*. What is the relationship of CONRAD** to CONRAD*? It is, of course, weaker than CONRAD*. We can view CONRAD* as following from CONRAD** with the addition of another axiom, which implements an "independence of hidden goods." The Independence of Hidden Goods Axiom, which I shall not write down, stipulates that two environments in Γ should be treated in the same manner if their lists of visible goods are the same, and their visible processing functions are the same, even if their lists of hidden goods differ or even if there are no hidden goods in one of the environments. That is, of course, precisely the contentious point with Scanlon. It is the "independence of hidden goods" that I used to motivate CONRAD as an information-economizing condition above.

If CONRAD* is replaced with CONRAD** in Theorem 2, the new theorem can be preserved by including the Independence of Hidden Goods as an axiom. This is just a formalization of Scanlon's criticism, not an answer to it. The criticism is that our beliefs, about whether compensation should be made to people because of the hidden attributes that contribute to determining their welfare, depend on what the hidden goods are. If the attributes are enzymes over which the agents have no control, perhaps they should be compensated; if the attributes are degrees of effort, or religious views, perhaps they should not be. To the extent that opponents of welfare egalitarianism base their argument on the identities of hidden goods, the Independence of Hidden Goods axiom is an important chink in the model's armor.

7. RESOURCE MONOTONICITY

The original resource monotonicity axiom (RMON) can be criticized as outcomist, because it ignores the names of goods. That objection is countered by the amendment to RMON*, which weakens the axiom and pays appropriate attention to named goods. Here, I address some other issues with respect to RMON and RMON*. I will refer to RMON, but the comments apply to either axiom.

RMON appears to be a reasonable requirement, but it is perhaps more powerful than our intuitions about resource egalitarianism warrant. For RMON compares a given economic environment to a continuum of other environments, ones which differ from each other in the size of their resource endowment. Our intuitions are based, I think, on making a finite number of comparisons – usually, comparing one world to some other benchmark world, some proposed counterfactual. Because our intuitions are poor when it comes to uncountable infinities, it is possible that RMON is not justified by the intuitions which recommend it.

This objection can be countered, as RMON can be replaced by another axiom that just compares a given world to one other benchmark world.[4] This axiom is mindful of Sen's (1973) weak equity axiom, and so it will be called:

Weak Equity Axiom (WE). Let $\xi = \langle n, \bar{x}, u, v \rangle$ be in Σ with $u(x) \geqslant v(x)$ for all x. Consider the benchmark environment $\xi^* = \langle n, \bar{x}, v, v \rangle$. Then the second agent in ξ should not get a lower outcome level under F's action then he does in ξ^*.

The Weak Equity Axiom says that an agent who is "handicapped" in his ability to process resources into outcome, compared to another, should not suffer due to his being in a world with the more "talented" agent. If we postulate Symmetry, then in ξ^* the agents split the endow-

4. There is another detour possible around resource monotonicity. Suppose the domain of economic environments is taken to be all environments $\langle n; \bar{x}; u, v \rangle$ where u and v are restricted only to being monotonic, but not necessarily concave, functions. Call this domain Λ. On Λ, outcome egalitarianism is characterized by the axioms Sy, PO, and CONRAD. No monotonicity axiom of any kind is required! This surprising result shows the sensitivity of this class of theorems to the domain assumption. (The proof is available from the author.)

ment. Thus, Weak Equity says that the "handicapped" agent in ξ should get at least the outcome level that he derives from one-half of the aggregate resource bundle.

Consider the following axiom, which strengthens the symmetry axiom:

Axiom of Limited Self-Ownership (LSO). Let $\xi = \langle n, \bar{x}, u, v \rangle$ with $u(x) \geq v(x)$ for all x. Then $u(F^1(\xi)) \geq v(F^2(\xi))$.

LSO says that in a world with a "talented" and a "handicapped" agent, the talented agent should end up with at least as high a level of benefit as the handicapped one. The name of the axiom derives from the fact that the mechanism does not penalize the talented agent by virtue of his possession of a talent for processing resources. Note that LSO implies the Symmetry axiom.

If RMON is replaced by Weak Equity and Symmetry is replaced by LSO, then the outcome-egalitarian conclusion remains true:

THEOREM 3. *Let an allocation mechanism satisfy D^{Σ}, PO, LSO, CONRAD, and WE. Then F is outcome egalitarian on all environments.*

Weak Equity is more palatable than RMON in not committing us to a continuum of comparisons. I do not view the replacement of Symmetry by LSO as imposing a significant cost.

8. INTERPERSONAL COMPARABILITY

Interpersonal comparability of outcome has been assumed thus far; it is that comparability which motivates the symmetry axiom, and LSO just above. Dworkin objects to welfare egalitarianism as an ethic, because among other reasons, he believes people have incommensurable conceptions of the good. If utility is noncomparable, then welfare egalitarianism is meaningless, and any cogent egalitarianism, he says, must be resource egalitarianism. The interpretation of the model I have insisted upon is one in which the kind of welfare measured by the processing functions is the same for all agents, and so Dworkin's incommensurability argument does not apply. As I noted, this narrows the scope of the model, but it makes the assumption of interpersonal comparability easier to accept.

What happens if the outcome measured by the processing functions is postulated to be noncomparable? The symmetry axiom can be dropped and replaced with an axiom of "cardinal noncomparability," which requires the allocation mechanism to view the processing functions as being unique only up to linear transformations.

Axiom of Cardinal Non-Comparability (CNC). Let $\xi = \langle n, \bar{x}, u, v \rangle$ be an environment in Σ and let $\xi^* = \langle n, \bar{x}, \alpha u, \beta v \rangle$ be another environment in Σ where α and β are arbitrary positive constants. Then $F(\xi) = F(\xi^*)$.

Axiom CNC says that the allocation chosen by the mechanism is invariant when the outcome scales are transformed by arbitrary (and different) changes of units, for each individual.

THEOREM 4. *Let an allocation mechanism satisfy D^{Σ}, PO, CNC, RMON and CONRAD. Then F is dictatorial: for all environments, it assigns all the resources that both agents like to the first (or the second) agent.*

Of course, the dictatorial mechanisms are not egalitarian. We can justifiably eliminate them by insisting, for egalitarian reasons, that there should be at least one environment in Σ for which the mechanism assigns some universally liked resources to both agents. In this case, Theorem 4 immediately implies an impossibility theorem: there is no allocation mechanism that satisfies the axioms.

The interpretation of Theorem 4 is that unless interpersonal comparability of outcome is assumed, there is no coherent conception of resource equality. In terms of Dworkin's contention about incommensurability, this theorem argues that the assumption of noncomparability rules out both welfare and resource egalitarian ethics as meaningful.

9. FULL INFORMATION

In the model of this paper, the planner has a great deal of information: he knows the processing functions of the agents, and the resource bundle to be distributed. (He may not know the "hidden resources" that exist, but he does know the processing functions, which incorporate those resources.) The question of responsibility, with which I began, is related to the incompleteness of information concerning internal traits and processing functions. For some interpretations, this is less an issue than for others: the infant survival functions may be objectively computable, while utility functions may not be. I will suggest that the incompleteness of information concerning welfare functions, in particular, carves out a realm for personal responsibility, and thereby drives a wedge between welfare and resource egalitarianism.

I propose four reasons why we may deem a person to be responsible for an action he has done or a trait he has; two of these are intimately related to the incomplete information we have about people's internal states, a third may be related, while the fourth one derives its cogency from an anti-egalitarian premise. (1) Free will: A person is responsible for an action he has taken or a trait that he has acquired because he could have reasonably been expected to have behaved differently. (2) Incentive compatibility and moral hazard: We hold a person responsible because we cannot measure or verify what caused him to do what he did. (3) Value of choice: We allow a sphere of personal responsibility because there is value in letting people make choices for themselves. (4) Social cost: We declare a realm of personal responsibility because it is too costly for society to compensate people fully.

I think reasons (2) and (3) are founded on the incomplete information we have about people, while (1) may be. The incentive compatibility argument is most clearly so founded. We declare the murderer responsible if he cannot demonstrate to us that he was temporarily insane. To allow him simply to declare his insanity, without offering proof, would expose society to a possible moral hazard, an incentive for all murderers to escape responsibility by declaring their (unverifiable) insanity. Private information held by an actor motivates an assignment of personal responsibility by society to him.

The free will argument for responsibility also involves the lack of information, in some of its variants. We can make room for free will in the model by supposing that the processing function measures the potential welfare (outcome) level an agent could achieve with full application of his effort and faculties. In fact, a person with processing function $u(x)$ may expend some less than full degree of effort, in which case he achieves less than $u(x)$ as an outcome level, with consumption of resources x. Then the theorems state that the axioms imply equality of potential welfare, not equality of actual welfare, where the difference is due to the variable efforts expended by the agents exercizing their will.[5] If one is an incompatibilist, and if the variation in effort could be accounted for by a variation in an enzyme or a neurotransmitter over which the agents have no control, that chemical could be included as a resource, and effort would not be an act of free will.[6] To say an instance of effort is an act of free will implies, under incompatibilism, that in the causal tree preceding the act, there is a cause that is not reducible to material, physiological responses. If there is, in fact, no further physical reduction of this nonmaterial cause, then the description of the act's cause is complete. But a "soft" free will belief attributes an act to free will if we lack the information to specify physically some node in the act's causal tree. In this case, the link between free will responsibility and incomplete information is clear. For a compatibilist, on the other hand, it is possible that the causal tree be completely physically specified, yet the act be one of free will. In this case, there is no dependence of free will

5. I owe this argument to G. A. Cohen.
6. An incompatibilist believes determinism and free will are incompatible. Thus, if effort were physically determined, it could not be an instance of free will. See Van Inwagen (1983) for an excellent discussion of the various positions on determinism and free will.

responsibility on incomplete information; but see Van Inwagen (1983) for arguments against compatibilism.

The "value of choice" argument for reserving a realm of personal responsibility is due to Scanlon (1986b), who in turn attributes it in part to Hart. Even given a belief in the "Causal Thesis," Scanlon argues there is value in letting people choose, and a concomitant assignment of responsibility for the consequences of choice; he decomposes that value into three constituent values. There is (1) a predictive or instrumental value in letting people choose, as they will presumably choose what they prefer, and others might not be able to do that for them; (2) a demonstrative value in choice, as when I show my wife the quality of my feelings for her by the very act of choosing an anniversary gift for her; and (3) a symbolic value in personal choice, as when my choice from a menu of exotic Chinese dishes exhibits my competence to others. I think these three values of choice all derive from the incomplete information that is available to us. If I knew everything about you, there would be no predictive or instrumental value in letting you choose: your welfare could as well be fulfulled by my choosing for you, insofar as your getting your preferred option is concerned. If my feelings were transparent, there would be no demonstrative value in the act of my spending time and exercising judgment for my wife's present; she would know the quality of my feelings with certainty, and any such act would be either redundant or a (futile) attempt at dissemblance. Finally, if you knew everything about me, there would be no symbolic value in my choosing, for the choice only has such value to me if there is some doubt in your mind about my competence.[7]

The social cost argument maintains that people should be responsible for some aspects of themselves because it would require too much sacrifice on the part of others fully to compensate them for their handicaps or traits. Although there may be value to this position, it begs the question for the present discussion: for my purpose is to understand the demarcation of the sphere of personal responsibility in order to conclude what degree of social compensation is appropriate. The social cost argument concludes, conversely, that society has limited liability with

7. There remains the question of whether there is a value in choice for the sake of autonomy, which cannot be reduced to the three values discussed by Scanlon. It is hard to think clearly about whether autonomy would have value in a world with perfect information. It seems the "autonomy" value of choice has to do with the value I get from acting and participating in the determination of my own life: but would such a value exist if I knew everything about myself, and there were no uncertainty with regard to the outcomes of the various plans I might choose? The autonomy value of choice seems closely linked to the existence of these uncertainties: it is the value I get from testing and finding my limits, and charting a successful course through unknown seas. The problems posed by this question are deep: I relegate it to a footnote not because it is easily settled, but to acknowledge it.

respect to compensating me by virtue of some already conceived standard concerning how much sacrifice from others can be demanded. Personal responsibility is assigned because excessive social costs would otherwise be incurred. The preconceived standard is one which constrains egalitarianism by some independently arrived at notion of reasonable sacrifice.

10. CONCLUSION

I have argued that, with respect to the naming of resources and types of outcome, it is the latter which is important. Once the type of outcome is identified and fixed, then there is an argument for postulating the anonymity of goods, based on our feelings that the necessity to differentiate, for distributive purposes, among the treatment of goods of different types has to do with our inference that those different goods are important as inputs into outcomes of different types. If, however, our views about the outcome, say welfare, depend on what goods bring it about, then the anonymity of goods is not defensible.

It can be questioned whether the domain of economic environments that is posited is too large: even without naming goods, should it be the case that for any type of welfare (say, infant survival) a possible world exists with arbitrarily specified processing functions, with respect to some set of inputs? Probably not. There are certain "technological" constraints, coming from human biology and culture, which limit the domain to a smaller one than is postulated for the theorems. Thus, even if the anonymity of goods is defensible, the domain axiom is a chink in the model's armor, related to whatever inflexibility is characteristic of human nature.

CONRAD can be weakened to include naming goods, and to include a specification of the goods which are actually hidden in a given environment. If this is done, then an Independence of Hidden Goods axiom must be postulated, which requires the allocation mechanism to treat an environment independently of which goods (if any) are actually hidden in it. I provided a defense of this axiom, on grounds of informational simplicity. The independence of hidden goods assures the planner that the allocation he settles on is the right one, regardless of which goods are later revealed to be hidden in the environment. This is a pragmatic, not an ethical, defense of the axiom. The axiom can still be challenged, as by Scanlon, for not allowing us to distinguish among different internal causes of the same outcome functions, which may in turn imply different views about responsibility and compensation.

I argued that resource monotonicity is a strong axiom, but showed it could be replaced with an axiom of weak equity, which only requires comparing a given economic environment to one benchmark environment.

I find the most compelling criticism of the model to be its full information specification. I think our assignment of responsibility is in large part linked to the incomplete information that we have about how people actually process resources into outcomes. Yet this incompleteness is not represented in the model. More than any explicit axiom, this appears to me to be the key to the evaporation of responsibility in the melding of resource and outcome egalitarianism.

The criticisms provided of the Anonymity of Goods, the Independence of Hidden Goods, the Domain axioms, and the full information assumption are, if taken on board, sufficient to prevent the melding of resource and welfare egalitarianism. The investigation of the theorems presented here focuses the contest of resource versus welfare egalitarianism on these issues, which may not have been the clear issues before. In any case, more careful evaluation of the criticisms is possible, once they are stated in a formal and precise way.

REFERENCES

Cohen, G.A. 1986. "Self-Ownership, World Ownership, and Equality: Part II." *Social Philosophy and Policy* 3:77–96.

Dworkin, Ronald. 1981b. "What is Equality? Part I: Equality of Welfare." *Philosophy and Public Affairs* 10:185–246.

———. 1981a. "What is Equality? Part II: Equality of Resources." *Philosophy and Public Affairs* 10:283–345.

Rawls, John. 1971. *A Theory of Justice*. Cambridge, Mass.: Harvard University Press.

Roemer, John. 1986a. "Equality of Resources Implies Equality of Welfare." *Quarterly Journal of Economics* 101:751–54.

———. 1986b. "The Mismarriage of Bargaining Theory and Distributive Justice." *Ethics* 96:88–110.

Scanlon, Thomas. 1986a. "Equality of Resources and Equality of Welfare: A Forced Marriage?" *Ethics* 97:111–18.

———. 1986b. "The Significance of Choice." *The Tanner Lectures on Human Values*. Brasenose College, Oxford.

Sen, Amartya. 1973. *On Economic Inequality*. Oxford: Clarendon Press.

———. 1979. "Personal Utilities and Public Judgements: or, What's Wrong with Welfare Economics?" *Economic Journal* 89:537–58.

———. 1980. "Equality of What?" *The Tanner Lectures on Human Values*. Vol. I. Salt Lake City: University of Utah Press.

Steiner, Hillel. 1977. "The Natural Right to the Means of Production." *Philosophical Quarterly* 27:41–49.

Van Inwagen, Peter. 1983. *An Essay on Free Will*. Oxford: Oxford University Press.

Varian, Hal. 1975. "Distributive Justice, Welfare Economics and the Theory of Fairness." *Philosophy and Public Affairs* 4:223–47.

Yaari, Menachem, and Bar-Hillel, Maja, 1984. "On Dividing Justly." *Social Choice and Welfare* 1:1–24.

[15]

On the Currency of Egalitarian Justice

*G. A. Cohen**

I. INTRODUCTION

In his Tanner Lecture of 1979 called "Equality of What?" Amartya Sen asked what metric egalitarians should use to establish the extent to which their ideal is realized in a given society. What aspect(s) of a person's condition should count in a *fundamental* way for egalitarians, and not merely as cause of or evidence of or proxy for what they regard as fundamental?

In this study I examine answers to that question, and discussions bearing on that question, in recent philosophical literature. I take for granted that there is something which justice requires people to have equal amounts of, not no matter what, but to whatever extent is allowed by values which compete with distributive equality; and I study what a number of authors who share that egalitarian view have said about the dimension(s) or respect(s) in which people should be made more equal, when the price in other values of moving toward greater equality is not intolerable.

I also advance an answer of my own to Sen's question. My answer is the product of an immanent critique of Ronald Dworkin, one, that is, which rejects Dworkin's declared position because it is not congruent with its own underlying motivation. My response to Dworkin has been influenced by Richard Arneson's work in advocacy of "equality of opportunity for welfare," but my answer to Sen's question is not that Arnesonian one, nor is my answer as well formulated as Arneson's is.[1] It needs much further refinement, but I nevertheless present it here, in a

* I thank Jerry Barnes and Tim Scanlon for their generously extended and very incisive criticism of a draft of this article. And, for their many helpful comments, I also thank Richard Arneson, John Baker, Tim Besley, Ronald Dworkin, John Gardner, David Knott, Will Kymlicka, David Lloyd-Thomas, Grahame Lock, John McMurtry, Michael Otsuka, Derek Parfit, Joseph Raz, Amartya Sen, and Phillippe Van Parijs.

1. See Richard Arneson, "Equality and Equality of Opportunity for Welfare," *Philosophical Studies*, vol. 55 (1989). My criticisms of Dworkin were conceived without knowledge of Arneson's partly parallel ones, but it was reading Arneson which caused me to see what positive view my criticisms implied, even though that view is not the same as Arneson's.

Ethics 99 (July 1989): 906–944

rough and ready form, because of its association with relatively finished criticisms of others which I think are telling. If this study contributes to understanding, it does so more because of those criticisms than because of the positive doctrine it affirms.

In Section II of the article I distinguish between egalitarian theses of different strengths, and I indicate that certain (not all) counter-examples to stronger sorts of theses fail to disturb correlative weaker ones.

Section III scrutinizes two Rawlsian criticisms of equality of welfare. The first says that an uncorrected welfare metric wrongly equates pleasures and preferences which differ in moral character. It puts the pleasure of domination, for example, on a par with pleasure from an innocent pastime, where the two are equal in intensity. And the second criticism says that the welfare metric caters unjustifiably to expensive tastes which are generated by, for example, their bearer's lack of self-discipline. Those criticisms defeat equality of welfare, but, so I claim, they do not, as Rawls thinks, also induce support for a primary goods metric, and the second criticism is, moreover, hard to reconcile with Rawls's views on effort and desert.

Ronald Dworkin refines and extends both Rawlsian criticisms of equality of welfare, although primary goods are replaced by resources in the Dworkinian development of the Rawlsian view. In Section IV I show that much of Dworkin's critique of equality of welfare will be met if egalitarians allow deviations from equality of welfare which reflect people's choices: that is, Arneson's *equal opportunity for welfare* theory. But some of Dworkin's objections to equality of welfare cannot be handled in Arneson's way, and the right response to them is to affirm what I call *equal access to advantage,* where "advantage" is understood to include, but to be wider than, welfare. Under equal access to advantage, the fundamental distinction for an egalitarian is between choice and luck in the shaping of people's fates. I argue that Dworkin's different master distinction, between preferences and resources, is less true to the motivation of his own philosophy than the one I favor is.

Thomas Scanlon argues, however, that the fact that a person chose to develop a certain taste is only superficially significant for distributive justice. The reason, he says, why egalitarians do not compensate people for chosen expensive tastes is that those tastes, being chosen, are ones which they might not have had. According to Scanlon, it is not their chosen but their peripheral or idiosyncratic character which explains why expensive tastes have no claim to be satisfied. In Section V I defend my emphasis on choice against Scanlon's skepticism, but I also significantly amend the choice-centered egalitarian proposal to cater to what seems undeniable in Scanlon's case against it.

Finally, in Section VI, I claim that Amartya Sen's writings on "capability" introduce two answers to his "Equality of What?" question, each of which has its attractions but which differ substantially in content, as I shall show at length elsewhere.[2]

II. METHODOLOGICAL PRELIMINARIES

A person is *exploited* when unfair advantage is taken of him, and he suffers from (bad) *brute luck* when his bad luck is not the result of a gamble or risk which he could have avoided.[3] I believe that the primary egalitarian impulse is to extinguish the influence on distribution of both exploitation and brute luck. To be sure, principled non- and antiegalitarians also condemn (what they consider to be) exploitation, but they do not have the same view of exploitation as egalitarians have, partly because they are less disturbed by brute-luck-derived asset differences which skew distributive outcomes.

On the foregoing sketch of the primary egalitarian impulse, a statement which purports to express and assert it is exposed to two kinds of challenge. First, such a statement might be criticized for misidentifying what should, in the light of the fundamental egalitarian aim, be equalized. I shall myself so criticize Dworkin's equality of resources proposal, since I think that (among other things) it penalizes people who have tastes for which they cannot be held responsible but which, unluckily for them, cost a lot to satisfy. But one might also reject equality of resources on the quite different ground that it conflicts with some important nonegalitarian values. One might say, for example, that while it is indeed brute luck which distributes children into rich and poor families, it would be wrong to seek rectification of the results of that luck, since that would undermine the institution of the family.

In this article I shall not discuss problems for egalitarian proposals of that second kind, problems, that is, of trade-off between equality and other values. That is because I shall treat the various egalitarian proposals to be reviewed below as *weak equalisandum claims.*

An *equalisandum* claim specifies that which ought to be equalized, what, that is, people should be rendered equal in. An unqualified or *strong equalisandum* claim, which is the sort that an uncompromising egalitarian asserts, says that people should be as equal as possible in the dimension it specifies. A qualified or *weak equalisandum* claim says that they should be as equal as possible in some dimension but subject to whatever limitations need to be imposed in deference to other values: those limitations are not specified by the claim in question.

2. See my "Equality of What? On Welfare, Good, and Capabilities," forthcoming in a volume of papers presented at the WIDER symposium on the Quality of Life held in Helsinki in July 1988, and for which not only my piece in the volume but also this one were originally prepared.

3. The latter kind of luck is *option luck.* The distinction between brute and option luck comes from Ronald Dworkin, "Equality of Resources," *Philosophy and Public Affairs* 10 (1981): 293.

Now, strong *equalisandum* claims face objections of the two kinds distinguished above, and which I shall now call *egalitarian* and *nonegalitarian* objections. An egalitarian objection rests on a view about the right way to treat people equally which differs from the one embodied in the strong *equalisandum* claim it challenges. The egalitarian objector thinks that people should be equal, to some or other extent, in something other than what the claim he opposes specifies, but he does not, qua egalitarian objector, object to the *strength* of that claim as such. By contrast, a nonegalitarian objection to a strong *equalisandum* claim says that, while the claim might (and might not) correctly identify what should be equalized, it wrongly fails to defer to nonegalitarian values which restrict the extent to which the form of equality it proposes should be pursued: because of those values, so the objection says, the *equalisandum* proposal is unacceptable (at least) in its strong form. An egalitarian objection to a strong *equalisandum* claim also applies to the weak one correlative to it, whereas a nonegalitarian objection challenges strong proposals only. Since mine will be a weak proposal, objections of a nonegalitarian kind will not detain me.

Taking welfare as a sample *equalisandum* proposal, I shall presently illustrate the distinction I have tried to draw by describing supposed objections to the welfare *equalisandum* which are (*a*) plainly not egalitarian, (*b*) arguably, and so I believe, egalitarian, and (*c*) problematic with respect to how they should be classified. But, before embarking on that exercise in differentiation, a word about what I shall mean by 'welfare' here, and throughout this study. Of the many readings of 'welfare' alive (if not well) in economics and philosophy, I am interested in two: welfare as enjoyment, or, more broadly, as a desirable or agreeable state of consciousness, which I shall call *hedonic welfare;* and welfare as *preference satisfaction,* where preferences order states of the world, and where a person's preference is satisfied if a state of the world that he prefers obtains, whether or not he knows that it does[4] and, a fortiori, whatever hedonic welfare he does or does not get as a result of its obtaining. A person's hedonic welfare increases as he gets more enjoyment, and his

4. These two readings of welfare correspond to Sen's "happiness" and "desire fulfilment" readings and exclude his "choice" reading (see Amartya Sen, "Well-Being, Agency and Freedom," *Journal of Philosophy* 82 [1985]: 187 ff.). It is reasonable to ignore the "choice" reading, since, as Sen shows, it comes from confusion about the relationship between preference and choice. My two readings also correspond to Dworkin's "conscious state" and "relative success" conceptions (see Ronald Dworkin, "Equality of Welfare," *Philosophy and Public Affairs* 10 [1981]: 191–94, 204–9, 220–21). I do not consider welfare as "overall success" (ibid., pp. 209 ff.) because it is very hard to handle, and in any case it is, arguably, undermotivated (see n. 34 below). I also set aside so-called objective theories of welfare (ibid., pp. 224–26), since most philosophers would consider them alternatives to any sort of welfare theory: Scanlon, for whom welfare is preference satisfaction, would describe his theory as antiwelfarist, yet it is an objective theory of welfare in Dworkin's sense. Finally, to complete the review of the five thinkers whose work is salient in this study, Arneson has the same understanding of welfare as Scanlon does, and Rawls has not specified a particular conception, which is not to say that he should have done.

preference satisfaction increases as more of his preferences, or his stronger preferences, are fulfilled. Note that one way to achieve more preference satisfaction is to cultivate, if you can, preferences that are easier to satisfy than those which you currently have.

It will sometimes be necessary to say which of those two ideas I mean by 'welfare,' but not always. For very often the debates on which I comment have a similar shape under either interpretation of welfare, so that I shall have each in mind (by which I do not mean some amalgam of the two) at once. Unless I indicate otherwise, my contentions are meant to hold under either of the two readings of welfare which I just distinguished, and the rest of the present section is a case in point.

a) Many people think that a policy of equalizing welfare is inconsistent with the maintenance of family values, because, so they say, those values endorse practices of benefiting loved ones which generate welfare inequalities.

Now, however penetrating that point may be, it does not represent an egalitarian objection to equality of welfare. Unregulated kinship generosity may be precious on other grounds, but it could not be thought to promote the result that people get an equal amount of something that they should have equal amounts of. Accordingly, if the family values objection indeed has force against equality of welfare, it is a reason for restricting the writ of that particular *equalisandum*, or form of equality, and not a reason for proposing another *equalisandum* in its stead. Family values do not challenge equality of welfare when the latter is construed as a qualified *equalisandum* proposal.

Another objection to unqualified equality of welfare which is not egalitarian is that implementing it would involve intolerably intrusive state surveillance.[5] ("Hi! I'm from the Ministry of Equality. Are you, by any chance, unusually happy today?") Gathering the information needed to apply unqualified equality of resources might well involve less intrusion, and that would be *a* reason for preferring unqualified equality of resources to unqualified equality of welfare, but not one which impugned the egalitarian character of equality of welfare.[6]

Still another nonegalitarian objection to equality of welfare is that, if priority were always given to relieving misery, then no resources could be devoted to maintaining cathedrals and other creations of inestimable

5. I do not have in mind the objection that the level of welfare a person enjoys is none of the state's business. I mean the objection that, whether or not welfare levels are any business of the state, the procedures necessary to find out what they are would be unacceptably invasive.

6. Recall that "an egalitarian objection *rests* on a view about the right way to treat people equally" (see p. 909 above). Hence, even if the "intrusion" objection to unqualified equality of welfare *issued in* support for unqualified equality of resources, it would not therefore be an egalitarian objection.

value. That powerful objection to uncompromising equality of welfare does not challenge the claim that, to the extent that equalization is defensible, welfare is the right thing to equalize.

b) Consider people who convert resources into welfare inefficiently, so that, if welfare is to be equalized, they must be given twice the resources that ordinary converters get. These bad converters divide into various subsets. Some of them are inefficient because they are negligent or feckless in a morally culpable way: they buy their food at Fortnum's because they cannot be bothered to walk up to the Berwick Street market. Others are blamelessly inefficient, because they are in some way disabled. They need twice the normal ration because half of such a double-share is required to overcome the illfare effects of a handicap from which they suffer. That half could be the cost of their renal dialysis.

Now there seems to me to be an egalitarian objection to a policy of ensuring that the Fortnum's customer's welfare level is as high as everybody else's. It seems to me that, when other people pay for his readily avoidable wastefulness, there is, *pro tanto,* an exploitative distribution of burden which egalitarians should condemn. Equality of welfare should here be rejected not because of other values but because it is inegalitarian.

But there could also be an objection to servicing kidney failure (and similar) sufferers to the extent required to equalize welfare: the policy could be said—*is* often said—to have too depressive an effect on the welfare of everybody else in society. Yet, while that may be right, it hardly represents an *egalitarian* objection to equality of welfare. Keeping aggregate welfare high at the expense of kidney sufferers is not a way of distributing something more equally.[7]

c) There are people whose inefficiency at turning resources into welfare is clearly their own fault, and others whose inefficiency is clearly bad luck. But, between these extreme types, there is a vast range of cases where it is unclear whether or not fault applies. It is very hard to say, with respect to many grumpy people, for example, whether they can be held to account for their grumpiness, whether, as we say, they are more to be pitied than blamed. Now grumpy people are bad converters, and, if we feel reluctant to service them with the extra resources they need to become a bit cheerful, then it is unclear whether the objection to equality of welfare associated with that reluctance is (at least in part) egalitarian, since it is unclear whether or not their conversion inefficiency is their own fault.

So much in illustration of different bases on which egalitarian claims might be challenged. Let us now take equality of welfare as a proposed solution to the *equalisandum* problem—it seems to me the most naive one, and therefore a natural one with which to start—and let us see how

7. I believe that I here display disagreement with what Dworkin says in "Equality of Welfare," p. 242, which I find obscure.

it must be modified in the light of egalitarian objections to it which have been raised in recent philosophical literature.

III. RAWLSIAN CRITICISM OF EQUALITY OF WELFARE

A good way to begin is by examining two objections to equality of welfare, in both its hedonic and its preference interpretations,[8] which derive from the work of John Rawls, and which I shall call the *offensive tastes* and *expensive tastes* criticisms. I believe that each criticism can be accommodated by a welfare egalitarian through a natural modification of his original view. In the case of the offensive tastes criticism, that would probably be conceded by Rawls (and by Ronald Dworkin, who develops the criticism more systematically and at some length). But the second criticism is supposed by Rawls and Dworkin to justify an abandonment of the terrain of welfare altogether, and, as I shall indicate, I do not think that it does. The second criticism also creates a problem for Rawls's system, which I shall describe in a brief digression.

Rawls adverts to offensive tastes in the course of his critique of utilitarianism, but, as Amartya Sen notes, he is at that point really criticizing welfarism as such, where welfarism is the view that just distribution is some or other function of nothing but the welfares of individuals.[9] It follows logically that the offensive tastes criticism also applies against a conception of justice in which equality of welfare is the only principle. And although a "weak" (see Sec. II above) egalitarian of welfare need not be a welfarist (save, of course, with respect to the metric of equality in particular), it is extremely unlikely that a good criticism of welfarism proper will not also apply to that restricted welfarism which acknowledges the relevance of no information but welfare in the context of equality, even if its proponent admits non-welfare information elsewhere. In any case, the offensive tastes criticism strikes me as powerful against even a weak welfare-egalitarian claim.

The offensive tastes criticism of welfarism is that the pleasure a person takes in discriminating against other people or in subjecting others to a lesser liberty should not count equally with other satisfactions in the calculus of justice.[10] From the point of view of justice, such pleasures deserve condemnation, and the corresponding preferences have no claim to be satisfied, even if they would have to be satisfied for welfare equality to prevail. I believe that this objection defeats welfarism, and, hence, equality of welfare. But the natural course for a welfare egalitarian to take in response to the offensive tastes criticism is to shift his favor to something like equality of *inoffensive* welfare. The criticism does not seem

8. For the difference between these interpretations, see above.

9. Amartya Sen, "Equality of What?" in *Tanner Lectures on Human Values*, ed. S. McMurrin (Cambridge: Cambridge University Press, 1980), p. 211.

10. John Rawls, *A Theory of Justice* (Cambridge, Mass.: Harvard University Press, 1971), pp 30–31.

to necessitate abandoning equality of welfare in a more fundamental way.[11]

The *expensive tastes* criticism is thought to necessitate such an abandonment. It occurs in the context of Rawls's advocacy of primary goods as the appropriate *equalisandum*: "Imagine two persons, one satisfied with a diet of milk, bread and beans, while the other is distraught without expensive wines and exotic dishes. In short one has expensive tastes, the other does not." A welfare egalitarian must, ceteris paribus, provide the epicure with a higher income than the person of modest taste, since otherwise the latter might be satisfied while the former is distraught. But Rawls argues powerfully against this implication of the welfare egalitarian principle:

> As moral persons citizens have some part in forming and cultivating their final ends and preferences. It is not by itself an objection to the use of primary goods that it does not accommodate those with expensive tastes. One must argue in addition that it is unreasonable, if not unjust, to hold such persons responsible for their preferences and to require them to make out as best they can. But to argue this seems to presuppose that citizens' preferences are beyond their control as propensities or cravings which simply happen. Citizens seem to be regarded as passive carriers of desires. The use of primary goods . . . relies on a capacity to assume responsibility for our ends.

People with expensive tastes could have chosen otherwise, and if and when they press for compensation, others are entitled to insist that they themselves bear the cost "of their lack of foresight or self-discipline."[12]

I believe that this objection defeats welfare egalitarianism but that it does not, as Rawls supposes, also vindicate the claims of the primary goods metric. The right way for an erstwhile welfare egalitarian to respond

11. In fairness to Rawls, one should recall that he presented the offensive tastes criticism as an objection not to equality of welfare but to utilitarianism, and for utilitarians a move to "inoffensive welfare" no doubt constitutes a pretty fundamental shift. From the fact that the same criticism applies against both views, and that each should be revised in the same way in the face of it, it does not follow that the distance between the original and the revised view is the same in both cases.

12. John Rawls, "Social Unity and Primary Goods," in *Utilitarianism and Beyond*, ed. Amartya Sen and Bernard Williams (Cambridge: Cambridge University Press, 1982), pp. 168–69. Compare John Rawls, "Fairness to Goodness," *Philosophical Review* 84 (1975): 553, "Justice as Fairness: Political Not Metaphysical," *Philosophy and Public Affairs* 14 (1985): 243–44. For a somewhat different explanation of why justice ignores expensive tastes, with less (not no) emphasis on the idea that they are subject to the agent's control and more on the idea that it is appropriate to hold him accountable for them, see the reply to Kenneth Arrow ("Some Ordinalist Notes on Rawls' Theory of Justice," in his *Collected Papers* [Cambridge, Mass.: Harvard University Press, 1983], 1:104 ff.) in Rawls's "Citizens' Needs and Primary Goods" (Philosophy Department, Harvard University, Cambridge, Mass., 1986, typescript). For interesting comment on and sympathetic development of Rawls's views on responsibility for preference, see Bruce Landesman, "Egalitarianism," *Canadian Journal of Philosophy* 13 (1983): 37.

to the objection seems to me to be the following: "To the extent that people are indeed responsible for their tastes, the relevant welfare deficits do not command the attention of justice. We should therefore compensate only for those welfare deficits which are not in some way traceable to the individual's choices. We should replace equality of welfare by equality of opportunity for welfare. It would be utterly unjustified to adopt a primary goods metric because of the expensive tastes counter-example."

I shall pursue that response further in the next section, in confrontation with Dworkin's extensive development of the theme of expensive taste. But, before turning to Dworkin, I want to indicate a serious problem for Rawls's system which his remarks about expensive tastes raise.

The problem is that the picture of the individual as responsibly guiding his own taste formation is hard to reconcile with claims Rawls elsewhere uses in a fundamental way to support his egalitarianism. I have in mind the skepticism which he expresses about extra reward for extra effort: "The effort a person is willing to make is influenced by his natural abilities and skills and the alternatives open to him. The better endowed are more likely, other things equal, to strive conscientiously, and there seems to be no way to discount for their greater good fortune. The idea of rewarding desert is impracticable."[13]

Now there are two ways of taking this passage. One way is as I think Rawls intended it, and the other is as Robert Nozick took it, and on the basis of which he entered strong criticism of Rawls. Nozick, I am sure, misread the passage, but his misreading of it constitutes a correct reading of what many socialists and egalitarians say about effort, so it will be worth our while to pause, digressively, to attend to Nozick's criticism. On either reading of the passage, it is hard to reconcile with what Rawls says about foresight, self-discipline, and expensive tastes. But I shall come to that point in a moment, for the passage can also be criticized independently, and I want to do that first.

The two readings of the passage divide with respect to how they take the word 'influenced' in Rawls's use of it here. In my reading of it, it means "influenced." In Nozick's, it means something like "wholly determined." There is difficulty for Rawls whichever way we take it, but not the same difficulty in each case.

In my reading of Rawls, in which he means "influenced" by 'influenced,' he does not say that the more effortful have no control over, and therefore deserve no credit for, the amount of effort they put in. His different point is that we cannot reckon the extent to which their above-par effort is attributable not to admirable striving but to "greater good fortune": there is "no way to discount" for the latter. That is a practical objection to trying to reward effort that deserves reward, not a claim that there is no such effort—see the final sentence of the passage.

13. Rawls, *A Theory of Justice*, p. 312.

If Rawls is right that not all effort is deserving, then, we might agree, not all effort deserves reward. But why should it follow that effort deserves no reward at all? The practical difficulty of telling how much of it merits reward hardly justifies rewarding it at a rate of 0 percent, as opposed to at a rate somewhere between 0 percent and 100 percent, for example, through a taxation scheme whose shape and justification escapes, because of its deference to effort, the writ of the difference principle.

But that criticism of Rawls is mild by comparison with the one to which he is exposed on Nozick's reading of his remarks. The plausibility of that reading is enhanced by Nozick's careless or mischievous omission of what follows "conscientiously" when he exhibits the *Theory of Justice* passage quoted above. Thereby, Nozick creates the impression that Rawls is presenting a familiar egalitarian determinist doctrine. Nozick's response to that doctrine is very powerful. He says that "denigrating a person's autonomy and prime responsibility for his actions is a risky line to take for a theory that otherwise wishes to buttress the dignity and self-respect of autonomous beings. . . . One doubts that the unexalted picture of human beings Rawls' theory presupposes and rests upon can be made to fit together with the view of human dignity it is designed to lead to and embody."[14] Nozick is pressing a dilemma: either people have real freedom of choice, in which case they may be credited (at least to some extent) with the fruits of their labors; or, there is no such thing as free choice, in which case liberals should take the purple out of the passages in which they set forth their conception of humanity, and—we can add—socialists should stop painting inspiring pictures of the human future (unless they believe that people lack free will under capitalism but that they will get it after the revolution).

On Nozick's reading of the "effort" passage, it is clearly inconsistent with the responsibility for taste formation with which Rawls credits citizens. That does not matter so much, since Nozick's reading is a misreading. But it is not easy to reconcile what Rawls says about effort with what he says about tastes even on my less creative reading of his text. On my reading of it, effort is partly praiseworthy and partly not, but we cannot separate the parts, and the indicated policy consequence is to ignore effort as a claim to reward. Now, the passage about tastes begins with the thought that "citizens have *some* part in forming and cultivating their final ends and preferences," though it ends by assigning a more wholesale responsibility for them to citizens. If we stay with the opening thought, then we can wonder why partial responsibility for effort attracts no reward at all while (merely) partial responsibility for expensive taste formation attracts a full penalty (and those who keep their tastes modest reap a welfare reward). And if we shift to the wholesale responsibility motif, then we can wonder why beings who are only in a limited way responsible

14. Robert Nozick, *Anarchy, State and Utopia* (New York: Basic, 1974), p. 214.

for the effort they put in may be held wholly responsible for how their tastes develop.

IV. RELOCATING DWORKIN'S CUT

A

Ronald Dworkin denies that equality of welfare provides the right reading of the egalitarian aim, and I agree with him about that. But I do not share his view that the demise of equality of welfare should prompt egalitarians to embrace equality of resources instead. Part of my reason for disagreeing with Dworkin on that score is my belief, to be defended in a moment, that one of his major objections to equality of welfare can be met by a revised form of that principle. The revised welfare principle, unlike equality of welfare, permits and indeed enjoins departures from welfare equality when they reflect choices of relevant agents, as opposed to deficient *opportunity* for welfare. If a person's welfare is low because he freely risked a welfare loss in gambling for a welfare gain, then, under the opportunity form of the principle, he has no claim to compensation. Nor does a person who frittered away welfare opportunities which others seized. Nor, to take a different kind of example, does a person who chose to forgo welfare out of devotion to an ideal which (expressly, or merely as it happened) required self-denial.

The revised principle can be called equality of opportunity for welfare.[15] It is not a principle that I shall endorse. Equality of opportunity for welfare is a better reading of egalitarianism than equality of welfare itself is, but it is not as good as what currently strikes me as the right reading of egalitarianism, namely, that its purpose is to eliminate *involuntary disadvantage,* by which I (stipulatively) mean disadvantage for which the sufferer cannot be held responsible, since it does not appropriately reflect choices that he has made or is making or would make.[16] Equality of opportunity for welfare eliminates involuntary welfare deficiencies, and welfare deficiencies are forms of disadvantage. Hence the principle I endorse responds to inequalities in people's welfare opportunities. But, as will be illustrated below, advantage is a broader notion than welfare. Anything which enhances my welfare is *pro tanto* to my advantage, but the converse is not true. And disadvantage is correspondingly broader than welfare deficiency, so the view I favor, which can be called *equal opportunity for advantage,* or, preferably, equal *access* to advantage, corrects for inequalities to which equal opportunity for welfare is insensitive.

Why is "equal *access* to advantage" a better name for the view than "equal *opportunity* for advantage" is? We would not normally regard meager personal capacity as detracting from opportunity. Your opportunities are the same whether you are strong and clever or weak and stupid: if you

15. For a clear articulation and persuasive defense of it, in its preference satisfaction interpretation, see Arneson's "Equality and Equality of Opportunity for Welfare."

16. The need to add that third disjunct is explained in Sec. V*A* below.

are weak and stupid, you may not use them well—but that implies that you have them. But shortfalls on the side of personal capacity nevertheless engage egalitarian concern, and they do so because they detract from access to valuable things, even if they do not diminish the opportunity to get them. Hence my preference for "access,"[17] but I still require this possibly unnatural stipulation: I shall treat anything which a person actually has as something to which he has access.[18]

Some of Dworkin's counter-examples to equality of welfare fail to challenge equality of opportunity for welfare, and they fail, a fortiori, to challenge the wider disadvantage principle. The Dworkin examples I here have in mind, which are to do with expensive tastes, not only do not challenge equality of opportunity for welfare: one can say the stronger thing that they bring its claims to the fore as a candidate reading of the egalitarian aim. But other counter-examples to equality of welfare presented by Dworkin necessitate movement beyond equality of opportunity for welfare to the broader conception of equality of access to advantage. One sort of counter-example that has that effect concerns handicaps, in the literal sense of the word, and I shall be presenting a handicap counter-example to equality of opportunity for welfare at the beginning of the next subsection.

In my view, however, equality of resources is subject to objections which are just as strong as those which defeat equality of welfare (and equality of opportunity for welfare). I shall now defend that conclusion, by describing the case of a doubly unfortunate person. I believe that egalitarians will be moved to compensate him for both of his misfortunes, but the fact that the first calls for egalitarian compensation challenges equality of welfare and the fact that the second does challenges equality of resources.

B

My unfortunate person's legs are paralyzed. To get around, he needs an expensive wheelchair. Egalitarians will be disposed to recommend that he be given one. And they will be so disposed before they have asked about the welfare level to which the man's paralysis reduces him. When compensating for disability, egalitarians do not immediately distinguish between the different amounts of misery induced by similar disabilities in people who have different (dis)utility functions. They propose

17. For analogous reasons, Arneson would have been better advised to call his theory "equality of access to welfare."

18. I am not entirely happy with the word 'advantage' in the title of the view I am espousing; I use the word only because I have been unable to find a better one. Its infelicity relates to the fact that it is so frequently used to denote competitive advantage, advantage, that is, *over* somebody else. But here 'advantage' must be understood shorn of that implication, which it does not always have. Something can add to someone's advantage without him, as a result, being better placed, or less worse placed, than somebody else, and the word will here be used in that noncompetitive sense.

compensation for the disability *as such*, and not, or not only, for its deleterious welfare effects. Insofar as we can distinguish compensation for resource deficiency from compensation for welfare deficiency, the first appears to enjoy independent egalitarian favor.

The egalitarian response to disability seems to defeat not only equality of welfare but also equality of opportunity for welfare. Tiny Tim is not only *actually* happy, by any standard. He is also, because of his fortunate disposition, blessed with abundant *opportunity* for happiness: he need not do much to get a lot of it. But egalitarians would not on that account strike him off the list of free wheelchair receivers. They do not think that wheelchair distribution should be controlled exclusively by the welfare opportunity requirements of those who need them. Lame people need them to be adequately resourced, whether or not they also need them to be, or to be capable of being, happy.

Note that I do not say that, whatever other demands they face, egalitarians will always service people like Tiny Tim. One could imagine him surrounded by curably miserable sound-limbed people whose welfare was so low that their requirements were judged to precede his. The essential point is that his abundant happiness is not as such decisive against compensating him for his disability.

In face of (what I say are) the intuitive phenomena, the only way of sustaining the view that equality of welfare is the right reading of the egalitarian aim is to claim that egalitarians propose assistance for disability without gathering welfare information because of a general correlation between disability and illfare which it is impossible or too costly to confirm in individual cases. Like Sen and Dworkin, I find that defense unpersuasive, and I consequently conclude that the egalitarian response to disability defeats equality of welfare.[19] And, as I argued, it also defeats equality of opportunity for welfare, since the response to disability is shaped by something other than the different costs in lost opportunity for welfare which disability causes in different people.

I have not completed my description of the man's misfortune. There is also something wrong with his arms. He is not less able to move them than most people are: I shall even assume, to make my point more vivid, that he is especially good at moving them. But there is, nevertheless, something seriously wrong with them, and it is this: after he moves them, he suffers severe pain in his arm muscles.

In the terms of a distinction which I once had occasion to make in a different context, it is not *difficult* for the man to move his arms, but it is very *costly* for him to do so.[20] What I call 'difficulty' and 'cost' are two

19. Dworkin, "Equality of Welfare," pp. 241–42, following Sen, "Equality of What?" pp. 217–18. Sen is surely right that it is his deficient capability as such which explains the claim to assistance of a contented crippled person who requires expensive prosthesis and who is not particularly poor. Compare Sen, "Well-Being, Agency and Freedom," pp. 195–97.

20. G. A. Cohen, *Karl Marx's Theory of History* (Oxford: Oxford University Press, 1978), p. 238.

widely conflated but importantly distinct ways in which it can be *hard* for a person to do something. (It is costly, but not difficult, for me to supply you with a check for £500, or for me to tell you some secret the revelation of which will damage me. It is extremely difficult for me to transport you to Heathrow on the back of my bicycle, but it is not costly, since I love that kind of challenge, and I have nothing else to do today. At the far end of the difficulty continuum lies the *impossible*, but it is the *unbearable* which occupies that position in the case of costliness.)[21]

Now there is an expensive medicine which, taken regularly, suppresses the pain that otherwise follows the man's arm movement, and this medicine is so expensive that it has no adverse side effects. Egalitarians would, I am sure, favor supplying our man with the medicine, even if it costs what a wheelchair does. But providing the medicine cannot be represented as compensating for a resource incapacity. The man's capacity to move his arms is, *in the relevant sense*, better (so I stipulated) than that of most people.

"In the relevant sense" does a lot of work here, so let me explain it. Someone might insist, and I do not have to deny, that there is *a* sense in which a typical normal person has a capacity which this man lacks. I need not deny that he lacks the capacity to move his arms without pain, or, if you prefer, to move his arms without pain without taking medicine. I can even agree that it is his lack of *that* capacity which is the egalitarian ground for compensating him. *But compensating for a lack of capacity which needs to be described in that way for the ground of the compensation to be revealed cannot be represented as compensating for incapacity when that is opposed to compensating for welfare opportunity deficiency.* A would-be resource egalitarian who said, "Compensation is in order here because the man lacks the resource of being able to avoid pain" would be invoking the idea of equality of opportunity for welfare even if he would be using resourcist language to describe it.

My example was medically fanciful, but a medically more ordinary example makes the same point, though you have to exercise slightly sharper perception to see it. It was fanciful in the foregoing case that the pain should wholly succeed and not also accompany the pain-inducing movement. Think now of a more ordinary case, in which arthritic pain accompanies movement, and suppose, what is likely, that the movement is not only painful but, consequently and/or otherwise, *also* difficult. That difficulty introduces a resource deficiency into the case, but the example nevertheless stands as a challenge to equality of resources. For it seems not coherently egalitarian to cater only to the difficulty of moving and not independently to the pain which moving occasions. So there is an irreducible welfare aspect in the case for egalitarian compensation in real-life disability examples.

21. A man otherwise like the one I described might find it difficult to move his arms for the psychological reason that he could not face the thought of what would follow their movement. But my man is psychologically robust: he can easily move his arms, though he often (coolly) decides not to on occasions when other people would move theirs.

Or just think of poor people in Britain who suffer discomfort in the winter cold. The egalitarian case for helping them with their electricity bills is partly founded on that discomfort itself. It does not rest entirely on the disenablement which the cold, both through discomfort and independently, also causes.

People vary in the amount of discomfort which given low temperatures cause them, and, consequently, in the volume of resources which they need to alleviate their discomfort. Some people need costly heavy sweaters and a great deal of fuel to achieve an average level of thermal well-being. With respect to warmth, they have what Dworkin calls *expensive tastes:* they need unusually large doses of resources to achieve an ordinary level of welfare. They are losers under Dworkin's equality of resources, because, as we shall see, it sets itself against compensation for expensive tastes.

The two grounds of egalitarian compensation which apply in the case of the disabled man have something in common. The man's straightforward inability to move his legs and his liability to pain when moving his arms are both disadvantages for which (I tacitly assumed) he cannot be held responsible, and, I suggest, that is why an egalitarian would compensate him for them. Both aspects of his plight represent unavoidable disadvantages, which he was unable to forestall and which he cannot now rectify. On my understanding of egalitarianism, it does not enjoin redress of or compensation for disadvantage as such. It attends, rather, to "involuntary" disadvantage, which is the sort that does not reflect the subject's choice. People's advantages are unjustly unequal (or unjustly equal) when the inequality (or equality) reflects unequal access to advantage, as opposed to patterns of choice against a background of equality of access. Severe actual disadvantage is a fairly reliable sign of inequality of access to advantage, but the prescribed equality is not of advantage per se but of access, all things considered, to it.

When deciding whether or not justice (as opposed to charity) requires redistribution, the egalitarian asks if someone with a disadvantage could have avoided it or could now overcome it.[22] If he could have avoided it, he has no claim to compensation, from an egalitarian point of view. If he could not have avoided it but could now overcome it, then he can ask that his effort to overcome it be subsidized, but, unless it costs more to overcome it than to compensate for it without overcoming it, he cannot expect society to compensate for his disadvantage.

I affirm equality of access to advantage, whatever advantage is rightly considered to be, but I cannot say, in a pleasingly systematic way, exactly what should count as an advantage, partly because I have not thought hard enough about this question, which is surely one of the deepest in normative philosophy.[23] What does appear clear is that resource deficiencies

22. The answers to those questions will not always be as simple as the sample answers that follow, but they are always the right questions to ask.

23. Another matter about which I cannot say anything systematic is the problem of how to compare the net advantage positions of different people. The right place to begin

and welfare deficiencies are distinct types of disadvantage and that each of them covers pretty distinct subtypes: poverty and physical weakness are very different kinds of resource limitation, and despondency and failure to achieve aims are very different kinds of illfare. Whatever the boundaries and types of welfare may be,[24] lack of pain is surely a form of it, and lack of disability, considered just as such, is not, *if* there is to be a contrast between equality of resources and equality of welfare. Those two classificatory judgments are reasonably uncontentious, and they are the ones I need to sustain the criticism of Dworkin which arises from reflection on the case of involuntary pain.

(I warned at the outset that my positive proposal would be crude. One thing that makes it so and makes me wish that it will be superseded is the unlovely heterogeneity of the components of the vector of advantage. One hopes that there is a currency more fundamental than either resources or welfare in which the various egalitarian responses which motivated my proposal can be expressed. But I certainly have not discovered it, so, at least for now, I stay with the appearances, which contradict welfare, resources, and opportunity for welfare readings of the egalitarian demand, and which point, in the first instance, to the theory [or semitheory: it is perhaps too close to the intuitive phenomena to merit the name 'theory'] I have affirmed.)

C

Whatever number of dimensions the space of disadvantage may have, egalitarianism, on my reading, cuts through each of its dimensions, judging certain inequalities of advantage as acceptable and others as not, its touchstone being a set of questions about the responsibility or lack of it of the disadvantaged agent.

In Ronald Dworkin's different reading of egalitarianism, people are to be compensated for shortfalls in their powers, that is, their material resources and mental and physical capacities, but not for shortfalls traceable to their tastes and preferences. What they get should reflect differences in what they want and seek, but not in their *ability* to get things.

Dworkin's "cut" contrasts with mine in two ways. First, it calls for compensation for resource deficiencies only, and not also for pain and other illfare considered as such. "There is no place in [Dworkin's] theory . . . for comparisons of the welfare levels of different people," nor, I infer, for catering to people whose pains do not diminish their capacity, since that service reflects a judgment about how their welfare, in one

would be with Amartya Sen's perspicacious discussion of the (at least) structurally analogous problem of how to order different capability-sets (see his *Commodities and Capabilities* [Amsterdam: North-Holland, 1985], chap. 5). (I say "[at least] structurally analogous" because it may turn out to be the same problem [see Sec. VI below].)

24. Dworkin's "Equality of Welfare" is a masterful exposé of ambiguities in the concept of welfare, even if it does not prove that egalitarian justice should ignore welfare comparisons.

relevant sense, compares with that of others.[25] My cut awards redress for both resource and welfare disadvantages, but, in Dworkin's theory, there is not even "some small room for equality of welfare," alongside other considerations.[26]

So, for purposes of egalitarian intervention, Dworkin-style, only one dimension of disadvantage is recognized. And the second difference between our cuts is that, within that single resource dimension, Dworkin does not put absence of responsibility in the foreground as a necessary condition of just compensation.

I say that the question of responsibility is not *foregrounded* in Dworkin's presentation, because I shall argue that, insofar as he succeeds in making his cut plausible, it is by obscuring both of the differences between it and the different cut that I have recommended. I shall also argue that the grounding idea of Dworkin's egalitarianism is that no one should suffer because of bad brute luck and that, since the relevant opposite of an unlucky fate is a fate traceable to its victim's control, my cut is more faithful to Dworkin's grounding idea than the one he ostensibly favors is.

For Dworkin, it is not choice but preference which excuses what would otherwise be an unjustly unequal distribution. He proposes compensation for power deficiencies, but not for expensive tastes,[27] whereas I believe that we should compensate for disadvantage beyond a person's control, as such, and that we should not, accordingly, draw a line between unfortunate resource endowment and unfortunate utility function.[28] A person with *wantonly* expensive tastes has no claim on us, but neither does a person whose powers are feeble because he recklessly failed to develop them. There is no moral difference, from an egalitarian point of view, between a person who irresponsibly acquires (or blamelessly chooses to develop) an expensive taste and a person who irresponsibly loses (or blamelessly chooses to consume) a valuable resource. The right cut is between responsibility and bad luck, not between preferences and resources.

The difference between those two cuts will have policy significance in the case of those expensive tastes which cannot be represented as reflecting choice. There will be no policy difference with respect to Dworkin's leading example of a person with expensive tastes. I refer to Louis, who requires ancient claret and plovers' eggs in order to reach an ordinary

25. The quoted material is from Dworkin, "Equality of Resources," p. 335.

26. Dworkin, "Equality of Welfare," p. 240.

27. On the hedonic conception of welfare, *X*'s taste is *pro tanto* more expensive than *Y*'s if more resources are needed to raise *X* to a given level of enjoyment. On the preference satisfaction conception of welfare, levels of preference satisfaction replace levels of enjoyment in the characterization of what makes a taste expensive. The discussion below of expensive tastes may be interpreted along either hedonic or preference lines.

28. An unfortunate utility function could itself be regarded as a resource deficiency, but not by someone concerned to contrast equality of resources and equality of welfare.

level of welfare. I treat Louis in practice the way Dworkin does, because, as Dworkin describes him, he did not just get stuck with his taste: he schooled himself into it. But, while Dworkin and I both refuse Louis's request for a special allowance, we ground our refusals differently. Dworkin says: sorry, Louis, we egalitarians do not finance expensive tastes; whereas I say: sorry Louis, we egalitarians do not finance expensive tastes which people choose to develop.

Now consider a case of expensive taste where there will be a policy difference. Paul loves photography, while Fred loves fishing.[29] Prices are such that Fred pursues his pastime with ease while Paul cannot afford to. Paul's life is a lot less pleasant as a result: it might even be true that it has less meaning than Fred's does. I think the egalitarian thing to do is to subsidize Paul's photography. But Dworkin cannot think that. His envy test for equality of resources is satisfied: Paul can afford to go fishing as readily as Fred can. Paul's problem is that he hates fishing and, so I am permissibly assuming, could not have helped hating it—it does not suit his natural inclinations. He has a genuinely involuntary expensive taste, and I think that a commitment to equality implies that he should be helped in the way that people like Paul are indeed helped by subsidized community leisure facilities. As this example suggests, there is between Dworkin's account of egalitarian justice and mine the difference that my account mandates less market pricing than his does.

I distinguish among expensive tastes according to whether or not their bearer can reasonably be held responsible for them. There are those which he could not have helped forming and/or could not now unform, and then there are those for which, by contrast, he can be held responsible, because he could have forestalled them and/or because he could now unlearn them. Notice that I do not say that a person who deliberately develops an expensive taste deserves criticism. I say no such severe thing because there are all kinds of reasons why a person might want to develop an expensive taste, and it is each person's business whether he does so or not. But it is also nobody else's business to pick up the tab for him if he does. Egalitarians have good reason not to minister to deliberately cultivated expensive tastes, and equality of welfare must, therefore, be rejected. But we should not embrace equality of resources instead, since that doctrine wrongly refuses compensation for involuntary expensive tastes, and it does not refuse compensation for voluntary ones for the right reason.

In Dworkin's view, only the principle of equality of resources can explain why Louis's expensive tastes should not be indulged by egalitarians. But his long discussion of Louis rejects the most obvious reason the egalitarian has for denying Louis the resources needed to service his taste: that he "sets out deliberately to cultivate" it.[30] It is crucial that, as

29. I thank Alice Knight for this example.
30. Dworkin, "Equality of Welfare," p. 229.

Dworkin acknowledges, "Louis has a choice": the taste is not instilled in him by a process which circumvents his volition.[31]

Instead of foregrounding the fact of Louis's choice, Dworkin asserts that he can be denied extra resources only if we think that, were Louis to demand them, he would be asking for more than his fair share of resources, where "fair share" is defined in welfare-independent terms. For Dworkin, it requires great "ingenuity" to "produce some explanation or interpretation of the argument in question—that Louis does not deserve more resources just because he has chosen a more expensive life—which does not use the idea of fair shares or any similar ideas."[32]

Now, it is certainly, because trivially, true that if we think that Louis should be denied the resources he demands, then we must believe that he would have more than his fair share if we gave them to him. But we could use equality of opportunity for welfare to define fair shares here: we could say that shares are fair when they equalize welfare opportunities. It is therefore false, and it scarcely takes ingenuity to show it, that only if we move toward equality of resources, toward fair shares in Dworkin's special sense, can we explain egalitarianism's lack of sympathy for Louis.

I conclude that while it is indeed true that "expensive tastes are embarrassing for the theory that equality means equality of welfare precisely because we believe that equality . . . condemns rather than recommends compensating for deliberately cultivated expensive tastes," the proposal that equality means equality of opportunity for welfare[33] glides by the Louis counter-example.[34]

31. The quoted material is from ibid., p. 237.

32. Ibid., p. 239.

33. Which must, on other grounds, be broadened into equality of access to advantage (see Secs. IV*B* and IV*D*). The quoted material is from Dworkin, "Equality of Welfare," p. 235.

34. Equality of opportunity for welfare and, a fortiori, equality of access to advantage, also supply what seems to me to be an adequate response to a complicated argument which Dworkin thinks contributes a great deal to this drive to subvert equality of welfare in favor of equality of resources. The argument first appears in the context of Dworkin's exploration of the hypothesis that equality of welfare be understood as equality of overall success—that hypothesis surfaces after the supposed wreckage of several previous ones. The argument has two premises, each of which I find hard to assess, but neither of which I shall here contest. The first premise is that "equality of overall success cannot be stated as an attractive ideal at all without making the idea of reasonable regret central" (ibid., p. 217): equality of overall success will seem defensible only if it promises to make people "equal in what they have reasonably to regret" (ibid., pp. 217, 218). And the second premise is that the idea of reasonable regret "requires an independent theory of fair shares of social resources . . . which would contradict equality of overall success" (ibid., p. 217). But if both premises are true, so that such a theory is indeed required, why can it not be a theory which says that shares are fair when they induce equality of opportunity for welfare, or equality of access to advantage? I do not find anything in Dworkin's dense ratiocination which appears to rule that out. It follows that the supposed self-destruction of equality of welfare on the altar of reasonable regret is much less of an argument for equality of resources than Dworkin appears to think it is. (For criticism of Dworkin's second premise, see James Griffin, "Modern Utilitarianism," *Revue Internationale de Philosophie* 36 [1982]: 365–66; and for an

D

While a proponent of equality of opportunity for welfare can readily deal with Louis, the case of Jude is much harder for him to handle.[35] I shall argue that Jude's case reflects credit on equality of access to advantage, by comparison with both equality of resources and equality of opportunity for welfare.

Jude has what might be called *cheap expensive tastes.* They are cheap in that he needs fewer resources to attain the same welfare level as others. But they are expensive in that he could have achieved that welfare level with fewer resources still, had he not cultivated tastes more expensive than those with which he began. Jude began with very modest desires, but then he read Hemingway and cultivated a desire to watch bullfights, and, once he had it, he needed more money than before to achieve an average level of welfare, though still less than what others needed.

A believer in equality of opportunity for welfare has to keep Jude poor, since he did not have to become a bullfight-lover (it is reasonable to suppose that he could have suppressed, at no great cost, his desire to cultivate that taste). A believer in Dworkin-style equality of resources ignores Jude's tastes, and their history, and finds no reason, in anything said so far, to grant him less income than anyone else. I reject both views. Pace equality of opportunity for welfare, I see no manifest injustice in Jude's getting the funds he needs to travel to Spain. He then still has fewer resources than others, and only the same welfare, so equality of access to advantage cannot say, on that basis, that he is overpaid. But, pace equality of resources, it seems not unreasonable to expect Jude to accept some deduction from the normal resource stipend because of his fortunate high ability to get welfare out of resources. Unlike either Dworkin's theory or Arneson's, mine explains why both gross underresourcing and gross "underwelfaring" (despite, respectively, a decent welfare level and a decent resource bundle) look wrong.[36]

E

There are some expensive tastes which Dworkin regards as "obsessions" or "cravings" and which he is prepared to assimilate to resource deficiency, for the purposes of distributive justice. This kind of taste is one that its bearer "wishes he did not have, because it interferes with what he wants to do with his life and offers him frustration or even pain if it is not

argument that the idea of overall success should never have been floated in the first place, see sec. 4 of Richard Arneson's "Liberalism, Distributive Subjectivism and Equal Opportunity for Welfare" [Department of Philosophy, University of California, San Diego, 1987, typescript].)

35. Dworkin, "Equality of Welfare," pp. 239–40.

36. I do not feel comfortable about this victory, since, in achieving it, I exploit to the hilt a feature of my theory which I regard as suspect: the heterogeneity of its conception of advantage (see latter part of Sec. IV*B* above).

satisfied."[37] Dworkin concludes that "these tastes are handicaps," and, since equality of resources redistributes for handicap, it will presumably do so (within the bounds of practicality) in the case of tastes which meet the quoted description.

Now, Dworkin's description of them assigns (at least) two features to "handicap" tastes, and he fails to say which feature makes them handicaps, or, equivalently, endows their owner with a claim to compensation. Is the crucial feature of the taste the fact that the person wishes he did not have it? Or is it his reason for wishing he did not have it, namely, that, among other things, it threatens to cause him frustration and pain?[38]

The latter proposal is unavailable to Dworkin. An involuntary liability to frustration and pain does indeed command compensation, but, as I urged in Section IV*B* above, that thought reflects egalitarian sensitivity to people's welfare, rather than to their resources position. Since Dworkin defends intervention in response to handicaps but not in response to shortfalls in welfare, he is not entitled to classify a taste as a handicap *because* it causes pain.

But perhaps the crucial feature of the tastes we are considering is that the individual whose tastes they are "wishes he did not have" them. He disidentifies with them, so that—we can attribute this thought to Dworkin—they are not inalienable aspects of his person (see Sec. IV*F* below), but more like unfortunate environing circumstances. They form no part of his *ambition,* in the special sense in which Dworkin uses that word, and that is why equality of resources can regard them as handicaps. I believe that this is indeed Dworkin's position, that the following regimented statement of it is not unfair: tastes are (subsidy-warranting) handicaps if and only if they represent obsessions, which they do if and only if the individual whose tastes they are disidentifies with them.

I have four comments on the thesis that it is the individual's alienation from his taste which makes it an obsession and therefore allows us to regard it as a handicap.

1. Some people in the grip of cravings are too unreflective to form the second-order preference-repudiating preference by reference to which Dworkin justifies the "handicap" epithet. But it would seem unfair to deny to them the assistance to be extended to others, just because of their deficient reflectiveness. So the disidentification criterion does not cover all compensation-worthy cravings.

2. Not all tastes which hamper the individual's life and therefore raise a case for compensation qualify either as obsessions or as tastes whose bearers, even if highly reflective, would repudiate. Paul (see Sec.

37. Dworkin, "Equality of Resources," p. 302.

38. This is one of several key places at which there is reason to regret that, in expounding his views, Dworkin abjures the device of canonical statement. Other cases in point are passages quoted at Sec. IV*F* below (on choosing tastes and choosing pursuits) and passages quoted at Secs. IV*F* and IV*G*, which give three materially different renderings of Dworkin's "master cut."

IV*C* above) might not want not to want to take pictures, and a person whose unhappy taste is "for music of a sort difficult to obtain" might well not disidentify with his desire for that music.[39] He has *a* reason to regret his musical preference, since it causes him frustration, but that is not a conclusive reason for wishing he did not have it. What he most likely regrets is not (as Dworkin stipulates) his musical preference as such, but the impossibility or expense of satisfying it. His taste is involuntary and unfortunate, but it is probably not an "obsession" or "craving": addiction is not the right model here.

A typical unrich bearer of an expensive musical taste would regard it as a piece of bad luck *not that he has the taste itself but that it happens to be expensive* (I emphasize those words because, simple as the distinction they formulate may be, it is one that undermines a lot of Dworkin's rhetoric about expensive tastes). He might say that in a perfect world he would have chosen to have his actual musical taste, but he would also have chosen that it not be expensive. He can take responsibility for the taste, for his personality being that way, while reasonably denying responsibility for needing a lot of resources to satisfy it.

3. By contrast with the more representative person described above, Dworkin's music craver prefers not to have his unfortunate preference yet, by hypothesis, persists in having it. That rather suggests that he cannot help having it, and that in turn raises the suspicion that it is its unchosen and uncontrolled, rather than its dispreferred, character, which renders compensation for it appropriate. Would not Dworkin's attitude to the music craver be less solicitous if he learned that he had been warned not to cultivate his particular musical interest by a sapient teacher who knew it would cause frustration?

4. Suppose that there was no such warning, that our unfortunate contracted his expensive taste innocently, and that we now offer him, gratis, an inexpensive unrepugnant therapy which would school him out of it. If he agrees to the free therapy, then, so I believe, the ideal of equality says that he should get it, regardless of whether he says farewell to his taste with unmixed relief or, instead, with a regret which reflects some degree of identification. This suggests that identification and disidentification matter for egalitarian justice only if and insofar as they indicate presence and absence of choice.[40]

F

The foregoing reflection brings me to the claim which I ventured in Section IV*C*, to wit, that, insofar as we find Dworkin's cut plausible, it is because we are apt to suppose that it separates presence and absence of

39. The quote comes from Dworkin, "Equality of Resources," p. 302.

40. For an amendment to that suggestion, see Sec. V*A* below, where, inter alia, I comment on the case, which is not addressed above, of a person who would refuse the offer of therapy because of his musical convictions.

choice. Choice is in the background, doing a good deal of unacknowledged work. Here is a passage which supports this allegation: "It is true that [my] argument produces a certain view of the distinction between a person and his circumstances, and assigns his tastes and ambitions to his person, and his physical and mental powers to his circumstances. That is the view of the person I sketched in the introductory section, of someone who *forms* his ambitions with a sense of their cost to others against some presumed initial equality of economic power, and though this is different from the picture assumed by equality of welfare, it is a picture at the center of equality of resources."[41]

This passage offers two characterizations of "tastes and ambitions" in putative justification of placing them outside the ambit of redistributive compensation. The first says that, by contrast with mental and physical powers, they belong to the person rather than to his circumstances. But, in the usual senses of those words, that classification cannot be sustained. Using language in the ordinary way, my mental powers are as integral to what I am as my tastes and ambitions are. The person/circumstances distinction must therefore be a technical one, which means that there must be another way of expressing it, and a possible different way emerges in the second sentence of the passage. That different way has to do with the suggestion that people *form* their preferences but not, presumably, their powers. But there are difficulties with this suggestion.

The first is that it proposes a false alignment. People certainly form some of their ambitions, but they arguably do not form all of them, and they certainly do not form all of their tastes, which are also supposed to belong to the person.[42] Dworkin emphasizes that people "decide what sort of lives to pursue," but they do not decide what in all pertinent respects their utility functions will be: pace Dworkin, they are extensively unable to "decide what sorts of lives they *want*."[43] So being "formed" by the person cannot be a necessary condition of being part of the person, if tastes and ambitions make up the person.

It confirms my claim that Dworkin's cut looks plausible because it seems to separate presence and absence of choice that he uses the two phrases "decide what sort of life to pursue" and "decide what sort of life

41. Dworkin, "Equality of Resources," p. 302, my emphasis. The word 'produces' in the first sentence of the passage should, Dworkin confirms, be 'presupposes': note the contrast with the picture "assumed" by equality of welfare. (But the question whether Dworkin has argued for, as opposed to from, his distinction does not matter here.) Dworkin does not describe the different picture which he thinks is assumed by equality of welfare. If it is a picture of the person as passive and unchoosing, that would help to justify my immanent critique of his view. For that picture, see Rawls, "Social Unity and Primary Goods," p. 169.

42. Dworkin does not actually say in the passage under scrutiny that people form their *tastes*: "tastes and ambitions" have shrunk to "ambitions" by the time that we get to the motif of self-formation. But unless Dworkin claims that tastes, too, are in general formed, on what basis is he here assigning them to a person's person?

43. The quotes are from Dworkin, "Equality of Resources," p. 288, my emphasis.

one wants" interchangeably, thus assimilating two very different kinds of process, only the first of which straightforwardly embodies choice, in the general case. Elsewhere, and similarly, "the choice between expensive and less expensive *tastes*" is put on the same level as "choosing a more [or a less] expensive *life*."[44] And we are also told, in another place, that, when "people choose plans or schemes for their lives," "their choices define a set of [resultant] preferences."[45] That formulation sweeps away the (often unchosen)[46] preferences which lie in the determining background of choice. A person in possession of his faculties always chooses (within the constraints he faces) what career to pursue, but he does not always choose what career to prefer, and the latter fact may reasonably restrict his responsibility for choosing to pursue an expensive one.

Being "formed" is not only not a necessary condition of belonging to what Dworkin calls the person: it is also not a sufficient one. For mental and physical powers fall outside the person, in his circumstances, and some of those powers are, unquestionably, formed. On either side of the preference/circumstance line people both find things and form things. Hence appeal to formedness does not show that distributive justice should ignore variations in preference and taste.

If, moreover, the false alignment (formed/not formed = person/circumstances) indeed worked, it would, surely, constitute a reduction of the person/circumstances distinction to the distinction between what is and what is not subject to choice. To repeat one of my main claims: it is only because Dworkin's preference/resource distinction *looks* alignable with the one it cannot in the end match that it commands appeal.

The idea that we *form* our ambitions is absent from a different formulation of the person/circumstances distinction, which comes soon after the one we have just studied: "The distinction required by equality of resources is the distinction between those beliefs and attitudes that define what a successful life would be like, which the ideal assigns to the person, and those features of body or mind or personality that provide means or impediments to that success, which the ideal assigns to the person's circumstances."[47] This proposal has different implications from the one (see above) which counterposes *tastes and ambitions* to circumstances, since

44. Ronald Dworkin, "Liberalism," in his *A Matter of Principle* (Oxford: Oxford University Press, 1985), p. 193, my emphases.

45. Dworkin, "Equality of Welfare," p. 206. I introduce 'resultant' to forestall the misinterpretation that Dworkin means that the choices *reflect* preferences.

46. "Many of a person's desires are indeed voluntary, since they derive simply from his own decisions. Someone typically acquires the desire to see a certain movie, for example, just by making up his mind what movie to see. Desires of this sort are not aroused in us; they are formed or constructed by acts of will that we ourselves perform, often quite apart from any emotional or affective state. However, there are also occasions when what a person wants is not up to him at all, but is rather a matter of feelings or inclinations that arise and persist independently of any choice of his own" (Harry Frankfurt, *The Importance of What We Care About* [Cambridge: Cambridge University Press, 1988], p. 107).

47. Dworkin, "Equality of Resources," p. 303.

not all ambitions, and few tastes, are informed by beliefs and attitudes: plenty of tastes and ambitions arise without being drawn forth by any sort of doxastic pull.[48] But I shall here set aside the problem of discrepancy between the "belief" cut and the "preference" one, in order to assess the belief cut in its own terms, in the light of Dworkin's larger purposes.

Within those purposes, the person/circumstances distinction is meant to be not only exclusive but (relevantly) exhaustive: we do not have to review anything beyond people's persons and circumstances to know how to treat them from an egalitarian point of view.[49] But, if that is so, then where are we to place the life-enhancing feature of cheerfulness, from the point of view of egalitarian justice? Cheerfulness raises two difficulties, one small and one big.

First, the small difficulty. Cheerfulness is not something that "defines what a successful life would be like." It should therefore count as a circumstance. But circumstances are elsewhere characterized as powers and incapacities, and cheerfulness is neither of those. It is not a power but a fortunate disposition which, for given inputs, generates higher than ordinary utility outputs. It is not something a person *exercises* when pursuing his goals, even if it tends often to improve his pursuit of them. Since it does the latter, the fact that it is not, strictly, a power is perhaps not a very important point. But there is another point which is certainly important.

The important point is that the value of cheerfulness is not merely, or mainly, that it raises the probability of a person's achieving what, by his lights, is "a successful life." Cheerfulness is a marvelous thing quite apart from that, and one different thing that it does is diminish the sadness of failure. It is a welfare-enhancer independently of being a goal-promoter. This makes it difficult for Dworkin to compensate cheerless people fully for their gloominess. But then there is an inconsistency between the criterion for determining what lies outside the person and the principle that disadvantages not deriving from the character of the person require compensation. Cheerlessness lies outside the person, but it is difficult to see how Dworkin can award appropriate compensation for it.

When I discussed gloominess with Dworkin he suggested that it was a borderline case with respect to the person/circumstances dichotomy and that the best way to cope with it would be to ask whether an individual

48. Frankfurt's sensitive distinction (see n. 46 above) between desires which do and desires which do not reflect decisions could be matched by a similar one between those which do and those which do not display attitude and commitment. For more on that differentiation within desire, see Sec. V*A* below.

49. At an Oxford seminar on economic justice of February 22, 1988, Dworkin was explicitly exhaustive. He spoke of his proposal requiring "a sharp distinction between personality (equals attachments, projects, etc.) and circumstances (equals everything else, the material with and against which people labour to achieve what their personality favours)."

would have insured against turning out to be gloomy, and to compensate him for his gloom if we think that the answer is "yes."

I think that the insurance device does have some appeal as a method of deciding whether or not to compensate for gloom. But its appeal seems to me to have nothing to do with the person/circumstances distinction: the individual who chooses to, or not to, insure against gloom is not thereby making *that* distinction. And if we suppose that he is indeed making it, then another problem arises. For in Dworkin's main use of the insurance device the individual *knows* what belongs to his person when he decides whether or not to insure: Dworkin's veil of ignorance is, in that important way, thinner than Rawls's.[50] But an individual who decides not to insure against gloominess remains, *ex hypothesi*, ignorant of whether or not he is gloomy.

The insurance device seems, then, unable to solve Dworkin's gloom problem. It is, nevertheless, independently attractive, especially when the veil of ignorance is indeed thickened, and that, I opine, is because it seems to sort out a big difference that really matters for egalitarian justice: between disadvantages that are and disadvantages that are not due to bad brute luck.[51] It is in the essential nature of insurance that luck is what we insure against, and genuine choice contrasts with luck. So anyone who, like Dworkin, is strongly drawn to the insurance test should consider accepting the choice/luck cut and giving up the attempt to defend the different cut of preferences/resources.

G

In my view, a large part of the fundamental egalitarian aim is to extinguish the influence of brute luck on distribution (see Sec. II above). Brute luck is an enemy of just equality, and, since effects of genuine choice contrast with brute luck, genuine choice excuses otherwise unacceptable inequalities.

Curiously enough, Dworkin advocates something very like the foregoing point of view in sketchy statements in "Why Liberals Should Care about Equality," but he is not faithful to it in "What Is Equality?" He says, in "Why Liberals Should Care about Equality," that we should attend to "which aspects of any person's economic position flow from his choices and which from advantages and disadvantages that were not matters of choice."[52] That is the compelling core idea, but it is misrendered in the

50. Dworkin's main use of the insurance device is to deal with handicaps and talents: see "Equality of Resources," secs. 3, 5, and 6 and see p. 296, and esp. p. 345 for the particular point that Dworkin insurers know what they think "is valuable in life."

51. If it is relevant that, given the chance, a person might have insured against cheerlessness, why is it not relevant that he might have insured against ending up with tastes that happen to be expensive? Compare L. Alexander and M. Schwarzchild, "Liberalism, Neutrality, and Equality of Welfare versus Equality of Resources," *Philosophy and Public Affairs* 16 (1987): 99 ff.

52. Ronald Dworkin, "Why Liberals Should Care about Equality," in *A Matter of Principle*, p. 208. ("What Is Equality?" is the joint title of "Equality of Welfare" and "Equality of Resources.")

cut between preferences and resources. Elsewhere in "Why Liberals Should Care about Equality," Dworkin also comes close to adopting genuine-choice/*luck* as the basic distinction. He says that the liberal "accepts two principles":

> The first requires that people have, at any point in their lives, different amounts of wealth insofar as the genuine choices they have made have been more or less expensive or beneficial to the community, measured by what other people want for their lives. The market seems indispensable to this principle. The second requires that people not have different amounts of wealth just because they have different inherent capacities to produce what others want, or are differently favored by chance. This means that market allocations must be corrected in order to bring some people closer to the share of resources they would have had but for these various differences of initial advantage, luck and inherent capacity.[53]

I say that Dworkin comes close to the basic distinction I favor here, but he does not quite get there, partly because luck (or chance) appears in his text as only one element in a set of unjust distributors, others being differences in initial advantage and in inherent capacity. And I find Dworkin's disjunctions of unjust distributors strange. For anyone who thinks that initial advantage and inherent capacity are unjust distributors thinks so because he believes that they make a person's fate depend too much on sheer luck: the taxa in Dworkin's disjunctions belong to different levels, and one of them subsumes the others.

Now, once we see the central role that luck should play in a broadly Dworkinian theory of distributive justice, Dworkin's own propensity to compensate for resource misfortune but not for utility function misfortune comes to seem entirely groundless. For people can be unlucky not only in their unchosen resource endowments but also in their unchosen liabilities to pain and suffering and in their unchosen expensive preferences. A willingness to compensate for deficiencies in productive capacity but not in capacity to draw welfare from consumption consequently leads to absurd contrasts.

Consider lucky Adrian and unlucky Claude.[54] "The desires and needs of other people" mean that unlike Claude, Adrian can pursue "a satisfying [gainful] occupation." People are happy to buy what Adrian, but not Claude, can enjoy producing, and that, for Dworkin, gives Claude a claim to redress quite separate from the one arising from the income difference between him and Adrian. But now suppose that, with respect to their leisure preferences, Adrian is like fisherman Fred, and Claude is like would-be photographer Paul,[55] and that the reason why fishing is cheap and photography is expensive is that many want to fish and few want to

53. Dworkin, "Why Liberals Should Care about Equality," p. 207.
54. Dworkin, "Equality of Resources," p. 308.
55. See Sec. IV*C* above.

take pictures, so that economies of scale are realized in the production of fishing, but not of photographic, equipment. It would follow that "the desires and needs of other people" mean that, unlike Claude, Adrian can pursue "a satisfying [leisure] occupation." Yet Dworkin will not redistribute for that luck-derived discrepancy, since it lies in the domain of consumption and not that of production.[56] But that is not a good basis for redistributive reluctance. It is quite absurd to regard Adrian's opportunity to pursue a satisfying profession as an enviable "circumstance," justifying redistribution,[57] without extending the same treatment to his opportunity for satisfying leisure.[58]

We must eschew Dworkin's preferences/resources distinction in favor of a wider access-oriented egalitarianism. We can agree with him that "it is perhaps the final evil of a genuinely unequal distribution of resources that some people have reason for regret just in the fact that they have been cheated of the chances others have had to make something valuable of their lives."[59] But equalizing those chances requires a discriminating attention to what is and is not chosen, not to what belongs to preference as opposed to endowment. In a brilliant exposition of how Dworkin's theory corrects deficiencies in Rawls's, Will Kymlicka remarks that "it is unjust if people are disadvantaged by inequalities of their circumstances, but it is equally unjust for me to demand that someone else pay for the costs of my choices."[60] That expresses Dworkin's fundamental insight very well, but a proper insistence on the centrality of choice leads to a different development of the insight from Dworkin's own. Dworkin has, in effect, performed for egalitarianism the considerable service of incorporating within it the most powerful idea in the arsenal of the anti-egalitarian right: the idea of choice and responsibility.[61] But that supreme effect of his contribution needs to be rendered more explicit.

56. Dworkin's refusal to redistribute for the discrepancy is explicit at "Equality of Resources," p. 288.

57. Ibid., p. 308.

58. The foregoing criticism depends on Dworkin's classification (ibid., p. 304) of a satisfying occupation as, so described, a resource. In his 1988 Oxford University B.Phil. thesis on "Justice and Alienation," Michael Otsuka argues that that was a superficial error on Dworkin's part. But I do not think that Dworkin can declassify occupation as a resource—and thereby escape my argument in the text—except at the severe cost of losing his argument against throwing people's powers to produce into his island auction, since that argument rests on the idea that, with people's powers to produce up for auction, the talented would end up envying the package of occupation and income enjoyed by the ungifted (see Dworkin, "Equality of Resources," pp. 311–12).

59. Dworkin, "Equality of Welfare," p. 219.

60. His 1987 Princeton lecture notes on Contemporary Political Philosophy, section on Rawls, subsection called "Subsidizing People's Choices" (Philosophy Department, University of Toronto, 1987, typescript), p. 5.

61. It is an idea much less deniable than the different idea of self-ownership, which is also central to right-wing thought. See the closing pages of G. A. Cohen, "Are Freedom and Equality Compatible?" in *Alternatives to Capitalism*, ed. Jon Elster and Karl O. Moene (Cambridge: Cambridge University Press, 1989).

Someone might say that to make choice central to distributive justice lands political philosophy in the morass of the free will problem. The distinction between preferences and resources is not metaphysically deep, but it is, by contrast, awesomely difficult to identify what represents *genuine* choice. Replacing Dworkin's cut by the one I have recommended subordinates political philosophy to metaphysical questions that may be impossible to answer.

To that expression of anxiety I have one unreassuring and one reassuring thing to say. The unreassuring thing is that we may indeed be up to our necks in the free will problem, but that is just tough luck. It is not a reason for not following the argument where it goes.

Now for the reassuring point. We are not looking for an absolute distinction between presence and absence of genuine choice. The amount of genuineness that there is in a choice is a matter of degree,[62] and egalitarian redress is indicated to the *extent* that a disadvantage does not reflect genuine choice. That extent is a function of several things, and there is no aspect of a person's situation which is wholly due to genuine choice.

Let me illustrate this point. One of the things that affects how genuine a choice was is the amount of relevant information that the chooser had. But we do not have to ask, Exactly what sort and amount of information must a person have to count as having genuinely chosen his fate? All that we need say, from the point of view of egalitarian justice, is: the more relevant information he had, the less cause for complaint he now has.

It seems to me that this plausible nuancing approach reduces the dependence of political philosophy on the metaphysics of mind.[63]

H

In a theory of distributive justice whose axis is the distinction between luck and choice, the positive injunction is to equalize advantage, save where inequality of advantage reflects choice. Now that sounds rather like equalizing the scope of genuine choice, of what, one might perhaps equivalently say, people are capable of doing. But, if those assimilations are correct, then the position latent in Dworkin looks close to the "capability equality" espoused by Amartya Sen, to which I shall turn after first facing a challenge to the emphasis I have placed on choice in articulating my conception of egalitarianism. The challenge will induce a needed revision of that conception.

62. This point corresponds to Dworkin's point that there is a continuum between brute and option luck (see "Equality of Resources," p. 293).

63. Thomas Scanlon's recent Tanner Lectures on "The Significance of Choice" present a liberatingly nonmetaphysical approach to choice in the context of, among other things, distributive justice. I have not yet had the time to determine to what extent what he offers can be used to improve the statement of a broadly Dworkinian theory of distributive justice.

V. SCANLON'S DOUBTS ABOUT VOLUNTARINESS

A

According to Thomas Scanlon, when we examine a person's condition with a view to determining what distributive justice owes him, we treat some of his interests as commanding more attention than others on a basis which is independent of his own ranking of those interests. It follows that we do not pursue a policy of equality of welfare, where welfare is understood as preference satisfaction (and it will be so understood throughout this section).

Scanlon does not address the view that justice should concern itself with opportunity for welfare, as opposed to welfare *tout court.* But the fact that he rejects the sovereignty, from the point of view of justice, of the subject's own preference ordering means that he would also reject an opportunity form of egalitarian welfarism.

Now, the features of Scanlon's position described above produce no conflict with the view I have espoused, since equality of access to advantage is not identical with equality of opportunity for welfare; and, in deciding both what qualifies as an advantage and the relative sizes of advantages, it is necessary to engage in objective assessment of the kind that Scanlon emphasizes. I nevertheless find two challenges to the view I have adopted in Scanlon's writings.[64]

As thus far developed, that view favors compensation for *all* deficits in ("inoffensive")[65] welfare which do not reflect the subject's *choice.* On this reading of the egalitarian attitude, it recommends a two-stage procedure. First, any deficit in welfare is treated as a possible case for compensation; then, whether it actually constitutes such a case is decided by facts about choice.[66] I discover in Scanlon's writings an objection to each stage of that procedure. First, he adduces examples of welfare deficit where the idea of compensation seems excluded from the start. Second, he offers a train of reasoning whose conclusion is that choice lacks the importance for distributive justice which it initially appears to have. If Scanlon is right, choice is just a surface indicator of something different and deeper.

According to Scanlon, (certain?) welfare deficits which reflect the subject's adherence to a religion raise no prima facie case for compensation:

> Differences in religious belief are one thing that can produce differences in utility level, and someone who regarded equality of welfare as the standard of interpersonal justification would have to regard these differences as being grounds for compensation: com-

64. There are further challenges in his Tanner Lectures, which I have not yet been able to study with care. See, in particular, the second lecture's critique of the "Forfeiture View," with which my own has affinities.

65. See Sec. III above. I shall henceforth take the parenthesized qualification as read.

66. I do not here mean a *conclusive* case: not only the distribution of nonwelfare advantages but also nonegalitarian considerations might defeat the welfare deficit claim.

pensation for having acquired a particularly onerous or guilt-inducing religion or one particularly unsuited to one's own personal strengths and weaknesses. This strikes me as distinctly odd. Quite apart from the fact that it might destroy the point of religious burdens to have them lightened by social compensation, the idea that these burdens are grounds for such compensation (a form of bad luck) is incompatible with regarding them as matters of belief and conviction which one values and adheres to because one thinks them right.[67]

Scanlon's powerful example forces me to choose among the following strategies: (1) to argue that it is because the burdens of religion so manifestly reflect choice that compensation for them is out of the question; (2) to argue that it is not as odd as Scanlon maintains to compensate a person for those burdens; (3) to revise my view that all burdens which do not reflect choice raise a case for compensation.

Before exploring these alternatives, I want to remark on a difference between the two kinds of religiously derived burdens mentioned by Scanlon in the passage quoted above. First, there is the burden of religiously induced guilt. And then there is the burden of one's religion being unsuited to one's strengths and weaknesses. Those two burdens seem to me to be relevantly different. It does seem, at least at first, "distinctly odd" to compensate for religiously induced guilt, but there are *some* discrepancies between a person's religion and his repertoire of capacity for which it is not similarly peculiar to offer compensation. I do not think that it is strange for a lame or poor person to request the cost of transport for a pilgrimage mandated by his religious convictions. And even if Scanlon means "strengths and weaknesses" of an intimately psychological kind only, there would still, I think, be cases falling under that description where compensation did not look so odd. I shall, however, focus on the particularly powerful guilt example.

Strategy 1 for dealing with that example is to represent the person's guilt as due to his choice of religion and as not raising a case for compensation for that reason. But people often no more choose to acquire a particular religion than they do to speak a particular language: in most cases, both come with upbringing. And when upbringing instills a religion which, like the one Scanlon describes, has a doxastic character (it is not just a way of life but, centrally, a set of beliefs), then we cannot regard its convinced adherent as choosing to retain it, any more than we can regard him as choosing to retain his belief that the world is round.

Strategy 2 says that compensating a person for religious guilt is not as strange as Scanlon maintains. To be sure, it would be strange for the subject himself to request compensation for his painful guilt feelings, since he believes that he *should* feel guilty: although he has in no sense

67. Thomas Scanlon, "Equality of Resources and Equality of Welfare: A Forced Marriage?" *Ethics* 97 (1986): 116–17.

chosen to have the feelings, *he would not choose not to have them if he could.*[68] It is, however, far less clear that those of us who reject his religion should have no inclination to compensate him for his guilt. If a person suffers because of (what we think is) a *plainly* false belief that God has commanded him to suffer, and we cannot persuade him that he is under an illusion, should we do nothing for him because he believes that he is owed nothing? If his belief is sapping his life, might we not give him priority when we distribute scarce recreational facilities? Why should *his* belief be sovereign here?[69]

When our own convictions match those of the believer's there is no purchase for the main claim of strategy 2, which is that the demands of justice may exceed the demands a person could intelligibly make on his own behalf. Strategy 3 does not employ that claim. This final strategy is to revise the view I have defended, as follows. Instead of saying, "compensate for disadvantages which are not traceable to the subject's choice," say, "compensate for disadvantages which are not traceable to the subject's choice *and* which the subject would choose not to suffer from." The revisionary element is the second clause. In the revised view, choice appears at two levels, actual and counterfactual. The revision seems to me not ad hoc but a natural development of the original view in the face of Scanlon's example.

The amendment is natural because it is true to the grounding idea that disadvantage is to be redressed when it reflects either exploitation or bad luck. Up to now, I have treated choice as the only relevant opposite of luck, but the Scanlon example shows that some of the costs of unchosen commitments (and they are commitments because one would not choose not to have them) are also not bad luck: they are not bad luck when they are so *intrinsically connected* with his commitments that their bearer would not choose to be without them.

The strong requirement of intrinsic connection establishes a contrast between Scanlon's believer and people whose expensive preferences engage my concern but not Dworkin's. The believer differs from a person whose preferences are not governed by belief at all and which a fortiori represent no commitment, such as someone who prefers plovers' eggs to hens' because the former were household fare in childhood. And the costs the believer incurs also differ relevantly from those sustained by the committed lover of expensive esoteric music (see Sec. IV*E* above), since the high

68. I do not mean that if, contrary to fact, he could choose not to have them, he would not so choose: ". . . if he could" is within the scope of the description of what he would not (now) choose. In saying "I would not give it up if I could" he is not making a prediction.

69. One might say: because it would destroy the point for him of his religious commitment to compensate him for the burdens associated with it. But that answer is here out of place; I am responding to the part of Scanlon's case which he represents as "quite apart" (see the last sentence of the passage quoted on p. 936 above) from the foregoing consideration.

price of satisfying the latter's preference is not integral to the commitment mandating that preference: that Berg is more expensive than be-bop is no part of what makes Berg better for most Berg lovers. It is just an unfortunate fact, and Berg lovers consequently do not break faith with their commitment to what they think is good music when they campaign for a Lincoln Center in which to hear it. Most would not choose to lack their esoteric taste, but they would certainly choose not to sustain the frustration that happens to accompany it, and that produces a relevant disanalogy with the case of the guilty religious believer. It means that we might think it right to provide a Lincoln Center even for those who forgo an offer to be schooled out of their high-brow musical tastes (see comment 4 in Sec. IV*E* above).

It follows from those contrasts that the Scanlon-inspired amendment enforces no retreat from anything ventured above in critique of Dworkin's view. I do not, however, want to understate the amendment's significance. Its policy implications are entirely negligible, but it does introduce a conceptual element very different from anything required to resist Dworkin. For counterfactual choice is *not* a kind of choice, even though, like choice, it is strictly inconsistent with luck. It is neither because of his choice nor because of bad luck that Scanlon's believer suffers.

Since the Scanlon amendment charges only for the intrinsic costs of commitments, it is not engaged by the pilgrimage case introduced earlier in this section. That case is similar to the example of the monument, which Scanlon uses in prosecution of his opposition to welfarism:

> The strength of a stranger's claim on us for aid in the fulfillment of some interest depends upon what that interest is and need not be proportional to the importance he attaches to it. The fact that someone would be willing to forgo a decent diet in order to build a monument to his god does not mean that his claim on others for aid in his project has the same strength as a claim for aid in obtaining enough to eat (even assuming that the sacrifices required of others would be the same). Perhaps a person does have some claim on others for assistance in a project to which he attaches such great importance. All I need maintain is that it does not have the weight of a claim to aid in the satisfaction of a truly urgent interest even if the person in question assigns these interests equal weight.[70]

I see no glaring oddity in a believer's claim that, since all should be equally able to worship as they will, his own worship, because it requires what happens to be expensive, warrants public subsidy.[71] Note that even

70. Thomas Scanlon, "Preference and Urgency," *Journal of Philosophy* 72 (1975): 659–60. Since Scanlon later (p. 666) assigns a special urgency to religious concern, one must charitably read the suggestion above that the need for a monument is not a "truly urgent interest" as a too strong way of saying that it is less urgent than a person's interest in a decent diet.

71. Compare Arneson, "Equality and Equality of Opportunity for Welfare."

Scanlon allows that, unlike the man burdened with a sense of sin, the monument builder might well have *a* claim on us. But, under the suggested amendment to my view, and as I am sure Scanlon would agree, the man's claim would lapse if his religion required him to build a monument *because* it was expensive, and therefore onerous to supply, for its cost to him would not then be a disadvantage which he would choose to have removed: it would be intrinsic to his religious commitment.

B

I turn to Scanlon's second challenge to the position I have espoused. I have in mind his argument against the importance of beliefs about choice in the explanation of our unwillingness to cater to expensive preferences.

Citing Rawls's suggestion that distributive justice does not attend to desire as such because desires are subject to our control, Scanlon provisionally hypothesizes that it is because preferences are "too nearly voluntary" that they are not "an appropriate basis for the adjudication of competing claims."[72]

Scanlon then asks in what way or sense preferences could be considered voluntary. He notes that they are not voluntary in the sense of being immediately subject to the will but allows that there is scope for volition "in the malleability of preferences over time."[73] So "perhaps the force of the voluntariness objection[74] lies in that it is possible for unusually strong or unusually expensive preferences" not, indeed, to be chosen at will, but "to be 'manufactured' by the person who has them."[75] But Scanlon proceeds to reject this account of the matter:

> But if this were the whole basis for the voluntariness objection one would expect that, at least in principle, the actual genesis of a person's preferences would be relevant to the strength of their claim to be satisfied. The very same intense interest might have arisen out of a conscious decision to "take up" a certain activity, or it might have grown almost unnoticed as the result of a series of chance encounters. Which of these is the case does not, however, seem to matter for the purposes of determining the strength of the person's claim on others for aid in the satisfaction of this interest. (Although it may be relevant to the assessment of his claim to aid in getting rid of the interest should he come to regard it as an obsession which cripples him in the pursuit of his normal activities.)[76]

I do not agree with Scanlon's contention that "the actual genesis of a person's preferences" is irrelevant to the strength of his claim to have

72. Scanlon, "Preference and Urgency," pp. 663–64. Scanlon cites John Rawls, "A Kantian Conception of Equality," *Cambridge Review* 96 (1975): 97. See, too, the passage from Rawls, "Social Unity and Primary Goods," quoted in Sec. III above.

73. Scanlon, "Preference and Urgency," p. 664.

74. To, i.e., the idea that distributive justice should track preference strength as such.

75. Scanlon, "Preference and Urgency," p. 664.

76. Ibid., pp. 664–65.

them satisfied. Suppose that each of two people have developed an expensive interest, and it is of a kind which, once contracted, cannot be extinguished, so that there is no question of any claim for assistance in getting rid of it. One of them, however, made a "conscious decision" to develop the interest, with full foreknowledge of the cost of satisfying it, while the other just happened to come by it, unawares, or developed it before it became expensive for wholly unforeseeable reasons. Then, so I believe, we should extend more sympathy and favor to the second persons. We might say of the first, "we must, in all charity, help him"; but it would be much harder to say in his case than in the case of the other, "we must, in all justice, help him." I therefore dissent from Scanlon's reasoning at this point. But it will nevertheless prove instructive to see how it continues.

Scanlon holds that there is something quite different from voluntariness underlying the reference to voluntariness. It is the very "fact that an interest, given its content, *could* have arisen" either voluntarily or not which is crucial, for that fact shows that the interest in question might not have arisen at all.[77] And, since it might not have arisen, Scanlon concludes that, from an objective point of view, it is of "peripheral importance," whatever may be the importance it has to the individual himself.[78] Hence, by a roundabout route, the suggestion that expensive tastes have no claim on us because they are deliberately cultivated is transmuted into the idea that they are of objectively secondary significance, however high the person himself may rank them: in a word, justice should not cater to *idiosyncrasy*, whatever its genesis may be.

One may say that, according to Scanlon, the liaison between interest and volition has implications for justice because of the following argument:

1. Sometimes people choose to develop a certain interest.

∴2. It is the sort of interest that a person could develop as a matter of choice.

∴3. It is an interest that might not develop: it is objectively peripheral.

∴4. It is an interest not commanding the urgent attention of justice (whether or not it was developed as a result of choice).

The final inference in this argument appears to me to be questionable. Scanlon himself raises a question about it: "Could there be an interest which . . . people might or might not happen to have—but which, if a person had it, would be the basis for urgent claims? . . . I cannot come up with an example. . . . Religion might seem to be an example. In our society some people are concerned with religion, others are not. Yet the claims of one's religious preferences not to be interfered with are thought to have a special urgency. But would this be so if it were not thought that religion *or something like it* has a central place in anyone's life?"[79]

77. Quoted material from ibid., p. 665, my emphasis.

78. Ibid.

79. Ibid., pp. 665–66.

In assessing Scanlon's claim that there is no urgent interest which is not universally shared, we have to be careful about the level of generality at which interests are individuated. Faced with the putative counter-example of religion, Scanlon regresses to a higher level of generality: he says that we think religion merits certain forms of protection because "religion *or something like it* has a central place in anyone's life." But now one has to ask: like religion in what way? And the answer cannot be: like it in mattering so much to the person in question, for that would return us to the subjective welfare ordering which Scanlon is seeking to eschew: "central place," at the end of the foregoing passage, has to be taken objectively. But then I cannot see what thing relevantly similar to religion appears in every normal person's life. And I therefore disagree with Scanlon's suggestion that religion fails to provide a counter-example of the required kind.

I do not, in conclusion, disacknowledge the need for objective assessment in arriving at distributive decisions: I recognized its inescapability at the beginning of this section. It is necessary for the purpose of deciding what an advantage is. My more limited conclusion is that the apparent importance for justice of facts about volition with respect to the genesis of a disadvantage deriving from preference is not a confused surface reflection of the priority of objective assessment.

VI. SEN ON CAPABILITY

How does *equality of access to advantage* relate to what Amartya Sen has called *capability equality?*

As I am using 'access,' a person enjoys access to something which he does not have only if he has both the *opportunity* and the *capacity* to obtain it, in the ordinary senses of those words, under which they name distinct requirements, neither of which entails the other. Now, even if 'capability,' in its ordinary meaning, differs from "capacity," it too nevertheless fails to entail "opportunity" (one might be capable of swimming without having the opportunity to swim), and from that one might conclude that my access is more demanding than Sen's capability and that our readings of equality consequently differ. But Sen's capability is not ordinary capability. It requires possession of external wherewithal, and it covers opportunity too: sometimes, indeed, Sen uses the very word 'opportunity,' in an extended sense, to mean what he more usually uses the word 'capability' to mean.[80] Hence the ordinary meanings of the words 'access' and 'capability' do not establish that our two readings of equality are distinct.

80. Immediately after introducing the notion of "*capability* to function" in his Dewey lectures, Sen shifts to the alternative language of "opportunity" to express the same idea (see "Well-Being, Agency and Freedom," pp. 200–201). Compare Sen, *Commodities and Capabilities*, p. 59, *The Standard of Living* (Cambridge: Cambridge University Press, 1987), p. 36.

It would, however, be premature to conclude that they are identical, for several reasons. One of them is that there is a substantial ambiguity in Sen's use of the term 'capability,' which makes it hard to be sure exactly what his conception of equality implies. For in his seminal "Equality of What?" Sen identified two ways of assessing a person's condition under the single name "capability," and the unnoticed and confusing duality has persisted in his subsequent writings. Both dimensions of assessment should attract egalitarian interest, but at most one of them merits the name "capability." The identification of the other dimension constitutes a striking contribution to normative understanding, but just that dimension is hard to perceive in Sen's exposition, because it is not felicitously described in the language (of "functioning" and "capability") which Sen uses to characterize it.

Sen arrived at what he called 'capability' through reflection on the main candidates for assessment of well-being which were in the field when he gave his 1979 lecture, to wit, utility, or welfare, and Rawlsian primary goods.[81] Sen pleaded for a metric of well-being which measured something falling *between* primary goods and utility, in a sense that will presently be explained, a something which had, amazingly, been largely neglected in previous literature. He called that something 'capability.'

Right from the start, however, 'capability' was used to denote two things, one of which was larger than the other, and 'capability' was not a felicitously chosen name for the larger one.

Sen said that "what is missing in all this framework[82] is some notion of 'basic capabilities': a person being able to do certain basic things."[83] But that relatively narrow characterization of the missing dimension was different from another which he offered in the same text, and which was more in keeping with his *argument* for the new perspective.

Sen's argument against the primary goods metric was that differently constructed and situated people require different amounts of primary goods to satisfy the same needs, so that "judging advantage purely in terms of primary goods leads to a partially blind morality."[84] It is, Sen rightly said, a "fetishist handicap" to be concerned with goods as such

81. A notable further candidate not yet then in print was Dworkin's equality of resources. Dworkinian resources differ from Rawlsian primary goods in a number of ways. One is that they include a person's mental and physical powers. It would be a worthwhile—and difficult—exercise to distinguish each of the two Sen dimensions I shall describe from the Dworkin resources dimension. (For pertinent remarks, see Sen's excellent rebuttal, all of which strikes me as correct, of Dworkin's criticism of Sen's view, at pp. 321–23 of "Rights and Capabilities," in his *Resources, Values and Development* [Oxford: Basil Blackwell, 1984].)

82. That is, the framework of discussion restricted to the rival claims of primary goods and utility as measures of well-being, and, within "primary goods," to goods in the ordinary sense. That is the relevant subset of primary goods here, and also in Rawls's discussion of expensive tastes.

83. Sen, "Equality of What?" p. 218.

84. Ibid., p. 216.

to the exclusion of what goods "*do* to human beings."[85] Both hedonic and preference-satisfaction welfarists are free of that particular fetishism, since they are concerned "with what these things do to human beings, but they use a metric [utility] that focusses not on the person's capabilities but on his mental reaction."[86] And that mental reaction is an unsuitable guide to policy, if only because people adjust their expectations to their conditions. The fact that a person has learned to live with adversity, and to smile courageously in the face of it, should not nullify his claim to compensation.[87]

Capabilities were thereby identified with what goods do to (or for) human beings, in abstraction from the utility they confer on them. But that identification was a mistake. For, even when utility has been set aside, it remains untrue that all that goods do for people is confer capability[88] on them, or that the uniquely important thing they do for them is that, or that that is the only thing they do for them which matters from an egalitarian point of view. In naming his view "Capability Equality" Sen failed to recognize the true shape and size of one of the dimensions he had uncovered.

It is indeed false that the normatively relevant effect on a person of his bundle of primary goods depends entirely on his mental reaction to what they do for him. There is also what welfarists ignore: what they do for him, what he gets out of them, apart from his mental reaction to or personal evaluation of that service. Consequently, Sen was right that, in the enterprise of assessing a person's well-being, we must consider his condition or state in abstraction from its utility for him. We must look at something which is "posterior" to "having goods" and "prior" to "having utility."[89] We must look, for example, at his nutrition level, and not just, as Rawlsians do, at his food supply, or, as welfarists do, at the utility he derives from eating food.[90]

85. Ibid., p. 218. Compare this statement: "What people get out of goods depends on a variety of factors, and judging personal advantage just by the size of personal ownership of goods and services can be very misleading. . . . It seems reasonable to move away from a focus on goods as such to what goods do to human beings" (Amartya Sen, "Introduction," in his *Choice, Welfare and Measurement* [Oxford: Basil Blackwell, 1982], pp. 29–30). Compare Amartya Sen, "Ethical Issues in Income Distribution," in *Resources, Values and Development*, p. 294, *Commodities and Capabilities*, p. 23, and *The Standard of Living*, pp. 15–16, 22.

86. Sen, "Equality of What?" p. 218. "Mental reaction" must here cover not only a kind of experience but also a subjective valuation, to cater for the preference form of welfarism.

87. This argument against the utility metric was not fully explicit in Sen, "Equality of What?" It appears at *Commodities and Capabilities*, pp. 21–22, 29, "Rights and Capabilities," pp. 308–9, "Introduction," in *Resources, Values and Development*, p. 34, "Goods and People," in *Resources, Values and Development*, p. 512, *The Standard of Living*, pp. 8–11.

88. Even in Sen's acceptably extended sense of the term—see earlier in this section—which is the sense in which I use it here.

89. Sen, *Commodities and Capabilities*, p. 11.

90. Sen, "Introduction," in *Choice, Welfare and Measurement*, p. 30.

But this significant and illuminating reorientation is not equivalent to focusing on a person's capability, where that is what he is able, all things considered, to do. Capability, and exercises of capability, form only part of the neglected intermediate (between primary goods and utility) state. *What goods do to or for people is not identical with what people are able to do with them,* nor even with what they actually do with them. To be sure, it is usually true that a person must do something with a good (take it in, put it on, go inside it, etc.) in order to be benefited by it, but that is not always true, and, even when it is true, one must distinguish what the good does for the person from what he does with it.

Not all that matters and is not utility is capability or an exercise of capability or a result of exercising capability. And many states which are indeed a result of exercising capability have a (nonutility) value which is unconnected with their status as effects of capability exercise, and which is not clearly exhibited in its true independence of capability (properly so-called) by Sen. A further development and defense of these critical contentions will appear elsewhere.[91]

91. See n. 2 above.

[16]

EQUALITY AND EQUAL OPPORTUNITY FOR WELFARE

Richard J. Arneson

(Received 2 January, 1988)

Insofar as we care for equality as a distributive ideal, what is it exactly that we prize? Many persons are troubled by the gap between the living standards of rich people and poor people in modern societies or by the gap between the average standard of living in rich societies and that prevalent in poor societies. To some extent at any rate it is the gap itself that is troublesome, not just the low absolute level of the standard of living of the poor. But it is not easy to decide what measure of the "standard of living" it is appropriate to employ to give content to the ideal of distributive equality. Recent discussions by John Rawls[1] and Ronald Dworkin[2] have debated the merits of versions of equality of welfare and equality of resources taken as interpretations of the egalitarian ideal. In this paper I shall argue that the idea of equal opportunity for welfare is the best interpretation of the ideal of distributive equality.

Consider a distributive agency that has at its disposal a stock of goods that individuals want to own and use. We need not assume that each good is useful for every person, just that each good is useful for someone. Each good is homogeneous in quality and can be divided as finely as you choose. The problem to be considered is: How to divide the goods in order to meet an appropriate standard of equality. This discussion assumes that some goods are legitimately available for distribution in this fashion, hence that the entitlements and deserts of individuals do not predetermine the proper ownership of all resources. No argument is provided for this assumption, so in this sense my article is addressed to egalitarians, not their opponents.

I. EQUALITY OF RESOURCES

The norm of equality of resources stipulates that to achieve equality the

Philosophical Studies **56**: 77–93, 1989.

agency ought to give everybody a share of goods that is exactly identical to everyone else's and that exhausts all available resources to be distributed. A straightforward objection to equality of resources so understood is that if Smith and Jones have similar tastes and abilities except that Smith has a severe physical handicap remediable with the help of expensive crutches, then if the two are accorded equal resources, Smith must spend the bulk of his resources on crutches whereas Jones can use his resource share to fulfill his aims to a far greater extent. It seems forced to claim that any notion of equality of condition that is worth caring about prevails between Smith and Jones in this case.

At least two responses to this objection are worth noting. One, pursued by Dworkin,[3] is that in the example the cut between the individual and the resources at his disposal was made at the wrong place. Smith's defective legs and Jones's healthy legs should be considered among their resources, so that only if Smith is assigned a gadget that renders his legs fully serviceable in addition to a resource share that is otherwise identical with Jones's can we say that equality of resources prevails. The example then suggests that an equality of resources ethic should count personal talents among the resources to be distributed. This line of response swiftly encounters difficulties. It is impossible for a distributive agency to supply educational and technological aid that will offset inborn differences of talent so that all persons are blessed with the same talents. Nor is it obvious how much compensation is owed to those who are disadvantaged by low talent. The worth to individuals of their talents varies depending on the nature of their life plans. An heroic resolution of this difficulty is to assign every individual an equal share of ownership of everybody's talents in the distribution of resources.[4] Under this procedure each of the N persons in society begins adult life owning a tradeable 1/N share of everybody's talents. We can regard this share as amounting to ownership of a block of time during which the owner can dictate how the partially owned person is to deploy his talent. Dworkin himself has noticed a flaw in this proposal, which he has aptly named "the slavery of the talented."[5] The flaw is that under this equal distribution of talent scheme the person with high talent is put at a disadvantage relative to her low-talent fellows. If we assume that each person strongly wants liberty in the sense of ownership over his own time (that is, ownership over his own body for his entire lifetime), the high-talent person finds that his taste for liberty is very expensive, as his time is socially valuable and very much in demand, whereas the low-talent person finds that his taste for liberty is cheap, as his time is less valuable and less in demand. Under this version of equality of resources, if two persons are identical in all respects except that one is more talented than the other, the more talented will find she is far less able to achieve her life plan than her less talented counterpart. Again, once its implications are exhibited, equality of resources appears an unattractive interpretation of the ideal of equality.

A second response asserts that given an equal distribution of resources, persons should be held responsible for forming and perhaps reforming their own preferences, in the light of their resource share and their personal characteristics and likely circumstances.[6] The level of overall preference satisfaction that each person attains is then a matter of individual responsibility, not a social problem. That I have nil singing talent is a given, but that I have developed an aspiration to become a professional opera singer and have formed my life around this ambition is a further development that was to some extent within my control and for which I must bear responsibility.

The difficulty with this response is that even if it is accepted it falls short of defending equality of resources. Surely social and biological factors influence preference formation, so if we can properly be held responsible only for what lies within our control, then we can at most be held to be partially responsible for our preferences. For instance, it would be wildly implausible to claim that a person without the use of his legs should be held responsible for developing a full set of aims and values toward the satisfaction of which leglessness is no hindrance. Acceptance of the claim that we are sometimes to an extent responsible for our preferences leaves the initial objection against equality of resources fully intact. For if we are sometimes responsible we are sometimes not responsible.

The claim that "we are responsible for our preferences" is ambiguous. It could mean that our preferences have developed to their present state due to factors that lay entirely within our control. Alternatively, it could mean that our present preferences, even if they have arisen through processes largely beyond our power to control, are now within our control in the sense that we could now undertake actions, at greater or lesser cost, that would change our preferences in ways that we can foresee. If responsibility for preferences on the first construal held true, this would indeed defeat the presumption that our resource share should be augmented because it satisfies our preferences to a lesser extent than the resource shares of others permit them to satisfy their preferences. However, on the first construal, the claim that we are responsible for our preferences is certainly always false. But on the second, weaker construal, the claim that we are responsible for our preferences is compatible with the claim that an appropriate norm of equal distribution should compensate people for their hard-to-satisfy preferences at least up to the point at which by taking appropriate adaptive measures now, people could reach the same preference satisfaction level as others.

The defense of equality of resources by appeal to the claim that persons are responsible for their preferences admits of yet another interpretation. Without claiming that people have caused their preferences to become what they are or that people could cause their preferences to change, we might hold that people can take responsibility for their fundamental preferences in the sense of identifying with them and regarding these preferences as their own, not as alien intrusions on the self. T. M. Scanlon has suggested the example of religious preferences in this spirit.[7] That a person was raised in one religious tradition rather than another may predictably affect his lifetime expectation of preference satisfaction. Yet we would regard it as absurd to insist upon compensation in the name of distributive equality for having been raised fundamentalist Protestant rather than atheist or Catholic (a matter that of course does not lie within the individual's power to control). Provided that a fair (equal) distribution of the resources of religious liberty is maintained, the amount of utility that individuals can expect from their religious upbringings is "specifically not an object of public policy."[8]

The example of compensation for religious preferences is complex, and I will return to it in section II below. Here it suffices to note that even if in some cases we do deem it inappropriate to insist on such compensation in the name of equality, it does not follow that equality of resources is an adequate rendering of the egalitarian ideal. Differences among people including sometimes differences in their upbringing may render resource equality nugatory. For example, a person raised in a closed fundamentalist community such as the Amish who then loses his faith and moves to the city may feel at a loss as to how to satisfy ordinary secular preferences, so that equal treatment of this rube and city sophisticates may require extra compensation for the rube beyond resource equality. Had the person's fundamental values not altered, such compensation would not be in order. I am not proposing compensation as a feasible government policy, merely pointing out that the fact that people might in some cases regard it as crass to ask for indemnification of their satisfaction-reducing upbringing does not show that in principle it makes sense for people to assume responsibility (act as though they were responsible) for what does not lie within their control. Any policy that attempted to ameliorate these discrepancies would predictably inflict wounds on innocent parents and guardians far out of proportion to any gain that could be realized for the norm of distributive equality. So even if we all agree that in such cases a policy of compensation is inappropriate, all things considered, it does not follow that so far as distributive equality is concerned (one among the several values we cherish), compensation should not be forthcoming.

Finally, it is far from clear why assuming responsibility for one's preferences and values in the sense of affirming them and identifying them as essential to one's self precludes demanding or accepting compensation for these preferences in the name of distributive equality. Suppose the government has accepted an obligation to subsidize the members of two native tribes who are badly off, low in welfare. The two tribes happen to be identical except that one is strongly committed to traditional religious ceremonies involving a psychedelic made from the peyote cactus while the other tribe is similarly committed to its traditional rituals involving an alcoholic drink made from a different cactus. If the market price of the psychedelic should suddenly rise dramatically while the price of the cactus drink stays cheap, members of the first tribe might well claim that equity requires an increase in their subsidy to compensate for the greatly increased price of the wherewithal for their ceremonies. Advancing such a claim, so far as I can see, is fully compatible with continuing to affirm and identify with one's preferences and in this sense to take personal responsibility for them.

In practise, many laws and other public policies differentiate roughly between preferences that we think are deeply entrenched in people, alterable if at all only at great personal cost, and very widespread in the population, versus preferences that for most of us are alterable at moderate cost should we choose to try to change them and thinly and erratically spread throughout the population. Laws and public policies commonly take account of the former and ignore the latter. For example, the law caters to people's deeply felt aversion to public nudity but does not cater to people's aversion to the sight of tastelessly dressed strollers in public spaces. Of course, current American laws and policies are not designed to achieve any strongly egalitarian ideal, whether resource-based or not. But in appealing to commmon sense as embodied in current practises in order to determine what sort of equality we care about insofar as we do care about equality, one would go badly astray in claiming support in these practises for the contention that equality of resources captures the ideal of equality. We need to search further.

II. EQUALITY OF WELFARE

According to equality of welfare, goods are distributed equally among a group of persons to the degree that the distribution brings it about that each person enjoys the same welfare. (The norm thus presupposes the possibility of cardinal interpersonal welfare comparisons.) The considerations mentioned seven paragraphs back already dispose of the idea that the distributive equality worth caring about is equality of welfare. To bring this point home more must be said to clarify what "welfare" means in this context.

I take welfare to be preference satisfaction. The more an individual's preferences are satisfied, as weighted by their importance to that very individual, the higher her welfare. The preferences that figure in the calculation of a person's welfare are limited to self-interested preferences — what the individual prefers insofar as she seeks her own advantage. One may prefer something for its own sake or as a means to further ends; this discussion is confined to preferences of the former sort.

The preferences that most plausibly serve as the measure of the individual's welfare are hypothetical preferences. Consider this familiar account: The extent to which a person's life goes well is the degree to which his ideally considered preferences are satisfied.[9] My ideally considered preferences are those I would have if I were to engage in thoroughgoing deliberation about my preferences with full pertinent information, in a calm mood, while thinking clearly and making no reasoning errors. (We can also call these ideally considered preferences "rational preferences.")

To avoid a difficulty, we should think of the full information that is pertinent to ideally considered preferences as split into two stages corresponding to "first-best" and "second-best" rational preferences. At the first stage one is imagined to be considering full information relevant to choice on the assumption that the results of this ideal deliberation process can costlessly correct one's actual preferences. At the second stage one is imagined to be considering also information regarding (a) one's actual resistance to advice regarding the rationality of one's preferences, (b) the costs of an educational program that would break down this resistance, and (c) the likelihood that anything approaching this educational program will actually be implemented in one's lifetime. What it is reasonable to prefer is then refigured in the light of these costs. For example, suppose that low-life preferences for cheap thrills have a large place in my actual conception of the good, but no place in my first-best rational preferences. But suppose it is certain that these low-life preferences are firmly fixed in my character. Then my second-best preferences are those I would have if I were to deliberate in ideal fashion about my preferences in the light of full knowledge about my actual preferences and their resistance to change. If you are giving me a birthday present, and your sole goal is to advance my welfare as much as possible, you are probably advised to give me, say, a bottle of jug wine rather than a volume of Shelley's poetry even though it is the poetry experience that would satisfy my first-best rational preference.[10]

On this understanding of welfare, equality of welfare is a poor ideal. Individuals can arrive at different welfare levels due to choices they make for which they alone should be held responsible. A simple example would be to imagine two persons of identical tastes and abilities who are assigned equal resources by an agency charged to maintain distributive equality. The two then voluntarily engage in high-stakes gambling, from which one emerges rich (with high expectation of welfare) and the other poor (with low welfare expectation). For another example, consider two persons similarly situated, so they could attain identical welfare levels with the same effort, but one chooses to pursue personal welfare zealously while the other pursues an aspirational preference (e.g., saving the whales), and so attains lesser fulfillment of self-interested preferences. In a third example, one person may voluntarily cultivate an expensive preference (not cognitively superior to the preference it supplants), while another person does not. In all three examples it would be inappropriate to insist upon equality of welfare when welfare inequality arises through the voluntary choice of the person who gets lesser welfare. Notice that in all three examples as described, there need be no grounds for finding fault with any aims or actions of any of the individuals mentioned. No imperative of practical reason commands us to devote our lives to the maximal pursuit of (self-interested) preference satisfaction. Divergence from equality of welfare arising in these ways need not signal any fault imputable to individuals or to "society" understood as responsible for maintaining distributive equality.

This line of thought suggests taking equal opportunity for welfare to be the appropriate norm of distributive equality.

In the light of the foregoing discussion, consider again the example of compensation for one's religious upbringing regarded as affecting one's lifetime preference satisfaction expectation. This example is urged as a reductio ad absurdum of the norm of equality of welfare, which may seem to yield the counterintuitive implication that such differences do constitute legitimate grounds for redistributing people's resource shares, in the name of distributive equality. As I mentioned, the example is tricky; we should not allow it to stampede us toward resource-based construals of distributive equality. Two comments on the example indicate something of its trickiness.

First, if a person changes her values in the light of deliberation that bring her closer to the ideal of deliberative rationality, we should credit the person's conviction that satisfying the new values counts for more than satisfying the old ones, now discarded. The old values should be counted at a discount due to their presumed greater distance from deliberative rationality. So if I was a Buddhist, then become a Hindu, and correctly regard the new religious preference as cognitively superior to the old, it is not the case that a straight equality of welfare standard must register my welfare as declining even if my new religious values are less easily achievable than the ones they supplant.

Secondly, the example might motivate acceptance of equal opportunity for welfare over straight equality of welfare rather than rejection of subjectivist conceptions of equality altogether. If equal opportunity for welfare obtains between Smith and Jones, and Jones subsequently undergoes religious conversion that lowers his welfare prospects, it may be that we will take Jones's conversion either to be a voluntarily chosen act or a prudentially negligent act for which he should be held responsible. (Consider the norm: Other things equal, it is bad if some people are worse off than others through no voluntary choice or fault of their own.) This train of thought also motivates an examination of equal opportunity for welfare.

III. EQUAL OPPORTUNITY FOR WELFARE

An opportunity is a chance of getting a good if one seeks it. For equal opportunity for welfare to obtain among a number of persons, each must face an array of options that is equivalent to every other person's in terms of the prospects for preference satisfaction it offers. The preferences involved in this calculation are ideally considered second-best preferences (where these differ from first-best preferences). Think of two persons entering their majority and facing various life choices, each action one might choose being associated with its possible outcomes. In the simplest case, imagine that we know the probability of each outcome conditional on the agent's choice of an action that might lead to it. Given that one or another choice is made and one or another outcome realized, the agent would then face another array of choices, then another, and so on. We construct a decision tree that gives an individual's possible complete life-histories. We then add up the preference satisfaction expectation for each possible life history. In doing this we take into account the preferences that people have regarding being confronted with the particular range of options given at each decision point. Equal opportunity for welfare obtains among persons when all of them face equivalent decision trees — the expected value of each person's best (= most prudent[11]) choice of options, second-best, . . . nth-best is the same. The opportunities persons encounter are ranked by the prospects for welfare they afford.

The criterion for equal opportunity for welfare stated above is incomplete. People might face an equivalent array of options, as above, yet differ in their awareness of these options, their ability to choose reasonably among them, and the strength of character that enables a person to persist in carrying out a chosen option. Further conditions are needed. We can summarize these conditions by stipulating that a number of persons face *effectively* equivalent options just in case one of the following is true: (1) the options are equivalent and the persons are on a par in their ability to "negotiate" these options, or (2) the options are nonequivalent in such a way as to counterbalance exactly any inequalities in people's negotiating abilities, or (3) the options are equivalent and any inequalities in people's negotiating abilities are due to causes for which it is proper to hold the individuals themselves personally responsible. Equal opportunity for welfare obtains when all persons face effectively equivalent arrays of options.

Whether or not two persons enjoy equal opportunity for welfare at a time depends only on whether they face effectively equivalent arrays of options at that time. Suppose that Smith and Jones share equal opportunity for welfare on Monday, but on Tuesday Smith voluntarily chooses or negligently behaves so that from then on Jones has greater welfare opportunities. We may say that in an extended sense people share equal opportunity for welfare just in case there is some time at which their opportunities are equal and if any inequalities in their opportunities at later times are due to their voluntary choice or differentially negligent behavior for which they are rightly deemed personally responsible.

When persons enjoy equal opportunity for welfare in the extended sense, any actual inequality of welfare in the positions they reach is due to factors that lie within each individual's control. Thus, any such inequality will be nonproblematic from the standpoint of distributive equality. The norm of equal opportunity for welfare is distinct from equality of welfare only if some version of soft determinism or indeterminism is correct. If hard determinism is true, the two interpretations of equality come to the same.

In actual political life under modern conditions, distributive agencies will be staggeringly ignorant of the facts that would have to be known in order to pinpoint what level of opportunity for welfare different persons have had. To some extent it is technically unfeasible or even physically impossible to collect the needed information, and to some extent we do not trust governments with the authority to collect the needed information, due to worries that such authority will be subject to abuse. Nonetheless, I suppose that the idea is clear in principle, and that in practise it is often feasible to make reliable rough-and-ready judgments to the effect that some people face very grim prospects for welfare compared to what others enjoy.

In comparing the merits of a Rawlsian conception of distributive equality as equal shares of primary goods and a Dworkinian conception of equality of resources with the norm of equality of opportunity for welfare, we run into the problem that in the real world, with imperfect information available to citizens and policymakers, and imperfect willingness on the part of citizens and officials to carry out conscientiously whatever norm is chosen, the practical implications of these conflicting principles may be hard to discern, and may not diverge much in practise. Familiar information-gathering and information-using problems will make us unwilling to authorize government agencies to determine people's distributive shares on the basis of their preference satisfaction prospects, which will often be unknowable for all practical purposes. We may insist that governments have regard to primary good share equality or resource equality as rough proxies for the welfarist equality that we are unable to calculate. To test our allegiance to the rival doctrines of equality we may need to consider real or hypothetical examples of situations in which we do have good information regarding welfare prospects and opportunities for welfare, and consider whether this information affects our judgments as to what counts as egalitarian policy. We also need to consider cases in which we gain new evidence that a particular resource-based standard is a much more inaccurate proxy for welfare equality than we might have thought, and much less accurate than another standard now available. Indifference to these considerations would mark allegiance to a resourcist interpretation of distributive equality in principle, not merely as a handy rough-and-ready approximation.

IV. STRAIGHT EQUALITY VERSUS EQUAL OPPORTUNITY; WELFARE VERSUS RESOURCES

The discussion to this point has explored two independent distinctions: (1) straight equality versus equal opportunity and (2) welfare versus resources as the appropriate basis for measuring distributive shares. Hence there are four positions to consider. On the issue of whether an egalitarian should regard welfare or resources as the appropriate standard of distributive equality, it is important to compare like with like, rather than, for instance, just to compare equal opportunity for resources with straight equality of welfare. (In my opinion Ronald Dworkin's otherwise magisterial treatment of the issue in his two-part discussion of "What Is Equality?" is marred by a failure to bring these four distinct positions clearly into focus.[12])

The argument for equal opportunity rather than straight equality is simply that it is morally fitting to hold individuals responsible for the foreseeable consequences of their voluntary choices, and in particular for that portion of these consequences that involves their own achievement of welfare or gain or loss of resources. If accepted, this argument leaves it entirely open whether we as egalitarians ought to support equal opportunity for welfare or equal opportunity for resources.

For equal opportunity for resources to obtain among a number of persons, the range of lotteries with resources as prizes available to each of them must be effectively the same. The range of lotteries available to two persons is effectively the same whenever it is the case that, for any lottery the first can gain access to, there is an identical lottery that the second person can gain access to by comparable effort. (So if Smith can gain access to a lucrative lottery by walking across the street, and Jones cannot gain a similar lottery except by a long hard trek across a desert, to this extent their opportunities for resources are unequal.) We may say that equal opportunity for resources in an extended sense obtains among a number of persons just in case there is a time at which their opportunities are equal and any later inequalities in the resource opportunities they face are due to voluntary choices or differentially negligent behavior on their part for which they are rightly deemed personally responsible.

I would not claim that the interpretation of equal opportunity for resources presented here is the only plausible construal of the concept. However, on any plausible construal, the norm of equal opportunity for resources is vulnerable to the "slavery of the talented" problem that proved troublesome for equality of resources. Supposing that personal talents should be included among the resources to be distributed (for reasons given in section I), we find that moving from a regime of equality of resources to a regime that enforces equal opportunity for resources does not change the fact that a resource-based approach causes the person of high talent to be predictably and (it would seem) unfairly worse off in welfare prospects than her counterpart with lesser talent.[13] If opportunities for resources are equally distributed among more and less talented persons, then each person regardless of her native talent endowment will have comparable access to identical lotteries for resources that include time slices of the labor power of all persons. Each person's expected ownership of talent, should he seek it, will be the same. Other things equal, if all persons strongly desire personal liberty or initial ownership of one's own lifetime labor power, this good will turn out to be a luxury commodity for the talented, and a cheap bargain for the untalented.

A possible objection to the foregoing reasoning is that it relies on a vaguely specified idea of how to measure resource shares that is shown to be dubious by the very fact that it leads back to the slavery of the talented problem. Perhaps by taking personal liberty as a separate resource this result can be avoided. But waiving any other difficulties with this objection, we note that the assumption that any measure of resource equality must be unacceptable if applying it leads to unacceptable results for the distribution of welfare amounts to smuggling in a welfarist standard by the back door.

Notice that the welfare distribution implications of equal opportunity for resources will count as intuitively unacceptable only on the assumption that people cannot be deemed to have chosen voluntarily the preferences that are frustrated or satisfied by the talent pooling that a resourcist interpretation of equal opportunity enforces. Of course it is strictly nonvoluntary that one is born with a particular body and cannot be separated from it, so if others hold ownership rights in one's labor power one's individual liberty is thereby curtailed. But in principle one's self-interested preferences could be concerned no more with what happens to one's own body than with what happens to the bodies of others. To the extent that you have strong self-interested hankerings that your neighbors try their hand at, say, farming, and less intense desires regarding the occupations you yourself pursue, to that extent the fact that under talent pooling your own labor power is a luxury commodity will not adversely affect your welfare. As an empirical matter, I submit that it is just false to hold that in modern society whether any given individual does or does not care about retaining her own personal liberty is due to that person's voluntarily choosing one or the other preference. The expensive preference of the talented person for personal liberty cannot be assimilated to the class of expensive preferences that people might voluntarily cultivate.[14] On plausible empirical assumptions, equal opportunity for welfare will often find tastes compensable, including the talented person's taste for the personal liberty to command her own labor power. Being born with high talent cannot then be a curse under equal opportunity for welfare (it cannot be a blessing either).

V. SEN'S CAPABILITIES APPROACH

The equal opportunity for welfare construal of equality that I am espousing is similar to a "capabilities" approach recently defended by Amartya Sen.[15] I shall now briefly sketch and endorse Sen's criticisms of Rawls's primary social goods standard and indicate a residual welfarist disagreement with Sen.

Rawls's primary social goods proposal recommends that society should be concerned with the distribution of certain basic social resources, so his position is a variant of a resource-based understanding of how to measure people's standard of living. Sen holds that the distribution of resources should be evaluated in terms of its contribution to individual capabilities to function in various ways deemed to be objectively important or valuable. That is, what counts is not the food one gets, but the contribution it can make to one's nutritional needs, not the educational expenditures lavished, but the contribution they make to one's knowledge and cognitive skills. Sen objects to taking primary social goods measurements to be fundamental on the ground that persons vary enormously from one another in the rates at which they transform primary social goods into capabilities to function in key ways. Surely we care about resource shares because we care what people are enabled to be and do with their resource shares, and insofar as we care about equality it is the latter that should be our concern.

So far, I agree. Moreover, Sen identifies a person's well-being with the doings and beings or "functionings" that he achieves, and distinguishes these functionings from the person's capabilities to function or "well-being freedom."[16] Equality of capability is then a notion within the family of equality of opportunity views, a family that also includes the idea of equal opportunity for welfare that I have been attempting to defend. So I agree with Sen to a large extent.

But given that there are indefinitely many kinds of things that persons can do or become, how are we supposed to sum an individual's various capability scores into an overall index? If we cannot construct such an index, then it would seem that equality of capability cannot qualify as a candidate conception of distributive equality. The indexing problem that is known to plague Rawls's primary goods proposal also afflicts Sen's capabilities approach.[17]

Sen is aware of the indexing problem and untroubled by it. The grand theme of his lectures on "Well-being, Agency and Freedom" is informational value pluralism: We should incorporate in our principles all moral information that is relevant to the choice of actions and policies even if that information complicates the articulation of principles and precludes attainment of a set of principles that completely rank-orders the available alternative actions in any possible set of circumstances. "Incompleteness is *not* an embarrassment," Sen declares.[18] I agree that principles of decision should not ignore morally pertinent matters but I doubt that the full set of my functioning capabilities does matter for the assessment of my position. Whether or not my capabilities include the capability to trek to the South Pole, eat a meal at the most expensive restaurant in Omsk, scratch my neighbor's dog at the precise moment of its daily maximal itch, matters not one bit to me, because I neither have nor have the slightest reason to anticipate I ever will have any desire to do any of these and myriad other things. Presumably only a small subset of my functioning capabilities matter for moral assessment, but which ones?

We may doubt whether there are any objectively decidable grounds by which the value of a person's capabilities can be judged apart from the person's (ideally considered) preferences regarding those capabilities. On what ground do we hold that it is valuable for a person to have a capability that she herself values at naught with full deliberative rationality? If a person's having a capability is deemed valuable on grounds independent of the person's own preferences in the matter, the excess valuation would seem to presuppose the adequacy of an as yet unspecified perfectionist doctrine the like of which has certainly not yet been defended and in my opinion is indefensible.[19] In the absence of such a defense of perfectionism, equal opportunity for welfare looks to be an attractive interpretation of distributive equality.

NOTES

[1] John Rawls, 'Social Unity and Primary Goods,' in Amartya Sen and Bernard Williams, eds., *Utilitarianism and Beyond* (Cambridge: Cambridge University Press, 1982), pp. 159—185.

[2] Ronald Dworkin, 'What Is Equality? Part 1: Equality of Welfare,' *Philosophy and Public Affairs* **10** (1981): 185—246; and 'What Is Equality? Part 2: Equality of Resources,' *Philosophy and Public Affairs* **10** (1981): 283—345. See also Thomas Scanlon, 'Preference and Urgency,' *Journal of Philosophy* **72** (1975): 655—669.

[3] Dworkin, 'Equality of Resources.'

[4] Hal Varian discusses this mechanism of equal distribution, followed by trade to equilibrium, in 'Equity, Envy, and Efficiency,' *Journal of Economic Theory* **9** (1974): 63—91. See also John Roemer, 'Equality of Talent,' *Economics and Philosophy* **1** (1985): 151—186; and 'Equality of Resources Implies Equality of Welfare,' *Quarterly Journal of Economics* **101** (1986): 751—784.

[5] Dworkin, 'Equality of Resources,' p. 312.

It should be noted that the defender of resource-based construals of distributive equality has a reply to the slavery of the talented problem that I do not consider in this paper. According to this reply, what the slavery of the talented problem reveals is not the imperative of distributing so as to equalize welfare but rather the moral inappropriateness of considering all resources as fully alienable. It may be that equality of resources should require that persons be compensated for their below-par talents, but such compensation should not take the form of assigning individuals full private ownership rights in other people's talents, which should be treated as at most partially alienable. See Margaret Jane Radin, 'Market-Inalienability,' *Harvard Law Review* **100** (1987): 1849—1937.

[6] Rawls, 'Social Unity and Primary Goods,' pp. 167—170.

[7] Thomas Scanlon, 'Equality of Resources and Equality of Welfare: A Forced Marriage?', *Ethics* **97** (1986): 111—118; see esp. pp. 115—117.

[8] Scanlon, 'Equality of Resources and Equality of Welfare,' p. 116.

[9] See, e.g., John Rawls, *A Theory of Justice* (Cambridge, MA: Harvard University Press, 1971), pp. 416—424; Richard Brandt, *A Theory of the Good and the Right* (Oxford: Oxford University Press, 1979), pp. 110—129; David Gauthier, *Morals by Agreement* (Oxford: Oxford University Press, 1986), pp. 29—38; and Derek Parfit, *Reasons and Persons* (Oxford: Oxford University Press, 1984), pp. 493—499.

[10] In this paragraph I attempt to solve a difficulty noted by James Griffin in 'Modern Utilitarianism,' *Revue Internationale de Philosophie* **36** (1982): 331—375; esp. pp. 334—335. See also Amartya Sen and Bernard Williams, 'Introduction' to *Utilitarianism and Beyond*, p. 10.

[11] Here the most prudent choice cannot be identified with the choice that maximizes lifelong expected preference satisfaction, due to complications arising from the phenomenon of preference change. The prudent choice as I conceive it is tied to one's actual preferences in ways I will not try to describe here.

[12] See the articles cited in note 2. Dworkin's account of equality of resources is complex, but without entering into its detail I can observe that Dworkin is discussing a version of what I call "equal opportunity for resources." By itself, the name chosen matters not a bit. But confusion enters because Dworkin neglects altogether the rival doctrine of equal opportunity for welfare. For a criticism of Dworkin's objections against a welfarist conception of equality that do not depend on this confusion, see my 'Liberalism, Distributive Subjectivism, and Equal Opportunity for Welfare.'

[13] Roemer notes that the person with high talent is cursed with an involuntary expensive preference for personal liberty. See Roemer, 'Equality of Talent.'

[14] As Rawls writes, ". . . those with less expensive tastes have presumably adjusted their likes and dislikes over the course of their lives to the income and wealth they could reasonably expect; and it is regarded as unfair that they now should have less in order to spare others from the consequences of their lack of foresight or self-discipline." See 'Social Unity and Primary Goods,' p. 169.

[15] Amartya Sen, 'Well-being, Agency and Freedom: The Dewey Lectures 1984,' *Journal of Philosophy* **82** (1985): 169—221; esp. pp. 185—203. See also Sen, 'Equality of What?', in his *Choice, Welfare and Measurement* (Oxford: Basil Blackwell, 1982), pp. 353—369.

[16] Sen, 'Well-being, Agency and Freedom,' p. 201.

[17] See Allan Gibbard, 'Disparate Goods and Rawls' Difference Principle: A Social Choice Theoretic Treatment,' *Theory and Decision* **11** (1979): 267—288; see esp. pp. 268—269.

[18] Sen, 'Well-being, Agency and Freedom,' p. 200.

[19] However, it should be noted that filling out a preference-satisfaction approach to distributive equality would seem to require a normative account of healthy preference formation that is not itself preference-based. A perfectionist component may thus be needed in a broadly welfarist egalitarianism. For this reason it would be misguided to foreclose too swiftly the question of the possible value of a capability that is valued at naught by the person who has it. The development and exercise of various capacities might be an important aspect of healthy preference formation, and have value in this way even though this value does not register at all in the person's preference satisfaction prospects.

Department of Philosophy,
University of California, San Diego,
La Jolla, CA 92093,
U.S.A.

[17]

FAIRNESS

by John Broome

This paper presents a theory about fairness, as it applies to the distribution of goods between people. I shall concentrate particularly on random lotteries. Sometimes a lottery is the fairest way of distributing a good, and my theory explains, better than any other theory I know, why this is so. That is the main evidence I offer for it. But the theory is not limited to lotteries; it is intended to apply whenever goods are distributed between people. I shall use the fairness of lotteries as a guide to fairness in general.[1]

I

It often happens that there are several candidates to receive a good, but the good cannot be divided up to go round them all. The good may be very important; it may even amount to the saving of the candidate's life. For instance, not enough kidneys are available for everyone who needs one. As a result, some people are denied treatment for their kidney failure, and consequently die.

For each candidate, there will be reasons why she should have the good, or some of it. (I mean *prima facie* reasons, which may be defeated by other reasons.) Amongst them will be the benefits, to the candidate herself and to other people, that will result from this candidate's receiving the good. When the good is the saving of life, these benefits will depend on how much the candidate enjoys her life, what responsibilities she has to other people, and so on. Then there may also be other reasons. One may be desert: some of the candidates may deserve the good, perhaps because of services they have performed in the past. For the moment, suppose all these reasons can be weighed against each other. (I shall question this later.) Then for some candidates, the reasons

* Meeting of the Aristotelian Society, held at the Senior Common Room, Birkbeck College, London on Monday 3rd December, 1990 at 8.15 p.m.

[1] Elsewhere, I have applied the theory to the distribution of divisible goods such as income. See my 'What's the good of equality?' in John Hey (ed.), *Current Issues in Microeconomics*, Macmillan, 1989, pp. 236–62, and my *Weighing Goods*, Blackwell, 1991, Chapter 9.

why they should have the good will be stronger, on balance, than for others. Let us call one person a 'better' candidate than another if she has stronger reasons in her favour.

How should it be decided which of the candidates should get the good? Several procedures might be used. One is to have some authority judge the merits of the candidates, and select the best. But this procedure has its costs. The job of assembling and assessing the necessary information may be expensive and time consuming. The responsibility of deciding who is to live and who to die (if that is in question) may be an intolerable emotional burden. Furthermore, the authority may not actually succeed in picking the best candidates. It may choose the candidates who best meet corrupt or prejudiced criteria, rather than the ones who are actually the best.

One procedure that avoids the costs and dangers of deliberate selection by an authority is to apply some fixed rule. (There is a risk of corruption or prejudice in setting up the rule, but not once it is set up.) And it may be possible to devise a rule that goes some way towards selecting the best candidates. For life saving, the rule of picking the youngest will do this. Age will certainly be one of the factors that helps determine which candidates are the best. Other things being equal, it is better to save a younger person than an older, because it does more good to the person who is saved: it gives her, on average, more years of life. So there is some correlation between a person's youth and how good a candidate she is.

A lottery is another procedure that avoids the costs and dangers of deliberate selection. Unlike a well-chosen fixed rule, though, it is no more likely to pick the best candidates than any others. So what advantage can it possibly have over a fixed rule? Plainly, only that it is sometimes fairer. But how can this be so? How can a lottery be fairer than a rule such as picking the youngest, which has a tendency to select the better candidates? Answering this question is the main test that has to be passed by any account of the fairness of lotteries. To answer it properly demands a particular theory of fairness in general; only this theory, which I shall describe in Sections III and IV, is able to explain adequately the fairness of a lottery.

II

Before coming to the theory, I shall first set out what I think it needs to account for: the facts about the fairness of lotteries that need to be explained.

First: a lottery is by no means always fair. It would not, for instance, be a fair way of choosing whom to award the prize in a violin competition. So in explaining the fairness of lotteries we shall need a criterion for distinguishing when lotteries are fair from when they are not.

Second: our account of the fairness of lotteries cannot simply be that lotteries are good tie breakers, appropriate only when the reasons in favour of different candidates are exactly balanced. The two examples below show that it is sometimes right to hold a lottery even when reasons are not exactly balanced. In any case, if a lottery were appropriate only for breaking a tie, its value would be insignificant. It will hardly ever happen in practice that reasons balance exactly. And if ever they do, the slightest change in one of them would mean they were no longer balanced. Then, if it was right to hold a lottery only for breaking a tie, it would no longer be right to hold one. So the value of a lottery would be lexicographically dominated by other values. (Section VI, however, qualifies this point.)

Furthermore, to say that lotteries are good tie breakers fails to explain their fairness. When there is a tie, it does not matter which candidate is chosen. What is required is simply a means of getting the decision made. A lottery is a handy means, even when no issue of fairness arises. When I cannot decide between two restaurants for dinner, I may toss a coin. This is not in order to be fair to the restaurants, but simply to avoid the fate of Buridan's Ass. When it comes to a choice, not between restaurants, but between candidates for some good, a lottery is sometimes more than just a handy means of getting the decision made when there is a tie. It is sometimes a better means than others because it is fairer. We, therefore, need a separate explanation of why it is fairer.

Thirdly: the fairness of a lottery does not consist solely in the fact that it overcomes the costs and dangers of deliberate selection by an authority. I have already explained that selection by a fixed rule is likely to be a better way of doing that. And even when it is possible to choose the best candidates deliberately, without cost and without corruption or prejudice, there is still sometimes a case for a lottery. The following two examples make this point, and also the second point mentioned above.

The first example is about games. Most games begin by holding a lottery to settle which player starts in the most favourable position (playing white, say). Fairness requires this. But normally some players will be better candidates for the favourable position than others, as I defined 'better candidate' in Section I. For instance, usually more joy will be caused in total by the victory of one player rather than another, so a greater expectation of benefit would result from giving that player a favourable start. Let us suppose there is a referee who, without prejudice or corruption, is easily able to pick out the best candidate. It would still be wrong to leave the decision to the referee rather than a lottery.

The second example is a dangerous mission. Someone has to be sent on a mission that is so dangerous she will probably be killed. The people available are similar in all respects, except that one has special talents that make her more likely than others to carry out the mission well (but no more likely to survive). This fact is recognized by her and everyone else. Who should be sent? Who should receive the good of being left behind? It could plausibly be thought that the right thing is simply to send the talented person. But it is also very plausible that doing so would be unfair to her, and that fairness requires a lottery to be held amongst all the candidates. These two views are not incompatible. It may be that fairness requires a lottery, so that it would be unfair not to hold one, but that in this case fairness is outweighed by expediency, so that on balance it is right to send the talented candidate without a lottery. This depends on the circumstances. If it is vital that there should be no slip in the execution of the mission, the unfairness will be tolerable. But if a less than perfect performance is acceptable, more importance can be given to fairness. In some circumstances, fairness will win, and a lottery should be held.

III

Those, then, are the facts. How can they be explained? In this section and the next, I shall present my theory of fairness. I mean it to apply to the distribution of any sort of good, whether indivisible or not. In Section V, I shall come back to indivisible goods and lotteries.

When a good is to be distributed, for each candidate there are reasons why she should have some of it. These reasons together determine what ought to be done: how the good should be distributed. But how, exactly, do the reasons combine together to determine what ought to be done? As I shall put it: how do reasons *work*? There are various views about this.

One is *teleology*. Teleology claims that the good ought to be distributed in whatever way maximizes overall benefit.[2] So the only sort of reasons it recognizes for a particular candidate to get the good is a benefit that would result. Imagine the good being distributed one unit at a time. Each unit should go to the candidate whose receiving it would produce the most benefit; this will normally ensure that overall benefit is maximized when all the units are eventually distributed. At each stage, the reason for giving a particular unit to one candidate is the benefit that would result; the reason for giving it to the next candidate is the benefit that would result from that; and so on. All these reasons should be weighed against each other, and the unit allocated to the candidate for whom the reason is strongest. So we can say that reasons are combined together by *weighing up*. This is how reasons work in teleology. Weighing up goes along with maximizing.

Other views disagree with teleology. One, for instance, claims that some reasons are *side constraints*. A side constraint determines directly what ought to be done; it is not subject to being weighed against other reasons. *Rights* are often thought to be side constraints. Suppose that, amongst the candidates for a good, one has a right to some part of it. Suppose it is her income, for instance, which she has earned. Then side-constraint theory says simply that she should have it; no question of weighing arises. The theory may acknowledge the existence of teleological reasons too, which work by weighing up. It may allow that weighing up is appropriate amongst other candidates, but not for a candidate who has a right.

[2] There are non-maximizing versions of teleology; see Michael Slote, 'Satisficing consequentialism', *Aristotelian Society Supplementary Volume*, 58 (1984), pp. 139-63. But for simplicity I shall ignore them here.

I am going to describe a third type of reason, which works in a third way. To introduce it, I shall first draw a distinction of a different sort amongst the reasons why a candidate should get the good: some of these reasons are duties *owed to the candidate herself*, and others are not. I shall call the former *claims* that the candidate has to the good.

The distinction between claims and other reasons is easy to grasp intuitively. Take the dangerous mission, for example. One candidate is more talented than the others. This is a reason for allotting to the others the good of staying behind. But the other candidates' lack of talent gives them no *claim* to this good. It may be right to leave them behind, but it is not owed *them* to do so. Whatever claim they have to this good, the talented candidate has it also.

The distinction can appear even within teleology—indeed within utilitarianism. All utilitarians think that if a person would benefit from having some particular good, that is a reason why she should have it. But some utilitarians think this reason is a duty owed to the person—a claim—and others think it is not. William Godwin, for one, thought it was a claim. 'Every man', he said, 'has a right to that, the exclusive possession of which being awarded to him, a greater sum of benefit or pleasure will result than could have arisen from its being otherwise appropriated'.[3]

The difference is nicely brought out by the attitude of utilitarians to changes in the world's population. Henry Sidgwick[4] believed an action was right if it maximized the total of good enjoyed by people in the world. So he believed one should promote growth in population if the extra people brought into existence will have good lives, and no harm will be done to people already living. But this is clearly not a duty owed to the people who will be brought into existence. One cannot owe anyone a duty to bring her into existence, because failing in such a duty would not be failing anyone. Sidgwick, then, evidently thought that the duty to benefit people is not owed to those people themselves. On the other hand, a utilitarian view promulgated by Jan Narveson[5] is that one should promote the

[3] *Political Justice*, Penguin Edition, 1976, p. 703.
[4] *The Methods of Ethics*, Macmillan, 1907, pp. 414-6.
[5] 'Utilitarianism and new generations', *Mind*, 76 (1967), pp. 62-72.

good of existing people or people who will exist, but there is no reason to increase the total of good in the world simply for its own sake. So the fact that the extra people will enjoy good lives is no reason to increase the world's population. Narveson is evidently motivated by the thought that, whatever duty there is to promote a person's good, it must be owed to the person herself. Consequently, there can be no duty to bring a person into existence.

It is clear, then, that there is a distinction between claims and other reasons. It is not so clear which particular reasons are claims and which are not. Even utilitarians, I have been saying, disagree about this. And if we recognize nonutilitarian reasons, there is further scope for disagreement. If we accept *desert* as a reason why a person should have a good, it is perhaps an uncontroversial further step to take it as a claim. But *need* is more controversial. If a person could benefit from a good, that is no doubt a reason why she should have it, but, despite Godwin, we may be reluctant to accept it is a claim. If, however, the person needs the good, perhaps we should accept that. Perhaps, for instance, a person who needs a kidney has a claim on it. But this is controversial.

In this paper, I am not going to engage in controversy over which reasons are claims and which are not. I shall take it for granted that some are: that some reasons why a person should have a good are duties owed to the person. And I shall concentrate on asking how these reasons, whichever they are, *work*. How do claims combine with each other and with other reasons, in determining what should be done?

IV

Some teleologists, as I say, recognize the existence of claims. But they suppose claims work by weighing up, just like other reasons. They think that the right thing to do, and the right way to distribute a good, is determined by the balance of reasons, whether claims or not. They throw claims and other reasons all together on to the same scales, in the same maximizing calculation.

But the fact that conflicting claims are duties owed to different people gives rise to an alternative intuition. Simply weighing claims against each other may not seem enough. Weighing up is the treatment we would naturally give to conflicting duties owed to a single person. Applying it between different people may not seem to be giving proper recognition to the people's separateness.[6]

In particular, weighing up claims does not seem to give proper attention to *fairness*. Take the example of the dangerous mission again. All reasons are evenly balanced, apart from the special reason for sending the talented candidate: she will perform the mission better. So weighing up reasons must conclude in favour of sending this candidate. But that seems unfair to her. It might be the right thing to do under pressure of expediency, but nevertheless it seems unfair. The talented candidate has a claim to the good of being left behind, and her claim is as strong as anyone else's. Yet when it is weighed against other people's claims, and the further reason that she will perform the mission better, her claim is overridden. Weighing up seems to override claims, rather than respect them.

It is fairness that matters here because the particular business of fairness is to mediate between the conflicting claims of different people. But I need to qualify this remark slightly. Certainly, fairness is *only* concerned with claims, and not with other reasons. Suppose there is some reason why a person should have a good, but she has no claim to it. Then if she does not get the good, that may be wrong, but she suffers no unfairness. It cannot be unfair to deny her a good she had no claim to in the first place. On the other hand, it is possible that some claims are outside the domain of fairness, and work in different ways from the one I shall be describing. I shall say more about this possibility later, and for the time being I shall ignore it. I shall assume that all claims are mediated by fairness.

Weighing up claims is not enough, then, because it does not give proper attention to fairness. It would not even be enough to give claims extra *heavy* weight in the course of weighing up. The example of the dangerous mission shows this too. However much weight is given to claims, each person's claim to the good of staying behind is still the same. So the claims will all balance, and the talented person will still be sent, because of the extra reason. But this is unfair to her.

[6] The *locus classicus* for this view is John Rawls, *A Theory of Justice*, Oxford University Press, 1972, pp. 22-27.

What, then, *does* fairness require? It requires, I suggest, that *claims should be satisfied in proportion to their strength.* I do not mean 'proportion' to be taken too precisely. But I do mean that equal claims require equal satisfaction, that stronger claims require more satisfaction than weaker ones, and also—very importantly—that weaker claims require some satisfaction. Weaker claims must not simply be overridden by stronger ones.

This suggestion merely extends and tightens up a principle that is often taken for granted: that people identically situated should be treated identically. Economists call this the principle of 'horizontal equity'.[7] It is, like my generalization of it, inconsistent with teleological maximizing. To see why, imagine two people have equal claims to some good, but that, if the good is divided between them, less benefit will be produced in total than if it is all given to one. Then maximizing implies it should all go to one, but horizontal equity says it should be divided.

The heart of my suggestion is that fairness is concerned only with how well each person's claim is satisfied *compared with* how well other people's are satisfied. It is concerned only with relative satisfaction, not absolute satisfaction. Take a case where all the candidates for a good have claims of equal strength. Then fairness requires equality in satisfaction. So if all the candidates get the same quantity of the good, then fairness has been perfectly achieved, even if they get very little, or indeed none at all.

To be sure, all is not well if they get none at all. For each claimant there is at least one reason why she should have some of the good: the reason that constitutes her claim. Claims should be satisfied, therefore. But it is not *unfair* if they are not, provided everyone is treated proportionally.

Everyone's claim to a good should, *prima facie*, be satisfied. Indeed, if there is any reason, whether a claim or not, for a person to have some of a good, she should have some. Call this the 'satisfaction requirement'. Normally, this requirement cannot be fully met for everyone. What does it require then? I suggest it requires maximizing of satisfaction. This implies that, to meet this requirement, claims will have to be weighed against

[7] See, for instance, Anthony B. Atkinson and Joseph E. Stiglitz, *Lectures on Public Economics*, McGraw-Hill, 1980, pp. 353–5.

each other and against other reasons; I think weighing up and maximizing are appropriate for the satisfaction requirement. But then *also* fairness requires that claims should be satisfied in proportion to their strength. Claims, therefore, give rise to two separate requirements: they should be satisfied, and they should be satisfied proportionally.

It will normally be impossible to fulfil both requirements completely. Consequently, the two will themselves have to be combined together in some way, to determine what should be done, all things considered. Here again, I suggest that weighing up is appropriate: the demands of fairness should be weighed against the demands of overall satisfaction. In some circumstances, no doubt, it will be very important to be fair, and in others fairness may be outweighed by expediency.

In summary, claims work like this. Together with other reasons, they go to determine the satisfaction requirement by weighing up. And claims together determine the fairness requirement by the proportionality rule. Then the fairness requirement is itself weighed against the satisfaction requirement.

Evidently, claims in my theory do not work as side constraints; they do not necessarily prevail. This may be a limitation of the theory. I defined claims as duties owed to people, and it may be that within this class there are some claims that are genuinely side constraints. If some claims are side constraints, they are not covered by my theory. My theory is limited to the subclass of claims that work in the way I have described. Call these 'fairness-claims'. It might be a convenient piece of terminology to say that fairness is a subdivision of *justice*, and that justice is concerned with all claims, but fairness only with fairness-claims.

Consequently, I cannot pretend to have defined claims independently of the notion of fairness, and then shown how fairness applies to them. The subclass of claims I am talking about is partly identified by the way they work, and this is itself determined by the theory of fairness. Nevertheless, I believe the subclass of fairness-claims picked out this way is an important one. It may even include all claims. And for brevity I shall continue to use the term 'claim' for fairness-claims only.

The merit of the theory is that it shows a way claims can work, without simply being weighed up in the manner of teleology, and also without being treated as side constraints. Robert Nozick argues for side-constraint theory largely on the grounds that teleology is mistaken. He concedes that these grounds are inadequate if there is a third alternative.[8] My theory of fairness offers one.

It shows how a claim can stop short of a *right*, considered as a side constraint. This fills a significant gap. It seems implausible that anyone has a right to a research grant from, say, the Ford Foundation. But if the Ford Foundation decides to distribute research grants, it should surely deal fairly with the applicants. Someone who was rejected on inadequate grounds would have a just complaint. But how can this be, if she had no right to a grant in the first place? My theory explains how. If her application is good enough, she has a fairness-claim. Consequently, *if* other people are receiving a grant, she should receive one too. In 'Claims of need',[9] David Wiggins considers just what sort of a claim is generated by need. Again, it seems implausible that a person has a right to whatever she needs. So what can her claim be? I suggest it might be a fairness-claim, which implies that *if* needed resources are being distributed, the person should have a share.

V

Now let us concentrate once more on cases where the good to be distributed is indivisible, and there is not enough to go round.

Take a case, first, where all candidates have equal claims. It would be possible to satisfy their claims equally, as fairness requires, by denying the good to all of them. There may be occasions when it is so important to be fair that this is the right thing to do. But it would totally fail to meet the satisfaction requirement, and normally the demands of fairness will not be enough to outweigh this requirement completely. It will be better to use as much of the good as is available.

In that case, the candidates' claims cannot all be equally satisfied, because some candidates will get the good and others will not. So some unfairness is inevitable. But a sort of partial equality in satisfaction can be achieved. Each person can be

[8] *Anarchy, State and Utopia*, Basic Books, 1974, note on p. 29.

[9] In Ted Honderich (ed.), *Morality and Objectivity*, Routledge and Kegan Paul, 1984, pp. 149–202.

given a sort of surrogate satisfaction. By holding a lottery, each can be given an equal *chance* of getting the good. This is not a perfect fairness, but it meets the requirement of fairness to some extent.

It does so, of course, only if giving a person a chance of getting the good counts as a surrogate satisfaction of her claim. This seems plausible to me. After all, if you have a chance of getting the good you may actually get it. It is quite different from merely giving the claim its proper weight against other reasons; that does not satisfy it in any way. Suppose, in the example of the dangerous mission, that the talented candidate was sent because of her talents. She could make the following complaint. She has as strong a claim to staying behind as anybody else. Her claim was weighed against other reasons. But this overrode her claim rather than satisfied it. It was never on the cards that she might actually get the good she has a claim to. But if she was sent because a lottery is held and she lost, she could make no such complaint.

Next, take a case where several people have claims to a good that are roughly, but not exactly, equal. Perhaps, for instance, they all need the good, but not exactly equally. And suppose again that there is not enough to go round them all. Fairness requires satisfaction in proportion to their claims. So if the good goes to the people with the strongest claims, the others will not have been fairly treated; their claims will have been overridden. And if it goes to other people, the unfairness will be worse. So unfairness is once again inevitable. But once again it can, if the circumstances are right, be mitigated by giving everyone a chance of getting the good. Ideally, each person's chance should be in proportion to the strength of her claim: the lottery should be unequally weighted. (At first, it is particularly puzzling how a weighted lottery could be fair.[10] If it is fair for some people to have a greater chance than others, that means they more ought to have the good. So why not let them have it without a lottery? My theory explains why not.) But even a lottery at equal odds may be fairer than giving the good directly to the candidates with the strongest claims. This depends on a complicated

[10] In 'Taming chance', *The Tanner Lectures*, Volume 9, Utah University Press, Jon Elster mentions two examples where weighted lotteries have been used in practice.

judgement. The result of a lottery will generally be that the good goes to candidates who do not have the strongest claims. This is less fair than the result of giving it directly to those who do. The likelihood of this less fair result will have to be weighed against the contribution to fairness of the lottery itself. But it is clear that, if claims are close to equality, holding a lottery will be fairer than not.

A subsidiary point. We have agreed that fairness requires everyone to have an equal chance when their claims are exactly equal. Then it is implausible it should require some people to have no chance at all when their claims fall only a little below equality.

When claims are equal or roughly equal, then, a lottery is *fair*. Whether it is *right* to hold one is then a matter of weighing the fairness it achieves against the likelihood that it will not meet the satisfaction requirement, which in this case requires the best candidates to be selected. The conclusion will depend on how important fairness is in the circumstances. But there will certainly be some circumstances where it is better to hold a lottery than to choose the best candidates deliberately.

A lottery should be held when, first, it is important to be fair and, second, the candidates' claims are equal or roughly equal. These conditions may occur quite often. They do not require an exact balance of all considerations; claims may be equal or roughly equal even when other considerations are not balanced at all. Consider, for instance, life-saving medical treatment such as kidney replacement. It seems plausible that, in these matters of life and death, fairness is particularly important. And it seems plausible that everyone has a claim to life, even if on other grounds some are much better candidates than others. Maybe older candidates have weaker claims than younger, since they have already received a greater share of life. But even so, the candidates' claims may be nearly enough equal to make a lottery appropriate.[11] This explains why a lottery may be better than the rule of picking the youngest. If an older person has a claim to the treatment, even if it is a weaker claim than a

[11] The arguments of Lewis Kornhauser and Lawrence Sager in 'Just lotteries', *Social Science Information*, are closely parallel to mine in many ways. The main difference is that their arguments permit these authors to recommend a lottery only when claims are exactly equal.

younger person's, it demands proportional satisfaction. A lottery provides at least a surrogate satisfaction: a chance. But the rule of picking the youngest gives no sort of satisfaction at all. It simply overrides the claims of older people. So it is less fair.

That is how my theory of fairness explains the value of lotteries. It satisfactorily accounts for the facts set out in Section II.

VI

I know no alternative theory that explains the value of lotteries as successfully as mine. I cannot review all the alternatives here, but I do need to deal with one that may seem promising at first.[12]

In Section I, I spoke of the 'best' candidates for a good, as though the notion was clear cut. But when the judgement between candidates depends on a comparing reasons of different sorts, it often seems impossible to weigh the reasons against each other in a precise way. How, for instance, when comparing candidates for life-saving treatment, should one's *joie de vivre* be weighed against another's family responsibilities? The impossibility might be in the nature of things: some reasons might simply be incommensurable with each other. Or it might be practical: we might have no practical way of making the comparison accurately, even though in principle the reasons might be commensurable.

This indeterminacy suggests the following defence of lotteries. A group of candidates might not be exactly tied—all equally as good as the others—but even so none might be definitely a better candidate than the others. Or it may be that some members of the group are actually better candidates than others, but we cannot in practice know which. Suppose there is only enough of the good for some of this group. Then, just as a lottery has a natural role as a tie breaker when there is an exact tie, it may be appropriate here for the same reason. Here we have a tie within the limits of comparability. And whereas I said in Section II that an exact tie will be very rare, a tie within the limits of comparability may be common. For life-saving medical treatment, for instance, once the medically unsuitable candidates, and

[12] An argument like this is used by Jonathan Glover in *Causing Death and Saving Lives*, Penguin, 1977, pp. 203-27, and by Nicholas Rescher in 'The allocation of exotic life saving therapy', *Ethics*, 79 (1969), pp. 173-86.

perhaps the very old, have been eliminated, it may be that all the remaining candidates are tied within the limits of comparability. We may not be competent to judge between them.

However, I do not think this argument accounts adequately for the value of lotteries. For one thing, it does not explain their *fairness.* As I said in Section II, the role of a tie breaker is simply as a device for getting the decision made. No question of fairness need arise. The new argument merely extends this role to a wider domain: a device is needed to get the decision made when the weighing up of reasons has gone as far as it can.

Furthermore, if there is no separate reason why a lottery is fair, it is doubtful that it is even going to be the best way of breaking the tie. A fixed rule may well do better, for the reason I gave in Section I: it has some tendency to pick better candidates. Picking the youngest may well do better in the case of life-saving treatment. To be sure, this reason is more questionable in our present context. I said in Section I that, in an arbitrary group of candidates for life saving, the younger ones are more likely to be better candidates than the older. Now, though, we are not dealing with an arbitrary group, but with a group that is tied within the limits of comparability. A candidate's youth is one of the considerations that should already have been taken into account in admitting her to this group. Within the group, therefore, the younger people should generally have fewer other considerations in their favour than the older ones; on balance they should be more likely to be good candidates. However, I doubt that in practice, when a lottery is defended on grounds of incomparability, it will often be for a group of people chosen in this finely balanced way. For instance, the group may consist of all the candidates except the medically unsuitable and the very old. For such a group, picking the youngest would be a better tie breaker than a lottery. In any case, this argument from incomparability provides no reason why a fixed rule should be *worse* than a lottery. It fails the test I mentioned at the end of Section I.

Department of Economics
University of Bristol
40 Berkeley Square
Bristol BS8 1HY.

Part III
Overview

[18]

Journal of Economic Literature
Vol. XXXI (June 1993), pp. 671–731

Taking Ethics Seriously: Economics and Contemporary Moral Philosophy

By DANIEL M. HAUSMAN
University of Wisconsin-Madison

and

MICHAEL S. MCPHERSON
Williams College

We are especially indebted to John Roemer for proposing this project and for offering extensive criticisms of earlier drafts. Richard Arneson, Henry Bruton, Eric Kramer, Philippe Mongin, Morty Shapiro, Amartya Sen, Julius Sensat, Hamish Stewart, Gordon Winston, and anonymous referees corrected many mistakes and led us to additional sources. Anne McEachern and John McEachern provided valuable research assistance. Hausman gratefully acknowledges the support of a Vilas Associate award from the University of Wisconsin-Madison.

TO BE A GOOD PERSON, one must take ethics seriously. But can the same be said about being a good *economist?* Does morality matter to economic analysis? It would be idle to suggest that economists should spend a large part of their time studying moral philosophy, and moral sophistication may be more important in some areas of economics, such as political economy, than in others, such as econometrics. Yet we would argue that a moderate dose of reflection on the relations between economics and morality could help many economists work more effectively. We should emphasize our concern to show the relevance of moral thinking to the conduct of *both* positive and normative economics. Not only do moral principles bear on issues concerning evaluation and policy, but they also influence the questions positive economists ask and the answers they find plausible.

The present essay surveys recent work by economists and moral philosophers that borders the two disciplines. It aims to provide an overview for a broad audience of working economists and to suggest possibilities for research to those with specific interests in "ethics and economics." (Book length treatments with similar goals include Allen Buchanan 1985 and Alan Hamlin 1986; see also Sen 1987a.) After the introductory and motivational remarks of Section 1, Section 2 will develop the relations between morality and rationality and the problems of modeling moral commitments. Section 3, the longest section in the essay, presents a number of different perspectives for the ethical evaluation of economic processes and outcomes. Section 4 is concerned with the moral relevance and presuppositions of social choice theory and game theory.

1. *Economics and Moral Theory*

Before beginning, a few abstract words on the relations between economics and ethics are in order. Those who deny that economics and ethics having anything in particular to do with one another rarely deny that economics is relevant to policy. They maintain instead that the relevance of economics is purely technical. It provides causal knowledge of the consequences of policies to enable policy makers to choose effective means toward their ends. Ethics determines the ends, and economics determines the means. They are both crucial to policy, but they have nothing much to do with one another.

The simple picture of the economist who provides value-free technical information to the decision maker is at best a useful caricature. It fits the activity of an economist who calculates the revenue losses from a proposed tax reduction, but it does not fit the activity of an economist who is asked for advice. For the political process never formulates all the relevant goals and constraints explicitly or specifies how to weight them (Fritz Machlup 1969, pp. 119–24).[1] If President Carter had asked Milton Friedman or Paul Samuelson, "What is the 'best' way to reduce inflation?" neither economist would have had a well-defined technical problem until he figured out what other objectives Carter had and what their relative weights were. At some point they would almost certainly have had to rely on some of their own values, too. The same issue arises in selecting problems to study: economists who refuse to "dirty their hands" with ethical matters will not know what technical problems to investigate.

Positive and normative questions may interact in the conduct of research as well as in deciding what problems to study or what advice to give. As some moral views "fit" familiar patterns of economic modeling more easily than others, economists may focus on the moral views that best mesh with their theoretical preconceptions, or distort other moral views to make them fit. Better understanding of moral views that are hard to link to familiar patterns of economic reasoning, such as those that emphasize rights or needs, could influence the development of economics, as theoretical categories are modified to provide other ways of organizing experience. Working out the implications of different moral views may also suggest novel economic problems or theoretical formulations.[2] The traffic need not all go from philosophy to economics. Theoretical results in economics such as Kenneth Arrow's impossibility theorem or Sen's liberal paradox force moral theorists to rethink their principles. Economic theorists have developed many analytical tools—in game theory, social choice theory, and the measurement of welfare, among others—that have challenged moral philosophers to articulate their views better and have

[1] We are indebted to Samuel Weston (forthcoming) for this reference.

[2] It may be that development of "property rights economics" has been influenced in this way by the liberatarian orientation of some its practitioners, just as Marxian commitments have influenced the development of theories of exploitation by John Roemer and others.

helped them to do so.[3] Intellectual progress is either moral philosophy or economic theory may stimulate workers in the other discipline.

1.1 *Why Should Economists Be Interested in Moral Questions?*

Economists should care about moral questions for at least the following four reasons:

1. The morality of economic agents influences their behavior and hence influences economic outcomes. Moreover, economists' own moral views may influence the morality and the behavior of others in both intended and unintended ways. Because economists are interested in the outcomes, they must be interested in morality.
2. Standard welfare economics rests on strong and contestable moral presuppositions. To assess and to develop welfare economics thus requires attention to morality.
3. The conclusions of economics must be linked to the moral commitments that drive public policy. To understand how economics bears on policy thus requires that one understand these moral commitments, which in turn requires attention to morality.
4. Positive and normative economics are frequently intermingled. To understand the moral relevance of positive economics requires an understanding of the moral principles that determine this relevance.

[3] There are concerns among some contemporary philosophers that the influence of economic theory on the development of modern moral philosophy has been all too great, leading to a neglect both of social history and of the history of philosophy as sources of understanding in this realm. See Michael Walzer (1983) and Charles Taylor (1989) for sustained attempts to carve out other paths.

1.1.1 *The Economic Importance of Morality.* Morality influences economic outcomes. The morality accepted by economic agents influences how they behave. It is among the causal factors that economists need to study. For example, as Fred Hirsch (1976) and others have noted, economic efficiency and economic policy depend crucially upon ethical values which may be undermined by the development of market economies (Karl Polanyi 1944; Albert Hirschman 1985; Sen 1977a; Arrow 1974). Without honesty, trust, and goodwill, economic life would grind to a halt. Insofar as economists seek to explain economic outcomes and to promote economic efficiency, they need to be concerned with the nature and sources of useful or harmful moral virtues or vices. Can economically useful virtues be sustained by rational self-interest, or does the success of economies depend crucially upon non-self-interested moral commitments? The role of moral norms in accounting for economic outcomes has received increasing attention in the areas of labor economics, economics of organization, and economic development. These developments are surveyed in Section 2.2 below.

For a striking example of the economic importance of moral norms, consider the work of Richard Titmuss (1971) concerning systems for acquiring and distributing blood for transfusions. Titmuss claims to show that volunary blood donation systems, such as Great Britain's, are more efficient than are commercial systems, and he argues that they embody and cultivate altruistic communitarian values. In a thoughtful and lengthy review, Arrow endorses much of Titmuss' case. In particular, Arrow underscores the serious drawbacks of commercial provision when the testing of blood for infectious agents is imperfect. Altruistic donors have no incentive to lie about whether their blood is safe, but commercial donors plainly do.

Arrow does, however, question Titmuss' ambitious claim that the commercial option for donors in the United States undermines the willingness of U.S. citizens to give blood altruistically (1972, esp. pp. 350–51). In Arrow's view markets increase freedom and enable us not ". . . to use up recklessly the scarce resources of altruistic motivation" (1972, p. 355). Arrow can make little sense of Titmuss' claim that markets "deprive men of their freedom to choose to give or not to give" (1972, p. 350). But as Peter Singer (1973, 1977) and Hirschman (1985) have noted, it can be misleading to regard altruism as a scarce resource, for, like a skill, its quantity can be increased by its use. And although Titmuss' language is puzzling, commercialization can discourage giving. To give blood, when it cannot be purchased, is to give something that is literally priceless, something which the donors themselves describe as "the gift of life." To give blood when it can be purchased is to give the equivalent of $50 (Singer 1977). Whether or not these attitudes are rationally justified, their potential economic effects are evident, and they can only be understood if economists are willing to study some ethics.

Even if economists should attend to the "sociological" influence of moral commitments on economic outcomes, it does not follow that they need to worry about the substantive "truth" or validity of those moral commitments. But it seems to us that economists may be able to advance their work by appraising people's moral behavior and ideas as well by tracing their causal consequences. It is natural, illuminating, and virtually unavoidable for economists to inquire whether people's observed (or alleged) moral commitments "make sense." Part of Arrow's discomfort with the Titmuss argument was that there seemed to him to be no good *reason* why people's willingness to donate blood should be influenced by the existence of a market. If an alleged preference or moral attitude is irrational, its existence and stability are cast into doubt. Descriptions of moral motivations and judgments are likely to be evaluations too, and are not always less useful for that.

Furthermore, as the examples suggest, the moral convictions of economic agents, unlike causal factors such as scarcities, can be influenced by the way in which they are analyzed and described by economists. Saying that human behavior can be modeled as if it were entirely self-interested (as the Chicago economists in particular do) or defining rationality as self-interest (as in Robert Frank 1988, p. 2) legitimizes and fosters self-interested behavior. In experiments on human cooperation, economics and business students are uniquely uncooperative (Gerald Marwell and Ruth Ames 1981). Learning economics, it seems, may make people more selfish.[4] A causal factor that depends upon the way in which it is described by economists is a tricky thing to study.

The facts that economists can rarely describe moral commitments without evaluating them and that economists affect what they see by how they describe it, provide reason for them to think about not just the morality in fact accepted in the society they study but about the morality they think should be accepted. Moral reflection is important for positive economics, not just normative economics. The moral principles accepted by positive economists matter empirically because they are economic agents as well as theorists. Their theorizing reflects their moral commitments and influences the actions and moral commitments of others.

1.1.2 *Morality and Standard Welfare*

[4] Or at least more caluclating. It has been suggested that economists are more "selfish" in laboratory "prisoners' dilemma" experiments because they grasp the situation better. Their unwillingness to cooperate could also reflect previous self-selection.

Economics. Welfare economists have sometimes thought that their techniques are virtually morally neutral, because they rest on innocuous and uncontroversial moral premises such as the Pareto principle. But the standard definition of a social optimum compares social alternatives exclusively in terms of the goodness of their *outcomes* (rather than the rightness of their *procedures*) and identifies the goodness of outcomes with satisfaction of individual preferences. These commitments to value only outcomes and to measure outcomes only in terms of individual utilities are neither neutral nor uncontroversial (see Sen 1979b; and Sen and Bernard Williams 1982).

Economists do not of course limit their contributions to policy discussions to identifying Pareto improvements. Familiar practices such as cost-benefit analysis and routine preferences for competitive markets cannot be defended in purely Paretian terms. In fact, developments within welfare economics itself over the last fifty years, including the theory of the second-best (Richard Lipsey and Kelvin Lancaster 1956) and the criticism of the so-called "compensation principle" (Samuelson 1950a) have made clear that no single all-purpose defense of these familiar practices and judgments is available (see Section 3.2.1 below). Yet the strategy of retreating into silence whenever the search for pure Pareto improvements comes up empty is not a plausible one. Because normative economists must make further evaluations of economic processes and outcomes, they cannot avoid moral assessment of the techniques and principles they rely on. It may be possible to reinforce standard policy conclusions by articulating a broader range of values, as in arguing for competition on grounds of its contributions to personal liberty as well as to efficiency.[5] Or it may be possible to improve on familiar techniques and to reach somewhat different policy conclusions. For example, one can correct for the possible distributional inequities of an unconstrained cost-benefit analysis (Anthony Atkinson 1970; Arnold Harberger 1978). Controversial moral commitments are unavoidable when the arguments are deepened in these ways.

Much applied welfare economics factors normative questions into questions of efficiency and of equity. This factoring is motivated by two things.[6] First, theoretical economics provides apparently precise and tractable notions of efficiency, while some notions of equity are vague, and most have little connection to the terms in which economists theorize. Second, the values that support greater efficiency have seemed less controversial than those supporting greater equity. So problems of efficiency are seen as manageable and uncontroversial, while problems of equity are seen as alien, controversial, and theoretically intractable. An unsurprising consequence is that standard welfare economics focuses on efficiency.

This circumstance already presupposes a great deal of moral theory. What is the moral basis of a concern with efficiency? Is it really less controversial than the moral commitments that lie behind notions of equity? What do economists presuppose when they factor questions of economic welfare into questions of efficiency and questions of equity? Can these moral presuppositions be sustained? Think about the extreme example of applying cost-benefit analysis to decide whether to build nuclear power

[5] Such arguments are stressed by authors as different as Friedman (1962), John Rawls (1971), and Robert Nozick (1974) as well as in the tradition of classical liberalism, for instance John Stuart Mill (1871, book 11, ch. 1) and Frank Knight (1935).

[6] For an excellent early discussion and critique of the alternative ways in which economists employ and defend the partitioning of normative questions into equity and efficiency components, see Paul Streeten (1953). See also Ian Little (1957).

plants. How should the interests of future people be reflected? What (if any) discount rate is morally appropriate to use? What is the right way of dealing with the tremendous uncertainties of the distant future? (Partha Dasgupta 1982; Isaac Levi 1980; Robert Lind et al. 1982; Douglas Maclean and Peter Brown 1983; Dennis Mueller 1974; Derek Parfit 1984, pp. 480–86; Peter Warr and Brian Wright 1981.)

1.1.3 *Making Economics Relevant to Policy*. When politicians and noneconomists think about problems of welfare, they employ concepts that do not easily translate into the language of standard economic theory. The Reagan administration spoke about preserving a "safety net." Panhandlers speak to us of their *needs*, not their preferences. Notions of fairness, opportunity, freedom, and rights are arguably of more importance in policy making than are concerns about moving individuals up their given preference rankings. Insofar as economists want to assist in the formulation of policy toward such ends, they must link economic theory to such concerns. Doing so requires understanding what these vague things are that people apparently value so much.

Consider, for example, the question of whether government should provide food or health care in kind, or whether it should instead provide a cash supplement to those in need. Most economists would offer a simple argument why the government should supply cash:[7] Construct an indifference map for an individual with quantity of health care on one axis and some composite consumption commodity on the other. Increased income raises the budget line. If the income increase is as large as the value of the in-kind health care provision, then the individual can purchase what the government would have provided if he or she prefers, or the individual can instead consume more of something else. The cash supplement makes individuals at least as well off as does the in-kind provision. Cash supplements are not only Pareto-superior to in-kind provision, but they also serve freedom by increasing the range of individual choice. And lower administrative costs would permit lower taxes or more health care.

Although this analysis brings in the value of freedom, it works mainly within the terms set by orthodox economic theory. There is no mention of needs, of the presuppositions of individual dignity, of opportunity, of rights, or of fairness. There is no concern with the normative commitments that support taxing individuals to provide such benefits (Steven Kelman 1986; Harold Hochman and James Rogers 1969). Not all the arguments in favor of in-kind provision that might follow from these points are paternalistic, but serious attention to questions of justified paternalism are begged from the beginning by equating recipients' welfare with the satisfaction of their preferences (which may be short-sighted or ill-informed).[8] So even if the simple argument were valid, it would be inconclusive. How much weight it ought to have in policy making cannot be considered without a much broader concern with ethical questions.

[7] For criticisms of this argument, see Lester Thurow (1977) and Arthur Okun (1975). This argument is faulty, for it leaves out of consideration the preferences of the donors. Asymmetric information also gives rise to serious problems (Charles Blackorby and David Donaldson 1988). If cash rather than medical care is provided to those in poor health, people will have an incentive to pretend to be sick.

[8] Notice that one might acknowledge the possibility that persons' preferences are flawed indications of their welfare and still argue on grounds of liberty against paternalistic intervention. Mill's classic critique of paternalism in *On Liberty* does not assume that individuals are always the best judge of their own good. For assessments of apparently paternalistic interventions, see Gerald Dworkin (1971, 1988), and Joel Feinberg (1986).

For another illustration, think about the apparently irrational way in which most societies allocate resources to the preservation of life and health. If the money spent on neonatal intensive care units were devoted instead to better health care for pregnant women and less precarious newborns, infant mortality could be reduced significantly. If the heroic efforts to rescue victims of coal-mine cave-ins were devoted instead to mundane mine safety, fewer miners would die. Hundreds of thousands of dollars were spent to rescue Baby Jessica, who fell into an abandoned well, money which could instead have been used to prevent dozens of avoidable deaths of other little children. According to some moral theories, such as utilitarianism, these choices are apparently as indefensible as most economists would find them. But what sort of a social world would we live in, if our humanitarianism were always under the control of rational calculation, if we said to Baby Jessica's mother or to the families of trapped coal miners that the victims could be saved, but it would cost too much to save them? Does rational beneficence (a virtue according to almost all moral theories) demand that we "humanely" pump down poison gas to shorten the suffering? While these examples dramatize life-and-death dilemmas, a great many economic choices require weighing numbers of deaths against other values, or weighing the deaths of some people against the deaths of others (perhaps in future generations). Economists who work on such matters need to understand the strongly felt moral values that govern such choices and to form a sensible appraisal of these values.

1.1.4 *On the Intermixture of Positive and Normative Economics.* Many economists would maintain that questions of positive economics—of how economies actually function, of what the consequences of policies will be—are entirely distinct from questions of normative economics—of what values economic arrangements should promote and of what policies should be adopted. Philosophers have, with good reason, questioned whether a sharp distinction can be maintained (John McDowell 1978; Hilary Putnam 1981, ch. 6; Richard Rorty 1982, ch. 11). But even if philosophers are wrong and there is in principle a sharp distinction to be drawn, the fact is that one often finds positive and normative concerns intermingled in economics.

For example, Paul Samuelson's influential essay, "An Exact Consumption-Loan Model of Capital and Interest" begins with a positive question concerning the effects on interest rates of the desire to save for retirement, but shifts midway to the normatively charged and highly theoretical question of the efficiency of competitive markets in infinite economies. And the two major initial comments on Samuelson's paper by William Meckling (1960) and Abba Lerner (1959) stem respectively from a concern to defend competitive markets and a concern to defend the welfare state. Normative issues have continued to play an important role in the development and assessment of overlapping-generations models (Hausman 1992, ch. 7).

Given shared moral commitments, theories that appear to be purely positive can have sharp normative consequences. For example in "The Economic Consequences of Cognitive Dissonance" (1982), George Akerlof and William Dickens offer a positive model of what will happen if individuals are able to adjust their beliefs to reduce cognitive dissonance. But the possibility of such adjustments casts doubt upon the identification of well-being with the satisfaction of preferences and consequently has immediate ethical consequences. If in order to reduce cognitive dissonance individuals adjust their beliefs concerning, for example, the hazards of their work, there is a stronger case to be made for government safety regulations. One can understand how positive theorizing about cognitive dissonance or other features of individual decision making can have so much normative importance only if one appreciates the ethical presuppositions from which its normative punch derives.

The same point can be put in a different way. Despite (or perhaps because of) their insistence that they need to make no controversial moral commitments, economists often speak on policy questions with an appearance of great moral *authority*. What are the moral foundations of that apparent authority? What sort of moral principles do most economists accept? Why do they seem so uncontroversial?

So there are a number of good reasons why economists need to think about morality. For only by thinking about morality can they understand why positive theory can be of so much moral importance, what values govern actual policy making, what moral presuppositions govern welfare economics, and what moral factors influence economic outcomes.

1.2 *What Does Moral Philosophy Have to Contribute?*

That economists face ethical questions does not imply that they will find answers in the scholarly work of moral philosophers. Because economics is a specialized discipline, with its own tools and outlook, one suspects economists will have to work out many of the answers on their own. Still, economists may be pleasantly surprised by how much work in contemporary philosophy is useful to them. Apart from systematic theorizing, such as new elaborations and defenses of utilitarian or contractualist theories, there is a wealth of narrowly focused work that may be of use to economists. Some contemporary moral philosophy will be familiar and usable precisely because it builds with tools philosophers have borrowed and adapted from economists. Reading some moral philosophy may also help exorcise unjustifiable skeptical doubts (to which economists have been prone) about the possibility of rational argument concerning values. Finally, the literature of moral philosophy will be useful as a warning against reducing the many dimensions of moral appraisal to one or two and as a reminder of how many different dimensions of moral appraisal there are.

The last point is worth elaborating. Philosophers have attended to many complexities of moral thought to which economists have paid little attention. Unless moral philosophy is to be seen as a purely a priori discipline, which is neither a plausible view nor a popular one among philosophers, part of its task must be to make sense of, and bring some order to, everyday moral experience.[9] On some issues (such as abortion) people have strong convictions. On others (such as animal rights), they may have mostly doubts. On some moral questions (should the homeless be allowed to starve?) people reach agreement easily, while on others controversy rages. Moral judgments are made about a variety of kinds of "ob-

[9] This is not to say that moral philosophers must be uncritical of "commonsense morality." There is some analogy here to natural science: scientists must start from everyday observations in building up a scientific picture of the world, but their conclusions may wind up being critical of some commonsense beliefs about the world. They could not, however, be critical of all everyday observations at once: everyday observation is the raw material of science. Similarly, everyday moral judgments are the raw material of moral philosophy, which moral theory has to connect up with, but does not in every case have to endorse. This is a rough statement of the view of moral justification Rawls has called "reflective equilibrium" (1951, 1971). It is helpfully discussed in Norman Daniels (1979), and Henry Sidgwick's classic discussion of moral intuitions (1901) is still of value.

jects": we may pronounce a person, an outcome, an action, an emotion "good" or "bad" in a moral sense. The complexity and fragmentation of actual moral judgments poses an important challenge to theory, one that is very familiar to economists in other contexts. There is an apparently inescapable trade-off between simplicity, generality, and theoretical precision on the one hand, and plausibility and recognition of complexity and "messiness" on the other.

This challenge is felt by economists as well as moral philosophers. But philosophers can perform a real service for economists to the extent that their work calls attention to the complications and multiple dimensions of moral judgment. The service is in part the negative one of discouraging economists from premature or overly sweeping generalization. But it includes as well the positive service of presenting economists with a variety of normative phenomena to which they may contribute their modeling skills. Indeed, it seems reasonable to suppose that both economists and philosophers may contribute as much to improving our understanding of moral problems by analyzing limited pieces of the puzzle as by advancing more general theories of morality. Much of the work we shall discuss is of the former kind.

2. *Morality and Rationality*

In their everyday usages, both "moral" and "rational" are normative and expressive terms: to characterize a choice as irrational or immoral is to condemn it, and not simply to describe it (Allan Gibbard 1990). Because modern economics is heavily committed to a specific characterization of rational conduct, it is committed to certain norms of rational individual choice. How are these norms related to moral norms, and how do moral norms influence what people do? Attempting to bring moral notions "into the picture" of the economic actor clearly raises a number of questions.

In sorting all this out, it may be useful to follow two separate lines of inquiry. One involves attempts by economists to take account empirically of the influence of moral norms on people's behavior. This approach starts from the apparent fact that people's economic behavior is influenced by their moral beliefs, and it looks to see what impact these beliefs have on economic outcomes. At least to begin with, one can pursue this approach in a purely "positive" light—asking not whether these moral beliefs are justified, but simply whether they are behaviorally effective. Rather quickly, however, such work turns to the question of whether the observed moral commitments are economically beneficial or pernicious, and at that point the normative and positive dimensions intertwine. Work on these lines tends to use rough and ready conceptions of economic rationality and of morality—the aim is to find categories that help sort out empirical phenomena.

The other line of inquiry is more self-consciously conceptual and theoretical. Viewed abstractly, what is the relation between a morality and a preference relation? Can one or should one offer a conception of economic rationality that makes sense of a distinction between acting morally and maximizing utility? If there are cases where the two can be said to diverge, does this imply that it is sometimes irrational to act morally or immoral to act rationally?

It will be useful before pursuing these two lines of inquiry to review briefly the main features of the standard view of economic rationality.

2.1 *Economic Rationality*

Economics portrays agents as choosing rationally. Many generalizations concerning how people do in fact choose are also claims about how agents *ought rationally* to choose. This fact distinguishes economics from the natural sciences, whose particles do not choose at all, and who theories have no similar normative dimension. Economists take choice as arising from constraints, preferences, and expectations or beliefs. Economists typically take preferences as givens and not themselves subject to rational appraisal. But choices and *sets* of beliefs and preferences may be rational or irrational. Choice is rational when it is determined by a rational set of beliefs and preferences. The rationality of sets of preferences and beliefs is defined within utility theory.

2.1.1 *Certainty and Ordinal Utility Theory.* In circumstances of certainty, agents are conventionally taken to have rational preferences if their preferences are complete and transitive, and to choose rationally if their preferences are rational and there is no feasible option that they prefer to the chosen option. Many economists, in accordance with the theory of revealed preference, equate preference with choice definitionally (provided that consistency requirements are met). But identifying preference and choice cuts off too many questions. Keeping them distinct is useful both for clarity about what preference and choice mean, and to leave space for the formulation of alternative views of rationality that allow for the possibility of choosing an action that does not maximally satisfy preferences (see Sen 1973a, 1977a, and p. 688 below). This notion of rationality, as weak as it seems, may be too demanding, and there are a variety of weaker concepts, which we cannot discuss here.[10]

Completeness and transitivity together establish a weak ordering of any finite set of alternatives, and one can assign numbers to options so that preferred options get higher numbers, and indifferent options get the same number. Any such assignment of numbers is an ordinal utility function. The *ordinal representation theorem* states that if an individual's preferences are complete, transitive, and continuous, then they may be represented by a continuous real-valued utility function (proved by Gerard Debreu 1959, pp. 54–59).[11]

To be a utility maximizer is merely to choose the available option one most prefers (or, in the case of ties, to choose one among the set of maximally preferred options). Although the utility language was inherited from the utilitarians, some of whom thought of utility as a sensation with a certain intensity, duration, purity, or propinquity (Jeremy Bentham 1789, ch. 4), there is no such implication in contemporary theory. To speak of individuals as *aiming to* maximize utility or as *seeking* more utility may suggest misleadingly that utility is an object of choice, some ultimately good thing that people want in addition to healthy children or better television. But the theory of rational choice specifies no distinctive aims. This fact is of considerable importance to moral theory, for utility theory as such is detached from any hedonistic psychology.

It is worth emphasizing that, despite the fact that it recommends no substantive aims, utility theory remains a normative theory rather than a positive theory or merely a model or definition. It is not

[10] See Sen (1971) and Edward McClennen (1990, ch. 2). Some of these views of rationality, as we shall repeatedly see—in the next footnote, for example—are more congenial to particular ethical theories than others.

[11] The assumption of continuity is arguably innocuous, but it is worth noting that at least one formal argument for utilitarianism (Marcus Fleming 1952) collapses without continuity of social or moral preference, and one formal argument for something akin to Rawls' difference principle turns crucially on rejecting continuity. See Steven Strasnick (1976, 1981); Peter Hammond (1976b); Claude d'Aspremont and Louis Gevers (1977).

a positive theory without further assumptions concerning the extent to which people are rational, and it is not merely a model or definition, because rationality is itself a normative notion. To define what rational preference and choice are, is ipso facto to say how one *ought* rationally to prefer and to choose. As utility theory places no constraints on what individuals may want, it has a much wider scope than economic theories.

2.1.2 *Expected Utility Theory*. Although the theory of rationality in circumstances of certainty is a central part of microeconomics, it is a thin theory. But the theory can be extended to cover cases of risk and uncertainty.[12] When actions do not lead with certainty to any particular outcome, they may be regarded as *lotteries* with outcomes as prizes. In offering a normative theory of decision making under risk and uncertainty, one then asserts that preferences among lotteries are complete, transitive, and continuous. In addition, one needs a reduction postulate identifying complex lotteries with simple lotteries that have the same probabilities and prizes (John Harsanyi calls it a "notational convention" 1977b, p. 24). Second (and last!) one needs the so-called "independence" or "sure-thing" principle, which says that if two lotteries differ only in one prize, *A*'s preferences between the lotteries match *A*'s preferences between the prizes. The (cardinal) representation theorem[13] says that if an agent's preferences are complete, transitive, and continuous and satisfy the reduction postulate and the independence principle, then those preferences may be represented by a utility function that possesses the expected utility property and is unique up to a positive affine (linear) transformation. A utility function possesses the expected utility property if and only if the (expected) utility of any lottery is equal to the utilities of its outcomes weighted by their probabilities. The representation theorem establishes that comparisons of utility *differences* are independent of the scale chosen. Although expected utilities are cardinal, they are not (at least without further argument) interpersonally comparable. As in the case of utility theory concerning choice under certainty, one relates choice to preference by asserting that individuals choose whatever feasible option is highest in their preference ranking—or, in the case of ties, a member of the maximal set of options. The probabilities in expected utility theory may be objective frequencies (as in von Neumann and Morgenstern 1947), but more commonly, they are subjective, representing the degrees of belief of individuals, and the axioms for rational choice under conditions of uncertainty imply that these degrees of belief will satisfy the axioms of the probability calculus. Moreover, it can be shown that if one's degrees of belief do not satisfy the axioms of the probability calculus, then one can be led to accept a series of bets on some chance event leading to a certain loss whether the event occurs or not.[14] Expected utility theory is thus not only a theory of rational preference and choice, but it may also provide a thin theory of rational belief.

2.1.3 *Questions about Utility Theory*. Expected utility theory imposes more structure on individual rationality than

[12] We follow Knight (1921), in speaking of situations of *risk* when outcomes have known probabilities and of situations of *uncertainty* when the probabilities of the outcomes of actions or even the range of outcomes is not known. See R. Duncan Luce and Howard Raiffa (1957, ch. 2).

[13] See Harsanyi (1977b, ch. 3). proofs of similar theorems can be found in Israel Herstein and John Milnor (1953); Niels Jensen (1967); and John von Neumann and Oskar Morgenstern (1947). See also Frank Ramsey (1926) and Leonard Savage (1972).

[14] See Frederic Schick (1986) for critical discussion of this so-called "Dutch-Book Argument."

does utility theory under certainty, and it has proved much more controversial. Psychologists and economists have subjected expected utility theory to experimental tests, with results that are often unfavorable to the theory. Some results suggest not merely that people are not always rational, but that expected utility theory is flawed as a theory of rationality. These empirical anomalies, along with general critiques of expected utility (see Maurice Allais 1952; Daniel Ellsberg 1961; Sen 1985b; Levi 1986b; McClennen 1990), have stimulated the formulation of several less demanding alternative theories of rationality under uncertainty (Farouk Gul 1991; Graham Loomes and Robert Sugden 1982; Mark Machina 1987, 1989; Amos Tversky and Daniel Kahneman 1979; Levi 1980).

Although we cannot survey the controversies concerning expected utility theory and its competitors here, they are directly relevant to moral philosophy as well as to economics. For expected utility theory is involved in arguments for moral conclusions, such as Fleming's (1952) Harsanyi's (1955), and William Vickrey's (1945, 1960) remarkable "proofs" of utilitarianism or David Gauthier's (1986) bargaining theory of justice. Alternative theories of rationality not only undercut these arguments, but in some instances, such as Levi (1980, 1986a), undercut the feasibility and attractiveness of specific moral views such as utilitarianism. Some of the more speculative of these alternative views of rationality, such as McClennen's "resolute choice" (1990, esp. chs. 9, 12), offer new possibilities for conceptualizing and overcoming conflicts between individual rationality and social optimality. McClennen defends the rationality of "resolutely" committing oneself to a course of action, such as cooperating in a series of prisoners' dilemma games (p. 719 below), and refusing (unless one is presented with unforeseen information) to make optimizing changes in one's plans. So resolute choosers might not defect in what they know to be the last round of an iterated prisoners' dilemma, and the "backwards induction" argument purportedly establishing the rationality of defecting on every move (p. 721 below) cannot get started. Faced with the possibility of dynamic inconsistency in one's actions (Robert Strotz 1956; Hammond 1976a, 1988), one need not adjust one's current decisions in the light of what one will prefer later. One can also decide on a course of action and stick to it.

Furthermore, although the issues concerning expected utility theory are highly theoretical, they are of imediate practical importance, as alternative theories may yield different recommendations about the rational thing to do. For example, in the case of nuclear power mentioned above (which obviously involves uncertainty, rather than merely risk), should we rely on our best guess as to the future consequences and maximize expected utility or should we recognize our ignorance of relevant probabilities and use some other principle of choice (Levi 1980)?

In addition to these controversies some moral philosophers have maintained that there are such things as irrational preferences, quite apart from any questions about consistency.[15] Parfit, for example, holds that, "It is irrational to desire something that is in no respect worth desiring . . ." (1984, p. 123). He gives the example of a person who prefers a greater pain on a future Tuesday over a lesser pain on a Wednesday, merely because he or she does not care what happens on future Tuesdays. Parfit remarks, ". . . the fact that the agony will be on a Tuesday is

[15] This is a classical view found in Aristotle and especially Plato. More recent defenders include Thomas Nagel (1970) and McDowell (1978).

no reason for preferring it. Preferring the *worse* of two pains for *no* reason, is irrational" (1984, p. 124). James Griffin (1986, chs. 3, 4) insists that certain classes of things such as accomplishment, pleasure, and "deep personal relations" should be among the objects of preference for all rational human beings, while other preferences are only rational if they can be shown to have some connection to such "objective" values. Such views are at odds with the way in which economists think about utility theory, though one might treat them merely as further constraints, rather than as a repudiation of the skeletal view of rationality espoused by economists.[16]

Indeed, even a philosopher such as Gauthier, who builds a theory of value on expected utility theory and who is a forceful critic of an objective view of value, insists that expected utility theory is too weak. Gauthier argues (1986, ch. 2) that rational preferences should reflect experience and survive reflection, and that the preferences one reveals in behavior should match the attitudes one enunciates verbally. On the basis of criteria such as these, Gauthier distinguishes *values* from mere *tastes*.

Accepting utility theory also gives rise to a deep problem for both prudence and morality whenever preferences change. As Richard Brandt (1979, ch. 13) and Parfit (1984) point out, to consider the good for an individual requires more than attention to his/her given preferences, no matter how purified. For if a given preference ranking changes, then it is unclear whether an individual is made better off by satisfying or frustrating the original preferences.[17] It seems that an acceptable view of rationality and welfare will have to look beyond, behind, or beneath given preferences (Stewart 1989). This point has clear policy relevance if institutions or policies have systematic effects on the preferences people form. For then assessment of policy requires either deciding which preferences to promote or deciding on procedural grounds that certain kinds of institutions provide a suitable framework within which desirable preferences will develop (McPherson 1982, 1983b). One should also consider whether there are conflicts between first-order preferences (for example for cigarettes) and so-called "metapreferences" or preferences for preferences (see page 688 below).

2.2 *Incorporating Moral Behavior into Economic Theory*

We can now discuss how moral features of conduct might be related to the standard view of rationality. A useful starting point is with the recent literature that attempts to incorporate moral dimensions of behavior into positive accounts of economic phenomena.[18] This

[16] The relation between preference satisfaction and well-being is further discussed in Section 3.1.1 below.

[17] Indeed, one faces within an agent's life something akin to the problem of interpersonal utility comparisons (Gibbard 1986).

[18] Some economists have adopted the view that purported explanations of economic phenomena that presuppose non-self-interested conduct are necessarily superficial and ad hoc. An adequate explanation must show that the apparently moral behavior can, on deeper analysis, be shown to be consistent with—and indeed can bederived from—self-interest. This position is examined by Jon Elster (1979, ch. 3). The research strategy of which this is an example is, of course, much more general in economics. Many contributions to macroeconomics, for example, have been similarly criticized as ad hoc unless they can be derived from the familiar equilibrium model of economics (Douglas Wade Hands 1988). About this general strategy it is perhaps worth making these three observations. First, at any stage in the development of economic understanding, it seems rash to reject theories outright because they appear superficial or ad hoc, simply on the hope that more adequate theories will become available later. Second, there cannot be any general guarantee that the attempt to reduce superficial theories to ones that are consistent with familiar microeconomic assumptions will work—we have no a priori guarantee that this set of axioms is true and complete. But third, it is per-

literature draws eclectically on generalizations about moral behavior from sociology, history, observation, or even experiment to develop modified theories about the behavior of households, firms, and hence economies. Many of these studies have emphasized that moral constraints on behavior may be *instrumentally* important to good economic performance, although one can also study how moral practices might hinder economic development (Diego Gambetta 1988; Edward Banfield 1958). And the effects of moral commitments on the character of economic outcomes can be of interest even if there is no effect on efficiency.

2.2.1 *The Effects of Moral Commitments.* Moral norms may have significant impacts on the provision of public goods, voting, and activities involving the production of externalities (Michael Taylor 1987; Thomas Schelling 1978; Jane Mansbridge 1990; and Elster 1989a). But perhaps the most sustained and illuminating treatments of moral influences on economic behavior have been concerned with work motivation and the organization of the firm. Since at least Marx and Mill, economists have recognized that worker performance is closely related to workers' perception of the legitimacy of authority and the fairness of distribution.

Recent research on these issues begins with the recognition that contracts for labor are unavoidably incomplete, and monitoring of worker performance is imperfect and costly. Any sort of performance-based contract is subject to moral hazard problems on both sides—with workers attempting to supply less effort than is agreed and employers trying to understate worker performance levels. A variety of devices for overcoming these problems have been examined, some of them relying strictly on self-interested motivation by all parties (Akerlof and Janet Yellen 1986). But both everyday experience and a substantial body of sociological research suggest that norms and moral dispositions have an important influence.[19] Akerlof (1983, 1984) has emphasized the role of norms of fairness—"a fair day's work for a fair day's pay"—in governing effort levels, and argues that sustaining these norms requires that workers and employers view part of the exchange between them as an exchange of "gifts"—a gift of work effort above what can be enforced and a gift of pay above what the market demands (see also Harvey Leibenstein 1976, 1979). A related but distinct point is the role of *trust* in governing worker-employer relationships (Roland McKean 1975; Arrow 1974; Gambetta 1988). Trust is particularly important in long-term work relationships, where the rewards for reliable service may be long delayed. Commentators on the Japanese economy have identified distinctive cultural norms regarding cooperation and work effort as important to the functioning of Japanese firms (Ronald Dore 1987; Michio Morishima 1982).

Economists have also noted that moral norms influence the comparative efficiency of alternative ways of organizing the productive enterprise (Oliver Williamson 1980; Alan Fox 1974; Hans Nutzinger 1976; McPherson 1984). Workers' rights to control over work decisions and workers' beliefs about distributive fairness have been alleged to play an important role in determining the relative

fectly reasonable for some economists to devote energy to searching for such reductions in particular cases: sometimes such reductions may work, and, if persistent efforts fail, the efforts may constitute grounds to take the apparently ad hoc claims seriously (Hausman 1992, esp. ch. 6).

[19] George Baker, Michael Jensen, and Kevin Murphy (1988) provide a helpful review of observed labor market phenomena that are hard to explain on standard economic assumptions and that seem to indicate an important role for moral norms in influencing the labor market.

productivity of entrepreneurial and worker-controlled firms. The general proposition, which dates back to Mill, is that workers will be more willing to supply effort in circumstances where they have a say in the rules governing the enterprise and where there is good reason to believe that a strong common effort will result in larger rewards for members of the group (Louis Putterman 1984; Samuel Bowles 1985; McPherson 1983a; Michael Reich and James Devine 1981; Bowles and Herbert Gintis 1990).

Sociological and normative aspects of work relations may also influence labor markets.[20] Indeed, social norms in the workplace may help explain "sticky wages" and persistent unemployment. "Gift exchange" or more generally normatively governed wage relations explain the existence of a wage that persists above the market clearing equilibrium as a means of providing workers with an incentive to perform well on the job (Akerlof 1984; Solow 1981; Alan Blinder and Don Choi 1990; Bowles 1985). Such an "efficiency wage" may explain a persistent excess supply of labor, but the persistence of such a wage itself raises problems. Why don't unemployed workers seek to undercut this wage by offering to work for less than those with jobs? Why don't employers actively seek such workers? Solow (1990, ch. 2) and Jörgen Weibull (1987) suggest that further social norms come into play—a norm among workers against bidding against their fellows for jobs and a norm among employers against seeking to undercut their existing workforce.

These lines of analysis point to the importance of normatively governed restraints on individual maximizing in explaining the performance of firms and the behavior of labor markets. They also raise further questions about how such norms originate and persist and about whether adherence to the norms is economically efficient and/or morally justified (Elster 1989a, 1989b; Sugden 1989).

If moral dispositions of economic agents influence outcomes, then economists concerned with public policy and social welfare may want to say something about whether public policies ought to encourage certain kinds of moral behavior. Attending empirically to moral dimensions of individual behavior may thus affect economists' evaluation of institutions or policies. A simple example is provided by Melvin Reder's (1979) analysis of the economics of honesty. Reder proposes to measure a person's honesty by the size of the reward required to induce him or her to lie.[21] Ceteris paribus, more honesty will reduce contracting and policing costs, and therefore policies that promote honesty will raise net economic output. Reder suggests that social investment in schools and churches may have this economic justification.[22]

This analysis makes the value of moral dispositions and of institutions which promote them instrumental to given eco-

[20] As Robert Solow (1990) emphasizes, this thought has a distinguished history in such works as Alfred Marshall (1887) and John Dunlop (1957).

[21] There is an anecdote, whose origins we have been unable to trace, of someone who attempted to bribe Abraham Lincoln. Lincoln kept brushing him off genially and the briber kept increasing his price. When the price got very high, Lincoln clouted him. When asked why he suddenly got so aggressive, Lincoln responded—because you were getting close to my price! It would be hard to model this sort of honesty in Reder's way.

[22] The instrumental or functional *justification* of some moral dispositions, or of institutions that promote morality, does not, without much further argument, *explain* their existence. As Elster has argued, pointing to the favorable consequences of a social practice does not explain its existence or persistence in the absence of an account of the mechanisms by which the favorable consequences produce or sustain the practice. In biology, natural selection provides such a mechanism. In the social sciences functional explanations are more dubious. (See G. A. Cohen 1982; Friedrich von Hayek 1988; Elster 1989a; Viktor Vanberg 1986; and Geoffrey Hodgson 1991.)

nomic ends. The advantages of embedding moral behavior into the familiar scheme of economic evaluation in this way are substantial, and this approach is compatible with influential philosophical accounts of the role of morality in social life. Philosophers within both utilitarian and contractualist traditions have argued that moral restraints are justified by the fact that the pursuit of self-interest may lead to nonoptimal social outcomes (Kurt Baier 1958; John Mackie 1977; Gauthier 1986).[23]

There are various ways in which moral beliefs and dispositions might be assessed instrumentally. Perhaps the simplest way would be to take economic efficiency to be the relevant goal (as Reder does). Yet the moral dispositions of economic actors may also influence distributive outcomes, so equity as well as efficiency judgments may figure in instrumental assessment of moral conduct. Questions of power also intrude, as would be stressed by radical economists who have argued that the tendency for workers to "shirk" under capitalist productive arrangements is a justifiable reaction to the oppressive circumstances of their work (Harry Braverman 1974; Richard Edwards 1979).

Viewing moral rules as promoting social welfare is useful in linking them to familiar modes of economic analysis, and it has also given rise to striking evolutionary speculations (Gibbard 1990). Yet this way of looking at moral rules broaches deep questions about the relation between rationality and morality. As McKean (1975) notes, this instrumental outlook takes moral dispositions as means to advance the satisfaction of given preferences. But where does the inclination to follow moral rules fit into the actors' preferences? If it is part of their preference system, then there seems to be an element of circularity in influencing the strength of the inclination (preference) for following moral rules as part of a strategy for maximizing overall preference satisfaction. But if moral dispositions are not part of the preference system, then the fact that a general practice of following the norms serves a useful social function leaves open whether it is *individually* rational for persons to adhere to moral norms.

2.2.2 *Modeling Moral Commitment.* These conundrums lead back to conceptual issues concerning the relations between morality and rationality. The central question is whether there is any *inconsistency* between economically rational action and morally motivated conduct. There seems offhand to be no inherent incompatbility between utility theory and the demands of morality. For utility theory places no constraints on the objects of preferences. Preferences can just as well reflect the dictates of conscience as the promptings of the libido.[24]

Despite the flexibility of utility theory, it is questionable whether the full range of familiar moral phenomena can be accommodated within it. Transitivity and completeness require that people have a clear view of what is the right thing to do in every situation and of how much weight to give moral concerns in every choice. As problems of moral backsliding, of weakness of will, and of doubt are familiar features of everyone's moral

[23] Historically, David Hume's analysis of justice is an important progenitor of this tradition. And, indeed, it can be argued that Hume's young friend Adam Smith gave substantial credit to this view of morality both in *The Theory of Moral Sentiments* and *The Wealth of Nations*.

[24] It is, however, important to appreciate that the *objects* over which preferences are defined may have to be quite different from the familiar range of economic commodities if the preferences are to rationalize moral choices. To cite a trivial example, a delicious piece of apple pie that was known to be stolen would not be the same object as a physically similar piece of pie that came as a gift. Susan Hurley (1981, part I) argues that values inevitably constrain which descriptions of the objects of preference are "eligible" (and that consequently values and preferences are interdependent).

experience, it is hard to believe that the choices of actors who are influenced by moral concerns can be rationalized by a complete and transitive preference function, nor is it obvious that it is reasonable to demand that they can be.[25]

But even if utility maximization and morally motivated conduct are formally consistent, one might still question how *helpful* utility theory is in analyzing moral conduct. As Sen (1977a) has argued, even though utility theory may be too demanding in some regards, it may at the same time impose *too little* structure on problems of choice to allow productive analysis of moral conduct. For example, the question with which we concluded the last section—Is moral norm-following consistent with individual rationality?—is drained of significance if people's moral concerns are automatically built in to their preference functions. The vocabulary in which preferences and choices are described needs enrichment.

One obvious step in this direction is to distinguish *self-regarding* or *egoistic* from *other-regarding* or *altruistic* preferences. No special formal difficulties arise in including either the utility or consumption levels of other individuals in a person's utility function.[26] Terminologically, it is useful to mark the distinction by referring to the satisfaction of self-regarding preferences by some term such as "personal interests" or "standard of living," recognizing that this differs from the person's overall level of satisfaction, including the satisfactions of sympathy.[27] However, not all nonegoistic concerns are well-captured by such notions of sympathy or altruism. First, one may be concerned not only with the level of another person's welfare or consumption, but with how it is attained. One may wish to be an active contributor to another's well-being. As Arrow has noted, the desire to contribute may have substantially different implications than mere altruism. If many affluent people prefer a higher level of consumption for "the poor," then the poor's consumption level is a public good to the affluent. If instead each wishes to contribute to helping the poor, the public-goods problem goes away (Hochman and Rodgers 1969). More generally, this *agency* aspect of individual motivation—the desire to *do* certain things rather than simply to enjoy the consequences of their being done—has important implications in modeling preference and choice (Sen 1982b, 1987a).

Sen proposes another distinction between sympathy and "commitment." Consider the example of a soldier on sentry duty. Her motives in staying alert may include a self-interested fear of punishment and a sympathetic concern for the welfare of those she is guarding. But she may be motivated as well by a desire to do her duty, to live up to a code she has acknowledged as binding on her. Sen proposes to define "commitment" in terms of her willingness to undertake an

[25] There is an interesting current literature questioning whether a specifically deontological moral system (one that specifies what is right or wrong without regard to the consequences) can be consistent with utility theory (John Broome 1991b). Many question whether a truly deontological ethics— particularly one employing "agent-centered constraints" (p. 705 below) is defensible (Samuel Scheffler 1982, 1988; Shelly Kagan 1989).

[26] Arrow (1972), Gary Becker (1981), Kenneth Boulding (1973), David Collard (1978). There is no reason in principle why the sign on other people's utility has to be positive. Things are particularly simple if what enters one person's utility function is the level of satisfaction of the *self-regarding* preferences of someone else. If instead what enters is the other person's overall level of satisfaction, including satisfactions obtained from the welfare of others, tricky strategic issues arise owing to the feedback effects between different people's welfare (see Elster 1989a).

[27] There is no canonical usage here. For a helpful discussion of alternative ways of distinguishing among the various categories of matters "an agent has reason to favour or promote" (Williams 1987, p. 95) see Sen's essay, Williams's comment, and Sen's reply in Sen et al. (1987). What is important is not the precise names given to different concepts here, but an awareness of distinctions among those concepts.

action (in this case staying alert) even if her welfare—including both self-interested and sympathetic components—were reduced by doing so.[28] Economists schooled by the theory of revealed preference may be tempted to insist that if the agent chooses to stay alert, then she must have preferred to; and staying alert makes her better off. But identifying preference, choice, and welfare begs too many important questions. Even though it may be possible formally to model the committed agent as maximizing utility, it seems enlightening not to do so. For then one can begin to consider just what sort of role morality might play in constraining choices, and one can recognize the special problems of self-control and weakness of will to which duties give rise.

Should a person who acts against her narrow personal interests out of sympathy or duty be said to act irrationally? Elaborating the structure of internal motivations has the helpful effect of making that question dissolve. If one stipulates that acting rationally requires acting in accord with selfish preferences, then the answer is "yes." If sympathetic but not "committed" concerns are captured in what the agent maximizes, then the answer concerning commitment is still "yes." But if one says most generally that acting rationally means acting on reasons that seem to be good ones, then the answer is "no."[29] It is important to be able to draw these distinctions, if only because the alleged "irrationality" of moral commitment needs to be distinguished from the irrationality of passion, vendetta, or schizophrenia.

The preceding pertains to making sense of the actions of a person with a set of complex but presumably settled motivations. But one may also need to make sense of the phenomena of reflecting on, assessing, and sometimes revising one's motives or reasons for acting. The devices of multiple preference systems and of higher-order preferences may be particularly useful in this regard. Multiple preference systems very naturally model internal conflict concerning such personal choices as whether or not to smoke (Schelling 1984, pp. 57–112) as well as more clearly moral choices such as whether to contribute to charity (Amitai Etzioni 1986, pp. 177–80; Harry Frankfurt 1971). Indeed some scholars have argued that the choices of morally influenced persons are in general better modeled through a multiple-utility framework (Howard Margolis 1982; Etzioni 1988). However, this approach also raises difficult questions, for it is not clear within the multiple-utility framework how to explain which ranking scheme will prevail in which circumstances. Indeed, if that determination is itself made by a consistent preference scheme that exists at a higher level, then it may make sense to reinvoke standard utility theory at this higher level.

The "homo economicus" of contemporary economics is "homo rationalis." This fact embodies a commitment both to a certain mode of modeling and to a normative theory of prudence. The theory of rationality is already a fragment of a theory of morality. But the view of rationality economists endorse—utility theory—may not even be compatible with moral behavior, and it does not provide a rich enough picture of individual choice to permit one to discuss the character, causes, and consequences of moral behavior. Of course economists need not

[28] Notice that this definition (like Reder's view of honesty, p. 685 above) involves a subjunctive. Duty or more generally committed behavior may happen to coincide with personal welfare; but the defining characteristic is that the committed action would be carried out *even if* this were not so.

[29] Or anyway, "not necessarily." Clearly a person could be misinformed or confused and be irrational for that reason at the same time she was being altruistic or dutiful.

aspire to provide a general theory of human action. Yet they should not shrug their shoulders at the difficulties in meshing moral behavior with economic rationality. For it seems that moral behavior may have important consequences for economic outcomes, and the propagation of utility theory has moral implications.

3. *Evaluating Economic Arrangements*

Distinguishing better from worse economic policies and outcomes is a central purpose of normative economics, and one that inescapably relies on moral judgments. Moral evaluations of economic arrangements are built into welfare economics and into the terms of policy debate. Because they permeate economics, it is worthwhile to make these moral appraisals as sensible as possible.

3.1 *Dimensions of Evaluation*

When people think of moral philosophy, they think of attempts to lay out and apply a general framework of moral principles and methods. This is a reasonable picture of landmark work such as Kant's ethics or utilitarianism, and of many modern theories, including Rawls' theory of justice, Nozick's entitlement theory, and neoclassical welfare economics. Because such theories are broad and systematic, and because each theory provides its own interpretation of important concepts such as "well-being" or "equality" or "rights," such theories are difficult to analyze and compare. In our view, the parts of ethical theories we shall survey here may be of more interest to economists than are the whole systems.

3.1.1 *Utility Theory and Human Good.* All plausible moral views assign an important place to conceptions of individual good, welfare, or well-being. This is most obviously true of utilitarianism, which takes morality as maximizing some function of the welfare of individual members of society. But even nonutilitarian views that emphasize notions of rights, fairness, and justice need a conception of human well-being. These views not only recognize the virtue of benevolence, which requires some notion of human good, but even their core notions make reference to well-being. Thus, for example, justice or fairness is understood in terms of treating the *interests* of different persons properly, and acting rightly will often involve avoiding *harm* to other individuals. And notions of harm and of interest are plainly connected to notions of human well-being.

Given economists' commitments to utility theory in *explaining* human choices, it is natural that they would look to levels of utility or of preference-satisfaction as the fundamental measure of human well-being for evaluative purposes as well.[30] In applied work, it is true, economists often rely on more objective measures of "real income" rather than utility measures. This, however, is typically viewed simply as a compromise with data limitations: real income is regarded as a proxy for preference satisfaction (and a highly imperfect one at that—see John Hicks 1940; Samuelson 1950a; Sen 1976b; and Jan de Van Graaff 1957).

However, it is questionable whether preference satisfaction is an adequate conception of individual well-being. Measurements of well-being have many purposes—to establish benchmarks for equality, to assess progress over time, to compare living standards across communities, to weigh the comparative

[30] If these explanations of choices are, as they appear to be, accounts of the *reasons* of *rational* agents, then what is chosen must, given the agent's beliefs, serve his or her interests best. If one assumes, as is common, self-interest and full information, the theoretical temptation to identify well-being with the satisfaction of preferences becomes overwhelming. Concerns about rationality link positive and normative economics (Hausman 1992, chs. 4, 15).

claims that different persons may justifiably make on social resources, and so on. Different conceptions may suit different purposes, and for some purposes central to moral reasoning, preferences may not form a suitable basis (Sen 1987b, 1987c).

A variety of reasons have been advanced for why, quite apart from measurement difficulties, preference satisfaction cannot serve some of these purposes well. First, there are reasons to doubt whether there is any context at all in which one can correctly identify well-being with the satisfaction of preferences. For preferences may be based on false beliefs. One does not make a person better off by satisfying a preference for a glass of poison based on the false beliefs that it is water or that it will make one immortal. Most philosophers who associate well-being with preference satisfaction consequently require that the preferences be suitably "corrected." This introduces an objective element of well-grounded or true belief into a preference-based standard.[31]

But problems remain. For preferences that are not based on indisputably false beliefs may nevertheless be idiosyncratic or based on highly contestable beliefs. Even if the preferences of a starving person who begs for money to make a sacrifice to his god are well informed, one may not believe that satisfying them will make this person better off. If the notion of individual well-being is to be employed in weighing the strength of claims for social provision, it must permit reasoned social agreement on basic components of well-being and on the relative "urgency" of claims to different goods (Thomas Scanlon 1975). One might thus acknowledge a moral obligation to feed the person, but not to finance his worship.[32] Notice that a subjectivist might claim that this resistance to honoring idiosyncratic preferences is purely practical: we would open ourselves to all kinds of manipulation and misrepresentation if we let people's subjective reports of their needs govern public distribution of benefits.[33]

There are further reasons to question whether the conception of well-being as the satisfaction of preferences is suitable for assessing claims to scarce resources. For example, those with expensive tastes may make unfairly large demands. A person who has cultivated a taste for "prephylloxera claret and plover's eggs" (Arrow 1973, p. 254) may be miserable without them and, in one sense, worse off than someone in similar circumstances who delights in beans and franks (see also Ronald Dworkin 1981). But one may question whether social policy should be responsive to such preferences. Defenders of a preference-satisfaction view may argue that what is at issue is fairness rather than the conception of well-being: the person *is* worse off without the plover's eggs, but policy makers don't have to care. In reply, defenders of more objective views of well-being can simply deny that the fancy eater's standard of living or level of well-being is lower at all; there is no need to explain away our indifference to his or her "plight." Similarly, as Harsanyi among others has argued, it is questionable whether satisfying racist, sadistic, and other such

[31] The satisfaction of some preferences, such as preferences for the prosperity of comparative strangers, seem to have nothing to do with an individual's own well-being and many have argued that other-regarding preferences should not be included in our understanding of individual well-being. (See Brian Barry 1965, pp. 11–15, 61–66, 71–72; Ronald Dworkin 1977, pp. 234f; D. W. Haslett 1990; and Thomas Schwartz 1982.)

[32] Scanlon (1975). See also Mark Sagoff (1986). One can see here one reason for preferring in-kind provision to transfer payments.

[33] One might also object that it is paternalistic not to respect the worshipper's preferences. But paternalism and antipaternalism are views about what it is permissible to *do;* they are not views about what individual welfare is. See footnote 8 above.

antisocial preferences should count as contributing to individual well-being.[34]

A final difficulty concerns the effects of culture on preferences and the problem of "adaptive preferences" (Elster 1983; Sen 1987b, 1990). For example women who are systematically denied roles in public life or equal shares of consumption goods may learn (à la Sinead O'Connor) not to want what they have not got. Their utility may be reasonably high, but objectively their standard of living or level of well-being may be low.

The difficulties with a subjective preference-satisfaction view of well-being have elicited two broad types of responses. One response has been to hang on to preference-satisfaction, and, on the one hand, to deflect or defeat some of these objections or, on the other hand, to "launder" preferences of these disagreeable features. Whether these responses succeed is a controversial question.[35] An alternative strategy is to propose a different conception of well-being. Not only are there traditional hedonistic views and hybrids such as Sidgwick's (1901, bk. 2, ch. 2), but there are also "perfectionist" views (Griffin 1986, ch. 4; Parfit 1984, ch. 6; Joseph Raz 1986, ch. 12) in which the desires that count and their weight depend on the objective value of their objects. Indeed what Parfit calls "objective-list" views (1984, Appendix I) jettison most links to agent's desires or aims.

For an objective view that may be more relevant to economists, consider John Rawls' *A Theory of Justice*. Although Rawls sees well-being as the satisfaction of rational preference or desire, he does not regard this conception as appropriate for the purposes of a theory of justice. Rawls proposed instead that well-being be measured by an index of "primary social goods." Goods such as education or income are all-purpose means or, as Rawls put it, things that you want, whatever else you want (1971, p. 92). Rawls does not regard primary social goods as proxies for utility levels. On the contrary, in his view they offer an alternative basis for a more settled social agreement on what is important to well-being (1982). Rawls' approach avoids the expensive tastes and antisocial preferences problems and, he argues, also provides a more impartial perspective for comparing how well-off different individuals are than a preference standard does.

Amartya Sen (1985c, 1987b, 1987c, 1992) criticizes the primary-goods approach because it focuses on the external means that permit people to attain various functionings rather than on "capabilities," or abilities to achieve functionings.[36] In focusing on external goods it leaves out more internal features of persons' circumstances, such as physical handicaps, which may profoundly affect well-being. In focusing on *primary* social goods, Rawls' account also may not work well for comparing the well-being of persons who are much above the mini-

[34] 1977a, p. 56. One may be able to deflect the claims of those with expensive or antisocial preferences without questioning the identification of well-being and the satisfaction of preferences. Not only can one claim (as noted in the text) that some moral issue distinct from the concept of well-being is involved, but one can also note that preferences are malleable, and expressions of preferences respond to incentives. The frustration of expensive and antisocial preferences may contribute to changing them and would discourage their expression, which would enable more preferences to be satisfied.

[35] Griffin (1986) provides an extended defense of an informed preference satisfaction view of individual well-being. For a critical summary of arguments against the preference-based approach to measuring well-being, see the introduction to Sen and Williams (1982), and for a powerful general reply, see Arneson (1990).

[36] A capability is the ability to achieve a certain sort of functioning—literacy is a capability; reading is a "functioning." People may value capabilities for their own sake as well as for the functionings they permit—you're glad to know you can walk around even if you are inclined to stay put.

mum. Sen's alternative is to define well-being in terms of the set of "functionings" a person achieves. Being well nourished is an example of a functioning whose achievement may be impaired either by internal obstacles (such as a digestive disorder) or external ones (a lack of money to buy food). Functionings are of course a vector (being well nourished, reading books, sleeping well) and combining them into a measure of well-being raises a serious index-number problem, the solution to which requires settling on the relative weight to be given to different capabilities and functionings.[37]

Even if the problems of weighting and measuring the components of well-being are greater for these more "objective" approaches than for standard utility theory (which is not clear), it can still be argued, following Sen, that "it is better to be vaguely right than precisely wrong." In particular, these approaches focus research on well-being in different directions, which link up more naturally to the normative terms in which policy is debated.

A further important advantage of more objective approaches is that they avoid the problems of interpersonal comparison that derive from identifying well-being and utility (construed as an index of preference satisfaction). Formerly, economists such as Pigou argued that overall welfare would be maximized by equalizing incomes as much as was consistent with retaining incentives to produce. Citing diminishing marginal utility of income, they maintained (not implausibly), that an extra one hundred dollars contributes less to the well-being of someone with an income of $50,000 than to the well-being of someone with an income of $5,000. Other things being equal, a more equal distribution of income would increase total welfare.

Whatever merits this argument may have if welfare is interpreted as some sort of general material well-being, it has (without further ethical premises) little worth if welfare is interpreted as preference satisfaction (Robert Cooter and Peter Rappoport 1984). Lionel Robbins argued compellingly that because preference rankings are entirely subjective and introspective, there is no way to compare where *A* is in *A*'s preference ranking with where *B* is in *B*'s ranking (1935, ch. 6). The fact that people nevertheless make interpersonal comparisons of well-being depends, Robbins argues, on the value judgment that the preferences of people in similar circumstances are similarly satisfied. (One might—in our view more plausibly—instead question whether these comparisons of well-being are comparisons of preference satisfaction.)

Yet Robbins did not convince everyone. Adopting a view similar to Arrow (1978) and Serge-Christophe Kolm (1972), Harsanyi (1955 and especially 1977b, ch. 4), for example, has argued that there is, in effect, a single utility function that depends not only on the objects of choice, but on causal variables affecting and in effect identifying the chooser. Because psychological theory cannot yet specify this underlying utility function, one employs one's empathic abilities to determine one's "extended" preferences between ordered option-agent pairs such as <*x*,Norma> and <*y*,Grover>. Judgments resulting from putting yourself in someone else's shoes in this way can be used to construct inter-

[37] This issue of weighting might seem to bring preferences in through the back door—ultimately, it might be said, the importance of different functionings would depend simply on the weight they are given in people's subjective preferences. However, while people's preferences for functionings and the capabilities they presuppose are relevant to their weight, it is by no means clear that a reasoned public discussion over these weights would wind up concluding that individuals' subjective preferences about them were their only or most important determinant.

personal comparisons.[38] It is also possible to find a foothold for making interpersonal comparisons of utility if one interprets utility in psychological terms, rather than as bare preference. Thus, if a high utility level corresponds to a certain state of mind (or set of possible states of mind), it may be possible to make sense of at least partial interpersonal comparability (Sen 1979d; see also Elster and Roemer 1991).

The identification of well-being with the satisfaction of preferences is questionable in itself. It gives rise to intractable problems of interpersonal comparisons, it is biased by adaptive preferences, and it fails to link up with the normative terms of policy debate. Moreover, the standard notion of utility is not easily measurable, and even if it were, economists cannot defend a measure of individual well-being as a good operational proxy without having some conception of what it is supposed to be a proxy for. The only real advantage of identifying well-being with the satisfaction of preferences is that it apparently links welfare problems immediately to fundamental economic theory. But the link is bogus unless the theoretical "welfare" problems are truly problems of human welfare or well-being.

3.1.2 *Liberty and Rights*. The concept of human well-being is crucial in moral theory, but it is not the only morally significant concept; and even if economists had a more cogent construal of well-being, they would still be hard pressed to evaluate economic outcomes without bringing in other notions.

One of these other important notions is liberty. Many people, including many economists, have the conviction that the protection of certain liberties is of great moral importance regardless of whether such protection always increases well-being. For example, many object to paternalistic laws, such as laws requiring the use of seat belts, as infringements on freedom regardless of whether these laws increase welfare. Social deliberation, unlike welfare economics, often treats protecting freedom and enhancing welfare as independent goals.

It is ironic that welfare economics focuses almost exclusively on the Pareto efficiency concepts. For economists typically value individual freedom; and much of the traditional case for capitalism was not so much in terms of its capacity to "deliver the goods" as in terms of the protection that the separation of economic and political power offers to individual liberty (Hayek 1960; Friedman 1962). Economists favor effluent taxes over direct state regulation of pollution not only because the taxes are purportedly Pareto superior to the regulation, but also because the regulation is a threat to freedom. Yet the efficiency case has been a part of "scientific" welfare economics, because it has appeared to rely only on uncontroversial moral premises, while the argument in terms of freedom has been for essayists or ideologues, because its moral premises have appeared more "philosophical."

To the extent that concerns about liberty underpin economists' normative judgments, they should be incorporated systematically into economists' methods for evaluating states of affairs. Doing so raises problems of *definition*, of *moral justification* and of *integration*. In other words, (1) What is freedom? (2) How can claims about the moral importance of freedom be defended? and (3) How can liberties be incorporated along with other values into a coherent scheme of ethical evaluation?

The term, "freedom," is notoriously slippery. Isaiah Berlin (1969) distinguished what he called "negative" from

[38] For a critique of this "mental shoehorn" tactic, see Alfred MacKay (1986) and Griffin (1986, ch. 7).

"positive" liberty. Negative liberty is liberty from interference, the freedom to act without deliberate negative social sanctions. Berlin defined positive liberty as autonomy or self-determination, while others have thought of positive liberty more in terms of the range and quality of alternatives open to an individual.[39]

It is hard to separate a concern with negative liberty from concerns with freedom in a wider sense. Rawls has attempted to cope with this complexity by distinguishing "liberty," understood as a formal notion, from the "worth of liberty"; others have distinguished "formal" from "effective"liberty. Sen's capabilities (p. 691 above) provide one construal of a sort of positive freedom. Autonomy, which is often seen as the central notion of positive liberty, is a complex notion that draws on other notions of freedom.[40] Moreover, one can distinguish between autonomy as an achievement and the capacity for autonomy (Raz 1986, pp. 204f). Two concepts of liberty are not enough to capture all the dimensions of interest.

Why is liberty in these several senses morally important? Negative liberties are important because they help people get what they want. They promote not only welfare but also integrity, dignity, and autonomy itself. One can make a similar instrumental case for positive freedoms. Some classic defenses of liberty, including Mill's (1859) and Hayek's (1960), are almost entirely instrumental: coercion is costly and dangerous and likely to be misapplied. In the long run, progress depends on individuality, which can only flourish in circumstances of liberty.

Although one can thus value freedom, without regarding it as intrinsically valuable, many would go further and maintain that positive freedom, construed as self-determination or autonomy, is itself intrinsically valuable (Griffin 1986, ch. 4; Raz 1986, ch. 15; Sen 1985a, 1985c). Indeed, autonomy, as rational self-legislation, is, in Immanuel Kant's (1785) view, perhaps the central moral value. The fact that liberty, and, relatedly, the prevention of rights violations, may be valued intrinsically as well as instrumentally, leads to complications in including liberty and rights in overall schemes of ethical valuation. We will return to these issues after saying something about the definition and justification of *rights*.

Although rights and justice obviously contribute to welfare, many people, including many economists, believe that the moral force of rights is not exhausted by their instrumental role. Even if permitting slavery might somehow make us richer, such a practice violates rights and is not to be tolerated.

Rights are often linked to liberties—and for good reason. For one kind of right (such as the right of ambulances to speed) simply *is* a liberty, and liberties constitute an important part of standard "claim-rights."[41] *P*'s (claim-)right to *X* involves both liberties of seeking, acquiring, possessing, or using *X* along with a set of duties on *others*, which may include positive duties such as performing a contracted service as well as negative duties of noninterference. Legal rights define what a person is permitted to do without incurring a threat of legal punishment, what personal claims are legally protected, and consequently what other per-

[39] In speaking of the quality of alternatives, one brings individuals' welfare back into the picture. George Stigler argued on this basis that "liberty" and "wealth" are really synonymous—both index the quality of your options assessed in welfarist terms (1978). But there is a real loss in liberty if you are locked in your house for the day, even if there is no place you would rather be (see Elster 1983 and Sen 1987a, ch. 3).

[40] Feinberg (1986, ch. 18) distinguishes many different aspects of autonomy and draws a helpful analogy to national sovereignty.

[41] The terminology is from Wesley Hohfeld (1923). For general discussions of rights see Feinberg (1973, chs. 4–6) and the introduction to Jeremy Waldron (1984).

sons or governments are prohibited from doing or are required to do. Moral rights similarly define permissions, guarantees, prohibitions, and requirements as matters of moral principle rather than law.

Liberties are important not only to the definition of rights, but also, at least within the Kantian tradition, to the specification and justification of rights. In the view of philosophers such as Herbert L. A. Hart (1955), the limitations imposed on others by *P*'s claim-rights must be justified by their contribution to *P*'s freedom. Rights determine the distribution of freedom. The libertarian considerations that justify placing control with *P*, justify the duties the right implies for others. Even if trespassers on *P*'s property pay fees that restore *P* to the same level of welfare, they have on this view still violated *P*'s property rights. "Isn't the very idea of a forced transfer contrary to the autonomy or liberty thought constitutive of rights?"[42]

But many philosophers would assert that other interests besides *P*'s interests in liberty can also ground *P*'s rights and the consequent duties of others. There is an intricate consequentialist case to be made for moral rights going back to Sidgwick and Mill. (For relevant contemporary work, see Roy Harrod 1936; Rawls 1955; David Lyons 1977; Donald Regan 1980; and Russell Hardin 1988.) From a utilitarian perspective, rights serve as rules that should be crafted to promote welfare. But even nonutilitarians often ground rights in terms of a wider set of individual interests. For example, in Raz's view, "if an individual has a right then a certain aspect of his well-being is a reason for holding others to be under a duty" (1986, pp. 171–72). Such a "benefit" view of rights is compatible with a utilitarian account, but it leaves open the question of when an interest of a potential rights-holder is sufficient to justify imposing duties on others. Rights may, depending on the circumstances, justify imposing a variety of duties on different individuals. Consider, for example, the array of duties that might be justified in terms of a child's right to an education. Notice that a right to education could be justified on grounds of the child's interest not only in future welfare but also in autonomy.

The remaining problem concerning rights and liberty is incorporating them systematically in schemes of moral evaluation. This problem takes different forms in different accounts of why liberty or rights are valuable. On instrumental or consequentialist views, the problem of rights articulation can be formulated as one of selecting rules that maximize good consequences. This is straightforward in principle, although difficult problems of strategic coordination may arise in devising effective rules. The choice of rules may also be influenced by limitations on persons' ability to calculate.

What about cases where rights protections are viewed as intrinsically valuable? One option here is simply to embed instances of rights protections (or of rights violations or losses of liberty) in the consequences, weighting them according to some scheme that reflects their importance relative to other aspects of outcomes. This approach seems to capture only part of the value of rights-protection. For in a situation in which committing one serious wrong, such as torturing a child, will prevent others from perpetrating two equally serious wrongs, this

[42] Jules Coleman and Jody Kraus (1986, p. 31). See also Guido Calabresi and Douglas Melamed (1972). On this view, sometimes called the "choice" view of rights because of the emphasis on the need for the right-holder's voluntary consent to any invasion of the right, only what Calabresi and Melamed call "property rules" (which rest control with the right-holder) serve to define true legal *rights*. Coleman and Kraus argue persuasively that "liability rules," which address themselves to the right-holder's welfare rather than to the right-holder's control, also define legal rights.

approach would mandate carrying out the torture. But many would say that such actions are simply *wrong*, regardless of the consequences or, at any rate, that the moral pressure on me not to do this evil thing goes beyond an impersonal weighing of the consequences. The consequentialist view does not capture the sense that the moral imperative on me is that *I* should not torture a child.[43]

One way to preserve a more thoroughly nonconsequentialist version of rights-protection is to adopt Robert Nozick's view of moral rights as absolute "side-constraints" on action.[44] On this view, an individual's obligation is not to strive for a minimum of rights violations, or a maximum of any social welfare function. Rather, agents may do as they wish, within the constraints imposed by rights. If everyone acts morally, then there will be no rights violations. It is not, however, permissible for anyone to violate rights in order to prevent other rights violations. Rights are simply not to be violated. This absolute lack of trade-offs not only of rights against other good things, but of lesser violations of rights against greater ones, is an implication of Nozick's view which has been found disturbing by many philosophers (for example Nagel 1983), and we suspect most economists would agree.

Amartya Sen has proposed another way to incorporate concern for moral rights into individuals' assessments of how they should act, which avoids the rigid repudiation of trade-offs in Nozick's view. This is to allow the evaluation of the goodness or badness of a state of affairs (or set of consequences) to vary with the perspective of the person doing the evaluating. In the torture example, an onlooker might readily conclude that it is morally better for one child rather than two to be tortured. But *from the standpoint of the person who is doing the torturing*, what is at stake is that person's own action—whether he or she tortures a child. One may act on one's own commitment to rights and judge that despite the good consequences of torturing a child, the act is wrong. Everyone might agree with both these judgments: from a neutral point of view, two tortures are worse than one; but from the point of view of one facing the prospect of torturing a child, carrying out the torture is morally worse than failing to prevent two tortures from happening. This account remains consequentialist but makes the evaluation of the consequences relative to the position of the evaluator (Sen 1982b, 1983a).

Some of these complications are probably unavoidable in any theory that takes rights seriously. However, for public policy purposes, the evaluator-relativity that Sen identifies is less likely to be a consideration than in personal morality, as the aim will be to appraise rights-systems from a suitably impersonal point of view. For this purpose, it may often prove adequate either to treat rights instrumentally or to embed their protection as an intrinsically valuable goal in an evaluator-neutral consequentialist moral framework.

3.1.3 *Equality*. An energetic debate about conceptions of equality has recently emerged that conforms roughly to the distinction between preference-based and more objective conceptions of well-being described in Section 3.1.1. Corresponding to the preference-based view of well-being are conceptions of

[43] It's more unsettling to note that I should in fact be willing to torture the child, on this consequentialist view, if doing so will prevent the torturing of one other child and will also produce some trivial moral gain, say raising somebody's utility by a tiny amount (Williams 1973). For a powerful defense of the importance of this nonconsequentialist aspect of judgments of right and wrong, see Nagel (1980).

[44] 1974, pp. 28–35. A moral view that emphasizes right action independent (or at least partly independent) of consequences is often called *deontological*.

equality of welfare, while corresponding to more objective views is a conception (or a family of conceptions) of equality of resources.[45] The correspondence is rough, because welfare need not be identified with the satisfaction of preferences, and resources may be conceived of as the raw materials out of which individuals achieve a level of well-being rather than as a part of a more objective notion of well-being itself.[46]

Despite these nuances, the intuitive contrast between equality of welfare and equality of resources is clear enough (Ronald Dworkin 1981a, 1981b). "Welfarist" views argue that what ultimately counts in moral evaluation are levels of welfare (usually understood as preference satisfaction), and therefore to the extent that there is concern with equality it should be concern for equalizing welfare. "Resourcist" views maintain that the levels of welfare people achieve depend on personal choices and characteristics that are no concern of social policy or public moral judgment. The proper concern of an egalitarian should not be welfare, but the resources people have available to pursue their own ends, whatever they happen to be.[47] "Resource egalitarianism" plainly appeals to some of the same intuitions as the somewhat vague notion of equal opportunity (see Arneson 1989). As resource and welfare egalitarians can hold different theories of welfare, there are many distinguishable positions in the debate.

Part of the complexity stems from the need to analyze both external and internal resources. Equal distribution of resources such as rice or tractors can be achieved by dividing the commodities themselves up equally. The resulting distribution will generally not be efficient, but competitive trade from an equal division starting point might be taken to preserve equality of resources. In fact, when all resources are external and alienable, a competitive equilibrium arising in this way can be shown to be both Pareto optimal and "envy free" in the sense that no one will prefer another's bundle of commodities to his own. Hal Varian (1974, 1975) has proposed the label "fair" for envy-free Pareto optima, and has defended this conception of fairness as ethically appealing (see also Duncan Foley 1967 and William Baumol 1986). An important stimulus to the study of envy-free allocations of resources has been their apparent ability to provide a standard of equity that does not involve interpersonal comparisons of welfare.

It is not so clear how to define equality of resources when some resources are internal. Consider differences in talent. Equal division of talent is plainly not possible. One might say that resources are equal whenever people have equal amounts of goods and equal amounts of leisure.[48] Unfortunately, if people's tastes differ, this outcome will generally not be efficient, and trade from this equal division starting point may disrupt equality, in the sense that the competitive equilibrium resulting from trade will not be envy free. (For examples, a proof, and

[45] The interplay between conceptions of well-being and conceptions of equality has gone both ways. Sometimes conceptions of well-being are defended on the ground that they give more adequate conceptions of equality.

[46] Thus, Rawls' conception of primary goods connects up with a resourcist view of equality, with primary goods as the resources. Sen's capabilities view is like resourcist views in being concerned with objective features of persons' existence rather than with their subjective satisfactions, but unlike more strictly resourcist views, it emphasizes outcomes (in the form of functionings) and freedom to achieve outcomes, rather than inputs.

[47] Ronald Dworkin (1990) is an ambitious attempt to provide moral foundations for this kind of view as part of a defense of a conception of liberal equality.

[48] If everyone has the same tastes, this will be a fair distribution—Pareto optimal and envy free. See Varian (1974, 1985). (This assumes that problemns of monitoring work effort to prevent shirking do not arise.)

further discussion, see David Schmeidler and Elisha Pazner 1974 and Varian 1985.) This difficulty has led economists to put forward two alternative definitions of equal resources, whose egalitarian properties will not be disrupted by trade.

The first of these is the notion of a "contribution-fair" distribution.[49] Imagine equalizing people's external resources but allowing them to retain the fruits of their differential talents. The resulting competitive equilibrium will not be envy-free, as those with more talent will tend to have consumption-leisure bundles that others envy. The equilibrium is, however, envy free over a space of consumption-output bundles. That is, no agent will want to trade places with another where trading places entails getting the other's consumption bundle but also producing as much as the other person. Contribution fairness essentially leaves talents or internal resources out of the package of things to be equalized, and accepts inequalities due to competitive rewards for talent as fair. This seems to fall short of what many people would think of as equality of resources.

Alternatively, one can define an "income-fair" distribution (Varian 1974, 1975; Schmeidler and Pazner 1974; Baumol 1986). The easiest way to think of this is to imagine everyone owning equal partial shares in the labor power (and hence the talents) of everyone. These shares and all external resources are divided equally. If one wants more leisure than the share of one's own labor power one happens to own (a very small share in a large society), one will have to buy it back from others. If we define a person's "full income" to include the market value of his or her leisure, the resulting competitive equilibrium will equalize full incomes—hence the name "income-fair." Notice, however, that the leisure of the talented is a high-priced commodity. It will cost a talented person more to obtain any given level of leisure than it will cost others. Thus, if tastes are constant across the community, the talented, with equal full incomes and more expensive leisure, wind up worse off—equality of resources in this sense winds up overcompensating the untalented in terms of equality of welfare![50]

If resources can include internal qualities like talents, why stop there? As Roemer (1985a) notes, Ronald Dworkin argues for redistribution of the fruits of unequal talent, but finds inequalities resulting from unequal amibition acceptable. Yet differences in persons' willingness to expend effort must ultimately be traceable to some set of differences in their biological and personal histories, just as for talents. Why not treat the capacity to be ambitious as a resource? For that matter, some people may possess enzymes that allow them to extract more nutrition from a meal, or more satisfaction from a movie. Might we not think of these differences too as hidden resources? It is easy to see that, following this route, one might argue that any dif-

[49] This terminology is due to Baumol (1986). Varian (1974, 1975) has labeled the same notion "wealth-fair."

[50] Ronald Dworkin (1981b), aware of this problem, proposed instead to define equality of resources in terms of a hypothetical insurance scheme that would guard against the misfortune of low productive abilities. Dworkin argued that insurance would produce more palatable results than would the mutual ownership of talents, but economists have criticized his analysis of the hypothetical insurance market (Varian 1985; Roemer 1985a). Developing suggestions of Bruce Ackerman (1981, pp. 116, 132–33), Philippe van Parijs has defended a weaker egalitarian notion of "undominated diversity" (1989, pp. 50–54). Undominated diversity obtains if for each pair of individuals *A* and *B* there is at least one individual who prefers *A*'s total package of internal and external endowments to *B*'s and at least one individual who prefers *B*'s total endowments to *A*'s. Arguing from a commitment to undominated diversity and other moral principles, van Parijs has made a persistent case for an unconditional grant to be paid to every adult citizen (1989, 1990, 1991).

ference in achieved welfare levels resulting from apparently equal resources really is the product of hidden differences in resources.

Roemer (1985a, 1986a, 1986b, 1987) has proved a remarkable set of theorems showing that the only distribution meeting several reasonable-looking requirements for a resource-equalizing mechanism is equality of welfare. Roemer rightly presents this result not as a proof that equality of welfare is the only proper standard, but rather as an effort to clarify the underlying issues involved in distinguishing resourcist from welfarist views. He argues that these issues are of two kinds. One concerns the gap between ideal reasoning about just distribution and realistic limits on information. Equalizing welfare requires enormous amounts of information not only about resource distributions but also about what is going on in people's heads. When we add to these problems the incentives for misrepresentation created by any system for equalizing welfare, some simplified version of resource egalitarianism may be a suitable compromise.

The second issue is more philosophical. The distinction between those internal resources society may wish to compensate for and those other internal differences which it should not compensate for must turn on views about the nature of individual responsibility and about the nature of the person. We may wish to compensate people for being born blind, but not for being born without ambition. We may regard it as appropriate to compensate a person for being stuck with an affliction that brings constant pain, but not appropriate to compensate someone for being stuck with religious beliefs that induce him to starve himself. Articulating and defending these distinctions in a coherent way is a large project, which is far from being done (Scanlon 1975, 1986).

From this standpoint, relying on preferences even to the extent presupposed by the notion of envy-free allocations seems problematic. The whole project of deciding what counts as a resource and of deciding the relative weights to be given to different resources in assessing departures from equality demands more objectivity. The list of resources and appraisal of their relative weights need to be objects of public moral deliberation. As with Rawls' primary goods or Sen's capabilities, the valuation of these resources should depend on assessment of the importance of their role in facilitating a range of good lives. Evidence about the amount of preference satisfaction or the level of market value attaching to a particular resource should influence, but not determine judgments about the resource's value.

In addition to this rapidly developing literature addressed to the question of what to equalize, discussions of whether, why, and to what extent to equalize continue. Judgments about how much to equalize are plainly dependent on the role of equality in overall schemes of moral evaluation. A commitment to moral and political equality is deeply embedded in American political traditions and in Kantian moral philosophy, but the implications of that commitment for *economic* equality as such are controversial. Some theorists, including Ronald Dworkin and Rawls, argue in effect that the same fundamental commitments that rationalize support for moral or political equality should lead us to accept economic equality as a baseline standard, valuable in its own right and to be departed from only at a cost. For these theorists, underlying moral principles of impartiality and mutual respect carry implications for the degree of economic inequality that is morally acceptable. Other theorists, however, deny that economic equality as such is of any moral importance (Raz 1986, ch. 9; Frankfurt 1987). Notice that it is compatible with a skeptical view about the intrinsic moral value of economic equality to hold that it may have substantial instrumental value, on the grounds that economic inequality tends to give rise to other serious evils, such as widespread poverty, inequality in political power, and political or social instability. These instrumental questions give rise to empirical questions about, for example, the political influence of wealth and the influence of economic inequality on social stability, as well as to theoretical questions involved in the very separation of political and economic life. Although Michael Walzer, for example, argues in defense of a pluralistic society in which political equality and economic inequality coexist, he maintains that the authoritarian structure of economic corporations is political rather than economic and is as inconsistent with political equality as are towns that are owned and controlled by corporations (1983, ch. 12). Given the striking increase in economic inequality over the last decade and the evident influence of wealth on election results, these questions are bound to become an increasingly important part of the normative agenda of economists.

3.1.4 *Justice*. The last of the dimensions of evaluation we shall survey is justice, which some take as an umbrella term incorporating all dimensions of evaluation besides efficiency. But the focus here is on issues of justice apart from those touched on in the previous discussions of equality, rights, and liberty.

People in our society are committed to a large number of principles of justice with which they evaluate economic institutions and outcomes. Consider, as a first example, some of the many prima facie principles that influence whether employees regard a given wage structure as fair:

1. More difficult, unpleasant, or dangerous work should be better paid.
2. Jobs that carry a great deal of responsibility should be better paid.
3. Hard work should be rewarded.
4. Seniority is fair. Those who have worked for a given employer for a long time should be better paid.
5. Wages should not depend on race, sex, or arbitrary whim.

These are only a few of many such principles, and there are other principles establishing priorities in case of conflict among these. Moreover, not all of these principles link up easily to positions in moral philosophy, and economists and philosophers may want to dispute some of them or particular attempts to apply them.[51] Some economists might question whether it is any more appropriate to offer a moral evaluation of wages than to offer a moral evaluation of the price of scissors or of the amount of snowfall in Buffalo, New York. But it is plain that moral judgments about wages on the lines enumerated above are frequently made by workers (if not by employers as well), and evaluation of such moral judgments may be relevant to the study of the weight and tenacity of the agents' commitments. A repudiation of this kind of moral evaluation itself rests on substantive principles of justice, and these require a defense.

Principles of justice influence evaluations of other aspects of economic life. Consider for example, equality of opportunity. While no one will dispute its importance, there is great disagreement on what equality of opportunity consists of. Is affirmative action implied by equality of opportunity or inconsistent with it?

[51] For example, Joseph Carens (1985) argues that despite the intuitive appeal of the principle that dangerous and unpleasant work should be better paid, the principle is better served by reducing inequalities in wealth and income than by direct attention to relative wages.

Does equality of opportunity require that more resources be devoted to the education of the relatively disadvantaged? Does equality of opportunity require some more substantial egalitarianism, such as equality of resources? Questions about the extent to which economic policies contribute to equality of opportunity can scarcely be broached until the concept itself is clarified.

There is also a strong consensus in favor of providing a basic "safety net," some minimal support to those who cannot support themselves. One might maintain that this consensus rests mainly on principles of benevolence, but Rawls has offered a powerful contractual argument for, in effect, the highest attainable social minimum. In his view (discussed further in Section 3.2.4 below), impartial rational individuals would choose to maximize the lifetime expectation of primary goods for the least well-off representative individual. If one takes income as a proxy for primary goods, this means that the income of the least well-off representative individual should be maximized. Although this distributive principle, called by Rawls "the difference principle," has some objectionable features, Rawls has provided an important form of argument defending the justice and not merely the charitableness, of a social minimum.

For one last example, consider exploitation. What seems wrong about exploitation is that some people unfairly take advantage of others. But the traditional theories of economic exploitation have not made clear how the sort of exploitation they discuss involves anyone unfairly taking advantage of others. Marxian exploitation is reflected in the fact that wages are less than total revenue net of the costs of nonlabor inputs. But it has not been obvious why exploitation in this sense is a bad thing. The same difficulty applies to extensions of neoclassical theory such as Joan Robinson's conception of exploitation (1933, book IX) whereby owners of factors of production are exploited if they are paid less than the values of their factors' marginal products.

Both in clarifying the traditional Marxian notions of exploitation and in offering an explication or replacement in terms of property rights, John Roemer has greatly clarified discussion of these issues. In his view capitalist exploitation (and there are other kinds) occurs if some group (the workers) would do better if they were to withdraw from society with their per capita share of the means of production, while some other group (the capitalists) would do worse.[52] This view of exploitation, like the others, is open to the question, "So what's wrong with it?" Roemer gives the striking answer, "It depends on how it comes about." It is not capitalist exploitation itself, but the unequal initial distribution that is morally objectionable. If capitalist exploitation were to arise pristinely through the voluntary transactions of individuals whose initial holdings are morally legitimate, then there may be nothing wrong with it (1985b). In Roemer's view a moral concern with exploitation leads one toward a historical view of justice, such as Nozick's (Section 3.2.2 below) and away from a "patterned" view.

3.2 *Four Bases for Overall Moral Judgments*

Although treatments of detailed moral concepts and problems are, we believe, most likely to be of immediate use to economists, no survey could omit a discussion of the moral theories that economists and others use to guide their overall assessment of economic institutions and outcomes. Not only are there

[52] 1982, ch. 7; 1988, ch. 9. This is a first approximation, and in his 1989 article Roemer accepts a suggestion of Erik Olin Wright that the greater benefits of the capitalists have to be linked to the effort exerted by the workers.

many specific moral theories, but they are of many kinds. To limit our survey, we shall focus on specimens of only four kinds of moral theories: (1) those which focus on efficiency, (2) libertarian theories, (3) utilitarian or consequentialist theories, and (4) contractarian theories.[53]

3.2.1 *Efficiency and Pareto Optimality*. If one is minimally benevolent and favors making people better off, then, other things being equal, one should accept the principle (which John Broome calls "the principle of the personal good") that "If two prospects are equally good for everyone, they are equally good, and if one of two prospects is better for someone than the other and at least as good for everyone, then it is better" (1989, p. 11). If in addition one identifies being better off with having a higher utility, then (other things being equal) one will endorse Pareto improvements and efficient (or Pareto optimal) allocations. Moreover, one can offer an argument in terms of these concepts for regarding a perfectly competitive equilibrium as a sort of moral ideal, other things being equal. Because competitive equilibria without externalities, public goods, informational limits, etc. are, by the first welfare theorem, Pareto efficient, they will be (other things being equal) morally good economic states, and market failures will be bad. Furthermore, the second welfare theorem shows that an efficient economic outcome producing any desired distribution of welfare can be attained by the workings of a competitive market, given the right initial distribution of endowments to agents. So with no ethical premise more controversial than minimal beneficence, albeit with a controversial conception of individual well-being, economists can offer moral evaluations along one significant dimension.

However, the Pareto principle may be unappealing when it involves honoring people's "nosy" preferences regarding others' conduct (see the discussion of Sen's liberty paradox below in Section 4.1). Moreover it has been shown that the Pareto principle is inconsistent with the conjunction of individual and collective rationality in conditions of uncertainty (Hammond 1983; Teddy Seidenfeld, Joseph Kadane, and Mark Schervish 1989). The problem lies in the fact that unanimity in individual rankings may rest on disagreements in subjective probability judgments and disagreements in preferences among options involving no uncertainty.[54]

Quite apart from these problems, the Pareto principle or variants appropriate to different views of well-being have very limited applicability, as economic changes usually involve winners and losers. Economists have been reluctant to accept the severe limitations on efficiency judgments imposed by the Pareto criterion and have struggled for many years over the issue of whether some device could be found that would permit judgments in cases involving trade-offs among individuals without invoking interpersonal utility comparisons. The hope was that one could find a way to endorse "potential Pareto improvements," in which the gains to the winners

[53] Recently there has been a good deal of striking criticism of liberal moral theorizing on the grounds that it illegitimately abstracts from the "rich" or "thick" moral discourse that characterizes communities. Authors such as Alastair MacIntyre (1981), Michael Sandel (1982), Charles Taylor (1979), and Walzer (1983) allege that moral theories of these kinds neglect or undervalue the values of community or public life, or that they presuppose a mistaken conception of the self abstracted from communal values and commitments. For a compact critical overview see Allen Buchanan (1989).

[54] For example, suppose the bourgeoisie and proletariat both prefer an armed worker's revolt, because they form different estimates of its likely consequences. The fact of their agreement does not establish that an armed revolt would be socially *better*. See also Levi (1990).

were sufficient to compensate the losers in utility terms, *without actually making the compensation* (Hicks 1939; Nicholas Kaldor 1939). The conclusion has been that no such blanket endorsement is possible, partly owing to technical failings in the proposed devices for identifying improvements, but more fundamentally because there simply is no way to judge changes that affect distributions while remaining neutral on distributive questions (Little 1957; Streeten 1953; Samuelson 1950). But to stop here would leave welfare economists with virtually nothing to say, and practical applications of welfare economics in the form of cost-benefit analysis need to go on. The difficulties seem to have been dealt with in two somewhat unsatisfactory ways. One is by increasing modesty: one cannot always endorse potential Pareto improvements, but at least economists can identify them and leave the endorsing to politicians. Second, it seems that welfare economists have perhaps moved implicitly toward reuniting considerations of efficiency and equity. Blanket endorsements of potential Pareto improvements are unjustifiable, but as there are various theoretical ways to adjust such measures for equity concerns, one can suggest that equity-adjusted potential Pareto improvements can consistently be endorsed. But economists are queasy about the final step of actually endorsing any one way of adjusting for equity concerns.[55]

3.2.2 *Libertarianism.* Libertarianism is both a political program and a philosophical position, and the latter is our main concern. The last two decades have seen a revival of philosophical libertarianism, "the doctrine that the only relevant consideration in political matters is individual liberty" (Jan Narveson 1988, p. 7; see also Tibor Machan 1982, p. vii). In libertarian writings, liberty—the fundamental value—is typically linked to a rights-based view of justice. Acts and policies are just if and only if they do not violate anyone's rights. Moreover, the duties that rights imply are taken to be almost exclusively negative duties not to interfere. The right to life, for example, is a right not to be killed, not a right to be given subsistence. In holding such a view, libertarians are not necessarily endorsing selfishness, although some, such as Ayn Rand's (1964) "objectivist" followers, are. Most libertarians value beneficence and charity as virtues. They only insist that individuals must not be forced to be beneficent or charitable. And some, such as Loren Lomasky, even defend some minimal rights to positive assistance, such as a right to be given a fair trial or an infant's right to nurture (1987, pp. 164, 260). But Lomasky wants to limit such rights narrowly. The duties to provide these particular benefits are, like the duties not to interfere, easy to comply with without compromising the character of one's projects, and the benefits are crucial to the possibility of pursuing any projects at all.

It is not obvious that taking liberty to be the fundamental value automatically commits one to a rights-based view of morality or to the view that rights rarely obligate others to give positive assistance. Indeed, Raz argues extensively that valuing autonomy commits one to an extensive role for government in providing the public goods that facilitate the achievement of autonomy (1986, ch. 8). But the arguments are complex and the libertarian case turns on the interpretation of the problematic notion of liberty.

In Robert Nozick's well-known version of libertarianism, natural rights—rights that do not depend on consequences—secure individual autonomy. Justice is respecting rights. According to Nozick's entitlement theory of justice, an outcome

[55] See also the discussion of "fair" allocations above pp. 697–98.

is just if and only if it arises from just acquisition of what was unowned or by voluntary transfer of what was justly owned. Just acquisition is acquisition that violates no rights, and transfers are, in the relevant sense, voluntary just in case none of the limitations on individual choices arise from rights violations.[56] Justice is a matter of entitlement and depends on the actual history, not at all on the resultant pattern. Only the need to rectify past injustices justifies redistribution. Some of Nozick's most striking arguments in favor of this "entitlement view" involve attempts to show that even minimal efforts to regulate the patterns of distributive outcomes involve much more extensive interference in people's lives than is at first apparent. The libertarian system of rights is presented as having an appealing coherence and integrity. Because the point of rights for Nozick and most other libertarians is to secure liberty and to permit individuals to pursue their own projects, considerations of welfare never justify interferences with individual liberty. Nozick argues that only an extremely minimal state can be justified.[57]

The (philosophical) libertarian's commitment to liberty is, in principle, independent of any consequences for human welfare, but libertarians would like it to be the case that protecting freedom also makes people better off, and libertarians need to show that some of their more extreme proposals, such as privatizing all streets and highways (Walter Block 1982) would not lead to disastrous consequences. Moreover, some theorists who are not libertarians in the strongly anti-consequentialist sense discussed above might be classified as libertarian on policy grounds. Friedrich Hayek, for example, argues that a broad range of important values, including economic prosperity, social innovation, and political democracy, are best advanced by keeping governmental action to a minimum (Hayek 1967, 1976). Most libertarian economists are probably less influenced by distinctive philosophical commitments than by specific reasons for doubting the efficacy of government intervention to improve efficiency or effect income redistribution.[58]

3.2.3 *Utilitarianism and Consequentialism Reborn*. Consequentialism is the ethical theory that an action, rule, or policy is morally permissible or right if and only if there is no alternative with better consequences. Different varieties of consequentialism differ about what "better consequences" are. "Welfarist" moral theories take the view that only consequences for individual well-being ultimately matter, with other items such as rights or virtues viewed strictly as means to promoting welfare. Utilitarianism is, in turn, a subspecies of welfarism in which only the sum or average of individual welfare levels matter. The major 19th century utilitarians (especially Bentham, Mill, and Sidgwick) took utility to be happiness or pleasure.[59] But one can also regard utility, as economists do, as an index of preference or desire satisfaction.

[56] A view such as Nozick's thus places heavy demands on a theory of rights, which Nozick leaves largely undeveloped. See Nagel (1983).

[57] Notice that the libertarian political program does not follow automatically, as a more-than-minimal state might serve liberty better than a minimal state.

[58] "[T]hose who toil in the libertarian fields devote the lion's share of their efforts to persuading us that the alleged benefits of the State are illusory . . ." (Narveson 1988, p. 183). For example, the literature on property rights and transaction costs that derives from Ronald Coase's arguments in "The Problem of Social Cost" (1960) usually reaches conclusions that are congenial to libertarians, but principled libertarians would emphatically reject the consequentialist view of rights as devices to reduce transactions costs and thereby to alleviate the suboptimalities caused by externalities.

[59] As Broome (1991a) points out, they actually took utility to be that property of objects that *causes* happiness or pleasure, but this complication is not germane to the discussion here.

During the decades that preceded the 1980s, utilitarianism appeared to be almost dead. Systematic moral philosophy had fallen from favor with the rise of logical positivism and its subjectivist and noncognitive view of ethics, and utilitarianism had the additional stigma of George E. Moore's (1903) critique of the so-called "naturalist fallacy" (the claim that the good can be defined in "natural" or nonethical terms). Although utilitarianism continued to influence policy makers, most philosophers did not take it seriously as a moral philosophy. Even economists abandoned utilitarianism in the face of the difficulties posed by interpersonal utility comparisons. And to pound the final nails in the coffin, John Rawls, in *A Theory of Justice* (1971) offered not only systematic criticism, but an alternative theory that was suitable for guiding policy. The resurgence in practical moral philosophizing that was so prominent in the 1970s usually took for granted some sort of rights perspective rather than any sort of consequentialism.

Yet by the end of the 1980s utilitarianism and consequentialism were alive again and arguably dominant in both theoretical and applied moral philosophy. In the diverse works of authors such as Brandt (1979); Broome (1991b); Griffin (1986); Hardin (1988); Richard Hare (1981); Harsanyi (1977a); Kagan (1989); Parfit (1984); Peter Railton (1984); and Sen (1982b, 1983a), consequentialism has been resurrected and transformed. Although these authors defend very different ethical theories, with Brandt, for example, developing a sophisticated mental-state variant of utilitarianism and Sen developing a consequentialism in which rights, capabilities, and functionings play a more central part than happiness, there are common traits which make this work especially interesting and appealing to economists.

1. Most of these authors draw a specific connection between ethics and the theory of rationality. There has been a widespread recognition that refusing to make trade-offs among different objectives and to maximize some sort of objective opens one to charges of irrationality. In Samuel Scheffler's terminology, deontological (nonconsequentialist) ethical theories employ both "agent-centered prerogatives" (they sometimes *permit* agents not to act so as to maximize the good) and "agent-centered constraints" (they sometimes *prohibit* agents from acting so as to maximize the good). Although Scheffler argues that values such as integrity justify agent-centered prerogatives, which Kagan disputes at length, agent-centered constraints seem indefensible to both of them.

In any event the discussion has the nonconsequentialist on the defensive, and the charms of maximizing theories, to which economists have long since succumbed, have been seducing philosophers as well. Thus a good part of this new ethical theorizing is both more congenial to economists and more easily integrated into normative economics. None of this work is, to be sure, *easily* operationalized, but the difficulties of putting it to work in applied normative theorizing are not insuperable, either. Indeed some of this work, such as Harsanyi's, would in many cases justify returning to old-fashioned utilitarian policy analysis.

2. With the exception of Richard Brandt, no prominent theorist now defends a hedonistic conception of utility. All of the other specifically utilitarian theorists on the list join economists in taking utility not as an object of reference, but as an index of preference satisfaction. Yet none of them join economists in regarding utility to be an index of satisfaction of *actual* preferences. Although the refusal to identify welfare with the satisfac-

tion of actual preferences sets moral theorists off from most welfare economists, the distance is much smaller than in the case of rights theorists or hedonists, and there are greater opportunities for building bridges. It might, for example, be possible to operationalize some of the conditions moral theorists have placed on "rational" (Harsanyi) and "well-informed" (Griffin, Railton) preferences and thereby to strengthen the moral basis for the conclusions of welfare economics.

3. Some of this new work on utilitarianism and consequentialism is informed and influenced by developments in economics and game theory, and more of it could be. In Russell Hardin's utilitarianism, for example, human ignorance of consequences and the difficulties of measuring and comparing utilities hold center stage, and various concepts from both cooperative and noncooperative game theory are put to work in generating the outlines of a utilitarian theory of property rights and of their limits. But the game theory Hardin employs and his derivations are informal. There are important opportunities for collaboration between economists and philosophers in developing institutional implications of utilitarianism in circumstances of scarcity, uncertainty, opportunism, and so forth. We shall have a little more to say about these opportunities in Section 4 below.

4. Of particular interest in this resurgence of consequentialism has been the development of consequentialist moral theories that are not utilitarian—of theories that take the good consequences to be maximized to be other things than happiness or the satisfaction of preferences (esp. Parfit 1984). Although it is difficult to find empirical proxies for some of these good consequences, the more objective the goods to be maximized the more opportunity (other things being equal) for empirical application. If philosophers can specify a well-defined and clearly measurable good to be achieved, then the welfare economist can step in and discuss how best to achieve it.

One important objective good in many of these theories is the satisfaction of needs, and even utilitarians emphasize it, though not, of course, as a fundamental and intrinsic good. For example, although James Griffin is a preference utilitarian, he argues that needs should have a great importance in social policy making on the grounds that governments can more easily tell what people need, than what will satisfy their informed preferences (1986, ch. 3). This emphasis on the empirical tractability of needs is somewhat ironic, given the traditional aversion economists have felt to distinguishing needs from mere wants. But this aversion seems not to have stemmed mainly from empirical difficulties in studying needs. It has arisen instead from qualms about the complexity that such a distinction would introduce into economic theory and from *theoretical* objections to drawing the distinction and giving needs any special weight. It seems to us that here is a case where moral philosophers are more practical than economists! In political discussions of economic policy, concern about human needs is already ubiquitous, and if philosophers can provide both a rationale for taking needs seriously in practical social decision making and a principled way of drawing the distinction between needs and wants in such contexts (David Braybrooke 1987; Garrett Thomson 1987), then economists can put their modeling tools to work in helping to devise policies that will satisfy needs.

Utilitarianism has, of course, been subject to many criticisms. Some of these, such as the view that it is a "pig philosophy," were unfair even when directed to traditional hedonistic versions, and do not apply to the preference utilitarianism that is now most common. Difficulties concerning interpersonal utility comparisons continue, however, to plague utilitarians. Yet the most powerful objections to utilitarianism have always been intuitive. It is morally impermissible to murder one's nasty neighbor Max, even if it is obvious that total happiness would be greater without Max. Although these objections cannot be entirely defused, philosophers have done a great deal to undercut them. In his celebrated essay, "Two Concepts of Rules" (1955), Rawls pointed out that one must distinguish questions about the design of institutions from questions concerning the enforcement of institutional norms. Even if murdering Max would maximize utility, murder is forbidden by law and custom, and new laws and customs permitting murder whenever one conscientiously believed that doing so would maximize utility would not be favored by a utilitarian (or anybody else). Indeed Richard Hare (1981) argues that one should distinguish sharply between a critical level of moral thinking (which is typically beyond human capacities) in which, like an archangel, one considers all the consequences of alternative actions, and an intuitive level in which moral thinking is governed by rough principles to which people have strong emotional commitments. Hare argues persuasively that a utilitarian would want individuals to develop the sort of intuitions that would condemn even a utility-maximizing murder. Furthermore, as Hardin (1988) points out, such hypothetical examples usually presuppose knowledge that is simply unattainable. Utilitarianism remains unpalatable to most people (though perhaps not to most economists), but its difficulties are not obviously greater than those of alternative ethical theories.

Traditionally, most consequentialist ethical theories have offered very limited construals of the goodness of consequences. They have also imposed, implicitly or explicitly, various kinds of neutrality constraints—for example, that the evaluation of a state of affairs should be independent of who is evaluating it or of who has brought the state of affairs about. Thus, for example, a utilitarian should not care whether Desdemona was run over by an ox-cart or stabbed by Othello, except insofar as the causal consequences of these ways of dying differ.

As we noted earlier, Amartya Sen (1982b, 1983a) has argued forcefully that there is no conceptual reason why consequentialist views have to be so abstemious. In principle, any feature that can be embedded in a description of a state of affairs can be an object of consequential moral evaluation. Consequences can include such items as rights violations (compare Section 3.1.2 above) and numbers and distribution of functionings achieved by members of society. There is similarly no conceptual difficulty in allowing such evaluations to vary among evaluators, so that Othello need not assess Desdemona's death from a neutral point of view.

One reason this broadening of the notion of consequentialism is important is that some prominent nonutilitarian moral theories have large consequentialist components. John Rawls' theory of justice, for example, is concerned with selecting that set of institutions which will maximize the achievement of equal basic liberty and, subject to that constraint, maximize the primary goods of the least well-off group in society—both of which are perfectly well-defined consequentialist goals.

It is important to distinguish the *conceptual* possibility of incorporating an extremely wide range of considerations in a consequentialist view from the *moral* question of what considerations belong in a moral evaluation. It is, for example, possible to define a consequentialist view in which murders that happen on Tuesdays are morally permissible, unlike murders on other days. But it is morally unacceptable to permit evaluations to be sensitive to such arbitrary matters. The objections to deontological views noted by theorists as different as Kagan (1989) and Scheffler (1982) might well also be lodged against some extended forms of consequentialism.[60]

3.2.4 *Contractualism.* "Contractualism" refers more to a method of arriving at moral judgments than to a substantive moral theory. The core idea of a contractual approach to morality is that an acceptable moral view for a society should, in some sense, reflect an agreement among the members of that society. The appeal of this core idea derives partly from the attractions of consent (James Buchanan 1975)—that persons should be bound only by what they have agreed to—and partly from an appeal to rationality—a morality that rational agents are willing to agree to under the appropriate circumstances is itself rational. It is useful to follow Barry (1989) in distinguishing two broad types of contractualist moral theory, especially as it applies to theories of justice. The first, exemplified by Thomas Hobbes and Hume, tends to identify rationality with self-interest and agreement with the outcome of bargaining, leading thus to a view of justice as *mutual advantage*. The second, exemplified by Kant and Rousseau, tends to identify rationality with the autonomous pursuit of ends (which need not be self-interested) and agreement with the outcome of a shared pursuit of common principles, leading thus to a view of justice as *impartiality*.[61] Theories of both kinds have found much use for economic reasoning.

Thus, an early and influential attempt to formalize the notion of justice as impartiality came from Harsanyi's (1955) and Vickrey's (1945, 1960) independent derivations of utilitarianism. They captured the notion of impartiality by asking what moral principles rational agents would agree to (a) if they were deprived of knowledge of which people in society they were and (b) if (as a consequence of applying the principle of indifference) they believed they were equally likely to be anybody. People in this position, it was argued, would maximize expected utility by adopting the utilitarian principle for society as a whole: maximizing the average welfare of its members.[62] Such a contractual approach leads naturally to average utilitarianism—maximizing average welfare—rather than classical utilitarianism—maximizing total welfare.[63] The exercise involves deciding how self-interested people would choose in this hypothetical situation, but the decision to conform one's conduct to the resulting principles in real life is *not* to be explained by self-interest: there is no

[60] Sen (1977b, 1985c, 1986b) has proposed that moral theories can be usefully classified and appraised in terms of the kinds of information they allow to count from a moral point of view. See also Charles Beitz (1986). On the particular question of whether different evaluators can legitimately come to different moral evaluations depending on their position see Sen (1982b, 1983a), Regan (1983), Kagan (1989), and Scheffler (1982).

[61] The differences are not perfectly sharp, as those who see justice as mutual advantage also see their principles of justice as impartial, while those who regard justice as impartiality also see adherence to their principles as mutually advantageous. But the difference in emphasis is important enough to be regarded as a difference in kind.

[62] Though one might well wonder, as Gauthier (1982) does, how agents are supposed to maximize expected utility without knowing their preferences.

[63] These versions of utilitarianism will differ in their analysis of optimal population—with total utilitarians wanting to increase population until the marginal utility of another life is zero, while average utilitarians stop where the average utility of a life is maximized. The classical version is more naturally gotten not from a contractual argument but the perspective of a benevolent impartial spectator who sees utility, pleasure, or desire satisfaction of individuals as the only intrinsically valuable things in the world, and therefore seeks to maximize them.

claim that *my* interest is always best served by maximizing the *average* utility.[64]

Since the classic articles by Harsanyi and Vickrey, various refinements of and objections to their stipulation of the initial situation in which impartial agreement is to be reached have been put forward. The most famous has been that of John Rawls. Rawls argued that rational actors behind a "veil of ignorance" about their individual identities would not choose utilitarianism. Rawls specifies the conditions of the initial situation—and the character of the actors in that situation—in more detail than Harsanyi and Vickery do, and he makes two especially important modifications. First, Rawls suggests that agents behind the veil of ignorance will choose among principles that determine their life chances on the basis of which will best secure the basic means (primary goods) required to live out any of a number of rational life plans. Not knowing who they are nor what their preferences are, they are not and cannot be utility maximizers. Second, Rawls argues that rational actors in what he styles "the original position" will not rely on the principle of indifference, thus further shortcircuiting the argument for utilitarianism.

Rather than electing to maximize utility, claims Rawls, actors subjected to the radical uncertainty of the original position, and aware of their fundamental interest in securing the means to a decent life, would adopt a "safety first" strategy in agreeing to principles of justice. They would seek first to safeguard their basic political and personal liberties and then, subject to that constraint, they would judge basic social and economic institutions according to their tendency to promote the interests of those least well off in society. The motivation for this maximin outlook is that it guards against the unhappy accident of being a member of that disadvantaged group.

In their full elaboration, Rawls' principles of justice are:

> First, each person is to have an equal right to the most extensive basic liberty compatible with a similar liberty for others. (1971, p. 60)
>
> [Second] Social and economic inequalities are to be arranged so that they are both (a) to the greatest benefit of the least advantaged and (b) attached to offices and positions open to all under conditions of fair equality of opportunity. (1971, p. 83)

In addition, Rawls specifies that the first principle is, in social conditions such as ours, lexically prior to the second. These principles pose questions concerning the relations between liberties and economic welfare, concerning the role of market vs. nonmarket institutions in allocating goods, and concerning savings for future generations. The "priority of liberty," as the first principle is sometimes labeled, is not easy to capture in economic models, and the lexicographic ranking of this principle is not the sort of thing economists find easy to swallow (but see Cooter 1989). However, part (a) of the second principle—that society should maximize the well-being of the least advantaged—has an elegant formal interpretation as a "maximin" standard. It implies that (subject to the first principle and part (b) of the second principle) society should maximize the primary goods of the least well-off. Although a focus on only this dimension of Rawls' theory yields a somewhat

[64] Scepticism about interpersonal comparisons might lead a contractualist to stop short of average utilitarianism, instead arguing that a rational person in this situation would at least endorse the Pareto principle. Some have tried to squeeze a defense of the "compensation principle" (roughly, attain all potential Pareto improvements) on the (empirically dubious) grounds that in the long run gains and losses from individual potential Pareto improvements will tend to even out, so that everyone would rationally agree to all such changes, in the absence of specific knowledge of his or her own situation (Richard Posner 1979). See also Streeten (1953) for discussion of such views.

distorted picture of Rawls' actual view, this "maximin" interpretation of Rawlsian justice has led to some simple and valuable comparisons between Rawlsian and utilitarian analyses of ideal economic arrangements (for example, Edmund Phelps 1973; Sidney Alexander 1974; and Richard Musgrave 1974).

Both utilitarianism and Rawlsian justice as fairness provide substantial scope for redistributive activity by governments to raise average welfare or to protect the least well off. This result is characteristic of theories that emphasize justice as impartiality. Notice, again, that the argument is not that redistributive taxation is in the interest of those who must pay the taxes, but rather that taxpayers should acknowledge that, looked at impartially, it is fair that they should pay. What motivates people to support such taxation is not, on this kind of account, rational self-interest, but some form of moral concern.[65]

Theories of justice as mutual advantage give self-interest a larger role. The rules of justice are conceived as the result of rational bargaining among well-informed and self-interested actors. Gauthier, for example, argues that if we suppose that such agents lack the means to make interpersonal utility comparisons, then they would agree to distribute the gains from cooperation in accordance with a principle of "minimax relative concession."[66] Gauthier argues that this principle would fairly distribute the gains from social interaction relative to the situation that would prevail in the absence of agreement. As, in Gauthier's view, this nonagreement point would itself reflect substantial inequalities, which are largely preserved in the just society (else it would not be in everyone's interest), the scope for redistributive governmental activities is substantially less than on Rawlsian or utilitarian views.

Gauthier, like others who want to characterize justice as the outcome of a mutually self-interest bargain, wishes to avoid reliance on an independent moral motivation in explaining people's willingness to comply with justice. The problem is a challenging one, as the presence of rules of justice creates a classic prisoners' dilemma: even if you and I jointly benefit from the rules, I will do still better if you obey them and I violate them when it suits me. Gauthier argues that, under certain circumstances, it will be in my rational self-interest to cultivate the kind of character that will lead me to obey the rules of justice, even if having that kind of character sometimes robs me of opportunities to free-ride. It is crucial to this solution that other members of society be able to detect, often enough, what kind of character I have, and to reward or punish me suitably, in terms of their willingness to interact with me, depending on what they discern. The issue here—of when it may be self-interestedly rational to cultivate dispositions that interfere with acting on self-interest—has received valuable treatment from economists (Akerlof 1983 and Frank 1988).

From a somewhat different perspective, James Buchanan and his collaborators argue that, as an empirical matter, self-interested agents who are concerned about "constitutional" choices—choices involved in setting the general rules of the game—face so many uncertainties that they might as well be behind Rawls' veil of ignorance. Because the gains from constitutional design may be very large,

[65] Scanlon suggests that the basic motivation for complying with contractualist moral principles is a desire to "justify one's actions to others on grounds that they could not reasonably reject—reasonably, that is, given the desire to find principles which others similarly motivated could not reasonably reject" (1982, p. 116).

[66] This is the Kalai and Smorodinsky bargaining solution, which is discussed below, page 722. In most circumstances minimax relative concession coincides with equal relative concession.

self-interested agents should be concerned about such problems, and they thus have reason to step behind "the veil of uncertainty" (as Geoffrey Brennan and James Buchanan 1985 style it). But in Buchanan's view rational agents behind the veil of uncertainty will be much more cautious about redistribution, because they will model both economic and political behavior as self-interested. They will make this assumption partly on grounds of realism and partly on the Humean grounds that in designing constitutions "every man ought to be supposed a knave" (quoted in Brennan and J. Buchanan 1985, p. 59). Thus, even supposing that redistribution of market incomes toward the poor is desirable, it it not obvious that political institutions such as majoritarian democracy will produce such redistribution (Brennan and J. Buchanan 1985). Given the vagaries of politics, individuals adopting a constitutional perspective would not want to leave redistribution to the discretion of self-interested politicians. If they favor equalizing measures at all, they may prefer to embed particular distributive rules, say a negative income tax financed by a flat rate tax, directly into the constitution. Such constitutional distributive rules should not in fact be considered *re*distributive, as they would figure into the underlying definition of property rights.

The general idea that moral principles or social norms can be usefully interpreted as the outcome of self-interested bargains is receiving wide attention. Along with Gauthier and James Buchanan, Jean Hampton (1986) and Gregory Kavka (1986) have outlined general theories of justice that adopt this Hobbesian starting point. The same general idea has also been employed to consider what sorts of detailed rules or conventions would become established among agents in various relations to one another. Thus Andrew Schotter (1981), Sugden (1986), and Michael Taylor (1987) consider the recurrent problems of coordination and conflict individuals face and the sorts of institutions and conventions they will come to accept to resolve them. Ken Binmore (1990) argues that imperfectly rational agents will be led to a utilitarian solution to recurrent bargaining problems. This sort of disaggregative contractualism places heavy demands on the tools of game theory (see Section 4.2 below). Its findings may have both explanatory and normative force.

Even economists who are not interested in the foundational questions raised by contractarian theories of justice are likely to be interested in the implications for economic policy and institutions of competing contractarian views. There has been considerable interest in recent years in working out the implications for tax policy of alternative versions of both Rawlsian and utilitarian distributive principles (James Mirrlees 1976; Phelps 1973; Atkinson and Joseph Stiglitz 1980, chs. 12, 13, and 14). The brand of contractarian argument advanced by James Buchanan (and having its origin in J. Buchanan and Gordon Tullock 1962) has encouraged analytical work in more of a "political economy" vein, involving efforts to work out the equilibrium behavior of alternative constitutional regimes under the assumption that actors are self-interested in both politics and economics (see Brennan and J. Buchanan 1985, ch. 8).

3.3 *Concluding Words on Evaluation*

Few economists can avoid ever making appraisals of economic outcomes or institutions, and in making such appraisals they unavoidably rely on some moral philosophy. The most obvious strategy for economists to employ is to rely on the most robust and least controversial moral premises that they can. For many purposes this strategy is a good one, although economists' perceptions of what is uncontroversial and what is not may be skewed by their theoretical commitments. But for those economists with a deep concern with evaluation, this policy of laying as few hostages as possible to the vicissitudes of arguments in moral philosophy is bound to be unsatisfying. Very little in ethics is completely uncontroversial, and very little can be said about economics that relies on only uncontroversial moral premises. Economists concerned with evaluation are going to have to get their feet wet in the swamps of moral philosophy. We've tried to provide a rough map of the terrain, but we make no guarantees that those who venture in will not find some surprises. It's tough and tangled territory.

4. *Technical Aspects of Applied Moral Theory*

Over the last four decades economists and decision theorists have made exciting progress in the development of formal characterizations of individual and social choice, strategic interactions, and related concepts. A good deal of this work seems to be linked to moral philosophy. Formal models of rationality and game theoretic studies of incentives hold out the hope of superseding the ancient puzzles concerning the relations between morality, rationality, and self-interest. Concepts of "fair" or envy-free allocations, discussed in Section 3.1.3 above, facilitate the articulation and evaluation of egalitarianism. Solution concepts in game theory may enrich the contractarian perspective that morality arises from or can be justified in terms of agreement. Formal work in social choice theory tests the consistency of traditional principles concerning how social policies should respond to individual interests and respect individual rights. We face an embarrassment of riches and can only offer a highly selective survey of relations between a few of these developments and moral philosophy.

4.1 *Social Choice Theory*

Social choice theory grew out of Abram Bergson's (1938) and Samuelson's (1947) formulations of the "social welfare function," and was given its decisive formulation by Arrow in his *Social Choice and Individual Values* (1951). Social choice theory has had a major impact on the way economists conceive normative problems and on contemporary moral philosophy as well. However, the interpretation of theorems in social choice, and even the definition of the subject, have been elusive and controversial.

As Sen (1986a) has suggested, social choice theory might be defined either by its approaches or by its subject matter. Sen defines its subject matter as follows: "Social choice problems arise in aggregating the interests, or preferences, or judgments, or views, of different persons (or groups) in a particular society" (1986a, p. 214). Because aggregating interests and resolving conflicts is central to moral philosophy, a large part of the subject matter of social choice theory *is* moral philosophy. But the methods of social choice theory are distinctively formal and axiomatic. Most works in social choice theory are devoted to proving theorems.

Although one might usefully regard social choice theory, as Sen suggests, as the union of its subject matter and approach, what most people think of as social choice theory is the intersection: the proof and interpretation of theorems concerning the social aggregation of preferences, judgments, and interests. The relevance of social choice theorems to morality depends on exactly *which* attitudes or judgments are being aggregated, and *for what purpose*. Sen has hopefully distinguished two broad purposes of aggregation, namely *deciding* and *evaluating*. Thus, one might want an aggregation mechanism for deciding which movie a group of people was going to see, and also an aggregation mechanism for determining which among a set of movies the group has seen was best, from an aesthetic, moral, political, or comic point of view. The criteria for judging whether a mechanism was good from the first point of view might be very different from those that should govern in the latter context.[67] For example, it seems more imperative for social evaluations than for social decisions to be transitive, while the Pareto principle is more compelling for social decisions (Broome 1989).

As the movie example suggests, *what* is being aggregated also differs among cases. Sen distinguishes among "interests, preferences, judgments, and views" as objects of aggregation exercises. No doubt this list could be extended to other items including capabilities, resource endowments, and so on. Any of these properties of individuals might be aggregated either for purposes of arriving at a social decision or an evaluative judgment. A good deal of the social choice literature treats the items to be aggregated as preferences.

Insofar as social choice theory attempts to provide a social evaluation based on profiles of individual welfare, it is a branch of moral philosophy, and its theorems can reveal to moral philosophers ambiguities or hidden implications of accepted principles. A simple illustration of an interest-aggregation mechanism based on a normative principle is a utilitarian social welfare function, which defines the socially best outcome as that which maximizes the sum of individual utilities (where the appropriate measure of individual utility may differ among different versions of utilitarianism). It is important to be clear on the point that what is involved here is not an attempt to aggregate individual normative *judgments* about what is socially best into a social judgment; rather utilitarianism presupposes the judgment that the best state is that which maximizes aggregate utility.[68]

Moral reasoning has crucial roles in appraising particular social choice theorems. The most obvious role involves the assessment of the axioms. Do they express plausible normative principles? But moral presuppositions can also be embodied in subtler features of a formal setup. For example, treating the relation between profiles of individual preferences and social choices as a *function* implies the uniqueness of social choice. Furthermore, one's moral scrutiny need not be limited to individual features of the formal system. One can question whether a particular aggregation mechanism as a whole is a morally justifiable way of arriving at either a decision or an evaluative judgment. One may, for example, object to a process for aggregating interests for purposes of decision making as *unfair*, perhaps because of the way it responds to minority interests. And one may object to a process for aggregating individual normative judgments into a collective judgment because it is *unwise*, in that it fails to respond to the quality of the arguments supporting a particular judgment. Finally, moral reasoning may also enter into the scru-

[67] Decisions and evaluative judgments are obviously related, but they are identical only on the strong assumption that the operative decision rule is always to choose the best alternative according to the given evaluative standard. But there can be more than one evaluative standard, and decision rules may have procedural virtues.

[68] What if individuals get satisfaction from having their view of justice or of moral goodness prevail? Coherent and plausible versions of utilitarianism are unlikely to allow the measure of individual utility that goes into the social welfare function to be defined so broadly.

tiny of the individual objects that are fed into the aggregation mechanism. We reviewed earlier the likelihood that individual preferences may need to be "laundered" before becoming suitable objects to be accorded moral weight, and some similar process might be applied on moral grounds to interests, views, or judgments. One might, for example, want to make sure that the informational basis of these items was adequate.

If the axioms and formal set-up pass preliminary scrutiny, one can reverse the order of dependence and argue from the results of social choice theory to moral conclusions. Proofs are, after all, arguments. And if the axioms of a particular social theory are morally correct and the proof is valid, then the theorem must be morally correct as well. Axiomatic arguments of this kind have been proposed for ethical conclusions as different as utilitarianism (Fleming 1952; Harsanyi 1955; Vickrey 1945, 1960), "leximin" utility (Steven Strasnick 1976; d'Aspremont and Gevers 1977; Hammond 1976b), and welfare egalitarianism (Roemer 1988). Harsanyi, for example, demonstrates that if (1) personal and moral preferences satisfy the axioms of expected utility theory, (2) the preferences of different people are treated symmetrically, and (3) the Pareto principle is satisfied, then social choice must be utilitarian.[69]

Although a good deal of social choice theory seems to consist of formal arguments for moral principles, we doubt that this is the best way to appreciate this work. Logically valid arguments only show that one cannot both accept all their premises and reject any of their conclusions. If one is convinced of the correctness of the premises, they can persuade one to accept the conclusions, but it is equally true that if one is convinced of the incorrectness of the conclusions, one will have reason to doubt the premises. As Kotaro Suzumura (1983, p. 3) quotes Samuelson (1977, p. 85): "the classic phrase 'by their fruit must ye know them' applies above all to axiom systems." In general, our confidence in the axioms will derive both from how reasonable they seem to be in their own right and from our sense of the reasonableness and moral attractiveness of the theorems they lead to. If the axioms are shown to entail a moral conclusion that we find disturbing, we will be motivated to scrutinize them more closely, as well as to reflect on whether our negative reaction is really justified.

We suspect that the most important role of purported demonstrations of moral principles by social choice theorists has been to reveal the ambiguities and difficulties in apparently plausible moral principles. These ambiguities and difficulties have been highlighted even more conclusively by demonstrations that sets of plausible principles may be logically inconsistent. Arrow's General Possibility Theorem is the most famous of these demonstrations. Arrow showed that there is no possible method of aggregating individual rankings of social alternatives that meets certain apparently innocuous criteria. Exactly what moral lessons should be drawn from this celebrated theorem is not however easy to say.

Much depends on how the individual rankings are interpreted. One possibility is to take the rankings as showing how social alternatives affect individual wel-

[69] For a recent challenge to the cogency of this interpretation of Harsanyi's theorem, see John Weymark (1991). Among other difficulties, the cardinal representation theorem (p. 681 above) only says that preferences satisfying the axioms *may* be represented by a cardinal utility function, U, with the expected utility property. The preferences may also—and apparently equally well—be represented by a utility function such as U^3, which does not possess the expected utility property. Harsanyi needs to explain why the representation that yields cardinal expected utilities is the right one to use for ethical comparisons.

fare levels. Then what Arrow shows is that individual ordinal rankings cannot provide an acceptable basis for reconciling conflicts among individual interests or for making decisions about how welfare should be distributed. But as Sen has observed, this failure is not particularly surprising, because individual ordinal rankings provide little information concerning the relative importance of different interests. If interpersonal comparisons of preference intensity are permitted, or if nonpreference information (say on comparative income or resource levels) is permitted, the impossibility result may no longer hold (Sen 1970a, chs. 7, 8).

A different interpretation is that individual rankings reflect individual judgments about what is best for society to do. We might take these to be individuals' *moral* judgments over social alternatives. It seems less appropriate than in the case of interest aggregation to avoid the Arrow problem by introducing some kind of interpersonal comparison—in particular, it is not clear that the intensity with which a person holds a certain view should necessarily add to its weight in social judgment or decision making. What the Arrow theorem then tells us is that no acceptable scheme for aggregating these individual moral judgments will produce a consistent set of judgments for the community as a whole. Here again the result is not really surprising, when it is remembered that one of Arrow's conditions is that an aggregation scheme must work for all possible preference profiles. The theorem then says that no aggregation scheme can produce a consistent set of moral judgments over the social alternatives facing a society, no matter what individuals' moral judgments are. The Arrow conditions do not allow any sets of moral rankings to be ruled out as improper, and they do not allow for any modification of individual moral views in response to discussion.[70] When constraints such as "single-peakedness" are imposed on preference profiles, the impossibility results no longer hold. Arrow's general possibility theorem does not, then, undercut such familiar practices in making moral judgments on public matters as weighing the importance of competing interests or deliberating over the persuasiveness of particular people's moral judgments and arguments (and Arrow has never suggested otherwise).

Sen's remarkable "Paretian liberal" paradox arguably has even more bearing on issues of social morality than Arrow's impossibility result. Sen showed that an apparently weak necessary condition of respecting individual liberty—that two individuals each be decisive over their own single pair of alternatives, which differ only with respect to some purely private matter—is incompatible with the achievement of Pareto optimality when people hold certain plausible rankings of social alternatives (Sen 1970b, 1976a, 1983b, and 1986a). His motivating example is one in which each of two people is acknowledged to have the right to read or not to read any given book and the two have conflicting preferences about what the other should do in regard to an erotic novel. The lewd would most like that both he and his counterpart, the prude, read *Lady Chatterley's Lover*. If only one should read it, however, Lewd wishes it to be his prudish friend, because it would loosen him up. Prude would best prefer the book not be read at all, but would rather read it himself than further his friend's corruption. Plainly, the Pareto-preferred solution is for Prude to read the book, but the exer-

[70] For criticisms of this conception of politics and advocacy of more deliberative views of democratic decision, see Joshua Cohen (1986, 1989), Jules Coleman and John Ferejohn (1986), Elster (1986), and David Estlund (1990).

cise of rights will result in Lewd reading it.

Allan Gibbard pointed out that if one strengthens Sen's minimal liberty condition to permit two individuals to be decisive over all pairs of alternatives that only differ with respect to purely personal matters, then certain combinations of preferences will rule out the possibility of any social choice, regardless of questions of Pareto optimality. In Gibbard's example of the nonconformist and Mrs. Grundy (1974, p. 389), the nonconformist wants his bedroom walls to be a different color from Mrs Grundy's, while she wants her bedroom walls to be the same color as the nonconformist's. If each is decisive over social alternatives that differ only with regard to the color of his or her bedroom walls, every possible outcome will be vetoed by somebody.

In interpreting the significance of Sen's result, and of the extensive response to it, it is worth noting that both the example and the theorem are aimed only at one type of liberty, namely personal liberty over "private" matters (Jonathan Riley 1989, 1990). One essential feature that generates the paradox is then the fact that people are assumed to have preferences over outcomes that properly—according to the liberty principle—belong in someone else's protected sphere. Indeed, Julian Blau (1975) shows that Sen's paradox does not arise in the two-person case unless at least one person has "meddlesome" preferences in a technically defined sense. The Pareto principle, as applied in this context, treats these preferences on a par with personally oriented ones.

A number of responses to the paradox have attempted to dissolve it by introducing devices that modify the libertarian rights so as to preserve the Pareto principle in the face of these "nosy" preferences. Blau (1975) has proposed, for example, that libertarian rights should only hold for a particular person when others' preferences over the outcomes within that person's "protected sphere" are not too strong. Gibbard (1974), Nozick (1974), Peter Gardenfors (1981), Sugden (1985), and Wulf Gaertner, Prasanta Pattanaik, and Suzumura (forthcoming) have all argued that the paradox arises from a misconstrual of rights. To have a privacy right is to have a certain freedom to do as one pleases, not to be decisive over social choices. Rights should be modeled as "game forms" (Gibbard 1974) rather than as a constraint on social choices. I have a right to determine the color of my walls if certain strategies are open to me. The fact that Mrs. Grundy will copy me is no violation of my rights. The game-form construal of rights would not only dissolve Gibbard's paradox, but it would permit individuals to enter into trades or contracts that allow them to arrive at Pareto optima. In the Prude/Lewd example, Prude might contract to read the book on condition that Lewd doesn't. Such optima may not be reached because of imperfect information and transaction costs, but the general incompatibility between liberty and efficiency would dissolve.

But there would be serious enforcement problems, for as Riley has shown (1989; see also Kaushik Basu 1984), in games corresponding to the social choice problems in which there is a clash between rights and Pareto optimality, the outcomes that respect rights will not be Nash equilibria (see footnotes 73 and 77 below). As Sen notes, there are questions whether such contracts or their enforcement is morally desirable, particularly because enforcement would require close supervision of what are agreed to be private matters. And, as Sen (unpublished) argues, the game-form interpretation of rights may be too weak. It is hard to see how any system of rights that provided genuine protection to individual liberty could fail to satisfy Sen's minimal liberty condition—to make at least two individuals decisive over a single separate pair of social alternatives. The moral of the story in Sen's view is that normative social policy cannot be based only on preferences.

The other obvious direction to look for resolution of the liberal paradox is through relaxation of the Pareto principle. There is no evident moral requirement that preferences regarding other people's private activities should be accorded the same moral importance as those regarding one's own activities or public matters.[71] Indeed, acknowledgement of a private sphere of activity for a person creates a presumption that those preferences should receive less weight. Other moral arguments have been offered for discounting other-regarding preferences in making public decisions (Ronald Dworkin 1977, ch. 12). It does not follow from these doubts about the Pareto principle that nosy preferences should be ignored entirely, nor that a simple formula can determine the weight they should receive in every case. But Sen's paradox does underscore the importance of permitting other things besides preferences to count. In particular, one may want to examine the *motivation* behind preferences in deciding on the role they should play in social decisions and moral judgments—a point we have noticed elsewhere in this essay.

What do examples such as the Arrow and Sen paradoxes, and the proofs of alternative moral systems from sets of axioms tell us about the fruitfulness of social choice theory in illuminating moral issues? While its subject matter—the problem of assembling individual judgments or interests into social evaluations—is unavoidable, the axiomatic approach which has characterized most work on social choice theory leaves us more ambivalent.

It is clear that the precision of formulation and the rigor in argument induced by the formal approach can lead to important clarifications, and can stimulate a new awareness of the depth of problems—as the literature on the liberal paradox shows. At the same time, the abstractness of these methods has pitfalls. To quote Sen: "Arrow was undoubtedly right in saying that 'one of the great advantages of abstract postulational methods is the fact that the same system may be given several different interpretations, permitting a considerable saving of time' (Arrow 1951, p. 87). But *that* probably is *also* one of the great disadvantages of these methods" (Sen 1977c, p. 190). Considerable confusion has been generated, particularly in discussions of the Arrow theorem, by a failure to distinguish among alternative interpretations of both the *objects* being aggregated and the *purposes* of aggregation. It is difficult to spend much time with the social choice literature without becoming aware of the disparity between the large amount of attention lavished on the derivation of theorems and the small amount devoted to interpretation of the assumptions and of the point of the exercises. Unless guided by ethical sophistication, social choice theory can degenerate into empty formal exercises. But it would be unfair to single out social choice theorists for blame. Moral philosophers ought to be more involved with this work, too. For if formalizations of plausible moral principles lead to inconsistencies or to unacceptable conclusions, then those moral principles may need revamping.

4.2 *Game Theory*

Game theory is concerned with strategic interactions among individuals who

[71] For other grounds to question the ethical appeal of the Pareto principle, see Section 3.2.1 above.

are to some extent rational. An interaction among individuals is strategic if the choices of some individuals depend on the choices of others. Most game theory employs standard conceptions of rationality.

There is almost an unlimited variety of strategic environments in which individuals can interact. To make the problems formally tractable, game theorists typically suppose that the only relevant properties of individual strategies[72] are (a) their causal consequences for the plays made by others and (b) the utilities of the outcomes of different combinations of strategies—the "payoff structure." In game theory the players come with a knowledge of what the possible strategies are and at least a probability distribution over the possible utility consequences. Much of game theory also includes a "common knowledge" assumption—that players know what others know, including that others know that they have this knowledge, and so on.

Most game theory is not addressed to moral questions, and moral philosophy is less directly relevant to the scrutiny of particular axiom systems than it was in social choice theory. But moral questions concerning prudence, benevolence, and justice remain relevant. Not only does most game theory specify the values and choices of agents in terms of preference satisfaction, but game theoretic analyses of social interactions carry an implicit commitment to a highly contestable set of answers to some of the deepest questions in normative social and political philosophy—to the view that the only (and hence the proper) perspective for individuals to adopt in their social interactions is individual maximization. This perspective does not rule out altruism or sympathy, and it need not in principle rule out "commitment" (p. 688 above), but it does rule out a collective perspective, a perspective that considers what *we* should do and what the consequences will be for *us*. And it has been argued that such a collective perspective is essential to the very notion of social interaction (Margaret Gilbert 1990) and to the explanation for why real individuals play simple games so differently than game theory would prescribe and predict (Robyn Dawes, Alphons van de Kragt, and John Orbell 1990; see also Hurley 1989, p. 145 and Regan 1980, ch. 8).

The relevance of game theory to moral philosophy is most obvious in normative applications of game theory to determine the "right" or "best" solution to problems of strategic interaction.[73] But positive applications of game theory to determine how more or less rational individuals will solve strategic problems may also be morally relevant. Because contractarians believe that what is morally right is what rational agents would agree to under appropriate circumstances, and game theory may determine the content of such agreements, game theory may have a role in determining what is morally right. We shall shortly see how David Gauthier employs game theory to argue for principles of justice, and as mentioned before (p. 711) game theory is central in attempts to see specific moral principles as solutions to detailed interaction problems. Game theory also bears on the question of the compatibility between the dictates

[72] A *strategy* is a complete recipe for how a player will respond to any possible sequence of eventualities in the game.

[73] Work in game theory is also a crucial adjunct to social choice theory, for even if there are solutions to the problems of aggregation with which social choice theory is concerned, there are important questions to be asked about how such solutions can be attained (Dasgupta, Hammond, and Eric Maskin 1979; Bezalel Peleg 1984). Indeed, as we noted briefly above in discussing Sen's paradox, many of the aggregation problems translate into difficulties concerning the solutions of games (Maskin 1985).

of individual rationality and the demands of morality.

Human flourishing requires social cooperation, but, as philosophers have long recognized, such cooperation is problematic. In Hobbes' state of nature, where there is little cooperation, "the life of man [is] solitary, poor, nasty, brutish, and short" (1651, p. 107). The theory of games is particularly relevant to moral philosophy in its revelation of the sorts of interaction problems with which moral principles have to deal.[74] Suppose that individuals *J* and *K* each have a choice of two actions, *A* and *B*, and that *J*'s and *K*'s utilities are as follows:

		K	
		A	*B*
J	*A*	3,3	0,4
	B	4,0	2,2

In this case, *J* and *K* have a dominant strategy: to play *B*, and one has a prisoners' dilemma game. Each pursuing what is best for himself or herself results in a suboptimal outcome. Prisoners' dilemmas have proven to be not only a particularly salient way of representing problems of social cooperation, free-riding, and public goods provision, but they have also been a fruitful tool for formulating problems concerning moral cooperation. For example, Derek Parfit (1979) has argued that the underlying prisoners' dilemma structure arises not only in contrasting moral to self-interested action, but also within the structure of moral thought itself. Each mother trying to save her own child from drowning in a beach accident, for example, may do less well than all would do if they cooperated in saving all the children. The collectively self-defeating character of moral commitments that are subject to this problem (like the paradoxes of humanitarianism discussed above, p. 677) is disturbing, and one might want to require that acceptable moral views not be collectively self-defeating. But many familiar moral maxims seem to fail in just this way.

Not all problems of social interaction have the structure of a prisoners' dilemma. There are also pure coordination problems (David Lewis 1969; Schelling 1978), such as determining which side of the road to drive on. These problems are easier in the sense that they may have self-enforcing solutions that can arise spontaneously. But they also have less bearing on moral problems, in which there are conflicts of interest to resolve. Conflicts of interest, however, are not always prisoners' dilemmas (Michael Taylor 1987, ch. 2; Hampton 1987; Hardin 1982). For example, suppose that *J*'s and *K*'s utilities are as follows:

		K	
		A	*B*
J	*A*	4,4	0,2
	B	2,0	1,1

For example, *J* and *K* might both want to do their part toward providing some collective good that requires both their efforts. One has here an "Assurance Problem" (Sen 1967; 1973b, pp. 96–99), in which the obstacles in the way of social cooperation are slighter than in a prisoners' dilemma and in which the prospects

[74] For example, Hardin (1988) argues that an appreciation of the difficulties of strategic interaction throws a wrench into both simple applications and criticisms of utilitarianism. A sophisticated utilitarianism that recognizes these problems may be able to defend certain constellations of rights assignments as devices to simplify strategic interactions and to avoid suboptimal outcomes.

for reconciling individual rationality and social optimality are much brighter. In fact, one strategy for coping with the social consequences of prisoners' dilemmas is to convert them into assurance problems by changing either incentives or personal motivations.

Suppose instead that the utilities look like this:

		K	
		A	*B*
J	*A*	3,3	2,4
	B	4,2	0,0

As in the assurance game *J* and *K* have no dominant strategy, but now they prefer to play *A* if and only if the other plays *B*. This game of "chicken" can arise easily when, for example, conflicts over possessions are costly. Both *J* and *K* might like the same fishing ground all to themselves. But sharing is better than ceding the fishing ground to the other, and fighting is worst of all. In such games, cooperation may be individually rational, particularly if, as Sugden (1986) has argued, the positions of the interactors are not fully symmetrical, so that conventions can arise directing those who occupy different positions to play different strategies. Property rights might be regarded as just such conventions, although they have of course been shaped by explicit legislation.

Indeed even a prisoners' dilemma structure of interactions need not prevent self-interested rational agents from cooperating if the interactions are iterated. Suppose that players in a prisoners' dilemma game are likely to play again. Defection is no longer a dominant strategy, as the ersatz cooperation of these entirely self-interested agents can elicit like cooperation from others. Though the formal analysis of repeated games is complex (Michael Taylor 1987, ch. 3, 4), computer simulations have shown that simple strategies such as "tit-for-tat" (cooperate on the first move, then do whatever one's opponent did on the previous move do well against a wide range of alternatives (Robert Axelrod 1984). Indeed, provided that the probability of repeated play is high enough, a small group of individuals who play tit-for-tat can "invade" a population of players who defect on every move and, if "survival" depends on success, eventually drive those who always defect to extinction.[75] So cooperation can evolve among rational self-interested agents, and one might be tempted to regard much of morality as the conventional outcome of iterated games with various structures.

But one may question how useful game theory really is for the purposes of moral philosophy. Not only are there legitimate concerns about the assumption of common knowledge, but the use of game theory to address ethical questions also runs afoul of Sen's critique of welfarism—of the reliance on nothing but information about the utilities of outcomes. Game theory is not strictly welfarist, for nonpreference information determines what the possible strategies are and what their utility consequences will be. But one might reasonably say that it is quasi-welfarist, for other ethically relevant factors—rights, capabilities, needs, and reasons—make no explicit appearance, and their role is heavily truncated (Roemer 1986a). For example, if the strategic problem is to distribute some set of commodities, then the solution will be the

[75] Tit-for-tat is in these circumstances an evolutionarily stable strategy. The biological terminology is not merely metaphor. Animal traits and behavior can be regarded as strategies, and game theory can be applied to the study of evolution. See Axelrod (1984, ch. 5).

same regardless of what the commodities are, if the feasible allocations and utility functions are the same. But people's judgments about just distributions depend on what the goods to be distributed are, and, as we shall see below the outcomes reached in experimental tests of bargaining theory depend on nonwelfarist information.[76]

Ethical applications of game theory are also going to be precarious, because game theory itself is in turmoil. If controversy simmers in the theory of rational choice in circumstances of uncertainty, it boils in game theory. Not only are there the problems involved in incorporating imperfect knowledge and imperfect rationality, but there is disagreement about what solution concepts are appropriate, even in circumstances of perfect knowledge and rationality. The traditional solution concept for noncooperative game theory is the Nash equilibrium.[77] Most game theorists (for one exception, see Giacomo Bonnano 1991) would continue to hold that it is a reasonable necessary condition that solutions should be Nash equilibria. But it is not a sufficient condition: not all Nash equilibria are rational solutions (Reinhart Selten 1975). But there is no agreement on what stronger solution concepts to accept.

Furthermore, standard game theory has paradoxical implications. In a finitely iterated prisoners' dilemma game with a known number of iterations, the so-called backwards-induction argument apparently demonstrates that the uniquely rational strategy is defection on every move. Real people do not play this way, and they wind up doing much better than if they played this purportedly uniquely rational strategy. The practical irrelevance of the backward induction argument may conceivably be explained by uncertainty about the number of plays parties will be engaged in. But experiments show that if individuals are permitted to form personal connections (which do not, however, involve any promises or contractual arrangements concerning their play), then they typically cooperate even in a one-shot prisoners' dilemma game (Dawes, van de Kragt, and Orbell 1990). The backwards induction argument is also itself puzzling, because it relies on apparently inconsistent counterfactual reasoning. Given common knowledge of perfect rationality, one is supposed to consider how an opponent would behave in a counterfactual situation that could not be reached by perfectly rational players with common knowledge of their perfect rationality (David Kreps et al. 1982; David Kreps and Robert Wilson 1982; Binmore 1987, 1988; Cristina Bicchieri 1988, 1990; Philip Pettit and Sugden 1989; Bonnano 1991). Most of game theory is currently too controversial to permit drawing ethical implications with any confidence.

Let us focus on one sort of game theory, which is subject to controversies of its own, but which has been applied to ethical issues: two-person cooperative bargaining theory. In John Nash's classic analysis, the two parties are supposed to have cardinal and interpersonally noncomparable utilities. The bargaining problem is to select a point from a closed convex set, S, of utility outcomes, containing a threat point, d, consisting of the utilities the two individuals receive if no bargain is reached. Nash proved that if the solution to the bargaining problem satisfies four explicit conditions (Pareto optimality, symmetry, indepen-

[76] Indeed Menachem Yaari and Maja Bar Hillel (1984) show that people have different ethical views about how to distribute avocados and grapefruits depending on whether they are told that the fruits are wanted for their taste or for their vitamins.

[77] A set of strategies is a Nash equilibrium if each strategy is a best reply to the others—that is, if no one can benefit by playing some other strategy given the strategies of others.

dence of irrelevant alternatives, and independence of positive linear utility transformations), then the solution maximizes the product of the utility gains from bargaining.[78] Although the Nash solution has many defenders, it has awkward consequences, for if the feasible set of utility outcomes expands in person *A*'s favor, the result may be that person *A* will get less than before (Elster 1989a, p. 66). The Nash solution may also be morally objectionable in the extent to which it disadvantages the poor and risk averse.

A further problem is that, in empirical studies, the bargains individuals reach systematically diverge from the Nash solution, even when both individuals have perfect knowledge of their utility functions. In so-called binary lottery games, individuals bargain over the distribution of lottery tickets. Because the utility functions are not interpersonally comparable, one can stipulate that each individual's utility is zero when he or she has no tickets—that is, no probability of winning—and that the utility for each of winning the prize is 1. The utility of each player then equals the percentage of the lottery tickets each has. The Nash solution (this is the Kalai and Smorodinsky solution, too) is a fifty-fifty split of the lottery tickets. This is true regardless of whether the prizes the individuals can win are the same. When the prizes differ, the actual solutions to the bargaining games are bimodal with both the Nash solution and the solution that equalizes monetary returns as the two modes (Alvin Roth and Michael Malouf 1979). Roth, Malouf, and J. Keith Murnighan (1981) argue persuasively that moral norms concerning just distributions affect the bargaining solutions. The person who stands to win the larger prize is seen as having a weaker moral claim on lottery tickets than the less advantaged person. So it seems that even purely positive bargaining theory must take cognizance of the moral commitments of the bargainers, and it is by no means obvious how this is to be accomplished formally (Gibbard 1990, esp. p. 262; Pettit 1990).

An alternative to the Nash solution developed by Kalai and Smorodinsky forms the core of Gauthier's (1986) ambitious contractarian effort to derive justice from rational choice. Kalai and Smorodinsky substitute a monotonicity requirement for Nash's independence of irrelevant alternatives, and their solution is called by Gauthier "minimax relative concession." The relative concession of each bargainer is $(u_{max} - u)(u_{max} - u_d)$, where u_{max} is the largest feasible utility attainable by the individual, u is the utility if a given bargain were made, and u_d is the utility at the threat point—the utility that would result if no bargain were struck. Minimax relative concession minimizes the largest concession anybody has to make. If equal relative concession is Pareto optimal, it coincides with minimax relative concession. Gauthier argues that rational individuals who are aware of their own rationality and the rationality of others and who are aware of the utility consequences of their bargaining will accept the minimax relative concession solution (1986, ch. 5). In Gauthier's view this argument suffices to establish that such a solution is just, although Gauthier also maintains that this solution satisfies conditions that have been thought reasonable to impose on conceptions of justice, such as impartiality (1986, ch. 8). As we discussed on page 710 above, Gauthier argues further that it is individually rational to constrain

[78] Nash (1950). Luce and Raiffa (1957, pp. 124–37). A valuable recent study which emphasizes the normative uses of bargaining theory is William Thomson and Terje Lensberg (1989). In a striking recent development, Binmore (1990) shows how utilitarianism can be an evolutionarily stable solution to Nash's bargaining game with less than perfectly rational agents (see p. 710 and footnote 75 above).

one's individual maximization and to adhere to such bargains (1986, ch. 6).

Gauthier's argument has been strongly contested[79], and its difficulties highlight the complex interconnections between game theory and moral philosophy. For the characterization of individual rationality that Gauthier relies on is controversial, the relevance of solutions to a bargaining problem under conditions of complete information questionable, the particular solution concept dubious, and the limitation to quasi-welfarist information objectionable. This list of difficulties is not intended as a criticism of Gauthier's pathbreaking efforts or as an argument against employing game theory to tackle moral problems. Indeed it is only through Gauthier's efforts that these dimensions of a contractualist argument for principles of justice could be clearly seen. Even though game theory is in no condition at present to solve moral problems, it may some day do so, and even in its current state, it provides a rigorous setting in which to pose and ponder the problems.

5. *Concluding Remarks*

In the last twenty years, economists and moral philosophers have renewed a conversation that was interrupted during the heyday of positivist methodology in both disciplines. Although there remain considerable gaps between the modes of expression and habits of thought of moral philosophers and economists—as those who have read this far can no doubt confirm—we hope our presentation has also shown that there is considerable room for productive interdisciplinary communication. For those who aim to make scholarly contributions in this area, our review suggests a number of promising avenues of inquiry. These range from relatively technical investigations in areas such as game theory and social choice to conceptual and empirical questions about morally important notions such as equality and well-being. Although we have not stressed them here, applications of moral reasoning to controversial areas of public policy, including for example affirmative action, environmental regulation, and social welfare measures, are also lively areas of inquiry.

A better appreciation of the connections between moral theory and economics may also prove helpful to the many economists who will never do research on moral subjects directly. A clearer understanding of the moral perspectives that lie in the background of much of economic analysis can help economists to address the value-relevant aspects of their work. What Marshall said about economics—that it is "not a body of concrete truth, but an engine for the discovery of concrete truth" (1885, p. 159)—may be said about moral reasoning as well. An economics that is engaged actively and self-critically with the moral aspects of its subject matter cannot help but be more interesting, more illuminating, and ultimately more useful than one that tries not to be.

[79] See Kraus and Coleman (1987), Alan Nelson (1988), Ellen Paul et al. (1988), and also the more technical critiques of Roemer (1986a) and Sugden (1990).

References

Ackerman, Bruce. *Social justice in the liberal state.* New Haven: Yale U. Press, 1981.

Akerlof, George. "Loyalty Filters," *Amer. Econ. Rev.*, Mar. 1983, *73*(1), pp. 54–63.

______. "Gift Exchange and Efficiency-Wage Theory: Four Views," *Amer. Econ. Rev.*, May 1984, *74*(2), pp. 79–83.

Akerlof, George and Dickens, William T. "The Economic Consequences of Cognitive Dissonance," *Amer. Econ. Rev.*, June 1982, 72(3), pp. 307–19.

Akerlof, George and Yellen, Janet. "Introduction," in *Efficiency wage models of the labor market.* Eds.: George Akerlof and Janet Yellen. NY: Cambridge U. Press, 1986, pp. 1–21.

Alexander, Sidney S. "Social Evaluation through

Notional Choice," *Quart. J. Econ.*, Nov. 1974, *88*(4), pp. 597–624.

ALLAIS, MAURICE. "The Foundations of a Positive Theory of Choice Involving Risk and a Criticism of the Postulates and Axioms of the American School," 1952; reprinted in *Expected utility hypotheses and the Allais paradox*. Eds.: MAURICE ALLAIS AND OLE HAGEN. Dordrecht: Reidel, 1979, pp. 27–145.

ARNESON, RICHARD. "Equality and Equal Opportunity for Welfare," *Philosophical Studies*, May 1989, *56*(1), pp. 77–93.

______. "Liberalism, Distributive Subjectivism, and Equal Opportunity for Welfare," *Philosophy and Public Affairs*, Spring 1990, *19*(2), pp. 158–94.

ARROW, KENNETH. *Social choice and individual values*. NY: Wiley, 1951; 2nd ed., 1963.

______. "Gifts and Exchanges," *Philosophy and Public Affairs*, Summer 1972, *1*(4), pp. 343–62.

______. "Some Ordinalist-Utilitarian Notes on Rawls's Theory of Justice," *J. Philosophy*, May 1973, *70*(9), pp. 245–63.

______. *The limits of organization*. 1st ed. NY: Norton, 1974.

______. "Extended Sympathy and the Possibility of Social Choice," *Philosophia*, June 1978, *7*, pp. 223–37.

D'ASPREMONT, CLAUDE AND GEVERS, LOUIS. "Equity and the Informational Basis of Collective Choice," *Rev. Econ. Stud.*, June 1977, *44*(2), pp. 199–209.

ATKINSON, ANTHONY B. "On the Measurement of Inequality," *J. Econ. Theory*, Sept. 1970, *2*(3), pp. 244–63.

ATKINSON, ANTHONY B. AND STIGLITZ, JOSEPH E. *Lectures on public economics*. NY: McGraw-Hill, 1980.

AXELROD, ROBERT. *The evolution of cooperation*. NY: Basic Books, 1984.

BAIER, KURT. *The moral point of view: A rational basis of ethics*. Ithaca: Cornell U. Press, 1958.

BAKER, GEORGE P.; JENSEN, MICHAEL C. AND MURPHY, KEVIN J. "Compensation and Incentives: Practice vs. Theory," *J. Finance*, July 1988, *43*(30), pp. 593–616.

BANFIELD, EDWARD. *The moral basis of a backward society*. Glencoe, IL: Free Press, 1958.

BARRY, BRIAN M. *Political argument*. London: Routledge, 1965.

______. *A treatise on social justice*. Vol. 1. *Theories of justice*. Berkeley, CA: U. of California Press, 1989.

BASU, KAUSHIK. "The Right to Give Up Rights," *Economica*, Nov. 1984, *51*(204), pp. 413–22.

BAUMOL, WILLIAM. *Superfairness: Applications and theory*. Cambridge, MA: MIT Press, 1986.

BECKER, GARY. *A treatise on the family*. Cambridge, MA: Harvard U. Press, 1981.

BEITZ, CHARLES. "Review of Amartya Sen's *Resources, Values, and Development*," *Econ. Philos.*, Oct. 1986, *2*(2), pp. 282–91.

BENTHAM, JEREMY. *An introduction to the principles of morals and legislation*. Ed.: W. HARRISON. Oxford: Basil Blackwell, [1789] 1967.

BERGSON, ABRAM. "A Reformulation of Certain Aspects of Welfare Economics," *Quart. J. Econ.*, Feb. 1938, *52*(2), pp. 310–34.

BERLIN, ISAIAH. "Two Concepts of Liberty," in *Four essays on liberty*. Oxford: Oxford U. Press, 1969, pp. 118–72.

BICCHIERI, CRISTINA. "Self-Refuting Theories of Strategic Interaction: A Paradox of Common Knowledge," *Erkenntnis*, Feb. 1988, *29*(1), pp. 69–85.

______. "Paradoxes of Rationality," *Midwest Studies in Philosophy*, 1990, *15*, pp. 65–79.

BINMORE, KEN. "Modeling Rational Players: Part I," *Econ. Philos.*, Oct. 1987, *3*(2), pp. 179–214.

______. "Modeling Rational Players: Part II," *Econ. Philos.*, Apr. 1988, *4*(1), pp. 9–56.

______. "Evolution and Utilitarianism," *Constitutional Political Economy*, Spring/Summer 1990, *1*(2), pp. 1–26.

BLACKORBY, CHARLES AND DONALDSON, DAVID. "Cash versus Kind, Self-selection, and Efficient Transfers," *Amer. Econ. Rev.*, Sept. 1988, *78*(4), pp. 691–700.

BLAU, JULIAN H. "Liberal Values and Independence," *Rev. Econ. Stud.*, July 1975, *42*(3), pp. 395–401.

BLINDER, ALAN S. AND CHOI, DON H. "A Shred of Evidence on Theories of Wage Stickiness," *Quart. J. Econ.*, Nov. 1990, *105*(4), pp. 1003–15.

BLOCK, WALTER. "A Free Market in Roads," in MACHAN 1982, pp. 164–83.

BONNANO, GIACOMO. "The Logic of Rational Play in Games of Perfect Information," *Econ. Philos.*, Apr. 1991 *7*(1), pp. 37–66.

BOULDING, KENNETH. *The economy of love and fear: A preface to grants economics*. Belmont, CA: Wadsworth, 1973.

BOWLES, SAMUEL. "The Production Process in a Competitive Economy: Walrasian, Neo-Hobbesian and Marxian Models," *Amer. Econ. Rev.*, Mar. 1985, *75*(1), pp. 16–36.

BOWLES, SAMUEL AND GINTIS, HERBERT. "The Democratic Firm: An Agency-Theoretic Evaluation." Amherst: Dept. of Economics, U. of Massachusetts, May 1990.

BRANDT, RICHARD B. *A theory of the right and the good*. Oxford: Oxford U. Press, 1979.

BRAVERMAN, HARRY. *Labor and monopoly capital*. NY: Monthly Review Press, 1974.

BRAYBROOKE, DAVID. *Meeting needs*. Princeton: Princeton U. Press, 1987.

BRENNAN, GEOFFREY AND BUCHANAN, JAMES. *The reason of rules: Constitutional political economy*. NY: Cambridge U. Press, 1985.

BROOME, JOHN. "Should Social Preferences Be Consistent?" *Econ. Philos.*, Apr. 1989, *5*(1), pp. 7–17.

______. "Utility," *Econ. Philos.*, Apr. 1991a, *7*(1), pp. 1–12.

______. *Weighing goods*. Oxford: Basil Blackwell, 1991b.

BUCHANAN, ALLEN E. *Ethics, efficiency, and the market*. Totowa, NJ: Rowman & Allanheld, 1985.

______. "Assessing the Communitarian Critique of Liberalism," *Ethics*, July 1989, *99*(4), pp. 852–82.

BUCHANAN, JAMES M. *The limits of liberty: Between*

anarchy and leviathan. Chicago: U. of Chicago Press, 1975.

BUCHANAN, JAMES M. AND TULLOCK, GORDON. *The calculus of consent*. Ann Arbor: U. of Michigan Press, 1962.

CALABRESI, GUIDO AND MELAMED, DOUGLAS. "Property Rules, Liability Rules, and Inalienability: One View of the Cathedral," *Harvard Law Rev.*, Apr. 1972, 85(6), pp. 1089–1128.

CARENS, JOSEPH. "Compensatory Justice and Social Institutions," *Econ. Philos.*, Apr. 1985, *1*(1), pp. 39–67.

COASE, RONALD. "The Problem of Social Cost," *J. Law Econ.*, Oct. 1960, *3*(1), pp. 1–44.

COHEN, GERALD ALLEN. "Functional Explanation, Consequence Explanation, and Marxism," *Inquiry*, Mar. 1982, 25(1), pp. 27–56.

COHEN, JOSHUA. "An Epistemic Conception of Democracy," *Ethics*, Oct. 1986, 97(1), pp. 26–38.

______. "Deliberation and Democratic Legitimacy," in *The good polity: Normative analysis of the state*. Eds.: ALAN HAMLIN AND PHILIP PETTIT. NY: Basil Blackwell, 1989, pp. 17–34.

COLEMAN, JULES AND FEREJOHN, JOHN. "Democracy and Social Choice," *Ethics*, Oct. 1986, 97(1), pp. 6–25.

COLEMAN, JULES L. AND KRAUS, JODY. "Rethinking the Theory of Legal Rights," *Yale Law Rev.*, June 1986, 95(7), pp. 1335–71; reprinted in *Markets, morals and the law*. Cambridge: Cambridge U. Press, 1988, pp. 28–63.

COLLARD, DAVID. *Altruism and economy: A study in non-selfish economics*. NY: Oxford U. Press, 1978.

COOTER, ROBERT. "Rawls's Lexical Orderings Are Good Economics," *Econ. Philos.*, Apr. 1989, 5(1), pp. 47–54.

COOTER, ROBERT AND RAPPOPORT, PETER. "Were the Ordinalists Wrong About Welfare Economics?" *J. Econ. Lit.*, June 1984, 22(2), pp. 507–30.

DANIELS, NORMAN. "Wide Reflective Equilibrium and Theory Acceptance in Ethics," *J. Philosophy*, May 1979, 76(5), pp. 256–82.

DASGUPTA, PARTHA. *The control of resources*. Cambridge: Harvard U. Press, 1982.

DASGUPTA, PARTHA; HAMMOND, PETER AND MASKIN, ERIC. "The Implementation of Social Choice Rules: Some General Results on Incentive Compatibility," *Rev. Econ. Stud.*, Apr. 1979, *46*(143), pp. 185–216.

DAWES, ROBYN; VAN DE KRAGT, ALPHONS AND ORBELL, JOHN. "Cooperation for the Benefit of Us—Not Me, or My Conscience," in *Beyond self-interest*. Ed.: JANE J. MANSBRIDGE. Chicago: U. of Chicago Press, 1990, pp. 97–110.

DEBREU, GERARD. *Theory of value*. NY: Wiley, 1959.

DORE, RONALD. *Taking Japan seriously: A Confucian perspective on leading economic issues*. London: The Athlone Press, 1987.

DUNLOP, JOHN T. "The Task of Contemporary Wage Theory," in *The theory of wage determination*. Ed.: JOHN T. DUNLOP. NY: St. Martin's Press, 1957, pp. 3–27.

DWORKIN, GERALD. "Paternalism," in *Morality and the law*. Ed.: RICHARD WASSERSTROM. Belmont, CA: Wadsworth Pub. Co., 1971, pp. 107–36.

______. *The theory and practice of autonomy*. Cambridge: Cambridge U. Press, 1988.

DWORKIN, GERALD; BERMANT, GORDON AND BROWN, PETER G., eds. *Markets and morals*. Washington: Hemisphere Pub. Corp.; NY: distributed solely by Halsted Press, 1977.

DWORKIN, RONALD. *Taking rights seriously*. Cambridge: Harvard U. Press, 1977.

______. "What is Equality? Part 1: Equality of Welfare," *Philosophy and Public Affairs*, Spring 1981a, *10*(3), pp. 185–246.

______. "What is Equality? Part 2: Equality of Resources," *Philosophy and Public Affairs*, Summer 1981b, *10*(4), pp. 283–345.

______. "Foundations of Liberal Equality," in *The Tanner lectures on human values*, XI. Ed.: GRETHE B. PETERSON. Salt Lake City: U. of Utah Press, 1990, pp. 1–119.

EDWARDS, RICHARD. *Contested terrain: The transformation of the workplace in the twentieth century*. NY: Basic Books, 1979.

ELLSBERG, DANIEL. "Risk, Ambiguity, and the Savage Axioms," *Quart. J. Econ.*, Nov. 1961, 75(4), pp. 643–99.

ELSTER, JON. *Ulysses and the sirens: Studies in rationality and irrationality*. NY: Cambridge U. Press, 1979.

______. *Sour grapes: Studies in the subversion of rationality*. Cambridge: Cambridge U. Press, 1983.

______. "The Market and the Forum: Three Varieties of Political Theory," in ELSTER AND HYLLAND 1986, pp. 103–32.

______. *The cement of society: A study of social order*. Cambridge: Cambridge U. Press, 1989a.

______. "Social Norms and Economic Theory," *J. Econ. Perspectives*, Fall 1989b, 3(4), pp. 99–117.

ELSTER, JON AND HYLLAND, AANUND, eds. *Foundations of social choice theory*. NY: Cambridge U. Press, 1986.

ELSTER, JON AND ROEMER, JOHN, eds. *Interpersonal comparisons of well-being*. Cambridge: Cambridge U. Press, 1991.

ESTLUND, DAVID. "Democracy Without Preference," *Philosophical Rev.*, July 1990, 99(3), pp. 397–423.

ETZIONI, AMITAI. "The Case for a Multiple-Utility Conception," *Econ. Philos.*, Oct. 1986, 2(2), pp. 159–83.

______. *The moral dimension. Toward a new economics*. NY: Macmillan, 1988.

FEINBERG, JOEL. *Social philosophy*. Englewood Cliffs, NJ: Prentice-Hall, 1973.

______. *Harm to self*. Oxford: Oxford U. Press, 1986.

FLEMING, JOHN MARCUS. "A Cardinal Concept of Welfare," *Quart. J. Econ.*, Aug. 1952, 66(3), pp. 366–84.

FOLEY, DUNCAN. "Resource Allocation and the Public Sector," *Yale Econ. Essays*, Spring 1967, 7, pp. 45–98.

FOX, ALAN. *Beyond contract: Work, power and trust relations*. London: Faber, 1974.

FRANK, ROBERT. *Passions within reason: The strategic*

role of the emotions. NY: W. W. Norton, 1988.

FRANKFURT, HARRY. "Freedom of Will and the Concept of a Person," *J. Philosophy*, Jan. 1971, *68*(1), pp. 5–20.

______. "Equality as a Moral Ideal," *Ethics*, Oct. 1987, *98*(1), pp. 21–43.

FRIEDMAN, MILTON. *Capitalism and freedom*. Chicago: U. of Chicago Press, 1962.

GAERTNER, WULF; PATTANAIK, PRASANTA AND SUZUMURA, KOTARO. "Individual Rights Revisited," *Economica*, forthcoming.

GAMBETTA, DIEGO, ed. *Trust: Making and breaking cooperative relations*. Oxford: Basil Blackwell, 1988.

GARDENFORS, PETER. "Rights, Games and Social Choice," *Nous*, Sept. 1981, *15*(3), pp. 341–56.

GAUTHIER, DAVID. "On the Refutation of Utilitarianism," in MILLER AND WILLIAMS 1982.

______. *Morals by agreement*. Oxford: Clarendon Press, 1986.

GIBBARD, ALLAN. "A Pareto-Consistent Libertarian Claim," *J. Econ. Theory*, Apr. 1974, 7(4), pp. 388–410.

______. "Interpersonal Comparisons: Preference, Good, and the Intrinsic Reward of a Life," in ELSTER AND HYLLAND 1986, pp. 165–94.

______. *Wise choices, apt feelings: A theory of normative judgment*. Cambridge, MA: Harvard U. Press, 1990.

GILBERT, MARGARET. "Walking Together: A Paradigmatic Social Phenomenon," in *Midwest Studies in Philosophy*, Vol. 15. *The Philosophy of the Human Sciences*. Eds.: PETER FRENCH, THEODORE UEHLING, AND HOWARD WETTSTEIN. Notre Dame, IN: U. of Notre Dame Press, 1990, pp. 1–14.

GRAAFF, JAN DE VAN. *Theoretical welfare economics*. Cambridge: Cambridge U. Press, 1957.

GRIFFIN, JAMES. *Well-being: Its meaning, measurement and moral importance*. Oxford: Clarendon Press, 1986.

GUL, FAROUK A. "A Theory of Disappointment Aversion," *Econometrica*, May 1991, *59*(3), pp. 667–86.

HAMLIN, ALAN. *Ethics, economics, and the state*. NY: St. Martin's Press, 1986.

HAMMOND, PETER J. "Changing Tastes and Coherent Dynamic Choice," *Rev. Econ. Stud.*, July 1976a, *43*(1), pp. 159–73.

______. "Equity, Arrow's Conditions, and Rawls' Difference Principle," *Econometrica*, July 1976b, *44*(4), pp. 793–804.

______. "Ex-Post Optimality as a Dynamically Consistent Objective for Collective Choice under Uncertainty," in *Social choice and welfare*. Eds.: PRASANTA PATTANAIK AND MAURICE SALLES. Amsterdam: North-Holland, 1983, pp. 175–205.

______. "Consequentialist Foundations for Expected Utility," *Theory and Decision*, Jan. 1988, *25*(1), pp. 25–78.

HAMPTON, JEAN. *Hobbes and the social contract tradition*. Cambridge: Cambridge U. Press, 1986.

______. "Free-Rider Problems in the Production of Collective Goods," *Econ. Philos.*, Oct. 1987, *3*(2), pp. 245–73.

HANDS, DOUGLAS WADE. "Ad Hocness in Economics and the Popperian Tradition," in *The Popperian legacy in economics*. Ed.: NEIL DE MARCHI. Cambridge: Cambridge U. Press, 1988, pp. 121–37.

HARBERGER, ARNOLD C. "On the Use of Distributional Weights in Social Cost–Benefit Analysis," *J. Polit. Econ.*, Apr. 1978, *86*(2), pp. S87–120.

HARDIN, RUSSELL. *Collective action*. Baltimore: Johns Hopkins U. Press, 1982.

______. *Morality within the limits of reason*. Chicago: U. of Chicago Press, 1988.

HARE, RICHARD M. *Moral thinking: Its levels, method, and point*. Oxford: Oxford U. Press, 1981.

HARROD, ROY. "Utilitarianism Revised," *Mind*, Apr. 1936, *45*(178), pp. 137–56.

HARSANYI, JOHN. "Cardinal Welfare, Individualistic Ethics and Interpersonal Comparisons of Utility," *J. Polit. Econ.*, Aug. 1955, *63*(4), pp. 309–21.

______. "Morality and the Theory of Rational Behavior," *Social Research*, Winter, 1977a, *44*(4), pp. 623–56; reprinted in SEN AND WILLIAMS 1982, pp. 39–62.

______. *Rational behavior and bargaining equilibrium in games and social situations*. Cambridge: Cambridge U. Press, 1977b.

HART, HERBERT L. A. "Are There any Natural Rights?" *Philosophical Review*, Apr. 1955, *64*(2), pp. 175–91; reprinted in WALDRON 1984, pp. 77–90.

HASLETT, D. W. "What is Utility?" *Econ. Philos.*, Apr. 1990, *6*(1), pp. 65–94.

HAUSMAN, DANIEL. *The inexact and separate science of economics*. Cambridge: Cambridge U. Press, 1992.

HAYEK, FRIEDRICH VON. *The constitution of liberty*. Chicago: U. of Chicago Press, 1960.

______. "The Moral Element in Free Enterprise," in *Studies in philosophy, politics and economics*. Chicago: U. of Chicago Press, 1967, pp. 229–36.

______. *The mirage of social justice*. Chicago: U. of Chicago Press, 1976.

______. *The fatal conceit: The errors of socialism*. Vol. 1. *Collected works of F. A. Hayek*. London: Routledge, 1988.

HERSTEIN, ISRAEL AND MILNOR, JOHN W. "An Axiomatic Approach to Measurable Utility," *Econometrica*, Apr. 1953, *21*(2), pp. 291–97.

HICKS, JOHN. "The Foundations of Welfare Economics," *Econ. J.*, Dec. 1939, *49*(196), pp. 696–712.

______. "The Valuation of Social Income," *Economica N.S.*, May 1940, 7, pp. 105–24.

HIRSCH, FRED. *Social limits to growth*. Cambridge: Harvard U. Press, 1976.

HIRSCHMAN, ALBERT O. "Against Parsimony: Three Easy Ways of Complicating Some Categories of Economic Discourse," *Econ. Philos.*, Apr. 1985, *1*(1), pp. 7–21.

HOBBES, THOMAS. *Leaviathan, or the matter, form and power of a commonwealth ecclesiastical and civil*. NY: Collier Books, [1651] 1962.

HOCHMAN, HAROLD M. AND ROGERS, JAMES D. "Pareto Optimal Redistribution," *Amer. Econ. Rev.*, Sept. 1969, *59*(4), pp. 542–57.

HODGSON, GEOFFREY M. "Hayek's Theory of Cultural Evolution: An Evaluation in the Light of Vanberg's Critique," *Econ. Philos.*, Apr. 1991, *7*(1), pp. 67–82.

HOHFELD, WESLEY. *Fundamental legal conceptions.* New Haven: Yale U. Press, 1923.

HURLEY, SUSAN L. *Natural reasons: Personality and polity.* Oxford: Oxford U. Press, 1989.

JENSEN, NIELS. "An Introduction to Bernoullian Utility Theory: I. Utility Functions," *Swedish J. Econ.*, Sept. 1967, *69*, pp. 163–83.

KAGAN, SHELLY. *The limits of morality.* Oxford: Oxford U. Press, 1989.

KALDOR, NICHOLAS. "Welfare Propositions of Economics and Interpersonal Comparisons of Utility," *Econ. J.*, Sept. 1939, *49*(195), pp. 549–52.

KANT, IMMANUEL. *Groundwork of the metaphysics of morals.* Trans.: H. PATON. NY: Harper & Row, [1785] 1948.

KAVKA, GREGORY S. *Hobbesian moral and political theory.* Princeton: Princeton U. Press, 1986.

KELMAN, STEVEN. "A Case for In-Kind Transfers," *Econ. Philos.*, Apr. 1986, *2*(1), pp. 55–73.

KNIGHT, FRANK H. *Risk, uncertainty and profit.* Chicago: U. of Chicago Press, [1921] 1971.

______. *The ethics of competition, and other essays.* NY and London: Harper & Brothers, 1935.

KOLM, SERGE-CHRISTOPHE. *Justice et equitè.* Paris: Editions du Centre National de la Recherche Scientifique, 1972.

KRAUS, JODY AND COLEMAN, JULES. "Morality and the Theory of Rational Choice," *Ethics*, July 1987, *97*(4), pp. 715–49.

KREPS, DAVID M. ET AL. "Rational Cooperation in the Finitely Repeated Prisoners' Dilemma," *J. Econ. Theory*, Aug. 1982, *27*(2), pp. 245–52.

KREPS, DAVID AND WILSON, ROBERT. "Sequential Equilibria," *Econometrica*, July 1982, *50*(4), pp. 863–94.

LEIBENSTEIN, HARVEY. *Beyond economic man: A new foundation for economics.* Cambridge, MA: Harvard U. Press, 1976.

______. "A Branch of Economics is Missing: Micro-Micro Theory," *J. Econ. Lit.*, June 1979, *17*(2), pp. 477–502.

LERNER, ABBA. "Consumption-Loan Interest and Money," *J. Polit. Econ.*, Oct. 1959, *67*(5), pp. 512–25.

LEVI, ISAAC. *The enterprise of knowledge.* Cambridge, MA: MIT Press, 1980.

______. *Hard choices: Decision-making under unresolved conflict.* Cambridge: Cambridge U. Press, 1986a.

______. "The Paradoxes of Allais and Ellsberg," *Econ. Philos.*, Apr. 1986b, *2*(1), pp. 23–53.

______. "Pareto Unanimity and Consensus," *J. Philosophy*, Sept. 1990, *89*(9), pp. 481–92.

LEWIS, DAVID. *Convention. A philosophical study.* Cambridge: Harvard U. Press, 1969.

LIND, ROBERT C. ET AL. *Discounting for time and risk in energy policy.* Washington, DC: Resources for the Future; distributed by Johns Hopkins U. Press, Baltimore, 1982.

LIPSEY, RICHARD AND LANCASTER, KELVIN. "The General Theory of Second Best," *Rev. Econ. Stud.*, Oct. 1956, *24*(1), pp. 11–32.

LITTLE, IAN. *A critique of welfare economics.* 2nd ed. Oxford: Oxford U. Press, 1957.

LOMASKY, LOREN. *Persons, rights and the moral community.* NY: Oxford U. Press, 1987.

LOOMES, GRAHAM AND SUGDEN, ROBERT. "Regret Theory: An Alternative Theory of Rational Choice under Uncertainty," *Econ. J.*, Dec. 1982, *92*(368), pp. 805–24.

LUCE, ROBERT DUNCAN AND RAIFFA, HOWARD. *Games and decisions.* NY: Wiley, 1957.

LYONS, DAVID. "Human Rights and the General Welfare," *Philosophy and Public Affairs*, Winter 1977, *6*(1), pp. 113–29.

MACHAN, TIBOR R., ed. *The libertarian reader.* Totowa, NJ: Rowman & Littlefield, 1982.

MACHINA, MARK. "Choice under Uncertainty: Problems Solved and Unsolved," *J. Econ. Perspectives*, Summer 1987, *1*(1), pp. 121–54.

______. "Dynamic Consistency and Non-Expected Utility Models of Choice Under Uncertainty," *J. Econ. Lit.*, Dec. 1989, *27*(4), pp. 1622–68.

MACHLUP, FRITZ. "Positive and Normative Economics," in *Economic means and social ends: Essays in political economics.* Ed.: ROBERT HEILBRONER. Englewood Cliffs, NJ: Prentice-Hall, 1969, pp. 99–129.

MACINTYRE, ALASTAIR C. *After virtue: A study in moral theory.* London: Duckworth, 1981.

MACKAY, ALFRED. "Extended Sympathy and Interpersonal Utility Comparisons," *J. Philosophy*, June 1986, *83*(6), pp. 305–22.

MACKIE, JOHN. *Ethics: Inventing right and wrong.* Harmondsworth: Penguin, 1977.

MACLEAN, DOUGLAS AND BROWN, PETER G., eds. *Energy and the future.* Totowa, NJ: Rowman & Littlefield, 1983.

MANSBRIDGE, JANE J. "Expanding the Range of Formal Modeling," in *Beyond self-interest.* Ed.: JANE MANSBRIDGE. Chicago: U. of Chicago Press, 1990, pp. 254–63.

MARGOLIS, HOWARD. *Selfishness, altruism, and rationality.* Cambridge: Cambridge U. Press, 1982.

MARSHALL, ALFRED. "The Present Position of Economics," 1885; reprinted in *Memorials of Alfred Marshall.* Ed.: A. C. PIGOU. London: Macmillan, 1925, pp. 152–74.

______. "A Fair Rate of Wages," 1887; reprinted in *Memorials of Alfred Marshall.* Ed.: A. C. PIGOU. London: Macmillan, 1925, pp. 212–26.

MARWELL, GERALD AND AMES, RUTH. "Economists Free Ride. Does Anyone Else? Experiments on the Provision of Public Goods. IV," *J. Pub. Econ.*, June 1981, *15*(3), pp. 295–310.

MASKIN, ERIC. "The Theory of Implementation in Nash Equilibrium," in *Social goals and social organization: Essays in memory of Elisha Pazner.* Eds.: LEONID HURWICZ, DAVID SCHMEIDLER, AND HUGO SONNENSCHEIN. Cambridge: Cambridge U. Press, 1985, pp. 173–204.

MCCLENNEN, EDWARD. *Rationality and dynamic choice: Foundational explorations.* Cambridge: Cambridge U. Press, 1990.

McDowell, John. "Are Moral Requirements Hypothetical Imperatives?" *Proceedings of the Aristotlian society supplementary volume*. 1978, pp. 13–29.

McKean, Roland N. "Economics of Trust, Altruism, and Corporate Responsibility," in *Altruism, morality and economic theory*. Ed.: Edmund S. Phelps. NY: Russell Sage Foundation, 1975, pp. 29–44.

McPherson, Michael. "Mill's Moral Theory and the Problem of Preference Change," *Ethics*, Jan. 1982, 92(1), pp. 252–73.

______. "Efficiency and Liberty in the Productive Enterprise: Recent Work in the Economics of Work Organization," *Philosophy and Public Affairs*, Fall 1983a, *12*(4), pp. 354–68.

______. "Want Formation, Morality, and Some 'Interpretive' Aspects of Economic Inquiry," in, *Social science as moral inquiry*. Eds.: Norma Haan et al. NY: Columbia U. Press, 1983b, pp. 96–124.

______. "Limits on Self-seeking: The Role of Morality in Economic Life," in *Neoclassical political economy*. Ed.: David Colander. Boston: Ballinger Press, 1984, pp. 71–85.

Meckling, William. "An Exact Consumption-Loan Model of Interest: A Comment," *J. Polit. Econ.*, Feb. 1960, *68*(1), pp. 72–76.

Mill, John Stuart. *On liberty*. 1859. Ed.: Currin V. Shields. NY: Macmillan, 1985.

______. *Principles of political economy*. 7th ed. Ed.: William J. Ashley [1871], 1909; reprinted NY: A. M. Kelley, 1976.

Miller, Harlan B. and Williams, William H. eds. *The limits of utilitarianism*. Minneapolis: U. of Minnesota Press, 1982.

Mirrlees, James A. "Optimal Tax Theory: A Synthesis," *J. Pub. Econ.*, Nov. 1976, *6*(4), pp. 327–58.

Morishima, Michio. *Why has Japan succeeded?* NY: Cambridge U. Press, 1982.

Moore, George Edward. *Principia ethica*. Cambridge: Cambridge U. Press, 1902; reprinted 1959, 1984.

Mueller, Dennis. "Intergenerational Justice and the Social Discount Rate," *Theory and Decision*, Oct. 1974, *5*(3), pp. 263–73.

Musgrave, Richard. "Maximin, Uncertainty, and the Leisure Trade-Off," *Quart. J. Econ.*, Nov. 1974, *88*(4), pp. 625–32.

Nagel, Thomas. *The possibility of altruism*. Oxford: Clarendon Press, 1970.

______. "The Limits of Objectivity," in *The Tanner lectures on human values*. Vol. I. Ed.: Sterling M. McMurrin. Salt Lake City: U. of Utah Press, 1980, pp. 75–139.

______. "Libertarianism Without Foundations," in *Reading Nozick: Essays on anarchy, state, and utopia*. Ed.: Jeffrey Paul. Oxford: Basil Blackwell, 1981, pp. 191–205.

Narveson, Jan. *The libertarian idea*. Philadelphia: Temple U. Press, 1988.

Nash, John. "The Bargaining Problem," *Econometrica*, Jan. 1950, *18*(1), pp. 155–62.

Nelson, Alan. "Economic Rationality and Morality," *Philosophy and Public Affairs*, Spring 1988, *17*(2), pp. 149–66.

von Neumann, John and Morgenstern, Oskar. *Theory of games and economic behavior*. 2nd ed. Princeton: Princeton U. Press, 1947.

Nozick, Robert. *Anarchy, state, and utopia*. NY: Basic Books, 1974.

Nutzinger, Hans G. "The Firm as a Social Institution: The Failure of a Contractarian Viewpoint." Working Paper No. 52, Alfred Weber Institute, U. of Heidelberg, 1976.

Okun, Arthur. *Equality and efficiency: The big tradeoff*. Washington, DC: Brookings Institution, 1975.

Parfit, Derek. "Prudence, Morality and the Prisoners' Dilemma," *Proceedings of the British Academy*, 1979.

______. *Reasons and persons*. Oxford: Oxford U. Press, 1984.

van Parijs, Philippe. "On the Ethical Foundations of Basic Income." Working Paper #CMID 32, Institut Supèrieur de Philosophie, Universitè Catholique de Louvain, 1989.

______. The Second Marriage of Justice and Efficiency," *J. Social Policy*, 1990, *19*, pp. 1–25.

______. "Why Surfers Should Be Fed: The Liberal Case for an Unconditional Basic Income," *Philosophy and Public Affairs*, Spring 1991, *20*(2), pp. 101–31.

Paul, Ellen Frankel et al., eds. *The new social contract: Essays on Gauthier*. Oxford: Blackwell, 1988.

Peleg, Bezalel. *Game theoretic analysis of voting in committees*. Cambridge: Cambridge U. Press, 1984.

Pettit, Philip. "*Virtus Normativa:* Rational Choice Perspectives," *Ethics*, July 1990, *100*(4), pp. 725–55.

Pettit, Philip and Sugden, Robert. "The Backward Induction Paradox," *J. Philosophy*, Apr. 1989, *86*(4), pp. 169–82.

Phelps, Edmund S. "Taxation of Wage Income for Economic Justice," *Quart. J. Econ.*, Aug. 1973, *87*(3), pp. 331–54.

Polyani, Karl. *The great transformation*. New York and Toronto: Farrar & Rinehart, 1944.

Posner, Richard. "Utilitarianism, Economics, and Legal Theory," *J. Legal Stud.*, Jan. 1979, *8*(1), pp. 103–40.

Putnam, Hilary. *Reason, truth and history*. Cambridge: Cambridge U. Press, 1981.

Putterman, Louis. "On Some Recent Explanations of Why Capital Hires Labor," *Econ. Inquiry*, Apr. 1984, *22*(2), pp. 171–87.

Railton, Peter. "Alienation, Consequentialism, and the Demands of Morality, "*Philosophy and Public Affairs*, Spring 1984, *13*(2), pp. 134–71.

Ramsey, Frank. "Truth and Probability," in *The foundations of mathematics and other logical essays*. Ed.: R. B. Braithwaite. London: Routledge & Kegan Paul, 1926, pp. 156–98.

Rand, Ayn. *The virtue of selfishness*. NY: Signet Books, 1964.

Rawls, John. "Outline of a Decision Procedure for

Ethics," *Philosophical Rev.*, Apr. 1951, *60*(2), pp. 177–97.

———. "Two Concepts of Rules," *Philosophical Rev.*, Apr. 1955, *64*(1), pp. 3–33.

———. *A theory of justice*. Cambridge, MA: Harvard U. Press, 1971.

———. "Social Unity and Primary Goods," in SEN AND WILLIAMS 1982, pp. 159–86.

RAZ, JOSEPH. *The morality of freedom*. Oxford: Oxford U. Press, 1986.

REDER, MELVIN. "The Place of Ethics in the Theory of Production," in *Economics and human welfare: Essays in honor of Tibor Scitovsky*. Ed.: MICHAEL BOSKIN. NY: Academic Press, 1979, pp. 133–46.

REGAN, DONALD. *Utilitarianism and cooperation*. Oxford: Clarendon Press, 1980.

———. "Against Evaluator Relativity: A Response to Sen," *Philosophy and Public Affairs*, Spring 1983, *12*(2), pp. 93–112.

REICH, MICHAEL AND DEVINE, JAMES. "The Microeconomics of Conflict and Hierarchy in Capitalist Production," *Rev. Radical Polit. Econ.*, Winter 1981, *12*(1), pp. 27–45.

RILEY, JONATHAN. "Rights to Liberty in Purely Private Matters, Part I," *Econ. Philos.*, Oct. 1989, *5*(2) pp. 121–66.

———. "Rights to Liberty in Purely Private Matters, Part II," *Econ. Philos.*, Apr. 1990, *6*(1), pp. 27–64.

ROBBINS, LIONEL. *An essay on the nature and significance of economic science*. 2nd ed. London: Macmillan, [1932] 1935.

ROBINSON, JOAN. *The economics of imperfect competition*. London: Macmillan, 1933.

ROEMER, JOHN. *A general theory of exploitation and class*. Cambridge, MA: Harvard U. Press, 1982.

———. "Equality of Talent," *Econ. Philos.*, Oct. 1985a, *1*(2), pp. 151–88.

———. "Should Marxists Be Interested in Exploitation?" *Philosophy and Public Affairs*, Winter 1985b, *14*(1), pp. 30–65.

———. "The Mismarriage of Bargaining Theory and Distributive Justice," *Ethics*, Oct. 1986a, *97*(1), pp. 88–110.

———. "Equality of Resources Implies Equality of Welfare," *Quart. J. Econ.*, Nov. 1986b, *101*(4), pp. 751–84.

———. "Egalitarianism, Responsibility, and Information," *Econ. Philos.*, Oct. 1987, *3*(2), pp. 215–44.

———. *Free to lose*. Cambridge: Harvard U. Press, 1988.

———. "What Is Exploitation? Reply to Jeffrey Reiman," *Philosophy and Public Affairs*, Winter 1989, *18*(1), pp. 90–97.

RORTY, RICHARD. *The consequences of pragmatism*. Minneapolis: U. of Minnesota Press, 1982.

ROTH, ALVIN AND MALOUF, MICHAEL. "Game Theoretical Models and the Role of Information in Bargaining," *Psych. Rev.*, Nov. 1979, *86*(6), pp. 574–94.

ROTH, ALVIN; MALOUF, MICHAEL AND MURNIGHAN, J. KEITH. "Sociological versus Strategic Factors in Bargaining," *J. Econ. Behav. Organ.*, June 1981, *2*(2), pp. 153–77.

SAGOFF, MARK. "Values and Preferences," *Ethics*, Jan. 1986, *96*(2), pp. 301–16.

SAMUELSON, PAUL. *Foundations of economic analysis*. Cambridge, MA: Harvard U. Press, 1947.

———. "Evaluation of Real National Income," *Oxford Econ. Pap., N.S.*, Jan. 1950, *2*(1), pp. 1–29.

———. "An Exact Consumption-Loan Model of Interest with or without the Social Contrivance of Money," *J. Polit. Econ.*, Dec. 1958, *66*(6), pp. 467–82.

———. "Reaffirming the Existence of 'Reasonable' Bergson-Samuelson Social Welfare Functions," *Economica N.S.*, Feb. 1977, *44*(173), pp. 81–88.

SANDEL, MICHAEL. *Liberalism and the limits of justice*. Cambridge: Cambridge U. Press, 1982.

SAVAGE, LEONARD. *The foundations of statistics*. NY: Dover, 1972.

SCANLON, THOMAS. "Preference and Urgency," *J. Philosophy*, Nov. 1975, *75*(22), pp. 655–70.

———. "Contractualism and Utilitarianism," in SEN AND WILLIAMS 1982, pp. 103–28.

———. "Equality of Resources and Equality of Welfare: A Forced Marriage?" *Ethics*, Oct. 1986, *97*(1), pp. 111–18.

SCHEFFLER, SAMUEL. *The rejection of consequentialism: A philosophical investigation of the considerations underlying rival moral conceptions*. Oxford: Clarendon Press, 1982.

———, ed. *Consequentialism and its critics*. Oxford: Oxford U. Press, 1988.

SCHELLING, THOMAS. *Micromotives and macrobehavior*. NY: Norton, 1978.

———. *Choice and consequence*. Cambridge: Harvard U. Press, 1984.

SCHICK, FREDERIC. "Dutch Bookies and Money Pumps," *J. Philosophy*, Feb. 1986, *83*(2), pp. 112–19.

SCHMEIDLER, DAVID AND PAZNER, ELISHA A. "A Difficulty in the Concept of Fairness," *Rev. Econ. Stud.*, July 1974, *41*(3), pp. 441–43.

SCHOTTER, ANDREW. *The economic theory of social institutions*. Cambridge: Cambridge U. Press, 1981.

SCHWARTZ, THOMAS. "What Welfare Is Not," in MILLER AND WILLIAMS 1982, pp. 195–206.

SEIDENFELD, TEDDY; KADANE, JOSEPH AND SCHERVISH, MARK. "On the Shared Preferences of Two Bayesian Decision Makers," *J. Philosophy*, May 1989, *86*(5), pp. 225–44.

SELTEN, REINHART. "Re-examination of the Perfectness Concept for Equilibrium in Extensive Games," *Int. J. Game Theory*, 1975, *4*, pp. 22–25.

SEN, AMARTYA. "Isolation, Assurance, and the Social Rate of Discount," *Quart J. Econ.*, Feb. 1967, *81*(1), pp. 112–24.

———. *Collective choice and social welfare*. San Francisco: Holden Day, 1970a.

———. "The Impossibility of a Paretian Liberal," *J. Polit. Econ.*, Jan./Feb. 1970b, *78*(1), pp. 152–57; reprinted in SEN 1982a, pp. 285–90.

———. "Choice Functions and Revealed Preference," *Rev. Econ. Stud.*, July 1971, 38(115), pp. 307–17.

———. "Behaviour and the Concept of Preference," *Economica N.S.*, Aug. 1973a, 40(159), pp. 241–59.

———. *On economic inequality*. Oxford: Clarendon Press, 1973b.

———. "Liberty, Unanimity and Rights," *Economica*, Aug. 1976a, 43(171), pp. 217–45.

———. "Real National Income," *Rev. Econ. Stud.*, Feb. 1976b, 43(1), pp. 19–39; printed in SEN 1982a, pp. 388–415.

———. "Rational Fools," *Philosophy and Public Affairs*, Summer 1977a, 6(4), pp. 317–44; reprinted in SEN 1982a, pp. 84–106.

———. "On Weights and Measures: Informational Constraints in Social Welfare Analysis," *Econometrica*, Oct. 1977b, 45(7), pp. 1539–72; reprinted in SEN 1982a, pp. 226–63.

———. "Social Choice Theory: A Re-examination," *Econometrica*, Jan. 1977c, 45(1), pp. 53–89; reprinted in SEN 1982a, pp. 158–200.

———. "Utilitarianism and Welfarism," *J. Philosophy*, Sept. 1979a, 76(9), pp. 463–89.

———. "The Welfare Basis of Real Income Comparisons," *J. Econ. Lit.*, Mar. 1979b, 17(1), pp. 1–45.

———. "Interpersonal Comparisons of Welfare," in *Economics and human welfare: Essays in honor of Tibor Scitovsky*. Ed.: MICHAEL BOSKIN. NY: Academic Press, 1979c, pp. 183–201; reprinted in SEN 1982a, pp. 264–81.

———. *Choice, welfare and measurement*. Cambridge, MA: MIT Press, 1982a.

———. "Rights and Agency," *Philosophy and Public Affairs*, Winter 1982b, 11(1), pp. 3–39.

———. "Evaluator Relativity and Consequential Evaluation," *Philosophy and Public Affairs*, Spring 1983a, 12(2), pp. 113–32.

———. "Liberty and Social Choice," *J. Philosophy*, Jan. 1983b, 80(1), pp. 5–28.

———. *Commodities and capabilities*. Vol. 7. *Professor Dr. P. Hennipman lectures in economics, theory, institutions, policy*. Amsterdam: North-Holland, 1985a.

———. "Rationality and Uncertainty," *Theory and Decision*, Mar. 1985b, 18(2), pp. 109–28.

———. "Well-being, Agency, and Freedom: The Dewey Lectures 1984," *J. Philosophy*, Apr. 1985c, 82(4), pp. 169–203.

———. "Foundations of Social Choice Theory: An Epilogue," in *Foundations of social choice theory*. Eds.: JON ELSTER AND AANUND HYLLAND. Cambridge: Cambridge U. Press, 1986a, pp. 213–48.

———. "Information and Invariance in Normative Choice," in *Social choice and public decision making: Essays in Honor of K. J. Arrow*. Vol 1. Eds.: WALTER HELLER, ROSS M. STARR, AND DAVID STARRETT. Cambridge: Cambridge U. Press, 1986b, pp. 29–55.

———. *On ethics and economics*. Oxford: Blackwell, 1987a.

———. "The Standard of Living: Lecture I, Concepts and Critiques," in SEN ET AL. 1987(b), pp. 1–19.

———. "The Standard of Living: Lecture II, Lives and Capabilities," in SEN ET AL. 1987(c), pp. 30–38.

———. "Gender and Cooperative Conflicts," in *Persistent inequalities*. Ed.: IRENE TINKER. London: Oxford U. Press, 1990, pp. 123–49.

———. *Inequality reexamined*. Cambridge, MA: Harvard U. Press, 1992.

———. "Minimal Liberty," *Economica*, forthcoming.

SEN, AMARTYA ET AL. *The standard of living*. Ed.: GEOFFREY HAWTHORN. Cambridge: Cambridge U. Press, 1987.

SEN, AMARTYA AND WILLIAMS, BERNARD, eds. *Utilitarianism and beyond*. Cambridge: Cambridge U. Press, 1982.

SIDGWICK, HENRY. *The methods of ethics*. 6th ed. London: Macmillan, 1901.

SINGER, PETER. "Altruism and commerce: A Defense of Titmuss against Arrow," *Philosophy and Public Affairs*, Spring 1973, 2(3), pp. 312–20.

———. "Freedoms and Utilities in the Distribution of Health Care," in DWORKIN, BERMANT, AND BROWN, eds. 1977, pp. 149–73.

SMITH, ADAM. *The theory of moral sentiments*. Eds.: D. D. RAPHAEL AND A. L. MACFIE. Oxford: Clarendon Press, 1976.

———. *An inquiry into the nature and causes of the wealth of nations*. Eds.: R. H. CAMPBELL AND A. S. SKINNER [1776]; Oxford: Clarendon Press, 1976.

SOLOW, ROBERT. 'Wage Bargaining and Unemployment," *Amer. Econ. Rev.*, Dec. 1981, 71(5), pp. 898–908.

———. *The labor market as a social institution*. Oxford: Basil Blackwell, 1990.

STEWART, HAMISH. "Taking Goals Seriously: A Reconsideration of Rationality in Economics." Ph.D. dissertation, Harvard U., 1989.

STIGLER, GEORGE. "Wealth and Possibly Liberty," *J. Legal Stud.*, June 1978.

STRASNICK, STEVEN. "Social Choice and the Derivation of Rawls's Difference Principle," *J. Philosophy*, Feb. 1976, 73(4), pp. 85–99.

———. "Neo-Utilitarian Ethics and the Ordinal Representation Assumption," in *Philosophy in economics: Papers deriving from and related to a workshop of testability and explanation in economics*. Ed.: JOSEPH C. PITT. Boston: D. Reidel, 1981, pp. 63–92.

STREETEN, PAUL. "Appendix: Recent Controversies," in *The political element in the development of economic theory*. By GUNNAR MYRDAL, translated by PAUL STREETEN. London: Routledge & Kegan Paul, 1953, pp. 208–17.

STROTZ, ROBERT. "Myopia and Inconsistency in Dynamic Utility Maximization," *Rev. Econ. Stud.*, 1956, 23(3), pp. 165–80.

SUGDEN, ROBERT. "Liberty, Preference, and Choice," *Econ. Philos.*, Oct. 1985, pp. 213–29.

———. *The economics of rights, co-operation, and welfare*. NY: Blackwell, 1986.

———. "Spontaneous Order," *J. Econ. Perspectives*, Fall 1989, 3(4), pp. 85–97.

_____. "Contractarianism and Norms," *Ethics*, July 1990, *100*(4), pp. 768–86.

SUZUMURA, KOTARO. *Rational choice, collective decisions, and social welfare*. NY: Cambridge U. Press, 1983.

TAYLOR, CHARLES. *Hegel and modern society*. Cambridge U. Press, 1979.

_____. *Sources of the self: The making of the modern identity*. Cambridge, MA: Harvard U. Press, 1989.

TAYLOR, MICHAEL C. *The possibility of cooperation*. NY: Cambridge U. Press, 1987.

THOMSON, GARRETT. *Needs*. London: Routledge, 1987.

THOMSON, WILLIAM AND LENSBERG, TERJE. *Axiomatic theory of bargaining with a variable number of agents*. NY: Cambridge U. Press, 1989.

THUROW, LESTER C. "Government Expenditures: Cash or In-Kind Aid," in GERALD DWORKIN, BERMAN, BROWN, eds. 1977, pp. 85–106.

TITMUSS, RICHARD. *The gift relationship: From human blood to social policy*. NY: Random House, 1971.

TVERSKY, AMOS AND KAHNEMAN, DANIEL. "Prospect Theory: An Analysis of Decision under Risk, *Econometrica*, Mar. 1979, *47*(2), pp. 263–91.

VANBERG, VIKTOR. "Spontaneous Market Order and Social Rules: A Critical Examination of F. A. Hayek's Theory of Cultural Evolution," *Econ. Philos.*, Apr. 1986, *2*(1), pp. 75–100.

VARIAN, HAL. "Equity, Envy, and Efficiency," *J. Econ. Theory*, Sept. 1974, *9*(1), pp. 63–91.

_____. "Distributive Justice, Welfare, Economics, and the Theory of Fairness," *Philosophy and Public Affairs*, Spring 1975, *4*(3), pp. 223–47.

_____. "Dworkin on Equality of Resources," *Econ. Philos.*, Apr. 1985, *1*(1), pp. 110–25.

VICKREY, WILLIAM. "Measuring Marginal Utility by Reactions to Risk," *Econometrica*, Oct. 1945, *13*(4), pp. 319–33.

_____. "Utility, Strategy, and Social Decision Rules," *Quart J. Econ.*, Nov. 1960, *74*(4), pp. 507–35.

WALDRON, JEREMY, ed. *Theories of rights*. Oxford: Oxford U. Press, 1984.

WALZER, MICHAEL. *Spheres of justice*. NY: Basic Books, 1983.

WARR, PETER G. AND WRIGHT, BRIAN D. "The Isolation Paradox and the Discount Rate for Benefit-Cost Analysis," *Quart. J. Econ.*, Feb. 1981, *96*(1), pp. 129–45.

WEIBULL, JÖRGEN. "Persistent Unemployment as Subgame Perfect Equilibrium." Seminar Paper No. 381 of the Institute for International Economic Studies, Stockholm, May 1987.

WESTON, SAMUEL. "Toward a Better Understanding of the Postitive/Normative Distinction in Economics," *Econ. Philos.*, forthcoming.

WEYMARK, JOHN. "A Reconsideration of the Harsanyi-Sen Debate on Utilitarianism," in ELSTER AND ROEMER, eds. 1991, pp. 255–320.

WILLIAMS, BERNARD. "A Critique of Utilitarianism," in *Utilitarianism: For and against*. Eds.: J. J. C. SMART AND BERNARD WILLIAMS. Cambridge: Cambridge U. Press, 1973, pp. 77–150.

_____. "The Standard of Living: Interests and Capabilities," in SEN ET AL. 1987, pp. 94–102.

WILLIAMSON, OLIVER. "The Organization of Work: A Comparative Institutional Assessment," *J. Econ. Behav. Organ.*, 1980, *1*(1), pp. 5–38.

YAARI, MENACHEM AND BAR-HILLEL, MAJA. "On Dividing Justly," *Soc. Choice Welfare*, 1984, *1*(1), pp. 1–24.

Name Index

The International Library of Critical Writings in Economics

1. Multinational Corporations
   Mark Casson
2. The Economics of Innovation
   Christopher Freeman
3. Entrepreneurship
   Mark Casson
4. International Investment
   Peter J. Buckley
5. Game Theory in Economics
   Ariel Rubinstein
6. The History of Economic Thought
   Mark Blaug
7. Monetary Theory
   Thomas Mayer
8. Joint Production of Commodities
   Neri Salvadori and Ian Steedman
9. Industrial Organization
   Oliver E. Williamson
10. Growth Theory (Volumes I, II and III)
    R. Becker and E. Burmeister
11. Microeconomics: Theoretical and Applied (Volumes I, II and III)
    Robert E. Kuenne
12. The Economics of Health (Volumes I and II)
    A.J. Culyer
13. Recent Developments in Macroeconomics (Volumes I, II and III)
    Edmund S. Phelps
14. Urban and Regional Economics
    Paul C. Cheshire and Alan W. Evans
15. Modern Public Finance (Volumes I and II)
    A.B. Atkinson
16. Exchange Rate Economics (Volumes I and II)
    Ronald MacDonald and Mark P. Taylor

17. The Economic Value of Education: Studies in the Economics of Education
Mark Blaug

18. Development Economics (Volumes I, II, III and IV)
Deepak Lal

19. The New Classical Macroeconomics (Volumes I, II and III)
Kevin D. Hoover

20. The Economics of the Environment
Wallace E. Oates

21. Post Keynesian Theory of Growth and Distribution
Carlo Panico and Neri Salvadori

22. Dynamic Labor Demand and Adjustment Costs
Giorgio Galeazzi and Daniel S. Hamermesh

23. The Philosophy and Methodology of Economics (Volumes I, II and III)
Bruce J. Caldwell

24. Public Choice Theory (Volumes I, II and III)
Charles K. Rowley

25. Evolutionary Economics
Ulrich Witt

26. Economics and Psychology
Shlomo Maital and Sharone L. Maital

27. Social Choice Theory (Volumes I, II and III)
Charles K. Rowley

28. Non-Linear Dynamics in Economic Theory
Marc Jarsulic

29. Recent Developments in Experimental Economics (Volumes I and II)
John D. Hey and Graham Loomes

30. Monopoly and Competition Policy (Volumes I and II)
F.M. Scherer

31. The Economics of Technical Change
Edwin Mansfield and Elizabeth Mansfield

32. The Economics of Exhaustible Resources
Geoffrey Heal

33. The Economics of Institutions
Geoffrey M. Hodgson

34. The Economics of Transport (Volumes I and II)
Herbert Mohring

35. Implicit Contract Theory
Sherwin Rosen

36. Foundations of Analytical Marxism (Volumes I and II)
John E. Roemer

37. The Economics of Product Differentiation (Volumes I and II)
Jacques-François Thisse and George Norman

38. Economic Growth in Theory and Practice: A Kaldorian Perspective
John E. King

39. Markets and Socialism
Alec Nove and Ian D. Thatcher

40. Recent Developments in the Economics of Education
Elchanan Cohn and Geraint Johnes

41. The Theory of Inflation
Michael Parkin

42. The Economics of Location (Volumes I, II and III)
Melvin L. Greenhut and George Norman

43. Financial Intermediaries
Mervyn K. Lewis

44. The Political Economy of Privatization and Deregulation
Elizabeth E. Bailey and Janet Rothenberg Pack

45. Gender and Economics
Jane Humphries

46. Macroeconomics and Imperfect Competition
Jean-Pascal Bénassy

47. Labor Economics (Volumes I, II, III and IV)
Orley C. Ashenfelter and Kevin F. Hallock

48. The Economics of Altruism
Stefano Zamagni

49. The Economic Analysis of Rent Seeking
Robert D. Tollison and Roger D. Congleton

50. Economics and Biology
Geoffrey M. Hodgson

51. The Economics of Ageing
John Creedy

52. Fiscal and Monetary Policy (Volumes I and II)
Thomas Mayer and Steven M. Sheffrin

53. The Economics of Information (Volumes I and II)
David K. Levine and Steven A. Lippman

54. Transaction Cost Economics (Volumes I and II)
Oliver E. Williamson and Scott E. Masten

55. Agricultural Economics
George H. Peters

56. International Debt (Volumes I and II)
Graham Bird and P. Nicholas Snowden

57. Economics and Discrimination (Volumes I and II)
William A. Darity, Jr

58. Business Cycle Theory
Finn E. Kydland

59. International Trade (Volumes I and II)
J. Peter Neary

60. The Money Supply in the Economic Process
Marco Musella and Carlo Panico

61. Small Firms and Economic Growth (Volumes I and II)
Zoltan J. Acs

62. Producer Cooperatives and Labor-Managed Systems (Volumes I and II)
David L. Prychitko and Jaroslav Vanek

63. Ethics and Economics (Volumes I and II)
Alan P. Hamlin

64. The Economics of the Family
Nancy Folbre

Future titles will include:

Long Wave Theory
Christopher Freeman

General Equilibrium Theory
Gerard Debreu

The Foundations of Public Finance
Peter Jackson

The Economics of Training
Robert J. LaLonde and Orley Ashenfelter

Economic Growth – Theory and Evidence
Gene M. Grossman

Chaotic Dynamics in Economics
W. Davis Dechert

The Economics of Communication and Innovation
Donald M. Lamberton

The Economics of Uncertainty
John D. Hey

International Finance
Robert Z. Aliber

Welfare Economics
William J. Baumol and Janusz A. Ordover

The Theory of the Firm
Mark Casson

The Economics of Inequality and Poverty
A.B. Atkinson

The Economics of Housing
John M. Quigley

Population Economics
Julian L. Simon

The Economics of Crime
Isaac Ehrlich

The Economics of Integration
Willem Molle

The Rhetoric of Economics
Donald McCloskey

Migration
Oded Stark

Economic Forecasting
Paul Ormerod

The Economics of Defence
Keith Hartley and Nicholas Hooper

Consumer Theory
Kelvin Lancaster

Law and Economics
Richard A. Posner and Francesco Parisi

The Economics of Business Policy
John Kay

The Economics of Productivity
Edward Wolff

Microeconomic Theories of Imperfect Competition
Jacques Thisse and Jean Gabszewicz

The Economics of Increasing Returns
Geoffrey Heal

The Balance of Payments
Michael J. Artis

Cost-Benefit Analysis
Arnold Harberger and Glenn P. Jenkins

The Economics of Unemployment
P.N. Junankar

Mathematical Economics
Graciela Chichilnisky

Economic Growth in the Long Run
Bart van Ark

Gender in Economic and Social History
K.J. Humphries and J. Lewis

The Economics of Local Finance and Fiscal Federalism
Wallace Oates

Privatization in Developing and Transitional Economies
Colin Kirkpatrick and Paul Cook

Input-Output Analysis
Heinz Kurz and Christian Lager

The Economics of Global Warming
Tom Tietenberg

Political Business Cycles
Bruno Frey

The Economics of the Arts
Ruth Towse

The Economics of Energy
Paul Stevens

The Economics of Intellectual Property
Ruth Towse

Ecological Economics
Robert Costanza, Charles Perrings and Cutler Cleveland

The Economics of Tourism
Clem Tisdell

The Economics of Organization and Bureaucracy
Peter Jackson